# Multinational Finance

# Multinational Finance

*Evaluating Opportunities, Costs, and Risks of Operations*

**Fifth Edition**

KIRT C. BUTLER
*Michigan State University*

WILEY
John Wiley & Sons, Inc.

Published by John Wiley & Sons, Inc., Hoboken, New Jersey.

First, Second, and Third Editions published by South-Western Pub in 1996, 1999, 2003. Fourth Edition published by Wiley-Blackwell in 2008.

Published simultaneously in Canada.



For general information on our other products and services or for technical support, please contact our Customer Care Department within the United States at (800) 762-2974, outside the United States at (317) 572-3993 or fax (317) 572-4002.

Wiley also publishes its books in a variety of electronic formats. Some content that appears in print may not be available in electronic books. For more information about Wiley products, visit our web site at www.wiley.com

**Library of Congress Cataloging-in-Publication Data**

Butler, Kirt Charles.
Multinational finance : evaluating opportunities, costs, and risks of operations / Kirt C. Butler.—5th ed.
p. cm.
Includes index.
ISBN 978-1-118-27012-7 (pbk.); ISBN 978-1-118-28276-2 (ebk); ISBN 978-1-118-28486-5 (ebk); ISBN 978-1-118-28516-9 (ebk)
1. International business enterprises–Finance. 2. Foreign exchange. 3. International finance. I. Title.
HG4027.5.B88 2012
658.15′99—dc23

2012008106

Printed in the United States of America

10 9 8 7 6 5 4

*For my family*

# Contents

# Preface

*Everything should be made as simple as possible, but not simpler.*
—Albert Einstein

*Multinational Finance* assumes the viewpoint of the financial manager of a multinational enterprise with investment or financial operations in more than one country. The enterprise could be a multinational corporation, but also could be a large financial institution or a small partnership or proprietorship. The book provides a framework for evaluating the many opportunities, costs, and risks of multinational operations in a manner that allows readers to see beyond the algebra and terminology to general principles.

Einstein's statement, "Everything should be made as simple as possible, but not simpler," is a perfect introduction to a text in multinational finance, because it captures the tension between simplicity and substance that is inherent in presenting a difficult subject in an accessible way.

Dealing with foreign cultures and currencies can be a dizzying experience, and it is essential to strive for a simple and intuitive approach to multinational finance. Yet some areas of multinational finance are inherently complex. Too much simplification in these areas would be a disservice to practitioners in the field, while too much detail can overwhelm the reader and obscure the forest for the trees. The goal of this text is thus to impart "just enough" knowledge in each of the most critical areas of multinational finance.

## MEETING YOUR OBJECTIVES

The text is organized into five Parts.

- **Part I: The International Financial Environment.** The text presents an in-depth treatment of the international financial environment, including international trade and the balance of payments, currency and Eurocurrency markets, and the international parity conditions. Chapters 3 and 4 on currency and Eurocurrency markets are a necessary prerequisite for most of the chapters that follow.

- **Part II: Derivative Securities for Financial Risk Management.** Chapters 5–7 contain detailed treatments of currency futures, options, and swaps because of the importance of these derivative instruments in financial risk management. The swaps chapter contains updated treatments of interest rate swaps, currency swaps, commodity swaps, and credit default swaps.
- **Part III: Managing the Risks of Multinational Operations.** Part III covers the rationale for hedging currency risks, operation of the multinational treasury, and the multinational corporation's management of transaction, operating, and translation exposures to currency risk.
- **Part IV: Valuation and the Structure of Multinational Operations.** Valuing and structuring the corporation's international assets is the heart of the text. Part IV begins with a discussion of country risk and its management. The cross-border capital budgeting chapter has far more depth than competing texts, covering the international parity case as well as disequilibrium situations in which the international parity conditions do not hold. Additional chapters cover multinational financing, taxation, real option valuation, and corporate governance.
- **Part V: International Portfolio Investment and Asset Pricing.** *Multinational Finance* takes a market-oriented view of the multinational corporation, with separate chapters on international capital markets, portfolio diversification, and asset pricing.

Most readers of *Multinational Finance* have a professional interest in international corporate finance. These readers will find that Part I, Part III, and Part IV provide a comprehensive coverage of key international corporate finance topics, with a managerial focus throughout.

Readers with an interest in international financial markets also will find a wealth of content in *Multinational Finance*. Part II provides a thorough and up-to-date coverage of currency futures, options, and swaps, and their use in financial risk management. These detailed and technical chapters provide a useful supplement to the risk management chapters in Part III of the text. Chapter 9, "Managing Transaction Exposure to Currency Risk," in Part III provides a simplified overview and comparison of the various financial derivatives.

Part V will prove useful to anyone with an interest in international investments, including students of corporate finance who want a deeper insight into investors' required returns, and the corporation's cost of capital, as well as readers with an interest in the international aspects of traditional investments.

## KEY FEATURES

This edition of *Multinational Finance* retains the classic features developed in earlier editions, as well as a wealth of new material on current and future topics of interest to practitioners of multinational finance.

- **Comprehensive and up-to-date coverage of traditional topics in multinational financial management.** Intended for advanced undergraduate and MBA classes, the text requires only a single preparatory course in finance. Chapters that extend material from the first course begin with a brief review of the fundamentals. Numerous graphs and figures assist the reader in understanding key financial concepts and techniques. Real-world updates, applications, and examples are used to illustrate how the financial concepts and techniques are used in practice. Advanced material is placed in chapter appendices, so that study can be tailored to each individual's objectives.

- **Distinctive chapters on key topics.** Distinctive chapters are devoted to topics of special interest to practitioners of multinational finance.
  - Chapters 5–7 provide detailed treatments of futures, options, and swaps. These specialized chapters are appropriate for students desiring a deep understanding of the financial tools available for currency risk management.
  - An optional Appendix 8A develops the rationale for hedging currency risk for those readers that desire a deeper understanding of the motives of the firm's stakeholders for managing currency risk, and the valuation consequences of currency risk management for the firm's stakeholders.
  - Chapter 16 takes a real options approach to valuing the flexibility in cross-border investments.
  - Chapter 17 describes differences in national corporate governance systems and their implications for the international market for corporate control. The chapter provides a survey of the rich and ongoing academic research into corporate governance and corporate control.
  - Chapter 20 on international asset pricing provides an up-to-date treatment of this interesting and important topic, including state-of-the-art international asset pricing models.
- **Exciting new material on topics of contemporary interest.** The text includes information on the best practices of multinational corporations, as well as the current thinking of top scholars in the field.
  - *Concepts*: Project valuation under equilibrium and disequilibrium conditions, time-varying expected returns and volatilities, hedge funds and private equity, agency costs, moral hazard, behavioral finance, home bias, the legal environment and investor protections, the diversification discount, asset allocation styles, the success of politically connected CEOs, and the impact of the 2008 financial crisis on the theory and practice of multinational finance.
  - *Tools*: All-in costs, the "Greeks" (deltas, gammas, vegas, and thetas), price elasticities, conditional and implied volatilities, exchange-traded funds (ETFs), hedge funds and private equity, credit derivatives, project finance, assets-in-place and growth options, and the no-arbitrage condition.
  - *Models*: Exchange rate forecasting, value-at-risk, conditional asset pricing models, currency option pricing models, factor models (e.g., currency; country vs. industry), the international value premium, and international momentum strategies.

## LEARNING AIDS

Several learning aids are used to highlight the main points in each chapter and assist the student in learning the material.

- Callouts in the text highlight key concepts and definitions.
- **Market Updates** and **Applications** appearing as boxed essays provide real-world examples and practical applications of the conceptual material.
- **Websites** appearing in the text link the chapter topics to the real world.
- **Key Terms** appear in boldface the first time they are used. Key terms are listed at the end of each chapter and defined in a comprehensive Glossary.
- An annotated list of **Suggested Readings** at the end of each chapter provides a gateway to the academic and practitioner literature in the area.
- More than 200 end-of-chapter **Conceptual Questions** summarize the key ideas in each chapter and allow readers to test their understanding of the material.
- More than 150 end-of-chapter **Problems** provide practice in applying the financial concepts, techniques, and strategies. Solutions to even-numbered problems are provided at the end of the text.

## SUPPLEMENTS FOR THE INSTRUCTOR

A comprehensive **Instructor's Manual** is available to instructors adopting the text for classroom use.

- More than 600 **PowerPoint** slides review the key elements in each chapter and illustrate how to apply the material. The accompanying **Notes Pages** provide additional anecdotes, insights, and examples for classroom use.
- A **Solutions Manual** provides answers to all of the end-of-chapter questions and problems.
- A comprehensive **Test Bank** includes more than one thousand test questions and solutions, including true-false and multiple-choice questions, numerical problems, and short essays.

Great care is taken in providing these supplements in order to reduce instructors' burden of preparation and allow them to spend their time where it is most needed—in teaching the students.

Kirt C. Butler
April 2012
East Lansing, Michigan

# Acknowledgments

At my "hombu" karate dojo in Lansing, Michigan, we begin and end each class session with the Japanese phrase "onegai shimasu," which means "please teach me." This is appropriate for both students and teachers. Although I have learned a great deal from my own teachers and colleagues, I have learned at least as much from my students. Their varied backgrounds and approaches to learning have enriched my life and made me a better teacher, scholar, and student.

I am particularly grateful to the following scholars, whose thoughtful comments and suggestions have helped make the writing of *Multinational Finance* an interesting and enjoyable journey:

Richard Ajayi, University of Central Florida
Anne Allerston, Bournemouth University
Richard Baillie, Michigan State University
Arindam Bandopadhyaya, University of Massachusetts–Boston
Jeffrey Bergstrand, University of Notre Dame
Shyam Bhati, University of Wollongong
Rita Biswas, SUNY–Albany
Gordon Bodnar, Johns Hopkins University
Donald J.S. Brean, University of Toronto
Rajesh Chakrabarti, Indian School of Business
Louis K.C. Chan, University of Illinois
David B. Cox, University of Denver
Adri de Ridder, Göteborg University
Miranda Detzler, University of Massachusetts–Boston
Mark Eaker, University of Virginia
Joseph E. Finnerty, University of Illinois
Julian Gaspar, Texas A&M
Thomas Gjerde, Butler University
Thomas Grennes, North Carolina State University
Dora Hancock, Leeds Metropolitan University
Roger D. Huang, University of Notre Dame
Kwang Nam Jee, Korea Development Bank
Kurt Jesswein, Sam Houston State University

Jun-Koo Kang, Nanyang Technological University
Andrew Karolyi, Ohio State University
Aditya Kaul, University of Alberta
Yong-Cheol Kim, University of Wisconsin–Milwaukee
Gerhard Kling, University of Southampton
Paul Koch, University of Kansas
Theodor Kohers, Mississippi State University
C.R. Krishnaswamy, Western Michigan University
Chuck Kwok, University of South Carolina
Christian Lundblad, University of North Carolina
Peter MacKay, Southern Methodist University
Thomas J. O'Brien, University of Connecticut
Barbara Ostdiek, Rice University
Ed Outslay, Michigan State University
Terry Pope, Abilene Christian University
Mitchell Ratner, Rider College
Jonathan Reeves, University of New South Wales
Ashok Robin, Rochester Institute of Technology
Antonio Rodriguez, Texas A&M International
Mehdi Salehizadeh, San Diego State University
Hakan Saraoglu, Bryant College
Vijay Singal, Virginia Tech
Jacky C. So, University of Macao
Michael Solt, San Jose State University
Wei-Ling Song, Louisiana State University
Richard Stehle, Humboldt University
Chris Stivers, University of Louisville
Philip Swicegood, Wofford College
Lawrence Tai, Zayed University
Tilan Tang, Clemson University
Dean Taylor, University of Colorado, Denver
Antoinette Tessmer, Michigan State University
Dosse Toulaboe, Fort Hays State University
Gwinyai Utete, Louisiana State University
Masahiro Watanabe, Rice University
Rohan Williamson, Georgetown University
Jiawen Yang, George Washington University
Ellen Yun Zhu, Oakland University

The Finance team at Wiley proved their mettle in bringing this project to fruition. My special thanks go to Executive Editor Bill Falloon, Developmental Editor Meg Freeborn, and Senior Production Editor Natasha Andrews-Noel for their support, encouragement, and conscientious attention to detail.

Ongoing inspiration and direction are provided by my parents, Bruce and Jean Butler, my children, Rosemarie and Vincent, and my Sensei, Seikichi Iha.

Finally, and most importantly, I wish to thank my wife, Erika, who travels the world in search of international business anecdotes, while I stay at home and work on yet another edition of *Multinational Finance*.

# PART One

# The International Financial Environment

*Even if you're on the right track, you'll get run over if you just sit there.*

—Will Rogers

CHAPTER 1

# An Introduction to Multinational Finance

*The more we learn of the possibilities of our world, and the possibilities of ourselves, the richer, we learn, is our inheritance.*

—H.G. Wells

This book assumes the viewpoint of the financial manager of a ***multinational corporation (MNC)*** with investment or financial operations in more than one country. Managers encounter new opportunities as they extend their operations into international markets, as well as new costs and risks. The challenge facing the multinational financial manager is to successfully develop and execute business and financial strategies in more than one culture or national business environment.

## 1.1 THE GOALS OF THE MULTINATIONAL CORPORATION

Figure 1.1 presents the ownership and control structure that is typical of companies in market economies. In these countries, the primary goal of the firm is to maximize shareholder wealth. However, shareholder wealth maximization is far from the only objective of the MNC. Many other ***stakeholders*** have an interest in the firm, including suppliers, customers, debtholders, managers, business partners, employees, and society at large. The objectives of these other stakeholders often are in conflict with shareholder wealth maximization, especially during periods of financial distress.

*Stakeholders include those with a stake in the firm.*

Figure 1.2 represents the value of the various claimants on the corporation's future revenues. In this view of the firm, the value of revenues can be allocated to operating expenses (labor and materials), the government (taxes), suppliers of debt and equity capital, and other potential claimants (e.g., litigants through local or foreign legal systems). Stakeholders sometimes are narrowly defined as the owners of the firm's debt and equity. These claims are paid out of operating income and are

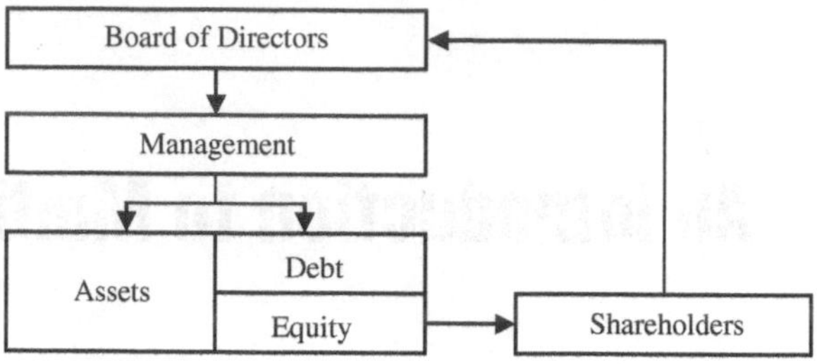


**FIGURE 1.1** Corporate Governance

represented by $V_{Debt}$ and $V_{Equity}$ in Figure 1.2. The values of these claims depend on the laws and conventions of the nations within which the MNC operates.

A broader definition of stakeholder includes anyone with an interest in the company, such as the firm's customers, suppliers, employees, host government(s), and anyone else with an actual or potential claim on the firm. The firm's customers help determine the value of revenues, $V_{Revenues}$. Suppliers and employees determine the value of operating expenses, $V_{Expenses}$. Governmental claims, $V_{Govt}$, represent the claims of society at large and include taxes, tariffs, and the costs of compliance with local laws and regulations (e.g., environmental and corporate governance rules).

The objectives of these other stakeholders are seldom the same as those of debt or equity. Labor is more concerned with wages and job security than with shareholder wealth. Customers and suppliers likewise are concerned with their own well-being. The objective of "maximize shareholder wealth" also can be in conflict with host countries' cultural, economic, political, environmental, or religious goals.

Managers have their own objectives, which are not the same as those of equity shareholders or other stakeholders. ***Agency costs*** refer to any loss in value from conflicts of interest between managers and other stakeholders, particularly

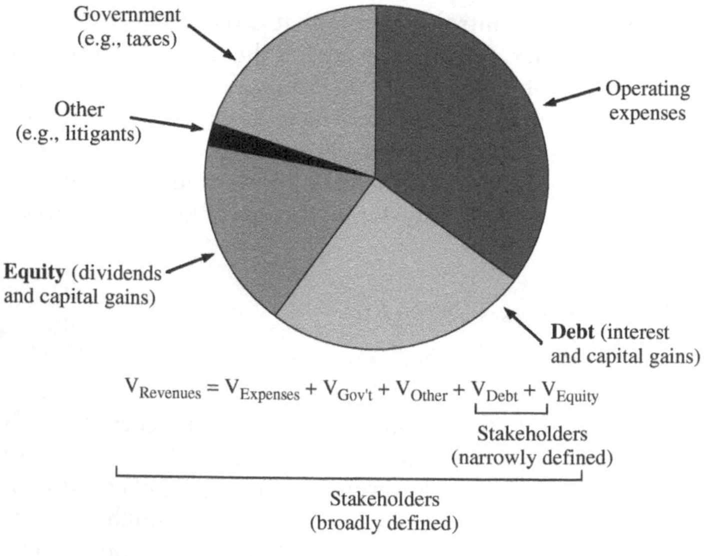


**FIGURE 1.2** Stakeholders and Their Claims on the Revenues of the Firm

equity shareholders. These costs include the costs of contracting and monitoring between the various stakeholders to reduce potential conflicts of interest. A good example of an agency cost from everyday life is the physician who recommends a costly procedure that may or may not be good for the patient—but is certainly good for the physician's pocketbook. The presence of agency costs does not mean that management will not act in the best interests of shareholders, only that it is costly to encourage managers to do so. As the residual owners of the firm, it is the shareholders who ultimately bear these agency costs.

*Agency costs arise from conflicts of interest.*

Not all of the firm's activities appear in the financial statements. Some of these activities can and do affect other stakeholders. For example, if the firm violates the laws of a host country, it may be liable for civil or criminal penalties. Union Carbide's disaster at its plant in Bhopal, India (see box ahead), resulted in huge claims that adversely affected all stakeholders.

Countries differ in the extent to which they protect each of these stakeholders. Countries with strong socialist movements place an emphasis on employee welfare. Some countries emphasize environmental concerns, while others actively promote their local economy to the detriment of the local—and global—environment. Most countries protect or subsidize key industries deemed to be of vital importance to the nation's economy or national identity. Protected industries often include products related to agriculture, such as rice in Japan, beer in Germany, and wine in France. In the United States, as in other countries, various agricultural products that are vulnerable to foreign competition are protected through price supports and tariffs.

Sovereign nations determine the nature of the playing field on which MNCs operate. Company representatives must work within the rules and respect the sensitivities of the societies in which they operate.[1] Businesses ignoring the local rules of the game do so at their own peril.

### MARKET UPDATE Union Carbide's Bhopal Disaster

Union Carbide (www.unioncarbide.com) is a diversified U.S. company with worldwide operations in a variety of industry segments. Union Carbide's 51%-owned subsidiary in India operated a chemical plant in Bhopal, India. In 1984, poisonous gases were inadvertently released from the plant, causing the death of more than 2,000 people and injuries to nearly a quarter of a million people. This disaster resulted in losses for nearly all of Union Carbide's stakeholders (broadly defined). Debt and equity lost value in anticipation of a class action suit that eventually was settled in India's courts. The careers and self-esteem of managers and employees involved in the Bhopal operation also suffered. The biggest losses were suffered by the Indian government (Union Carbide's equity partner) and the local population.

## 1.2 THE CHALLENGES OF MULTINATIONAL OPERATIONS

### Recognizing and Overcoming Cultural Differences

An English aristocrat once said, "The only trouble with going abroad is that you have to leave home to do it." True enough. People and their cultural norms vary widely. Managers and employees of the MNC must deal with unfamiliar business and popular cultures as they seek to extend the firm's competitive advantages into new and unfamiliar markets. Being able to understand, adapt to, and manage cultural differences can make the difference between a successful and an unsuccessful international venture.

> *Cultural differences can be a source of risk.*

Language is one of the more obvious differences between cultures. Literal translations of common words or phrases can create some amusing situations. If you've traveled, you'll no doubt have your own favorite anecdote. (I once announced to a class in Germany that "Ich bin warm"—only to discover that "I am warm" is German slang for "I am gay.") A little language can go a long way, but only if you are able to laugh about your lack of fluency with your hosts.

As if verbal language weren't enough of a barrier to communication, body language differs across cultures as well. In many settings, what we do with our bodies is even more important than what we say. (Voltaire wrote, "Words were given to man to enable him to conceal his true feelings.") Although some body language is universal, much of it is a reflection of our culture.

Eye contact is a good example. In the Western world, direct eye contact conveys confidence. Avoiding eye contact is taken as a sign of weakness and may even convey untrustworthiness. In Western countries, subordinates show respect by meeting the eyes of their superiors. In some Asian countries, subordinates show their respect by avoiding eye contact. In some Arab countries, excessive eye contact between a man and woman is thought to be disrespectful to the woman. The eyes are the windows to the soul, but be careful which windows you look through.

Another way to categorize differences in national business environments is along the functional areas of business. The following list characterizes some of the differences that MNCs encounter in their cross-border operations:

- *Differences in legal, accounting, and tax systems.* Successful multinational managers must learn unfamiliar tax laws, accounting and legal conventions, and business procedures. As an example, governments in developing countries sometimes offer tax benefits in the form of tax holidays as an investment incentive. Negotiating these benefits and ensuring that they are not revoked subsequent to investment can be a delicate and time-consuming task.
- *Differences in personnel management.* MNCs must adapt their human resource practices and organizational structures to accommodate the labor conditions

and conventions in foreign markets. Human resource policies developed at home often do not translate into other cultures.

- *Differences in marketing.* Cross-cultural differences in marketing extend well beyond differences in language. For example, Walt Disney owns and operates some of the world's most successful theme parks. At the heart of Disney's U.S. success is its family appeal. When it opened its EuroDisney theme park near Paris in the late 1980s, Disney tried to retain this family orientation and refused to sell alcoholic beverages. This unfortunately ensured that no self-respecting Frenchman would visit the park. EuroDisney was beset by other difficulties as well, including overly optimistic forecasts, labor strife, and popular opposition. Fortunately for Disney, its equity stake was kept to a minimum by bringing in other investors in a project finance arrangement. Disney's reputation did take a beating, along with several classes of foreign investors and the reputation of the French government of François Mitterrand.
- *Differences in distribution.* A prolonged stay in another country inevitably means shopping for groceries. Observant shoppers can detect many national differences in the ways in which foods are distributed. U.S. residents are accustomed to large grocery chains that offer wide selections of food and nonfood items. These large chains keep expenses low through efficient supply chain management. In many other parts of the world, groceries are sold in local mom-and-pop stores. Large discount stores are seen as impersonal and are not trusted by shoppers. The source of the local owners' advantage lies in their close relationships with their customers.
- *Differences in financial markets.* Financial market operations vary across countries. Although the most obvious differences are in the liquidity and volume of trade, other differences can be profound. For example, banking practices in many Islamic countries are conducted according to the teachings of the prophet Mohammed as found in the Koran and other Islamic holy scriptures. According to these Islamic banking customs, depositors do not receive a set rate of interest but instead share in the profits and losses of the bank. Western banks opening branch banks in Islamic countries must be cognizant of these local religious norms.
- *Differences in corporate governance.* Another difference between national business cultures lies in ***corporate governance***—the mechanisms by which major stakeholders exert control over the firm (and discussed at length in Chapter 17). The corporation is defined by a legal framework of contracts between customers, suppliers, labor, debt, equity, and management. Because each of these contracts is executed within the laws of the societies in which the firm operates, society itself helps determine the forms of these contracts and the rights and responsibilities of the various parties.

A foreign venture that does not respect local cultural sensibilities is destined for trouble. Multinational managers must learn new business systems and social behaviors, including what types of corporate behaviors are punished, what types are merely tolerated, and what types can lead to fruitful partnerships with foreign residents and their governments.

**APPLICATION ¿Que Hora Es?**

Mexico City, September 12, 11:50 A.M.: You are a New Yorker working for AT&T on a satellite communications deal with the Mexican telecom giant Telmex. You have scheduled lunch with Aldo Martinez of Telmex at a fashionable restaurant in Mexico City. Conscious of the importance of the proposed deal, you arrive early and secure a private table in a secluded area of the restaurant.

12:20 P.M.: Thirty minutes have passed since your arrival and still no sign of Aldo. Could he have been caught in one of Mexico City's infamous traffic jams? Should you try to contact him on your cell phone? The waiter doesn't seem concerned that you haven't begun to order. Should you order food for the two of you? Oh, dear.

12:35 P.M.: It has been over half an hour! Now you are really concerned. Your imagination starts to run away with you. Perhaps the deal has fallen through? No, you're just panicky. Perhaps he was overcome by smog? The delay is beginning to irritate you. You resolve to contact Aldo by phone—and just at that moment Aldo strolls calmly into the restaurant. Greeting you as if nothing is out of the ordinary, he takes a seat and inquires how you have been. Doesn't he realize the anxiety and inconvenience that he has caused?

Attitudes toward time vary across cultures, particularly in the precision with which time is measured. You are merely experiencing the difference between a New York minute and la hora Mexicana (Mexican time).

### Managing the Costs and Risks of Multinational Operations

Cross-border operations create additional costs. They also increase the MNC's risk exposures. ***Risk*** exists whenever actual outcomes can differ from expectations. The MNC has ***exposure*** to risk when its assets or liabilities can change in value with unexpected changes in business conditions. As individuals and businesses pursue cross-border opportunities, they expose themselves to a wide variety of new risks.

*Risk exists when outcomes can differ from the expected.*

An important new risk exposure arising from cross-border operations is ***country risk***—the risk that the business environment in a host country or the host country's relationship with another country will unexpectedly change. Important sources of country risk to which the MNC is exposed include political risks and financial risks.

***Political risk*** is the risk that the business environment in a host country will unexpectedly change due to political events. Political risk usually is determined within a country as local political forces influence the business environment. Sources of political risk include unexpected changes in the business environment arising from repatriation restrictions, taxes, local content and employment regulations, restrictions on foreign ownership, business and bankruptcy laws, foreign exchange controls, and expropriation.

> *Country risks include political and financial risks.*

***Financial risk*** refers to the risk of unexpected change in the financial or economic environment of a host country. Financial risk is influenced by political factors, but also by a myriad of financial and economic factors that are outside the control of local political forces. A particularly important financial risk exposure for MNCs with operations in more than one country is currency risk. The MNC is exposed to ***currency risk***—also called ***foreign exchange risk*** or ***forex (FX) risk***—if unexpected changes in currency values affect the value of the firm. Volatility in the world's currency markets can cause the value of the MNC to fluctuate in unexpected ways. Profits can be wiped out quickly by changes in currency values. For this reason, financial risk management is essential for both large and small firms competing in today's global marketplace.

## 1.3 THE OPPORTUNITIES OF MULTINATIONAL OPERATIONS

According to the ***discounted cash flow*** approach to valuation, asset value is equal to the present value of expected future cash flows discounted at an appropriate risk-adjusted discount rate.

$$V = \Sigma_t[E[CF_t]/(1+i)^t] \qquad (1.1)$$

This valuation equation has an important implication for the firm. If a corporate decision has no impact on the firm's expected future cash flows or discount rate, then the decision also has no impact on the value of the firm. Conversely, if a decision is to add value, then the decision must either increase expected cash flows or decrease the cost of capital.

### Multinational Investment Opportunities

The set of investments available to the corporation is called its ***investment opportunity set***. The corporation's investment objective is to identify, invest, and then manage the set of assets that maximizes the value of the firm to its key stakeholders. In terms of Equation 1.1, the objective is to choose the set of investments that maximizes the present value of expected future operating cash flows. This means accepting projects with expected returns that exceed investors' required return, and rejecting projects that do not meet this hurdle.

Multinational corporations have many opportunities that are not available to local firms for increasing operating cash flows.

**Enhancing Revenues** Multinational corporations enjoy higher revenues than local firms by providing goods or services that are not readily available in local markets. Here are a few examples of revenue-enhancing advantages that MNCs enjoy over domestic firms.

- *Global branding*. A global brand can provide an advantage over local competitors. For example, McDonald's and Coca-Cola have leveraged their internationally recognized brand names into marketing efficiencies that are unavailable to local competitors.
- *Marketing flexibility*. MNCs have more marketing flexibility than domestic firms, in that they can more easily shift sales efforts toward markets willing to pay higher prices for their products. For example, if Ford's Focus is in high demand in Europe, then Ford can shift its marketing efforts toward Europe and away from regions of lower demand or profitability.
- *Advantages of scale and scope*. Because of their size and the breadth of their operations, MNCs can exploit their competitive advantages on a larger scale and across a broader range of markets and products than domestic competitors. For example, Nike promotes its corporate brand—the Nike swoosh—in multiple international markets and across its product line.

**Reducing Operating Costs** Multinational operations can reduce operating expenses in a number of ways that are not available to domestic firms.

- *Low-cost raw materials*. MNCs seek low-cost raw materials to reduce costs and ensure supplies. The lure of low-cost resources can be powerful. In 1997, the French company Total secured a $2 billion deal to develop Iran's South Pars gas field. Political opposition from Tehran—as well as from other governments—had prevented foreign investment in Iran since its 1979 revolution. When Iran sought outside investment to increase production and overcome a budget deficit, MNCs such as Total were quick to respond, and economic necessity overcame two decades of political opposition.
- *Low-cost labor*. Labor costs vary widely around the world, and manufacturers have an incentive to buy their goods and services from low-cost sources. Rapid industrialization in Japan and Korea during the 1960s and 1970s was driven by their low labor costs and educated workforces. These countries rose to the first rank of international economies as they acquired technological expertise. In more recent years, the ascendance of China and India similarly has been fueled by low labor costs. The threat of low-cost foreign labor is a major fear of organized labor in industrialized countries. Indeed, labor unions are vocal opponents of efforts to promote international trade through organizations such as the European Union (EU), the North American Free Trade Agreement (NAFTA), and the World Trade Organization (WTO).
- *Flexibility in global site selection*. MNCs have greater flexibility than domestic firms in the location and timing of their investments. Competition between local, regional, and national governments for capital investment allows MNCs to "shop around" for the most attractive deal. For example, automobile manufacturers such as Toyota and General Motors routinely shop for tax incentives

before investing in new plants or product lines. Because of their size and international presence, multinational corporations are in a better position than local firms to manage their international site location decisions.

- *Flexibility in sourcing and production.* By having a diversified manufacturing base, MNCs can shift production to low-cost locations in response to currency movements or other factors. If changes in currency values make components less expensive from some countries than from others, then MNCs can use their global manufacturing network to increase production in the low-cost countries and decrease production in the high-cost countries. Local competitors typically do not enjoy this flexibility.
- *Economies of scale and scope.* Companies possess ***economies of scale*** when size itself results in lower average or per-unit production costs. Economies of scale arise as fixed development or production costs are spread over a larger output. For example, manufacturing integrated circuits entails high development costs and large fixed investment costs. Once a manufacturing plant is set up, variable production costs can be quite low. High start-up costs serve to insulate large MNCs from local competition. ***Economies of scope*** are similar, but refer to efficiencies that arise across product lines, such as when joint production results in lower per-unit costs.
- *Economies of vertical integration.* Firms possess ***economies of vertical integration*** when they enjoy lower costs through their control of a vertically integrated supply chain. Firms vertically integrate when it is more efficient to arrange the steps of a production process through internal rather than external markets. Vertical integration is popular in industries that need to protect their production processes or technologies from competitors. Mature MNCs often integrate their supply chains from labor and raw material inputs right through the final marketing, distribution, and after-sale service of their products.

**Multinational Business Strategy** Here are a few classic strategies for preserving or enhancing operating cash flows through multinational operations. Note these strategies are often influenced by local (foreign or domestic) factors.

- *Following the customer.* Service firms, such as banks and accounting firms, often follow their customers into foreign markets. Parts suppliers in industries such as automobile manufacturing also follow this strategy. As the nuances of operating in a foreign country are mastered, these firms can begin to pursue foreign clients as well.
- *Leading the customer.* Many firms try to attract foreign companies into their domestic market. This lead-the-customer strategy is a way of solidifying relations with foreign companies before they establish relations with other local competitors.
- *Following the leader.* When competitors are actively acquiring foreign assets, a common response is to similarly acquire foreign assets to reduce the threat of falling behind in global market share or production costs. This bandwagon phenomenon is especially common in industries enjoying high profitability.
- *Going local.* MNCs often build capacity directly in foreign markets to avoid quotas or tariffs on imported goods. This reduces the risk of protectionism, as

the MNC is seen as less of an outsider if it employs local workers. It also may increase sales, as customers are more receptive to locally produced goods.

## Multinational Financial Opportunities

The objective of financial policy is to maximize the value of the firm through its financing choices, given the firm's investment decisions. Financial policy includes decisions regarding the mix of debt and equity, the maturity structure of debt, the markets in which capital is raised and its currency of denomination, the method of financing domestic and foreign operations, and financial risk management.

Many financial opportunities arise from financial market imperfections, so it is sensible to first define a perfect financial market.

**The Perfect Market Assumptions and Concepts of Market Efficiency** The *perfect financial market assumptions* will prove useful at several points in the text.

> *In a perfect financial market, rational investors have equal access to market prices and information in a frictionless market.*

This definition has several components, summarized in Figure 1.3.

- *Frictionless markets.* A frictionless market has no transaction costs, taxes, government intervention, agency costs, or costs of financial distress. Some market frictions such as transaction costs are a function of market volume and liquidity. Other frictions such as taxes are externally imposed and independent of volume and liquidity.
- *Equal access to market prices.* If all market participants have equal access to market prices, then no single party can influence prices. Although this is a convenient assumption, it does not always hold. Many domestic and international actors can influence prices. Governments influence asset and currency values through their fiscal and monetary policies, cartels such as the Organization of

| Rational investors have equal access to market prices and information in a frictionless market. | |
|---|---|
| 1. Frictionless markets | No transactions costs<br>No government intervention<br>No taxes<br>No agency costs<br>No costs of financial distress |
| 2. Equal access to market prices | Perfect competition<br>No barriers to entry |
| 3. Rational investors | More return is good, and more risk is bad |
| 4. Equal access to costless information | Everyone has instantaneous and costless access to information |

**FIGURE 1.3** The Perfect Market Assumptions

Petroleum Exporting Countries (OPEC) influence commodity prices through their control of production, and hedge funds such as George Soros's Quantum Fund affect market prices through the sheer size of their trades.

- *Rational investors.* Rational investors price assets with a dispassionate eye toward expected returns and risks. Although this sounds great in theory, investors are not always rational, and there are significant cross-border differences in investors' behaviors. The study of the impact of psychological factors on behaviors and asset prices is referred to as behavioral finance, and is an active area of financial research.
- *Equal access to costless information.* Equal access to costless information puts market participants on an equal footing with one another. This assumption belies the fact that language serves as a very real barrier to the flow of information across (and sometimes within) national boundaries. Even with a common language, information is difficult to convey and can change in the telling. There are also wide differences in accounting measurement and disclosure requirements, and managers and other insiders benefit from their privileged access to information in both developed and developing markets.

The assumption of frictionless markets is an assumption of ***operational efficiency*** such that there are no drains on funds as they are transferred from one use to another. The last three assumptions are sufficient to ensure an ***informationally efficient*** market in which prices fully reflect all relevant information. Informational efficiency does not require frictionless markets, as prices can fully reflect information despite the existence of transaction costs. For example, a bid-ask spread on currency transaction would preclude costless ***arbitrage,*** although currencies could still be correctly priced within the bounds of transaction costs.[2] Similarly, stock and bond markets can be informationally efficient despite relatively high transaction costs.

Operational efficiency and informational efficiency together promote ***allocational efficiency***; that is, an efficient allocation of capital toward its most productive uses. Allocational efficiency—the basic objective of any financial market—is greatest when there is high liquidity and transaction volume in freely traded assets. Less liquid financial markets do not allocate capital between savers and borrowers as efficiently as more liquid markets.

In a perfect financial market, there is no need for government regulators, bank auditors, or attorneys. With no taxes, there is no need for tax collectors or tax accountants. With equal access to market prices and no transaction costs, there is no need for financial intermediaries such as banks and brokers, nor any market for finance graduates. And, with costless information, there is no need for finance professors or this text. The net result is that the price of a particular asset is the same all over the world. Although this is strictly true only in a perfect world, it has important implications for real-world financial policies.

**Implications of Perfect Financial Markets for Multinational Financial Policy** The perfect market assumptions provide a convenient starting point for investigating many difficult issues in finance. In particular, the corporation's financial policy is irrelevant in a perfect financial market because—with equal access to market prices and information in a frictionless market—individual investors can replicate or reverse any action that the firm can take.[3] In such a world, financial policy cannot affect firm value.

The converse of this irrelevance proposition also must be true.

> ***If financial policy is to increase firm value, then it must increase the firm's expected cash flows or decrease the discount rate in a way that cannot be replicated by individual investors.***

Financial market imperfections are more prominent in international than in domestic markets, so MNCs have more opportunities than comparable domestic firms to create value through their financial policies. Here are a few examples.

- *Financial market arbitrage.* Chapter 4 shows how market participants can take advantage of cross-border differences in asset prices, such as disequilibria in currencies and interest rates.
- *Hedging policy.* Chapter 8 shows how financial managers can create value by reducing drains on operating cash flows (e.g., by reducing expected bankruptcy costs) through the firm's hedging policy.
- *MNC cost of capital when there are capital flow barriers.* Chapter 14 discusses how MNCs can lower their cost of capital by selling debt or equity securities to foreign investors that are willing to pay higher prices than domestic investors.
- *Reducing taxes through multinational operations.* Chapter 15 shows how MNCs can reduce their tax burden through multinational tax planning. In particular, MNCs have an incentive to recognize income in low-tax countries and expenses in high-tax countries.
- *Barriers to the free flow of capital across international markets.* Chapter 18 surveys the world's debt and equity markets, and describes some of the barriers that impede the free flow of capital across national borders. Chapter 18 also discusses vehicles for diversifying across national boundaries in the presence of these capital flow barriers.
- *Currency risk and the cost of capital.* Chapter 20 discusses the multinational corporation's exposure to currency risk and the impact of this exposure on investors' required returns and the MNC's cost of capital.

Violations of any of the perfect financial market assumptions can lead to financial opportunities, particularly for multinational corporations with access to international financial markets.

### Multinational Opportunities and Firm Value

Figure 1.4 illustrates the potential increase in firm value provided by multinational opportunities. The downward-sloping lines represent the investment opportunity set of a domestic corporation and of a comparable multinational corporation. Each firm accepts its most lucrative projects first, so expected returns fall as more capital is invested. The expected return on the domestic firm's first dollar of investment

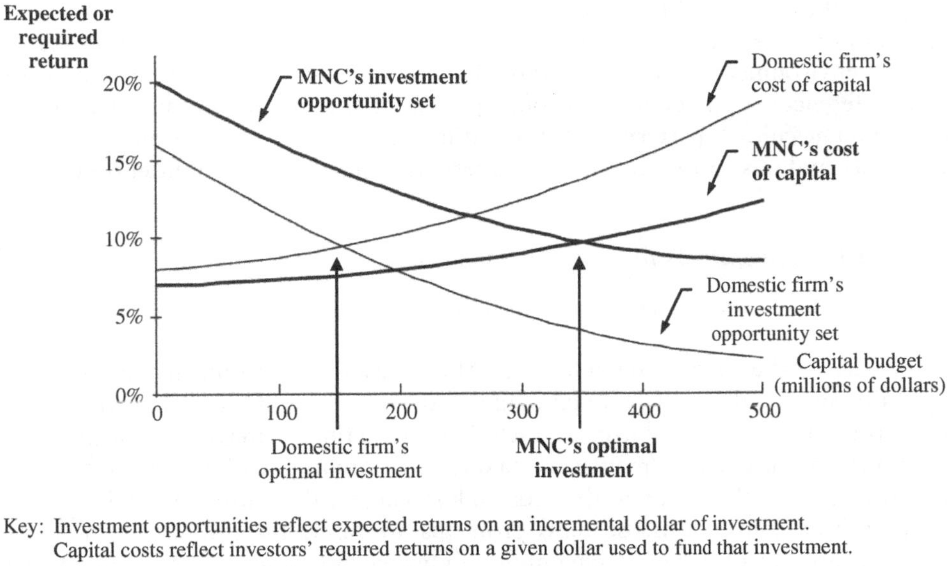


**FIGURE 1.4** The Potential Benefits of Multinationality

is 16 percent along the y-axis. With more attractive investment alternatives, the MNC's initial investments are displayed with an expected return of 20 percent.

The upward-sloping lines represent the required return or cost of capital on investment. Firms draw upon their lowest cost sources of funds first, so cost of capital is an increasing function of the capital budget. The domestic firm in Figure 1.4 has a cost of capital of 8 percent on the first dollar that it invests. With access to lower cost funds from international sources, the MNC in Figure 1.4 faces a required return of only 7 percent on its initial investment.

The MNC in Figure 1.4 earns an expected return of 20 percent at a required return of only 7 percent along the y-axis, so its first dollar of investment increases shareholder wealth by 13 cents. The MNC in Figure 1.4 will continue to invest until its expected return falls below its required return at a capital budget of approximately $350 million. With a larger and richer set of investments, this MNC will have a higher value than a comparable domestic firm.

The market value of a multinational corporation should reflect these expanded investment and financing opportunities. However, these opportunities come with additional costs and risks as well. Although an MNC's international experience places it in a better position than its domestic rivals to evaluate and manage these opportunities, costs, and risks, it is an open question whether multinational operations per se can increase the value of the firm.[4]

## 1.4 FINANCIAL MANAGEMENT OF THE MULTINATIONAL CORPORATION

At the heart of the opportunities, costs, and risks of multinational operations are the differences among the countries and peoples of the world. Local culture influences the conduct of business in profound and subtle ways, creating important cross-border differences in financial, economic, political, regulatory, accounting, and tax environments. The multinational financial manager must be sensitive to these differences in the conduct of both professional and personal life. Failing to accommodate cultural patterns and expectations can obstruct negotiations and result in hostility and mistrust even if both counterparties have the best of intentions.

*MNCs have operations in more than one country*

Because of the far-reaching influence of local business environments on multinational operations, the multinational financial manager must be well versed in each of the traditional fields of business, including marketing, management of physical and human resources, law, regulation, taxation, accounting, and finance. Successful operation in each of these areas depends on knowing local cultures and their written and unwritten conventions. Business problems are rarely the province of a single discipline, and the challenges facing multinational corporations are especially prone to be multidisciplinary.

To be able to recognize and develop business opportunities in foreign markets, the multinational financial manager also must be an expert in several fields within finance. Multinational financial managers must understand the capabilities and limitations of traditional investment analysis, have a plan of attack for entry into and exit from foreign markets, and value the flexibilities and real options presented by investment opportunities in foreign markets. The financial opportunities of the MNC also are richer than those of the domestic corporation, because of cross-border differences in investors' expectations, risk tolerances, and required returns. Multinational financial management requires a thorough knowledge of the international financial markets for equity securities, interest rate contracts, currencies, commodities, and derivatives (futures, options, and swaps). Today's multinational financial manager must be a jack-of-all-trades, as well as a master of finance.

## 1.5 SUMMARY

An understanding of multinational financial management is crucial to success in today's, and inevitably in tomorrow's, marketplace. This is unquestionably true for firms competing directly with foreign firms, such as domestic automakers in competition with foreign automakers. It is also true for domestic firms whose suppliers, customers, and competitors are increasingly likely to be from foreign countries.

In today's business environment, the success of a multinational corporation depends on its manager's abilities to recognize and exploit imperfections in national markets for products and factors of production, and to work effectively within the political and economic constraints imposed by host governments.

This book develops a framework for evaluating the opportunities, costs, and risks presented by the world's marketplaces. Although we usually take the perspective of the financial manager of a large multinational corporation, this framework works just as well for government entities, small businesses, and even individuals. Along the way, we provide a tour of business environments in many countries around the world. Bon voyage.

## KEY TERMS

*agency costs*
*allocational, informational, and operational efficiency*
*arbitrage*
*corporate governance*
*country risk*
*currency (foreign exchange) risk*
*discounted cash flow*
*economies of scale and scope*
*economies of vertical integration*
*financial risk*
*investment opportunity set*
*multinational corporation (MNC)*
*perfect financial market assumptions*
*political risk*
*risk versus risk exposure*
*stakeholders*

## CONCEPTUAL QUESTIONS

1.1 List the MNC's key stakeholders. How does each have a stake in the MNC?

1.2 In what ways do cultural differences affect the conduct of international business?

1.3 What is country risk? Describe several types of country risk one might face when conducting business in another country.

1.4 What is political risk?

1.5 What is foreign exchange risk?

1.6 What investment opportunities might MNCs enjoy that are not available to local firms?

1.7 How can MNCs reduce operating expenses relative to domestic firms?

1.8 What are the perfect financial market assumptions? What is their implication for multinational financial management?

1.9 Describe the ways in which multinational financial management is different from domestic financial management.

CHAPTER 2

# World Trade and the International Monetary System

*History is almost always written by the victors.*

—Jawaharlal Nehru

This chapter begins with a discussion of world trade and international efforts to reduce trade barriers in the world's markets for goods, services, and financial products. This is followed by a description of the balance-of-payments (BoP) accounting system used to measure cross-border trade flows. The rest of the chapter is devoted to the international monetary system; that is, to the global network of commercial and governmental institutions within which exchange rates are determined. The international monetary system is influenced by national laws, regulations, policies, and practices, and by supranational organizations such as the International Monetary Fund (IMF) and the World Bank.

## 2.1 INTEGRATION OF THE WORLD'S MARKETS

The world's markets for goods, services, and financial assets and liabilities have become increasingly integrated across national boundaries during the past several decades. An ***integrated market*** is one in which equivalent assets sell for the same price in every location. In ***segmented markets,*** the price of an asset is not necessarily the same in all markets. Factors that contribute to market segmentation include transaction costs, regulatory and institutional interference, informational barriers, and labor immobility. As barriers to trade progressively fall, foreign markets are playing an increasingly important role in the viability of domestic industries and the global economy.

*Markets are becoming more integrated across national borders.*

### Cross-Border Integration of Markets for Goods and Services

The pessimistic tone of daily news reports about efforts to integrate world trade highlights the substantial barriers to a truly global economy. Yet viewed through the long lens of history, trade barriers today are lower than ever. In the goods markets, the world's businesses are turning to foreign sales, foreign sourcing, foreign direct investment, and cross-border partnerships as paths toward business consolidation and expansion. The markets for services also have seen an explosion of cross-border trade, particularly in telecommunications, information technology, and financial services. This increasing globalization has been hastened by many trends and events.

- The global trend toward free-market economies and an international equity culture
- The rise of regional and global trade pacts, including the 1995 creation of the ***World Trade Organization (WTO)*** for the negotiation and resolution of trade disputes
- The 1991 breakup of the Soviet Union, the reunification of East and West Germany, and the migration of many Central and Eastern European countries toward the ***European Union (EU)***
- The emergence of China as a major economic power and international trading partner, symbolized by China's 2001 entry into the WTO
- The rapid industrialization of the Far East and Pacific Rim
- The 1999 creation of the euro, and its adoption by an expanding set of European countries

Foreign trade is a mainstay of industrialized economies as they struggle for market share in a competitive global marketplace. Foreign trade is equally important to emerging markets, as they strive to develop their industrial bases and increase local living standards. National governments reduce trade barriers through trade agreements that provide a forum for peacefully resolving trade disputes between member nations. These pacts promote economic growth and stability.

Figure 2.1 lists the world's major trade agreements. There are ongoing discussions aimed at extending these pacts. ***EU*** enlargement has expanded the EU to 27 countries, with a growing number of ***Eurozone*** nations adopting the euro (€) as their currency. There are ongoing efforts to link ***North America's Free Trade Agreement (NAFTA)*** with South America's ***Union of South American Nations (UNASUR)***. There are also active bilateral and regional trade talks in Africa, Asia, and the Middle East.

Developing economies often undergo a "life cycle" of industrial growth. In developing countries without a rich endowment of natural resources such as oil, early growth tends to be based on labor cost advantages. As countries industrialize and labor costs increase, labor-intensive industries begin to migrate toward countries with even lower labor costs, and developing economies find themselves directly competing with industrialized economies. This transition from a low-tech, labor-driven economy into a globally competitive, capital-intensive, high-tech economy is difficult, and these countries face vexing social and public policy issues as their workforce lays claim to the newfound wealth.[1]

Cross-border trade is becoming increasingly important to the world economy. Figure 2.2 shows the growth in U.S. imports and exports of merchandise trade from 1960–2010, restated in 2010 dollars. Other nations have experienced similar growth in cross-border trade, with some countries experiencing even more rapid growth.

| | |
|---|---|
| ASEAN – Association of South-East Asian Nations(www.aseansec.org) | Brunei Darussalam, Cambodia, Indonesia, Laos, Malaysia, Myanmar, Philippines, Singapore, Thailand, and Vietnam |
| APEC – Asia-Pacific Economic Cooperation (www.apec.org) | 21 Pacific Rim members including Australia, Canada, China, Indonesia, Japan, Korea, Malaysia, Russia, and the United States |
| AU – African Union (www.au.int) | Includes all 54 states on the African continent |
| CIS – Commonwealth of Independent States (www.cisstat.com/eng) | Several members of the former Soviet Union including Armenia, Azerbaijan, Belarus, Kazakhstan, Kyrgyzstan, Moldova, Russia, Tajikistan, Turkmenistan, Ukraine, and Uzbekistan |
| EU (http://europa.eu/index_en.htm) | 27 members in a pan-European market (see Figure 2.7)<br>17 countries use the euro (symbol €) as their currency |
| NAFTA | Canada, Mexico, and the United States |
| OPEC – Organization of Petroleum Exporting Countries (www.opec.org) | Algeria, Angola, Ecuador, Iran, Iraq, Kuwait, Libya, Nigeria, Qatar, Saudi Arabia, United Arab Emirates, and Venezuela |
| UNASUR (www.unasursg.org) | An agreement combining Mercosur (Argentina, Brazil, Paraguay, Uruguay) and the Andean Community (Bolivia, Colombia, Ecuador, and Peru) with several other states (Chile, Guyana, Suriname, and Venezuela) |
| WTO (www.wto.org) | In 1994, 121 nations signed the Uruguay Round of the General Agreement on Tariffs and Trade (GATT). GATT slashed tariffs, established intellectual property protection, and created a dispute resolution process. The WTO — with more than 150 members — now oversees the agreement. |

**FIGURE 2.1** The World's Major Economic Cooperation and Free Trade Agreements

Globalization has an enormous influence on individuals and their societies. Globalization increases interdependence among national economies and leads to business cycles that are regional or global in nature. Globalization also changes the business environment within and across a country's borders, creating both opportunities and challenges for multinational corporations.

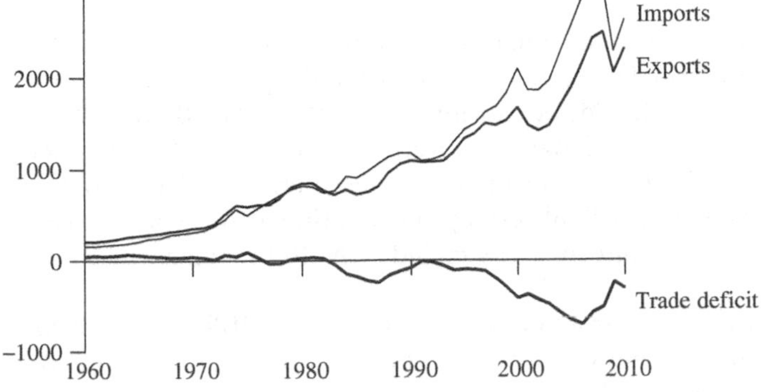


**FIGURE 2.2** U.S. Merchandise Trade (in billions of 2010 U.S. dollars)
*Source:* Trade figures from www.bea.gov are restated in 2010 dollars using CPI deflators from www.bls.gov.

### Cross-Border Integration of the World's Financial Markets

Integration is proceeding at an even faster pace in financial markets as advances in electronic communication and data processing reduce physical and institutional barriers to the free flow of capital. Developments in information technology (IT) and telecommunications have been especially important in hastening the integration of international financial markets. Trading in currency derivatives continues to enjoy explosive growth. Although some of this growth is a consequence of the growth in import and export trade, a considerable portion is due to the introduction of new financial markets and instruments that facilitate trade and the transfer of ownership, risks, and returns.

*IT assists financial market integration.*

Along with the reduction of barriers in the world's goods markets, the demise of capital flow barriers in international financial markets has had several consequences.

- An increase in cross-border financing as multinational corporations (MNCs) raise capital in whichever market and in whatever currency offers the most attractive rates (see Chapter 14)
- Increasingly interdependent national financial markets, including an increasing number of cooperative linkages among securities exchanges (see Chapters 5–7 and 18)
- An increasing number of cross-border partnerships, including many international mergers, acquisitions, and joint ventures (see Chapter 17)

The global financial crisis of 2008 provides a striking example of the interdependence of the world's financial markets and reminds us that we all live on the same small planet.

## 2.2 BALANCE-OF-PAYMENTS STATISTICS

In July 1944, representatives of the allied nations convened at Bretton Woods, New Hampshire, to create a postwar financial system that would promote world trade and avoid a repetition of the worldwide depression of the 1930s. The ***Bretton Woods Conference*** created the International Bank for Reconstruction and Development, now known as the ***World Bank,*** to help in the reconstruction and development of its member nations. The World Bank Group has continued to evolve since its establishment at Bretton Woods and currently includes the following agencies:

- International Bank for Reconstruction and Development (IBRD), which promotes development in poor-but-creditworthy countries through loans, guarantees, and advisory services
- International Development Association (IDA), which provides loans or credit to poor countries
- International Finance Corporation (IFC), which promotes private-sector investment

- Multilateral Investment Guarantee Agency (MIGA), which promotes investment in developing countries by offering political risk insurance
- International Centre for the Settlement of Investment Disputes (ICSID)

> ***The IMF and the World Bank were created at Bretton Woods in 1944.***

Bretton Woods also created the ***IMF*** to provide assistance to countries trying to defend their currencies against temporary trade or supply/demand imbalances. The IMF is a huge supranational organization with an annual budget of close to $1 billion. The IMF compiles and publishes a monthly summary of (***BoP***) **statistics** that track each country's cross-border flow of goods, services, and capital.

> ***BoP statistics track cross-border trade.***

Figure 2.3 presents BoP accounts for the United States on an annual basis. BoP statistics show a country's inflows (+) and outflows (−) of goods, services, and capital. The accounts of most interest are: (1) the trade balance, (2) the current account, and (3) the financial account.

The ***trade balance*** measures whether a country is a net importer or exporter of goods. Exports are a positive number while imports are negative, so a ***trade surplus***

| | 2000 | 2001 | 2002 | 2003 | 2004 | 2005 | 2006 | 2007 | 2008 | 2009 | 2010 |
|---|---|---|---|---|---|---|---|---|---|---|---|
| Goods: Exports f.o.b. | 772 | 719 | 683 | 713 | 808 | 895 | 1024 | 1164 | 1309 | 1073 | 1293 |
| Goods: Imports f.o.b. | −1224 | −1146 | −1167 | −1261 | −1473 | −1677 | −1860 | −1985 | −2141 | −1577 | −1937 |
| **Trade Balance** | −452 | −427 | −484 | −547 | −665 | −783 | −836 | −820 | −832 | −504 | −644 |
| Services: Credit | 292 | 279 | 289 | 309 | 344 | 381 | 413 | 484 | 530 | 498 | 541 |
| Services: Debit | −219 | −210 | −240 | −257 | −296 | −315 | −342 | −366 | −397 | −369 | −393 |
| Balance on Goods & Services | −379 | −358 | −436 | −495 | −618 | −717 | −765 | −702 | −699 | −375 | −496 |
| Income: Credit | 353 | 284 | 245 | 310 | 380 | 475 | 622 | 830 | 797 | 588 | 662 |
| Income: Debit | −331 | −269 | −257 | −264 | −349 | −463 | −629 | −730 | −645 | −467 | −499 |
| Balance on Goods, Services, & Income | −357 | −344 | −447 | −449 | −587 | −705 | −773 | −603 | −547 | −253 | −333 |
| Current transfers: Net | −53 | −49 | −56 | −71 | −81 | −86 | −84 | −116 | −122 | −125 | −137 |
| **Current Account** | −410 | −393 | −503 | −520 | −668 | −792 | −857 | −718 | −669 | −378 | −470 |
| Capital account: Net | 1 | 1 | 1 | −3 | −2 | −4 | −4 | 0 | 6 | 0 | 0 |
| Direct Investment Abroad | −178 | −128 | −124 | −141 | −252 | −9 | −249 | −414 | −351 | −269 | −346 |
| Direct Invest from Abroad | 308 | 131 | 30 | 67 | 107 | 110 | 184 | 271 | 328 | 135 | 194 |
| Portfolio Investment Assets | −278 | −109 | −26 | −180 | −251 | −224 | −322 | −391 | 286 | −393 | −144 |
| Portfolio Invest Liabilities | 552 | 482 | 388 | 430 | 601 | 704 | 827 | 1157 | 520 | 367 | 757 |
| Other Investment Assets | −150 | −134 | −6 | −8 | −352 | −193 | −475 | −671 | 226 | 574 | −533 |
| Other Investment Liabilities | 156 | 140 | 213 | 392 | 732 | 399 | 754 | 680 | −394 | −196 | 293 |
| **Financial Account** | 409 | 382 | 474 | 561 | 585 | 785 | 719 | 638 | 583 | 268 | 237 |
| Net Errors and Omissions | 0 | 11 | 29 | −38 | 85 | 10 | 141 | 80 | 85 | 163 | 235 |

**FIGURE 2.3** U.S. Balance of Payments (billions of U.S. dollars)
*Source:* IMF (www.imf.org). Figures may not add due to rounding. The term *f.o.b.* stands for "free-on-board" and indicates that the values of imports and exports are measured at the border of the exporting country.

(a balance greater than zero) indicates that residents are exporting more than they are importing. Conversely, a ***trade deficit*** (a trade balance less than zero) means that residents are importing more goods than they are exporting. The trade balance is important to fiscal and monetary authorities because higher exports mean higher employment in the domestic economy. During 2010, U.S. imports and exports of goods were $1,937 billion and $1,293 billion, respectively, for a trade deficit of $644 billion. The United States has run a trade deficit every year since 1978.

Figure 2.4 provides estimates of 2010 trade balances for a cross-section of countries. Gross domestic product (GDP) and GDP per capita also are shown for reference. Some countries, such as the United States (−$633 billion) and the United Kingdom (−$141 billion) were net importers during 2010. Other countries were net exporters, including Germany (+$217 billion), China (+$199 billion), Russia (+$139 billion), Saudi Arabia (+$136 billion), and Japan (+$128 billion).

The ***current account*** is a broader measure of import-export activity that includes the trade balance on goods, as well as services, royalties, patent payments, travel and tourism, employee compensation, individual investment income, gifts, and grants. The U.S. current account deficit was $470 billion in 2010 according to the U.S. Bureau of Economic Analysis (www.bea.gov). The United States has had a current account deficit every year since 1981.

The ***financial account*** covers cross-border transactions associated with changes in ownership of financial assets and liabilities. Within these accounts, the "direct investment" accounts include inflows and outflows of direct investment capital such as equity capital, reinvested earnings, and intercompany transactions between affiliated parties. "Portfolio investment" includes cross-border transactions associated with long-term debt and equity securities, money market instruments, and derivative instruments. "Other investment" reflects other financial transactions, including foreign currency deposits, loans, and trade credits. The financial account is the sum of these transactions. The United States has run a financial account surplus for many years, with more money being attracted to the United States than invested abroad.

| | Exports | Imports | Trade balance | GDP | GDP per capita | | Exports | Imports | Trade balance | GDP | GDP per capita |
|---|---|---|---|---|---|---|---|---|---|---|---|
| European Union | 1.952 | 1.690 | 0.262 | 14.910 | 29,645 | Indonesia | 0.146 | 0.111 | 0.035 | 1.033 | 4,206 |
| United States | 1.270 | 1.903 | −0.633 | 14.720 | 46,994 | Turkey | 0.117 | 0.166 | −0.049 | 0.958 | 12,163 |
| China | 1.506 | 1.307 | 0.199 | 9.872 | 7,385 | Australia | 0.211 | 0.200 | 0.010 | 0.890 | 40,870 |
| Japan | 0.765 | 0.637 | 0.128 | 4.338 | 34,299 | Iran | 0.079 | 0.059 | 0.020 | 0.864 | 11,086 |
| India | 0.201 | 0.327 | −0.126 | 4.046 | 3,402 | Taiwan | 0.275 | 0.251 | 0.023 | 0.824 | 35,697 |
| Germany | 1.337 | 1.120 | 0.217 | 2.960 | 36,332 | Poland | 0.161 | 0.167 | −0.007 | 0.725 | 18,865 |
| Russia | 0.377 | 0.237 | 0.139 | 2.229 | 16,066 | Netherlands | 0.451 | 0.408 | 0.043 | 0.680 | 40,387 |
| Brazil | 0.200 | 0.188 | 0.012 | 2.194 | 10,785 | Saudi Arabia | 0.235 | 0.099 | 0.136 | 0.623 | 23,822 |
| United Kingdom | 0.406 | 0.547 | −0.141 | 2.189 | 34,913 | Argentina | 0.068 | 0.053 | 0.015 | 0.596 | 14,269 |
| France | 0.509 | 0.578 | −0.069 | 2.160 | 33,072 | Thailand | 0.191 | 0.157 | 0.034 | 0.580 | 8,698 |
| Italy | 0.458 | 0.460 | −0.001 | 1.782 | 29,205 | South Africa | 0.077 | 0.077 | 0.000 | 0.528 | 10,764 |
| Mexico | 0.303 | 0.306 | −0.003 | 1.560 | 13,717 | Egypt | 0.025 | 0.000 | 0.025 | 0.501 | 6,103 |
| South Korea | 0.466 | 0.418 | 0.048 | 1.467 | 30,089 | Pakistan | 0.020 | 0.033 | −0.012 | 0.451 | 2,408 |
| Spain | 0.268 | 0.325 | −0.056 | 1.376 | 29,430 | Colombia | 1.506 | 1.307 | 0.199 | 0.432 | 9,657 |
| Canada | 0.407 | 0.406 | 0.000 | 1.335 | 39,229 | Malaysia | 0.210 | 0.174 | 0.036 | 0.417 | 14,505 |

**FIGURE 2.4** Trade Balances during 2010 by Country (trillions of U.S. dollars)
*Source:* CIA Factbook (www.cia.gov). The figure lists trade balances in the 29 countries with the largest 2010 GDP, with the EU added for comparison. All accounts except GDP per capita are in trillions of U.S. dollars.

As the name suggests, the BoP is a double-entry system that is intended to record both sides of every cross-border transaction. Because only one side of a transaction typically is reported to the local monetary authorities, the BoP includes a "net errors and omissions" account to ensure that inflows equal outflows. This account is an attempt to infer cross-border activity from imbalances elsewhere in the BoP. Illegal drug trafficking, for example, is unlikely to be reported by the traffickers. Purchases and sales of short-term financial claims also are often unreported and can account for a sizable proportion of the "net errors and omissions" account. Errors and omissions were \$235 billion in the United States during 2010, or about 1.6 percent of the \$14.72 trillion in U.S. GDP.

## 2.3 EXCHANGE RATE SYSTEMS

Figure 2.5 presents the IMF's classification of exchange rate arrangements. The IMF has had a difficult time creating this classification system because exchange rates interact with monetary policy, and exchange rate arrangements can be fluid and complex. Many governments intervene in the currency markets in the pursuit of their fiscal and monetary policy objectives, and policy objectives themselves change for political and economic reasons.

The IMF's current classification system identifies three broad categories: hard pegs, soft pegs, and floating arrangements.[2] A hard peg at one end of the spectrum reduces the ability of a nation's central bank to influence monetary policy. A floating arrangement at the other end relies on market forces to determine currency values in a competitive marketplace. Rather than delve into the nuances of the IMF's classification scheme, we'll focus on the two textbook extremes of fixed (pegged) and floating exchange rates.

**Fixed Exchange Rate Systems** In a fixed (or pegged) exchange rate system, governments try to force currency values on market participants. If they can be maintained, fixed rate systems reduce exposure to currency risk for companies conducting cross-border trade. For instance, if a domestic exporter agrees to supply goods to a foreign importer in exchange for an amount of foreign currency payable in three months, the exporter knows exactly how much the foreign currency will be worth in three months under a fixed exchange rate system.

> *Governments set exchange rates in pegged systems.*

Exchange rate changes in a fixed rate system are called ***devaluations*** when one currency falls in relation to another currency and ***revaluations*** when that currency rises in value. For example, if the Chinese government changes the official exchange rate from \$0.13095/CNY to \$0.13099/CNY, the Chinese new yuan (CNY) has had a revaluation against the dollar. At the same time, the dollar has had a devaluation from CNY7.6364/\$ (the reciprocal of \$0.13095/CNY) to CNY7.6341/\$ against

| | Hard pegs | Soft pegs | Floating arrangements |
|---|---|---|---|
| | Exchange arrangements with no separate legal tender, and currency board arrangements | Conventional peg arrangements, stabilized arrangements, crawling pegs, crawl-like arrangements, and pegs within horizontal bands | Floating (largely market determined and without exchange rate targets) Free floating (market determined with very infrequent intervention) |
| **Africa** | Djibouti | Angola, Bangladesh, Botswana, Cape Verde, Comoros, Eritrea, Ethiopia, Lesotho, Libya, Malawi, Morocco, Namibia, Rwanda, Seychelles, Sierra Leone, Swaziland, Tunisia, Yemen, Zimbabwe<br>*CAEMC*: Cameroon, Chad, Congo, Central African Rep., Gabon, Equatorial Guinea<br>*WAEMU*: Benin, Burkina Faso, Côte d'Ivoire, Guinea-Bissau, Mali, Niger, Senegal, Togo | Burundi, Congo, Egypt, Ghana, Kenya, Guinea, Liberia, Mauritania, Mauritius, Gambia, Madagascar, Mozambique, Nigeria, São Tomé & Príncipe, Somalia, South Africa, Sudan, Tanzania, Uganda, Zambia |
| **Asia & Pacific regions** | Brunei Darussalam, Kiribati, Micronesia, Marshall Islands, Palau, Timor-Leste, Hong Kong SAR | Bhutan, China, Fiji, Maldives, Mongolia, Nepal, Samoa, Solomon Islands, Sri Lanka, Tonga, Vietnam | Afghanistan, Australia, Cambodia, India, Indonesia, Japan, Korea, Laos, Malaysia, Myanmar, Pakistan, New Zealand, Papua New Guinea, Philippines, Singapore, Thailand, Vanuatu |
| **Europe** | Bosnia and Herzegovina, Bulgaria, Lithuania, Montenegro, San Marino | Azerbaijan, Belarus, Croatia, Denmark, Kazakhstan, Macedonia, Russian Fed., Tajikistan, Turkmenistan, Uzbekistan | Albania, Algeria, Armenia, Georgia, Czech Rep., Hungary, Iceland, Kyrgyz Rep., Moldova, Norway, Poland, Romania, Serbia, Sweden, Switzerland, Ukraine, United Kingdom<br>*Eurozone*: Austria, Belgium, Cyprus, Latvia, Slovakia, Finland, France, Germany, Greece, Ireland, Italy, Luxembourg, Malta, Netherlands, Portugal, Slovenia, Spain |
| **Middle East** | | Bahrain, Iran, Iraq, Jordan, Kuwait, Lebanon, Oman, Qatar, Saudi Arabia, Syria, United Arab Emirates | Israel, Turkey |
| **Americas** | Ecuador, El Salvador, Panama<br>*ECCU*: Dominica, Grenada, Antigua & Barbuda, St. Lucia, St. Kitts & Nevis, St. Vincent & the Grenadines | Argentina, Aruba, Bahamas, Barbados, Belize, Bolivia, Costa Rica, Guyana, Honduras, Netherlands Antilles, Nicaragua, Suriname, Trinidad & Tobago, Venezuela | Brazil, Canada, Chile, Colombia, Dominican Rep., Guatemala, Haiti, Jamaica, Mexico, Paraguay, Peru, United States, Uruguay |

**FIGURE 2.5** IMF Classifications of Exchange Rate Regimes
*Source:* IMF (www.imf.org). CAEMC—Central African Economic and Monetary Community. ECCU—Eastern Caribbean Currency Union. WAEMU—West African Economic and Monetary Union.

the yuan. Sometimes these changes are planned, such as when a pegged system automatically adjusts to inflation differences with the currency serving as the peg. At other times, the market might force a government to change its peg.

> *Fixed exchange rates link employment to inflation.*

There are two major drawbacks to a fixed exchange rate system. First, fixed exchange rates forge a direct link between inflation and employment. Suppose Chinese inflation is high relative to Indonesian inflation in a fixed exchange rate regime. The yuan prices of Chinese goods will rise at a fast rate with relatively high yuan inflation, while prices in Indonesia will increase at the lower rupiah inflation rate. With a fixed exchange rate between yuan and rupiah, Chinese products will become relatively more expensive than Indonesia's products in international markets. Eventually, consumers will shift purchases away from high-priced Chinese goods and toward low-priced Indonesian goods. This in turn shifts employment away from China and toward Indonesia, resulting in rising unemployment in China and rising employment in Indonesia. As employment shifts toward Indonesia, Chinese wages will fall and Indonesian wages will rise. In this way, a fixed exchange rate system links cross-country inflation differences to wage levels and employment conditions.

The second drawback of a fixed exchange rate system is the difficulty of sustaining fixed exchange rates when they diverge from market rates. By standing ready to buy or sell currencies at official exchange rates, governments are attempting to preempt the function of the forex (FX) market. If an official rate differs from the market rate, the government will suffer a loss of value as counterparties attempt to buy the undervalued currency and sell the overvalued currency at the official rate. If a government refuses to trade at the official exchange rate, it impedes the cross-border flow of goods, services, and capital. Governments cannot indefinitely impose their will on financial markets; the markets ultimately prevail. And when a devaluation arrives in a fixed rate system, it is often a whopper.

Governments are most adamant about maintaining fixed rates when their currency is under pressure because it is overvalued. Devaluations typically come on the heels of claims that the government has full confidence in the currency and will maintain the fixed rate system at all costs. This only encourages currency speculators to bet against the beleaguered currency. When overvalued currencies collapse, government officials are quick to blame currency speculators for precipitating the collapse. Because changes tend to come infrequently but in large increments in a fixed exchange rate system, the apparent absence of currency risk is an illusion.

***The apparent absence of currency risk in a fixed rate system is an illusion.***

Many governments nevertheless attempt to peg or manage their currency values in relation to another currency, such as the euro, U.S. dollar, or South African rand, or to a composite index. Denmark attempts to peg the value of the krone within a band around the value of the euro. Saudi Arabia tries to peg the value of the riyal to the dollar because oil—its major export—is globally priced in dollars. Other countries try to maintain a peg to the value of a composite index, such as the IMF's special drawing right. ***Special drawing rights (SDRs)*** are an international reserve account created by the IMF and allocated to member countries to supplement their foreign exchange reserves. SDRs are not actual currencies. Rather, they are bookkeeping units of account that are traded only between central banks as they manage their BoP and foreign exchange positions.

**Floating Rate Systems** Floating exchange rate systems allow currency values to fluctuate according to market supply and demand without direct interference by government authorities. In these systems, there are no official bounds on currency values. Nevertheless, government intervention in the foreign exchange markets can and does have an impact on currency values, especially in the short term. An increase in a currency value under a floating exchange rate system is called an ***appreciation*** and a decrease in a currency value is called a ***depreciation***. As under fixed exchange rates, when one currency rises in value, the other must fall.

*In floating rate systems, values are determined by supply and demand.*

The major advantage of a floating exchange rate system is that changes in inflation, wage levels, and unemployment in one country are not forced on another country, as they are in a fixed exchange rate system. Consider our earlier example of a fixed exchange rate system with higher inflation in China than in Indonesia. With a fixed exchange rate, international consumers eventually will see lower prices on Indonesian goods than on Chinese goods because of higher Chinese inflation and the fixed exchange rate. This will be good for the Indonesian economy and bad for the Chinese economy, unless China can either bring inflation under control or adjust the exchange rate. Floating exchange rates can adjust to the differential inflation, and allow a single worldwide price for goods from all countries. Floating rate systems tend to insulate domestic economies from changes in inflation, wage levels, and unemployment in other countries.

The major disadvantage of a floating rate system is the flip side of its major strength. Because exchange rates change continuously, it is difficult to know how much a future cash flow in a foreign currency will be worth in the domestic currency. The good news with floating rate systems is that the financial markets develop financial contracts (currency forwards, futures, options, and swaps) that allow market participants to hedge their exposures to currency risk.

## 2.4 A BRIEF HISTORY OF THE INTERNATIONAL MONETARY SYSTEM

The international monetary system refers to the global network of governmental and commercial financial institutions within which exchange rates are determined. Figure 2.6 highlights the key events in this system during the past 100 years. The system has evolved through several different exchange rate arrangements during this time. A review of this history will help you to understand how alternative exchange rate systems affect asset values across national borders. This is essential knowledge for managing the financial risks of an investment portfolio or a multinational corporation.

### The International Monetary System before 1944

*Currencies were pegged to gold prior to WWII.*

| Date | Event | Causes and repercussions |
|---|---|---|
| 1914 | Collapse of the classical gold standard | Prior to 1914, gold is used to settle trade balances in a pegged exchange rate system. Breakdown of the system leads to a period of floating exchange rates. |
| 1925 | Gold exchange standard | United Kingdom and United States hold gold reserves. Other currencies are convertible into gold, dollars, or pounds in a pegged exchange rate system. |
| 1930s | Global depression | The gold exchange standard fails and exchange rates begin to float. Protectionist trade policies and the breakdown of the gold exchange standard lead to a global depression. |
| 1944 | Bretton Woods Conference | Price of gold set at $35/ounce. Other currencies are convertible into dollars at pegged rates. The IMF and the World Bank also are created at Bretton Woods. |
| 1971 | Bretton Woods system collapses | Most currencies begin to float. Repeated attempts to resurrect a fixed rate system end in failure. |
| 1976 | Jamaica Agreement | Floating rates declared acceptable, officially endorsing the system in place. |
| 1979 | European Exchange Rate Mechanism (ERM) created | ERM created to maintain currencies within a band around central rates. European Currency Unit (Ecu) created. |
| 1991 | Treaty of Maastricht | European community members agree to pursue a broad agenda of reform leading to European monetary union (Emu) and a single European currency. |
| 1992 | Exchange rate volatility leads to ERM breakdown | Uncertainty over the outcome of Emu ratification votes leads to a breakdown of the ERM. Bands widened to ±15 percent as England and Italy fall out of the system. |
| 1995 | Mexican peso crisis | The peso plummets in value and is allowed to float. The stock market rebounds. |
| 1997 | Asian crisis | Falling currency and asset values in Asian countries cause political upheaval in Indonesia and economic difficulties throughout the region. |
| 1998 | Russia's currency crisis | The value of the ruble plummets along with the values of other Russian assets. The stock market recovers fairly quickly. |
| 1998 | Brazil's currency crisis | The real plummets in value and is allowed to float. The stock market rebounds. |
| 1999 | Euro replaces the Ecu | On January 1, 1999, the euro replaces the Ecu on a one-for-one basis. The currencies of participating Emu countries are pegged to the euro. |
| 2002 | Argentina's currency crisis | The peso plummets in value and is allowed to float. The stock market rebounds. |
| 2002 | Eurozone in force | The euro begins public circulation, replacing the currencies of Emu participants. The expectation is that all EU members eventually will adopt the euro once their economies meet the convergence criteria, although Denmark, Sweden, and the United Kingdom may continue to opt out. |
| 2008 | Global financial crisis | Real and financial asset prices fall in the worst financial crisis since the Great Depression. Governments intervene to provide liquidity to the markets. |

**FIGURE 2.6** A History of the International Monetary System

Prior to 1914, major countries operated on what is known as the ***classical gold standard*** in which gold was used to settle national trade balances. World War I upset this standard and threw the international monetary system into turmoil. In 1925, a ***gold exchange standard*** was instituted in which the United States and England held only gold reserves while other nations held gold, U.S. dollars, or pounds sterling as reserves. Reserves are used by central banks to manage their BoP and foreign exchange positions. The system lasted until 1931, at which time England withdrew under pressure from demands on its reserves as a result of an unrealistically high pound sterling value. To maintain competitiveness most other nations followed England in devaluing their currencies relative to the price of gold.

The global depression of the 1930s was fueled by this breakdown of the international monetary system and by the protectionist trade policies that followed. Currency speculation during this period was rampant, causing wild fluctuations in exchange rates. There was no way to hedge currency risk, because there was not an established forward exchange market at the time. Businesses were at the mercy of a very fickle monetary system.

### Bretton Woods: 1944–1971

In addition to creating the IMF and the World Bank, the Bretton Woods Conference created a fixed or pegged exchange rate system that lasted for 25 years. Under the Bretton Woods system, the price of an ounce of gold was set in U.S. dollars at $35 per ounce. Each nation agreed to maintain a fixed (or pegged) exchange rate for its currency in terms of the dollar or gold. For example, the German mark was set equal to 1/140 of an ounce of gold, or $0.25/DM. Under this form of gold exchange standard, only U.S. dollars were convertible into gold at the official par value of $35 per ounce. Other member nations were not required to exchange their currency for gold, but pledged to intervene in the foreign exchange markets if their currency moved more than 1 percent from its official rate.

*The post-WWII monetary system was relatively stable.*

The Bretton Woods system worked passably well until the late 1960s. Devaluations were common as the market periodically imposed its own values on the world's currencies, but by-and-large the system facilitated cross-border trade and economic development. During the 1960s, U.S. inflation rose as the U.S. government borrowed money to finance the war in Vietnam. High U.S. inflation caused the market price of gold to rise above $35 per ounce and the market value of the dollar to fall below the official rate relative to foreign currencies. A run on the U.S. dollar ensued as speculators (investors, financial institutions, and governments) rushed to buy gold with dollars at the price of $35 per ounce. Finally, on August 15, 1971, President Nixon surrendered to market forces and took the United States off the gold standard. Many currencies were already floating by this time. This date marked the end of the Bretton Woods exchange rate system.

### Exchange Rates after the Fall of Bretton Woods

**Efforts to Resurrect a Pegged Exchange Rate System during the 1970s** After the collapse of Bretton Woods, several unsuccessful attempts were made to resurrect a gold exchange standard. The first of these, the Smithsonian Agreement, was signed in Washington, D.C., by the Group of Ten in December 1971.[3] This agreement devalued the dollar to $38 per ounce of gold and revalued other currencies relative to the dollar. A 4.5 percent band was established to promote monetary stability.

*Currencies began to float in the early 1970s.*

In April 1972, members of the European Economic Community (EEC)—the predecessor to the EU—established a pegged system known as "the snake within the tunnel" or "the snake." The term snake refers to the fact that the pegged currencies floated as a group against non-EEC currencies. The tunnel refers to the band allowed around the central currency rates in the system.

Both the Smithsonian Agreement and the snake proved unworkable in the presence of continued exchange rate volatility. Countries frequently were forced to either devalue their currency or fall out of these pegged systems until an agreement could be reached on a new target price. Realignments were the rule of the day. The Bank of England allowed the pound sterling to float against other currencies in June 1972. The Swiss franc remained in the EEC's exchange rate mechanism until January 1973, at which time it, too, was allowed to float. In February 1973, the U.S. government devalued the dollar from \$38 to \$42.22 per ounce of gold. Currency values fluctuated even more severely following the 1973–1974 OPEC oil embargo.

This was a period of unprecedented financial risk. High volatility in floating exchange rates contributed to high levels of currency risk. Interest rate risk was on the rise as inflation grew in many countries. The OPEC oil embargo resulted in higher oil price risk. Market participants faced a nemesis—financial price volatility—for which they were ill-prepared.

In January 1976, the IMF convened a monetary summit in Jamaica to reach some sort of consensus on the monetary system. Exchange rate volatility was still too high and policy objectives too diverse for governments to form an agreement on a fixed rate or pegged system. However, participants did agree to disagree. Under the Jamaica Agreement, floating exchange rates were declared acceptable, officially acknowledging the system already in place and legitimizing the basis for the floating rate system still used by many countries today.

In 1979, the European snake was replaced by the ***ERM***. The ERM relied on central bank cooperation to maintain currency values within a ±2.25 percent band around ERM central rates. The United Kingdom (England, Northern Ireland, Scotland, and Wales) subsequently was admitted with a ±6 percent band around central rates. The ERM attempted to combine the best of the fixed and floating rate systems. First and foremost, currency risk was reduced because exchange rates tended to remain relatively stable within the ERM. The system did not require the highly restrictive monetary policies that accompany a fixed rate system, as the band allowed some movement around the central rate. Allowable currency movements varied in the ERM for different currencies and at different times. The German mark, historically the most stable of Europe's currencies, usually was kept within a band of ±2.5 percent around the central rate. If a currency moved outside its ERM range, EU central banks would either cooperate in buying the currency to keep it within its ERM band, reset the allowable band around the central exchange rate, or revalue the currency within the ERM.

**The U.S. Dollar during the 1980s** During the mid-1980s, the dollar rose in value relative to other currencies. During this time, foreign governments complained that the high value of the dollar was causing inflation in their economies because of the high prices of U.S. imports. The U.S. government complained of a widening trade deficit due to the poor competitive position of high-priced U.S. goods. The dollar reached its high in early 1985, climbing to DM3.50/\$ against the German mark.

In September 1985, the Group of Ten met in New York and agreed to cooperate in bringing down the value of the dollar and controlling exchange rate volatility. In fact, the dollar had already begun to devalue during the spring and summer of 1985. By February 1987, the dollar had fallen to what many believed to be its equilibrium value. At that time, the Group of Five (France, Germany, Japan, the United Kingdom, and the United States) met in France and agreed to promote stability in currency markets around current levels.

**The 1991 Treaty of Maastricht and European Monetary Union** The most important international monetary development of the past half century is the *Emu*, which aims for economic and monetary union within Emu countries. To achieve this objective, 17 EU countries have exchanged their currencies for the euro (€). Figure 2.7 displays the members of the EU and lists the ***Eurozone*** countries that have adopted the euro.

The timetable for Emu was established in the 1991 Treaty of Maastricht and included the following dates:

- 1999: The euro replaced the Ecu in the ERM, becoming a unit of account but not yet a physical currency. The exchange rates of participating countries were pegged to the euro at that time.
- 2002: The euro began public circulation alongside national currencies on January 1, and then replaced the currencies of participating countries on July 1, 2002.

Voters in Austria, Belgium, Finland, France, Germany, Ireland, Italy, Luxembourg, the Netherlands, Portugal, and Spain ratified the Maastricht Treaty. Voters

EU members (27)
Austria, Belgium, Bulgaria, Czech Republic, Cyprus, Denmark, Estonia, Finland, France, Germany, Greece, Hungary, Ireland, Italy, Latvia, Lithuania, Luxembourg, Malta, the Netherlands, Poland, Portugal, Romania, Slovakia, Slovenia, Spain, Sweden, United Kingdom

Participants in the Eurozone (€)
Austria, Belgium, Cyprus, Estonia, Finland, France, Germany, Greece, Ireland, Italy, Luxembourg, Malta, the Netherlands, Portugal, Slovakia, Slovenia, Spain

Planned expansion of the Eurozone
Bulgaria, Czech Republic, Hungary, Latvia, Lithuania, Poland, Romania

Chose to opt out of the Eurozone
Denmark, Sweden, United Kingdom

Not participating: Switzerland

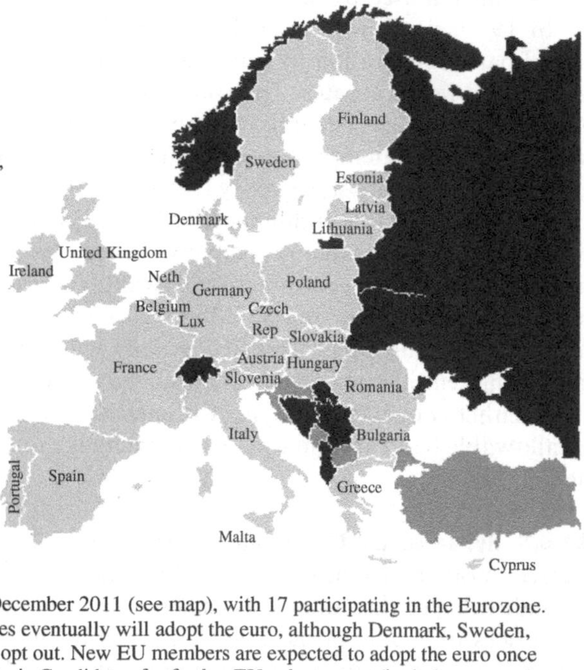


There were 27 members in the EU as of December 2011 (see map), with 17 participating in the Eurozone. The expectation is that all 27 member states eventually will adopt the euro, although Denmark, Sweden, and the United Kingdom may continue to opt out. New EU members are expected to adopt the euro once their economies meet the convergence criteria.Candidates for further EU enlargement (in dark gray on the map) include Croatia, Iceland (not shown), Macedonia, Montenegro, and Turkey.

**FIGURE 2.7** The European Union and the Eurozone
*Source:* European Union (http://europa.eu/index_en.htm).

in Denmark, Sweden, and the United Kingdom rejected the treaty, but retained the option of joining Emu at a later date.

A single-currency zone is viable only if the participating countries have similar economic and monetary policies. The Maastricht Treaty established the following ***convergence criteria*** for entry into the Eurozone to ensure relatively homogenous economic and monetary conditions in participating countries:

- Inflation rates within 1.5 percent of the three best-performing EU countries
- Budget deficits no higher than 3 percent of GDP
- Exchange rate stability within the ERM for at least two years
- Long-term interest rates within 2 percent of the three best-performing EU countries
- Government debt less than 60 percent of GDP

The most important criteria are low inflation, low budget deficits, and exchange rate stability.

By the end of 1997, there was convergence in inflation, interest rates, and budget deficits in the participating Emu countries. According to the European Commission, average EU inflation was 1.6 percent in 1997. The average budget deficit fell from 6.1 percent of GDP in 1993 to just 2.4 percent in 1997. Budget deficits were 3 percent or less in each participating country. There was less convergence in the amount of public debt outstanding. Only 3 of the 11 Emu participants met the 60 percent debt limit of the Maastricht Treaty, with Belgium (122.2 percent of GDP) and Italy (121.6 percent) the worst offenders. Greece did not meet any of the treaty's convergence criteria and was unable to join until 2001. New EU members are expected to adopt the euro once they have met the convergence criteria. Indeed, the Eurozone recently has been expanded to include Estonia, Malta, Slovakia, and Slovenia.

*Countries adopting the euro must meet convergence criteria.*

The largest impediments to Emu remain the divergent monetary, fiscal, political, and social conditions within participating countries. Some countries, such as Germany, enjoy high standards of living, while others have much lower average incomes. Workers in high-wage countries are vulnerable to competition from elsewhere within Europe as monetary union equalizes wages across the continent. Workers in less well-to-do countries that have been protected from foreign competition by their national government are also at risk. The hope is that increased trade and general consumer welfare will more than compensate for these local losses.

The EU is comparable to the United States in size and trading power; each contributes about one-fifth of the world's GDP. The next largest producer is China, accounting for about 13 percent of the world's GDP. The EU's 27 countries contain about 500 million people, compared with 1.3 billion in China, 1.2 billion in India, more than 300 million in the United States, and about 125 million in Japan.

## Currency Crises and the Role of the IMF

*The IMF's goal is to promote financial stability.*

According to the Bretton Woods agreement, the mission of the IMF is to make short-term loans to countries with temporary funding shortages. The IMF has assisted many countries in times of stress, such as during the oil shocks of the 1970s, the debt crises of the 1980s, and the currency crises of the 1990s. Proponents of the IMF claim that these interventions promote financial stability, while critics claim that the IMF's medicine—in the form of currency devaluations, austerity programs, or other arrangements—can be worse than the disease.

This section describes several currency and stock market crises that illustrate the role of the IMF in helping countries achieve economic stability. In each crisis, conditions were triggered by

- A fixed or pegged exchange rate system that overvalued the local currency
- A large amount of foreign currency debt

In each case, the government depleted its foreign currency reserves in defense of the currency and was unable to maintain the fixed exchange rate.

**The Mexican Peso Crisis of 1995** During December 1994 and January 1995, the Mexican peso lost nearly 50 percent of its value against the U.S. dollar. The stock market also fell by nearly half in local (peso) terms during this time. The combined effect of the peso depreciation and stock market crash was a 70 percent drop in the dollar value of Mexican stocks. Figure 2.8 displays the real (inflation-adjusted) value

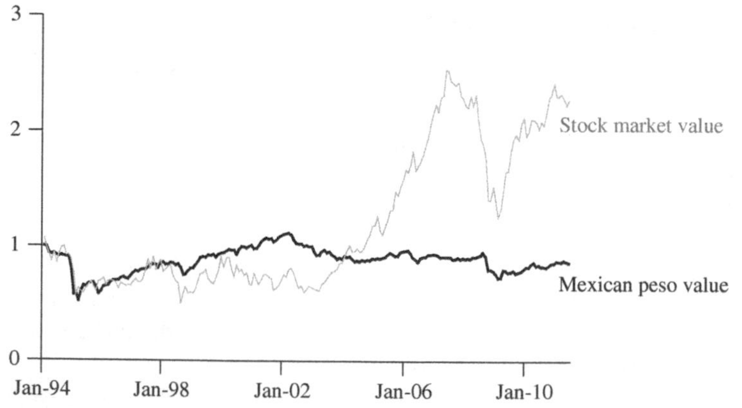


**FIGURE 2.8** The Mexican Peso Crisis of 1995
*Source:* The equity index (from www.msci.com) and exchange rate (from www.bis.org/statistics/eer/) are stated in real (inflation-adjusted) terms to adjust for relative changes in the purchasing power of the peso. (See Section 4.5 for an explanation.) Values start from a base of 1.00 on December 31, 1993.

of the peso from the Bank for International Settlements (www.bis.org). The value of the Mexican stock market also is inflation adjusted, based on monthly inflation from the IMF (www.imf.org).

The Mexican peso crisis caught many investors by surprise. The Mexican economy had been thriving during the 1980s and early 1990s as Mexico liberalized its economy in a series of economic and market reforms. The government had slashed its trade and investment barriers through agreements such as the NAFTA and had privatized nearly 1,000 companies in industries including petroleum and telecommunications. The government had maintained a balanced budget since 1987, and inflation had been reduced from 150 percent in 1987 to 27 percent in 1994. Despite these positive trends, the Mexican government made two critical mistakes that precipitated the crisis.

*Mexico's crisis was aggravated by foreign currency debt.*

- The government had maintained the value of the peso at artificially high levels by buying pesos on international markets. As a consequence, Mexico's foreign currency reserves fell from $30 billion in early 1994 to only $5 billion by November 1994.
- Mexican banks and the government had rolled over $23 billion of short-term, peso-denominated debt into short-term securities called tesebonos, whose principal was indexed to the value of the dollar. The peso value of these obligations rose and fell with the dollar.

With only $5 billion in foreign exchange reserves and $23 billion in short-term dollar-denominated liabilities, Mexico was deeply exposed to a fall in the value of the peso.

The peso came under increasing pressure in late 1994 as Mexico's foreign exchange reserves were depleted. Eventually, the government concluded that the exchange rate could not be sustained. On December 20, 1994, the government announced a 30 percent devaluation of the peso. The market value of the peso continued to fall as investors pulled out of Mexican assets. The resulting 50 percent fall of the peso against the dollar doubled the peso value of Mexico's short-term, dollar-denominated tesebono obligations.

Mexico's peso crisis was essentially a crisis of short-term liquidity; the economy and the underlying fiscal condition of the country were in relatively good shape. To assist Mexico in meeting its obligations, the United States and the IMF assembled a standby credit of $40 billion. With financial liquidity ensured, the Mexican economy rebounded in 1995. Although 1995 GDP was 7 percent below 1994 levels, the low value of the peso helped increase exports by 30 percent and decrease imports by 10 percent. As a result, Mexico's trade balance rose from a deficit of $18.5 billion in 1994 to a surplus of $7.4 billion in 1995. Mexico's peso crisis was severe but short-lived. The peso has been fairly stable since the crisis, and the devaluation of the peso allowed Mexico's stock market to soar relatively quickly after the 1995 peso crisis. Mexico paid the balance of its IMF loan in 2000.

**Continuing Troubles in South America** Brazil experienced a currency crisis beginning in 1998 (see Figure 2.9). Brazil is the world's fifth largest country both in population and in landmass. Like Mexico, Brazil had financed its budget deficits with foreign currency debt, accumulating a balance of more than $250 billion. Brazil spent $50 billion in support of the Brazilian real's crawling peg during 1998 in an attempt to support the value of the real. The government ran out of foreign currency reserves in November 1998 and negotiated a $42 billion IMF loan that called for fiscal and monetary restraint. The Brazilian real nevertheless was devalued in November 1998 and allowed to float shortly thereafter. By 2002, Brazil owed more than $16 billion to the IMF. After several years of severe recession, Brazil was able to weather the storm and repay the balance of its IMF loans in 2005.

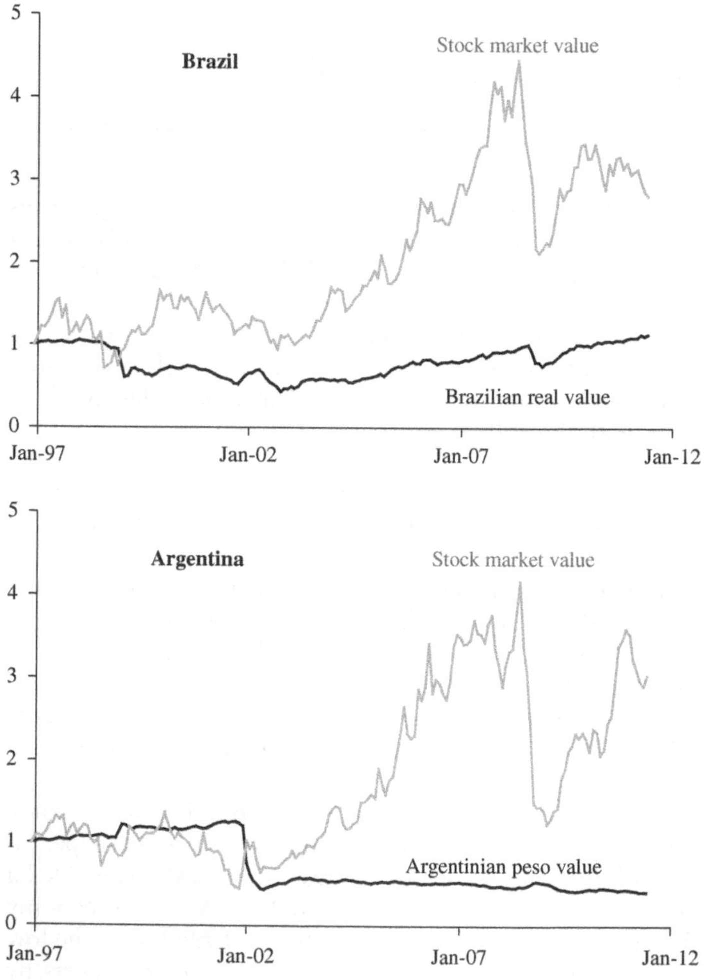


**FIGURE 2.9** Crises in Brazil and Argentina
*Source:* Equity indices (from www.msci.com) and exchange rates (from www.bis.org/statistics/eer/) are stated in real (inflation-adjusted) terms to adjust for relative changes in purchasing power. (See Section 4.5 for an explanation.) Values start from a base of 1.00 on December 31, 1996.

Argentina followed Brazil with a crisis of its own, shown in Figure 2.9. A currency board had pegged the peso one-for-one to the dollar since 1991. Although this had cured the country's hyperinflation (3000 percent in 1989), the overvalued peso contributed to a severe depression beginning in 1998 that is visible in Figure 2.9 as a plummeting stock market. As in Brazil, the government had financed its budget deficits with foreign currency debt, accumulating a balance of more than $150 billion. The government was forced to devalue the peso in January 2002 and eventually allowed the peso to float, despite an IMF-sponsored $40 billion standby line of credit. As its currency was devalued, Argentina added to its existing IMF loans, bringing its total indebtedness to more than $10 billion by 2003. The stock market rebounded during this time, eventually climbing back to its previous high. Argentina was able to repay its IMF loans in 2006.

**The Asian Contagion of 1997** In May 1997, the Thai baht came under pressure as speculators bet against the currency, which was pegged to a currency basket. Foreign currency reserves were exhausted as the Bank of Thailand defended the baht, falling from nearly $40 billion at year-end 1996 to less than $10 billion by July 1997. Thailand allowed the baht to float on July 2, 1997. By the end of 1997, the baht had lost nearly 50 percent of its value against the dollar (Figure 2.10).

Thailand suffered from several problems, including a current account deficit that was 8 percent of GDP, massive short-term foreign currency borrowings used to support speculative property ventures in Thailand, and declining competitiveness

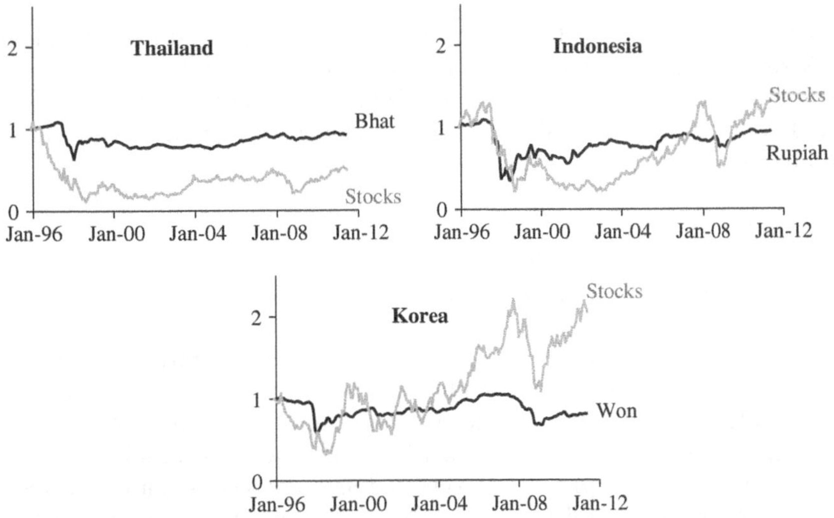


**FIGURE 2.10** The Asian Contagion of 1997
*Source:* Equity indices (from www.msci.com) and exchange rates (from www.bis.org/statistics/eer/) are stated in real (inflation-adjusted) terms to adjust for relative changes in purchasing power. (See Section 4.5 for an explanation.) Values start from a base of 1.00 on December 31, 1995. Equity values appear as a light line and currency values appear as a dark line.

brought on by rising wages. Faced with these problems, investors lost confidence and Thailand's property and stock markets fell. By the end of the year, the Thai stock market had lost more than 50 percent of its value. Because of the depth of the crisis, Thailand's stock market still has not recovered to its 1995 level.

The "Asian contagion" soon spread to Indonesia. Like Thailand, Indonesia had a pegged exchange rate, a large current account deficit, massive short-term foreign currency debt (much of it used for speculative property ventures in Indonesia), and declining competitiveness because of the inflated value of the rupiah. The rupiah fell steadily throughout the second half of 1997, losing more than 75 percent of its value against the dollar. Investors lost confidence in Indonesia's ability to repay its foreign debt, and Indonesia's stock market fell by 33 percent near the end of 1997. The lower value of the rupiah eventually reinvigorated Indonesia's economy, and the stock market is now up nearly 300 percent from its 1995 value.

South Korea's won was the next to fall in 1997. As in Thailand and Indonesia, South Korea's economic situation was undermined by a pegged exchange rate, a large current account deficit, and large short-term foreign currency obligations. In contrast to Thailand and Indonesia, the Korean economy was in relatively good shape. Much of the foreign currency debt had been invested in export industries that stood to gain from a drop in the won, as opposed to the speculative property ventures that were popular in Thailand and Indonesia. Despite the competitiveness of the Korean economy, the won lost nearly one-half of its value during the last several months of 1997, falling from \$0.00104/W in October to \$0.00059/W at the end of 1997. The Korean stock market lost more than 50 percent of its value between September 1997 and September 1998. The Korean economy has now largely recovered from the crisis, and the Korean stock market is about 250 percent higher than its value in 1995.

As in Mexico in 1995, the IMF came to the assistance of these troubled economies. With the support of the United States, Europe, and Japan, the IMF assembled standby credit arrangements of \$58 billion for Korea, \$43 billion for Indonesia, and \$17 billion for Thailand. These packages were tied to structural reforms that included:

- Fiscal and monetary restraint
- Liberalization of financial markets
- Increased competition, efficiency, and transparency

Korea implemented significant reforms in banking and corporate governance, and also enjoyed the quickest economic and financial rebound from the 1997 crisis. Thailand also implemented significant reforms, but had a hard time rebounding from the 1997 crisis. Unemployment remained high into the 2000s, and the stock market still has not regained its pre-1997 levels. Indonesia agreed to some reforms, but had less success in their implementation. Nevertheless, the Indonesian stock market quadrupled in value between 2003 and 2008. Each of these countries was able to repay its IMF loans in fairly short order; Korea in 2001, Thailand in 2003, and Indonesia in 2006.

**The Fall of the Russian Ruble in 1998** Russia embarked on a painful transition from a centrally planned to a market economy after the breakup of the Soviet Union in

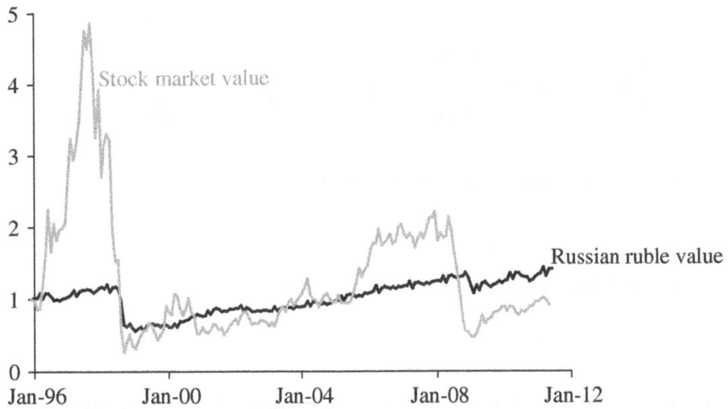

**FIGURE 2.11** Russia's Currency Crisis of 1998
*Source:* The equity index (from www.msci.com) and exchange rate (from www.bis.org/statistics/eer/) are inflation-adjusted. (See Section 4.5 for an explanation.) Values start from a base of 1.00 on December 31, 1995.

1991. Russia's difficulties during this period included hyperinflation, an undeveloped banking system, widespread tax avoidance, corruption, and huge budget deficits. These difficulties caused Russia's GDP to fall from $804 billion in 1991 to only $282 billion in 1998, with a budget deficit of nearly 10 percent of GDP.

In July 1993, Russia placed the ruble in a crawling peg. This stabilized the value of the ruble (Figure 2.11) and reduced inflation from 1700 percent in 1992 to 15 percent by 1997. It also resulted in high real (inflation-adjusted) ruble interest rates. Faced with declining tax revenues, the government financed its fiscal deficit by borrowing in the capital markets. In 1997, Russia began rolling over its ruble-denominated debt into dollar-denominated Eurobonds.

In 1998, the ruble came under speculative pressure as investors reassessed the viability of emerging market investments following the Asian crisis of 1997. By July 1998, Russia was finding it difficult to refinance its dollar debt as it matured. The IMF arranged a $23 billion loan package, but this was not enough to support the ruble. On August 17, 1998, Russia was forced to abandon its exchange rate peg and defaulted on more than $40 billion of debt. By April 1999, Russia owed the IMF nearly $13 billion. The devalued currency helped the Russian economy and stock market recover, and Russia was able to repay its IMF loans in 2004.

**The IMF, International Lending, and Moral Hazard** The IMF's evolution from short-term lender into lender of last resort has sparked an active debate about its proper role during currency crises. Both sides of this debate are interested in ensuring the stability of the international financial system. The sides differ in the means to this end. Proponents of the IMF's policies believe that short-term loans help countries overcome temporary crises, such as Mexico's 1995 peso crisis, and prevent these crises from spreading to other countries. Opponents argue the medicine prescribed by the IMF worsens these crises.[4] These critics believe that fiscal and monetary belt-tightening at the time of a crisis is counterproductive.

- Providing loans so that a government can try to support an unsustainable exchange rate is throwing good money after bad.
- Capital market liberalizations expose developing countries to even more risk.
- IMF remedies benefit creditors from developed countries and not the country in crisis.
- IMF loans can leave a legacy of debt that can last for decades.

*IMF loans influence lenders' and borrowers' expectations.*

Central to this debate from the perspective of the multinational financial manager is the notion of ***moral hazard***—the risk that the existence of a contract will change the behaviors of parties to the contract. In the absence of IMF bailouts, lenders must assess the risks and expected returns of their investments and then bear the consequences. The expectation of an IMF bailout creates a moral hazard in that it changes the expectations and hence the behaviors of borrowers, lenders, and governments. The challenge for the IMF is in developing policies that both promote economic stability and ensure that the consequences of poor investment decisions are borne by investors and not by taxpayers.

Meanwhile, the challenge for the multinational financial manager is in correctly anticipating both market events and the actions of national governments and supranational organizations.

## 2.5 THE GLOBAL FINANCIAL CRISIS OF 2008

The global stock market collapse of 2008 triggered the worst financial crisis since the Great Depression. Global equity values fell by 50 percent in the last half of 2008, although many national markets had recovered most of their value by mid-2011. This collapse and (partial) recovery are visible in Figure 2.8, Figure 2.9, Figure 2.10, and Figure 2.11, where only Brazil and Russia failed to recapture more than half of their equity value by mid-2011. Other asset prices such as real estate also fell at the time of the crisis, and unemployment jumped in most countries. Governments responded to the crisis by pumping liquidity into the financial system to ensure solvency in banking and commerce. Some governments also provided direct aid to key local businesses.

Financial crises are not new. Nations have experienced periods of financial crisis throughout history. These crises share many common elements, particularly plunges in equity and real estate markets.[5] The particular antecedents of the 2008 crisis included a relaxation in U.S. mortgage loan standards and an accompanying bubble in U.S. housing and real estate prices.

The U.S. government promotes affordable housing through easy access to mortgage credit through several government-sponsored enterprises. Two of these—Fannie Mae and Freddie Mac—together own or guarantee about half of the \$12 trillion U.S. mortgage market. Fannie Mae and Freddie Mac are corporations that operate under the guidance of the U.S. government to purchase and then securitize mortgages in the secondary market.

The U.S. government had encouraged lenders to relax credit requirements for homeowners in low- and medium-income brackets in the years preceding the crisis. These loans were securitized into ***collateralized debt obligations (CDOs)*** for resale to investors. A CDO is a special-purpose entity that owns a pool of mortgages as collateral and issues bonds against these assets, often in credit tranches of various maturities and credit risks. CDOs were created by Salomon Brothers and First Boston in 1983 so that Freddie Mac could provide liquidity to the mortgage market.

Unfortunately, securitization provided little incentive for lenders to carefully screen borrowers, as ***subprime loans*** (loans to poor credit risks) could be passed along to other investors through the securitization process rather than held as investments.

*Troubles in U.S. subprime lending triggered the 2008 crisis.*

Poor credit screening increased the default risk of CDOs, particularly after the crisis eroded borrowers' ability to pay. Although securitization provided liquidity to the mortgage market, it also raised housing prices and investors' expectations of further real estate gains. And when it rained, it poured.

***Liquidity*** refers to the ease with which an asset can be exchanged for another asset of equal value. Illiquidity in the subprime CDO market was the first and most visible symptom of the crisis. This illiquidity eventually spilled over to other markets, including real estate, stocks, bonds, commercial paper, and bank lending. Industrial output and employment fell in most major countries, although Brazil and China emerged relatively unscathed. Many countries experienced large budget deficits caused by the drop in tax revenues and the increase in expenses from fiscal stimulus programs. Asset illiquidity and an increase in default risk caused some government bonds—most notably those of Greece and Iceland—to drop sharply in price.

## 2.6 SUMMARY

Cross-border trade is vitally important to all nations. This chapter began by describing the ongoing globalization and integration of the world's markets for goods, services, and capital. We then presented a description of the IMF's BoP statistics that track the flow of goods, services, and capital into and out of each country. The BoP statistics allow multinational financial managers to identify opportunities as well as potential problem areas in the conduct of their foreign and domestic operations.

We then described the difference between fixed and floating exchange rate systems. Exchange rates under fixed rate and pegged systems have occasional large devaluations and revaluations, while exchange rates under a floating rate system have smaller but more continuous depreciations and appreciations.

The chapter concluded with a history of the international monetary system. The currencies of many developed countries have floated since the currency crises of 1971. Attempts to limit exchange rate fluctuations through mechanisms such as the ERM have met with some success, although in the long run currency values are determined by market forces and not by government fiat. This was made painfully obvious in a series of currency crises in Asia, Russia, and Latin America.

The most significant monetary innovation of the past several decades is undoubtedly the 1999 introduction of the euro in Austria, Belgium, Finland, France, Germany, Ireland, Italy, Luxembourg, the Netherlands, Portugal, and Spain. Additional countries were added to the Eurozone (Cyprus, Estonia, Greece, Malta, Slovakia, and Slovenia). The euro created a single-currency zone with GDP about equal to those of China and the United States, and more than twice that of Japan. EU enlargement is providing an avenue for other European states to join the single-currency Eurozone. The global crisis of 2008 is the most significant economic event since the Great Depression. This crisis brought to light the importance of liquidity in financial markets. Without liquidity, markets fail in their price discovery function and are unable to effectively allocate capital.

## KEY TERMS

*appreciation*
*balance-of-payments (BoP) statistics*
*Bretton Woods Conference*
*collateralized debt obligation (CDO)*
*convergence criteria*
*current account*
*depreciation*
*devaluation*
*euro*
*Eurozone*
*European Exchange Rate Mechanism (ERM)*
*European monetary union (Emu)*
*European Union (EU)*
*financial account*
*fixed exchange rate system*
*floating exchange rate system*
*integrated versus segmented markets*
*International Monetary Fund (IMF)*
*international monetary system*
*liquidity*
*moral hazard*
*North American Free Trade Agreement (NAFTA)*
*revaluation*
*special drawing right (SDR)*
*subprime loan*
*trade balance*
*Union of South American Nations (UNASUR)*
*World Bank*
*World Trade Organization (WTO)*

## CONCEPTUAL QUESTIONS

2.1 List one or more trade pacts in which your country is involved. Do these trade pacts affect all residents of your country in the same way? On balance, are these trade pacts good or bad for residents of your country?

2.2 Do countries tend to export more or less of their gross national product today than in years past? What are the reasons for this trend?

2.3 How has globalization in the world's goods markets affected world trade? How has globalization in the world's financial markets affected world trade?

2.4 What distinguishes developed, less developed, and newly industrializing economies?

2.5 Describe the IMF BoP accounting system.

2.6 How would an economist categorize exchange rate systems? How would the IMF make this classification? In what ways are these the same? How are they different?

2.7 Describe the Bretton Woods agreement. How long did the agreement last? What forced its collapse?

2.8 What factors contributed to the Mexican peso crisis of 1995 and to the Asian crises of 1997?

2.9 What is moral hazard, and how does it relate to IMF rescue packages?

2.10 What were the causes and consequences of the global financial crisis of 2008?

## PROBLEMS

2.1 Update the history of the international monetary system from Section 2.4. Have any new international treaties been signed? What currency or market crises have hit since the 2008 crisis? Which countries have struggled since the crisis, and which have rebounded?

## SUGGESTED READINGS

### Globalization and the role of the World Bank and the IMF are discussed in

Joseph Stiglitz, *Globalization and Its Discontents* (New York: Norton, 2002).

### The 2008 financial crisis is compared with earlier financial crises in

Carmen M. Reinhart and Kenneth S. Rogoff, "Is the 2007 U.S. Subprime Crisis So Different? An International Historical Comparison," *American Economic Review* 98 (May 2008), 339–344.

CHAPTER 3

# Foreign Exchange and Eurocurrency Markets

*There was a story about the quantum theorist Werner Heisenberg on his deathbed, declaring that he will have two questions for God: why relativity, and why turbulence. Heisenberg says, "I really think He may have an answer to the first question."*

—James Gleick, *Chaos*

At the heart of the international financial markets is a global network of commercial banks and other financial institutions that conduct markets in foreign exchange and Eurocurrency deposits and loans. The foreign exchange (or currency) market allows currencies to be exchanged at a point in time—either now or at some future date. The Eurocurrency market is a market in bank deposits and loans that allows funds to be borrowed or invested over time within a single currency. In combination, these markets allow capital to be moved across currencies and over time. An understanding of these markets—and of the global network of commercial banks and financial exchanges that link these markets—is essential for understanding the opportunities, costs, and risks of international business.

## 3.1 CHARACTERISTICS OF FINANCIAL MARKETS

***Financial markets*** are markets for financial (as opposed to real) assets and liabilities. Although there are many ways to classify financial markets, a market's most important characteristic is its liquidity. ***Liquidity*** refers to the ease with which you can capture an asset's value. Liquid assets can be quickly converted into their cash value. Liquidity is closely related to transaction volume, with high-volume markets being more liquid than low-volume markets. The interbank currency and Eurocurrency markets enjoy high liquidity in large part because of the high volume of trade.

> ***Liquid assets can be quickly converted into their cash value.***

Another dimension along which financial markets vary is according to maturity.

- ***Money markets*** are markets for financial assets and liabilities of short maturity, usually considered to be less than one year.
- ***Capital markets*** are markets for long-term financial assets and liabilities, typically with maturities of one year or more.

For many financial assets, the difference between short-term and long-term is an arbitrary distinction. For example, a 30-year Treasury bond is a long-term financial asset and is traded in the capital market at the time of its issue. But when the bond is three months from expiration, it is a money market instrument and is priced in the same way that 3-month Treasury bills are priced.

Despite the apparently arbitrary classification of financial markets according to maturity, the distinction is important because market participants tend to gravitate either toward short- or long-term instruments. Bond investors match the maturities of their assets to their liabilities or investment horizons, and so have strong maturity preferences. Banks tend to lend in the short- and intermediate-term markets to offset their short- and intermediate-term liabilities. Life insurance companies and pension funds invest in long-term assets to counterbalance their long-term obligations. The distinction between capital markets and money markets also is often encoded in national regulations governing public securities issues.

Another dimension along which financial markets can be categorized is according to whether they are regulated by a single country.

- Financial contracts in an ***internal market*** are issued in the currency of a host country, placed within that country, and regulated by authorities in that country.
- Financial contracts in an ***external market*** are placed outside the borders of any single country and can be regulated by more than one country or by none at all.

This is an important distinction because it determines regulatory jurisdiction; that is, the regulatory authority or government with jurisdiction over the market.

Finally, financial markets can be categorized according to their operational, informational, and allocational efficiency.

- **Operational efficiency** refers to how large an influence transaction costs have on a market's operation.
- **Informational efficiency** refers to whether market prices reflect information, and thus the "true" or intrinsic value of the underlying asset.
- **Allocational efficiency** refers to how well a financial market channels capital toward its most productive uses.

Because of their high volume and liquidity, the interbank currency and Eurocurrency markets are the most efficient markets in the world.

## 3.2 THE EUROCURRENCY MARKET

Figure 3.1 illustrates the linkages between the domestic credit markets of the United States, the United Kingdom, and Japan. For domestic banks, the bulk of

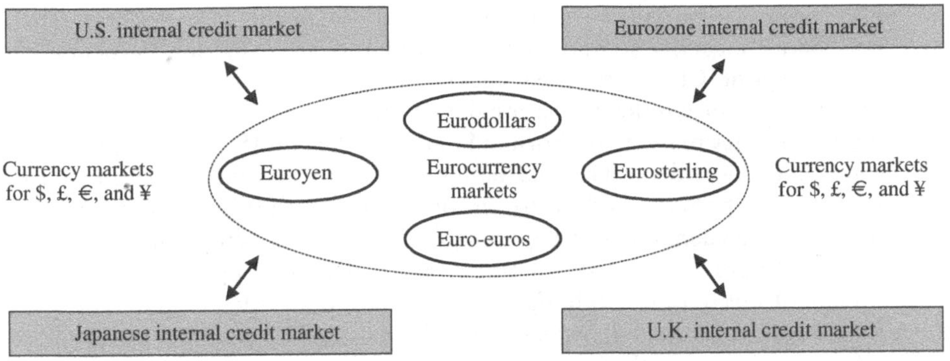


**FIGURE 3.1** Linkages between Domestic Credit and Eurocurrency Markets.

their transactions are with local depositors and borrowers in an internal credit market. Internal credit markets are markets for deposits and loans by domestic residents; hence, they are governed by the rules and institutional conventions of local authorities. A U.S. resident depositing dollars with a U.S. bank is an example of an internal market transaction. Another example of an internal transaction is a Japanese subsidiary of a U.S. firm borrowing Japanese yen from a Japanese bank. Local authorities regulate each of these transactions.

The need for international banking activities arose as commercial banks followed their customers into foreign markets. As cross-border investment became more common early in the 20th century, large banks developed financial services that facilitated the overseas trade of their customers. In addition to commercial credit, banks provide ancillary services such as cash collections, cash management, trade financing, and market-making in foreign exchange. More recently, commercial banks have developed markets in interest rate and currency derivatives, as well as risk management services. Because of their foreign exchange activities, international banks are well positioned to serve as financial intermediaries in multiple credit markets.

External credit markets trade deposits and loans that are denominated in a single currency but are traded outside the borders of the country issuing that currency. Because external credit markets grew up in Europe, they are referred to as ***Eurocurrency markets***.

> ***Eurocurrencies trade in an external credit market.***

Dollar-denominated deposits held in a country other than the United States are called ***Eurodollars***. Similarly, the ***Eurosterling*** credit market resides outside the United Kingdom, and the ***Euroyen*** market resides outside Japan. Eurocurrency markets remain relatively unencumbered by government regulation, because the government issuing the currency has no direct jurisdiction over the deposit, the depositor, or the Euromarket bank.

Eurocurrencies are usually variable rate time deposits with maturities of less than five years. There is an active secondary market for large-denomination Eurocurrency certificates of deposit (CDs) with face values of $100,000 and up. These markets are operated outside of, or parallel to, national credit markets.

The Eurocurrency market was born in London in the late 1950s. At the time, the Soviet Union held dollar deposits in U.S. banks to finance trade with the United States and feared these deposits would be frozen or seized for political reasons. Yet the Soviets needed dollar-denominated deposits to hedge against fluctuations in the value of the dollar. When the Soviets asked London banks to hold deposits denominated in dollars, the banks were only too happy to oblige. The dollar-denominated deposits allowed the banks to make dollar-denominated loans to their customers and helped solidify their dominance of the international banking industry.

Banks making a market in Eurocurrencies quote ***bid rates*** at which they will take deposits and ***offer rates*** or ***ask rates*** at which they will make loans to other Eurocurrency banks. The difference between a bank's offer and bid rates is called the ***bid-ask spread***, and is often less than 1/8 percent for large transactions in major currencies between large commercial banks. About 50 percent of all ***Forex (FX)*** transactions occur through London banks. Dealer quotes are available online from services such as *Quotronix* and *Reuters*.

The London Interbank Bid Rate (LIBID) and the London Interbank Offer Rate (LIBOR) are frequently quoted rates. LIBID and LIBOR are the average bid and offer rates that London banks quote for large transactions with other Euromarket banks. LIBID and LIBOR are quoted for all major currencies, including U.S. dollars, yen, euros, and pounds sterling. Another popular benchmark is the Euro Interbank Offered Rate or Euribor (www.euribor.org), which is based on euro-denominated term deposits between commercial banks within the Eurozone.

> ***LIBOR is a benchmark offer rate for interbank deposits.***

The Eurodollar market is by far the largest Eurocurrency market and is approximately the same size as the domestic U.S. credit market. Eurocurrency markets are active in other major currencies as well, including Eurosterling, Euroyen, and euro-denominated Eurocurrencies (sometimes called "Euro-euros"). Eurocurrency markets are dominated by domestic issuers. For example, U.S. banks and corporations are by far the largest issuers of Eurodollars. The rest of this section describes the most important features of the Eurocurrency market.

## An Absence of Government Interference

Eurocurrency transactions in the external market fall outside the jurisdiction of any single nation. This results in the Eurocurrency market's most distinctive feature: a near-total absence of outside regulatory interference. In most countries, Eurocurrency transactions have no withholding taxes, reserve requirements, interest rate regulations or caps, credit allocation regulations, or deposit insurance requirements. They also tend to have fewer disclosure requirements.

## MARKET UPDATE The Basel Accords on the Capital Adequacy of Commercial Banks

In 1988, the Bank for International Settlements (www.bis.org) convened a meeting of central bankers in Basel, Switzerland, to create a set of regulations governing the capital adequacy of financial institutions such as commercial banks. This accord—now called Basel I—required that banks set aside equity capital as a protection against unforeseen losses according to the credit risk of the borrower (e.g., a government, bank, or corporation). Banks with less than the required equity reserve had to raise capital or shed assets.

Basel II, adopted in 2004, more broadly assessed the various risks faced by commercial banks and introduced three elements or "pillars" of commercial bank regulation.

*Minimum capital requirements* to refine the framework set out in Basel I

*Supervisory review* of capital adequacy and internal assessment processes by regulatory bodies

*Market discipline* through accounting disclosure requirements to encourage sound banking practices

Basel II assessed credit risk based on external ratings (e.g., Standard and Poors (S&P) or Moody's) or on a bank's internal ratings. Unfortunately, Basel II may have contributed to the 2008 financial crisis by increasing capital requirements and thereby reducing bank lending just at the time that credit was most needed. The resulting credit crunch exacerbated the difficulties that companies faced because of their own deteriorating financial conditions.

The financial crisis of 2008 prompted a further review of bank capital adequacy, leverage, and liquidity. The Basel Committee on Banking Supervision (www.bis.org/bcbs) is proposing several changes in a newly proposed standard called Basel III to be implemented over the next several years.

- Strengthen bank capital reserve requirements
- Expand credit risk coverage to include derivatives and other financial securities
- Introduce a financial leverage ratio to supplement Basel II's risk-based framework
- Introduce measures to encourage the accumulation of capital buffers during good times
- Introduce a liquidity standard encompassing both short-term and long-term liquidity

A major thrust of Basel III is to create regulatory policies that are countercyclical to economic and financial fluctuations. Collectively, the three regulatory standards are referred to as the ***Basel Accords.***

Eurocurrencies are not entirely free from government interference. For example, the U.S. SEC Rule 144A on private placements imposes a reserve requirement on dollars deposited from a foreign bank to a U.S. bank. But for deposits and loans that remain offshore, this market remains essentially unregulated by domestic authorities. With market values in the trillions of dollars and few regulatory constraints, this is the world's most competitive and efficient credit market.

### Floating Rate Pricing

In most credit markets, lenders prefer short-term loans because of their liquidity and their lower exposures to interest rate risk and default risk. Consequently, borrowers that prefer long-term loans must pay a premium to attract funds. This supply and demand for loanable funds results in a ***term premium***, and in a term structure of interest rates or "yield curve" (the relation of fixed rate bond yields to bond maturities) that is typically upward sloping.

Eurocurrency deposits are no different, in that Eurocurrency lenders prefer to make short-term, low-risk loans. Because of this preference, Eurocurrencies typically have maturities shorter than five years and interest rates tied to a variable rate base. The short maturity keeps default risk to a minimum. The variable interest rate lowers interest rate risk relative to a fixed rate contract of comparable maturity. LIBOR is the most common variable rate base. Although fixed rate Eurocurrency deposits and loans and Eurocurrencies with maturities longer than five years are available, the interbank market conducts most of its transactions in floating rate Eurocurrency contracts with maturities shorter than five years.

> *Eurocurrencies have short maturities and floating rates.*

### Interest Rates in Domestic Credit and Eurocurrency Markets

Figure 3.2 displays the relation between interest rates in domestic credit markets and Eurocurrency bid and offer rates. The interbank Eurocurrency market is very competitive. The domestic lending rate is greater than LIBOR and the domestic

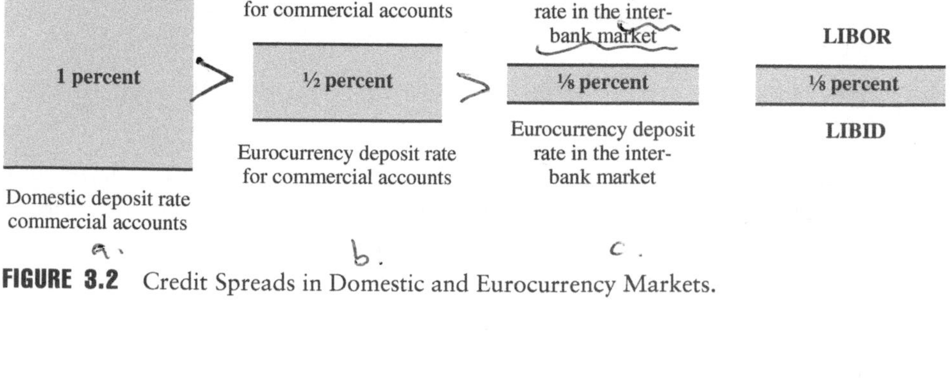


**FIGURE 3.2** Credit Spreads in Domestic and Eurocurrency Markets.

deposit rate is less than LIBID, so the Eurocurrency market pays more interest on deposits and accepts less interest on loans than on comparable transactions in domestic credit markets.

To make a profit, banks purchase funds at low rates and lend them out at higher rates. For example, a bank might pay 1.5 percent per year on the savings account of a depositor and lend these funds out to a small business at 2.5 percent per year. The 1 percent spread is the source of the bank's profit. For large loans to corporate customers in the external Eurocurrency market, the bank might charge 2.25 percent. For large deposits (greater than $1 million) in the external Eurocurrency market, the bank might be willing to pay 1.75 percent. In this case, the bank's spread falls to 0.5 percent (2.25−1.75). Corporate customers with large enough borrowing needs and good enough credit to be able to borrow in this market often find they can improve on the rates they would face in their domestic credit market.

Interest rates extended to corporate borrowers depend on the borrower's creditworthiness and the size of the loan. Interest rates on large loans to AAA-rated corporate borrowers typically are made at a minimum of 15 to 25 basis points (0.15 percent to 0.25 percent) over LIBOR. Larger spreads are charged on smaller loans and on loans to customers with lower credit quality.

Interest rate spreads often are quoted in ***basis points,*** where one basis point is 1/100$^{th}$ of 1 percent (or, sometimes, 1/100$^{th}$ of one cent).

> ***1 percent is equal to 100 basis points.***

A bank might quote borrowing and lending rates of 1.9375 percent and 2.0625 percent on a large transaction with another bank in the Eurocurrency market. At these rates, the bank's bid-ask spread is 0.125 percent, or 12.5 basis points. The bank can afford to quote such a small bid-ask spread for large transactions with a reputable counterparty. Larger spreads would be quoted for smaller amounts, for longer maturities, with banks of lower credit quality, and in volatile market conditions.

### Clearing and Settlement for International Transactions

Transfers between international financial institutions are cleared and settled through the *Society for Worldwide Interbank Financial Telecommunications (SWIFT)* (www.swift.com). SWIFT is an industry-owned cooperative with thousands of members from the commercial banking, asset management, securities, and insurance industries. SWIFT ensures low-cost, secure transmission of electronic messages between member institutions.

## 3.3 THE FOREIGN EXCHANGE MARKET

The *foreign exchange market* allows one currency to be exchanged for another. This market also is referred to as the *currency market* or the *FX market.* The foreign

## MARKET UPDATE Value-at-Risk

Most international banks assess credit risk using a method called ***value-at-risk (VaR)*** that estimates potential losses with a certain level of confidence and over a certain time horizon due to adverse price movements in an underlying asset. For example, a bank might estimate that there is a 5 percent probability of losing more than 20 percent of a loan portfolio's value over the next year. Today, internationally active banks commonly report VaR estimates in their financial reports in response to calls for increased disclosures of banks' risk exposures. There is evidence that these disclosures are indeed informative in that they predict subsequent variability in banks' revenues.[1]

VaR is often criticized because applications based on the normal distribution underestimate the probability of extreme negative events and fail to account for ***correlated default***; that is, the tendency of asset prices to fall in unison. Such events can have a disproportionate impact on economic life and the viability of the international financial system. Indeed, a major point of emphasis in Basel III is to foster the use of risk assessment tools that recognize the existence of correlated defaults. To this end, many contemporary applications of VaR eschew the normality assumption for models that incorporate fat tails and higher-than-normal co-movements in the tails of the return distribution.

exchange market is largely an interbank market that deals in spot and forward currency transactions.

- In the ***spot market,*** trades are made for immediate delivery.
- In the ***forward market,*** trades are made for future delivery according to an agreed-upon delivery date, exchange rate, and amount. The forward currency market can be further categorized into outright forwards and currency swaps.
  - ***Outright forwards*** are transactions involving a single delivery date.
  - ***Currency swaps*** involve multiple future delivery dates and are similar in form and function to portfolios of outright currency forward contracts.

Most interbank transactions are settled through CLS Group Holdings AG (CLS stands for continuous linked settlement), with each counterparty receiving one currency and delivering the other. Forward and swap transactions are settled on the agreed-upon delivery date or dates.

The foreign exchange market is at the heart of international trade and finance, because it permits the transfer of purchasing power from one currency to another—either today or in the future. When used in combination with the Eurocurrency market, spot and forward FX markets allow investors to move capital toward productive uses regardless of the timing of investment or currency of denomination.

The most important function of the foreign exchange market is to provide a means to defend or hedge against exposures to currency risks. ***Foreign exchange risk*** or ***currency risk*** is the risk of unexpected changes in exchange rates. The Multinational Corporation (MNC) is exposed to currency risk if unexpected changes in FX rates affect the value of the firm's assets or liabilities. Hedging can reduce the adverse consequences of currency risk by creating currency exposures that offset the MNC's underlying exposures.

> ***FX risk is the risk of unexpected change in an FX rate.***

The foreign exchange market also allows speculators to bet on changes in currency values. Currency speculation by international banks and hedge funds ensures that FX rates represent a consensus of market participants and provides additional liquidity to the FX markets.

## Foreign Exchange Transaction Volume

The *Bank for International Settlements* (www.bis.org) surveys central banks in April of every third year regarding wholesale foreign exchange activities conducted by that country's residents. Central banks from 53 countries reported foreign exchange transactions in the April 2010 survey.

Figure 3.3 displays the results of the last several surveys. FX transactions averaged nearly $4 trillion per day during April 2010. In comparison, gross domestic product around the world was about $62 trillion during 2010. About 37 percent of FX transactions were in the spot market, 12 percent in outright forwards, and 45 percent in foreign exchange or currency swaps.

Daily volume fell from $1.5 trillion in the 1998 BIS survey to $1.2 trillion in 2001. A small part of this decrease was attributable to the introduction of the euro (€) in 1999. The euro replaced the national currencies of Austria, Belgium, Finland, France, Germany, Greece, Ireland, Italy, Luxembourg, the Netherlands, Portugal, and Spain in 1999 as a step toward European monetary union (Emu). With the elimination of cross-currency trading within these countries, average daily

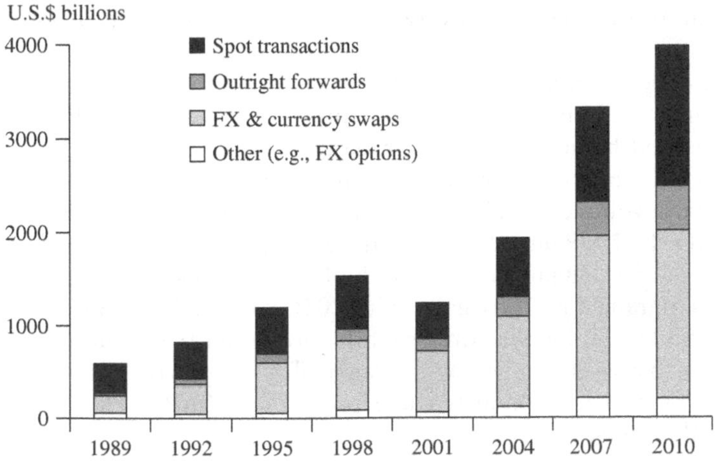


**FIGURE 3.3** Global Foreign Exchange Turnover.
*Source:* Bank for International Settlements Triennial Central Bank Survey, April 2010 (www.bis.org).

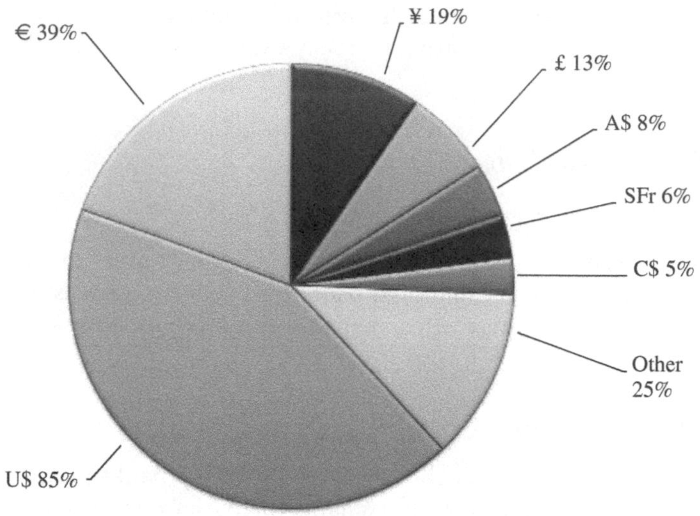


**FIGURE 3.4** Foreign Exchange Turnover by Currency.
*Source:* BIS Triennial Survey, April 2010 (www.bis.org). Percentages sum to 200 percent. Symbols represent Japanese yen (¥), U.K. pound (£), Swiss franc (SFr), Australian (A$), Canadian (C$), and U.S. dollars ($), and euros (€).

volume fell from $332 billion in the 1998 survey to $234 billion in 2001 within the Eurozone.

As shown in Figure 3.4, the U.S. dollar was involved in 84.9 percent of all FX transactions, followed by the euro (39.1 percent), Japanese yen (19.0 percent), British pound (12.9 percent), Australian dollar (7.6 percent), Swiss franc (6.4 percent), and Canadian dollar (5.3 percent). The next most actively traded currencies were the Hong Kong dollar (2.4 percent), Swedish krona (2.2 percent), New Zealand dollar (1.6 percent), Korean won (1.5 percent), Singapore dollar (1.4 percent), Norwegian krone (1.3 percent), and Mexican peso (1.3 percent). These percentages sum to 200 percent rather than 100 percent because two currencies are involved in each transaction.

Figure 3.5 displays the geographic distribution of volume in the five most active markets. London dominated trading with average daily volume of $1,854 billion during April 2010. The next highest volume of trade is in the United States, with average daily volume of $904 billion. Banks in Eurozone countries have a prominent place in the FX market with volume of $477 billion, despite losing trade in currencies within the Eurozone after the 1999 introduction of the euro. Japan's FX volume has rebounded in recent years after languishing during the 1990s because of a lingering recession. Switzerland maintained its 2007 gains with 2010 volume of $263 billion. Japan's daily volume of $312 billion was only slightly more than the $266 billion volume in Singapore, which actively trades a wider range of currencies than is traded in Tokyo. Active markets also are conducted in Hong Kong, Zurich, Frankfurt, Paris, and other regional centers.

## Foreign Exchange Market Participants

Commercial banks serve as *dealers* or *market makers* in the foreign exchange market by quoting ***bid*** and ***offer*** (or ***ask***) ***prices,*** earning their profit by buying at

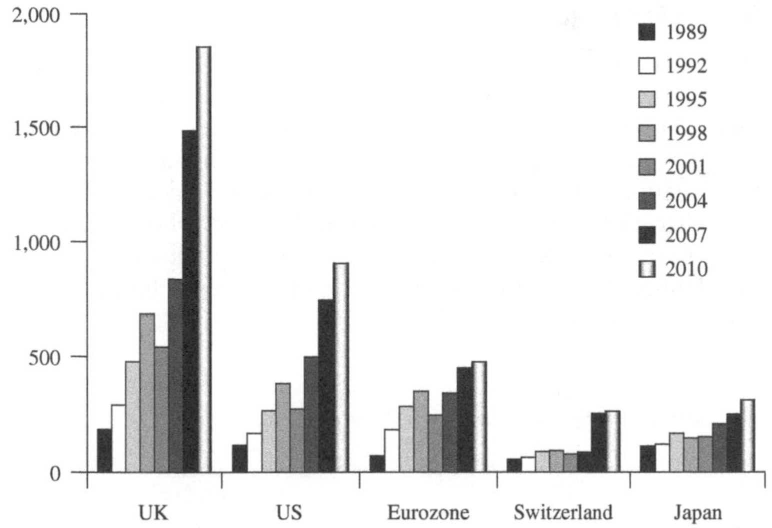


**FIGURE 3.5** Major Foreign Exchange Trading Centers (Average daily volume in billions of U.S. dollars during April).
*Source:* Bank for International Settlements Triennial Central Bank Survey (www.bis.org). Totals are adjusted for local double-counting, but not cross-border double-counting.

their bid price and selling at a slightly higher offer price. ***Bid-ask spreads*** (ask price minus bid price) depend on the size of the transaction, the liquidity and volatility of the currencies, and—for forward transactions—the creditworthiness of the counterparty. Spreads are often as low as a few basis points for large transactions between major banks in the active interbank currency market. Most customers settle the full amount on forward contracts, whereas others choose to settle only the gain or loss.

When a bank buys one currency, it simultaneously sells another currency. A bank has a long position in a particular currency when it has purchased that currency in the spot or forward market. Conversely, a bank is in a short position when it has sold that currency. By aggregating all of its expected future transactions at each forward date, the bank can identify its net position in each currency. In this way, banks can identify and manage their exposures to currency risks.

Whereas dealers take a position, foreign exchange ***brokers*** serve as matchmakers and do not put their own money at risk. Brokers monitor the quotes of major international banks through computerized quotation systems such as *Reuters*, and can quickly identify the banks offering the best rates. A major player, such as a central bank or a large commercial bank, can conceal its identity, and sometimes its intentions, through the use of a broker. For example, if the U.K. Chancellor of the Exchequer wants to dispose of an accumulated position in euros without signaling its activity to the market, it can use a broker to maintain anonymity.

***Banks serve as dealers in an active FX market.***

More than 85 percent of all FX transactions are conducted through commercial banks, credit card companies, or other financial institutions. The remaining business is with retail customers, including governments, businesses, smaller commercial customers, and individuals.

## Efficiency of the Foreign Exchange Market

**Operational Efficiency** The interbank wholesale market is the world's most operationally efficient market, with very low percentage costs for large transactions between major banks. Although the interbank market is operationally efficient, percentage fees on retail transactions can be large. Tourists face bid-ask spreads of 2 to 10 percent at international airports. Fees charged by local vendors outside of airports can be even higher. For example, a tourist might find that a shopkeeper in a resort location is more than happy to accept a nonlocal currency. However, unless she does a quick calculation, she might not notice the 20 percent surcharge hidden in the foreign currency price of a loaf of bread.

> *Operational efficiency refers to the influence of market frictions.*

One way to reduce these charges is to use an ATM card from your local bank. Most ATM cards have access to your local financial account through one or more international communications networks. A range of fees may apply to international cash withdrawals depending on the policies of your financial institution, but are often around 2 percent of the transaction amount. Fees charged by credit card providers such as *Visa* and *MasterCard* vary, but are typically about 3 percent plus applicable finance charges. Check the fees charged on your ATM and credit cards before you travel abroad. Credit card usage may not be advisable when traveling in countries with high rates of credit card fraud, such as Nigeria.

In all countries, you should keep an eye on your card during each transaction and get it back as quickly as possible to avoid losing your credit card information. You also should routinely save your ATM and credit card receipts and reconcile them with your billing statements.

**Informational Efficiency**

> *Informational efficiency refers to whether prices reflect value.*

Through their dealing and trading activities, international commercial banks ensure that currency values represent a consensus of informed opinions and thus promote the informational efficiency of the currency market. The international banks also provide a forum in which market participants can speculate on the direction of changes in currency values. Currency speculators take positions and seek to profit by anticipating the direction of future changes in currency values. Speculation is widely blamed by government officials for contributing to volatility and serving as a destabilizing influence in financial markets. Nevertheless, speculative activity by informed, profit-seeking participants promotes the informational efficiency of financial markets and ensures that prices reflect a consensus estimate of the value of the underlying instruments.

### APPLICATION The notation used in Multinational Finance

**UPPERCASE SYMBOLS ARE USED FOR PRICES Lowercase symbols are used for changes in a price**

- $P_t^d$ = price of an asset in currency d at time t
- $p^d$ = inflation rate (i.e., change in the consumer price index) in currency d
- $i^d$ = nominal interest rate in currency d
- $\text{R}^d$ = real (or inflation-adjusted) interest rate in currency d
- $S_t^{d/f}$ = spot exchange rate between currencies d and f at time t
- $s_t^{d/f}$ = change in the spot rate between currencies d and f during period t
- $F_t^{d/f}$ = forward exchange rate between currencies d and f for exchange at time t
- $f_t^{d/f}$ = change in the forward rate between currencies d and f during period t

Note: Time subscripts are dropped when it is unambiguous to do so.

**Allocational Efficiency** Because of its operational and informational efficiency, the interbank market in major currencies is the most allocationally efficient market in the world. Markets for less liquid currencies are less efficient in their allocation of capital. Fixed exchange rate systems also are less efficient, because governments intentionally disrupt the flow of capital in the pursuit of their policy objectives.

## 3.4 FOREIGN EXCHANGE RATES AND QUOTATIONS

Two simple rules will allow you to make sense of exchange rate quotations.

### Two Rules for Dealing with Foreign Exchange

In most markets, prices are stated as a currency value per unit of good or service. When you purchase a bottle of wine in Germany at a price of €20, the price is quoted as €20/bottle. The starting wage at a winery in Germany might be €10/hour. This is a natural way to state values, because a higher number in the numerator (euros) ascribes a higher value to the item being bought or sold in the denominator (a bottle of wine or an hour's wage).

Here's the rub. Currency transactions involve two currencies, either of which may appear in the denominator. As an example, an exchange rate of \$1.25/€ is equivalent to 1/(\$1.25/€) = €0.80/\$. At this rate of exchange, €10 can be exchanged for (€10)(\$1.25/€) = \$12.50. If you buy euros at \$1.25/€, you are simultaneously selling dollars at €0.80/\$. And, vice versa.

Because two currencies are involved in every currency transaction, it is essential that you keep track of the currency units. If you don't, you'll end up multiplying when you should be dividing. This seems simple enough now, but as our discussion of FX instruments and positions becomes more complex, it will become imperative to include the currency units wherever they appear in an equation. This is such an important point that it has its own rule.

**Rule #1**

Keep track of your currency units.

A related problem in currency trading is in keeping track of which currency is being bought and which is being sold. References to currency values invariably have the value of a single currency in mind. The statement, "The *dollar fell* against the yen," refers to the dollar. Conversely, the statement, "The *yen rose* against the dollar," refers to the yen. The currency that is being referred to is called the ***currency of reference,*** or the ***referent currency.***

Buying or selling currency is like buying or selling any other asset. It is easiest to think of the currency in the *denominator* as the asset being traded. Currency values are then just like the price of any other asset. For example, you could substitute "unit" for dollar and think of the euro price of the dollar as €0.80/unit (or, in this case, €0.80/$). You might just as well be buying bottles of wine.

**Rule #2**

Think of buying or selling the currency in the *denominator* of an exchange rate.

Figure 3.6 provides an example. Suppose you buy 1 million euros at a price of ¥115.4/€ and then sell 1 million euros at a price of ¥115.7/€. Remember, you are buying and selling euros—the currency in the denominator. The net result is that you spend (¥115.4/€)(€1,000,000) = ¥115,400,000 to buy 1 million euros and then sell them for (¥115.7/€)(€1,000,000) = ¥115,700,000, for a profit of ¥300,000.

The bottom panel of Figure 3.6 illustrates what can go wrong. Suppose euro-per-yen rates are quoted as 1/(¥115.7/€) ≈ €0.008643/¥ and 1/(¥115.4/€) ≈ €0.008666/¥. If you buy €1 million (in the numerator!) at the "low" price of €0.008643/¥, your cost is in fact (€1,000,000)(¥115.7/€) = ¥115,700,000. If you then sell at the "high" price of €0.008666/¥, your payoff in yen is (€1,000,000)(¥115.4/€) = ¥115,400,000. This results in a net *loss* of ¥300,000. The simplest way to avoid this pitfall is to follow Rule #2 and think of the denominator as the currency of reference.

Foreign exchange quotations can be easy to understand if you follow these two rules. Make sure that you conscientiously apply them as you practice the end-of-chapter problems. You'll see that following these rules will help you avoid

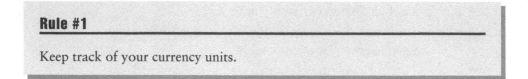

| | | |
|---|---|---|
| Exchange rates $S^{¥/€}$ = ¥115.400/€ | ⇔ | $S^{€/¥}$ = €0.008666/¥ |
| $S^{¥/€}$ = ¥115.700/€ | ⇔ | $S^{€/¥}$ = €0.008643/¥ |
| **An example following Rule #2** | | |
| "Buy €1 at a price of ¥115.400/€ and sell it for ¥115.700/€" | | |
| Buy €1 at ¥115.400/€ | ⇔ | Sell ¥s at €0.008666/¥ |
| Sell €1 at ¥115.700/€ | ⇔ | Buy ¥s at €0.008643/¥ |
| ⇒ ¥0.3/€ profit | | ⇒ €0.000023/¥ profit |
| **An example of what can go wrong** | | |
| "Buy ¥1 at a price of ¥115.400/€ and sell it for ¥115.700/€" | | |
| Buy ¥1 (sell euros) at ¥115.400/€ | ⇔ | Sell €s (buy yen) at €0.008666/¥ |
| Sell ¥1 (buy euros) at ¥115.700/€ | ⇔ | Buy €s (sell yen) at €0.008643/¥ |
| ⇒ ¥0.3/€ **LOSS!** | | ⇒ €0.000023/¥ **LOSS!** |

**FIGURE 3.6** Buying Low and Selling High.

| | Outright quote (European terms) | | Outright quote (American terms) | | Mid-rates quoted* in the financial press | |
|---|---|---|---|---|---|---|
| | Bid | Offer | Bid | Offer | SFr/$ | $/SFr |
| Spot rate | 1.7120 | 1.7130 | 0.5838 | 0.5841 | 1.7125 | 0.5839 |
| 1-month forward | 1.7169 | 1.7179 | 0.5821 | 0.5824 | 1.7174 | 0.5823 |
| 3-month forward | 1.7256 | 1.7267 | 0.5791 | 0.5795 | 1.7261 | 0.5793 |
| 6-month forward | 1.7367 | 1.7379 | 0.5754 | 0.5758 | 1.7373 | 0.5756 |

*Mid-rates are averages of bid and ask rates.

**FIGURE 3.7** Swiss Franc per Dollar Exchange Rate Quotations.

many careless mistakes as the problems become more complex in the chapters that follow.

### Foreign Exchange Quotation Conventions

In practice, FX quotations follow a variety of conventions. Because the referent currency is not always in the denominator, some of these conventions can be difficult to interpret. The two most common conventions distinguish either between the U.S. dollar and another currency, or between the domestic and a foreign currency. These two conventions are described in this section.

**European and American Quotes for the U.S. Dollar** Interbank quotations that include the U.S. dollar conventionally are given in ***European terms,*** which state the foreign currency price of one U.S. dollar, such as a bid price of SFr1.7120/$ for the Swiss franc in Figure 3.7.[2]

> *European terms state the foreign currency price of one U.S. dollar.*

The U.S. dollar is the most frequently traded currency, and this convention is used for all interbank dollar quotes except those involving the British pound or the currencies of a few former colonies of the British Commonwealth. The SFr1.7120/$ quote could be called "Swiss terms." It is convenient to the Swiss in that it treats the foreign currency (the U.S. dollar) just like any other asset. The "buy low and sell high" rule works for a resident of Switzerland that is buying or selling dollars in the denominator of the quote.

When this bank is buying dollars, it is simultaneously selling francs. Consequently, the dollar bid price must equal the Swiss franc ask price. Following Rule #2, we could treat the Swiss franc as the currency of reference and place it in the denominator.

$$S^{\$/SFr} = 1/S^{SFr/\$} = 1/(SFr1.7120/\$) \approx \$0.5841/SFr$$

Conversely, ***American terms*** state the dollar price of a unit of foreign currency. This is convenient to a U.S. resident because the foreign currency (the Swiss franc) is in the denominator.

European and American quotes are not possible for transactions that do not include the U.S. dollar. For these transactions, we need an alternative quotation convention, such as one based on domestic versus foreign (rather than U.S. versus non-U.S.) currencies.

**Direct and Indirect Quotes for Foreign Currency** The most straightforward way to quote bid and offer prices from a domestic perspective is with ***direct quotes,*** stating the price of a unit of foreign currency in domestic currency terms.

> *Direct quotes state the domestic currency price of one unit of foreign currency.*

This is a natural way to quote prices for a domestic resident, because the foreign currency is in the denominator. For a U.S. resident, a direct quote for the Swiss franc might be

$0.5838/SFr Bid and $0.5841/SFr Ask

This bank is willing to buy francs (and sell dollars) at $0.5838/SFr or sell francs (and buy dollars) at $0.5841/SFr. The bank's bid-ask spread is $0.0003/SFr.

Nevertheless, the convention in many countries is to use ***indirect quotes,*** which state the price of a unit of domestic currency in foreign currency terms, such as SFr1.7120/$ for a U.S. resident. For example, an indirect Swiss franc quote to a U.S. resident might be

SFr1.7120/$Bid and SFr1.7130/$ Ask

In this example, the bank is willing to buy dollars in the denominator (and sell francs in the numerator) at the SFr1.7120/$ price. It is also willing to sell dollars (and buy francs) at the SFr1.7130/$ price. The bank's bid-ask spread is SFr.0010/$.

**What If a Quote Doesn't Follow Rule #2?** In this example, the bank could quote

SFr1.7130/$ Bid and SFr1.7120/$ Ask

In this case, the bid is higher than the ask. Does this mean that the bank is willing to lose money on every purchase and sale? Not at all. By quoting a higher bid price than ask price, the bank is indicating that it is willing to buy francs (in the *numerator*!) at SFr1.7130/$ or sell francs at the SFr1.7120/$ rate. This is, of course, equivalent to buying dollars at SFr1.7120/$ and selling dollars at SFr1.7130/$. The rule for determining the currency that is being quoted is as follows:

- When the bid is lower than the offer, the bank is buying and selling the currency in the *denominator* of the quote.
- When the bid is higher than the offer, the bank is buying and selling the currency in the *numerator* of the quote.

Note that this indirect quote to a U.S. resident is equivalent to 1/(SFr1.7120/$) ≈ $0.5841/SFr and 1/(SFr1.7130/$) ≈ $0.5838/SFr. Swiss banks quoting these bid and offer prices to a Swiss resident with an indirect quote might quote

$0.5838/SFr Bid and $0.5841/SFr Ask

This bank is willing to buy Swiss francs (and sell dollars) at 58.38 cents per franc or sell Swiss francs (and buy dollars) at 58.41 cents per franc. Alternatively, the bank might quote

$0.5841/SFr Bid and $0.5838/SFr Ask

which means that the bank is willing to buy dollars (in the numerator) at the bid price and sell dollars (in the numerator) at the ask price. These quotes are equivalent.

Each of these examples makes sense if (and only if) you follow Rule #2 and think of the denominator as the currency of reference.

**The Special Case of the British Pound** Exchange rates for the British pound sterling (and of countries associated with the British empire, such as Australia) often are quoted as the foreign currency price per pound, such as $1.4960/£. The reason for this is historical. Prior to 1971, one British pound was worth 20 shillings and each shilling was worth 12 pence. The convention of keeping the pound in the denominator was convenient at that time because fractions of a pound were not easily translated into shillings and pence.

### Forward Premiums and Discounts

Forward premiums and discounts reflect a currency's forward price relative to its spot price. Again, it is easiest to keep the currency of reference in the denominator of the FX quote.

> *A forward premium is when a forward price is higher than the spot price.*

> - A currency is trading at a ***forward premium*** when the value of that currency in the forward market is *higher* than in the spot market.
> - A currency is trading at a ***forward discount*** when the value of that currency in the forward market is *lower* than in the spot market.

Forward premiums and discounts can be expressed as a basis point spread. If the Swiss franc spot rate is \$0.58390/SFr and the 6-month forward rate is \$0.57560/SFr, then the franc is selling at a 6-month forward discount of \$0.00830/SFr, or 83 basis points (in this case, a basis point is 1/100th of one Swiss cent). Common usage is to speak of the "forward premium" even when the forward rate is at a discount to the spot rate. This saves having to say "forward premium or discount" each time.

Forward premiums also are quoted as a per-period percentage deviation from the spot rate.

$$\text{Foreign currency premium (periodic)} = (F_t^{d/f} - S_0^{d/f})/(S_0^{d/f}) \qquad (3.1)$$

In the example with $S_0^{\$/SFr} = \$0.58390/SFr$ and $F_1^{\$/SFr} = \$0.57560/SFr$ where one period equals six months, the 6-month forward premium is calculated as

$$\begin{aligned}(F_t^{d/f} - S_0^{d/f})/(S_0^{d/f}) &= (\$0.57560/SFr - \$0.58390/SFr)/(\$0.58390/SFr)\\ &= -0.014215\end{aligned}$$

or −1.4215 percent per six months. Note this formula works only for the currency in the denominator.

This 6-month forward premium can be stated as an annual forward premium in several ways. The formula used in the United States and Canada is

$$\textit{Foreign currency premium (annualized)} = (n)[(F_t^{d/f} - S_0^{d/f})]/(S_0^{d/f}) \qquad (3.2)$$

where n is the number of compounding periods per year. Multiplying by n translates the forward premium into an annualized rate with n-period compounding. For example, a 6-month forward premium is annualized by multiplying the 6-month forward premium by n = 2 semiannual periods per year. Similarly, a 1-month forward premium is annualized by multiplying the 1-month forward premium by

$n = 12$. In the example with $S_0^{\$/SFr} = \$0.58390/SFr$ and $F_1^{\$/SFr} = \$0.57560/SFr$, the forward premium is calculated as

$$\begin{aligned}(n)[(F_t^{d/f} - S_0^{d/f})]/(S_0^{d/f}) &= (2)[(\$0.57560/SFr - \$0.58390/SFr)]/(\$0.58390/SFr)\\ &= (-0.014215/\text{period})(2\text{ periods})\\ &= -0.028430\end{aligned}$$

or −2.8430 percent on an annualized basis with semiannual compounding.

In much of the rest of the world, forward premiums are calculated as an effective annual rate, also called an *effective annual percentage rate* (APR), according to

$$\text{Foreign currency premium (APR)} = (F_t^{d/f}/S_0^{d/f})^n - 1 \qquad (3.3)$$

Under this convention, the annual forward premium is

$$\begin{aligned}(F_t^{d/f}/S_0^{d/f})^n - 1 &= ((\$0.57560/SFr)/(\$0.58390/SFr))^2 - 1\\ &= (0.985785)^2 - 1\\ &= -0.028227\end{aligned}$$

or an effective annual rate of −2.8227 percent. This is the same as −2.8430 percent with semiannual compounding, simply stated under an alternative compounding convention.

## Percentage Changes in Foreign Exchange Rates

In a floating exchange rate system, an increase in a currency value is called an *appreciation* and a decrease is a *depreciation*. Changes in currency values in fixed exchange rate systems are called *revaluations* or *devaluations*. Calculation of a percentage change in a FX rate is similar to that of a forward premium. The value of the currency in the denominator of an exchange rate quote changes according to the formula

$$\text{Percentage change in a foreign currency value} = (S_1^{d/f} - S_0^{d/f})/S_0^{d/f} \qquad (3.4)$$

Suppose the dollar-per-franc rate changes from $S_0^{\$/SFr} = \$0.5839/SFr$ to $S_1^{\$/SFr} = \$0.5725/SFr$ over a 6-month period. The percentage change in the Swiss franc in the denominator of the quote is

$$[(\$0.5725/SFr - \$0.5839/SFr)]/(\$0.5839/SFr) \approx -0.0195$$

The Swiss franc in the denominator depreciated 1.95 percent over the 6-month period.

If the franc falls, the dollar must rise. Rule #2 says that to find the dollar appreciation, we first should place the dollar in the denominator. The beginning spot rate is $1/(\$0.5839/\text{SFr}) \approx \text{SFr}1.7126/\$$ and the ending rate is $1/(\$0.5725/\text{SFr}) \approx \text{SFr}1.7467/\$$. The percentage rise in the dollar (in the denominator) is then

$$[(\text{SFr}1.7467/\$ - \text{SFr}1.7126/\$)]/(\text{SFr}1.7126/\$) \approx +0.0199$$

That is, the dollar appreciated 1.99 percent over the 6-month period.

Percentage changes in direct and indirect FX rates are related, as an appreciation in one currency must be offset by a depreciation in the other. Applying the equality $S_t^{d/f} = 1/S_t^{f/d}$ and simplifying the result yields

$$S_1^{d/f}/S_0^{d/f} = 1/(S_1^{f/d}/S_0^{f/d})$$

Alternatively, we can let $(S_1^{d/f}/S_0^{d/f}) = (1 + s^{d/f})$, where $s^{d/f}$ is the percentage change in the d-per-f spot rate during the period. This can then be rewritten as

$$(1 + s^{d/f}) = 1/(1 + s^{f/d}) \tag{3.5}$$

For a +1.99 percent change in the dollar that is offset by a −1.95 percent change in the Swiss franc, the algebra looks like this.

$$(1 + s^{\$/SFr}) = (1 - 0.0195) \approx 1/(1 + 0.0199) = 1/(1 + s^{SFr/\$})$$

Note that an appreciation in one currency is offset by a depreciation of smaller magnitude in the other currency. This asymmetry is an unfortunate but essential part of the algebra of holding period returns.[3]

### A Reminder: Always Follow Rule #2

The intuition "buy low and sell high" works only for the currency in the denominator of a foreign exchange quote. Thus, there is a simple remedy for keeping things straight—just follow Rule #2. If the currency that you would like to reference is in the numerator, simply move it to the denominator according to $S^{d/f} = 1/S^{f/d}$. Following this convention will help you avoid needless confusion. (Actually, this rule is entirely self-serving. If you conscientiously follow Rule #2, your teachers—me included—will be spending less time on the phone answering your questions!)

## 3.5 THE EMPIRICAL BEHAVIOR OF EXCHANGE RATES

### Changes in Exchange Rates

It is useful to describe how exchange rates change over time, because this behavior determines currency risk. A convenient starting point is the process called a random walk. If exchange rates follow a ***random walk,*** then exchange rate changes at a particular point in time are independent of previous changes and are equally likely to rise or fall. That is, there is an equal probability of an appreciation or a depreciation in currency value. There is no memory in a random walk, so once a rate is established there is again an equal probability of an appreciation or a depreciation.

*FX changes are close to a random walk.*

For daily measurement intervals, nominal spot rate changes are close to a random walk with a nearly equal probability of rising or falling. Because of this behavior, the best guess of tomorrow's exchange rate is simply today's exchange rate. The current spot rate outperforms most other exchange rate forecasts for forecasting horizons of up to one year in most currencies. At forecast horizons of longer than one year, forecasts derived from the international parity conditions (see Chapter 4) begin to outperform spot rates as predictors of future exchange rates.

### Time-Varying Exchange Rate Volatility

Empirical studies of exchange rates reject the simplest form of the random walk model. In its place, researchers have modeled exchange rates as a process in which the following is true.

*FX volatility is predictable.*

- Spot rate changes are approximately normally distributed at each point in time.
- Exchange rate volatility (or standard deviation) changes over time in a predictable way.

A time series exhibiting this behavior is frequently modeled as a GARCH process. *GARCH* stands for ***generalized autoregressive conditional heteroskedasticity*** and is a statistician's way of saying "variance (heteroskedasticity) depends (is conditional) on previous (autoregressive) variances." That is, today's variance depends on the recent history of exchange rate changes.

**A GARCH(1,1) Model** The conditional variance of a GARCH(1,1) process at time t is[4]

$$\sigma_t{}^2 = a_0 + a_1\sigma_{t-1}{}^2 + b_1 s_{t-1}{}^2 \tag{3.6}$$

where $a_0$, $a_1$, and $b_1$ are constants constrained so that the process is stable, and

$\sigma_{t-1}{}^2$ = the conditional variance estimate from period $t - 1$,

$s_{t-1}{}^2$ = the square of the percentage change in the spot rate during period $t - 1$.

At each point in time, this GARCH process is normally distributed with conditional (time-varying) variance $\sigma_t{}^2$. The GARCH variance is called an *autoregressive conditional variance* because it depends on last period's variance ($\sigma_{t-1}{}^2$) and the square of the most recent change in the spot exchange rate ($s_{t-1}{}^2$).

The GARCH process includes the random walk as a special case in which the parameters $a_1$ and $b_1$ are zero. In this case, variance $\sigma_t^2$ is a constant equal to $a_0$. Empirical studies of nominal FX rates have rejected the random walk model in favor of GARCH specifications for yearly, monthly, weekly, daily, and intra-day measurement intervals. The particular form of GARCH is not as important as the recognition that volatility is autoregressive; that is, exchange rate volatility depends on recent market history.

***RiskMetrics*' Conditional Volatility Model** The most widely known model for producing conditional volatility estimates is from *RiskMetrics*. The *RiskMetrics* system was created in 1992 by J.P.Morgan (www.jpmorgan.com) to assist clients in assessing and managing exposures to ***financial price risks,*** including currency, interest rate, and commodity price risk. *RiskMetrics* was spun off from J.P.Morgan in 2008 and then acquired by Morgan Stanley (www.msci.com) in 2010. The system provides users with daily data on more than 300 financial price indices including interest rates, exchange rates, commodity prices, and equity market indices. *RiskMetrics* uses a restricted form of Equation 3.6,

$$\sigma_t^{\,2} = a\sigma_{t-1}^{\,2} + (1-a)s_{t-1}^{\,2} \tag{3.7}$$

in which the intercept term is omitted, the autoregressive parameter "a" is bounded by $0 < a < 1$ to ensure that the process is stable, and the parameter weights sum to one: $a + (1 - a) = 1$. For monthly intervals, the standard *RiskMetrics* model assigns a weight of $a = 0.97$ on the most recent conditional variance and a weight of $(1 - a) = 0.03$ on the most recent squared spot rate change. For daily intervals, the model assigns weights of $a = 0.95$ and $(1 - a) = 0.05$. *RiskMetrics*' model is an exponentially weighted moving average in which the impact of past spot rate changes on conditional variance decays at a rate of $(1 - a)(a^t)$.

Figure 3.8 illustrates the *RiskMetrics* model. The left graph displays monthly spot rates $S_t^{¥/\$}$ in the floating rate era since 1971. The dollar tended to fall during this period because dollar inflation was higher than yen inflation. The right-hand graph displays absolute changes in the spot rate $|s_t^{¥/\$}|$ along with the *RiskMetrics* estimate

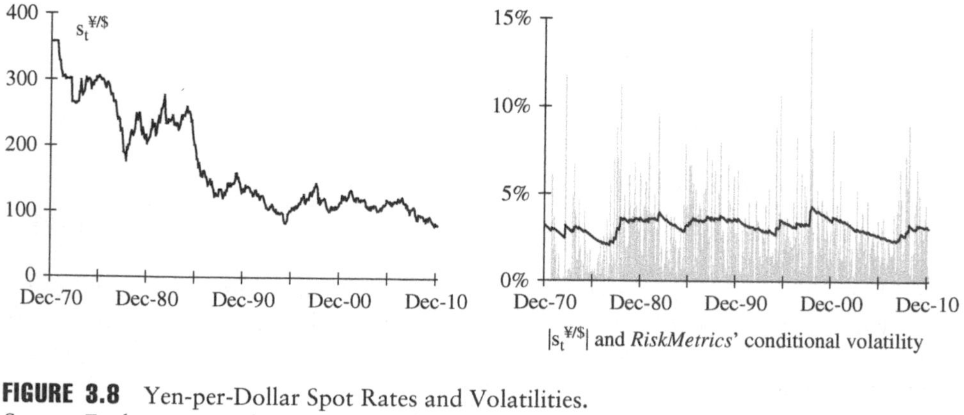


**FIGURE 3.8** Yen-per-Dollar Spot Rates and Volatilities.
*Source:* Exchange rates from www.oanda.com.

of conditional volatility as a black line. *RiskMetrics* conditional volatility rises in periods of high absolute monthly changes in the value of the dollar, such as when the dollar depreciated by 15 percent in October 1998. Conditional volatility falls during less volatile periods, such as in the early years of the 21st century. Conditional volatility estimates are sensitive to market conditions, and that is a useful attribute for a volatility measure that is used to manage exposures to currency risk.

## 3.6 SUMMARY

The interbank currency market is the most liquid and operationally efficient market in the world. Because of low transaction costs and high liquidity, the interbank market is also fairly efficient at pricing and allocating purchasing power across currencies. Exchange rates can be volatile, despite the informational efficiency of the FX market.

The Eurocurrency market is an external credit market in bank deposits and loans, usually in the form of variable rate time deposits with maturities of less than five years. Because they are traded in external markets, Eurocurrencies are not subject to many of the rules that regulatory authorities impose on national credit markets. The Eurocurrency market is the most efficient credit market in the world because of its high volume and liquidity. In combination, the currency and Eurocurrency markets allow capital to flow both across currencies and over time.

Finally, remember these two important rules for dealing in foreign exchange:

**Rule #1:** Keep track of your currency units.

**Rule #2:** Think of buying or selling the currency in the *denominator* of an exchange rate.

Following these rules will help you avoid careless mistakes when dealing with foreign exchange.

### APPLICATION Calculating Appreciations and Depreciations

Equation 3.5 provides a formula for calculating how much a currency appreciates when another depreciates. If you have trouble remembering formulas, here's an alternative method that might be useful.

Suppose $S_t^{¥/\$}$ starts out at ¥100/$ and rises to ¥125/$. This situation can be graphically displayed as

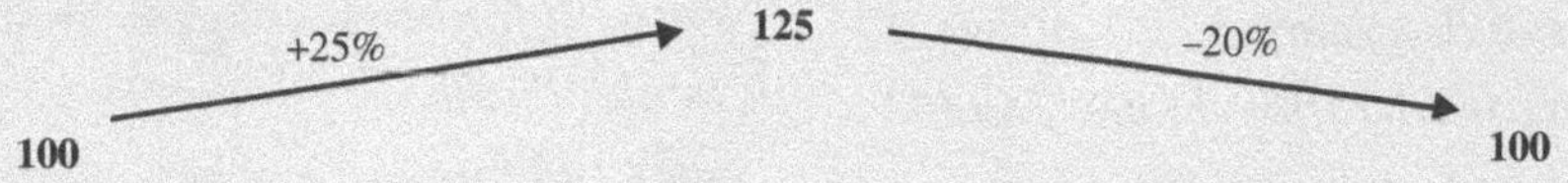


The dollar gains 25 percent on the way up. On the way down, the drop from 125 to 100 corresponds to a change of $(100 - 125)/125 = -0.20$, or

−20 percent in the value of the yen. If the dollar in the denominator appreciates by 25 percent, then the yen must depreciate by 20 percent. This can be verified with Equation 3.5.

$$s^{\$/¥} = 1/(1 + s^{¥/\$}) - 1 = 1/(1.25) - 1 = -0.20, \text{ or } -20 \text{ percent}$$

Let's try the example from the text in which the Swiss franc changes from $0.5839/SFr to $0.5725/SFr. The percentage change in the dollar-per-franc spot rate is

$$[(\$0.5725/\text{SFr} - \$0.5839/\text{SFr})]/(\$0.5839/\text{SFr}) \approx -0.0195$$

or −1.95 percent. If the franc in the denominator falls to (100.00 − 1.95) = 98.05 percent of its beginning value, then the dollar in the numerator must go up accordingly.

A dollar appreciation from 98.05 to 100 results in (100.00 − 98.05) / 98.05 ≈ +0.0199, or +1.99 percent. Although this yields the same result as Equation 3.5, you may find it easier to remember this method than the equation.

## KEY TERMS

*allocational, informational, operational efficiency*
*Basel Accords*
*basis points*
*bid and offer (ask) rates and the bid-ask spread*
*capital vs money markets*
*correlated default*
*currency of reference (referent currency)*
*dealers (market makers) vs brokers*
*direct vs indirect terms*
*Euro Interbank Offered Rate (Euribor)*
*Eurocurrency markets*
*Eurodollars, Eurosterling, and Euroyen markets*
*European vs American terms*
*external vs internal markets*
*financial markets*
*financial price risk*
*foreign exchange (currency) market*
*foreign exchange (currency) risk*
*forward premium or discount*
*GARCH*
*liquidity*
*London Interbank Bid and Offer Rates (LIBID and LIBOR)*
*outright forwards vs currency swaps*
*random walk*
*spot and forward market*
*SWIFT*
*term premium*
*value-at-risk (VaR)*

## CONCEPTUAL QUESTIONS

3.1 Define liquidity.

3.2 What is the difference between a money market and a capital market?

3.3 What is the difference between an internal and an external market?

3.4 What is the Eurocurrency market and what is its function?

3.5 In what way is the Eurocurrency market different from an internal credit market?

3.6 What is the LIBOR?

3.7 What are the Basel Accords? What effects have they had on international banks?

3.8 What is the difference between spot and forward markets for foreign exchange?

3.9 What is Rule #1 when dealing with foreign exchange? Why is it important?

3.10 What is Rule #2 when dealing with foreign exchange? Why is it important?

3.11 What are the functions of the foreign exchange market?

3.12 Define operational, informational, and allocational efficiency.

3.13 What is a forward premium? What is a forward discount?

3.14 Describe the empirical behavior of exchange rates.

## PROBLEMS

3.1 Citigroup quotes Danish kroner as "DKK5.62/$ Bid and DKK5.87/$ Ask."

a. Which currency is Citigroup buying at the DKK5.62/$ bid rate, and which currency is Citigroup selling at the DKK5.87/$ offer rate?
b. What are the bid and ask prices in American terms? Which currency is Citigroup buying at these prices and which currency is Citigroup selling?
c. With the foreign currency in the numerator, the "DKK5.62/$ Bid and DKK5.87/$ Ask" quotes are indirect quotes for a U.S. resident. What are the bid and ask prices in direct terms for a U.S. resident? At these prices, which currency is Citigroup buying and which currency is it selling?
d. If you sell $1 million to Citigroup at a bid price of DKK5.62/$ and simultaneously buy $1 million at their offer price of DKK5.87/$, how many Danish krona ("krona" is the plural of kroner) will you make or lose? What is Citigroup's kroner profit or loss on the transaction?

3.2 You want to buy Swedish krona (SKr). Your bank quotes "SKr7.5050/$ Bid and SKr7.5150/$ Ask." What would you pay in dollars if you bought SKr10,000,000 at the current spot rate?

3.3 The Canadian-U.S. spot rate $S_0^{C\$/\$}$ is quoted as "C$1.2340/$ Bid and C$1.2350/$ Ak." The 6-month forward rate $F_1^{C\$/\$}$ is quoted as "C$1.2382/$

Bid and C$1.2397/$ Ask." Assume you reside in the United States. Calculate forward quotes for the Canadian dollar as an annual percentage premium or discount. Would a FX trader in Canada get a different answer if asked to calculate the annual percentage premium or discount on the U.S. dollar for each forward rate? Why?

3.4 Today's spot rate is $S_0^{\$/¥} = \$0.009057355/¥$. The 90-day forward rate is $F_1^{\$/¥} = \$0.008772945/¥$.

a. Calculate the forward premium on Japanese yen in basis points and as a percentage premium or discount over the 90-day period.
b. Calculate the forward premium on Japanese yen as an annualized percentage premium following the U.S. convention.
c. Calculate the forward premium on Japanese yen as an effective annual percentage rate (APR).

3.5 In 1984, the number of German marks required to buy one U.S. dollar was 1.80. In 1987, the U.S. dollar was worth 2.00 marks. In 1992, the dollar was worth 1.50 marks. In 1997, the dollar was again worth 1.80 marks.

a. What was the percentage appreciation or depreciation of the dollar between 1984 and 1987? Between 1987 and 1992? Between 1992 and 1997?
b. What was the percentage appreciation of the mark between 1984 and 1987? Between 1987 and 1992? Between 1992 and 1997? (*Hint*: Follow Rule #2 and convert $S^{DM/\$}$ to $S^{\$/DM}$.)

3.6 A foreign exchange dealer in Warsaw provides quotes for spot and 3-month forward rates for the Polish zloty against the dollar.

| | Bid (PZ/$) | Ask (PZ/$) |
|---|---|---|
| Spot | 4.0040 | 4.0200 |
| 3-month forward | 3.9690 | 3.9888 |

a. What would you receive in dollars if you sold PZ 5 million at the spot rate?
b. What would it cost in dollars to purchase PZ 20 million forward three months. When would you make payment?

3.7 You have sold ¥104 million at a spot price of ¥104/$. One year later, you pay dollars to buy back ¥104 million at the prevailing spot rate of ¥100/$. How much have you gained or lost in dollars?

3.8 Euro bid and ask prices on the Japanese yen are quoted direct in Paris at €0.007634/¥ Bid and €0.007643/¥ Ask. What are the corresponding indirect quotes for euros?

3.9 Calculate appreciation or depreciation in each of the following:

a. If the dollar depreciates 10 percent against the yen, by what percent does the yen appreciate against the dollar?
b. If the dollar appreciates 1000 percent against the ruble, by what percent does the ruble depreciate against the dollar?

3.10 Dollars are trading at $S_0^{SFr/\$}$ = SFr0.7465/\$ in the spot market. The 90-day forward rate is $F_1^{SFr/\$}$ = SFr0.7432/\$. What is the forward premium on the dollar in basis point terms? What is the forward premium as an annualized percentage rate?

3.11 In what way are these quotes equivalent?

a. "$0.5841/SFr Bid and $0.5852/SFr Ask"
b. "$0.5852/SFr Bid and $0.5841/SFr Ask"

3.12 The Danish kroner is quoted in New York at $0.18536/DKK spot, $0.18519/DKK 30 days forward, $0.18500/DKK 90 days forward, and $0.18488/DKK 180 days forward. Calculate the forward discounts or premiums on the kroner.

3.13 At time $t = 0$ the dollar-per-yen spot rate $S_0^{\$/¥}$ is $0.0100/¥. The yen then appreciates 25.86 percent.

a. What is the closing spot rate in dollars per yen $S_1^{\$/¥}$?
b. By what percentage does the dollar depreciate against the yen?

3.14 Find a formula like Equation 3.1 for calculating a forward premium with currency d in the numerator. [*Hint*: Substitute $S_0^{d/f} = 1/(S_0^{f/d})$ and $F_t^{d/f} = 1/(F_t^{f/d})$ into Equation 3.1 to get currency d in the denominator, and then rearrange and simplify.]

3.15 Suppose you estimate a GARCH(1,1) model of monthly volatility in the value of the dollar and arrive at the following estimates:

$$\sigma_t^2 = 0.0034 + (0.40)\sigma_{t-1}^2 + (0.20)s_{t-1}^2 \tag{3.8}$$

where the conditional variance ($\sigma_{t-1}^2$) and the square of the percentage change in the spot exchange rate ($s_{t-1}^2$) are from the previous period. If $\sigma_{t-1} = 0.05$ and $s_{t-1} = 0.10$, what is the GARCH estimate of conditional volatility?

## SUGGESTED READINGS

### The function and operation of foreign exchange dealers are examined in

Richard K. Lyons, "Profits and Position Control: A Week of FX Dealing," *Journal of International Money and Finance* 17 (February 1998), 97–115.

### Accounting disclosure of value-at-risk estimates is assessed in

Philippe Jorion, "How Informative Are Value-at-Risk Disclosures?" *Accounting Review* 77 (October 2002), 911–931.

### The GARCH conditional volatility model is developed in

Timothy Bollerslev, "Generalized Autoregressive Conditional Heteroskedasticity," *Journal of Econometrics* 31 (April 1986), 307–328.

CHAPTER 4

# The International Parity Conditions and Their Consequences

*Though this be madness, yet there is method in it.*

—William Shakespeare

This chapter describes how prices in the currency and Eurocurrency markets are linked through a set of ***international parity conditions*** that relate forward premiums and expected spot exchange rate changes to cross-currency differentials in nominal interest rates and inflation. These parity relations are then used to develop a measure of a currency's purchasing power relative to other currencies, called the ***real exchange rate.*** The chapter concludes with a discussion of exchange rate forecasting from the international parity conditions and other predictors.

## 4.1 THE LAW OF ONE PRICE

The ***law of one price,*** also known as ***purchasing power parity*** or ***PPP,*** is the single most important concept in international finance and economics.

### The Law of One Price

Equivalent assets sell for the same price.

The implication for multinational finance is that an asset must have the same value regardless of the currency in which value is measured. If PPP does not hold within the bounds of transaction costs, then there is an opportunity to profit from cross-currency differences in price.

***Arbitrage ensures equivalent assets sell for the same price.***

### Arbitrage Profit

*Arbitrage profit has no net investment or risk.*

Although the popular press often uses the term "arbitrage" or "risk arbitrage" to refer to speculative positions, ***arbitrage*** is more strictly defined as a profitable position obtained with

- No net investment
- No risk

This "no money down and no risk" opportunity sounds too good to be true. In the high-stakes interbank currency and Eurocurrency markets, it usually is too good to be true once transaction costs are included. Arbitrage opportunities are quickly exploited, and just as quickly disappear as arbitrageurs drive prices back toward equilibrium.

Let $P^d$ denote the domestic currency price of an asset and $P^f$ denote the foreign currency price of the same asset. The law of one price requires that the value of an asset be the same whether value is measured in the foreign or in the domestic currency. This means that the spot rate of exchange must equate the value in the foreign currency to the value in the domestic currency.

$$\frac{P^d}{P^f} = S^{d/f} \Leftrightarrow P^d = P^f S^{d/f} \tag{4.1}$$

If this equality does not hold within the bounds of transaction costs, then there may be an opportunity for an arbitrage profit.[1]

As an example, suppose gold sells for $P^{\$} = \$1508.00/\text{oz}$ in New York and $P^{£} = £942.50/\text{oz}$ in London. The no-arbitrage condition requires that the value of gold in dollars must equal the value of gold in pounds, so $S^{\$/£} = P^{\$}/P^{£} = (\$1508.00/\text{oz})/(£942.50/\text{oz}) = \$1.6000/£$, or $S^{£/\$} = 1/S^{\$/£} = £0.6250/\$$. If this relation does not hold within the bounds of transaction costs, then there is an opportunity to lock in a riskless arbitrage profit in cross-currency gold transactions.

Transaction costs are relatively small for actively traded financial assets, such as currencies in the interbank market. PPP nearly always holds in these markets, because the potential for arbitrage ensures that prices are in equilibrium. PPP is less likely to hold in illiquid markets, or in markets where high transaction costs or financial market controls prevent arbitrage from enforcing the law of one price.

### Transaction Costs and the No-Arbitrage Condition

For there to be no arbitrage opportunities, PPP must hold within the bounds of transaction costs for identical assets bought or sold simultaneously in two or more locations. This ***no-arbitrage condition*** is the foundation upon which the law of one price is built. Whether PPP holds depends on the extent to which market frictions restrain arbitrage from working its magic. Some barriers to the cross-border flow of capital are generated in the normal course of business, as fees are charged for making a market, providing information, or transporting and delivering an asset. Other barriers are imposed by governmental authorities, including trade barriers, taxes, and financial market controls.

***The no-arbitrage condition ensures PPP holds within the bounds of transaction costs.***

Buying or selling real assets usually entails higher costs than trading a financial claim on the real asset. As an example, gold is costly to transport because of its weight, but a financial asset representing ownership of gold is easily transferred from one party to another and can be as simple as a piece of paper or a credit in an account. Although large amounts of gold are a nuisance to store, currency can be stored conveniently in the Eurocurrency market at a competitive interest rate. Because of this difference between financial and real assets, actively traded financial assets are more likely than similar real assets to conform to the law of one price.

Figure 4.1 illustrates how transaction costs influence the analysis. Suppose gold is quoted at "£930/oz bid and £940/oz ask" in London and "\$1,500/oz bid and \$1,516/oz ask" in New York. A forex (FX) dealer quotes pounds in the spot market as "\$1.599/£ bid and \$1.601/£ ask." Translated into pounds at the \$1.600/£ mid-rate, the New York dealer's mid-price is (\$1,508/oz)/(\$1.600/£) = £942.50/oz. This is slightly higher than the London dealer's mid-price of £935/oz, so if there is an arbitrage opportunity it would likely be to buy gold from the London dealer and sell gold to the New York dealer. Suppose you buy 1,000 ounces of gold for £940,000 at the London dealer's £940/oz ask price for gold. The FX dealer will sell £940,000 to you at the \$1.601/£ ask price for pounds for a payment of (£940,000)(\$1.601/£) = \$1,504,940. Selling the gold in New York yields only \$1,500,000 at the New Yorker dealer's bid price for gold. This leaves you with a net loss of \$4,940 (i.e., a cash inflow of \$1,500,000 and an outflow of \$1,504,940). Even though PPP does not hold exactly, it does hold within the bounds of transaction costs in this example. Unfortunately for your dreams of wealth, the dealers' bid-ask prices overlap each other and an arbitrage profit is not possible.

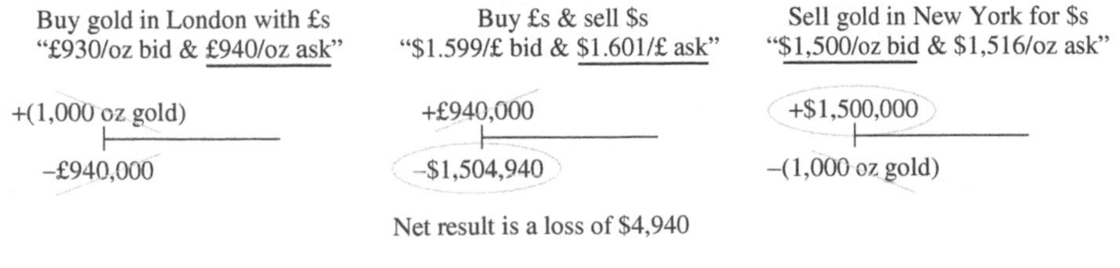


**FIGURE 4.1** The No-Arbitrage Condition in the Gold Market with Transaction Costs.

## 4.2 EXCHANGE RATE EQUILIBRIUM

Spot and forward contracts are traded in liquid interbank markets with few restrictions or market frictions. The potential for arbitrage using actively traded financial contracts ensures that the international parity conditions in Sections 4.2 and 4.3 will hold within the bounds of transaction costs in the interbank markets. These are international parity conditions that you can trust.

### Bilateral Exchange Rate Equilibrium and Locational Arbitrage

*Arbitrage ensures that FX rates are in equilibrium.*

In the absence of market frictions, the no-arbitrage condition for trade in spot exchange rates between two banks X and Y is

$$S^{d/f}(Y) = S^{d/f}(X) \Leftrightarrow \frac{S^{d/f}(Y)}{S^{d/f}(X)} = 1 \tag{4.2}$$

This ensures bilateral exchange rate equilibrium. If this relation does not hold within the bounds of transaction costs, then there is a ***locational arbitrage*** opportunity between the banks.

**An Example of Locational Arbitrage** Consider Figure 4.2, in which Bank X is quoting "A\$0.5838/€ Bid and A\$0.5841/€ Ask" and Bank Y is quoting "A\$0.5842/€ Bid and A\$0.5845/€ Ask." If you buy €1 million from X at its A\$0.5841/€ ask price and simultaneously sell €1 million to Y at its A\$0.5842/€ bid price, you can lock in an arbitrage profit of (A\$0.0001/€)(€1,000,000) = A\$100 with no net investment or risk. Transaction costs are built into the A\$0.0001/€ bid-ask spread, so this profit is free and clear.

If this is a good deal with €1 million, it is even better with a €1 billion transaction. The larger the trade, the larger is the profit. Trading €1 billion rather than €1 million would result in an A\$100,000 arbitrage profit. If you can find such an opportunity, you've likely earned your salary for the day.

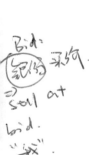

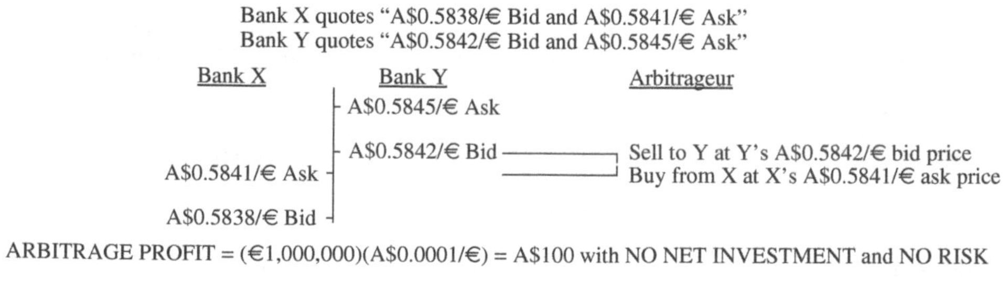


**FIGURE 4.2** Arbitrage Profit in the Foreign Exchange Market.

With FX volume around $2 trillion per day, you can bet your bottom dollar (euro, or yuan) that there are plenty of arbitrageurs looking for opportunities such as these. Dealers are just as vigilant in ensuring that their bid and offer quotes overlap those of other FX dealers. If a bank's bid or offer quotes drift outside of the band defined by other dealers' quotes, it quickly finds itself inundated with buy (sell) orders for its low-priced (high-priced) currencies. Even if banks' quoted rates do not allow arbitrage, banks offering the lowest offer (or highest bid) prices in a currency will attract the bulk of customer purchases (sales) in that currency.

### The Long and the Short of It

*A long position refers to a currency purchase.*

A ***long position*** is synonymous with ownership of an asset. A ***short position*** means the holder of the position has sold the asset with the intention of buying it back at a later time. Long positions benefit if the price of the asset goes up, whereas short positions benefit if the price of the asset goes down. For example, a bank is in a long euro position and a short dollar position when, on balance, it has purchased euros and sold dollars. Conversely, a bank is short euros and long dollars when it has sold euros and purchased dollars. Currency balances must be netted out; if a bank has bought €100 million and sold €120 million in two separate transactions, then its net position is short €20 million. Banks try to minimize their net exposures, because currency dealers operating with large imbalances risk big gains or losses if new information arrives and currency values unexpectedly change.

### Cross Rates and Triangular Arbitrage

An exchange rate that does not involve the domestic currency is called a ***cross exchange rate***, or simply a ***cross rate***. Financial newspapers such as *The Wall Street Journal* and the *London Financial Times* publish bilateral exchange rates in a cross-rate table like the one in Figure 4.3. Cross-rate tables report bid-ask midpoints, so these rates do not represent prices that actually can be traded in the market.

Suppose you are given bilateral exchange rates for currencies d, e, and f. The no-arbitrage condition for ***triangular arbitrage*** in the currency markets is

$$S^{d/e}S^{e/f}S^{f/d} = 1 \tag{4.3}$$

Equation 4.3 can be stated in its reciprocal form $(S^{d/e}S^{e/f}S^{f/d})^{-1} = S^{e/d}S^{f/e}S^{d/f} = 1$. Again, remember to follow Rule #1 and keep track of your currencies. If this condition does not hold within the bounds of transaction costs, then triangular arbitrage provides an opportunity for a riskless profit.

*Triangular arbitrage ensures that cross rates are in equilibrium.*

| Currency | | BRL | GBP | CNY | EUR | INR | JPY | CHF | USD |
|---|---|---|---|---|---|---|---|---|---|
| Brazilian real | BRL | 1 | 1.1804 | 0.2914 | 2.3633 | 0.0347 | 0.0239 | 1.9415 | 1.8357 |
| British pound | GBP | 0.8471 | 1 | 0.1021 | 0.8279 | 0.0122 | 0.0084 | 0.6801 | 0.6430 |
| Chinese new yuan | CNY | 3.4317 | 9.7965 | 1 | 8.1101 | 0.1191 | 0.0819 | 6.6627 | 6.2996 |
| Euro area | EUR | 0.4231 | 1.2079 | 0.1233 | 1 | 0.0147 | 0.0101 | 0.8215 | 0.7768 |
| Indian rupee | INR | 28.806 | 82.234 | 8.3942 | 68.078 | 1 | 0.6877 | 55.928 | 52.880 |
| Japanese yen | JPY | 41.890 | 119.58 | 12.207 | 98.998 | 1.4542 | 1 | 81.330 | 76.898 |
| Swiss franc | CHF | 0.5151 | 1.4703 | 0.1501 | 1.2172 | 0.0179 | 0.0123 | 1 | 0.9455 |
| U.S. dollar | USD | 0.5448 | 1.5551 | 0.1587 | 1.2874 | 0.0189 | 0.0130 | 1.0576 | 1 |

**FIGURE 4.3** Currency Cross Rates.
*Source:* www.federalreserve.gov (January 2012). Exchange rates in this table are left-over-top; that is, the left-hand currency divided by one unit of the currency at the top of the table. For example, the dollar-per-yen spot rate $S^{\$/¥} = \$0.0130/¥$ indicates one yen is worth \$0.0130. Similarly, the yen-per-dollar spot rate $S^{¥/\$} = ¥76.898/\$$ indicates one dollar is worth 76.898 yen. The relation between the two exchange rates is $S^{\$/¥} = 1/S^{¥/\$}$.

**An Example of Triangular Arbitrage** Suppose $S^{\$/¥} = \$0.0130/¥$ and $S^{¥/SFr} = ¥81.330/SFr$ as in Figure 4.3. However, rather than the equilibrium rate of $S^{SFr/\$} = SFr0.9455/\$$ as in Figure 4.3, suppose you can buy dollars (in the denominator of the quote) at a bargain price of $S^{SFr/\$} = SFr0.9400/\$$. The product of the spot rates is less than 1

$$S^{\$/¥}S^{¥/SFr}S^{SFr/\$} = (\$0.0130/¥)(¥81.330/SFr)(SFr0.9400/\$) = 0.9939 < 1$$

and $S^{SFr/\$}$ is too low relative to the cross-currency equilibrium in Figure 4.3. There is an arbitrage opportunity here, so long as transaction costs are not too high.

Suppose you start with \$1 million and simultaneously make the following transactions in a "round turn" (i.e., buying and then selling each currency in turn):

| | |
|---|---|
| Buy ¥ with | $\$(\$1{,}000{,}000)/(\$0.0130/¥) = ¥76{,}923{,}077$ |
| Buy SFr with ¥ | $(¥76{,}923{,}077)/(¥81.330/SFr) = SFr945{,}814$ |
| Buy \$ with SFr | $(SFr945{,}814)/(SFr0.9400/\$) = \$1{,}006{,}185$ |

There is no net investment if you execute these trades simultaneously. So long as your credit is good and your counterparties are trustworthy, each cash outflow in a given currency is covered by an offsetting cash inflow in that same currency. With no net investment and no time delay between trades, you have no money at risk. And, you'll have captured an arbitrage profit of \$6,185.

Suppose you go the wrong way on your round turn and start by purchasing Swiss francs.

| | |
|---|---|
| Buy SFr with \$ | $(\$1{,}000{,}000)(SFr0.9400/\$) = SFr940{,}000$ |
| Buy ¥ with SFr | $(SFr940{,}000)(¥81.330/SFr) = ¥76{,}450{,}200$ |
| Buy \$ with ¥ | $(¥76{,}450{,}200)(\$0.0130/¥) = \$993{,}853$ |

Oops! In this case, you've locked in an arbitrage *loss* of \$6,147. How can you tell which direction to go on your round turn? If you start with dollars, do you first convert them to Japanese yen or to Swiss francs?

**APPLICATION Significant Digits and Rounding Error**

The result of a foreign exchange calculation (indeed, any calculation) is only as precise as the least precise value in the calculation. Consider the following three spot exchange rates:

$$S^{\$/¥} = \$0.0130/¥ \quad S^{¥/SFr} = ¥81.330/SFr \quad S^{SFr/\$} = SFr0.9400/\$$$

Suppose the spot rate $S^{SFr/\$} = SFr0.9400/\$$ is precise. $S^{\$/¥} = \$0.0130/¥$ is then the least precise of these values because it is quoted with only three significant digits. As a consequence, any calculation based on these values will have rounding error in the third digit. An arbitrage profit based on a $1,000,000 initial transaction as in the example below is accurate only to about the nearest $10,000. In the example, triangular arbitrage yields a profit of $6,185, plus or minus a few thousand dollars. The precision implied by the seemingly precise answer of $6,185 is spurious unless you can trade at the exact prices in the quotes.

As a general rule, it is best to retain as many significant digits as possible in your calculations. The result of any calculation is only as accurate as your inputs.

**Which Way Do You Go?** The no-arbitrage condition is $S^{d/e}S^{e/f}S^{f/d} = 1$. If $S^{d/e}S^{e/f}S^{f/d} < 1$, then at least one of these exchange rates should increase as triangular arbitrage forces these rates back toward equilibrium. This suggests the winning arbitrage strategy should be to buy the currency in the denominator of each spot rate with the currency in the numerator.

Conversely, if $S^{d/e}S^{e/f}S^{f/d} > 1$ then at least one of the rates $S^{d/e}$, $S^{e/f}$, or $S^{f/d}$ must fall to achieve parity. In this case, you want to sell the high-priced currency in the denominator of each spot rate for the low-priced currency in the numerator.

Here's the rule for determining which currencies to buy and sell in triangular arbitrage.

- If $S^{d/e}S^{e/f}S^{f/d} < 1$, then $S^{d/e}$, $S^{e/f}$, and $S^{f/d}$ are too low relative to equilibrium.
  - Buy the currencies in the denominators with the currencies in the numerators.
- If $S^{d/e}S^{e/f}S^{f/d} > 1$, then $S^{d/e}$, $S^{e/f}$, and $S^{f/d}$ are too high relative to equilibrium.
  - Sell the currencies in the denominators for the currencies in the numerators.

In our example, $S^{\$/¥}S^{¥/SFr}S^{SFr/\$} = 0.9939 < 1$ at the disequilibrium rate $S^{SFr/\$} = SFr0.9400/\$$. One or more of these exchange rates must rise to return to equilibrium, so you should buy the currency in the denominator of each spot rate with the currency in the numerator. You should (1) buy yen with dollars at $S^{\$/¥}$, (2) buy francs with yen at $S^{¥/SFr}$, and (3) buy dollars with francs at $S^{SFr/\$}$. In this example, triangular arbitrage is worth doing so long as transaction costs on the round turn are less than $(1 - S^{\$/¥}S^{¥/SFr}S^{SFr/\$}) \approx 0.61$ percent of the transaction amount, or about $6,100.

Here's a complementary way of viewing the example. The inequality $S^{\$/¥}S^{¥/SFr}S^{SFr/\$} = 0.9939 < 1$ can be restated in its reciprocal form $(S^{\$/¥}S^{¥/SFr}S^{SFr/\$})^{-1} = (0.9939)^{-1}$, or $S^{¥/\$}S^{SFr/¥}S^{\$/SFr} \approx 1.0061 > 1$. The product of the exchange rates is greater than one, so you should (1) sell dollars for yen, (2) sell yen for francs, and (3) sell francs for dollars. Of course, whenever you sell the currency in the denominator you are simultaneously buying the currency in the numerator. Viewed in this way, the two inequalities for determining "which way to go" are equivalent. No matter which inequality you use, in our example you want to buy yen with dollars (sell dollars for yen), buy francs with yen (sell yen for francs), and buy dollars with francs (sell francs for dollars).

In actuality, all three exchange rates (as well as any related bilateral exchange rates) are likely to change as financial market arbitrage forces these prices toward equilibrium. Cross-rate tables must be internally consistent within the bounds of transaction costs to preclude arbitrage opportunities. Interbank currency markets for large transactions between major banks are highly competitive, and the no-arbitrage condition ensures that currency cross rates are in equilibrium at all times.

## 4.3 INTEREST RATE PARITY AND COVERED INTEREST ARBITRAGE

Let $F_t^{d/f}$ be the t-period forward exchange rate initiated at time 0 for exchange at time t. $S_0^{d/f}$ is the spot exchange rate at time 0. Nominal interest rates in the two currencies are denoted $i^f$ and $i^d$. The relation between spot and forward exchange rates and interest rates is called ***interest rate parity (IRP)*** or, equivalently, ***covered interest parity (CIP)***.[2]

$$\frac{F_t^{d/f}}{S_0^{d/f}} = \left[\frac{(1+i^d)}{(1+i^f)}\right]^t \qquad (4.4)$$

According to interest rate parity, the forward premium (or discount) reflects the interest rate differential on the right-hand side of Equation 4.4. For major currencies, nominal interest rate contracts are actively traded in the interbank Eurocurrency markets. Likewise, there are active spot and forward markets for major currencies. Because each contract in Equation 4.4 is actively traded, interest rate parity always holds within the bounds of transaction costs in these markets.

### Covered Interest Arbitrage

Locational arbitrage exploits a price discrepancy between two locations, and triangular arbitrage exploits price disequilibria across three cross rates. Through a similar mechanism, ***covered interest arbitrage*** takes advantage of an interest rate differential that is not fully reflected in the forward premium. In particular, disequilibrium in the interest rate parity relation provides an opportunity for arbitrageurs to borrow in one currency, invest in the other currency, and cover the difference in the spot and forward currency markets. The no-arbitrage condition then ensures that currency and Eurocurrency markets are in equilibrium within the bounds of transaction costs.

> ***Covered interest arbitrage forces markets into equilibrium.***

**An Example** Suppose you can trade at the following prices:

$S_0^{\$/£} = \$1.670800/£$ $F_1^{\$/£} = \$1.600000/£$ $i^{\$} = 1.000000\%$ $i^{£} = 1.500000\%$

IRP doesn't hold, because $F_1^{\$/£}/S_0^{\$/£} = 0.957625 < 0.995074 = (1 + i^{\$})/(1 + i^{£})$. Covered interest arbitrage is described ahead and illustrated in Figure 4.4.

1. Borrow £1 million at the prevailing Eurocurrency interest rate of $i^{£} = 1.5$ percent for one year. Your obligation will be £1,015,000 in one year.
2. Exchange the £1 million for $1.6708 million at the spot exchange rate. This leaves you with a net dollar inflow today and a pound obligation in one year.
3. Invest the $1.6708 million at $i^{\$} = 1$ percent. Your payoff will be $1,670,800 (1.01) = $1,687,508 in one year. Your net position is now an inflow of $1,687,508 and an outflow of £1,015,000, both at time t = 1.
4. To cover your time t = 1 obligation of £1,015,000, sign a 1-year forward contract in which you buy £1,015,000 and sell ($1.6/£)(£1,015,000) = $1,624,000 at the forward rate $F_1^{\$/£} = \$1.6/£$.

The net result is an arbitrage profit of $63,508. Although this example ignores bid-ask spreads, these could be included by using the appropriate bid or offer price when trading each contract.

**Which Way Do You Go?** Which currency do we borrow and which do we lend in order to lock in an arbitrage profit? Suppose $F_t^{d/f}/S_0^{d/f} > [(1 + i^d)/(1 + i^f)]^t$, so domestic interest rates are too low and foreign interest rates are too high to justify the forward premium. At least one of these rates must change if markets are to return to equilibrium.

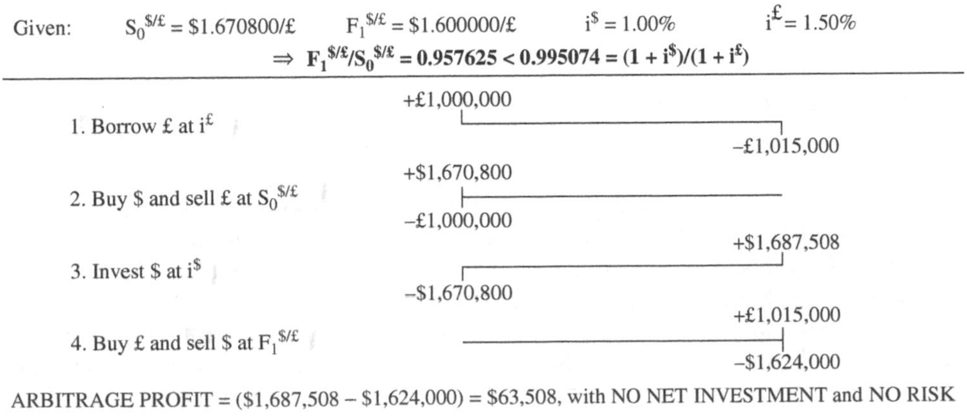


**FIGURE 4.4** Covered Interest Arbitrage and Interest Rate Parity.

- If the ratio $F_t^{d/f}/S_0^{d/f}$ is too high, then either $F_t^{d/f}$ must fall or $S_0^{d/f}$ must rise.
- If the ratio $[(1 + i^d)/(1 + i^f)]^t$ is too low, then either $i^d$ must rise or $i^f$ must fall.

If $F_t^{d/f}/S_0^{d/f} > [(1 + i^d)/(1 + i^f)]^t$, then the winning arbitrage strategy is to borrow at the relatively low rate $i^d$ and invest at $i^f$ while selling currency f at the relatively high forward rate $F_t^{d/f}$ and buying it spot at $S_0^{d/f}$. This locks in an arbitrage profit based on the difference between the two ratios.

Conversely, if $F_t^{d/f}/S_0^{d/f} < [(1 + i^d)/(1 + i^f)]^t$, then domestic interest rates are too high or foreign interest rates are too low to justify the forward premium. In this case, you want to borrow in the foreign currency and invest in the domestic currency. This leads to the following rules:

- If $F_t^{d/f}/S_0^{d/f} > [(1 + i^d)/(1 + i^f)]^t$, then borrow at $i^d$, buy $S_0^{d/f}$, invest at $i^f$, and sell $F_t^{d/f}$.
- If $F_t^{d/f}/S_0^{d/f} < [(1 + i^d)/(1 + i^f)]^t$, then borrow at $i^f$, buy $F_t^{d/f}$ , invest at $i^d$, and sell $S_0^{d/f}$.

As with triangular arbitrage, using indirect quotes leads to an equivalent set of rules.

FX traders will tell you that forward exchange rates are really just an interest rate play. Exchange rates are much more likely to adjust to disequilibria than are Eurocurrency interest rates. Nevertheless, these rules send you in the right direction in your search for arbitrage profits.

## Changes in Exchange Rates, Interest Rates, and Forward Premiums

*Forward premiums reflect interest rate differentials.*

Covered interest arbitrage ensures that the forward/spot ratio over each horizon is determined by the differential between foreign and domestic interest rates over that period. In this way, spot and forward rates are linked through the interest rate differential. Exchange rates are far more volatile than interest rates, so the spot and forward rates move up or down over time in tandem. If relative interest rates do not change, then neither does the forward premium. The forward premium changes only with a change in a foreign or domestic interest rate. The time horizon of the forward premium thus is determined by the relative yield curves in the foreign and domestic currencies.

## 4.4 LESS RELIABLE INTERNATIONAL PARITY CONDITIONS

Covered interest arbitrage is possible because each contract in the IRP relation is actively traded in interbank markets. Disequilibria involving contractual cash flows in these markets are quickly forced back to equilibrium. The parity conditions in this section are less reliable because they involve at least one noncontractual future price. Disequilibria in nontraded prices cannot be arbitraged and can persist for long periods of time. Nevertheless, speculative activity suggests that the parity relations described in this section should hold on average and in the long run.

### Relative Purchasing Power Parity

Recall that $P_t^d$ and $P_t^f$ represent the domestic and foreign prices of a single asset or of two identical assets at a particular point in time. Suppose the asset is a standardized basket of consumer goods and services, such as a consumer price index. Percentage change in a consumer price level during a period is given by

$$p_t = \frac{P_t - P_{t-1}}{P_{t-1}} = \frac{P_t}{P_{t-1}}$$

Relative to an arbitrarily defined base period at t = 0, the consumer price level at time t depends on inflation during the intervening periods according to

$$P_t = P_0(1 + p)^t$$

where p is a geometric mean inflation rate satisfying $(1 + p)^t = (1 + p_1)(1 + p_2) \ldots (1 + p_t)$.

The expected change in the spot exchange rate should reflect relative inflationary expectations in the two currencies if the currencies are to retain their relative purchasing power. This ***relative purchasing power parity (RPPP)*** relation

$$\frac{E[S_t^{d/f}]}{S_0^{d/f}} = \left[\frac{(1 + E[p^d])}{(1 + E[p^f])}\right]^t \tag{4.5}$$

states that expected spot rate changes reflect the currencies' expected inflation differential.[3]

This relation holds only on average, because neither expected inflation nor future spot exchange rates are traded contracts. Over measurement intervals of a few days or months, spot rates move in nearly a random fashion and Equation 4.5 has very little predictive power. For illustration, Figure 4.5 plots monthly changes in the yen-per-dollar spot rate against the previous month's inflation differential. The theory in Equation 4.5 predicts a one-to-one relation, when in fact the relation appears to be in the wrong direction. Moreover, the size of a typical change in the spot exchange rate is much larger than a typical inflation differential.

> ***Spot rate changes should reflect inflation differentials.***

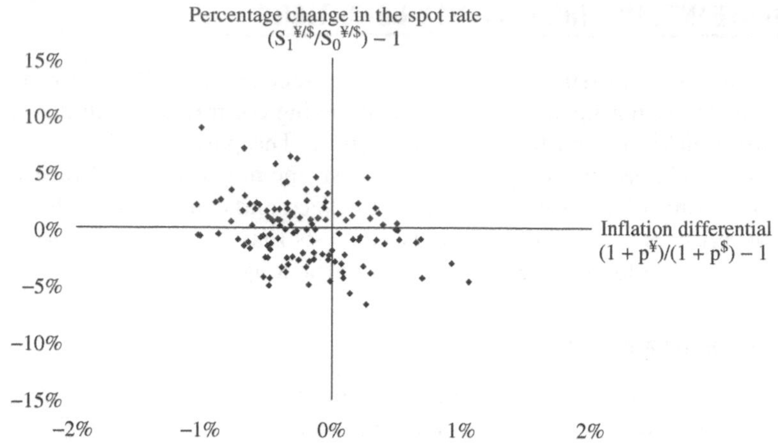


**FIGURE 4.5** RPPP: Japanese Yen versus U.S. Dollar.
*Source:* Monthly changes in exchange rates and relative inflation over 2001–2010 from International Monetary Fund (IMF) Statistics (www.imf.org).

In the long run, inflation differences do prevail eventually. Figure 4.6 graphs the mean annual change in the spot rate against inflation differentials relative to the U.S. dollar for several currencies over 5-year and 10-year forecast horizons. As predicted by RPPP, the dollar rose against currencies with high inflation. Moreover, the influence of inflation is more pronounced over 10-year than over 5-year horizons as RPPP begins to exert itself. RPPP holds in the long run, but is of little use in predicting daily or even quarterly changes in the spot exchange rate.

## Forward Rates as Predictors of Future Spot Rates

*Forward parity* asserts that forward exchange rates are unbiased predictors of future spot rates; that is, $F_t^{d/f} = E[S_t^{d/f}]$.

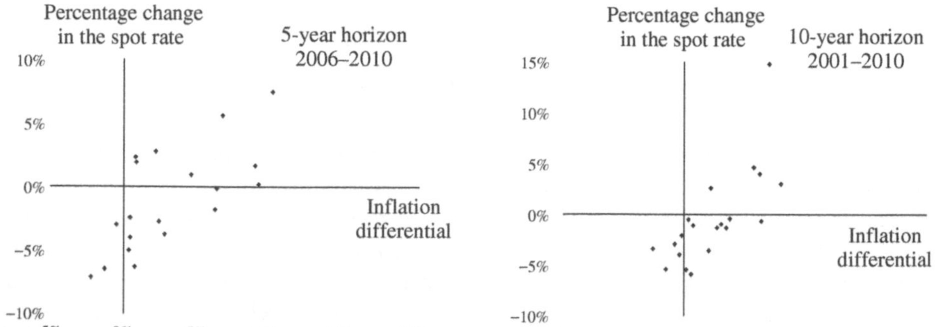


This figure displays average annual changes in the spot rate $s^{f/\$} = (S_1^{f/\$} - S_0^{f/\$})/S_0^{f/\$}$ against average annual inflation differentials relative to the dollar $(1 + p^f)/(1 + p^{\$}) - 1$ over 5-year (2006–2010) and 10-year (2001–2010) forecast horizons for Argentina, $(S_1^{f/\$} - S_0^{f/\$})$, Australia, Canada, Colombia, Egypt, the Eurozone, India, Indonesia, Japan, S. Korea, Malaysia, Mexico, New Zealand, Pakistan, Philippines, Singapore, South Africa, Sri Lanka, Switzerland, and the United Kingdom.

**FIGURE 4.6** RPPP in the Long Run.
*Source:* Exchange rates and inflation from IMF Statistics (www.imf.org).

*Forward rates should predict future spot rates.*

If forward parity holds, then forward premiums should reflect the expected change in the spot exchange rate according to

$$\frac{F_t^{d/f}}{S_0^{d/f}} = \frac{E[S_t^{d/f}]}{S_0^{d/f}} \tag{4.6}$$

Like the inflation differential in Equation 4.5, forward rates are poor predictors over short horizons. Figure 4.7 plots actual spot rate changes $s_t^{¥/\$} = (S_t^{d/f}/S_{t-1}^{d/f}) - 1$ against the forward premium $FP_t^{¥/\$} = (F_t^{d/f}/S_{t-1}^{d/f}) - 1$ for 1-month intervals. If forward parity accurately predicts future spot rates, then the actual and predicted changes in the spot rate should lie along a 45-degree line

$$s_t^{¥/\$} = \alpha + \beta FP_t^{¥/\$} + e_t \tag{4.7}$$

with $\alpha = 0$ and $\beta = 1$. Contrary to theory, there is no obvious relation between spot rate changes and forward premiums in Figure 4.7. The 1-month forward rate clearly is not a good predictor of the following month's spot exchange rate. Over longer forecast horizons, the forward parity relation gradually gains credence and begins to look more like the relations in Figure 4.6.

Froot and Thaler review 75 studies of this relation over short forecasting horizons and find a mean slope coefficient in Equation 4.7 of −0.88.[4] This finding is referred to as the ***forward premium anomaly*** and often is interpreted as evidence of a bias in forward rates. However, this bias (if it exists) is small in magnitude and

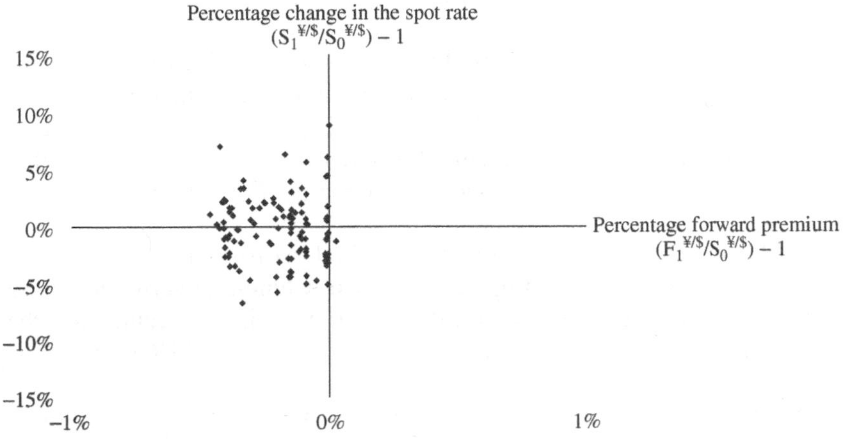


**FIGURE 4.7** Forward Parity: Japanese Yen versus the U.S. Dollar.
*Source:* This figure displays monthly yen-per-dollar forward premiums and spot rate changes over the period 2001–2010 based on spot and forward exchange rates from Bloomberg (www.bloomberg.com.)

unreliable as an exchange rate predictor. Moreover, some of the bias is caused by other factors, such as persistence in exchange rate volatility.[5]

*Forward premiums reflect relative opportunity costs of capital.*

In this book, we'll often use forward exchange rates as predictors of future spot rates. At the very least, the forward premium reflects the relative opportunity cost of capital in the two currencies through the interest rate parity relation. The good news is that the forecasting performance of forward rates improves considerably over longer horizons. Indeed, the long-run performance of forward rates as predictors of future spot rates is similar to the long-run performance of inflation differentials in Figure 4.6. For these reasons, forward rates are useful predictors of future spot rates in capital budgeting and other long-horizon forecasting problems.

## The International Fisher Relation

**The Fisher Equation** If investors care about real (inflation-adjusted) returns, then they will set nominal required returns to compensate them for real required returns and expected inflation. The ***Fisher equation*** relates the nominal interest rate i to inflation p and a real interest rate $\textsc{r}$.

$$(1 + \text{nominal interest rate}) = (1 + \text{inflation rate})(1 + \text{real interest rate})$$

$$\text{or} \qquad (1 + i) = (1 + p)(1 + \textsc{r})$$

*Real interest rates are inflation-adjusted.*

For example, if Chinese inflation is expected to be 5 percent and investors require a real return of 2 percent on a 1-year government discount bond, then the nominal required return on the bond will be $i^{CNY} = (1 + E[p^{CNY}])(1 + \textsc{r}^{CNY}) - 1 = (1.05)(1.02) - 1 = 0.071$, or $i = 7.1$ percent.[6] If the discount bond has a par value of 1 million Chinese new yuan, then it would sell for (CNY1,000,000/1.071) = CNY933,707.

Realized real return is determined by the nominal return earned during the period and realized inflation. For example, if a 1-year Chinese government bond yields $i = 7.1$ percent and realized inflation during the year is 3 percent, then the realized real return on the bond is $\textsc{r} = [(1 + i)/(1 + p)] - 1 = (1.071)/(1.03) - 1 \approx 0.0398$, or 3.98 percent.

The Fisher equation can be written alternatively as $i = (1 + p)(1 + \textsc{r}) - 1 = p + \textsc{r} + p\textsc{r}$. If real interest and inflation rates are low, then the cross-product term $p\textsc{r}$ is small and the approximation $i \approx p + \textsc{r}$ is close to the actual value. If $p = 0.05$ and $\textsc{r} = 0.02$, this approximation suggests a nominal required return of $i \approx 0.05 + 0.02 = 7$ percent, which is close to the exact answer of 7.1 percent.

Use the exact form of Equation 4.8 when real returns or inflation is high. For example, if expected inflation is 70 percent and required real return is 30 percent, the approximation suggests a nominal return of $i \approx 0.30 + 0.70 = 1.00$, or 100 percent. The true nominal required return is $i = (1.30)(1.70) - 1 = 1.21$, or 121 percent, which is quite a bit more than the approximation.

### Real Interest Parity and the International Fisher Relation

> ***Real interest parity requires*** $R^d = R^f$.

The Fisher equation has an important consequence for nominal interest rates in an international setting. In particular, substituting the Fisher equation into the ratio of nominal interest rates in Equation 4.4 leads to

$$(1 + i^d)/(1 + i^f) = [(1 + E[p^d])(1 + R^d)] \backslash [(1 + E[p^f])(1 + R^f)] \qquad (4.8)$$

According to the law of one price, real (inflation-adjusted) required returns on comparable assets should be equal across currencies so that $R^d = R^f$. This equality is called ***real interest parity.*** If real interest parity holds, then the $(1 + R^d)$ and $(1 + R^f)$ terms cancel and the nominal interest rate differential merely reflects the expected inflation differential. Over t periods, the relation is

$$\left[\frac{(1 + i^d)}{(1 + i^f)}\right]^t = \left[\frac{(1 + E[p^d])}{(1 + E[p^f])}\right]^t \qquad (4.9)$$

Equation 4.9 is called the ***international Fisher relation.***

Like other parity conditions based on nontraded assets, these two parity relations are unreliable over short horizons. The unreliability of these parity relations over short horizons is further confounded by volatility in realized inflation. Figure 4.8 illustrates the volatility of inflation relative to nominal interest rates with 1-month Euroyen and Eurodollar London Interbank Offer Rate (LIBOR) contracts over 1990–2010. The difference between the Eurocurrency yield and realized inflation is

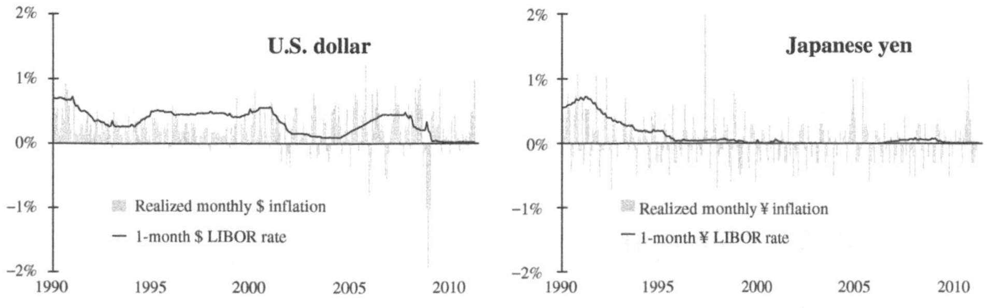


**FIGURE 4.8** Nominal Eurocurrency Interest Rates and Inflation.

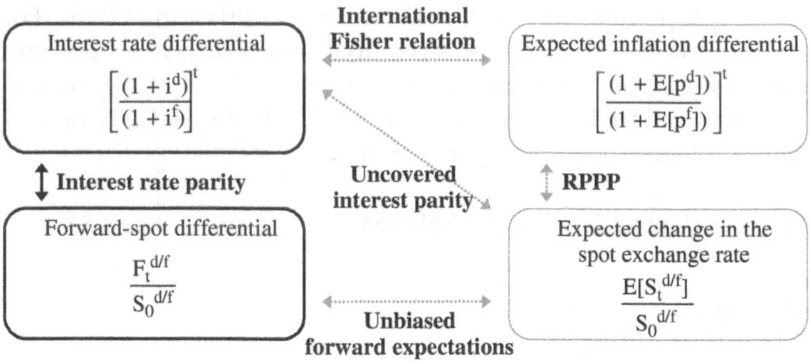


**FIGURE 4.9** The International Parity Conditions.

the realized real return in each currency. Real interest parity and the international Fisher relation do not hold over short horizons largely because of inflation volatility.

*Real rates are seldom equal across currencies.*

### Uncovered Interest Parity

Figure 4.9 summarizes the international parity conditions. Note that the ratios that lie diagonally across the figure also must be equal in equilibrium. Because interest rates are tied to the forward premium and the forward premium is a (long-run) predictor of changes in spot rates, then

$$\frac{E[S_t^{d/f}]}{S_0^{d/f}} = \left[\frac{(1+i^d)}{(1+i^f)}\right]^t \tag{4.10}$$

This is called ***uncovered interest parity*** and relates nominal interest rates to expected spot rate changes, and vice versa.[7]

Similarly, the other diagonal in Figure 4.9 should hold in equilibrium.

$$\frac{F_t^{d/f}}{S_0^{d/f}} = \left[\frac{(1+E[p^d])}{(1+E[p^f])}\right]^t \tag{4.11}$$

The inflation differential should predict future changes in the spot rate of exchange. This completes the circuit of international parity conditions.

## 4.5 THE REAL EXCHANGE RATE

Suppose you invest £100,000 in a 1-year certificate of deposit earning 5 percent. At the end of the year, you'll have £105,000 in the bank. This sounds great. But what if the inflation rate in pounds sterling was 8 percent during the year? Solving the Fisher equation, your real rate of return during the year was $R^{£} = (1 + i^{£})/(1 + p^{£}) - 1 = (1.05/1.08) - 1 = -0.028$, or $-2.8\%$. In real or purchasing power terms, you are worse off at the end of the year than you were at the beginning of the year. And you are a year older, if no wiser.

A similar phenomenon occurs with exchange rate changes. If you look only at nominal changes, you'll miss real changes in purchasing power across currencies. In order to identify real, as opposed to nominal, changes in spot rates of exchange, we need to adjust nominal exchange rates for the effects of inflation in the foreign and domestic currencies.

## Real Changes in Purchasing Power

Suppose the spot rate is $S_0^{¥/\$} = ¥100/\$$, as in Figure 4.10. Expected inflation is $E[p^{¥}] = 0$ in Japan and $E[p^{\$}] = 10$ percent in the United States. If nominal spot rate changes reflect changes in the relative purchasing power of the yen and the dollar, the expected spot rate in one period should be

$$E[S_1^{¥/\$}] = S_0^{¥/\$}\frac{(1+E[p^{¥}])}{(1+E[p^{\$}])} = (¥100/\$)\frac{(1.00)}{(1.10)} = ¥90.91/\$$$

according to RPPP in Equation 4.5.

Suppose that one year later the inflation estimates turn out to be accurate but the dollar has appreciated to $S_1^{¥/\$} = ¥110/\$$. This is a 10 percent dollar appreciation in nominal terms. In fact, this represents a 21 percent real (inflation-adjusted) appreciation of the dollar relative to the expected spot rate of ¥90.91/\$.

$$(\text{Actual} - \text{Expected})/\text{Expected} = \frac{(¥110/\$ - ¥90.91/\$)}{¥90.91/\$} = 0.21$$

This 21 percent real (inflation-adjusted) surprise in purchasing power is shown in the right panel of Figure 4.10. In this example, the dollar has experienced a 21 percent appreciation in purchasing power relative to the yen. The real exchange rate captures changes in the purchasing power of a currency relative to other currencies by backing out the effects of inflation from changes in nominal exchange rates.

## The Real Exchange Rate

We used the law of one price as our guiding principle in deriving the international parity conditions. This faith is well founded for actively traded financial contracts, such as currencies and Eurocurrencies traded in the interbank markets. For these assets, arbitrage is quick to eliminate deviations from PPP. For less actively traded assets, especially those with many barriers to trade such as land or labor, deviations from PPP can persist for many years.

The ***real exchange rate*** $X_t^{d/f}$ is the nominal exchange rate $S_t^{d/f}$ adjusted for relative changes in domestic and foreign price levels (i.e., adjusted for differential inflation) since an arbitrarily defined base period at time $t = 0$.

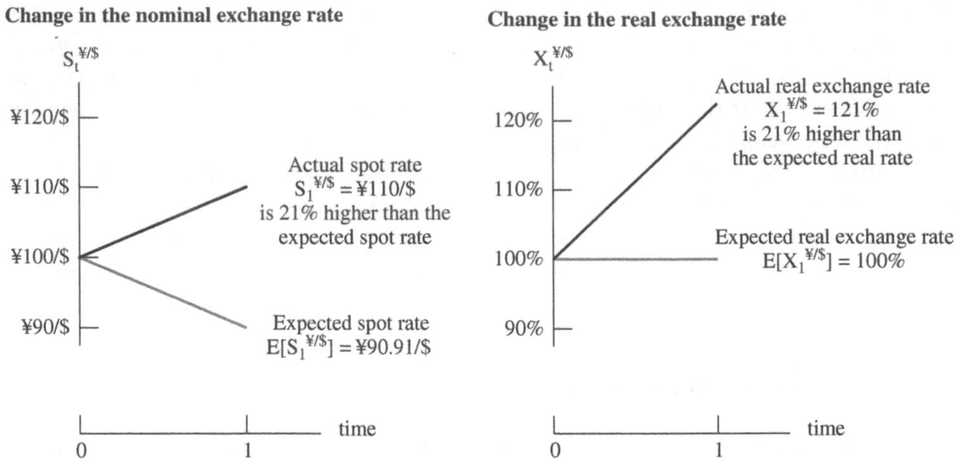


**FIGURE 4.10** Change in the Real Exchange Rate.

*Real exchange rates reflect changes in purchasing power.*

$$X_t^{d/f} = (S_t^{d/f}/S_0^{d/f})\{[(1+p_1^f)/(1+p_1^d)][(1+p_2^f)/(1+p_2^d)]\ldots[(1+p_t^f)/(1+p_t^d)]\}$$
$$= (S_t^{d/f}/S_0^{d/f})\left\{\prod_{\tau=1}^{t}[(1+p_\tau^f)/(1+p_\tau^d)]\right\} \quad (4.12)$$

The nominal spot exchange rate $S_t^{d/f}$ at time t divided by the base period spot rate $S_0^{d/f}$ equals one plus the percentage in the spot exchange rate. The inflation adjustment indicates whether this change in the nominal exchange rate reflects the accumulated inflation differential between the two currencies. If change in the nominal spot rate of exchange exactly offsets the mean inflation differential, then the real exchange rate will remain at 100 percent of its base level. Thus, the real exchange rate provides a measure of the purchasing power of two currencies relative to a base period.

The formula for the percentage change in the real exchange rate during a single period is

$$(1+x_t^{d/f}) = (X_t^{d/f}/X_{t-1}^{d/f}) = (S_t^{d/f}/S_{t-1}^{d/f})[(1+p_t^f)/(1+p_t^d)] \quad (4.13)$$

The percentage change in the real exchange rate depends only on change in the nominal exchange rate and the inflation differential during the period.

It is somewhat misleading to retain the currencies on the symbols for the real exchange rate, because the currency units cancel from the ratio $(S_t^{d/f}/S_0^{d/f})$ in Equations 4.12 and 4.13. Inflation rates also are unit-less. The measure $X_t^{d/f}$ is a number, such as 1.21, that represents the real value of the currency in the denominator *relative to the base period.* Currencies are retained as a reminder that this is a measure of the relative purchasing power of the currency in the denominator.

Let's return to Figure 4.10. The ratio $(S_1^{¥/\$}/S_0^{¥/\$}) = (¥110/\$)/(¥100/\$) = 1.10$ indicates that the dollar increased 10 percent in nominal terms during the period. This was despite the fact that dollar inflation was 10 percent higher than yen inflation. By construction, the level of the real exchange rate in the base period is $X_0^{¥/\$} = 1.00$. Equation 4.13 yields

$$(1 + x_1^{¥/\$}) = (X_1^{¥/\$}/X_0^{¥/\$}) = [(¥110/\$)/(¥100/\$)][(1.10)/(1.00)] = 1.21$$

or a real exchange rate that is 21 percent higher than at the start of the period. This represents a 21 percent increase in the purchasing power of the dollar during the period.

It is convenient to pick a base period in which the purchasing power of the two currencies is close to equilibrium. In this case, PPP holds and $S_0^{d/f} = P_0^d/P_0^f$ for a wide range of assets. Because any base period can be chosen, the level of the real exchange rate is not necessarily informative. In particular, it is inappropriate to claim that a currency is overvalued simply because the level of the real exchange rate is greater than 1. It may be that the currency was undervalued in the base period and remains undervalued. For example, the real exchange rate may have risen by 10 percent from 1.00 to 1.10, but if the "true" value of the currency in the base period was only 0.80 (80 percent of equilibrium), then a 10 percent real appreciation of the currency only brings it up to 0.88 (88 percent of its equilibrium value) and it remains undervalued relative to its equilibrium value. Further, there are cross-currency differences in asset prices, so that a currency can have more purchasing power in some assets than in others. *Change* in a real exchange rate is more informative than the level of the real exchange rate because of cross-currency differences in individual or national consumption baskets (and hence measures of inflation) and the arbitrary choice of the base period.

It is often convenient to place the domestic currency in the denominator:

$$(1 + x_t^{f/d}) = (X_t^{f/d}/X_{t-1}^{f/d}) = (S_t^{f/d}/S_{t-1}^{f/d})[(1 + p_t^d)/(1 + p_t^f)] \qquad (4.13)$$

to measure the relative purchasing power of the domestic currency. If currency f in the numerator is replaced by a basket of foreign currencies, then $x_t^{f/d}$ provides a measure of the purchasing power of the domestic currency relative to other currencies in the currencies basket.

Figure 4.11 plots the real value of the euro, yen, pound, and dollar in this way since the early 1970s. Most exchange rates began to float in early 1973, so only the period since early 1973 is relevant to the modern era. The dollar and the yen were grossly out of balance in the fixed exchange rate regime that preceded the 1973 float. The floating rate era brought currency values closer to equilibrium, but was unable to achieve true parity. For example, at times the yen has been 50 percent higher and at other times 20 percent lower than its average value. Figure 4.11 illustrates that there are large and persistent deviations from real PPP.

Academic studies confirm our casual interpretation of Figure 4.11.

- Deviations from real exchange rate parity can be substantial in the short run.
- Deviations from real exchange rate parity can last several years.

## APPLICATION Keeping Track of Your Currency Units

In the international parity conditions, the currency in the numerator (denominator) stays in the numerator (denominator) of the interest rates and exchange rates. For example, in RPPP,

$$E[S_t^{d/f}]/S_0^{d/f} = [(1+E[p^d])/(1+E[p^f])]^t \tag{4.5}$$

the currency in the numerator of each spot rate also is in the numerator of the inflation ratio. Conversely, the currency in the denominator of the left-hand side stays in the denominator on the right-hand side.

Real exchange rates are the only exception to this rule. With a real exchange rate, we want to *reverse* the effects of inflation on nominal exchange rates.

$$1 + x_t^{d/f} = (X_t^{d/f}/X_{t-1}^{d/f}) = (S_t^{d/f}/S_{t-1}^{d/f})[(1+p_t^f)/(1+p_t^d)] \tag{4.13}$$

The currency in the numerator of the real and nominal spot exchange rates moves to the denominator in the inflation ratio, and vice versa. The equation for change in the real exchange rate provides the only exception to the "numerator to numerator and denominator to denominator" rule.

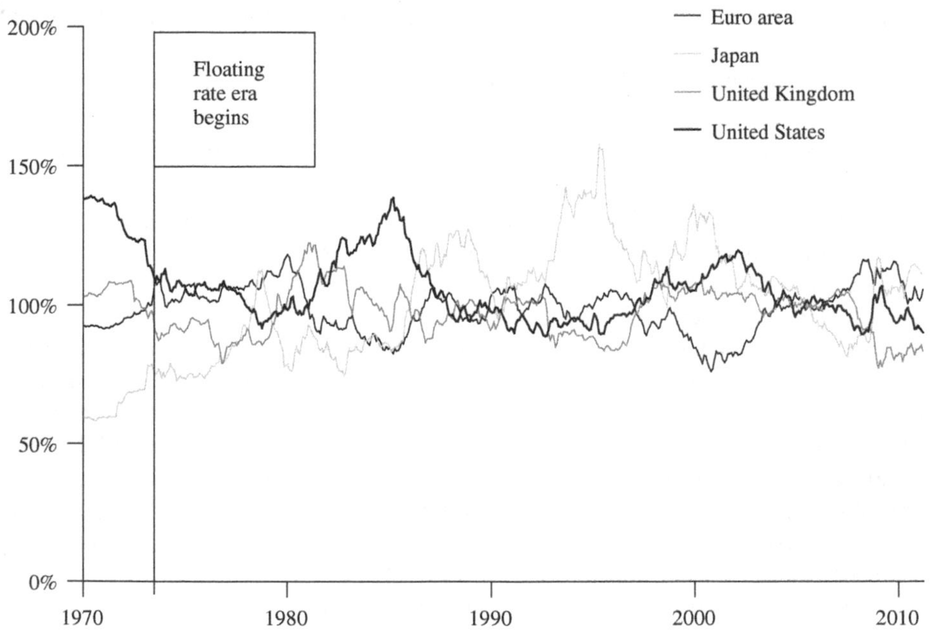


**FIGURE 4.11** Real Value of the Dollar.
*Source:* Based on Bank for International Settlements indices (www.bis.org/statistics/eer/).

Although real exchange rates tend to revert to their long-run average, in the short run there can be substantial deviations from the long-run average. In a study of real exchange rates over a 200-year sample period, Lothian and Taylor estimate that it takes between 3 and 6 years for a real disequilibrium in the exchange rate to be reduced by half.[8]

Deviations from parity in real exchange rates appear to be a consequence of differential frictions in the markets for real and financial assets, with goods prices adjusting more slowly than financial prices. PPP holds for actively traded financial assets, but seldom holds for inactively traded goods such as land or human labor. Consequently, PPP typically does not hold for general price levels, either. It can take the markets for real (nonfinancial) assets a long time to bring price levels back into equilibrium.

### The Effect of a Change in the Real Exchange Rate

If RPPP holds, then changes in nominal exchange rates should reflect the influence of foreign and domestic inflation. Moreover, nominal exchange rate changes that reflect merely the influence of inflation should have little economic significance of their own. Real changes in exchange rates, on the other hand, have a profound impact on the operations of multinational corporations (MNCs), as well as on a country's balance of trade. In particular,

- A **real appreciation** of the domestic currency raises the price of domestic goods relative to foreign goods.
- A **real depreciation** of the domestic currency lowers the price of domestic goods relative to foreign goods.

A real appreciation of the domestic currency is both good and bad news for the domestic economy. A real appreciation helps domestic importers and consumers because raw materials and imported goods cost less. This helps to hold down inflation. On the other hand, it hurts domestic exporters and their employees as the goods and services produced by domestic companies are relatively expensive in international markets. The effect on domestic producers is asymmetric, in that goods and services competing on the world market are hurt more than those competing solely on the domestic market. This shifts resources within the domestic economy from export-oriented firms toward firms that import goods or services from other countries or that compete primarily in the domestic market.

*A real appreciation of a currency reflects an increase in purchasing power.*

Consider the labor expense of a Japanese exporter that sells its goods in international markets. A real yen appreciation increases the Japanese exporter's labor costs relative to foreign competitors because its local wages are paid in yen. Conversely, the labor costs of non-Japanese competitors remain constant in their local currencies but decrease in terms of yen. Under these conditions, Japanese exporters face a real cost disadvantage.

Consider instead a Japanese investor such as an MNC that is seeking investment opportunities overseas. A real appreciation of the yen means that foreign assets become less expensive for the Japanese investor. If the investor is in the market to purchase real estate, a real appreciation of the yen makes California real estate relatively less expensive than it used to be. The value of the yen will fall as capital flows out of costly Japanese assets and into relatively less expensive foreign (non-Japanese) assets. Market equilibrium eventually will be restored, if only in passing.

A real depreciation of the domestic currency is the flip side of a real appreciation. A real depreciation of the domestic currency results in lower prices for domestic goods in foreign and domestic markets. This promotes domestic employment. On the downside, a real depreciation results in higher prices for imported goods and an increase in domestic inflation. Whether a real depreciation is good or bad for the domestic economy depends on which of these countervailing forces triumphs.

## 4.6 EXCHANGE RATE FORECASTING

The concept of informational efficiency is useful when asking whether exchange rates are predictable. In an informationally efficient market, currencies are correctly priced based on available information. In an informationally efficient market, it is not possible to consistently "beat the market" and earn returns beyond those obtainable by chance in positions of similar risk. The premise that markets are informationally efficient is called the ***efficient market hypothesis.***

### Forecasts Based on the International Parity Conditions

Exchange rate forecasts are provided by several of the international parity conditions.

*The international parity conditions provide useful FX forecasts.*

$E[S_t^{d/f}] = F_t^{d/f}$ forward parity

$E[S_t^{d/f}] = S_0^{d/f}\,[(1+i^d)/(1+i^f)]^t$ a combination of forward parity and IRP

$E[S_t^{d/f}] = S_0^{d/f}\,[(1+p^d)/(1+p^f)]^t$ RPPP

The first two equations are equivalent if interest rate parity holds, as it usually does in international currency and Eurocurrency markets.

The international parity conditions provide a signal as to in which direction a currency should change in equilibrium. The beauty of these forecasts is that anyone with access to a financial newspaper can make them. Unfortunately, these forecasts do not work well in the short term. The signal from the international parity conditions is weak relative to exchange rate volatility over daily or monthly intervals. As the forecasting horizon lengthens, the signal-to-noise ratio improves.[9] Beyond one year, cross-currency interest rate and inflation differentials begin to impose themselves, and the forward exchange rate begins to dominate the current spot rate as a predictor of nominal exchange rates. Forecasts based on the inflation differential in RPPP also are useful long-term predictors.

Although the international parity conditions are useful for forecasting long-term trends in nominal exchange rates, they are less helpful in forecasting real exchange rates because real exchange rates are assumed to be constant in the international parity relations. The best that can be said for the international parity conditions is that real exchange rates eventually will return to their long-run average.

## Model-Based Exchange Rate Forecasts

Professional forecasters use technical analysis or fundamental analysis to construct their forecasts. ***Technical analysis*** looks for recurring patterns in exchange rates and FX trading volumes that predict future exchange rates. Technical analysis can be effective for short-term exchange rate forecasts. ***Fundamental analysis*** tries to link exchange rate behavior to economic fundamentals and is useful for long-term forecasts. Some forecasters faithfully follow one approach and forswear the other. Others combine what they consider to be the best features of each approach.

> *Technical analysis uses price patterns to forecast FX rates.*

**Technical Analysis** Technical analysts believe that there are patterns in exchange rate movements, and that these patterns allow successful prediction of future exchange rates. This would not be possible in a ***weak form efficient market,*** in which prices fully reflect the information in past prices. Some technical forecasters use statistical measures such as autocorrelations or filter rules to identify patterns in the data. Others use heuristic rules of thumb or intuition. Some of these patterns are only in the eye of the beholder, but others can be useful predictors.

Although technical analysis often has been dismissed by an academic literature that presumes exchange rate movements are random, it nevertheless has always been popular among practitioners. A survey of foreign exchange dealers in London found that more than 90 percent of respondents placed some weight on technical analysis.[10]

A popular technical trading rule is to borrow in a currency with a low nominal interest rate and invest in a currency with a higher nominal interest rate. Exchange rates are close to a random walk over short intervals, so this should yield a positive return. Froot and Thaler estimated that borrowing for one year in one currency and investing these funds in another currency at a 1 percent higher interest rate yields an expected payoff of 2 percent per year.[11] Unfortunately, Froot and Thaler find that the standard deviation of this strategy is 36 percent, so the positive expected returns of this strategy are accompanied by a great deal of risk. Although most investors prefer more conventional investments, nominal interest rate differences can help improve exchange rate forecasts.[12]

**Fundamental Analysis** Fundamental analysts believe that the foreign exchange market is not semistrong form efficient. Prices in a ***semistrong form efficient market*** reflect all publicly available information, including past price histories and other publicly available information. Typically, an econometric model is used to predict exchange rates as a function of macroeconomic data, such as the balance of payments, money supply, industrial production, or consumer confidence. Fundamental analysts believe that this publicly available information can lead to superior exchange rate forecasts.

> *Macro-economic data helps forecast long-term trends.*

The link between currency values and fundamental information can be difficult to establish. A part of the reason is that exchange rates react only to new information. For example, if the market has already incorporated its expectations regarding inflation into exchange rates, then only that part of a government inflation report that is unexpected will cause a further change in exchange rates. Without a precise estimate of expected inflation, it is difficult to demonstrate a link between unexpected inflation and exchange rate changes. Further, exchange rates may respond to fundamental variables with a lag, or only in the long run. For these reasons, exchange rates do not respond to fundamental information in an easy-to-decipher way. Nevertheless, fundamental analysis can have good predictive power for long-term forecasts.[13]

## 4.7 SUMMARY

This chapter develops the implications of the law of one price (also known as PPP) for international currency and Eurocurrency markets. The law of one price states that

> **The Law of One Price**
>
> Equivalent assets sell for the same price.

The law of one price is enforced by the profit-making activities of market participants. Riskless arbitrage ensures that the following international parity conditions hold within the bounds of transaction costs in the interbank currency and Eurocurrency markets.

| | | |
|---|---|---|
| PPP | $P_t^d/P_t^f = S_t^{d/f}$ | (4.1) |
| Bilateral equilibrium | $S^{d/f}(Y)/S^{d/f}(X) = 1$ | (4.2) |
| Triangular equilibrium | $S^{d/e}S^{e/f}S^{f/d} = 1$ | (4.3) |
| IRP | $F_t^{d/f}/S_0^{d/f} = [(1 + i^d)/(1 + i^f)]^t$ | (4.4) |

The law of one price has implications for noncontractual prices as well, but only in the long run. International parity conditions that include expectations of future price and exchange rate levels include

| | | |
|---|---|---|
| Relative PPP | $E[S_t^{d/f}]/S_0^{d/f} = [(1 + E[p^d])/(1 + E[p^f])]^t$ | (4.5) |
| Unbiased forward expectations | $F_t^{d/f}/S_0^{d/f} = E[S_t^{d/f}]/S_0^{d/f}$ | (4.6) |
| International Fisher relation | $[(1 + i^d)/(1 + i^f)]^t = [(1 + E[p^d])/(1 + E[p^f])]^t$ | (4.7) |

Because they are based on nontraded contracts, these relations are less reliable than those in Equations 4.1 through 4.4.

Real exchange rates measure the relative purchasing power of two currencies. Change in the real exchange rate during period t is calculated as

$$(1 + x_t^{d/f}) = (X_t^{d/f}/X_{t-1}^{d/f}) = (S_t^{d/f}/S_{t-1}^{d/f})[(1 + p_t^f)/(1 + p_t^d)] \quad (4.13)$$

Changes in real exchange rates have the following effects:

- A **real appreciation** of the domestic currency raises the price of domestic goods relative to foreign goods.
- A **real depreciation** of the domestic currency lowers the price of domestic goods relative to foreign goods.

Empirical evidence indicates that deviations from PPP can be substantial in the short run and typically are returned to equilibrium only after a period of several years.

Changes in exchange rates are difficult to predict, being close to a random walk over daily or monthly intervals. Over longer forecasting horizons, cross-currency inflation differentials eventually have their way and the international parity conditions can provide useful exchange rate forecasts.

Despite the random nature of exchange rate changes, individuals and corporate financial managers will continue to demand exchange rate forecasts because of the potential for risk reduction and speculative gain. This is one forecast that you can trust.

## KEY TERMS

*arbitrage and the no-arbitrage condition*

*covered interest arbitrage*

*cross exchange rate (cross rate)*

*efficient market hypothesis*

*Fisher equation*

*forward parity (unbiased forward expectations)*

*forward premium anomaly*

*fundamental vs technical analysis*

*interest rate parity (IRP), or covered interest parity (CIP) international Fisher relation*

*international parity conditions*

*law of one price (purchasing power parity, PPP)*

*locational arbitrage*

*long vs short position*

*purchasing power parity (PPP)*

*real appreciation or depreciation*

*real exchange rate*

*relative purchasing power parity (RPPP)*

*real interest parity*

*strong form vs weak form efficient market*

*triangular arbitrage*

*uncovered interest parity*

## CONCEPTUAL QUESTIONS

4.1 What is the law of one price?

4.2 What is an arbitrage profit?

4.3 What is the difference between locational, triangular, and covered interest arbitrage?

4.4 Is interest rate parity a reliable relation in the interbank currency and Eurocurrency markets?

4.5 What is RPPP?

4.6 Are forward exchange rates good predictors of future spot rates?

4.7 What does the international Fisher relation say about interest rate and inflation differentials?

4.8 What are real changes in exchange rates?

4.9 Are real exchange rates in equilibrium at all times?

4.10 What is the effect of a real appreciation of the domestic currency on the purchasing power of domestic residents?

4.11 Will an appreciation of the domestic currency help or hurt a domestic exporter?

4.12 Describe the behavior of real exchange rates.

4.13 What methods can be used to forecast future spot rates of exchange?

4.14 How can the international parity conditions allow you to forecast next year's spot rate?

## PROBLEMS

4.1 Calculate the following cross exchange rates:

a. If exchange rates are 200 yen per dollar and 50 U.S. cents per Swiss franc, what is the exchange rate of yen per franc?

b. The dollar is trading at ¥100/$ and at SFr1.60/$. What is the yen per franc rate?

4.2 As a percentage of an arbitrary starting amount, about how large would transaction costs have to be to make arbitrage between the exchange rates $S_0^{SFr/\$}$ = SFr1.7223/$, $S_0^{\$/¥}$ = $0.009711/¥, and $S_0^{¥/SFr}$ = ¥61.740/SFr unprofitable?

4.3 Do Equations 4.2 and 4.3 hold for forward exchange rates in the interbank currency market? That is, are the equalities $Ft^{d/f}(Y)/F^{d/f}(X) = 1$ and $F_t^{d/e}F_t^{e/f}F_t^{f/d} = 1$ true in a market with few transaction costs?

4.4 Given $S_0^{£/\$}$ = £0.6361/$ and the 180-day forward rate $F_1^{£/\$}$ = £0.6352/$, what is the dollar forward premium? Based on the unbiased forward expectations hypothesis, by how much is the dollar expected to appreciate or depreciate over the next 180 days? Provide a forecast of the spot rate of exchange in 180 days.

4.5 The Mexican peso is quoted in direct terms at "¥28.74/MXN BID and ¥28.77/MXN ASK" in Tokyo. The yen is quoted in direct terms in Mexico City at "MXN0.0341600/¥ BID and MXN0.03420/¥ ASK."

a. Calculate the bid-ask spread as a percentage of the bid price from the Japanese and from the Mexican perspective.

b. Is there an opportunity for profitable arbitrage? If so, describe the necessary transactions using a ¥1 million starting amount. Take your profit in yen.

4.6 Industrial Bank of China is earning a nominal yuan return of 7.1 percent on a commercial loan. Expected inflation in CNY is 5 percent. What is the expected real return in yuan? (Be precise.)

4.7 The current spot exchange rate is $S_0^{¥/\$}$ = ¥190/$ and the 1-year forward rate is $F_1^{¥/\$}$ = ¥210/$. The prime rate in the United States is 15 percent.

a. What should the Japanese prime rate be?

b. According to forward parity, by how much should the dollar change in value during the next year?

4.8 Suppose $S_0^{\$/£}$ = $1.25/£ and the 1-year forward rate is $F_1^{\$/£}$ = $1.20/£. The real interest rate on a risk-free government security is 2 percent in both the United Kingdom and the United States. The U.S. inflation rate is 5 percent.

a. What is the U.K.'s inflation rate if the equilibrium relationships hold?

b. What is the U.K.'s nominal required return on risk-free government securities?

4.9 Suppose that for the same basket of goods the time zero price indices in countries D and F are $P_0^D$ = D100 and $P_0^F$ = F1, so that $S_0^{D/F} = P_0^D/P_0^F$ = D100/F. Inflation rates in countries D and F are expected to be 10 percent and 21 percent per period, respectively, over the foreseeable future.

a. What are the expected price levels $E[P_1^D]$ and $E[P_1^F]$ and the expected nominal spot rate of exchange $E[S_1^{D/F}]$ in one period?

b. Looking two years into the future, what are the expected future price levels $E[P_2^D]$ and $E[P_2^F]$ in these two countries?

4.10 A foreign exchange dealer in Tokyo provides the following quotes for spot exchange and 3-month forward exchange between the Malaysian ringgit (MR) and the U.S. dollar:

| | Bid (MR/$) | Ask (MR/$) |
|---|---|---|
| Spot | 4.0040 | 4.0200 |
| 3-month forward | 3.9690 | 3.9888 |

a. In New York, 3-month U.S. Treasury bills yield 7 percent per annum. What should be the annualized yield on 3-month Malaysian government bills? Use U.S. dollar ask quotes for simplicity.
b. Verify your answer to part a. with a hypothetical investment of $10 million for three months in each country. Use only ask quotes for simplicity and ignore other fees, charges, and taxes.

4.11 Quotes for the U.S. dollar and Thai baht (Bt) are as follows:

| | |
|---|---|
| Spot contract midpoint | $S_0^{Bt/\$}$ = Bt24.96/$ |
| 1-year forward contract midpoint | $F_1^{Bt/\$}$ = Bt25.64/$ |
| 1- year Eurodollar interest rate | $i^{\$}$ = 6.125% per year |

a. Your newspaper does not quote 1-year Eurocurrency interest rates on Thai baht. Make your own estimate of $i^{Bt}$.
b. Suppose that you can trade at $S_0^{Bt/\$}$, $F_1^{Bt/\$}$, and $i^{\$}$ and that you also can either borrow or lend at a Thai Eurocurrency interest rate of $i^{Bt}$ = 10 percent per year. Based on a $1 million initial amount, how much profit can you generate through covered interest arbitrage?

4.12 You can trade at the following prices:

| | |
|---|---|
| Spot rate, Mexican pesos per dollar | MXN10/$ |
| 6-month forward rate for Mexican pesos | MXN11/$ |
| 6-month Mexican interest rate | 18% |
| 6-month U.S. interest rate | 6% |

Is covered interest arbitrage worthwhile? If so, explain the steps and compute the profit based on an initial (time t = 0) transaction of $1 million. Calculate your profit in dollars in one period.

4.13 Currency exchange rates and Eurocurrency interest rates are as follows:

| | |
|---|---|
| Current Singapore dollar (S$) spot rate | $0.50/S$ |
| 1-year Singapore dollar (S$) forward rate | $0.51/S$ |
| 1-year Singapore dollar (S$) interest rate | 4.0% |
| 1-year U.S. interest rate | 6.0% |

In what direction will covered interest arbitrage force the quoted rates to change? Explain the steps and compute the profit based on a \$1 million initial position.

4.14 Suppose $P_0^D = 100$, $P_0^F = 1$, and $S_0^{D/F} = D100/F$. Inflation in countries D and F are expected to be $p^D = 10$ percent and $p^F = 21$ percent over the foreseeable future.

a. What are the expected price levels $E[P_1^F]$ and $E[P_1^D]$ and the expected nominal exchange rate $E[S_1^{D/F}]$ in one period?
b. What is the expected real exchange rate $X_1^{D/F}$ in one period using time zero as a base?
c. Looking two years into the future, what are the expected price levels in each country ($E[P_2^F]$ and $E[P_2^D]$) and the expected real exchange rate $E[X_2^{D/F}]$?

4.15 One year ago, the spot exchange rate between Japanese yen and Swiss franc was $S_{-1}^{¥/SFr} = ¥160/SFr$. Today, the spot rate is $S_0^{¥/SFr} = ¥155/SFr$. Inflation during the year was $p^{¥} = 2$ percent and $p^{SFr} = 3$ percent in Japan and Switzerland, respectively.

a. What was the percentage change in the nominal value of the Swiss franc?
b. One year ago, what nominal exchange rate would you have predicted for today based on the difference in inflation rates?
c. What was the percentage change in the real exchange rate, $x_0^{¥/SFr}$, during the year?
d. What was the percentage change in the relative purchasing power of the franc?
e. What was the percentage change in the relative purchasing power of the yen?

4.16 Do the following individuals use technical or fundamental analysis in forecasting currency values?

a. An investor uses charts of historical exchange rate movements to predict future exchange rate movements.
b. A hedger uses a computer program called a neural network to identify patterns in exchange rates. The neural network uses past price information to generate a signal indicating whether a particular currency exposure should be hedged.
c. A speculator gathers the most recent balance-of-payments data from European countries. She uses this data to make long-term forecasts of the value of the euro against the pound.
d. A currency has been trading in a narrow range during the past several months. The currency falls in value days after the government announces it has suspended payments on dollar-denominated loans. A hedge fund manager sells the currency after comparing the size of the dollar-denominated loans with the country's foreign exchange reserves.
e. A currency has been trading in a narrow range for several months. The currency falls in value after the government announces it has suspended payments on dollar-denominated loans. A hedge fund manager sells the

currency after noticing that the currency has fallen in value for three successive days.

## SUGGESTED READINGS

### The international parity conditions are investigated in

Richard T. Baillie and Tim Bollerslev, "The Forward Premium Anomaly Is Not as Bad as You Think," *Journal of International Money and Finance* 19 (August 2000), 471–488.

James R. Lothian and Mark P. Taylor, "Real Exchange Rate Behavior: The Recent Float from the Perspective of the Past Two Centuries," *Journal of Political Economy* 104 (June 1996), 488–509.

James R. Lothian and Liuren Wu, "Uncovered Interest-Rate Parity over the Past Two Centuries," *Journal of International Money and Finance* 30 (April 2011), 448–473.

Michael J. Moore and Maurice J. Roche, "Less of a Puzzle: A New Look at the Forward Forex Market," *Journal of International Economics* 58 (December 2002), 387–411.

Kenneth S. Rogoff, "The Purchasing Power Parity Puzzle," *Journal of Economic Literature* 34 (June 1996), 647–668.

### The performance of exchange rate forecasts and exchange rate forecasters is discussed in

Jamil Baz, Francis Breedon, Vasant Naik, and Joel Peress, "Optimal Portfolios of Foreign Currencies," *Journal of Portfolio Management* 28 (Fall 2001), 102–111.

Kenneth Froot and Richard Thaler, "Anomalies: Foreign Exchange," *Journal of Economic Perspectives* 4 (1990), 179–192.

Nelson C. Mark and Donggyu Sul, "Nominal Exchange Rates and Monetary Fundamentals: Evidence from a Small Post-Bretton Woods Panel," *Journal of International Economics* 53 (February 2001), 29–52.

Christopher J. Neely and Paul A. Weller, "Technical Trading Rules in the European Monetary System," *Journal of International Money and Finance* 18 (June 1999), 429–458.

Mark P. Taylor and Helen Allen, "The Use of Technical Analysis in the Foreign Exchange Market," *Journal of International Money and Finance* 11 (June 1992), 304–314.

## APPENDIX 4A: CONTINUOUS COMPOUNDING

Legend has it that many years ago the bankers of the world employed nearsighted men in green accountants' visors and armbands to compound interest continuously in the smoky back rooms of commercial banks. But no matter how fast they worked, it proved impossible for these unfortunate lackeys to compound interest on a continuous basis. One day, a particularly clever bank clerk discovered that holding period rates of return can be transformed into continuously compounded rates of return with a simple formula. Here's what he discovered.

### Continuously Compounded Rates of Return

As the number of compounding intervals within a period approaches infinity, returns are said to be compounded continuously. At any instant, the rate of return is then called the instantaneous rate of return. Henceforth, let's denote continuously compounded rates of return with *italics*, so that $i$ will represent the continuously compounded version of a holding period interest rate i.

Suppose you have an amount $V_0$ today and you want to know how large this value will be after T periods if it earns a continuously compounded rate of interest $i$. With continuous compounding, the value $V_T$ at time T is given by

$$V_T = V_0 e^{iT} \tag{4A.1}$$

where the number e is an irrational constant approximately equal to 2.718282. Conversely, the present value of a cash flow to be received at time T with continuous compounding is given by

$$V_0 = V_T / e^{iT} = V_T\, e^{-iT} \tag{4A.2}$$

The formula for converting a rate of return with periodic (e.g., annual) compounding into a continuously compounded rate is $i = \ln(1 + \mathrm{i})$, where ln is the natural logarithm function with base e. The equation follows from

$$(1 + i) = e^{i} \Leftrightarrow \ln(1 + i) = \ln(e^{i}) = i \tag{4A.3}$$

For example, the continuously compounded annual rate of return $i$ that is equivalent to a rate i = 12.64 percent with annual compounding is $i = \ln(1.1264) = 0.1190$, or 11.90 percent per year. That is, $e^{0.1190} = 1.1264$ and $\ln(1.1264) = 0.1190$. A 12.64 percent rate of return with annual compounding is equivalent to an 11.90 percent annual return with continuous compounding.

Let's review the properties of the natural logarithm and its inverse, the exponential function e. The following properties hold for positive values A, B, and C:

$$e^{\ln(x)} = \ln(e^{x}) = x \tag{4A.4}$$

$$\ln(AB) = \ln(A) + \ln(B) \tag{4A.5}$$

$$\ln(A/B) = \ln(A) - \ln(B) \tag{4A.6}$$

$$\ln(A^{C}) = C \ln(A) \tag{4A.7}$$

These properties make calculating the compound rate of return over a series of continuously compounded returns easy, because *continuously compounded rates are additive* rather than multiplicative over time.

$$\begin{aligned} \ln[(1 + \mathrm{i}_1)(1 + \mathrm{i}_2)\ldots(1 + \mathrm{i}_T)] &= \ln[e^{i_1} e^{i_2} \ldots e^{i_T}] = \ln[e^{(i_1 + i_2 + \ldots + i_T)}] \\ &= i_1 + i_2 + \ldots + i_T \end{aligned} \tag{4A.8}$$

Let's try an example. The average rate of return over three periods with annual holding period returns of 10 percent, 16 percent, and 12 percent is found with a geometric average as follows:

*Geometric mean return with periodic compounding*

$$(1 + i_{avg}) = [(1.10)(1.16)(1.12)]^{1/3}$$
$$= 1.1264, or 12.64\% \text{ per year (compounded annually)}$$

An equivalent answer can be found with continuously compounded rates of return.

*Arithmetic mean return with continuous compounding*

$$i_{avg} = [\ln(1.10) + \ln(1.12) + \ln(1.16)]/3 = [0.0953 + 0.1133 + 0.1484]/3$$
$$= 0.1190, \text{ or } 11.9\% \text{ per year (compounded continuously)}$$

This 11.9 percent continuously compounded return is, of course, equivalent to the 12.64 percent average rate of return with annual compounding.

## International Parity Conditions in Continuously Compounded Returns

The international parity conditions with continuously compounded returns are a straightforward application of natural logarithms. Over a single period, the parity conditions in holding period returns are

$$F_1{}^{d/f}/S_0{}^{d/f} = E[S_1{}^{d/f}]/S_0{}^{d/f} = (1 + i^d/(1 + i^f) = (1 + E[p^d])/(1 + E[p^f]) \quad (4A.9)$$

Using $i$ to indicate a continuously compounded interest rate and $p$ to indicate a continuously compounded inflation rate, the parity conditions over a single period can be restated as

$$\ln(F_1{}^{d/f}/S_0{}^{d/f}) = \ln(E[S_1{}^{d/f}]/S_0{}^{d/f}) = (i^d - i^f) = (E[p^d] - E[p^f]) \quad (4A.10)$$

Over t periods, we can apply the rule $\ln(A^C) = C \ln(A)$ to solve for the t-period international parity conditions in continuously compounded returns.

$$\ln(F_t{}^{d/f}/S_0{}^{d/f}) = \ln(E[S_t{}^{d/f}]/S_0{}^{d/f}) = t(i^d - i^f) = t(E[p^d] - E[p^f]) \quad (4A.11)$$

where the interest and inflation rates are continuously compounded arithmetic mean rates of return over the t periods.

Empirical tests of the international parity conditions generally are conducted in continuously compounded returns because they are additive and are more likely to satisfy assumptions of normality and linearity. We'll return to continuously compounded returns in the next chapter and in the chapters on currency options.

### Real Exchange Rates in Continuously Compounded Returns

Translating Equation 4.13 into continuously compounded returns, the continuously compounded change in the real exchange rate $x_t^{d/f}$ is

$$\begin{aligned} x_t^{d/f} &= \ln(1 + x_t^{d/f}) \\ &= \ln[(S_t^{d/f}/S_{t-1}^{d/f})(1 + p_t^f)/(1 + p_t^d)] \\ &= \ln(S_t^{d/f}/S_{t-1}^{d/f}) + \ln(1 + p_t^f) \\ &= \ln(1 + p_t^d) = s_t^{d/f} + (p_t^f - p_t^d) \end{aligned} \quad (4A.12)$$

for a continuously compounded change in the spot rate $s_t^{d/f} = \ln(S_t^{d/f}/S_{t-1}^{d/f})$. In continuously compounded returns, the change in the real exchange rate is equal to the change in the nominal exchange rate $s_t^{d/f}$ adjusted for the difference in inflation. This formulation is used commonly in empirical tests of PPP.

Consider the real exchange rate example from Section 4.5 in which $S_0^{¥/\$}$ = ¥100/\$, $S_1^{¥/\$}$ = ¥110/\$, $p^{¥}$ = 0 percent, and $p^{\$}$ = 10 percent. The continuously compounded change in the real rate of exchange during the period is

$$\begin{aligned} x_t^{¥/\$} &= \ln(S_1^{¥/\$}/S_0^{¥/\$}) + \ln(1 + p^{\$}) - \ln(1 + p^{¥}) \\ &= \ln((¥110/\$)/(¥100/\$)) + \ln(1.10) - \ln(1.00) \\ &= 0.09531 + 0.09531 = 0.19062 \end{aligned}$$

As in the original example, the real appreciation of the dollar is $i = (e^{0.19062}) - 1 = 0.21$, or a 21 percent change in the real value of the dollar during the period.

### Summary

Continuously compounded returns are convenient because they are additive rather than multiplicative. Continuously compounded returns $i$ are related to holding period returns i according to

$$(1 + i) = e^{i} \Leftrightarrow \ln(1 + i) = \ln(e^{i}) = i \quad (4A.3)$$

Over a single period, the international parity conditions are stated in continuously compounded returns as

$$\ln(F_1^{d/f}/S_0^{d/f}) = \ln(E[S_1^{d/f}]/S_0^{d/f}) = (i^d - i^f) = (E[p^d] - E[p^f]) \quad (4A.10)$$

where $i$ and $p$ represent continuously compounded interest and inflation rates, respectively. In words, the forward premium/discount to the currency spot rate and the expected change in the spot rate are determined by interest rate differentials between the two currencies. If real interest rates are constant across the two currencies, then interest rate differentials are, in turn, determined by inflation differentials. Finally, continuously compounded change in the real exchange rate during period t is given by

$$x_t^{d/f} = s_t^{d/f} + (p_t^f - p_t^d) \quad (4A.12)$$

where $p_t^{\,d} = \ln(1 + p_t^{\,d})$ and $p_t^{\,f} = \ln(1 + p_t^{\,f})$ are the continuously compounded inflation rates observed during the period, and $s_t^{\,d/f} = \ln(S_t^{\,d/f}/S_{t-1}^{\,d/f})$ is the continuously compounded change in the spot exchange rate.

## PROBLEMS

4A.1 Suppose you earn a 100 percent return in one period and then lose 50 percent in the next period. Compute your average periodic rate of return over the two periods using geometric holding period returns. Now, compute your average periodic rate of return using continuously compounded returns. Are these rates of return equivalent?

4A.2 Suppose $P_0^{\,D}$ = D100, $P_0^{\,F}$ = F1, and $S_0^{D/F}$ = D100/F. Inflation rates are $p^D$ = 10 percent and $p^F$ = 21 percent in holding period returns. Transform these inflation rates to continuously compounded returns and find $E[P_1^{\,D}]$, $E[P_1^{\,F}]$, $E[S_1^{D/F}]$, $E[P_2^{\,D}]$, $E[P_2^{\,F}]$, and $E[S_1^{\,D/F}]$ according to the international parity conditions. (Note that this is a repeat of Problem 4.9 using continuously compounded returns.)

# PART Two

# Derivative Securities for Financial Risk Management

*One must still have chaos in oneself to be able to give birth to a dancing star.*

—Nietzsche, Thus Spake Zarathustra

CHAPTER 5

# Currency Futures and Futures Markets

*The best thing about the future is that it comes only one day at a time.*
—Abraham Lincoln

*Currency futures* are similar to currency forward contracts in that each represents an exposure to exchange rates around a predetermined date and price. Whereas forward contracts are traded in an interbank market and are customized to fit the needs of each client, futures contracts are standardized contracts that trade on futures exchanges. Standardization means that futures come in only a limited number of currencies, transaction amounts, and expiration dates. Although this promotes liquidity, it comes at the price of flexibility. For a corporate treasurer, the choice of a forward or futures contract depends on the trade-offs between costs, flexibility, and liquidity.

Exchange-traded financial futures contracts are a major force in international markets. The principal users of the futures markets are large banks and corporations that use the markets to hedge their exposures to financial price risks. If an exposure can be approximately matched by a standardized futures contract traded on a futures exchange, the futures contract can be a low-cost substitute for a customized forward contract from a commercial bank.

## 5.1 FINANCIAL FUTURES EXCHANGES

Spot and forward markets for agricultural products and commodities, such as gold and silver, have been around as long as recorded history. Futures contracts are a relative newcomer, first appearing in Europe as the *lettre de faire* in medieval times. Organized commodity futures exchanges grew up somewhat later. One of the first known futures exchanges serviced the rice market at Osaka, Japan, in the early 1700s. This market bore many similarities to present-day futures markets. Rice futures contracts were standardized according to weight and quality, traded through a futures exchange clearinghouse, and had a specified contract life.

Figure 5.1 shows the growth in exchange-traded futures trading. Futures contracts are traded on derivatives exchanges that trade derivatives on a wide variety of financial and agricultural products and commodities. Much of the recent growth in derivatives trading has been driven by exchanges outside of North America, particularly in China, Korea, India, and Brazil.

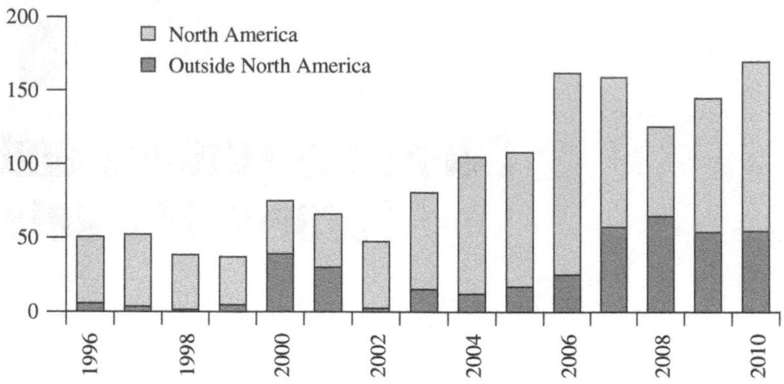


**FIGURE 5.1** Exchange-Traded Currency Futures Outstanding at Year-End (in $ billions).
*Source:* Bank for International Settlements (www.bis.org).

In the United States, the Chicago Board of Trade (CBOT) (www.cbot.com) began trading spot and forward contracts on agricultural products in 1848. Agricultural futures contracts were introduced on the CBOT during the 1860s. Another Chicago futures exchange, the Chicago Mercantile Exchange (CME) (www.cme.com), began trading currency futures contracts in 1972 in response to the dramatic increase in currency risk following the 1971 collapse of the Bretton Woods exchange rate agreement.

*Forex (FX) futures began on the CME in 1972.*

On U.S. exchanges, futures contracts expire on the Monday before the third Wednesday of each contract month. The previous Friday is the last day of trade. Contract sizes vary by exchange. Euro futures have a contract size of €125,000 on the CME and €10,000 on the Euronext exchange. Currency futures on most of the world's exchanges expire in March, June, September, and December.

Figure 5.2 ranks the world's top derivatives exchanges by contract volume. Volumes include futures on a range of products, including equity indices, bonds, interest rates, derivatives, commodities, and currencies. Futures exchanges trade a variety of currency futures contracts based on price quotations in the local currency. For example, the CME trades dollar prices on a variety of currency futures, including pounds, euros, and yen. Many exchanges also offer cross-rate futures contracts. The CME offers a wide variety, including euro futures contracts priced in pounds, yen, and Swiss francs.

Standardized futures contracts promote liquidity, but reduce the flexibility of futures contracts relative to forward contracts. If the amount of a futures contract does not evenly divide into an underlying exposure or if futures contracts do not expire on the same day as an underlying exposure, then futures will not permit a perfect hedge of currency risk.

| Rank | Exchange | 2010 volume | 2000 volume | National market(s) |
|---|---|---|---|---|
| 1 | Korea Exchange | 3,748,861 | 22,626 | Korea |
| 2 | CME Group (includes CBOT and Nymex) | 3,080,492 | 470,856 | U.S. |
| 3 | Eurex (includes ISE) | 2,642,093 | 289,952 | EU |
| 4 | NYSE Euronext | 2,154,742 | 201,686 | U.S. & EU markets |
| 5 | National Stock Exchange of India | 1,615,789 | - | India |
| 6 | BM&F Bovespa | 1,422,104 | 80,074 | Brazil |
| 7 | CBOE Group | 1,123,505 | 47,440 | U.S. |
| 8 | Nasdaq OMX | 1,099,437 | 20,918 | U.S. & Nordic markets |
| 9 | Multi-Commodity Exchange of India | 1,081,814 | - | India |
| 10 | Russian Trading Systems Stock Exchange | 623,992 | - | Russia |
| 11 | Shanghai Futures Exchange | 621,898 | 4,130 | China |
| 12 | Zhengzhou Commodity Exchange | 495,905 | - | China |
| 13 | Dalian Commodity Exchange | 403,168 | - | China |
| 14 | Intercontinental Exchange | 328,946 | - | U.S., U.K., & Canada |
| 15 | Osaka Securities Exchange | 196,350 | 8,708 | Japan |
| 16 | JSE (formerly Johannesburg Securities Exchange) | 169,899 | 22,397 | South Africa |
| 17 | Taiwan Futures Exchange (TFE) | 139,793 | 1,927 | Taiwan |
| 18 | Tokyo Financial Exchange | 121,210 | 50,852 | Japan |
| 19 | London Metal Exchange | 120,258 | 61,413 | U.K. |
| 20 | Hong Kong Exchanges and Clearing | 116,054 | 5,079 | Hong Kong |

Volume includes futures and options on a range of products, including equity indices, bonds, derivatives, commodities, and currencies. Futures on individual equities are excluded. Contract sizes and methods for counting volumes vary by exchange. Data unavailability is indicated with a hyphen ("–").

**FIGURE 5.2** Top 20 Derivatives Exchanges by Contract Volume (in thousands).
*Source:* Futures Industry Association (www.futuresindustry.org).

## 5.2 THE OPERATION OF FUTURES MARKETS

The movie *Trading Places* contains a scene involving the futures market for frozen concentrated orange juice (FCOJ). Eddie Murphy plays a down-and-out con artist named Billy Ray. Dan Aykroyd plays a rich, privileged Ivy-Leaguer named Louis, who trades commodity futures on behalf of a pair of brothers named Duke. The Duke brothers make a \$1 bet over which of these men—Louis (Dan Aykroyd) or Billy Ray (Eddie Murphy)—would prosper if their fortunes were reversed. To wit, is it heredity or environment that makes the man? In an ill-fated social experiment, the Dukes hire Billy Ray and fire Louis. Louis and Billy Ray eventually discover the Dukes' ruse and join forces to seek their revenge.

In the movie, the futures market is concerned over the effect of the winter weather on the orange harvest. A U.S. Department of Agriculture (USDA) report on the status of the orange juice crop finds that the winter was not as bad as expected. The Dukes conspire to steal the report before it becomes public. Louis and Billy Ray intercept the report and send the Duke brothers a false report stating that the winter's toll was worse than expected. On the exchange floor the morning of the report, Louis and Billy Ray orchestrate the following scene:

> *9 A.M. Frozen Concentrated Orange Juice futures open at \$102. The Dukes, thinking the orange harvest will be small, buy FCOJ futures in anticipation of a price rise. Observing the Dukes' behavior and suspecting insider information, other traders follow their lead and buy futures contracts. Louis and Billy Ray are only too happy to oblige and sell as many contracts as they can. By 10 A.M, the price has risen to \$142.*

*10 A.M. The USDA report is read over the television: "The cold winter has apparently not affected the orange harvest." While Louis and Billy Ray are short the orange juice futures contract, most traders (especially the Dukes) are long. Panic selling sets in, and the price starts to fall. Louis and Billy Ray have closed out their position by the time the price hits $29. With an initial margin of 2 percent, Louis and Billy Ray have earned up to [($142–$29)/$29]/(0.02) = 19483% on their investments in FCOJ futures. When the Duke brothers' margin call comes in at $394 million, the Dukes are bankrupt.*

This amusing scene faithfully represents two powerful forces moving the market.

- *Public information.* Information is valuable only when it differs from expectations. "The winter was bad" conveys no information to the market if the market already knew the winter was bad. "The winter was not as bad as expected" conveys much information that is relevant to the value of oranges and frozen concentrated orange juice futures contracts.
- *Private information.* The value of private information is clearly portrayed. Private information (if it is accurate!) can let investors buy before the price rises and sell before the price falls. Although the Dukes acquired their private information illegally, private information also can be obtained by legal means. (Hey, someone had to survey those orange groves.)

Although entertaining, this fanciful scene is unrealistic because of the exaggerated price movements of the FCOJ futures contract. Price movement from $102 to $142 and then back to $29 is highly unlikely, and trading would be halted in any case if the exchange has price limits in place. Many commodities trade within a ±1 percent band of opening price. Based on an opening price of $102, a 1 percent daily price limit would limit movement up or down by $1.02. This trading delay hopefully would have given the Duke brothers and the rest of the market a chance to incorporate information on the orange juice harvest in a more reasoned manner.

## 5.3 FUTURES CONTRACTS

The major problem with forward contracts is that forwards are pure credit instruments. Whichever way the spot rate of exchange moves, one party has an incentive to default. Consider a forward contract on pounds sterling at a rate of $1.5000/£. If the pound appreciates to $1.6000/£ on the expiration date, then whoever has agreed to sell pounds at the forward rate of $1.5000/£ has an incentive to default. If the pound depreciates to $1.4000/£, then the party obliged to buy pounds at the forward rate of $1.5000/£ has an incentive to default.

### The Futures Contract Solution

Futures contracts provide a remedy for the default risk inherent in forward contracts through the following conventions (see Figure 5.3):

| | Forwards | Exchange-traded futures |
|---|---|---|
| 1. Location | Bank | Exchange floor or electronic trading system |
| 2. Maturity | Negotiated; typically from 1 week to 10 years | CME contracts expire on the Monday before the third Wednesday of the month; last trading day is the previous Friday; seller chooses when to make delivery during the delivery month |
| 3. Amount | Negotiated | In increments of a contract amount, such as €125,000 for euros on the CME; "open interest" = number of contracts |
| 4. Fees | Bid-ask spread | Commissions charged per "round turn" (usually about $30 per contract on the CME) |
| 5. Counterparty | Bank | Exchange clearinghouse |
| 6. Collateral | Negotiated; depends on customer's credit risk | Purchaser must deposit an initial margin (bank letter of credit, cash, T-bills, etc.); contract is then "marked-to-market" daily; an initial margin and a maintenance margin ensure daily payment |
| 7. Settlement | Nearly all | Less than 5% settled by physical delivery; most positions are closed early by buying the opposite futures position; open interest is then netted out |
| 8. Trading hours | Banking hours (possibly 24 hours) | The CME's Globex trading platform allows 24-hour trading; open outcry trade is during exchange hours only |

**FIGURE 5.3** Forwards versus CME Futures Contracts.

- An exchange clearinghouse takes one side of every transaction.
- Futures contracts are marked-to-market on a daily basis.
- An initial margin and a maintenance margin are required.

> ***Futures have less default risk than forwards.***

With an exchange clearinghouse on one side of every transaction, futures market participants are ensured daily settlement of their contract by the clearinghouse. The exchange insures itself against loss through a ***margin requirement*** and by settling changes in the value of each contract on a daily basis, or ***marking-to-market.*** The clearinghouse matches buy and sell orders and then takes one side of each contract, so that it has a zero net position in each contract. Consequently, at any given time the clearinghouse faces at most one day's risk in each contract.

A margin account protects the broker, although margin accounts on futures perform this function in a different way than margin accounts on stock do. A margin account on an equity account allows an equity investor to borrow from the broker in order to buy additional shares of stock. A maintenance margin serves as a down payment on the price of the stock, with the difference between the price of the stock and the maintenance margin borrowed from the broker. The borrower must pay back the broker when the stock position is liquidated. On a futures contract, the margin is not a down payment on a loan; rather, it is a performance bond ensuring that the customer will make required payments as the contract is marked-to-market.

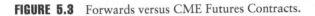

Suppose a €125,000 futures contract is purchased at a price of $1.1754/€ on the CME. The purchaser must deposit an initial margin, although no dollars or euros are exchanged upon purchase of the contract. If the futures price rises by $0.0010/€ to $1.1764/€ at the close of trading on the following day, then the clearinghouse adds ($0.0010/€)(€125,000) = $125 to the purchaser's margin account. If the contract price subsequently falls back to \$1.1754/€, \$125 is transferred from the customer's margin account to the clearinghouse. This daily marking-to-market ensures that the clearinghouse's exposure to currency price risk is limited to the gain or loss from a single day's change in price.

Maintenance margins and price limits for futures are determined by the individual futures exchanges and vary by contract and by exchange. The CME has no price limits during the first 15 minutes of trade. A schedule of expanding price limits follows the 15-minute opening period. Limits also are waived during the last 15 minutes of trade for expiring contracts. Margin requirements and daily price limits are revised periodically by the exchanges according to volatility in the underlying asset.

Suppose the maintenance margin is \$2,000 for a €125,000 futures contract on the CME. The minimum dollar price tick of one basis point (0.01 percent) on the CME euro futures contract is worth (\$0.0001/€)(€125,000/contract) = \$12.50 per contract. If the maximum price move before a limit is reached is 100 basis points (plus or minus 1 percent), then the value of the contract can move up or down by \$1,250. Since the \$2,000 maintenance margin is greater than the daily price limit of \$1,250, the clearinghouse can recoup 1-day price variations (up to the price limit) in the futures contract. Maintenance margins are set large enough to cover all but the most extreme price movements. If an investor cannot meet a margin call, the exchange clearinghouse cancels the contract and offsets its position in the futures market on the following day.

Don't be fooled by price limits. Just because futures prices are artificially limited to a trading band around the current price does not mean that true prices can't exceed these bounds. If the true price moves more than the price limit in a single day, default risk exists on the difference. Fortunately, since the exchange clearinghouse is on the other side of every transaction, the holder of a futures contract can rest assured payment will be received. The futures exchange clearinghouse further reduces its risk by requiring that futures be traded through a brokerage house (called a "futures commission merchant" in the United States) rather than an end customer. If an end customer cannot meet its margin call, it is the broker rather than the clearinghouse that bears the consequences.

### A Futures Contract as a Portfolio of One-Day Forward Contracts

Because futures are marked-to-market each day, a futures contract can be viewed as a bundle of consecutive 1-day forward contracts. Each day, the previous day's forward contract is replaced by a new 1-day forward contract with a delivery price equal to the closing (or settlement) price from the previous day's contract. At the end of each day, the previous forward contract is settled and a new 1-day forward contract is created. The purchaser of a futures contract buys the entire package. A 3-month futures contract, for instance, contains 90 renewable 1-day forward contracts. The futures exchange clearinghouse renews the contract daily until expiration so long as the maintenance margin is satisfied. On the investor's side of the futures contract, an offsetting transaction can be made at any time to cancel the position.

> *A futures contract is a portfolio of renewable 1-day forwards.*

Forward and futures contracts are equivalent once they are adjusted for differences in contract terms and liquidity. Indeed, the difference between a futures and a forward contract is operational rather than valuational, in that it depends on the contracts themselves (the deliverable asset, settlement procedures, maturity dates, and amounts) and not directly on prices.[1] As with forward contracts, the price $Fut_t^{d/f}$ of a futures contract is determined by relative interest rates and the current spot rate of exchange according to interest rate parity.

$$Fut_t^{d/f} = F_t^{d/f} = s_0^{d/f}[(1 + i^d)/(1 + i^f)]^t \qquad (5.1)$$

As with forwards, futures contracts allow you to hedge against nominal, but not real, changes in currency values. If inflation in the foreign currency is more than expected, then the forward rate won't buy as much purchasing power as you expected. Currency forward and futures contracts can eliminate currency risk, but not inflation or interest rate risk within any single currency.

## 5.4 FORWARD VERSUS FUTURES MARKET HEDGES

*Interest rate parity determines futures prices.*

Both futures and forward prices are determined according to interest rate parity. Suppose we denote futures and forward prices for a currency f in terms of currency d at time t for exchange at time T as $Fut_{t,T}^{d/f}$ and $F_{t,T}^{d/f}$, respectively. At expiration, both futures and forward prices converge to spot prices because

$$\begin{aligned} Fut_{t,T}^{d/f} &= F_{t,T}^{d/f} = S_t^{d/f}[(1 + i^d)/(1 + i^f)]^{T-t} \\ &= S_T^{d/f} \quad \text{as} \quad t \rightarrow T \end{aligned} \qquad (5.2)$$

This is the same as Equation 5.1, except that time is measured backward from the expiration date rather than forward from the present. This is a convenient representation of the convergence of the futures price to the spot price at expiration. The rest of this section compares futures and forward market hedges of currency risk.

### Exposure to Currency Risk and Currency Risk Profiles

Watanabe Distributing is a U.S. firm that buys Japanese electronics and resells them to a chain of retail stores in Europe. It is now the third Friday in December. Watanabe has promised to pay its Japanese supplier ¥37,500,000 on the third Friday in March (which happens to be the expiration date of a CME futures contract). A German retailer has promised to pay Watanabe €250,000 on the same date. Watanabe's expected cash flows are shown here.

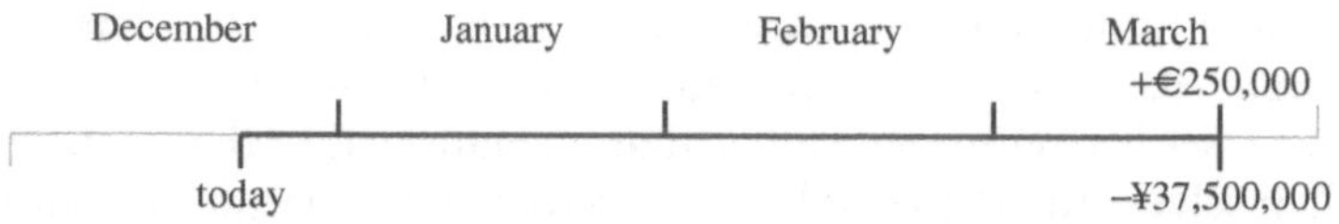


Watanabe is short yen and long euros three months forward. Watanabe's yen and euro cash flow exposures and ***risk*** (***payoff***) ***profiles*** are as follows:

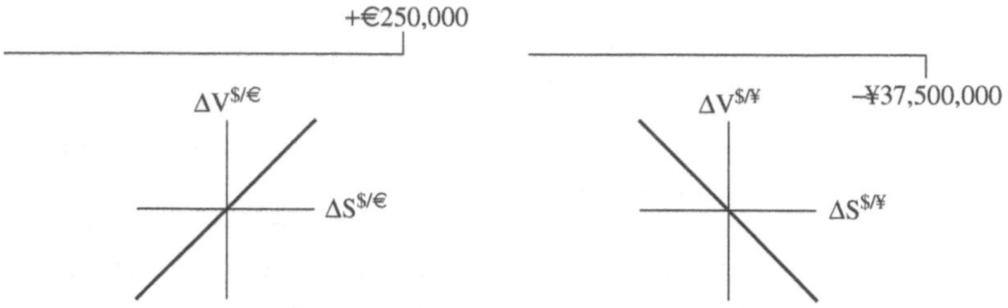


Depending on the exchange rates $S_t^{\$/¥}$ and $S_t^{\$/€}$, Watanabe might be spending some sleepless nights between now and March.

## Forward Market Hedges

Watanabe can hedge these exposures by buying ¥37,500,000 forward and selling €250,000 forward. Suppose forward rates are equal to current spot rates such that $S_0^{\$/¥} = F_{0,T}^{\$/¥} = \$0.00800/¥$ and $S_0^{\$/€} = F_{0,T}^{\$/€} = \$1.2000/€$. Buying yen forward is equivalent to selling (¥37,500,000)($0.00800/¥) = $300,000 forward. Selling euros forward is equivalent to buying (€250,000)($1.2000/€) = $300,000 forward. These forward contracts lock in the following cash flows and payoff profiles:

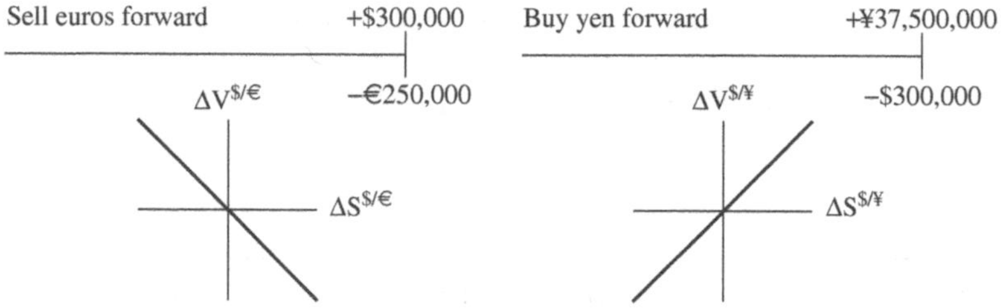


In this example, the $300,000 cash outflow of the long yen position exactly offsets the $300,000 inflow of the short euro position. When combined with Watanabe's underlying short yen and long euro positions, these transactions exactly neutralize Watanabe's exposures to the yen and euro.

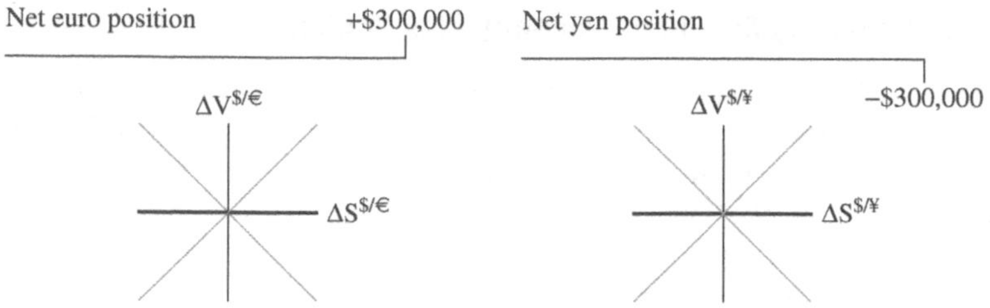

The net position has no exposure to currency risk, and Watanabe can now sleep soundly at night.

### Futures Market Hedges

These cash flows are an integer multiple of the CME futures contract and occur on a CME expiration date, so they can be hedged exactly. Watanabe needs to buy three CME 3-month yen futures contracts worth ¥37,500,000 and sell two CME 3-month euro futures contracts worth €250,000. Cash inflows in each currency will be exactly offset by outflows, and Watanabe has no net exposure to currency risk.

### Forwards versus Futures: Vivéla Différence

The biggest difference between futures and forwards is that changes in the underlying spot rate are settled daily in futures, whereas they are settled at maturity in a forward. Suppose the yen spot rate is $S_0{}^{\$/¥} = \$0.010000/¥$ and that 180-day interest rates are $i^{\$} = 4.03$ and $i^{¥} = 1.00$ percent. Today's futures and forward prices for exchange in six months are given by interest rate parity.

$$\begin{aligned} Fut_{0,1}{}^{\$/¥} = F_{0,1}{}^{\$/¥} &= S_0{}^{\$/¥}[(1+i^{\$})/(1+i^{¥})]^{1-0} \\ &= (\$0.010000/¥)[(1.0403)/(1.0100)]^1 \\ &= \$0.010300/¥ \end{aligned}$$

The yen is selling at a 3 percent forward premium because the ratio of Eurodollar and Euroyen interest rates is 3 percent.

> *Futures are marked-to-market daily.*

Suppose actual spot rates rise by \$0.000005/¥ per day over each of the next 180 days to $S_1{}^{\$/¥} = (\$0.010000/¥) + (\$0.000005/¥)(180) = \$0.010900/¥$. This is a 9 percent increase over the current rate of \$0.010000/¥. The purchaser of a yen forward would pay $F_1{}^{\$/¥} = \$0.010300/¥$ at expiration for yen worth \$0.010900/¥ in the spot market, for a gain of \$0.000600/¥ at expiration.

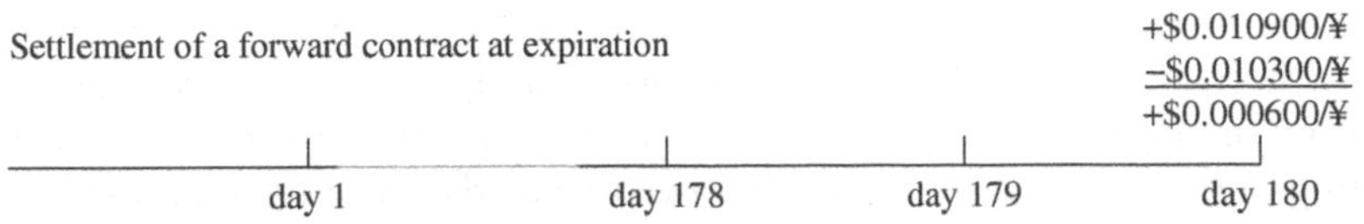


This is a profit of $(\$0.000600/¥)/(\$0.010000/¥) = 0.06$, or 6 percent on each yen purchased.

In contrast, the futures contract is settled one day at a time. According to interest rate parity, the spot price is expected to rise by $(\$0.0003/¥)/(180 \text{ days}) = \$0.000001\overline{6}/¥$ per day. If in fact the yen rises by $(\$0.0009/¥)/(180 \text{ days}) = \$0.000005/¥$ per day, there is a net gain at each daily settlement of (\$0.0006/¥)/(180 days) = $\$0.00000\overline{3}$/¥. Accumulated over 180 days, this equals a 6 percent gain. At expiration, the accumulated gain on the futures contract is the same as the gain on the forward contract. The difference is that the futures gain is received one day at a time.

Daily settlement of a futures contract (sum of all 180 days = $0.0006/¥)

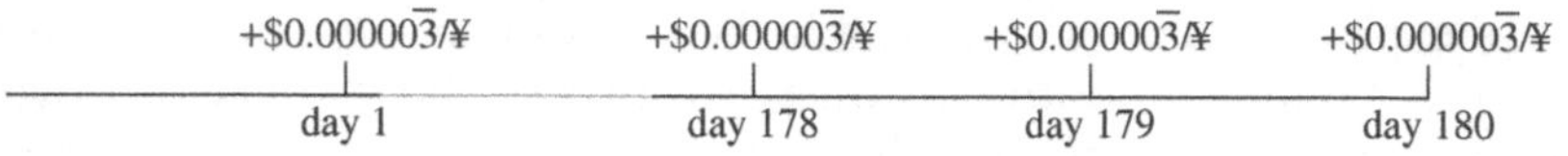


*The net gain or loss on futures is the same as on a forward.*

In the more general case in which exchange rates fluctuate randomly over time, the net gain at the expiration of the forward contract still equals the sum of the daily settlements on a comparable futures contract. Figure 5.4 shows spot and futures prices that begin at $S_0^{\$/¥}$ = \$0.010000/¥ and $Fut_{0,1}^{\$/¥}$ = \$0.0103000/¥ and then fluctuate randomly toward a spot price at expiration of $S_T^{\$/¥}$ = \$0.010900/¥. As in the previous example, day-to-day changes in the futures price are settled daily through the maintenance margin account as the contract is marked-to-market at each day's close. At the end of the contract, the futures price will have converged to the spot exchange rate. Since the beginning and ending points are the same as in the previous example, the sum of the payments to or from each customer's margin account over the life of the futures contract must equal the gain or loss at expiration on a comparable forward contract. The size and timing of the cash flows from the futures contract depend on the time path of the futures price, but the net gain or loss is the same as on the forward contract. This is the reason futures and forwards are near substitutes for hedging purposes and share the same risk profiles.

## Standardized or Customized: Which Do You Choose?

*A perfect hedge exactly offsets the underlying exposure.*

The size, timing, and currency underlying a forward contract are negotiated between the bank and its client, so the transaction exposure of a foreign currency cash inflow or outflow can be exactly matched with a forward contract. If the size and timing of the foreign currency cash flow are exactly offset by a forward contract, the forward provides a ***perfect hedge*** against currency risk.

Futures provide a perfect hedge against currency risk only when the underlying transaction falls on the same day and is in an integer multiple of a futures contract. To the extent that the amount or timing of cash flows does not match an exchange-traded contract, futures provide only an imperfect hedge. The size mismatch is a problem only for small transactions. The maturity mismatch can be important, because exchange-traded contracts cannot be tailored to the maturity date of the

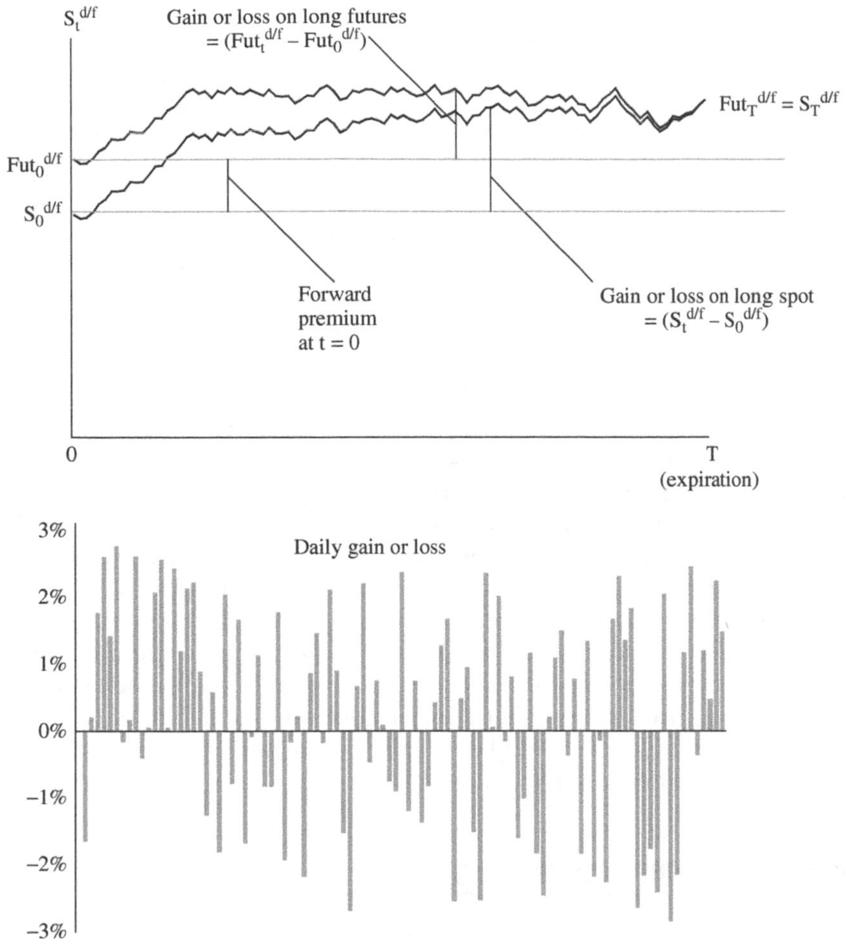


**FIGURE 5.4** Futures and Spot Price Convergence.

exposure. For the same reason, forward and futures contracts cannot be compared on cost alone unless the size and maturity of the forward and futures positions are identical.

## 5.5 FUTURES HEDGES USING CROSS-EXCHANGE RATES

Multinational Corporations (MNCs) with cash flows in multiple currencies should determine their net exposure in each currency and at each future date. Consider Watanabe Distributing's long euro and short yen cross-rate exposure from Section 5.4. If Watanabe hedges using CME futures contracts denominated in dollars as in the example, then the dollar cash flow on the yen contract exactly offsets the dollar cash flow on the euro contract. Total hedging costs might be reduced if Watanabe buys yen and sells euros directly using a ¥/€ cross-rate futures contract, rather than going through dollars as in the CME futures contracts. The underlying exposures and the futures cross hedge are shown here.

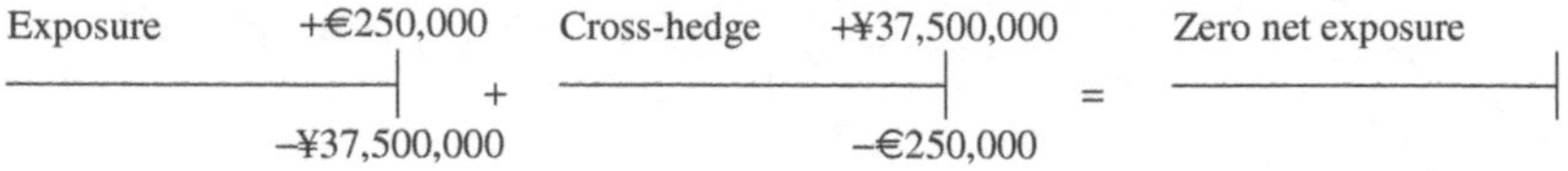


Watanabe can trade ¥/€ futures on the CME. Triangular arbitrage ensures that cross rates are in equilibrium, so the ¥/€ spot rate must be $S^{¥/€} = S^{¥/\$}S^{\$/€} = (\$1.2000/€)/(\$0.00800/¥) = ¥150/€$. At this price, each contract is worth $(¥150/€)(€125{,}000) = ¥18{,}750{,}000$. If Watanabe sells two ¥/€ futures, then Watanabe's euro exposure is $2(€125{,}000) = €250{,}000$ short. The offsetting exposure in yen is $2(¥18{,}750{,}000) = ¥37{,}500{,}000$ long. Watanabe's yen exposure is completely hedged with this position. The commission charged on two ¥/€ CME contracts is likely to be less than that on three CME futures contracts (one $/¥ and two $/€ contracts) when going through dollars.

Watanabe should shop around in order to hedge the exposure most effectively and at the least cost. For example, a ¥/€ futures hedge on the TFE (www.tfx.co.jp/en/) might be less expensive than a CME cross hedge, and just as effective. To execute this hedge, Watanabe would need to contact a futures broker (a "trading member" in Japan) authorized to trade futures on the TFE. Ideally, contract terms on the exchange would match the terms of the underlying exposure. Contract size is not a problem for Watanabe, because the TFE trades €10,000 contracts. TFE futures also mature in March, June, September, and December. The choice of a CME or a TFE futures hedge thus comes down to the cost of trade.

## 5.6 HEDGING WITH CURRENCY FUTURES

Forward contracts hedge foreign currency cash flows one-to-one when the forward contract matches the size, timing, and currency of the underlying exposure. Futures hedges also provide a perfect hedge against currency risk when the amount of a transaction that is exposed to currency risk is an even multiple of a futures contract and matures on the same date as a futures contract in the same currency. Exchange-traded futures contracts cannot be tailored to meet the unique needs of each customer because they come in only a limited number of contract sizes, maturities, and currencies. Figure 5.5 presents a classification of futures hedges as a function of the maturity and currency of the underlying exposure. The rest of this section discusses these futures hedges.

### Maturity Mismatches and Delta Hedges

A futures hedge is called a ***delta hedge*** when there is a mismatch between the maturity—but not the currency—of a futures contract and the underlying exposure. When there is a maturity mismatch, a futures hedge cannot provide a perfect hedge against currency risk.

| Hedge (hedge ratio estimation) | | Currency | |
|---|---|---|---|
| | | Exact match | Mismatch |
| Maturity | Exact match | Perfect hedge: $s_t^{d/f} = \alpha + \beta\, s_t^{d/f} + e_t$ (such that $\alpha = 0$, $\beta = 1$, and $r^2 = 1$) | Cross hedge $s_t^{d/f} = \alpha + \beta\, s_t^{d/f_2} + e_t$ |
| | Mismatch | Delta hedge $s_t^{d/f} = \alpha + \beta\, fut_t^{d/f} + e_t$ | Delta hedge $s_t^{d/f_1} = \alpha + \beta\, fut_t^{d/f_2} + e_t$ |

**FIGURE 5.5** A Classification of Future Hedges.

***A delta hedge has a maturity mismatch.***

Suppose that today is Friday, March 13 (time 0), and that Chen Machinery Company has a S\$10 million (Singapore dollar) obligation due on Friday, October 26. There are 227 days between March 13 and October 26, so with annual compounding this is $t = (227/365)$ of one year. The nearest CME Singapore dollar futures contracts mature on Friday, September 11, and on Friday, December 16. This maturity mismatch is shown here.

A hedge with the futures contract that expires on September 11 hedges only against currency risk through that date. Chen remains exposed to changes in currency values from the end of the contract through October 26. The December futures contract is a better choice because it can hedge currency risk through October 26 and can then be canceled. December 16 is 278 days after March 13, so the time until expiration of the December contract is $T = (278/365)$ of one year.

Suppose the spot rate is $S_0^{\$/S\$} = \$0.6010/S\$$ on March 13. Annual interest rates in the United States and Singapore are $i^{\$} = 6.24\%$ and $i^{S\$} = 4.04\%$, respectively. According to interest rate parity, the forward price for exchange on October 26 is

$$\begin{aligned} F_{0,t}^{\$/S\$} &= S_0^{\$/S\$}[(1+i^{\$})/(1+i^{S\$})]^t \\ &= (\$0.6010/S\$)[(1.0624)/(1.0404)]^{(227/365)} \\ &\approx \$0.6089/S\$ \end{aligned} \tag{5.3}$$

Chen can form a perfect hedge with a long forward for delivery of S\$10 million on October 26 in exchange for (\$0.6089/S\$)(S\$10,000,000) = \$6,089,000. As we shall see, a futures hedge using the December 16 futures contract can eliminate most—but not all—of Chen's S\$ exposure.

### The Basis Risk of a Delta Hedge

*Basis is the difference between nominal interest rates.*

In a futures hedge, the underlying position is settled in the spot market and the futures position is settled at the futures price. Although futures converge to spot prices at expiration, prior to expiration there is a risk that interest rates will change in one or both currencies. If interest rates change, the forward premium or discount also will change through interest rate parity.

The interest rate differential often is approximated by the simple difference in nominal interest rates ($i^d - i^f$). This difference is called the ***basis***. The basis changes as interest rates rise and fall. The risk of unexpected change in the relation between the futures price and the spot price is called ***basis risk***. When there is a maturity mismatch between a futures contract and the underlying exposure, basis risk makes a futures hedge slightly riskier than a forward hedge.

Using the Chen Machinery Company example, here is how basis is determined and how it can change prior to expiration. As with a forward contract, the price of the March 13 S$ futures contract for December delivery (i.e., at time T in 278 days) is determined by interest rate parity.

$$\begin{aligned}Fut_{0,T}{}^{\$/S\$} &= S_0{}^{\$/S\$}[(1+i^{\$})/(1+i^{S\$})]^T \\ &= (\$0.6010/S\$)[(1.0624)/(1.0404)]^{(278/365)} \\ &\approx \$0.6107/S\$ \qquad (5.4)\end{aligned}$$

When this price is set on March 13, the expectation is that on October 26 the spot price will not have risen by the full amount. The expectation of the October 26 spot price is the same as the price for forward delivery on that date.

*Basis risk: unexpected change in the relation between spot and futures prices.*

$$\begin{aligned}F_{0,t}{}^{\$/S\$} &= E[S_{0,t}\$/S\$] = S_0{}^{\$/S\$}[(1+i^{\$})/(1+i^{S\$})]^t \\ &= (\$0.6010/S\$)[(1.0624)/(1.0404)]^{(227/365)} \\ &\approx \$0.6089/S\$ \qquad (5.5)\end{aligned}$$

This expectation will hold over the life of the exposure only if the interest rate ratio $(1+i^{\$})/(1+i^{S\$}) = 1.0624/1.0404 = 1.0211$ remains constant. This ratio is the "basis" for changes in futures prices.

The convergence of futures prices to the spot price at expiration is almost linear over time, so the basis $(i^{\$} - i^{S\$}) = (6.24\% - 4.04\%) = 2.20$ percent often is used in lieu of the ratio of interest rates in the interest rate parity relation. Using the basis approximation, the spot price on October 26 is predicted to be

| time 0 | time t | time T |
|---|---|---|
| Mar 13 | Oct 26 | Dec 16 |
| | –S\$10 million | |

**Actual profit (loss) on long S\$ futures position:** $(Fut_{t,T}^{\$/S\$} - Fut_{0,T}^{\$/S\$})$

**Unexpected profit (loss) on short S\$ spot position:** $-(S_t^{\$/S\$} - E[S_t^{\$/S\$}])$ <u>Equation</u>

Time zero: $S_0^{\$/S\$} = \$0.6010/S\$$ with $i^{\$} = 6.24\%$ and $i^{S\$} = 4.04\%$

$\Rightarrow Fut_{0,T}^{\$/S\$} = S_0^{\$/S\$}[(1+i^{\$})/(1+i^{S\$})]^T$ (5.4)

$= (\$0.6010/S\$)\,[(1.0624)/(1.0404)]^{(278/365)} \approx \$0.6107/S\$$

$\Rightarrow E[S_t^{\$/S\$}] = S_0^{\$/S\$}[(1+i^{\$})/(1+i^{S\$})]^t$ and $[(1+i^{\$})/(1+i^{S\$})^t]$ (5.5)

$= (\$0.6010/S\$)\,[(1.0624)/(1.0404)]^{(277/365)} \approx \$0.6089/S\$$

Scenario #1: $S_t^{\$/S\$} = \$0.6089/S\$$ with $i^{\$} = 6.24\%$ and $i^{S\$} = 4.04\%$

$Fut_{t,T}^{\$/S\$} = (\$0.6089/S\$)\,[(1.0624)/(1.0404)]^{(51/365)} \approx \$0.6107/S\$$ (5.4)

| | | |
|---|---|---|
| Profit on long futures: | +(\$0.6107/S\$ – \$0.6107/S\$) | +\$0.0000/S\$ |
| Profit on short spot: | –(\$0.6089/S\$ – \$0.6089/S\$) | <u>–\$0.0000/S\$</u> |
| Net gain | \$0.0000/S\$ | |

Scenario #2: $S_t^{\$/S\$} = \underline{\$0.6255/S\$}$ with $i^{\$} = 6.24\%$ and $i^{S\$} = \underline{4.54\%}$ (5.4)

$\Rightarrow Fut_{t,T}^{\$/S\$} = (\$0.6255/S\$)\,[(1.0624)/(1.0454)]^{(51/365)} \approx \$0.6269/S\$$

| | | |
|---|---|---|
| Profit on long futures: | +(\$0.6269/S\$ – \$0.6107/S\$) | +\$0.0162/S\$ |
| Profit on short spot: | –(\$0.6255/S\$ – \$0.6089/S\$) | <u>–\$0.0166/S\$</u> |
| Net gain | –\$0.0004/S\$ | |

Scenario #3: $S_t^{\$/S\$} = \underline{\$0.5774/S\$}$ with $i^{\$} = \underline{6.74\%}$ and $i^{S\$} = 4.04\%$ (5.4)

$\Rightarrow Fut_{t,T}^{\$/S\$} = (\$0.5774/S\$)\,[(1.0624)/(1.0404)]^{(51/365)} \approx \$0.5795/S\$$

| | | |
|---|---|---|
| Profit on long futures: | +(\$0.5795/S\$ – \$0.6107/S\$) | –\$0.0312/S\$ |
| Profit on short spot: | –(\$0.5774/S\$ – \$0.6089/S\$) | <u>+\$0.0315/S\$</u> |
| Net gain | \$0.0003/S\$ | |

**FIGURE 5.6** An Example of a Delta Hedge.

$(0.0220)(227/365) = 0.0137$, or 1.37 percent above the March spot price. This suggests an October spot price of (\$0.6010/S\$)(1.0137) = \$0.6092/S\$, which is fairly close to the forward price of \$0.6089/S\$ from Equation 5.5.

On October 26, there are 51 days remaining on the contract. This contract provides a perfect hedge of Chen's exposure so long as the basis does not change. If the basis changes, then the hedge is imperfect and there will be some variability in the hedged payoffs. Figure 5.6 provides an example using three scenarios.

**Scenario #1** Scenario #1 reflects the market's expectation. In this scenario, the basis $(i^{\$} - i^{S\$})$ has not changed and the spot rate on October 26 turns out to be the \$0.6089/S\$ rate predicted by Equation 5.5. On October 26, the futures price for December delivery is based on the prevailing spot exchange rate of \$0.6089/S\$, the basis of 2.20 percent per year, and the $(T - t) = (278 - 227) = 51$ days remaining on the futures contract according to Equation 5.4.

$$Fut_{t,T}^{\$/S\$} = S_t^{\$/S\$}[(1+i^{\$})/(1+i^{S\$})]^{T-t}$$
$$= (\$0.6089/S\$)[(1.0624)/(1.0404)]^{(51/365)}$$
$$\approx \$0.6107/S\$$$

This is the same time T price expected at time t = 0. In this scenario, there are no gains or losses on the long futures position or on the underlying short position in spot currency.

$$\text{Profit on long futures: } (Fut_{t,T}^{\$/S\$} - Fut_{0,T}^{\$/S\$}) = (\$0.6107/S\$ - \$0.6107/S\$)$$
$$= \$0.00/S\$$$
$$\text{Profit on short spot: } -(S_t^{\$/S\$} - E[S_t^{\$/S\$}]) = -(\$0.6089/S\$ - \$0.6089/S\$)$$
$$= \$0.00/S\$$$

Consequently, in this scenario there is no gain or loss on the combined position.

**Scenario #2** In this scenario, the S\$ interest rate rose to $i^{S\$} = 4.54\%$ and the Singapore dollar rose to $S_t^{\$/S\$} = \$0.6255/S\$$ on October 26. With these new rates, the October futures price for December delivery is

$$Fut_{t,T}^{\$/S\$} = S_t^{\$/S\$}[(1 + i^{\$})/(1 + i^{S\$})]^{T-t}$$
$$= (\$0.6255/S\$)[(1.0624)/(1.0454)]^{(51/365)}$$
$$\approx \$0.6269/S\$$$

The gains (losses) on the futures and spot positions are now as follows:

$$\text{Profit on long futures: } (Fut_{t,T}^{\$/S\$} - Fut_{0,T}^{\$/S\$}) = (\$0.6269/S\$ - \$0.6107/S\$)$$
$$= +\$0.0162/S\$$$
$$\text{Profit on short spot: } -(S_t^{\$/S\$} - E[S_t^{\$/S\$}]) = -(\$0.6255/S\$ - \$0.6089/S\$)$$
$$= -\$0.0166/S\$$$

The net position is then +(\$0.0162/S\$) – (\$0.0166/S\$) = –\$0.0004/S\$, or –\$4,000 based on the S\$10 million underlying positions. This loss arises because of a change in the Singapore dollar interest rate and not because of change in the spot exchange rate.[2]

**Scenario #3** In this scenario, dollar interest rates rose to $i^{\$} = 6.74$ percent and the spot rate fell to $S_t^{\$/S\$} = \$0.5774/S\$$. Singaporean interest rates remain unchanged at $i^{S\$} = 4.04$ percent. The October futures price for December delivery is

$$Fut_{t,}^{\$/S\$} = S_t^{\$/S\$}[(1 + i^{\$})/(1 + i^{S\$})]^{T-t}$$
$$= (\$0.5774/S\$)[(1.0674)/(1.0404)]^{(51/365)}$$
$$\approx \$0.5795/S\$$$

In this instance, the gains (losses) on the two positions are

$$\text{Profit on long futures: } (Fut_{t,T}{}^{\$/S\$} - Fut_{0,T}{}^{\$/S\$}) = (\$0.5795/S\$ - \$0.6107/S\$)$$
$$= -\$0.0312/S\$$$
$$\text{Profit on short spot: } -(S_t{}^{\$/S\$} - E[S_t{}^{\$/S\$}]) = -(\$0.5774/S\$ - \$0.6089/S\$)$$
$$= +\$0.0315/S\$$$

The net gain is (−\$0.0312/S\$ + \$0.0315/S\$) = +\$0.0003/S\$, or \$3,000 based on the S\$10 million short and long positions. Again, it is basis risk that spoils the futures hedge.

Chen's underlying short position in Singapore dollars is exposed to considerable currency risk. If the range of spot rates is from \$0.5774/S\$ to \$0.6255/S\$, as in Scenarios #2 and #3, then the range of dollar obligations is \$481,000 (from −\$5,774,000 to −\$6,255,000) on the underlying exposure in the spot market. This risk arises from *variability in the level of the exchange rate.* A forward contract can reduce the variability of the hedged position to zero. The futures hedge does almost as well, producing a \$7,000 range of outcomes (from −\$4,000 to +\$3,000). The remaining risk in the futures hedge arises from *variability in the basis*—the risk that interest rates in one or both currencies will change unexpectedly. The futures hedge transforms the nature of Chen's currency risk exposure from a bet on exchange rates to a bet on the difference between domestic and foreign interest rates.

### Futures Hedging Using the Hedge Ratio

The optimal ***hedge ratio*** $N_F{}^*$ of a forward position is defined as

$$N_F{}^* = \text{Amount in forward position/Amount exposed to currency risk} \quad (5.6)$$

In a perfect forward hedge, the forward contract is the same size as the underlying exposure, and the optimal hedge ratio is $N_F{}^* = -1$. The minus sign indicates that the forward position is opposite (short) the underlying exposure. A forward contract provides a perfect hedge because gains (losses) on the underlying position are exactly offset by losses (gains) on the forward position.

**The Futures Hedge** As with forward contracts, most of the change in the value of a futures contract is derived from change in the underlying spot rate. However, because futures contracts are exposed to basis risk, there is not a one-to-one relation between spot prices and futures prices. For this reason, futures contracts generally do not provide perfect hedges against currency exposure. However, futures contracts can provide very good hedges, because basis risk is small relative to currency risk.

The relation between spot and futures price changes can be viewed as a regression equation

$$S_t{}^{\$/S\$} = \alpha + \beta \, fut_t{}^{\$/S\$} + e_t \quad (5.7)$$

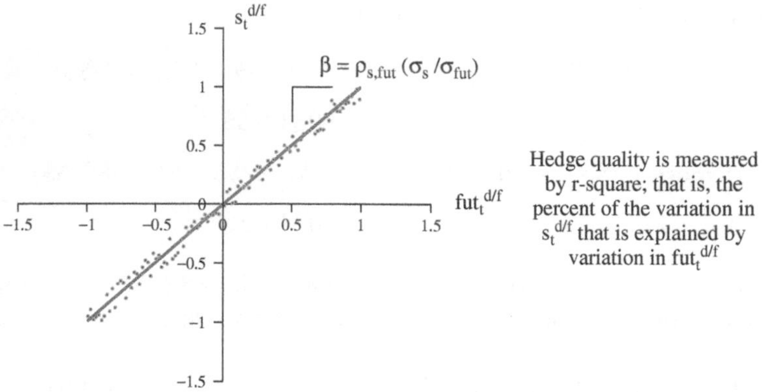


**FIGURE 5.7** Linear Regression and the Hedge Ratio.

where $s_t^{\$/S\$} = (S_t^{\$/S\$} - S_{t-1}^{\$/S\$})/S_{t-1}^{\$/S\$}$ and $fut_t^{\$/S\$} = (Fut_t^{\$/S\$} - Fut_{t-1}^{\$/S\$})/Fut_{t-1}^{\$/S\$}$ are percentage changes in spot and futures prices during period t. In the Chen example, this regression should be estimated using futures contracts that mature in 7½ months (e.g., from March through October). The regression then provides an estimate of how well changes in futures prices predict changes in spot prices over 7½-month maturities.

The regression in Equation 5.7 is shown graphically in Figure 5.7. Since spot and futures prices are close to a random walk, the expectations of both $Fut_t^{\$/S\$}$ and $s_t^{\$/S\$}$ are zero and the intercept term $\alpha$ in this regression is usually ignored. As in any regression, the slope $\beta$ in Equation 5.7 is equal to

$$\beta = (\sigma_{s,fut})/(\sigma_{fut^2}) = \rho_{s,fut}(\sigma_s/\sigma_{fut}) \tag{5.8}$$

The slope coefficient $\beta$ measures changes in futures prices relative to changes in spot prices. The error term $e_t$ captures any variation in spot rate changes $s_t^{\$/S\$}$ that is unrelated to futures price changes $fut_t^{\$/S\$}$.

If the historical relation between spot prices and futures prices is a reasonable approximation of the expected future relation, then this regression can be used to estimate the number of futures contracts that will minimize the variance of the hedged position. Let $N_S$ be the size of the underlying exposure to currency risk and $N_{Fut}$ the amount of currency to be bought or sold in the futures market to offset the underlying exposure. The optimal amount in futures to minimize the risk of the futures hedge is

$$\begin{aligned} N_{Fut}^* &= \text{Amount in futures contracts/Amount exposed to currency risk} \\ &= -\beta \end{aligned} \tag{5.9}$$

In this context, the hedge ratio provides the optimal amount in the futures hedge per unit of value exposed to currency risk. A futures hedge formed in this fashion is called a delta hedge because it minimizes the variance (the $\Delta$, or delta) of the hedged position.[3]

## MARKET UPDATE Megallgesellschaft's Oil Futures Hedge

Metallgesellschaft A.G. was a large MNC based in Germany with interests in engineering, metals, and mining. In 1991, Metallgesellschaft's U.S. subsidiary MG Refining and Marketing (MGRM) nearly drove Metallgesellschaft into bankruptcy through an ill-fated hedging strategy in crude oil futures.* MGRM had arranged long-term contracts to supply U.S. retailers with gasoline, heating oil, and jet fuel. Many of these were fixed rate contracts that guaranteed a set price over the life of the contract.

To hedge the risk of these delivery obligations, MGRM formed a "rolling hedge" of long positions in crude oil futures contracts of the nearest maturity. Each quarter, the long position was rolled over into the next quarter's contract. MGRM used a one-to-one hedging strategy in which long-term obligations were hedged dollar-for-dollar with positions in near-term crude oil futures contracts.

Although the intent of this hedging strategy was well-intentioned, the mismatch between the long-term short positions in delivery contracts and the short-term long positions in oil futures created havoc for MGRM. Futures price fluctuations resulted in wildly fluctuating short-term cash flows in MGRM's margin account that did not match the maturity of MGRM's long-term delivery contracts. Metallgesellschaft nearly went bankrupt in 1991 as a result of a $1.4 billion loss from its hedge. Metallgesellschaft's experience is a reminder that the exposure (i.e., maturity) of a financial hedge must match the exposure of the underlying transaction.

* Metallgesellschaft's difficulties are described in the Spring 1995 issue of the *Journal of Applied Corporate Finance.* Metallgesellschaft is now a part of Germany's GEA Group AG.

***Hedge quality*** is measured by the ***r-square*** of the regression in Equation 5.7. R-square is the square of the correlation coefficient (i.e., $\rho_{s,fut}{}^2$) and also is called the "coefficient of determination" or "$r^2$." It is bounded by zero and one, and measures the percentage of the variation in $s_t^{\$/S\$}$ that is explained by variation in $Fut_t^{\$/S\$}$. A high r-square indicates low basis risk and a high-quality delta hedge. A low r-square means that basis risk is high relative to the underlying currency risk.

***R-square measures hedge quality.***

The regression in Equation 5.7 is designed to estimate basis risk over the maturity of a proposed hedge. Unfortunately, it is difficult to construct a sample of futures prices of constant maturity t because exchange-traded futures come in only a limited assortment of maturities. In the Chen example, this would be a 7½-month maturity. Exchange-traded futures expire only every three months, and the futures prices on any single contract converge to the spot rate at maturity. Fortunately, interest rate parity determines both the forward price and the futures price for a given maturity. It is much easier to construct a sample of forward prices of constant maturity than a sample of futures prices of constant maturity, so the hedge ratio conventionally is estimated from the relation of forward price changes to spot changes over the desired maturity.

**An Example of a Delta Hedge** Suppose the regression in Equation 5.7 yields a regression coefficient of $\beta = 1.025$. The futures hedge should then consist of

$$N_{Fut}^{*} = (\text{Amount in futures contracts})/(\text{Amount exposed}) = -\beta$$

$$\Rightarrow (\text{Amount in futures contracts}) = (-\beta)(\text{Amount exposed})$$

For Chen's underlying S\$10 million short exposure, this requires a long position of

$$\text{Amount in futures contract} = (-1.025)(-\text{S\$}10{,}000{,}000) = \text{S\$}10{,}250{,}000$$

Variability in the hedged position can be minimized with S\$10,250,000 of December futures. On the CME, this would be worth (S\$10,250,000)/(S\$125,000/contract) = 82 futures contracts.

## Cross Hedges and Delta-Cross Hedges

A ***delta-cross hedge*** is used when there are both maturity and currency mismatches between the underlying exposure and the futures hedge. The regression in Equation 5.7 must be modified for a delta-cross hedge to include both basis risk from the maturity mismatch as well as currency cross-rate risk from the currency mismatch. The general form of the regression equation for estimating the optimal hedge ratio of a delta-cross hedge is

> *Delta-cross hedges have FX and maturity mismatches.*

$$s_t^{d/f_1} = \alpha + \beta\, fut_t^{d/f_2} + e_t \tag{5.10}$$

for an underlying transaction exposure in currency $f_1$ and a futures hedge in currency $f_2$. The interpretation of the slope coefficient as the optimal hedge ratio is the same as in Equation 5.9; that is, buy futures contracts according to the ratio $N_{fut}^{*} = -\beta$.

A ***cross hedge*** is a special case of the delta-cross hedge. As discussed earlier, in a cross hedge there is a currency mismatch but not a maturity mismatch. The optimal hedge ratio of a cross hedge is estimated from

$$s_t^{d/f_1} = \alpha + \beta\, s_t^{d/f_2} + e_t \tag{5.11}$$

This is identical to Equation 5.10 except that $Fut_t^{d/f_2}$ is replaced by $s_t^{d/f_2}$. Spot rate changes $s_t^{d/f_2}$ can be substituted for $fut_t^{d/f_2}$ because futures prices converge to spot prices at maturity, and the maturity of the futures contract is the same as that of the underlying transaction exposure in the spot market.

If futures are not available in the currency that you wish to hedge, a cross hedge using a futures contract on a currency that is closely related to the desired currency can at least partially hedge against currency risk. As an example, a U.K.-based corporation can hedge a Canadian dollar (C$) obligation with a long U.S. dollar futures contract because the pound values of the U.S. dollar and the Canadian dollar are highly correlated. For a U.S. dollar hedge of a Canadian dollar obligation, the spot exposure is in Canadian dollars and the futures exposure is in U.S. dollars as in the following regression:

*A cross hedge has a currency mismatch.*

$$s_t^{£/C\$} = \alpha + \beta\ fut_t^{£/\$} + e_t \tag{5.12}$$

The quality of this cross-rate futures hedge is only as good as the correlation between the pound sterling values of the U.S. and Canadian dollars.

When both the maturity and the currency match that of the underlying obligation, Equation 5.10 reduces to

$$s_t^{d/f} = \alpha + \beta\ s_t^{d/f} + e_t \tag{5.13}$$

Since the correlation of $s_t^{d/f}$ with itself is +1, this is a perfect hedge (r-square = 1) and the optimal hedge ratio is $N_{Fut}^* = -\beta = -1$. In this circumstance, the futures hedge is equivalent to a forward market hedge. There is no basis risk and currency risk can be completely eliminated.

## 5.7 SUMMARY

Forward contracts are pure credit instruments and are therefore subject to default risk. Futures contracts reduce the risk of default relative to forward contracts through the following conventions:

- An exchange clearinghouse takes one side of every transaction.
- Initial and maintenance margins are required.
- Futures contracts are marked-to-market on a daily basis.

Because they are marked-to-market daily, futures contracts are essentially a bundle of consecutive one-day forward contracts. This means that they are functionally equivalent to forward contracts and, aside from contractual differences, are priced in the same way. Whereas forward contracts can form perfect hedges

## MARKET UPDATE Competition between International Exchanges

Competition between derivatives exchanges has spawned a number of mergers, acquisitions, and alliances in the industry. One of the most active futures exchanges is the Eurex (www.eurexchange.com), which trades futures and options on indices and individual stocks, bonds, and currencies. Eurex was created in 1998 through a merger of Frankfurt's DTB (Deutsche Terminbörse) and Zurich's SOFFEX (Swiss Options and Financial Futures Exchange). Eurex subsequently formed alliances with derivatives exchanges in Vienna (Austria), Dublin (Ireland), and the CBOT (United States).

The other large European futures exchange, Euronext (www.euronext.com), was created in 2001 through a merger of the Amsterdam, Brussels, and Paris exchanges. Euronext trades stocks, bonds, commodities, and derivatives. Euronext acquired London's LIFFE (London International Financial Futures Exchange) in 2001 for €907 million, a 100 percent premium to LIFFE's pre-acquisition share price. Euronext subsequently signed deals with exchanges in Helsinki (Finland), Lisbon (Portugal), Warsaw (Poland), and Luxembourg. Euronext LIFFE then merged with the New York Stock Exchange in 2007 to form NYSE Euronext.

Exchanges also are forming alliances in the battle for market share. For example, the CME's Globex trading system links derivatives trading from the CME, Euronext, Singapore (SGX), Spain (MEFF), Montreal, and Brazilian (BM&F) exchanges. Globex provides a 24-hour electronic trading platform for a variety of global derivatives contracts. Nearly 75 percent of the CME's trading volume is conducted through Globex, with the remainder via open outcry on the exchange floor. The CME purchased the CBOT in 2006 for $8 billion in stock with the intention of further extending its Globex platform.

against transaction exposure, futures hedges are imperfect when there is a mismatch between the size, maturity, or currency of the underlying exposure and of the futures contract used to hedge the exposure. The choice between a forward or futures contract depends on the cost of each contract and on how close the underlying risk profile is to that of a standardized futures contract.

A delta hedge is used when the timing of the transaction exposed to currency risk is not the same as the maturity of available futures contracts. Although a delta hedge can eliminate currency risk, it typically cannot eliminate basis risk; that is, the risk that the relation of futures prices to spot prices will change. This is because spot and futures prices do not move in unison when there are changes in the basis—the difference in nominal interest rates between the foreign and domestic currencies. The hedge ratio of a delta hedge can be estimated from

$$s_t^{d/f} = \alpha + \beta \, fut_t^{d/f} + e_t \tag{5.7}$$

where $s_t^{d/f}$ and $Fut_t^{d/f}$ are percentage changes in spot and futures prices, respectively. The hedge ratio

$$N_{Fut}{}^{*} = \text{Amount in futures contracts/Amount exposed} \qquad (5.9)$$
$$= -\beta$$

minimizes the risk of the hedged position.

Similarly, futures do not provide a perfect hedge when there is a currency mismatch. A futures hedge with a maturity match and using a currency that is closely related to the exposed currency is called a cross hedge. For an underlying exposure in currency $f_1$ and a futures hedge using currency $f_2$, the hedge ratio is estimated from the regression

$$s_t^{d/f_1} = \alpha + \beta\, s_t^{d/f_2} + e_t \qquad (5.11)$$

where d is the hedger's currency of reference.

A futures hedge for which there are both currency and maturity mismatches is called a delta-cross hedge. This is the most general form of futures hedge. The hedge ratio is estimated from

$$s_t^{d/f_1} = \alpha + \beta\, fut_t^{d/f_2} + e_t \qquad (5.10)$$

If the underlying exposure and the futures contract are in the same currency, then $f_1 = f_2 = f$ and the hedge is a delta hedge. If there is a maturity match but a currency mismatch, then $fut_t^{d/f_2} = s_t^{d/f_2}$ and the hedge is a cross hedge. If there is a match on both maturity and currency, then a futures hedge is equivalent to a forward market hedge and can completely eliminate currency risk so long as the underlying transaction exposure is an even increment of the futures contract size.

## KEY TERMS

*basis*
*basis risk*
*cross hedge*
*currency futures contract*
*delta-cross hedge*
*delta hedge*
*hedge quality*
*hedge ratio*
*margin requirement*
*marking-to-market*
*perfect hedge*
*risk profile (or payoff profile)*
*r-square (coefficient of determination or $r^2$)*

## CONCEPTUAL QUESTIONS

5.1 How do currency forward and futures contracts differ with respect to maturity, settlement, and the size and timing of cash flows?

5.2 What is the primary role of the exchange clearinghouse?

5.3 Draw and explain the payoff profile associated with a currency futures contract.

5.4 What is a delta hedge? A cross hedge? A delta-cross hedge?

5.5 What is the basis? What is basis risk?

5.6 How do you measure the quality of a futures hedge?

## PROBLEMS

5.1 Suppose that at time zero the spot rate equals the 90-day forward rate at $S_0^{\$/S\$} = F_{90}^{\$/S\$} = \$0.65/S\$$. Assume that the spot rate increases by \$0.0002/S\$ each day over the ensuing 90 days. You buy Singapore dollars in both the forward and futures markets. Draw a time line for each contract showing the cash inflows/outflows arising from the daily change in the spot rate.

5.2 On September 11, a U.S.-based MNC with a customer in Singapore expects to receive S\$3 million. The current spot exchange rate is \$0.5950/S\$. The transfer will occur on December 10. The current S\$ futures price for December delivery is \$0.6075/S\$. The size of the CME futures contract is S\$125,000. How many futures contracts should the U.S. multinational buy or sell in order to minimize the variance of the hedged position? What is the MNC's net profit (or loss) on December 10 if the spot rate on that date is \$0.5900/S\$?

5.3 Snow White Manufacturing makes snowmobiles, some of which it sells to Japan for recreation in the wilderness of the northern islands. Snow White is expecting a payment of ¥9 million in six months.

a. Draw a time line illustrating the transaction.
b. Draw a payoff profile with dollars-per-yen on the axes.
c. Suppose Snow White takes out a forward contract to hedge this transaction. Describe this contract.
d. Describe the advantages/disadvantages to Snow White if Snow White takes out a futures contract instead of a forward contract.

5.4 Suppose Cotton Bolls, Inc. does business with companies in Israel and Singapore. Cotton Bolls expects to pay 500,000 Israeli shekels and receive 125,000 Singapore dollars on the Friday before the third Wednesday of April. Forward rates for that date are $F_T^{\$/\text{shekel}} = \$0.1625/\text{shekel}$ and $F_T^{\$/S\$} = \$0.65/S\$$.

a. Show time lines illustrating each transaction.
b. How would Cotton Bolls hedge these transactions with \$/shekel and \$/S\$ futures contracts?
c. Suppose the forward rate is S\$0.2500/shekel. Describe a cross hedge that would accomplish the same objective as the two hedges in part b.

5.5 You work for Texas Instruments in the United States and are considering ways to hedge a 10 billion Danish kroner (DKK) obligation due in six months. Your currency of reference is the U.S. dollar. The current value of the kroner is $S_0^{\$/DKK} = \$0.80/DKK$ in dollars and $S_0^{€/DKK} = €0.75/DKK$ in euros.

a. A futures exchange in Copenhagen trades futures contracts on the U.S. dollar that expire in seven months with a contract size of \$50,000. You estimate $\beta = 1.025$ based on the regression $s_t^{\$/DKK} = \alpha + \beta\, fut_t^{\$/DKK} + e_t$. The r-square of the regression is 0.98. How many futures contracts should you buy to minimize the risk of your hedged position?

b. A commercial bank in Chicago is willing to sell a customized euro (€) futures contract in any amount and maturing on the date that your obligation is due in six months. Based on the regression $s_t^{\$/DKK} = \alpha + \beta\, s_t^{\$/€} + e_t$, you estimate $\beta = 1.04$. The r-square of the regression is 0.89. How large a position in this euro futures contract should you take to minimize the risk of your hedged position?

c. Euronext in Frankfurt trades €/\$ futures contracts that expire in seven months and have a contract size of \$50,000. Based on the regression $s_t^{\$/DKK} = \alpha + \beta\, fut_t^{\$/€} + e_t$, you estimate $\beta = 1.05$. The r-square of this regression is 0.86. How many futures contracts should you buy to minimize the risk of your hedged position?

d. Which of these futures market hedges provides the best quality?

5.6 Refer to Figure 5.6. It is now March 13 and the current spot exchange rate between U.S. dollars (\$) and Singapore dollars (S\$) is \$0.6010/S\$. You have a S\$10 million obligation due on October 26. The nearest S\$ futures contract expires on December 16. Interest rates are 6.24 percent in the United States and 4.04 percent in Singapore.

a. Suppose the spot exchange rate on October 26 is \$0.6089/S\$. Fill in the three scenarios in Figure 5.6 assuming (1) $i^{\$} = 6.24\%$ and $i^{S\$} = 4.04\%$, (2) $i^{\$} = 6.24\%$ and $i^{S\$} = 4.54\%$, and (3) $i^{\$} = 6.74\%$ and $i^{S\$} = 4.04\%$.

b. Suppose interest rates do not change (so that $i^{\$} = 6.24\%$ and $i^{S\$} = 4.04\%$) but that the spot exchange rate does change. Fill in the three scenarios in Figure 5.6 assuming (1) $S_t^{\$/S\$} = \$0.6089/S\$$, (2) $S_t^{\$/S\$} = \$0.6255/S\$$, and (3) $S_t^{\$/S\$} = \$0.5774/S\$$.

## SUGGESTED READINGS

### A comparison of futures and forward contracts appears in

Kenneth R. French, "A Comparison of Futures and Forward Prices," *Journal of Financial Economics* 12, No. 3 (November 1983), 311–342.

### The properties of the delta hedge ratio are developed in

Louis Ederington, "The Hedging Performance of the New Futures Markets," *Journal of Finance* 34, No. 1 (1979), 157–170.

### Appropriate and inappropriate hedging strategies surrounding Metallgesellschaft's crude oil futures hedges appear in

Christopher L. Culp and Merton H. Miller, "Metallgesellschaft and the Economics of Synthetic Storage," *Journal of Applied Corporate Finance* 7 (Winter 1994), 62–76.

### And in the following articles from the Journal of Applied Corporate Finance 8 (Spring 1995):

Franklin R. Edwards and Michael S. Canter, "The Collapse of Metallgesellschaft: Unhedgeable Risks, Poor Hedging Strategy, or Just Bad Luck?" *Journal of Applied Corporate Finance* 8 (Spring 1995), 86–105.

Antonio S. Mello and John E. Parsons, "Maturity Structure of a Hedge Matters: Lessons from the Metallgesellschaft Debacle," *Journal of Applied Corporate Finance* 8 (Spring 1995), 106–121.

Christopher L. Culp and Merton H. Miller, "Hedging in the Theory of Corporate Finance: A Reply to Our Critics," *Journal of Applied Corporate Finance* 8 (Spring 1995), 121–128.

CHAPTER 6

# Currency Options and Options Markets

*There are two times in a man's life when he should not speculate: when he can't afford it and when he can.*

—Mark Twain

Governance of the multinational corporation involves creating and managing a wide variety of options. Options are embedded in the firm's real assets, including options to expand, contract, suspend, or abandon the firm's investments. Human resource management employs options as rewards in executive compensation contracts and in employment termination clauses. Options are attached to corporate securities in the form of call and convertibility options and interest rate caps and floors. Options insure the firm against property and casualty risks. Understanding how these options affect the firm is both a challenge and an opportunity for the financial manager.

Currency options are a useful tool for managing the multinational corporation's exposures to currency risk. Currency options are derivative securities, in that their value is derived from the value of an underlying exchange rate. As exchange rates change, so do the values of options written on the exchange rate. This chapter employs simple graphs to develop the intuition behind option valuation and their use in hedging currency risks. The technical details of option valuation are presented in the appendix to the chapter.

## 6.1 WHAT IS AN OPTION?

The difference between an option and a forward or futures contract comes down to choice. Currency options are like currency forward contracts in that they allow two parties to exchange currencies according to a prearranged date, amount, and rate of exchange. In a forward contract, both sides have an obligation to perform. In an option contract, one side has the option of forcing the exchange while the other side has an obligation to perform if the option holder exercises the option. One side of the agreement has the option, and the other side of the agreement has the obligation. This is the fundamental difference between option and forward contracts.

*One side has the option; the other an obligation.*

### Types of Currency Options

There are two types of options—calls and puts.

- A currency ***call option*** is the right to buy the underlying currency at a specified price and on a specified date.
- A currency ***put option*** is the right to sell the underlying currency at a specified price and on a specified date.

If you sell or *write* a currency call option, the buyer of the option has the right to buy one currency with another currency at the contract's ***exercise price***, or ***strike price***. The option writer has the obligation to sell currency to the option holder. A currency put option holder has the right to sell a specified amount of currency at the exercise price. A currency put option writer has the obligation to buy the currency from the put option holder, should the option be exercised.

### Markets in Currency Options

Currency option contracts are traded on financial exchanges, as well as over-the-counter (OTC) through commercial and investment banks.

**Exchange-Traded Currency Options** Currency options were first traded on an organized exchange in 1983 at the Philadelphia Stock Exchange (PSE, now a part of NASDAQ OMX). Currency options now trade at a large number of derivatives exchanges around the world. Option contracts often are written on an underlying futures contract rather than on the spot exchange rate because options are more easily settled with futures contracts than with cash. Figure 6.1 shows the growth of

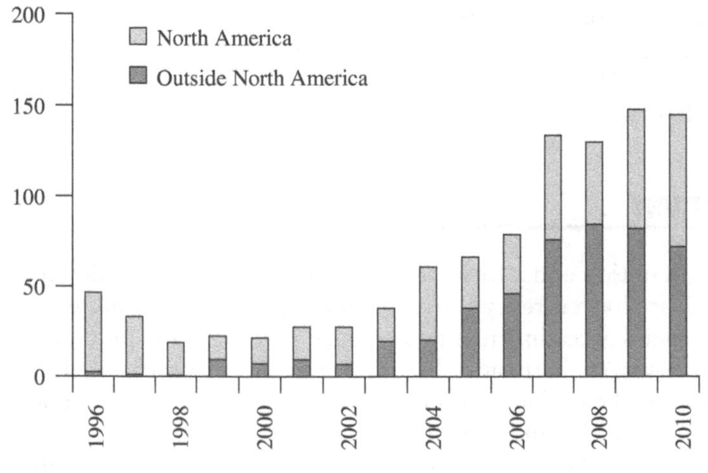


**FIGURE 6.1** Exchange-Traded Currency Options Outstanding at Year-End (in $ billions).
*Source:* Bank for International Settlements (www.bis.org).

| | PSE<br>"British pound Dec 145 call (European)" | Chicago Mercantile Exchange (CME)<br>"British pound Dec 1450 put (American)" |
|---|---|---|
| Underlying asset | British pound sterling | British pound sterling |
| Type of option | Call option | Put option |
| Expiration date | Third Wednesday in December | Third Wednesday in December |
| Rule for exercise | European – exercisable only at expiration | American – exercisable before expiration |
| Settlement | Spot currency | Nearest CME futures contract |
| Pounds-per-contract | £31,250 | £62,500 |

**FIGURE 6.2** Currency Option Contract Terms.

exchange-traded currency options based on the end-of-the-year value of outstanding contracts. As with currency futures trading, much of the recent growth has been driven by derivatives exchanges outside of North America.

*Options on spot and futures are essentially the same.*

Figure 6.2 describes the contract terms of a "British pound Dec 145 call" traded on the PSE and a "British pound Dec 1450 put" from the CME. The underlying asset or deliverable instrument of the option is the currency being bought or sold. The PSE call is an option to buy pounds. The CME put is an option to sell pounds. PSE contracts are settled in spot currency. The deliverable instrument of the CME contract is the CME futures contract expiring one week after the ***expiration*** of the option contract. Options on spot and futures are nearly identical in their ability to hedge currency risk because futures prices converge to spot prices at expiration (see Chapter 5) and spot and futures price volatilities are nearly the same.

Each PSE contract is worth £31,250. The holder of this option has the right to buy £31,250 pounds at $K^{\$/£}$ = \$1.45/£ on the contract's expiration date, where the symbol $K^{d/f}$ is used to indicate the exercise price in domestic currency per foreign currency unit. The option holder pays £31,250(\$1.45/£) = \$45,312.50 and receives £31,250 upon exercise. Both PSE and CME options expire on the Saturday before the third Wednesday of the month, so the last day of trade is the previous Friday. The third Wednesday of the month is the settlement date on which currencies are exchanged. The PSE contract is a ***European option***, exercisable only at expiration.

The CME option is an example of an American option; that is, an option that can be exercised prior to expiration. Holders of American options are usually better off if they leave their options unexercised. Because early exercise options are seldom exercised, European and American currency options are nearly equivalent in their ability to hedge currency risk.[1]

**Over-the-Counter Currency Options** Financial institutions conduct an active OTC market in currency options. Whereas exchange-traded options are standardized, OTC options are customized to fit the needs of individual customers. Expiration dates and contract amounts are specified by the customer, and prices and fees are then quoted by the bank.

> *OTC options are custom-tailored.*

Retail clients include corporations and financial institutions that have a need to manage their currency risk exposures. These clients value the right to exercise a currency option and typically do not want the obligation from writing option contracts. International commercial and investment banks are the principal writers (sellers) of currency options. This asymmetry between buyers and sellers is not seen in currency forward and futures markets. International banks also maintain an active wholesale market in which they hedge—or reinsure—the currency risk exposures in their asset/liability portfolios.

## 6.2 OPTION PAYOFF PROFILES

The value of an option can be illustrated with a *payoff profile*—a graph of an option's value against the value of its underlying asset.

### A Zero-Sum Game

In an efficient market, option transactions are a zero-sum game in which the gain-or-loss on one side of a contract exactly offsets the loss-or-gain on the other side of the contract.

**Currency Call Options** The left-hand graph below plots the dollar value of a long pound call option as a function of the spot rate between dollars and pounds at expiration. The time subscript T on the call option value and on the spot rate are reminders that these are values at expiration.

> *Calls are options to buy.*

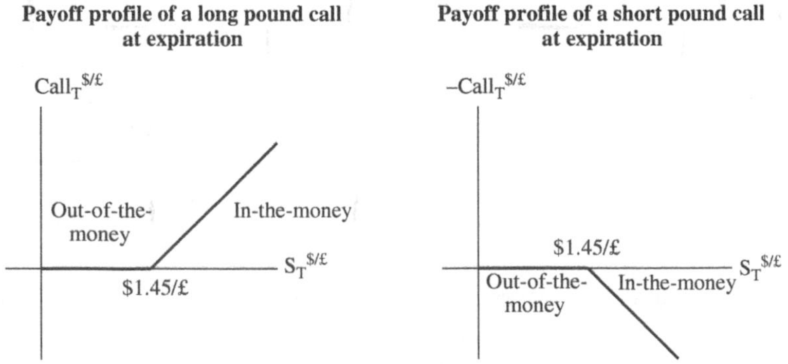


The deliverable instrument is the pound. This call option is ***out-of-the-money*** when the spot rate is below the exercise price. In this case, it is cheaper to buy pounds in the spot market than at the exercise price of \$1.45/£. The call is ***in-the-money*** when the spot rate is above the exercise price. Suppose the spot rate at expiration is \$1.50/£ on a £62,500 CME option. The option holder has the right to buy pounds at a price of \$1.45/£. The option holder can then sell this £62,500 in the spot market at \$1.50/£ for a five-cents-per-pound profit, or (£62,500)(\$0.05/£) = \$3,125.

The right-hand graph plots call value from the perspective of the option writer. This contract is a zero-sum game, in that any value gained by the option holder is a loss to the option writer. The risk profile—or *payoff profile*—of a short call is the mirror image of the long call.

**Currency Put Options** The payoff profile of a long pound put option at expiration is shown below on the left, with its corresponding short position on the right.

> *Puts are options to sell.*

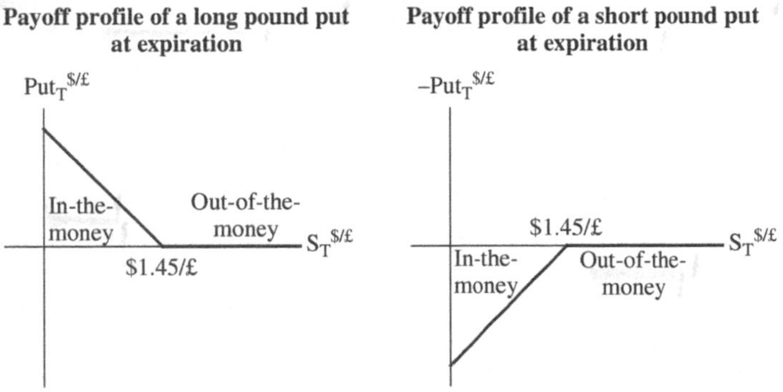


Put options are options to sell the underlying asset, so currency put options are in-the-money when the exercise price is greater than the underlying exchange rate. If the exercise price on a £62,500 CME put option is \$1.45/£, then the option holder will exercise the option at expiration when the underlying exchange rate is below \$1.45/£. For example, if the spot rate at expiration is \$1.40/£, then the option holder can buy £62,500 in the spot market for \$1.40/£ and simultaneously exercise the option to sell £62,500 to the option writer for \$1.45/£, for a net profit of (£62,500)(\$0.05/£) = \$3,125. As in the case of a call option, any gain in value to the option holder in the left-hand graph is a loss to the option writer in the right-hand graph.

### Profit and Loss on a Currency Option at Expiration

Options to buy or sell currencies are not free; option sellers demand an ***option premium*** for writing an option. The premium depends on the writer's expected losses should the option expire in-the-money. The effect of this premium on the profit or loss of an option is obtained by superimposing the premium on the option's payoff profile, as described below.

**CME option quotation "A$ Dec 6400 call" selling for $0.0120/A$ on an A$100,000 contract**

Exercise price $K^{\$/A\$}$ = $0.6400/A$ => Exercise price = ($0.6400/A$)(A$100,000) = $64,000
Option premium = $0.0120/A$ => Premium cost = ($0.0120/A$)(A$100,000) = $1,200

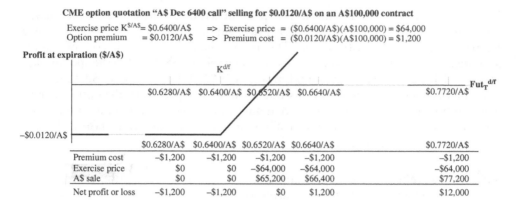

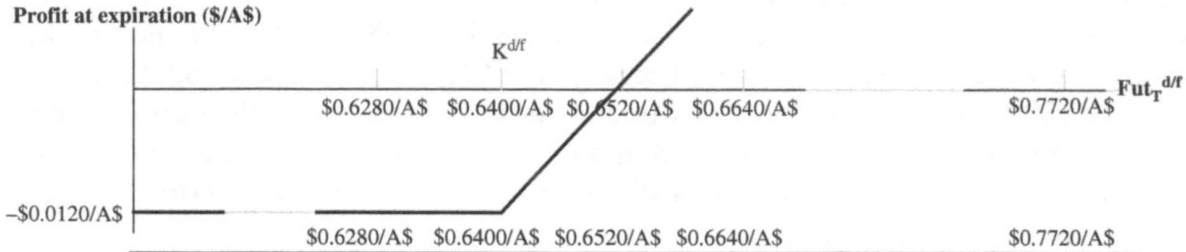

| | $0.6280/A$ | $0.6400/A$ | $0.6520/A$ | $0.6640/A$ | $0.7720/A$ |
|---|---|---|---|---|---|
| Premium cost | –$1,200 | –$1,200 | –$1,200 | –$1,200 | –$1,200 |
| Exercise price | $0 | $0 | –$64,000 | –$64,000 | –$64,000 |
| A$ sale | $0 | $0 | $65,200 | $66,400 | $77,200 |
| Net profit or loss | –$1,200 | –$1,200 | $0 | $1,200 | $12,000 |

**FIGURE 6.3** Profit or Loss on a Call Option at Expiration.

*The option premium is the price of the option.*

**Currency Call Options** Figure 6.3 displays the profit or loss at expiration of an Australian dollar call option quoted as "A$ Dec 6400 call" and selling on the CME at an option premium of $0.0120/A$. This option has an exercise price of $0.6400/A$ and expires on the third Wednesday in December. The deliverable instrument of a CME currency option is the corresponding CME futures contract. Each Australian dollar option contract on the CME is worth A$100,000, so this option costs $64,000 = ($0.6400/A$)(A$100,000) to exercise. At a price of $0.0120/A$, the option costs $1,200 = ($0.0120/A$)(A$100,000) to purchase.

The value of this option at expiration depends on the difference between the futures price and the exercise price. Profit or loss at expiration is shown in Figure 6.3 at several exchange rates. This graph combines option value at expiration with the initial cost of the option. For example, if the actual futures price is $0.6520/A$ at expiration, then selling A$100,000 in the futures market yields $65,200, which just covers the $64,000 exercise price and the $1,200 option premium.

This is a zero-sum game between the option writer and the option holder, as the writer's payoff is a mirror image of the seller's. The option holder gains (and the writer loses) whenever the futures price closes above $0.6520/A$. The option holder loses (and the writer gains) whenever the futures price closes below $0.6520/A$.

**Currency Put Options** Figure 6.4 shows the profit or loss at expiration on a CME "A$ Dec 6400 put" selling at an option premium of $0.0160/A$. At this price, one A$100,000 contract costs $1,600 = ($0.0160/A$)(A$100,000). The cost of exercise is again $64,000 at the $0.6400/A$ exercise price. The option writer's payoff is the mirror image of the option holder's payoff. The option holder gains when the exchange rate closes at any price below $0.6240/A$. The option writer gains whenever the exchange rate closes above $0.6240/A$. Again, currency options are a zero-sum game; the option holder's gain equals the option writer's loss.

**CME option quotation "A$ Dec 6400 put" selling for $0.0160/A$ on an A$100,000 contract**

Exercise price $K^{\$/A\$}$ = $0.6400/A$ => Exercise price = ($0.6400/A$)(A$100,000) = $64,000
Option premium = $0.0160/A$ => Premium cost = ($0.0160/A$)(A$100,000) = $1,600

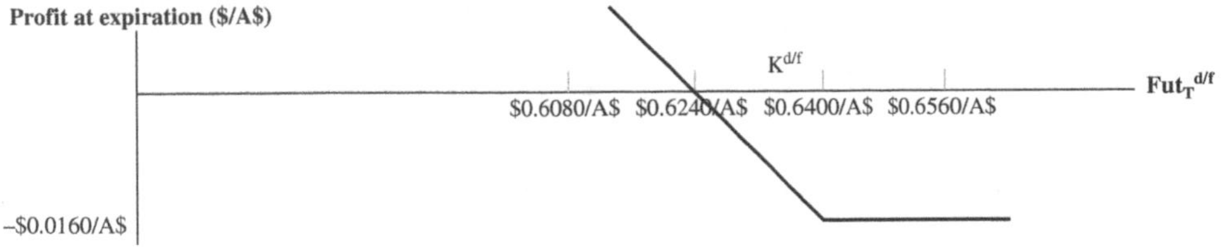


| | $0.6080/A$ | $0.6240/A$ | $0.6400/A$ | $0.6560/A$ |
|---|---|---|---|---|
| Premium cost | –$1,600 | –$1,600 | –$1,600 | –$1,600 |
| A$ purchase | –$60,800 | –$62,400 | $0 | $0 |
| Exercise price | +$64,000 | +$64,000 | $0 | $0 |
| Net profit or loss | +$1,600 | $0 | –$1,600 | –$1,600 |

**FIGURE 6.4** Profit or Loss on a Put Option at Expiration.

## At-the-Money Options and Asset Pricing Relations

Suppose a currency option is ***at-the-money***, with an exercise price equal to the current exchange rate. If exchange rates are a random walk, then the current spot rate and the exercise price equal the expected future spot rate at expiration. Centering the origin of a payoff profile on the exercise price provides a graph of changes in option values against changes in exchange rates, as shown below for a call option on pounds sterling. The deliverable instrument is the pound, so it is convenient to use dollar-per-pound prices.

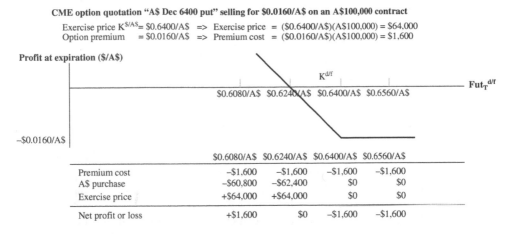

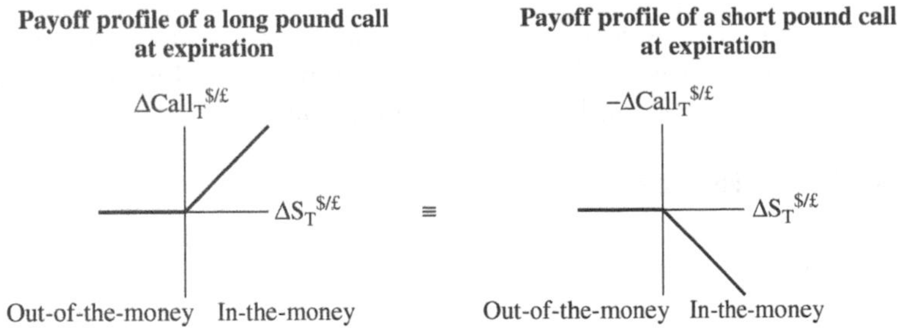


**A Call Option by Any Other Name** Buying pounds at $S^{\$/£}$ means that you are simultaneously selling dollars at $S^{£/\$}$. For this reason, an option to buy pounds at a price of $K^{\$/£}$ is the same contract as an option to sell dollars at $K^{£/\$}$. That is, *a call option to buy pounds sterling is equivalent to a put option to sell dollars.* The payoff profiles of a pound call and its counterpart, the dollar put, are shown here.

> *A call option on a currency is a put option on another currency.*

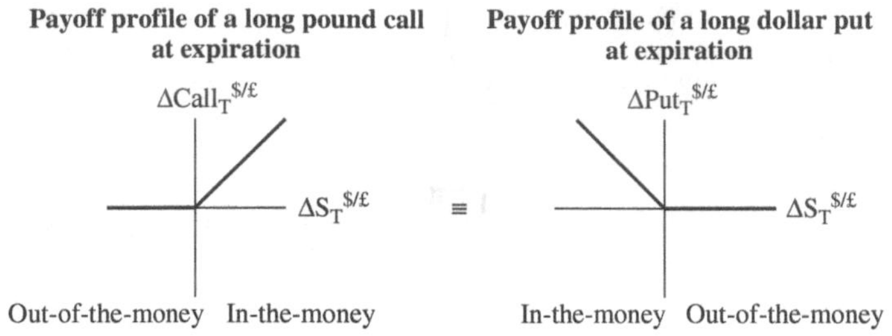


Prices in these figures are related according to $P^{\$/£} = (P^{£/\$})^{-1}$. This option is in-the-money when the spot rate $S^{\$/£}$ is above the exercise price $K^{\$/£}$ or, equivalently, when the spot rate $S^{£/\$}$ is below the exercise price $K^{£/\$}$. Since a call option to buy pounds with dollars is equivalent to a put option to sell dollars for pounds, these payoff profiles are equivalent. In this sense, a currency option is simultaneously both a put and a call.

On the other side of the contract, the option writer has an obligation to sell pounds and buy dollars. From the option writer's perspective, an obligation to sell pounds for dollars is equivalent to an obligation to buy dollars with pounds. These equivalent payoffs are shown next.

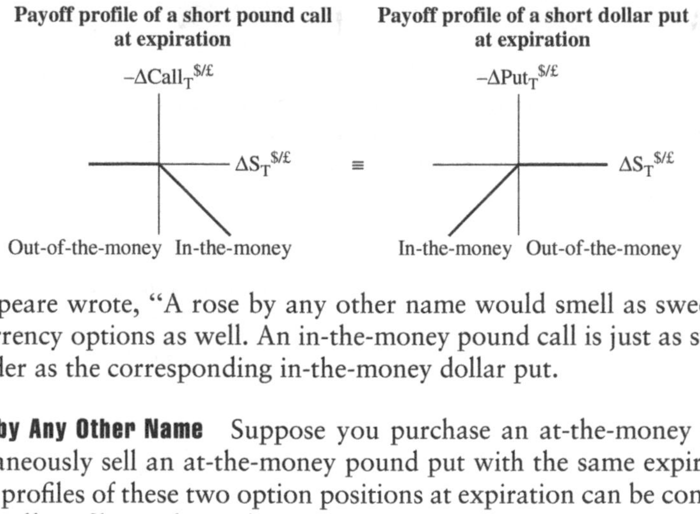


Shakespeare wrote, "A rose by any other name would smell as sweet." This is true for currency options as well. An in-the-money pound call is just as sweet to the option holder as the corresponding in-the-money dollar put.

**A Forward by Any Other Name** Suppose you purchase an at-the-money pound call and simultaneously sell an at-the-money pound put with the same expiration date. The payoff profiles of these two option positions at expiration can be combined into a single payoff profile, as shown here.

> *A forward is the same as a long call and a short put.*

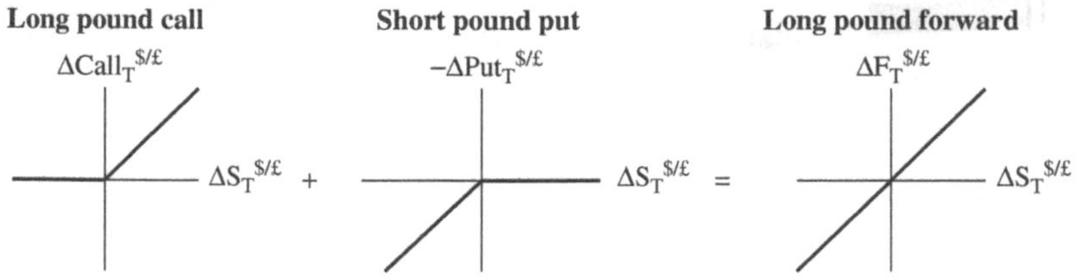

Does the graph on the right look familiar? It should. A combination of a long pound call and a short pound put with the same exercise price and expiration date creates the same payoff at expiration as a long forward position on pounds sterling.

Conversely, a short pound call and a long pound put with the same exercise price and expiration date is equivalent to a short forward position in pounds sterling at expiration.

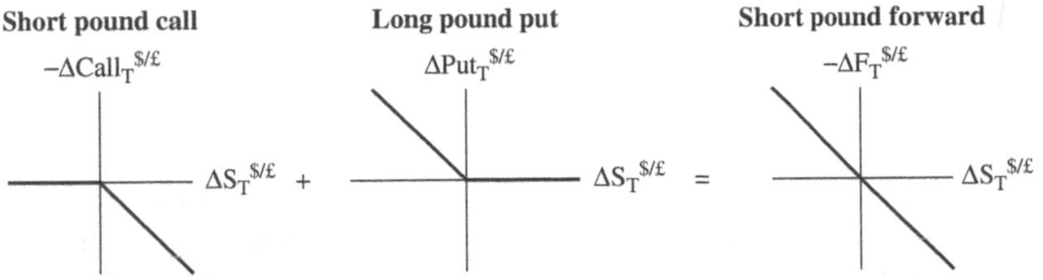


If the value of the pound is below the exercise price at expiration, the long put allows you to sell pounds at the above-market exercise price. If the value of the pound is above the exercise price at expiration, the short call forces you to buy pounds at the below-market exercise price. The resulting payoff profile exactly matches that of a short pound forward position with the same contract price and expiration date.

**Put-Call Parity** The previous section showed that the exposure of a long forward position can be replicated with a long call and a short put on the underlying asset. Conversely, the exposure of a short forward position can be replicated with a short call and a long put. Thus, the no-arbitrage condition ensures that the values of puts and calls at a particular exercise price must be related to the value of a forward contract on the underlying asset. The general case of this relation is called ***put-call parity.***

> ***Put and call values are related to forward rates.***

Suppose a call and a put option are written on currency f with a single exercise price $K^{d/f}$ and an expiration date in T periods. Put-call parity relates the option values $Call^{d/f}$ and $Put^{d/f}$ to the discounted present values of the exercise price and the forward price

$$Call^{d/f} - Put^{d/f} = (F_T^{d/f} - K^{d/f})/(1 + i^d)^T \tag{6.1}$$

where $i^d$ is the risk-free rate of interest in the domestic currency. Arbitrage between markets in these currency derivatives ensures that the put-call parity relation holds within the bounds of transaction costs.

## 6.3 CURRENCY OPTION VALUES PRIOR TO EXPIRATION

Option payoff profiles can make even the most complex option positions seem transparent. Yet these graphs only give option values at expiration. The put-call parity relation in Equation 6.1 suggests it is useful to estimate option values *prior* to expiration.

| Δ | Option value determinant | | $\Delta Call^{d/f}$ | $\Delta Put^{d/f}$ |
|---|---|---|---|---|
| ↑ | Underlying exchange rate ($S^{d/f}$ or $Fut^{d/f}$) | ⇒ | ↑ | ↓ |
| ↑ | Exercise price ($K^{d/f}$) | ⇒ | ↓ | ↑ |
| ↑ | Risk-free rate of interest in currency d ($i^d$) | ⇒ | ↑ | ↓ |
| ↑ | Risk-free rate of interest in currency f ($i^f$) | ⇒ | ↓ | ↑ |
| ↑ | Volatility in the underlying exchange rate ($\sigma$) | ⇒ | ↑ | ↑ |
| ↑ | Time to expiration (T) | ⇒ | ↑ | ↑ |

**FIGURE 6.5** The Determinants of Currency Option Values.

Currency option values are a function of the six variables shown in Figure 6.5. The price of an American currency call or put option will respond as indicated when each of these determinants is increased while holding the other determinants of option value constant.[2] With the exception of volatility, each of these determinants of option value is readily observable for currency options quoted on major exchanges. The exercise price and expiration date are stated in the option contract, and the underlying exchange rate and the foreign and domestic interest rates are quoted in the financial press. The volatility of the underlying asset is not directly observable, which makes it an extremely important ingredient in option valuation. ***Volatility*** refers to the standard deviation of continuously compounded returns to the underlying asset or exchange rate. (Section 6.5 discusses volatility in more detail.)

> *Volatility must be estimated.*

Options have two sources of value prior to expiration: the *intrinsic value* of immediate exercise and the *time value* reflecting the value of waiting until expiration before exercise.

## APPLICATION An Application of Put-Call Parity

The CME trades a call option on U.K. pounds sterling with an exercise price of $K^{\$/£} = \$1.7500/£$ and an expiration date in six months. The risk-free rates of interest are $i^{£} = 4.08$ percent and $i^{\$} = 0.50$ percent per annum. The spot exchange rate is $S_0^{\$/£} = \$1.7600/£$. The call option sells for an option premium of \$0.0717/£.

Put-call parity allows us to calculate the value of a pound put with the same exercise price and expiration date as the pound call. The forward rate from interest rate parity is $F_T^{\$/£} = S_0^{\$/£}[(1+i^{\$})/(1+i^{£})]^T = (\$1.7600/£)[(1.0408)/(1.0050)]^{1/2} = \$1.7911/£$. Solving Equation 6.1 for the value of the put leads to $Put^{\$/£} = Call^{\$/£} - (F_T^{\$/£} - K^{\$/£})/(1+i^{\$})^{1/2} = \$0.0717/£ - (\$1.7911/£ - \$1.7500/£)/(1.0408)^{1/2} = \$0.0314/£$.

### The Intrinsic Value of an Option

The ***intrinsic value*** of an option is the value of the option if it is exercised today. Consider the currency call and put options presented here.

*Intrinsic value is the value of immediate exercise.*

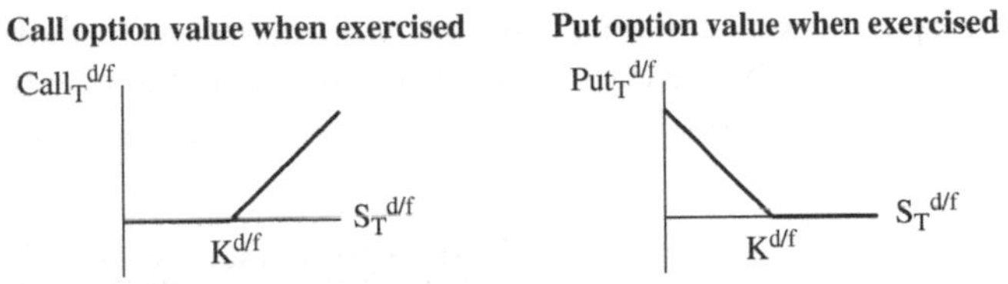


If an option is out-of-the-money, its intrinsic value is zero. If an option is in-the-money, its intrinsic value is equal to the difference between the exercise price and the value of the underlying asset. Option values at exercise on the spot exchange rate are determined as follows:

$$\text{Call option value when exercised} = \text{Max}[(S_t^{d/f} - K^{d/f}),0]$$

$$\text{Put option value when exercised} = \text{Max}[(K^{d/f} - S_t^{d/f}),0]$$

These are the intrinsic values of the call and put options, respectively. Every graph that has appeared up to this point in the chapter has been a graph of intrinsic value.

As the underlying asset value moves away from the exercise price, option values follow a one-way path. Currency call option holders gain when the underlying exchange rate rises above the exercise price, but cannot lose more than the option premium as the underlying exchange rate falls below the exercise price. Put option holders gain as the underlying exchange rate falls below the exercise price, but lose, at most, the option premium as the exchange rate rises. It is this asymmetry that gives options their unique role as a disaster hedge.

### The Time Value of an Option

The ***time value*** of an option is the option's market value minus its intrinsic value. Two important variables in determining the time value of an option are the volatility in the underlying exchange rate and the time to expiration. Volatility in the underlying (spot or futures) exchange rate determines how far in- or out-of-the-money an option is likely to expire. Time to expiration has an effect that is similar to volatility, in that more time until expiration results in more variable outcomes at expiration. Here's the general rule for American options.

*Time value is market value less intrinsic value.*

That is, American option values are greater if volatility in the underlying asset (e.g., the exchange rate for a currency option) increases or if the time to expiration is longer.

> ***As time to expiration or volatility increases, the values of American call and put options increase.***

Consider the payoffs to a dollar call and a dollar put option, each with an exercise price of $K^{¥/\$}$ = ¥100/$. Suppose the spot rate at expiration will be either ¥90.484/$ or ¥110.517/$ with equal probability.[3] Payoffs to these options are as follows:

| | Closing spot exchange rate $S_T^{¥/\$}$ | |
|---|---|---|
| | ¥90.484/$ | ¥110.517/$ |
| Value of a call at expiration | ¥0/$ | ¥10.517/$ |
| Value of a put at expiration | ¥9.516/$ | ¥0/$ |

Suppose the volatility of the spot rate increases such that the spot rate at expiration can be as low as ¥81.873/$ or as high as ¥122.140/$.[4] The values of a dollar call and a dollar put at these spot rates and with an exercise price of ¥100/$ are as follows:

| | Closing spot exchange rate $S_T^{¥/\$}$ | |
|---|---|---|
| | ¥81.873/$ | ¥122.140/$ |
| Value of a call at expiration | ¥0/$ | ¥22.140/$ |
| Value of a put at expiration | ¥18.127/$ | ¥0/$ |

Because option holders continue to gain on one side of the exercise price but do not suffer continued losses on the other side, options become more valuable as the end-of-period exchange rate distribution becomes more dispersed. For this reason, prior to expiration there are more good things than bad that can happen to option value.[5]

The figure below illustrates how at-the-money call options gain from an increase in volatility. An at-the-money call gains if the spot rate closes above the exercise price, but does not lose if the spot rate closes farther below the exercise price. As volatility increases as in the distribution at the right, more good things can happen for the call as it can close even farther in-the-money.

**Exchange rate volatility and at-the-money call option value**

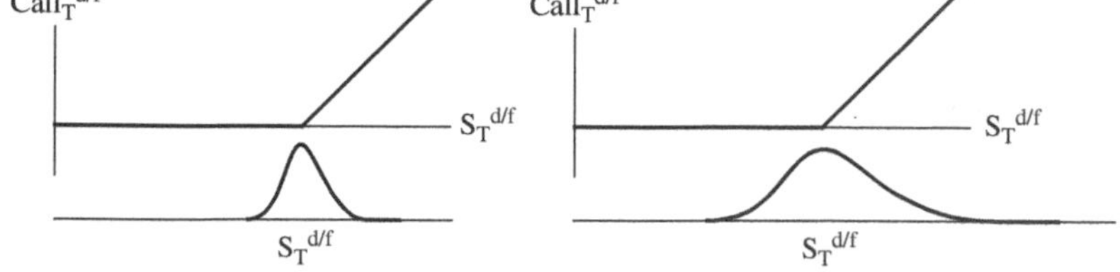

The same principle holds for out-of-the-money call options, as shown below. At expiration, only that portion of the distribution that expires in-the-money has value. The out-of-the-money call option on the left has little value because there is little likelihood of the forex (FX) rate climbing above the exercise price. As the variability of end-of-period FX rates increases in the graph on the right, there is an increasing probability that the spot rate will close above the exercise price.

**Exchange rate volatility and out-of-the-money call option value**

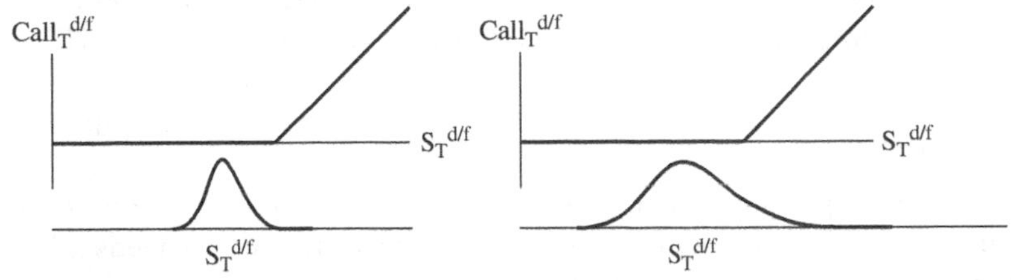


The same general principle holds for the in-the-money call options shown below. If an underlying exchange rate is below the exercise price at expiration, the option has zero value regardless of how far the closing price falls below the exercise price. On the other hand, the call option continues to increase in value as the spot rate increases. Thus, in-the-money call options also benefit from higher volatility in the underlying asset.

> *Option values gain from volatility.*

**Exchange rate volatility and in-the-money call option value**

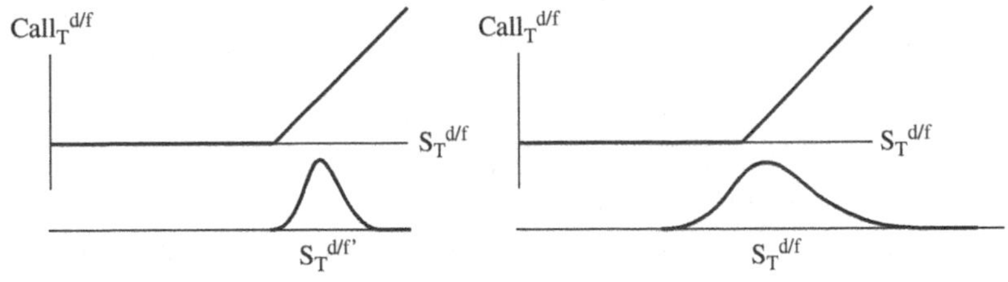


Similarly, currency puts gain more in value from exchange rate decreases than they lose in value from increases of the same magnitude. The general rule is that currency options gain from increasing variability in the distribution of end-of-period exchange rates regardless of whether the option is in-the-money, at-the-money, or out-of-the-money. In turn, variability in the distribution of end-of-period exchange rates depends on exchange rate volatility and on the time to expiration.

## 6.4 HEDGING WITH CURRENCY OPTIONS

Currency option hedges can be either static or dynamic in nature, depending on the objectives and resources of the hedger.

### Static Hedging Strategies That Match on Expiration

Suppose the Japanese firm Toyota anticipates a £1 million cash inflow from a U.K. customer on December 13, which happens to be a Friday on which CME currency options expire. If left unhedged, the yen value of this cash flow will depend on the spot rate at expiration. Toyota can use a currency option as a form of insurance or "disaster hedge" against an unfavorable change in the value of the pound. Suppose interest rates in yen and pounds are equal, and the spot rate is equal to the forward rate at $S_0^{¥/£} = F_T^{¥/£} = ¥200/£$. The CME yen-per-pound cross-rate futures contract has a contract size of £62,500, so it will take 16 CME futures to hedge the £1 million cash inflow. The CME pound option with a striking price of $K^{¥/£} = ¥200/£$ is at-the-money, and the price of both call and put options are $Call^{¥/£} = Put^{¥/£} = ¥40/£$.

Toyota's long pound exposure is shown on the left in the following graph. Toyota needs to offset the downside risk of this exposure, and so needs a hedge with a negative exposure below the ¥200/£ exercise price. The long pound put option in the middle graph does the trick. When combined with the underlying long pound exposure, the long pound put transforms the payoffs to Toyota's net position as shown on the right.

**A long pound exposure hedged with a long pound put**

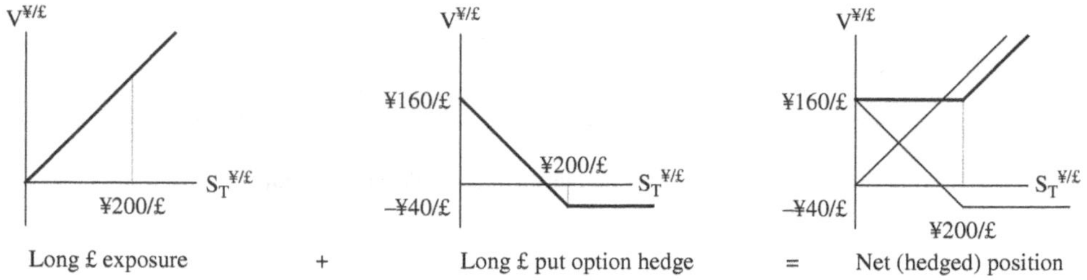


The net position is found by adding the y-axis values of the underlying position and its hedge at each point along the x-axis. For example, at a closing spot price of $S_T^{¥/£} = ¥0/£$, the underlying position is worthless while the pound put pays ¥160/£. Between $S_T^{¥/£} = ¥0/£$ and $S_T^{¥/£} = ¥200/£$, for every increase in value on the underlying exposure there is a corresponding decrease in value from the long put, so the payoff on the combined position remains ¥160/£. Above a closing price of $S_T^{¥/£} = ¥200/£$, the option is out-of-the-money while the long exposure continues to gain in value. In essence, Toyota has paid an option premium (in this case, an insurance premium) of ¥40/£ to ensure that it'll receive at least ¥160/£ on its net position.

As with other forms of insurance, Toyota would prefer that it not have to exercise its option. Toyota benefits when the pound rises above ¥200/£. This is the preferred outcome. Just like auto insurance that is exercised only when there is an accident, the option insurance is exercised only when bad events unfold; that is, when the pound falls in value and erodes the value of the underlying position.

Suppose Toyota has a short euro exposure of €10 million due on December 13, as shown on the left in the figure below.

**A short euro exposure hedged with a long euro call**

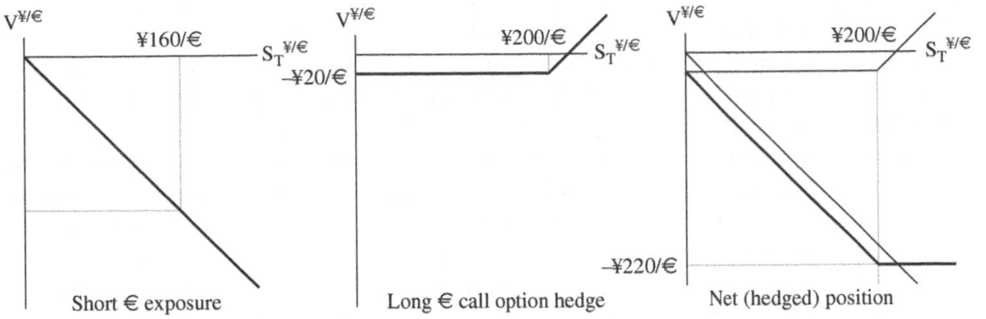


The CME trades a €125,000 cross-rate contract against the yen, so (€10 million) ÷ (€125,000/contract) = 80 contracts will offset Toyota's underlying position. The spot and forward rates are $S_0^{¥/€} = F_T^{¥/€}$ = ¥160/€. Toyota decides to hedge the short euro exposure with a long euro call at an exercise price of $K^{¥/€}$ = ¥200/€. The option premium on this contract is $Call^{¥/€}$ = ¥20/€, as shown in the middle graph.

The combined or net position is shown on the right. If the spot rate closes at ¥160/€, Toyota will owe (€10 million)(¥160/€) = ¥1,600 million on its underlying exposure. It'll lose even more on its underlying exposure if the euro appreciates above ¥160/€. The long euro call at $K^{¥/€}$ = ¥200/€ protects Toyota against a euro increase of more than ¥200/€, but the cost of this hedge is the option premium of ¥20/€. The net result is that Toyota has hedged against an increase in the value of the euro above ¥200/€ at a cost of ¥20/€. At worst, Toyota will pay (€10 million)(¥220/€) = ¥2,200 million to fulfill its obligation. At best, the yen-per-euro spot rate will fall and Toyota's obligation will correspondingly decrease in value.

## Dynamic Hedging Strategies with Rebalancing

Individual transactions can be hedged against currency risk. However, it is more cost-effective to first offset transactions within the firm and then hedge the firm's net exposures to currency risks. Thus, exposures evolve over time and dynamic hedging strategies need to adapt to these changing circumstances. This section presents several measures that are useful in dynamically managing the firm's evolving exposures to currency risk.

**Delta Hedges** The sensitivity of option value to change in the value of the underlying asset is called ***option delta.*** Call option deltas are positive, as indicated by the slope of option value in the call option payoff profiles. The delta of a call option increases as the underlying asset increases in price. For deep-in-the-money calls, the slope of option value approaches a delta of one (i.e., a 45-degree line). The delta of a put option is negative and approaches zero from below as the price of the underlying asset increases.

> *Option delta is the sensitivity of option value to the underlying asset.*

Option delta also is called the ***hedge ratio*** because it indicates the number of options required to offset one unit of the underlying asset and minimize the variance of the hedged position.[6] This measure is useful when hedging an underlying spot, forward, or futures position. Suppose the delta of a currency call option on the yen/dollar futures price is +0.50. For a given (small) change in the futures price, option value increases by exactly 50 percent of that amount.

To form a *delta-neutral hedge* of a forward position with an option position, an offsetting position is taken according to the hedge ratio. For example, a Japanese firm can hedge a future dollar obligation of $1 million with a long dollar call option. For a long call with a delta of +0.50, the firm should take a $2 million option position to offset the underlying $1 million obligation. A small increase in the yen value of the dollar will result in a loss in value on the underlying forward obligation. This loss is offset by a gain in value on the long call position. Note that the expiration date of this option does not need to match that of the underlying forward obligation.

The $1 million forward obligation also could be offset by writing a $4 million put option with a delta of −0.25. An increase in the value of the dollar futures price then increases the yen value of the forward obligation at the same time that it decreases the yen obligation on the short put option.

Conversely, a future cash inflow of $1 million can be delta-hedged with (1) a short position of $1.25 million on a dollar call option with a delta of +0.80, or (2) a long position of $3 million on a dollar put option with a delta of −0.33.

**More Funny Greek Letters** Option delta is a measure of the rate of change or sensitivity of option value to change in the underlying asset value. A delta hedge uses this measure to offset an underlying exchange rate exposure with a currency option position that has the same sensitivity to an exchange rate change. However, option delta changes as the underlying price changes. As delta changes, so does the hedge ratio that matches the sensitivities of the option and the underlying positions.

When the delta of an option hedge changes at a different rate than that of the underlying position, even small changes in an underlying exchange rate can quickly throw a delta hedge out of balance. The option pricing methods in the appendix to this chapter assume continuous rebalancing. In practice, option hedges must be closely monitored to make sure they do not become too unbalanced.

Option ***gamma*** is the rate of change of delta with a change in underlying asset price; that is, the *curvature* of option value in the option payoff profiles.[7] Many option hedges are designed to be gamma-neutral as well as delta-neutral. Matching on gamma usually means forming a hedge with payoffs that match those of the underlying position. Hedges that are both delta-neutral and gamma-neutral are far less likely to become unbalanced with changes in underlying asset values.

Another useful measure of option sensitivity is ***vega***, which is the sensitivity of option value to changes in the volatility (or standard deviation) of the underlying asset. Option vega is greatest for long-term options, all else being constant. As time to expiration decreases, so too does option vega. Vega also is larger for near-the-money options than for deep in-the-money or deep out-of-the-money options.

Finally, ***theta*** is the sensitivity of option value to change in the time to expiration. All else being constant, theta increases in absolute value as the time to expiration decreases, so that currency options lose most of their value just prior to expiration.

Theta is also greater in absolute value for near-the-money than for deep in-the-money or deep out-of-the-money options.

## Combinations of Options

Two or more option positions can be combined by snapping together the corresponding option payoff profiles. This is a simple yet powerful technique for understanding the risks and potential payoffs of even the most arcane option positions.

Here's an example. In early 1995, a rogue trader named Nick Leeson drove the United Kingdom's Barings Bank into bankruptcy through unauthorized speculation in Nikkei stock index futures on the Singapore and Osaka stock exchanges. Leeson sold *option straddles* on the Nikkei index at a time when volatility on the index was low. A long option straddle is a combination of a long call and a long put on the same underlying asset and with the same exercise price, as shown below.

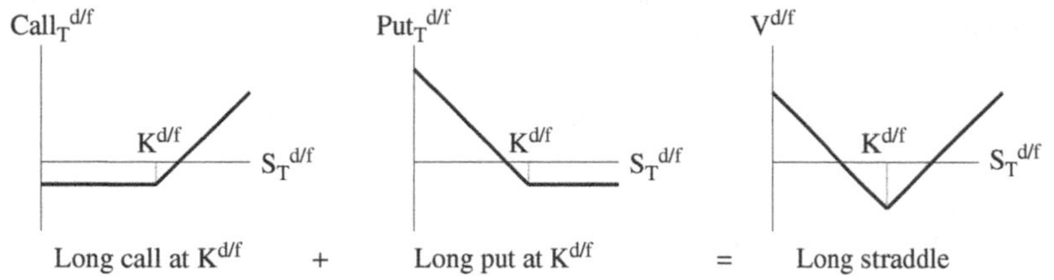


Leeson formed a short straddle by selling calls and puts. After including the proceeds from these option sales, the profit/loss diagram on the short straddle position at expiration is as follows:

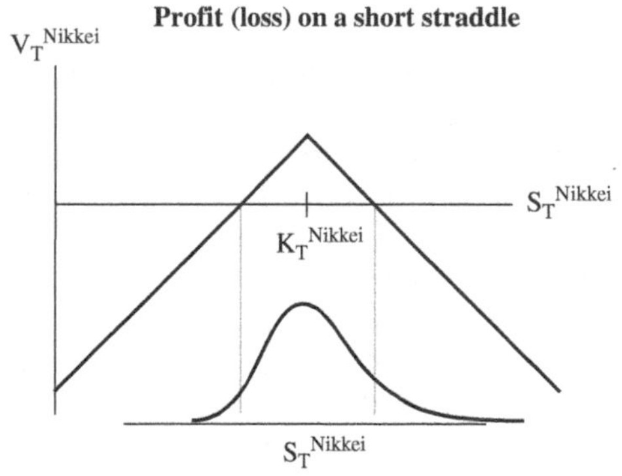


Leeson placed a bet on the volatility of the Nikkei index. In option parlance, Leeson "sold volatility." So long as the Nikkei index did not vary too much, Leeson would have won his bet. As seen in the diagram, Leeson wins if the end-of-period Nikkei index falls between the two points at which the profit/loss pyramid crosses the x-axis. Leeson loses if the Nikkei index rises too high or falls too low. Volatility on the Nikkei index was low at the time Leeson sold his position, so the proceeds from the sale were small (and Leeson's gamble was large) relative to what would have been received on this position in a high-volatility market. As it turned out, the Nikkei index fell below the profitable range. Leeson incurred further losses by buying futures on the Nikkei index in the hopes of a recovery that, to Barings' regret, never occurred.

## 6.5 EXCHANGE RATE VOLATILITY REVISITED (ADVANCED)

The behavior of exchange rates—as well as options on exchange rates—is best examined in continuously compounded returns, so let's start this section with a brief review. If you find the algebra to be unfamiliar, try to follow the intuition behind the algebra. If necessary, skip the numeric examples altogether. You don't really need the algebra of continuous compounding to follow the subsequent discussion of exchange rate volatility.[8]

### Continuously Compounded Returns and the Normal Distribution

Continuously compounded changes in exchange rates *s* (in italics) are related to holding period changes s according to

$$s = \ln(1+s) \quad \text{or} \quad e^{s} = e^{\ln(1+s)} = 1+s \tag{6.2}$$

For example, if the yen-per-dollar spot rate appreciates from $S_0^{¥/\$} = ¥100/\$$ to $S_1^{¥/\$} = ¥110.517/\$$, then the holding period rate of change $s_1^{¥/\$} = 10.517$ percent is equivalent to a continuously compounded change of $s_1^{¥/\$} = \ln(1+s_1^{¥/\$}) = \ln(1.10517) = 0.10000$, or 10 percent. Conversely, if the spot rate depreciates a continuously compounded 10 percent from an initial price of ¥100/\$, then the holding period rate of change of $s_1^{¥/\$} = e^{(-0.10)} - 1 = -0.09516$, or $-9.516$ percent, will result in an end-of-period spot rate of $(¥100/\$)e^{(-0.10)} = ¥90.484/\$$.

Because the normal distribution has convenient statistical properties, continuously compounded returns often are assumed to be independently and identically distributed (i.i.d.) as normal with mean $\mu$ and variance $\sigma^2$, or $N(\mu,\sigma^2)$. The parameter $\sigma^2$ is the ***instantaneous variance*** and often is assumed to be a constant. Whether returns are i.i.d. normal is an empirical question that we shall examine shortly. For now, let's develop the statistical properties of i.i.d. normal distributions.

The term *identically* in the phrase "independently and identically distributed" means that returns are drawn from the same distribution at every instant of time. The term *independently* means that the return realized at each instant of time does not depend on previous returns or influence future returns. The assumption of i.i.d. returns implies that the return series is ***stationary***, in that the process generating returns is identical at every instant of time. A snapshot of the return distribution at one instant yields the same snapshot as at every other instant.

Return variance increases linearly with time in an i.i.d. normal return series. That is, the end-of-period variance after T periods is T times the instantaneous variance

$$\sigma_T^2 = T\sigma^2 \tag{6.3}$$

where $\sigma^2$ is the instantaneous (or continuously compounded) variance measured over a single period and $\sigma_T^2$ is the variance of continuously compounded return measured over T periods. This implies $\sigma_T = (\sqrt{T})\sigma$, so standard deviation increases with the square root of time. Equation 6.3 identifies the manner in which volatility $\sigma$ and time to expiration T interact to increase the variability of the end-of-period return distribution $\sigma_T$ in an i.i.d. normal return series.

Volatility can be estimated in several ways. The two most prominent methods are historical volatility and implied volatility. Historical volatility is a backward-looking measure that captures observed variations over the recent past in the hope that history will repeat itself. Implied volatility is a forward-looking measure that uses current option prices to estimate volatility in the underlying asset. Because it is based on current prices, implied volatility reflects the expectations of participants in the options markets.

## Historical Volatility

***Historical volatility*** is the actual volatility of an exchange rate realized over some historical period. For changes in currency values, historical volatility can be estimated by calculating the observed standard deviation of continuously compounded changes $s_t$ sampled over T periods.

$$\sigma = \sqrt{[(1/T)\Sigma_t(s_t - \mu)^2]} \qquad (6.4)$$

> *Historical volatility is realized over some historical period.*

As an example, suppose the standard deviation of continuously compounded daily changes in the yen/dollar spot rate is estimated from Equation 6.4 to be $\sigma = 0.00645 = 0.645$ percent per trading day over the 252 business days in a particular calendar year. Assuming zero volatility on nontrading days, such as weekends and holidays, the annual standard deviation of continuously compounded changes in the exchange rate is $\sigma = (\sqrt{T})\sigma_T = (\sqrt{252})(0.00645) = 0.1024$, or 10.24 percent per year. If instantaneous changes in exchange rates are normally distributed, plus or minus one standard deviation results in plus or minus 10.24 percent per year in continuously compounded returns.

Suppose the spot rate is ¥130/$, as in Figure 6.6. Plus two standard deviations of 10.24 percent in continuously compounded returns is $2\sigma = (2)(0.1024) = 0.2048$, or 20.48 percent. The periodic rate of change over the period is $s_1^{¥/\$} = e^{(2\sigma\sqrt{t})} - 1 = e^{(+0.2048)} - 1 = 22.73$ percent. Two standard deviations above the ¥130/$ spot rate is thus $S_1^{¥/\$} = S_0^{¥/\$}e^{(+0.2048)} = (¥130/\$)(1.2273) = ¥159.55/\$$. In periodic returns, this is a 22.73 percent increase in the spot rate.

Similarly, two standard deviations below the spot rate is $S_1^{¥/\$} = S_0^{¥/\$}e^{(-0.2048)} = (¥130/\$)(0.8148) = ¥105.93/\$$. This is equivalent to $s_1^{¥/\$} = (0.8148-1) = -0.1852$, or an 18.52 percent decrease in the spot rate. About 95 percent of the normal distribution falls within two standard deviations of the mean, so there is a 95 percent chance that the actual spot rate in one year will fall between ¥105.93/$ and ¥159.55/$.

As a check, let's back out continuously compounded changes implied by a change in the spot rate from ¥130/$ to either ¥105.93/$ or ¥159.55/$. If the spot rate moves

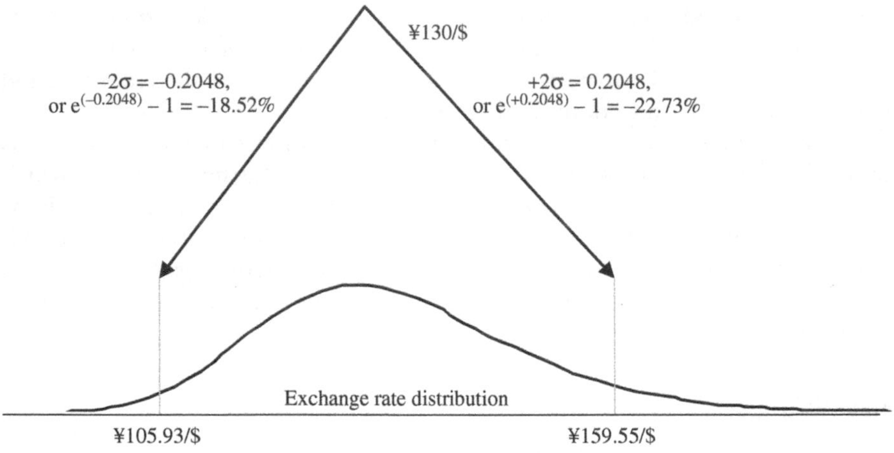


**FIGURE 6.6** Exchange Rate Volatility.

from ¥130/$ to ¥159.55/$, the percentage change is $s_1^{¥/\$} = (¥159.55/\$)/(¥130/\$) - 1 = 0.2273$, or 22.73 percent. In continuously compounded returns, this is equal to $s^{¥/\$} = \ln(1.2273) = 0.2048$, or 20.48 percent. Conversely, a move from ¥130/$ to ¥105.93/$ results in a continuously compounded return of $s_1^{¥/\$} = \ln(S_1^{¥/\$}/S_0^{¥/\$}) = \ln((¥105.93/\$)/(¥130/\$)) = -0.2048$, or $-20.48$ percent.

Another useful fact is that volatility measured in continuously compounded returns does not depend on the currency of reference. To verify this, let's perform the same calculations using dollar-per-yen quotes. The yen-per-dollar exchange rates convert into dollar-per-yen spot rates according to $S^{\$/¥} = 1/S^{¥/\$}$.

$$1/S^{¥/\$} = 1/(¥159.55/\$) = \$0.0062676/¥ = S^{\$/¥}$$

$$1/S^{¥/\$} = 1/(¥130.00/\$) = \$0.0076923/¥ = S^{\$/¥}$$

$$1/S^{¥/\$} = 1/(¥105.93/\$) = \$0.0094402/¥ = S^{\$/¥}$$

A 22.73 percent dollar appreciation from ¥130/$ to ¥159.55/$ is equivalent to a 19.52 percent yen depreciation from ($0.0076923/¥) to ($0.0062676/¥). A 19.52 percent dollar depreciation from ¥130.00/$ to ¥105.93/$ is the same as a 22.73 percent yen appreciation from ($0.0076923/¥) to ($0.0094402/¥). Alternatively, in dollars per yen

$$s_1^{\$/¥} = \ln(S_1^{\$/¥}/S_0^{\$/¥}) = \ln[(\$0.0062676/¥)/(\$0.0076923/¥)] = \ln(0.8148)$$
$$= -0.2048$$

and

$$s_1^{\$/¥} = \ln(S_1^{\$/¥}/S_0^{\$/¥}) = \ln[(\$0.0094402/¥)/(\$0.0076923/¥)] = \ln(1.2273)$$
$$= +0.2048$$

Sure enough, these represent ±20.48 percent changes in continuously compounded returns.

A variant of historical volatility called ***realized volatility*** is becoming increasingly popular.[9] Realized volatility is formed by cumulating squared returns measured over short (e.g., 15-minute) intervals throughout the day. Realized volatility estimates are relatively good predictors of future volatility over short forecasting horizons because the average of recent high-frequency squared returns closely approximates true variance at a given point in time. They are less useful in predicting volatilities over longer forecast horizons. For long-horizon forecasts of volatility, the market-based "implied volatility" estimate described in the next section has proven useful.

## Implied Volatility

There are six determinants of a currency option value: (1) the spot rate $S^{d/f}$, (2) the exercise price $K^{d/f}$, (3) the domestic risk-free rate $i^d$, (4) the foreign risk-free rate $i^f$, (5) time to expiration T, and (6) the volatility of the underlying asset $\sigma$. For publicly traded options, the values of five of the six determinants, as well as the option value itself, are published in the financial press. The only unobservable determinant is the volatility of the underlying asset.

> ***Implied volatility is implied by an option price.***

Suppose you know the equation specifying how option values are related to these six variables. Then, given five of the six inputs and the option price, the value of the single unknown determinant (exchange rate volatility) can be found by trial and error. Volatility estimated in this way is called ***implied volatility***, because it is implied by the option price and the other option value determinants.

As an example, consider a "December A\$ 73 call" trading on the PSE. Suppose the following values are known:

| **Value of call option** | $\mathbf{Call^{\$/A\$}}$ | = | **\$0.0102/A\$** | |
|---|---|---|---|---|
| Price of underlying asset | $S^{\$/A\$}$ | = | \$0.7020/A\$ | |
| Exercise price | $K^{\$/A\$}$ | = | \$0.7300/A\$ | |
| Domestic risk-free rate | $i^{\$}$ | = | 4% per year | (continuously compounded) |
| Foreign risk-free rate | $i^{A\$}$ | = | 0% per year | (continuously compounded) |
| Time to expiration | T | = | 2½ months | |
| Volatility of the spot rate | $\sigma$ | = | ? | |

Solving the currency option pricing model (OPM) from the appendix to the chapter for the standard deviation of the spot rate yields an implied volatility of 0.148, or 14.8 percent per year. When combined with the five other inputs, this is the only standard deviation that results in an option value of \$0.0102/A\$.

### A Cautionary Note on Implied Volatilities

> *Beware of prices in thinly traded markets.*

Let's look at another quote, a "December A$ 63 call" on the PSE. Suppose the following prices are quoted in *The Wall Street Journal*:

| Value of call option | $Call^{\$/A\$}$ | = | $0.0710/A$ | |
|---|---|---|---|---|
| Price of underlying asset | $S^{\$/A\$}$ | = | $0.7020/A$ | |
| Exercise price | $K^{\$/A\$}$ | = | $0.6300/A$ | |
| Domestic risk-free rate | $i^{\$}$ | = | 4% per year | (continuously compounded) |
| Foreign risk-free rate | $i^{A\$}$ | = | 0% per year | (continuously compounded) |
| Time to expiration | T | = | 2½ months | |
| Volatility of the spot rate | $\sigma$ | = | ? | |

Both options are based on the December U.S.-per-Australian spot rate, so the implied volatility of this option should be the same as that of the previous option. However, trying to find an implied volatility for the $0.63/A$ call based on these prices is futile. There is no value for volatility that yields a call price of $0.0710/A$. What's wrong?

*The Wall Street Journal* reports prices from the last trade of the previous day. The call option's time of last trade may or may not correspond to the time of last trade of the exchange rate underlying the option. Suppose the last time this option traded on the PSE was at noon, at which time the spot rate was $0.6900/A$. The implied volatility of the "December A$ 63 call" at that instant is determined from the following:

| Value of call option | $Call^{\$/A\$}$ | = | $0.0666/A$ | |
|---|---|---|---|---|
| Price of underlying asset | $S^{\$/A\$}$ | = | $0.6900/A$ | |
| Exercise price | $K^{\$/A\$}$ | = | $0.6300/A$ | |
| Domestic risk-free rate | $i^{\$}$ | = | 4% per year | (continuously compounded) |
| Foreign risk-free rate | $i^{A\$}$ | = | 0% per year | (continuously compounded) |
| Time to expiration | T | = | 2½ months | |
| Volatility of the spot rate | $\sigma$ | = | ? | |

The implied volatility for this "December A$ 63 call" is 14.8 percent per year, the same as in the "December A$ 73 call." There was no solution to the previous example because the end-of-day exchange rate was used to price an option that last traded at noon. This example suggests a general result: *Beware of prices in thinly traded markets*. In this example, we were comparing apples and oranges. Or, more precisely, we were comparing apples (or options) at two different times of the growing season.

## Volatility and Probability of Exercise

Let's go back to the example of a December A$ 73 call on the PSE.

| Value of call option | $Call^{\$/A\$}$ | = | $0.0102/A$ | |
|---|---|---|---|---|
| Price of underlying asset | $S^{\$/A\$}$ | = | $0.7020/A$ | |
| Exercise price | $K^{\$/A\$}$ | = | $0.7300/A$ | |
| Domestic risk-free rate | $i^{\$}$ | = | 4% per year | (continuously compounded) |
| Foreign risk-free rate | $i^{A\$}$ | = | 0% per year | (continuously compounded) |
| Time to expiration | T | = | 2½ months | |
| Volatility of the spot rate | $\sigma$ | = | 14.8% | |

What is the probability of this option being in-the-money on the expiration date in December? The spot rate would have to go from $S_0^{\$/A\$} = \$0.7020/A\$$ to $S_T^{\$/A\$} = \$0.73/A\$$ for a continuously compounded change of $s_T^{\$/A\$} = \ln[(\$0.73/A\$)/(\$0.7020/A\$)] = 0.039$, or 3.9 percent. The standard deviation over 2.5 months is $\sigma_T = (\sqrt{T})\sigma = (2.5/12)^{(1/2)}(0.148) = 0.0676$, or 6.76 percent per 2.5 months. The continuously compounded change in the spot rate must be $s_T^{\$/A\$}/\sigma_T = (0.039)/(0.067) = 0.58$, or 58 percent of one standard deviation above the current spot rate. The probability mass of the normal distribution above $0.58\sigma$ is about 0.40. Thus, there is about a 40 percent chance of this option expiring in-the-money.

## Time-Varying Volatility

Recall that empirical investigations of exchange rate behavior reject the simple random walk model. Instead, researchers have found that exchange rates can be described as having ***generalized autoregressive conditional heteroskedasticity (GARCH).***[10]

- At each point in time, instantaneous returns are normally distributed.
- The instantaneous variance at each point in time depends on whether exchange rate changes in the recent past have been large or small.

The fact that foreign exchange volatility is not a constant means that OPMs that assume stationary price changes (such as the binomial and Black-Scholes models) are misspecified. Implied volatility is actually a time-weighted average of the instantaneous variances prevailing over the life of the option. For this reason, implied volatilities option values may not represent the instantaneous volatility at any point in time during the life of the option.

As an example, implied volatilities can be as large as 20 percent per year during turbulent periods in the foreign exchange markets. A 20 percent implied volatility on a 5-month currency option might represent a 40 percent standard deviation over the first month and a 10 percent standard deviation over the remaining four months.[11] Because of time-varying volatility, foreign exchange volatilities estimated from OPMs are at best imprecise estimates of current and expected future exchange rate volatility.

## 6.6 SUMMARY

An option represents a choice. Holders of options can exercise options at their discretion. Sellers (or writers) of options have an obligation to perform at the option of the option holders.

Currency options are useful for hedging or speculating because, in contrast to forward and futures contracts, their payoffs are asymmetric. This asymmetry allows currency options to serve as a disaster hedge against unfavorable changes in the value of a currency, or as a bet on the direction or volatility of foreign exchange rates.

Options can be categorized along several dimensions. The most important is whether the option is a call or a put.

- A call option is the right to buy the underlying asset.
- A put option is the right to sell the underlying asset.

Whenever you buy one currency you simultaneously sell another, so a call option on one currency is simultaneously a put option on another currency.

There are six determinants of a currency option value: (1) the value of the underlying exchange rate, (2) the exercise price of the option, (3) the risk-free rate in the domestic currency, (4) the risk-free rate in the foreign currency, (5) the time to expiration on the option, and (6) the volatility of the underlying exchange rate. With the exception of volatility, each of these determinants is readily observable for currency options quoted on major exchanges. The most important determinant—and the only one that typically is not listed in the financial section of a newspaper—is the volatility of the underlying exchange rate.

Option values can be decomposed as follows:

$$\text{Option value} = \text{Intrinsic value} + \text{Time value}$$

The intrinsic value of a currency option is its value if it is exercised immediately. Intrinsic value depends on the difference between the underlying exchange rate and the exercise price. The time value of a currency option comes from the possibility that currency values will move further in-the-money and the intrinsic value of the option will increase prior to expiration of the option.

There are two ways to estimate the volatility of exchange rates. Historical volatility is calculated from the time series of exchange rate changes. Implied volatility is the exchange rate volatility that is implied by the value of an option, given a particular OPM and the other determinants of option value.

## KEY TERMS

*American option*
*at-the-money*
*call option*
*European option*
*exercise price (or strike price)*
*expiration date*
GARCH
*hedge ratio*
*historical volatility*
*implied volatility*
*in-the-money*
*instantaneous variance*
*intrinsic value*
*option delta*
*option gamma*
*option premium*
*option theta*
*option vega*
*out-of-the-money*
*payoff (risk) profile*
*put option*
*put-call parity*
*realized volatility*
*stationary series*
*time value*
*volatility*

## CONCEPTUAL QUESTIONS

6.1 What is the difference between a call option and a put option?

6.2 What are the differences between exchange-traded and OTC currency options?

6.3 In what sense is a currency call option also a currency put option?

6.4 In what sense is a currency forward contract a combination of a put and a call?

6.5 What are the six determinants of a currency option value?

6.6 What determines the intrinsic value of an option? What determines the time value of an option?

6.7 Currency volatility is a key determinant of currency option value, but it is not directly observable. In what ways can you estimate currency volatility?

## PROBLEMS

6.1 You work at the currency desk at Barings Bank in London. As the middleman in a deal between the U.K. and Danish governments, you have paid £1,000,000 to the U.K. government and have been promised DKK8,438,000 from the Danish government in three months. You wouldn't mind leaving this long krone position open. However, next month's referendum in Denmark may further delay Denmark's adoption of the euro as its currency. If this happens, you expect the krone to drop on world markets. As a hedge, you are considering purchasing a call option on pounds sterling with an exercise price of DKK8.4500/£ that sells for DKK0.1464/£. Fill in the call option values at expiration in the following table. Refer to the long call in Figure 6.3 for reference.

| | 8.00 | 8.40 | 8.42 | 8.44 | 8.46 | 8.48 |
|---|---|---|---|---|---|---|
| Spot rate at expiration (DKK/£): | | | | | | |
| Call value at expiration (DKK/£): | | | | | | |

6.2 Based on the information in Problem 6.1, draw the payoff profile for a long krone put option at expiration. Note that these exchange rates are reciprocals of those in Problem 6.1.

| | 0.12500 | 0.11905 | 0.11876 | 0.11848 | 0.11820 | 0.11792 |
|---|---|---|---|---|---|---|
| Spot rate at expiration (£/DKK): | | | | | | |
| Put value at expiration (£/DKK): | | | | | | |

6.3 Label your axes and plot each of the points. Draw a profit/loss graph for this long krone put at expiration. Refer to the long put in Figure 6.3 for reference.

6.4 Based on the prices and exchange rates in Problem 6.1 and 6.2, use graphs to show how a short pound call is equivalent to a short krone put.

6.5 Construct an option position (i.e., some combination of calls and/or puts) with the same risk profile ($\Delta\text{Call}^{\$/A\$}$ versus $\Delta S^{\$/A\$}$) as a forward contract to buy A\$ at a forward price of $F_1^{\$/A\$} = \$0.75/A\$$. Use both words and graphs.

a. Label the axes.
b. Identify the asset underlying the option(s).
c. Indicate whether each option is a put or a call.
d. Indicate whether you are buying or selling the option.
e. Indicate the exercise price.

6.6 Section 6.3 used graphs to show how volatility affects the time value of out-of-the-money, at-the-money, and in-the-money call options. Use similar graphs to show how volatility affects the time value of out-of-the-money, at-the-money, and in-the-money put options.

6.7 Suppose you believe that the market has underestimated the volatility of the yen-per-dollar exchange rate. You are not sure whether the dollar will rise or fall in value, only that it probably will rise or fall by a larger amount than expected by other market participants. Consider forming a "purchased straddle" by combining a purchased dollar call and a purchased dollar put with the same exercise price $K^{¥/\$}$ and expiration date. Diagram the payoff profile of this position at expiration.

6.8 Suppose the yen value of a dollar is ¥100/\$ and that this exchange rate has an equal probability of moving to either ¥90.484/\$ or ¥110.517/\$ in one period. To what continuously compounded rates of return do these changes correspond?

6.9 Suppose the spot rate is ¥105/\$ and there is an equal chance that it will fall to ¥70.38/\$ or rise to ¥156.64/\$. To what continuously compounded rates of return do these changes correspond?

6.10 Using one year (252 trading days) of historical data, you have estimated a daily standard deviation of 0.00742 = 0.742 percent for the $S^{\$/A\$}$ exchange rate.

a. What is the annual standard deviation of the $S^{\$/A\$}$ exchange rate if continuously compounded exchange rate changes $s^{\$/A\$}$ are i.i.d. as normal?
b. Suppose the current spot rate of exchange is A\$1.40/\$. Find the exchange rates that are plus or minus two standard deviations from this rate after one year based on annual volatility in part a.
c. Verify that $S^{\$/A\$}$ volatility is equal to $S^{A\$/\$}$ volatility by (1) translating your $\pm 2\sigma$ of the spot exchange rate and (2) finding the annual standard deviation implied by these rates from $s^{A\$/\$} = \ln(S_1^{A\$/\$}/S_0^{A\$/\$})$.

## SUGGESTED READINGS

### "Realized volatility" estimates are introduced in

T.M. Andersen and T. Bollerslev, "Answering the Skeptics: Yes, Standard Volatility Models Do Provide Accurate Forecasts," *International Economic Review* 39 (1998), 885–905.

## APPENDIX 6A: CURRENCY OPTION VALUATION

Option valuation involves the mathematics of stochastic processes. The term ***stochastic*** means random, and stochastic processes model randomness. Since its introduction in the 1970s, study of stochastic processes has revolutionized asset valuation. Although the mathematics of stochastic processes can be intimidating, the good news is that it doesn't take a rocket scientist to use options to hedge financial price risks, such as currency risk, using the option payoff profiles in the body of this chapter. The OPM in this appendix will help those with an interest in options to develop a deeper understanding of how option prices move with changes in the option value determinants.[12]

### The binomial option pricing model

In the body of the chapter, we concentrated on option values at expiration. To value options prior to expiration, we need to develop an OPM. The simplest way to do this is with the binomial OPM.

The ***binomial OPM*** begins with the simplest possible (nontrivial) circumstance in which there are only two possible outcomes in the underlying exchange rate. To illustrate, let's take the perspective of a Japanese resident purchasing a European call option to buy U.S. dollars in one period through a Japanese investment bank. The currency of reference is the U.S. dollar, so we'll keep dollars in the denominator. For convenience, the option contract size is assumed to be one dollar. The option is exercisable in one period with an exercise price equal to the expected future spot exchange rate of $E[S_1^{¥/\$}] = K^{¥/\$} = ¥100/\$$. The current spot rate is also ¥100/\$.

Suppose that the exchange rate at expiration of the option in one period will be either ¥90.484/$ or ¥110.517/$ with equal probability. The payoff on this foreign currency call option will be zero if the exchange rate closes out-of-the-money at ¥90.484/$. An option holder would be better off buying dollars in the spot market at ¥90.484/$ than at the exercise price of ¥100/$, so the option will remain unexercised at expiration. If the spot rate closes in-the-money at ¥110.517/$, a call option holder can exercise the option to buy dollars from the option writer at the ¥100/$ exercise price and then sell dollars in the foreign exchange market at the market rate of ¥110.517/$. The payoff at expiration on this call option position is $(S_1^{¥/\$} - K^{¥/\$}) = (¥110.517/\$ - ¥100/\$) = ¥10.517/\$$. These alternatives are depicted graphically as follows:

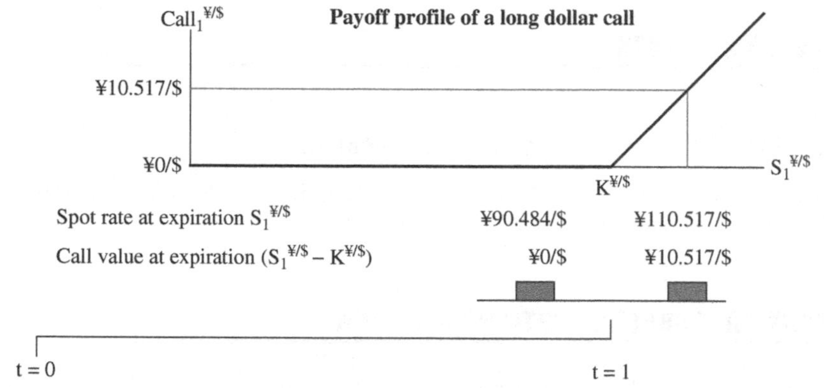


To value this option prior to expiration, we'll replicate the call option payoffs with money market instruments and then find the value of the position in the money market.

**"Buy a Dollar and Borrow Yen"** Compare this option payoff profile with that of buying one dollar today at the current spot rate of ¥100/$ and borrowing (¥90.484)/1.05 = ¥86.175 from a bank at the 5 percent Japanese rate of interest. The yen value of the dollar will fluctuate, depending on the spot exchange rate $S^{¥/\$}$. In contrast, the yen value of the loan repayment is –¥90.484, regardless of the spot rate of exchange. In sum, the "buy a dollar and borrow yen" strategy replicates the call option payoff. This is represented graphically here:

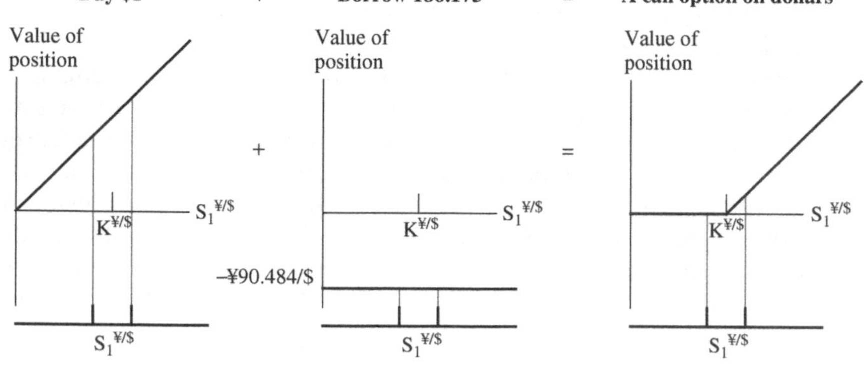

Algebraically, the payoffs on these strategies as a function of the end-of-period spot rate are

| Closing spot rate $S_1^{¥/\$}$ | ¥90.484/\$ | ¥110.517/\$ |
|---|---|---|
| Yen value of \$1 | ¥90.484 | ¥110.517 |
| Loan repayment | −¥90.484 | −¥90.484 |
| Net payoff | ¥0 | ¥20.033 |

These values represent the spread of possible values in the "buy a dollar and borrow yen" strategy, given the two possible spot rate outcomes. The value of this position at today's ¥100/\$ spot rate is

*Value of "buy a dollar and borrow yen"*

= present value of the "buy \$1 and borrow ¥86.175" strategy

= ¥100 − ¥86.175 bank loan

= ¥13.825

This money market strategy is a multiple of the call option strategy. The next section values the call option prior to expiration by scaling down the "buy a dollar and borrow yen" strategy until the payoffs on the two strategies are equal.

**Using the Hedge Ratio to Value Currency Options** The *option delta* or *hedge ratio* indicates the number of call options required to replicate the payoff from buying one unit of the underlying asset.

Option delta = (Spread of possible option prices)/(Spread of possible asset values)

= number of call options required to replicate one unit of the underlying asset

For our example, this is equal to (¥10.517)/(¥20.033) = 0.52498 call options per dollar. The payoff on the dollar call option is 52.498 percent of the value of the "buy a dollar and borrow yen" strategy, regardless of the future spot rate of exchange, so the value of the call must be 52.498 percent of the value of the "buy a dollar and borrow yen" strategy.

Instead of buying \$1, suppose you buy \$0.52498 and borrow (¥86.175/\$)(\$0.52498) = ¥45.240 at the 5 percent yen interest rate.[13] In one period, you'll owe ¥45.240(1.05) = ¥47.502 on the loan. Your payoff on the "buy \$0.52498" strategy will be 52.498 percent of the "buy a dollar" strategy; that is, either ¥47.502 or ¥58.019 with equal probability. Your net payoffs on this money market position are

| Closing spot rate $S_1^{¥/\$}$ | ¥90.484/\$ | ¥110.517/\$ |
|---|---|---|
| Yen value of \$0.52498 | ¥47.502 | ¥58.019 |
| Loan repayment | −¥47.502 | −¥47.502 |
| Net payoff | ¥0 | ¥10.517 |

A position that replicates the payoffs of an option contract is called a ***replicating portfolio***. For the dollar call in the example, the replicating portfolio consists of buying \$0.52498 and borrowing ¥47.502/(1.05) = ¥45.240. Since the payoffs to the option and its replicating portfolio are identical, arbitrage will ensure that their values are equal as well.[14]

***Value of a one-dollar call option***

= 52.498 percent of the value of a "buy \$1 and borrow ¥86.175" strategy
= value of "buy \$0.52498 and borrow ¥45.240"
= ¥52.498−¥45.240
= ¥7.2578

Voilà! You've valued your first call option. If payoffs are binomially distributed, the payoffs to a foreign currency call option can be replicated by borrowing the domestic currency and buying the foreign currency according to the proportion in the hedge ratio.

**A General Case of the Binomial Model** In this example, there are two possible outcomes for the end-of-period exchange rate. The model can be extended to an arbitrary number of outcomes by allowing the exchange rate to bifurcate (or split) several times in succession. Suppose the underlying exchange rate diverges from ¥100/\$ by ±1 percent twice in succession. After the first split, the exchange rate is (¥100/\$)$e^{(\pm.01)}$ = ¥99.005/\$ or ¥101.005/\$ with equal probability.

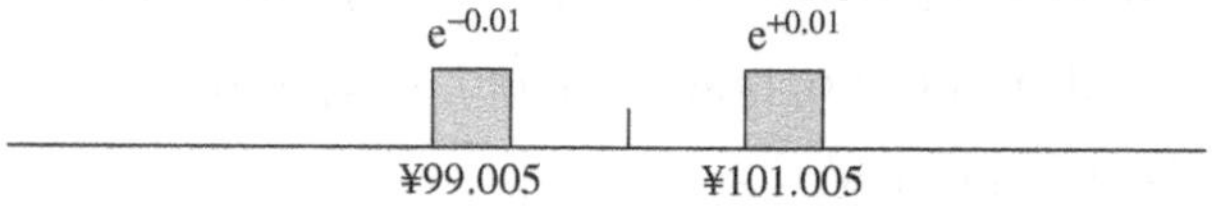


There are three possible outcomes when outcomes diverge by an additional ±1 percent: ¥100/\$ (with 50 percent probability), and ¥98.020/\$ and ¥102.020/\$ (each with a 25 percent probability).

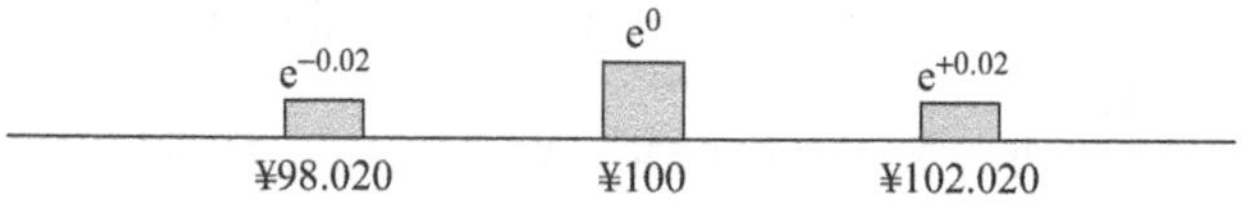


These outcomes correspond to −2 percent, 0 percent, and +2 percent in continuously compounded returns. Another round of ±1 percent changes results in ±3 percent (each with 1/8 probability) and ±1 percent (each with 3/8 probability) as follows:

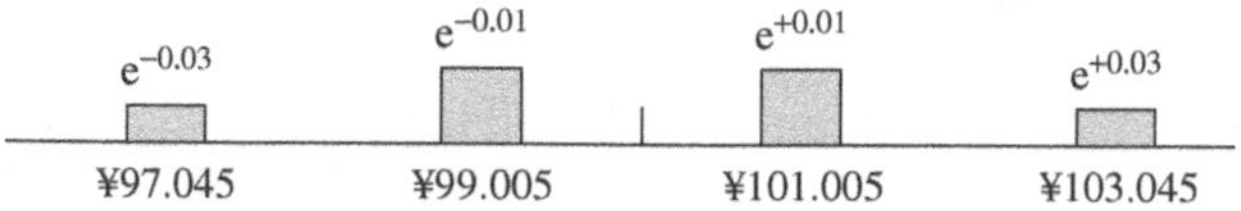


*The* next bifurcation results in five possible outcomes, and so on. This type of repetitive bifurcation can be summarized in a tree diagram.

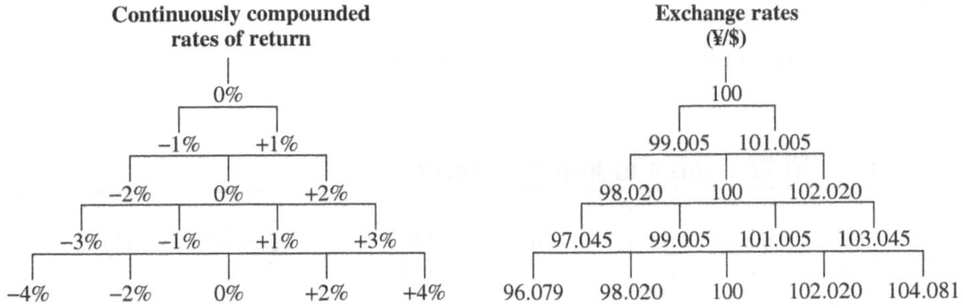


If the probabilities and distances of up and down movements are equal at each bifurcation, then the continuously compounded end-of-period rate of return approaches the normal distribution as the number of bifurcations increases. The corresponding distribution in prices (or, in this case, in exchange rates) is said to ***lognormal*** and is positively skewed and bounded by zero from below.

The binomial model can be generalized by allowing the process generating up and down movements to bifurcate over shorter and shorter intervals. As an example, the standard deviation created by eight yen-per-dollar exchange rate bifurcations of ±1 percent each is 3.75 percent, or ¥3.75/$ based on the ¥100/$ starting value.[15] In the limit, the distribution of continuously compounded exchange rates approaches the normal distribution. The binomial model is then equivalent to the currency OPM presented in the next section.

## Currency Option Pricing

In 1973, Fischer Black and Myron Scholes borrowed a model from fluid dynamics to solve for the value of a European option on a non-dividend-paying stock. This innovation triggered a worldwide boom in options trading on financial assets, including currencies.

**The Black-Scholes Option Pricing Model** A key assumption in the ***Black-Scholes OPM*** is that continuously compounded returns are normally distributed with constant mean $\mu$ and standard deviation $\sigma$.[16] The Black-Scholes formula for the value of a European call option on a share of non-dividend-paying stock is

$$\text{Call} = \text{P}\,\text{N}(\text{d}_1) - e^{(-i\text{T})}\text{K}\,\text{N}(\text{d}_2) \qquad (6\text{A}.1)$$

where

Call = the value of a call option on a share of non-dividend-paying stock

P = the current share price

K = the exercise price of the call option

$i$ = a constant risk-free rate of interest in continuously compounded returns

$\sigma$ = the instantaneous standard deviation of return on the stock

T = the time to expiration of the option expressed as a fraction of one period

$\text{d}_1 = [\ln(\text{P}/\text{K}) + (i + (\sigma^2/2))\text{T}]/(\sigma\sqrt{\text{T}})$

$d_2 = (d_1 - \sigma\sqrt{T})$

$N(\cdot)$ = the standard normal cumulative distribution function

## APPLICATION The Holes in Black-Scholes

Although the option pricing formulas presented in this appendix work well in most circumstances, you should be aware of their limitations.

1. The most important input in any option pricing formula is volatility. For exchange-traded options, volatility is also the only input that cannot be read directly out of a financial newspaper. Regardless of how sophisticated the OPM, option values are only as reliable as the estimate of volatility.
2. Most OPMs assume continuously compounded returns are normally distributed and stationary over time. Empirical studies have found that returns to most assets (including currencies) are ***leptokurtic,*** with more probability mass around the mean and in the tails and less probability mass in the shoulders than the normal distribution. Assets also have volatilities that vary over time. Differences between a model's assumptions and actual returns create a bias in option values calculated with an option pricing formula.
3. Although the formulas in this appendix are for European options, many exchange-traded and OTC options are American options. The early-exercise feature of American currency options can make them worth slightly more than European currency options at the same exercise price.

*Source:* See Black, "How to Use the Holes in Black-Scholes," *Journal of Applied Corporate Finance* (1989).

The value of a put option on a share of stock can be found from put-call parity, which is stated in continuously compounded returns as

$$\text{Call} - \text{Put} = \text{P} - e^{(-iT)}\text{K} \Leftrightarrow \text{Put} = \text{Call} - \text{P} + e^{(-iT)}\text{K} \qquad (6\text{A}.2)$$

The call and put values and the price of the underlying asset are already in present value terms, and the term $e^{(-iT)}K = K/(1+i)^T$ discounts the exercise price back to the present at the risk-free rate i (or $i = \ln(1+i)$ in continuously compounded returns). As in the binomial model, this equation is enforced through risk-free arbitrage with a replicating portfolio.

Here is the intuition behind the Black-Scholes formula. At expiration, time value is equal to zero and call option value is composed entirely of intrinsic value.

$$\text{Call}_T = \text{Max}[0, P_T - K]$$

Prior to expiration, the closing price is a random variable that will not be known until expiration. To value a call option prior to expiration, we need to find the expected value of $[P_T - K]$ given the option expires in-the-money (i.e., given $P_T > K$). In the Black-Scholes formula, $N(d_1)$ is the probability that the call option will expire in-the-money. This probability is shown below.

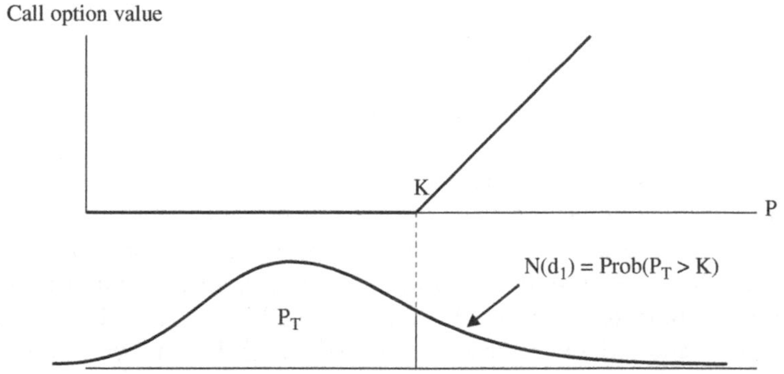


The term $P_N(d_1)$ in Equation 6A.1 is the expected value of share price at expiration, given $P_T > K$. Similarly, $KN(d_2)$ is the expected value of the exercise price at expiration, given $P_T > K$. The $e^{(-iT)}$ term in Equation 6A.1 discounts the expected exercise price to the present at the risk-free rate of interest. Option value is thus the present value of the option's expected value at expiration.

**A Currency Option Pricing Model** Biger and Hull applied the Black-Scholes framework to European currency options by replacing stock prices with exchange rates and assuming constant interest rates in the foreign and domestic currencies.[17] Biger and Hull's European currency option pricing formula can be stated either in terms of spot exchange rates or in terms of forward exchange rates.

$$Call^{d/f} = e^{(-i^d T)}[F_T^{d/f} N(d_1) - K^{d/f} N(d_2)] \qquad (6A.3)$$

$$\Leftrightarrow Call^{d/f} = e^{(-i^f T)}[S_0^{d/f} N(d_1)] - e^{(-i^d T)}[K^{d/f} N(d_2)] \qquad (6A.4)$$

Where

$Call^{d/f}$ = the value of a call option on one unit of foreign currency

$S_0^{d/f}$ = today's spot exchange rate

$F_T^{d/f}$ = today's forward exchange rate for delivery at time T

$S_0^{d/f} = e^{(+i^d T)} e^{(-i^f T)}$ in continuously compounded returns

$K^{d/f}$ = the exercise price on one unit of foreign currency

$i^d$ = the domestic risk-free interest rate in continuously compounded returns

$i^f$ = the foreign risk-free interest rate in continuously compounded returns

$\sigma$ = the instantaneous standard deviation of the exchange rate

$T$ = the time to expiration of the option expressed as a fraction of one period

$d_1 = [\ln(S^{d/f}/K^{d/f}) + (i^d - i^f + (\sigma^2/2))T]/(\sigma\sqrt{T})$

$d_2 = (d_1 - \sigma\sqrt{T})$
$N(\cdot)$ = the standard normal cumulative distribution function

Equations 6A.3 and 6A.4 are related through interest rate parity in continuously compounded returns. The value of a put option on foreign currency is found from put-call parity.

$$\text{Call}^{d/f} - \text{Put}^{d/f} = e^{(-idT)}(F_T^{d/f} - K^{d/f}) \tag{6A.5}$$

$$\Leftrightarrow \text{Put}^{d/f} = \text{Call}^{d/f} - e^{(-ifT)}S_0^{d/f} + e^{(-idT)}K^{d/f} \tag{6A.6}$$

where interest rate parity again ensures that $F_T^{d/f} = S_0^{d/f}e^{(+idT)}e^{(-ifT)}$.

As in the Black-Scholes OPM, $N(d_1)$ is the probability of a call option expiring in-the-money. Because a put option with the same exercise price is in-the-money whenever a call is out-of-the-money, and vice versa, the probability of a put option expiring in-the-money is $1 - N(d_1)$. $N(d_1)$is also the hedge ratio; that is, the number of call options required to replicate the payoff from buying one unit of foreign currency. Because the probability of a put being exercised is 1 minus the probability of a call being exercised, the hedge ratio for a put option is equal to $1 - N(d_1)$.

The CME, as well as many other options exchanges around the world, trades options on futures rather than options on spot exchange rates. The volatilities of futures and spot prices are nearly identical and futures prices converge to spot prices at expiration, so the differences between options on futures and options on spot exchange rates are minor.[18] Equations 6A.3 and 6A.5 work with forward exchange rates as well as with futures prices.

Solution of the option pricing problem proved to be a turning point in the evolution of finance. The OPM set the stage for the subsequent introduction and growth of options trading on a variety of assets, including stocks, bonds, commodities, interest rates, and exchange rates. The OPM also made a course in stochastic processes a required part of doctoral programs in finance.

## KEY TERMS

*binomial option pricing model (OPM)*
*Black-Scholes option pricing model (OPM)*
*hedge ratio (option delta)*
*leptokurtic*
*lognormal distribution*
*replicating portfolio*
*stochastic*

## PROBLEMS

6A.1 What is the value of a European call option on U.S. dollars with an exercise price of ¥100/$ and a maturity date six months from now if the current spot rate of exchange is ¥80/$ and the continuously compounded risk-free rate in both Japan and the United States is 5 percent? You have estimated the instantaneous standard deviation of the yen/dollar exchange rate as 10 percent per year based on the variability of past currency movements.

6A.2 Suppose that in Problem 6A.1 the currency markets are undergoing a period of unusually high volatility. If the true standard deviation of the yen/dollar spot rate is 20 percent, by how much have you under- or overestimated the value of the dollar call option?

6A.3 Consider the following "December Yen 84 call" on the Philadelphia exchange:

| | |
|---|---|
| Current call price | \$0.000118/¥ |
| Price of underlying asset | \$0.008345/¥ |
| Exercise price | \$0.008400/¥ |
| Risk-free rate in dollars | 4% (continuously compounded) |
| Risk-free rate in yen | 4% (continuously compounded) |
| Time to expiration | 2½ months |

What is the volatility of the dollar-per-yen exchange rate implied by the currency OPM?

6A.4 As head of currency trading at Ball Bearings Bank in London, you need to price a series of options of various maturity on Danish kroner. The current spot rate is DKK8.4528/£. Risk-free interest rates in the United Kingdom and in Denmark are 1.74 percent and 1.30 percent in continuously compounded returns per three months, respectively. Instantaneous volatility on the pound/krone spot rate is 5 percent per three months. The international parity conditions hold.

a. Assume an exercise price of $K^{DKK/£}$ = DKK8.5000/£. Fill in the following table based on the international parity conditions and the currency option pricing formulas in Equations 6A.4 and 6A.6:

| | Maturities | | | |
|---|---|---|---|---|
| | 1 month | 3 months | 6 months | 1 year |
| Forward rate (DKK/£) | | | | |
| Call option value | | | | |
| Put option value | | | | |

b. Repeat part a using the currency option pricing formula in Equations 6A.3 and 6A.5.

c. Draw a payoff profile that includes all four call options on the same graph.

d. Draw a payoff profile that includes all four put options on the same graph.

6A.5 Rather than varying the maturity of the options as in Problem 6A.4, let's vary the exercise price. Fill in the following table, assuming a 3-month time to expiration and the information from Problem 6A.4:

| | Exercise prices (DKK/£) | | | |
|---|---|---|---|---|
| | 8.200 | 8.400 | 8.600 | 8.800 |
| Call option value | | | | |
| Put option value | | | | |

## SUGGESTED READINGS

### The Black-Scholes option pricing model was introduced in

Fischer Black and Myron Scholes, "The Pricing of Options and Corporate Liabilities," *Journal of Political Economy* 81 (May–June 1973), 637–659.

### Fischer Black modified the original model to value options on futures in

Fischer Black, "The Pricing of Commodity Options," *Journal of Financial Economics* 3, No. 1/2 (1976), 167–179.

### The option pricing model was adapted to currency options in

Nahum Biger and John Hull, "The Valuation of Currency Options," *Financial Management* 12 (Spring 1983), 24–28.

Mark Garman and Steve W. Kohlhagen, "Foreign Currency Option Values," *Journal of International Money and Finance* 2, No. 3 (1983), 231-237.

### Practical aspects of option use are discussed in

Fischer Black, "How to Use the Holes in Black-Scholes," *Journal of Applied Corporate Finance* 1, No. 4 (1989), 67–73.

# CHAPTER 7

# Currency Swaps and Swaps Markets

*Never take a job for which you have to change clothes.*

—Henry David Thoreau

A *swap* is a derivative instrument in which counterparties exchange one stream of cash flows for another. In a ***currency swap,*** the cash flows are in two different currencies. The most common form of currency swap trades a fixed interest rate in one currency for a floating interest rate in another. Although both principal and interest payments could be exchanged, in most currency swaps the principal is not exchanged and only a ***difference check*** recognizing the difference in the interest payments is exchanged. The principal amount in a swap is called ***notional principal*** because it determines the size of the interest payments on the two sides of the swap. An ***interest rate swap*** is a similar transaction except the principal amounts are in the same currency.

Suppose British Petroleum (BP) has a U.S. oil refinery that generates cash flows in U.S. dollars. Although BP's functional currency is the British pound and much of its debt is denominated in pounds, fixed rate dollar debt could hedge the operating cash flows of BP's U.S. refinery. A floating-for-fixed currency swap with a commercial or investment bank could accomplish this hedge without having to incur the costs of issuing new dollar-denominated debt. Swap contracts such as these provide cost-effective vehicles for quickly transforming one's exposures to financial price risks including interest rates, exchange rates, and commodity prices.

## 7.1 THE GROWTH OF THE SWAPS MARKET

*Counter-parties exchange cash flow streams in a swap.*

Currency swaps evolved out of a 1970s financial arrangement called a parallel loan in which two firms from different countries borrowed in their domestic currency and then agreed to pay each other's debt. Similar to a parallel loan agreement, the currency swap contract identifies the currencies of denomination and the amount and timing of cash inflows and outflows. The swap contract releases each party from its obligation should the other party default on its obligation. In the event of default, the aggrieved party simply can stop making interest payments on its side of the contract and, if necessary, seek compensation in court.

In 1981, Salomon Brothers (now a part of Citigroup) engineered the first currency swap between the World Bank and International Business Machines, which, because of the stature of the participants, served to legitimize the swaps market. By the early to middle 1980s, investment bankers such as Salomon Brothers were nurturing an increasingly active market in currency and interest rate swaps. These early swaps were customized, low-volume, high-margin deals. As volume and liquidity grew, international commercial and investment banks began serving as swap dealers and the market turned into a high-volume, low-margin business. This market for "plain vanilla" swaps uses standardized contracts that follow the conventions of the *International Swaps and Derivatives Association* (www.isda.org). Today, commercial and investment banks are the major dealers in a liquid international swaps market.

Swaps combine a liability (a firm's commitment to pay the counterparty) with an asset (the counterparty's commitment to pay the firm), and so could distort a firm's apparent financial leverage if these largely offsetting positions were capitalized on the balance sheet. For this reason, accounting and regulatory conventions in most countries treat swaps as off-balance sheet transactions that appear in the footnotes to financial statements. The swap's impact is felt on the income statement through interest expense and, in the case of currency swaps, through foreign currency gains and losses.

Figure 7.1 displays the phenomenal growth in derivatives trading based on a survey by the Bank for International Settlements (www.bis.org) of swap dealers in the over-the-counter (OTC) derivatives market. Interest rate derivatives (interest rate swaps and options, and interest rate forward contracts called *forward rate agreements*) were by far the most commonly traded contracts, with $465 trillion in notional principal outstanding in December 2010. Currency contracts (forwards, swaps, and options) were second in notional outstanding, with $58 trillion. Credit default swaps (CDSs) accounted for $30 trillion and are the fastest growing segment of the market. Equity derivatives have held a fairly steady share of the market for the past decade, and accounted for $7 trillion in notional principal. Commodity derivatives accounted for another $7 trillion. CDSs, commodity swaps, and equity swaps are described later in this chapter.

## 7.2 SWAPS AS PORTFOLIOS OF FORWARD CONTRACTS

You've taken a fast-track job as a junior analyst with International Notions Company, Inc. It's your first day on the job and Hiromi Ito, Notions' CFO, brings you into her office to discuss the currency exposure of Notions' operations. You only get one chance to make a first impression, and you are eager to demonstrate that your time at school was well spent.

*Ito:* "I want to get your opinion on a persistent problem that we face here at Notions. We have sales in more than 140 countries worldwide. Yet 70 percent of our research and development expenses, the bulk of our production

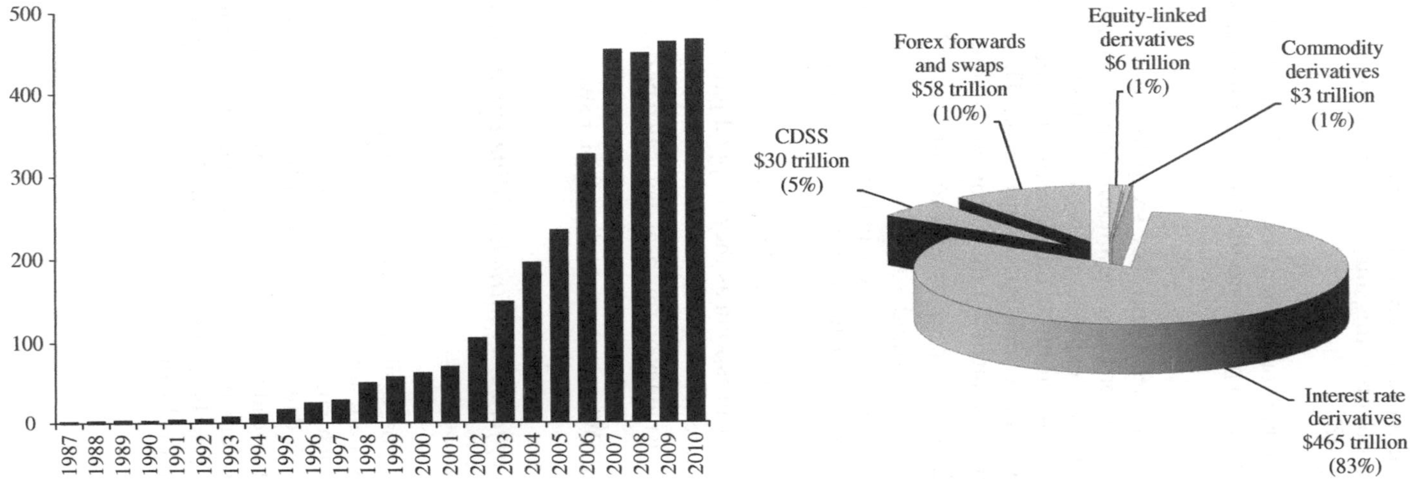


**FIGURE 7.1** Notional Amounts Outstanding in OTC Derivatives Markets ($ trillions).
*Sources*: International Swap Dealers Association (www.isda.org) and Bank for International Settlements (www.bis.org).

expenses, and all of our interest expenses are in dollars. Our dividends also are paid in dollars. I'm particularly concerned about our exposure to the countries of the European Union. A high percentage of our sales come from these countries, yet our operating and financial expenses are largely in dollars. What do you suggest?"

(Okay . . . now what was it that you studied in school? Think fast! Ah, yes. A currency swap might be just the thing. Stepping into the breach, you suggest a dollar-for-euro currency swap.)

*You*: "Well, we might consider a currency swap for euros. We could swap our dollar debt for euro debt on the same amount of notional principal and thereby convert some of our dollar expenses to euro expenses. Our counterparty would pay the dollar interest payments on our debt and we would pay the euro interest payment on a comparable amount of euro debt. This would form a hedge against revenues from countries in the European Union."

*Ito*: "Hmm . . . and who do you propose as a counterparty?"

*You*: "This should be a fairly standard financial transaction, so I'd suggest an international bank making a market in currency swaps. I have a classmate in the swaps department at UBS in New York. I'm sure she could give us a quote."

*Ito*: "What if they default on their side of the deal?"

*You*: "We'd stop paying them as soon as they stopped paying us. At most, we'd be out a few months' interest on the notional principal."

*Ito*: "If Notions loses any money on this deal, we'll also be out one junior analyst!"

How do you respond? What *is* the default risk of a swap contract?

> ***A swap is a portfolio of forward contracts of different maturity dates.***

Ms. Ito's question is most easily answered by comparing the swap contract with a futures contract. Futures are nothing more than a bundle of consecutive one-day forward contracts in which changes in wealth due to changes in exchange rates are marked-to-market each day. Swaps are also a bundle of forward contracts. But instead of being laid end-to-end as renewable one-day forwards contracts, a swap is a bundle of *simultaneous* forward contracts, each with a different maturity date.

Suppose a domestic firm borrows an amount $X^d$ in a T-period nonamortizing loan with periodic (fixed or floating rate) interest payments $C_t^d = i_t^d X^d$ throughout the life of the loan.

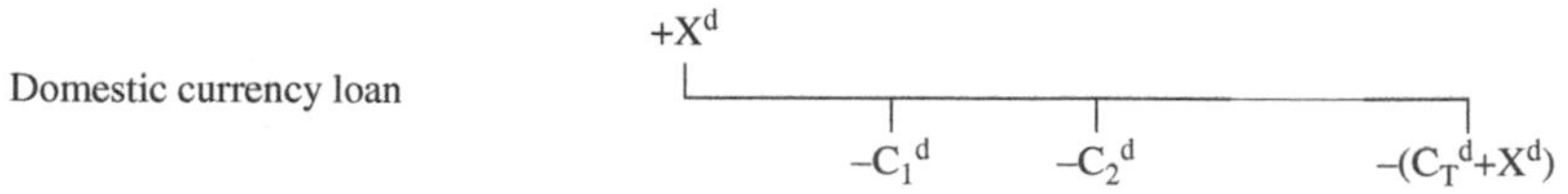

If the company has a need to hedge revenues from a foreign subsidiary, it can swap this domestic currency loan for a foreign currency loan of equal value ($X_t^f = X_t^d / S_t^{d/f}$) paying interest payments $C_t^f = i_t^f X^f$. If the principal being received is set equal in value to the principal being paid, there is no reason to exchange the principal amounts, and the principal is called notional principal. Rather than exchange the full amount of the interest payments, only the difference check need be exchanged. This difference check is equal to ($C_t^d - C_t^f S_t^{d/f}$) after translating the foreign currency interest payment into domestic currency at the prevailing spot rate. The net cash flows look as follows:

| | | | |
|---|---|---|---|
| Net cash flows of a currency swap | $+C_1^d$ <br> $-C_1^f S_1^{d/f}$ | $+C_2^d$ <br> $-C_2^f S_2^{d/f}$ | $+C_T^d$ <br> $-C_T^f S_T^{d/f}$ |

This is equivalent to a portfolio of T forward contracts each with successively longer maturities.

| | | | |
|---|---|---|---|
| One-period forward contract | $(C_1^d - C_1^f S_1^{d/f})$ | | |
| Two-period forward contract | | $(C_2^d - C_2^f S_2^{d/f})$ | |
| T-period forward contract | | | $(C_T^d - C_T^f S_T^{d/f})$ |

Currency swaps are essentially bundles of currency forward contracts of different maturities. Ms. Ito's concern is at least partially justified because swap contracts, like forward contracts, are subject to default risk. Although the risk and consequences of default are somewhat more than in a comparable futures contract with a futures exchange clearinghouse, they are far less than for straight debt.

A futures contract reduces default risk relative to a forward contract by: (1) requiring a margin, (2) having an exchange clearinghouse as the counterparty, and (3) marking-to-market daily. Swaps can be compared with futures along these same three dimensions. First, swaps do not generally require a performance bond, such as a margin requirement, and this tends to give swaps slightly more default risk than comparable futures contracts. Second, a commercial or investment bank making a market in swaps is generally the counterparty. To the extent that the bank is more prone to default than a clearinghouse, this may slightly increase default risk. Third, whereas the entire gain or loss on a futures contract is marked-to-market daily, the performance period between payments is longer (e.g., six months) than in a futures contract and only the current interest payment is settled in a swap. The default risk of a swap contract thus falls somewhere between the risk of a comparable futures contract (which is negligible) and the risk of the longest maturity forward contract in the swap contract.

Swaps are far less risky than straight debt because if one side defaults, the other side is released from its obligations as well. Further, the entire principal is not at risk as it is in a loan because of the exchange of actual or notional principals at the beginning and at the end of the contract. The interest payments are less at risk than in straight debt, because the difference check depends on the difference between the interest rates rather than on the level of one of the interest rates. For these reasons, currency and interest rate swaps are far less risky than comparable straight debt.[1]

## 7.3 CURRENCY SWAPS

***Financial engineering*** is a buzzword on Wall Street that aptly describes the "name of the game" in investment banking. The rapid pace of financial innovation to meet both old and new financing needs is truly extraordinary. This high rate of technological innovation is both a blessing and a curse for multinational financial managers. The blessing is that access to capital markets is far greater today than at any time in history. The curse is that it is difficult to keep abreast of innovations in new financial products. Value can easily be destroyed without a thorough understanding of the benefits, costs, and risks of financial contracting. Fortunately, products that at first appear to be new contracts are in most cases new versions of established contracts. This section shows how currency swaps can be used to quickly and effectively transform the nature of the firm's assets and liabilities.

The most common form of currency swap is the ***currency coupon swap,*** a fixed-for-floating rate nonamortizing currency swap traded primarily through commercial banks. In a nonamortizing loan, the entire principal is repaid at maturity and only interest is paid during the life of the loan. Currency swaps also come with amortizing loans in which periodic payments spread the principal repayment throughout the life of the loans. Currency swaps can be structured as fixed-for-fixed, fixed-for-floating, or floating-for-floating swaps of either the nonamortizing or amortizing variety.

> *Currency coupon swaps are fixed-for-floating currency swaps.*

Swap dealers such as Citigroup quote ***swap pricing schedules*** for actively traded swaps. Figure 7.2 shows a nonamortizing fixed-for-floating currency coupon swap pricing schedule between Australian (A$) and U.S. ($) dollars with annual interest payments and a maturity of five years. Citigroup's position is summarized at the

A$/$ Currency Coupon Swap Pricing Schedule

| Maturity | Bid (in A$) | Ask (in A$) |
|---|---|---|
| 5 years | 6.63% | 6.73% |

Quotes are against 1-year London Interbank Offer Rate (LIBOR)` Eurodollar flat.

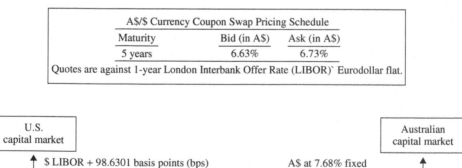

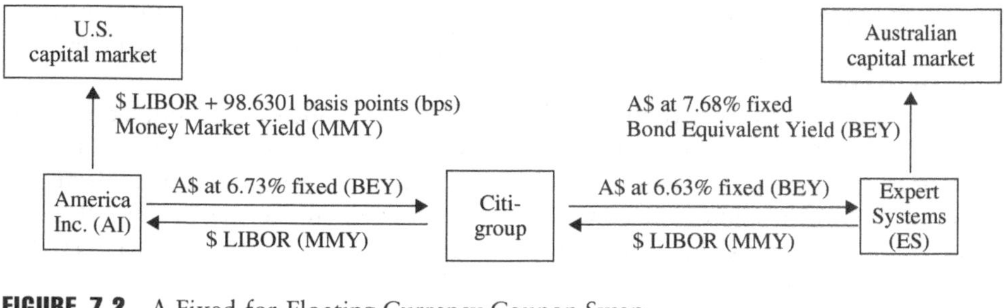


**FIGURE 7.2** A Fixed-for-Floating Currency Coupon Swap.

bottom of the figure. By setting the floating rate side of each swap to the 1-year Eurodollar LIBOR rate, Citigroup has zero net exposure to U.S. dollars so long as the bank's swap book is in balance. Floating rate interest payments on a swap usually are determined at one settlement date and then paid at the next. On the fixed rate side, Citigroup pays its bid rate of 6.63 percent and receives its ask rate of 6.73 percent, and so earns a bid-ask spread of 10 bps on the notional principal.

## A Note on Day Count Conventions

Before using this swap pricing schedule, we need to introduce one technical detail. Floating rate Eurocurrency interest rates such as LIBOR are quoted on an "Actual/360" or ***MMY*** basis, assuming 360 days in a year and interest that accrues over the actual number of calendar days between two payment dates. In contrast, many fixed rate instruments including U.S. Treasury bonds are quoted as a ***BEY*** (either "Actual/365" or "Actual/Actual") based on 365 days in a year. This ***day count*** convention defines the way in which interest accrues over time.

This difference means that a MMY on the floating rate side of a swap is not equivalent to the BEY on the fixed rate side. The approximate relation between the two is

$$\begin{aligned} \text{MMY} &= \text{BEY}(360/365) \\ \text{or, equivalently,}\quad \text{BEY} &= \text{MMY}(365/360) \end{aligned} \tag{7.1}$$

For example, a 4.40 percent BEY on a U.S. Treasury bond is approximately the same as a $(4.40\%)(360/365) \approx 4.34\%$ MMY on a Eurodollar deposit pegged to LIBOR. This transformation allows you to compare floating rate yields based on a 360-day year with fixed rate yields based on a 365-day year. No adjustment is necessary when the fixed and floating rate sides of the swap have the same day count convention.

## An Example of a Currency Coupon Swap

Suppose the current spot rate is $S_0^{A\$/\$} = A\$1.25/\$$ and the U.S. dollar is selling at a forward premium of $F_t^{A\$/\$}/S_0^{A\$/\$} = [(1+i^{A\$})/(1+i^{\$})]^t = (1.02)^t$, or 2 percent per year. Assuming a flat term structure in both U.S. and Australian dollars, the U.S. dollar interest rate that corresponds to the 6.68 percent Australian dollar swap mid-rate in the swap pricing schedule is $i^{\$} = (1+i^{A\$})/(F_1^{A\$/\$}/S_0^{A\$/\$}) - 1 = (1.0668)/(1.02) - 1 = 0.04588235$, or about 4.59 percent per year.

**The Swap Bank Receives the Fixed Rate** Writes software for the artificial intelligence industry. AI has \$50 million of 5-year debt at a 1-year Eurodollar floating rate of LIBOR + 98.6301 bps (MMY). AI wants to exchange its floating rate U.S. dollar debt for fixed rate Australian dollar debt to fund its operations in Australia. Citigroup agrees to pay AI a floating rate U.S. dollar payment in exchange for a fixed rate Australian dollar payment. At the current spot rate of $S_0^{A\$/\$} = A\$1.25/\$$, the \$50 million principal is equal in value to A\$62.5 million.

Based on the swap pricing schedule in Figure 7.2, AI would pay Citigroup fixed rate A$ interest payments at a rate of 6.73 percent in BEY on the notional principal. Citigroup pays the floating LIBOR Eurodollar rate to AI. AI's original cost of floating rate U.S. debt was 98.6301 bps over the LIBOR Eurodollar rate. Citigroup only pays LIBOR flat, so AI still must pay this spread (or premium) to LIBOR.

The *approximate* cost of this swap to AI will be the 98.6301 bp spread over LIBOR plus the 6.73 percent payment to Citigroup, or $(0.00986301 + 0.0673) = 7.716301$ percent of the notional principal. There are two reasons why this is only an approximation. First, the 98.6301 bp spread over LIBOR is a MMY and is not directly comparable to the BEY on the fixed rate side of the swap. Second, the 98.6301 bp spread is in U.S. dollars and will not be equal in present value to a 98.6301 bp spread in Australian dollars if interest rates over various maturities are not equal in the two currencies.

*Spreads on each side of a fully covered swap are equal in present value.*

In practice, swap banks provide "fully covered" quotes in which a bp adjustment is made to both the fixed- and the floating rate side of the swap so that customers can exactly match their cash flow needs. In the example shown in Figure 7.3, AI wants to fully cover its floating rate dollar payments at LIBOR + 98.6301 bps (MMY). In order to prevent arbitrage, swap dealers set the interest payments on the fixed rate side so that they are equal in present value to the interest payments on the floating rate side of the swap, given current spot and forward exchange rates and Eurocurrency interest rates. That is, for the present value of an interest rate spread (or premium) $r^d$ in currency d to equal the present value of an interest rate spread $r^f$ in currency f, given periodic Eurocurrency interest rates $i^d$ and $i^f$, requires

$$\sum_{t=1}^{T} \frac{r^d}{(1+i_t^d)^t} = \sum_{t=1}^{T} \frac{r^f}{(1+i_t^f)^t} \tag{7.2}$$

over the term (T) of the swap. To preserve the equality of Equation 7.2, the currencies with higher interest rates must have larger spreads.

AI's existing floating rate debt is at the LIBOR Eurodollar rate plus 98.6301 bps (MMY). LIBOR is quoted as a 360-day money market yield, so over 365 days the 98.6301 bps spread pays (98.6301 bps)(365/360) = 100 bps in BEY, which corresponds to an annual interest payment of (0.0100)($50 million) = $500,000 over the LIBOR Eurodollar rate.

In order to fully cover AI's floating rate payment, the swap dealer will ensure that the 100 bp (BEY) spread to the LIBOR dollar rate is equal in present value to the A$ (BEY) spread on the fixed rate side of the swap. Assuming a flat term

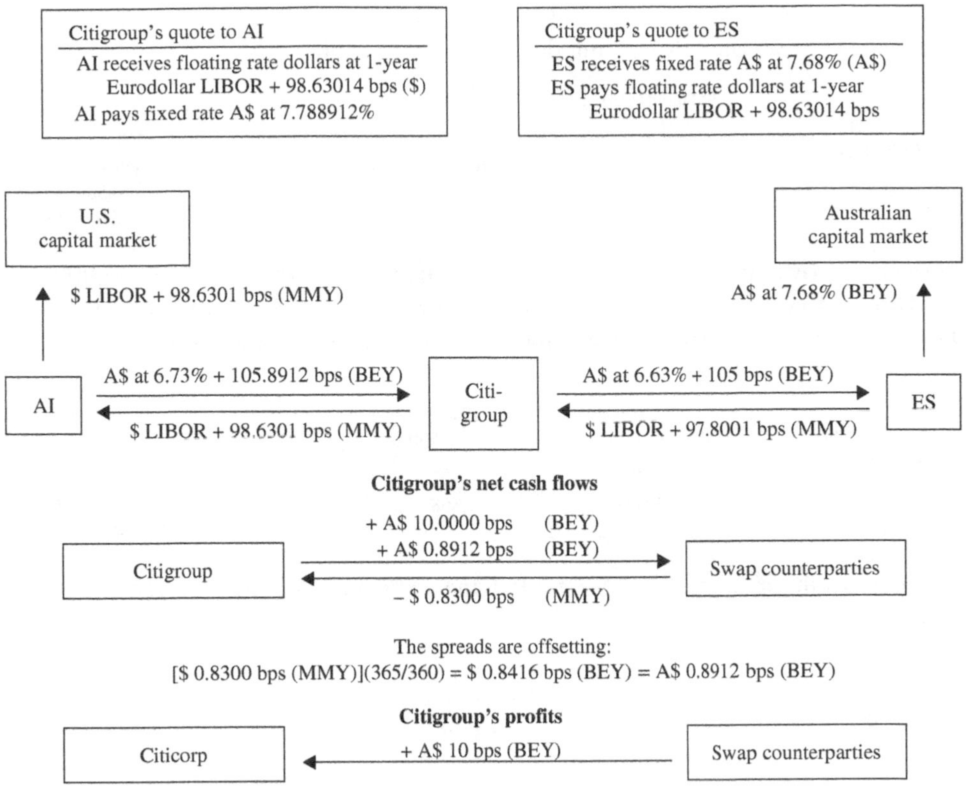


**FIGURE 7.3** A "Fully Covered" Fixed-for-Floating Currency Coupon Swap.

structure in each currency, this requires

$$\sum_{t=1}^{5} \frac{100 \text{ bps}(\$)}{(1.0459)^t} = \sum_{t=1}^{5} \frac{r^{A\$}}{(1.0668)^t}$$

from Equation 7.2. The present value factors for the discount rates are present value interest factors for annuities (PVIFA)(4.588235%, 5 yrs) = 4.3792036 and PVIFA(6.68%, 5 yrs) = 4.1355691, so the spread $r^{A\$}$ is

$$r^{A\$} = [100 \text{ bps}(\$)](4.3792036)/(4.1355691) = 105.8912 \text{ bps}(A\$)$$

in BEY. Multiplied by the A$ notional principal, this results in an A$ payment of (0.01058912)(A$62,500,000) = A$661,820 per year for five years. This must be added to the (0.0673)(A$62,500,000) = A$4,206,250 from the swap pricing schedule, for a total annual payment of (A$4,206,250 + A$661,820) = A$4,868,070. This is an ***all-in cost*** of (A$4,868,070)/(A$62,500,000) = 0.07788912, or about 7.79 percent of the notional principal.[2]

> ***Currencies with high interest rates have large swap spreads.***

In order to see the effect on AI's net position, it's convenient to start with the annual cash flows on AI's existing dollar-denominated debt.

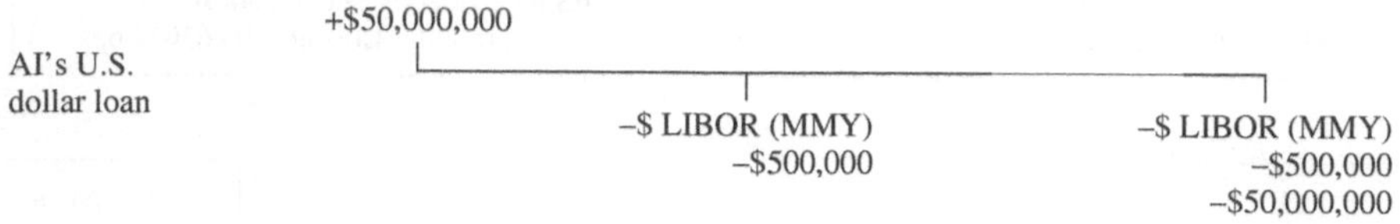


In the fully covered swap, AI receives the LIBOR Eurodollar rate plus \$500,000 and pays an A\$ fixed rate interest payment of A\$4,868,070 to the swap bank each year. The cash flows of the swap are as follows, assuming an exchange of principals:

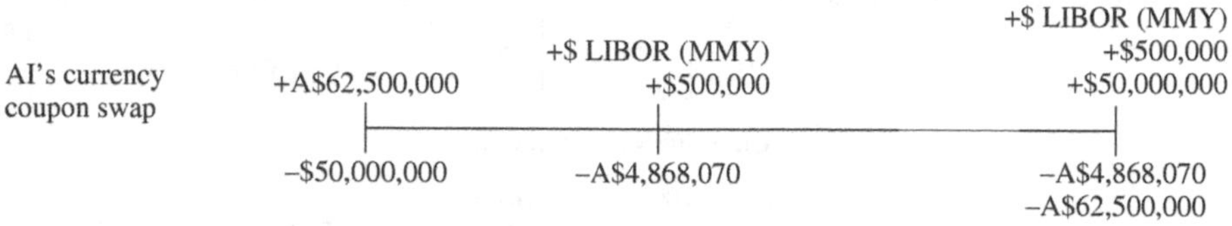


The net result of combining the underlying exposure with the currency coupon swap is

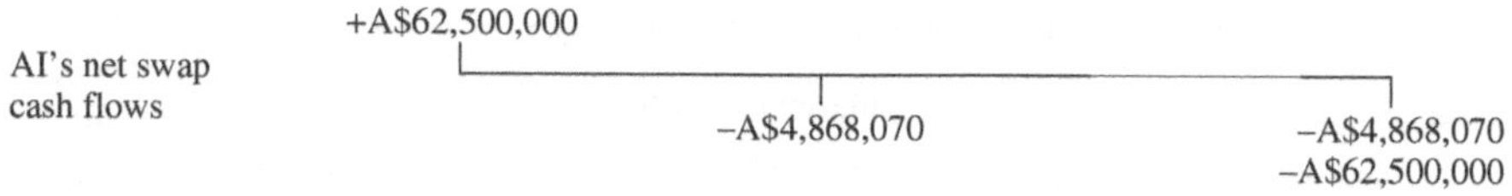


The swap transaction effectively cancels the floating rate U.S. dollar interest payments and leaves an all-in cost in fixed rate Australian dollars of 7.79 percent (BEY) based on the notional principal.

**The Swap Bank Pays the Fixed Rate** ES, a software developer based in Australia, has A\$62.5 million of 5-year fixed rate debt with a 7.68 percent BEY. ES wants floating rate dollar debt to fund its U.S. operations. Citigroup agrees to pay ES's fixed rate A\$ debt in exchange for floating rate U.S. dollar payments. The A\$62.5 million notional principal is worth \$50 million at the $S^{A\$/\$} = A\$1.25/\$$ spot rate. ES pays (0.0768)(A\$62,500,000) = A\$4,800,000 in annual interest on its A\$ debt. This is 105 bps (in BEY) more than the 6.63 percent Australian dollar bid rate in the swap pricing schedule.

In order to fully cover ES's fixed rate A\$ interest payments, the swap bank will solve Equation 7.2 for the corresponding U.S. dollar spread over LIBOR.

$$\sum_{t=1}^{5} \frac{r^{\$}}{(1.0459)^t} = \sum_{t=1}^{5} \frac{105 \text{ bps(A\$)}}{(1.0668)^t}$$

Solving for the U.S. dollar spread using the 5-year present value annuity factors yields a BEY of

$$r^{\$} = [105 \text{ bps(A\$)}](4.1355691)/(4.3792036) = 99.1584 \text{ bps(\$)}$$

## APPLICATION Finding the All-In Cost of a Currency Coupon Swap

### Floating rate to fixed rate

Follow this recipe to go from a floating rate in currency d to a fixed rate in currency f.

1. If necessary, convert the spread over the floating rate domestic currency interest rate index (e.g., LIBOR) from a 360-day MMY into a 365-day spread $r^d$ in BEY according to

$$\text{MMY} = \text{BEY}\ (360/365)$$
$$\text{or, equivalently, BEY} = \text{MMY}(365/360) \tag{7.1}$$

2. Find the spread $r^f$ (BEY) over the fixed rate foreign currency contract that has the same present value as the floating rate domestic currency spread $r^d$ (BEY) according to

$$\sum_{t=1}^{T} \frac{r^d}{(1+i_t^d)^t} = \sum_{t=1}^{T} \frac{r^f}{(1+i_t^f)^t} \tag{7.2}$$

for Eurocurrency interest rates $i_t^d$ and $i_t^f$ over the term of the swap. As a rule, the percentage spread in Equation 7.2 is larger in the currency with the higher interest rates.

If the two yield curves are flat, then the present value summations can be replaced by the corresponding PVIFA($i^d$, T) and PVIFA($i^f$, T), such that

$$(r^d)\text{PVIFA}(i^d, T) = (r^f)\text{PVIFA}(i^f, T) \tag{7.3}$$

3. Add the spread from step 2 to the swap ask rate to calculate the fixed rate payment in currency f.

### Fixed rate to floating rate

Reverse these steps to go from a fixed rate in one currency to a floating rate in another currency.

1. Calculate the fixed rate spread to the swap bid rate from step 3.
2. Find the equivalent spread in the other currency as in step 2.
3. Convert to a MMY (if necessary) as in step 1.

The all-in cost is the variable rate base (e.g., LIBOR) plus this spread.

This is an annual interest payment of (0.0097801)($50,000,000) = $495,792, or a dollar spread of (99.1584 bps)(360/365) = 97.8001 bps in MMY. The all-in cost of ES's floating rate dollar financing is thus LIBOR + 97.8001 bps (MMY).

ES's underlying exposure in annual Australian dollar cash flows is

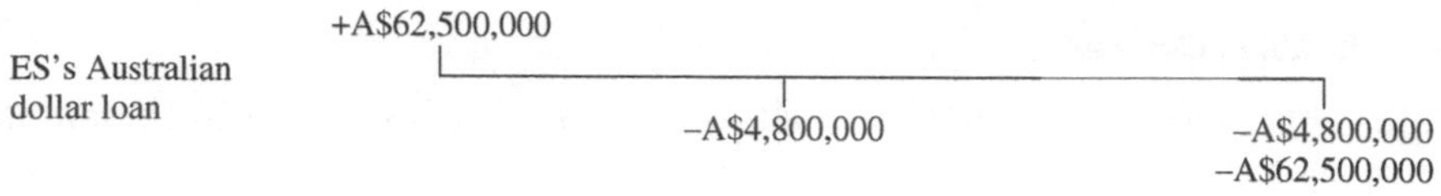


The cash flows attached to ES's currency coupon swap are

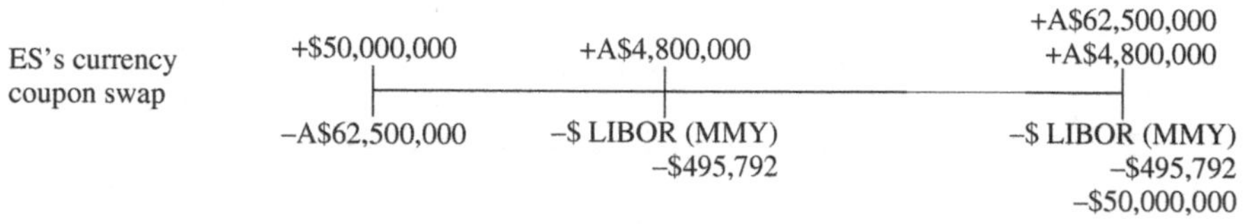


This leaves net cash flows to ES of

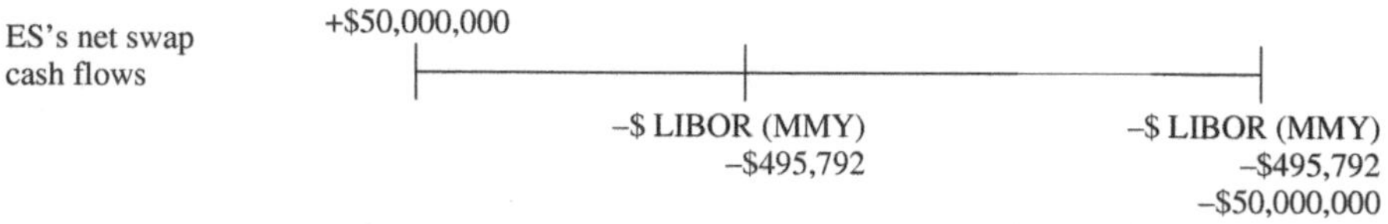


The all-in cost of ES's floating rate debt is the LIBOR Eurodollar rate plus the bp spread of ($495,792)/($50,000,000) = 0.00991584, or about 99.16 bps in BEY. Stated as a MMY, ES's cost of U.S. dollar debt is LIBOR plus 97.8001 bp.

**The Swap Bank's Gains** From Citigroup's perspective, the two swaps with AI and ES offset each other and leave a 10 bp spread, just as in the swap pricing schedule. On the floating rate side, Citigroup pays 98.6301 bps (MMY) to AI and receives 97.8001 bps (MMY) from ES for a net dollar payment of (98.6301 bps – 97.8001 bps) = 0.8300 bps (MMY). This is equivalent to (0.8300 bps)(365/360) = 0.8416 bps (BEY) in U.S. dollar BEY. The corresponding A$ BEY is the solution to

$$\sum_{t=1}^{5} \frac{0.8416 \text{ bps}(\$)}{(1.0459)^t} = \sum_{t=1}^{5} \frac{r^{A\$}}{(1.0668)^t}$$

Solving for the A$ spread using the 5-year present value annuity factors yields

$$r^{A\$} = [0.8412 \text{ bps}(\$)](4.3792036)/(4.1355691) = 0.8912 \text{ bps}(A\$)$$

This U.S. dollar liability on the floating rate side of the swaps is exactly offset in present value by the Australian dollar surplus of (105.8912 bps – 105 bps) = 0.8912 bps on the fixed rate side of the swaps. The net result is a 10 bp profit.

This can be verified from the swap cash flows (assuming an exchange of principals).

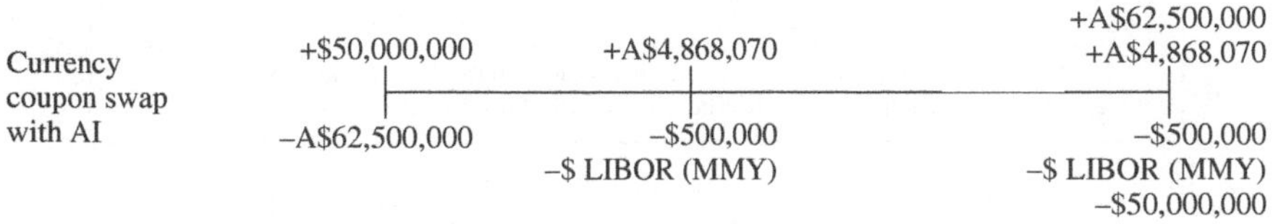


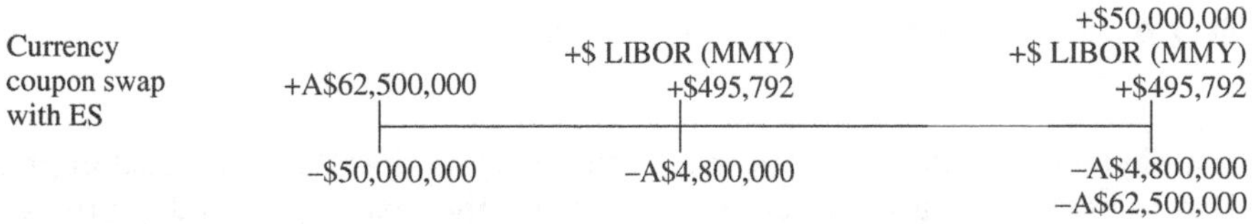


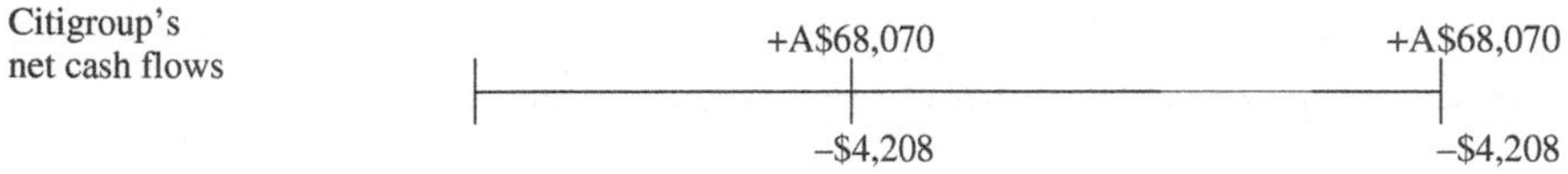


Subtracting the 10 bps spread on the A\$62,500,000 notional principal yields a surplus of (A\$68,070 – A\$62,500) = A\$5,570 on the fixed rate side. As the present value of a 5-year annuity at the 6.68 percent A\$ mid-rate, the A\$ surplus is worth (A\$5,570)(4.1355691) = A\$23,035. On the floating rate U.S. dollar side of the swap, the present value of the \$4,208 shortfall is (\$4,208)(4.3792036) = \$18,428, or $V_0^{A\$} = V_0^{\$} S_0^{A\$/\$}$ = (A\$1.25/\$)(\$18,428) = A\$23,025. The Australian dollar surplus exactly offsets the U.S. dollar shortfall in present value. The net result is a 10 bp spread on the notional principal.

Note that Citigroup does have a small residual exposure to the A\$/\$ exchange rate, which it will combine with other positions in its swap book before it decides whether to hedge its net position.

## 7.4 INTEREST RATE SWAPS

An interest rate swap is a variant of the currency swap in which both sides of the swap are denominated in the same currency.[3] Because the principal amounts are in the same currency, the principal needn't be exchanged and is hence notional. Only the difference check between the interest payments is exchanged when interest payments are due. The notional principal is used only to calculate the interest payments.

The most common interest rate swap is a fixed-for-floating ***coupon swap*** that offsets fixed rate interest payments on a notional principal with floating rate interest payments pegged to a floating interest rate index, such as a 6-month LIBOR Eurocurrency rate. Coupon swaps in major currencies are quoted by commercial and investment banks in maturities of 1 to 20 years. Citigroup might quote the prices in Figure 7.4 on a U.S. dollar coupon swap with a 5-year maturity. As in the currency coupon swap, to satisfy the no-arbitrage condition the swap dealer will set

| Maturity | Bank Pays Fixed Rate | Bank Receives Fixed Rate | Current TN Rate |
|---|---|---|---|
| 5 years | 5 yr TN sa + 33bps | 5 yr TN sa + 60bps | 4.92% |

This schedule assumes nonamortizing debt and semiannual rates (sa). Quotes are against 6-month dollar LIBOR flat. TN = U.S. Treasury note rate.

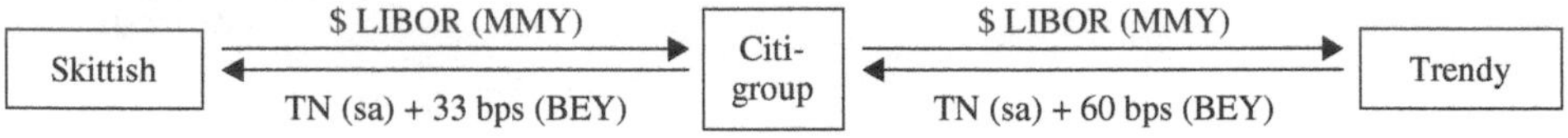


**FIGURE 7.4** A Fixed-for-Floating Coupon Swap ($s).

interest payments on the fixed rate side of the swap so that they are equal in present value to the expected future interest payments on the floating rate side of the swap, given current Eurocurrency interest rates.

*Coupon swaps are fixed-for-floating interest rate swaps.*

Although swap banks are willing to quote fully covered interest rate swaps, it is not a critical selling point for interest rate swaps because all cash flows are in the same currency. Only the difference in interest payments—the difference check—need be exchanged.

## An Example of an Interest Rate Swap

An example illustrates the cash flows and pricing of a coupon swap.

**The Swap Bank Pays the Fixed Rate** Skittish Co. has $50 million of nonamortizing 5-year debt with a BEY of 8 percent compounded semiannually, or semiannual interest payments of (0.08/2)($50,000,000) = $2 million based on the $50,000,000 notional principal.

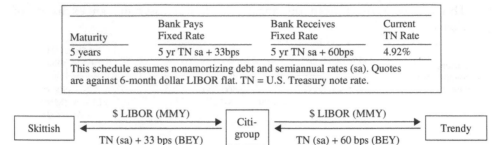

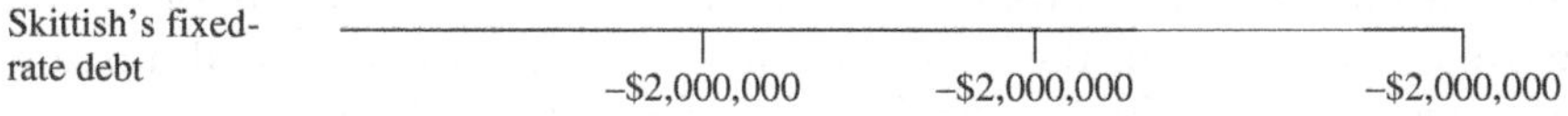


This is 3.08 percent over the current 5-year T-note yield of 4.92 percent. Skittish prefers floating rate debt because its cash flows are sensitive to interest rates.

Skittish agrees to a fixed-for-floating swap with Citigroup. According to the swap pricing schedule in Figure 7.4, Citigroup will pay Skittish a fixed rate 5-year note with semiannual compounding at 33 bps over the 5-year T-note rate. With the T-note at 4.92 percent, this means a BEY of $0.0492 + 0.0033 = 0.0525$, or 5.25 percent with semiannual compounding, for an annualized yield of $[1 + (0.0525/2)]^2 - 1 \approx 0.0532$, or 5.32 percent. Semiannual interest payments are (0.0525/2)($50 million) = $1,312,500. On the other side of the coupon swap,

Skittish pays Citigroup a floating rate 5-year note at LIBOR with semiannual interest payments.

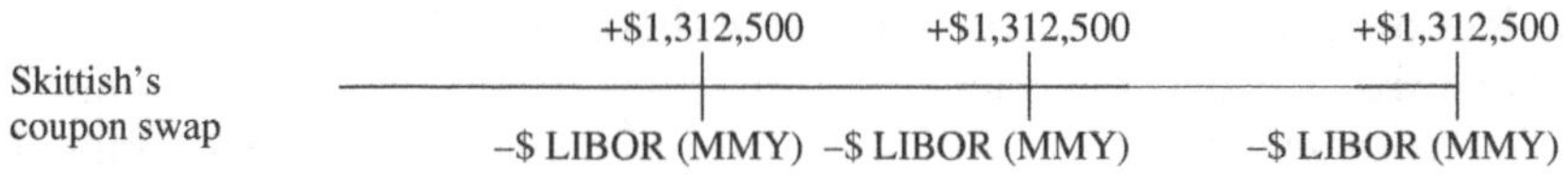


On the original loan, Skittish pays 8 percent fixed. After the swap, Skittish receives 5.25 percent fixed from Citigroup and pays LIBOR floating to Citigroup. The difference between Skittish's 8 percent fixed rate payments and 5.25 percent fixed rate receipts leaves a net cost of 275 bps on the fixed rate side, or a semiannual payment of (0.00275/2)($50 million) = $687,500.

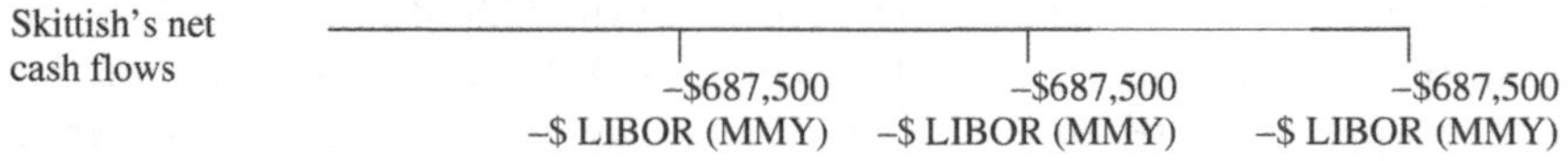


Stating this as a MMY on the notional principal, Skittish's net cost on the fixed rate side is (275 bps)(360/365) $\approx$ 271 bps (MMY) per year with semiannual compounding. Skittish's all-in cost of floating rate funds is then LIBOR + 271 bps per year in semiannually compounded MMY.

**The Swap Bank Receives the Fixed Rate** Trendy Co. has $50 million of 5-year debt with a cost of 6-month LIBOR + 125 bps in MMY. Trendy prefers fixed rate debt, but doesn't want to issue new debt because of the high commission fees that would be charged by its investment banker. Citigroup comes to the rescue with the fixed-for-floating coupon swap in Figure 7.4.

The 125 bps (MMY) spread to LIBOR is equivalent to (125 bps)(365/360) = 126.7361 bps as BEY a with semiannual compounding, or (126.7361 bps)/2 = 63.3681 bps per six months. Trendy also pays a (4.92% + 60 bps) = 5.52 percent fixed rate to Citigroup according to the swap pricing schedule. Trendy's all-in cost of fixed rate funds is then (5.52% + 1.267361%) = 6.787361%, or about 6.79 percent in BEY with semiannual compounding.

## APPLICATION Risk Management at Daimler A.G.

Daimler A.G. is a German holding company with 2010 earnings of €5.4 billion on revenues of €97.8 billion, primarily from vehicle sales in its Daimler and Mercedes lines. The global nature of Daimler's operations exposes the firm to a wide variety of currency, interest rate, and commodity price risks. Here are the notional values of Daimler's hedges of financial price risks at year-end 2010 from its 2010 annual report.

| | Notional value |
|---|---|
| Hedges of currency risks from receivables/liabilities | |
| Forward exchange contracts | €7.2 billion |
| Currency swaps | €9.5 billion |
| Hedges of currency risks from forecasted transactions | |
| Forward exchange contracts and currency options | €24.0 billion |
| Hedges of interest rate risks from receivables/liabilities | |
| Interest rate swaps | €21.3 billion |
| Hedges of commodity price risks from forecasted transactions | |
| Forward commodity contracts | €0.8 billion |

Daimler's biggest currency exposure is to the U.S. dollar, with U.S. sales accounting for 21 percent of 2010 revenues. Sales to China accounted for another 9 percent of revenues. Daimler hedges about 75 percent of its currency exposures with a variety of derivative instruments including currency forwards, options, and swaps. Daimler designates many of its derivative positions as hedges for accounting purposes according to International Financial Reporting Standards (see Chapter 11).

Like many other Multinational Corporations (MNCs), Daimler uses *value-at-risk* to estimate its potential losses from unexpected changes in financial prices. Daimler reported the following value-at-risk estimates at year-end 2010 based on a 99 percent confidence interval and a 5-day horizon.

Estimated loss with a 1 percent probability over a 5-day horizon Value-at-risk

| | Value-at-risk |
|---|---|
| Exchange rate risk | €21 million |
| Interest rate risk | €49 million |
| Commodity price risk | €52 million |

That is, Daimler estimates that at year-end 2010 there was a 1 percent probability of losing more than 21 million over a 5-day period from adverse changes in exchange rates. These exposures are designed to offset Daimler's exposures to the underlying financial price risks, such as dollar-denominated accounts receivables.

*Source:* Daimler A.G., 2010 Annual Report (www.daimler.com).

This all-in cost can be verified with the cash flows of the swap. The 63.3681 bp (BEY) semiannual spread adds interest payments of (0.00633681)($50 million) = $316,840 over LIBOR.

| | | | |
|---|---|---|---|
| Trendy's floating-rate loan | –$ LIBOR (MMY)<br>–$316,840 | –$ LIBOR (MMY)<br>–$316,840 | –$ LIBOR (MMY)<br>–$316,840 |

According to the swap pricing schedule, Citigroup pays Trendy the 6-month LIBOR rate and Trendy pays Citigroup the 5-year T-note rate plus 60 bps for a semiannually compounded BEY of 0.0492 + 0.0060 = 0.0552, or 5.52 percent. The 5.52/2 = 2.76 percent semiannual rate results in semiannual interest payments of (0.0276)($50,000,000) = $1,380,000 from Trendy to Citigroup.

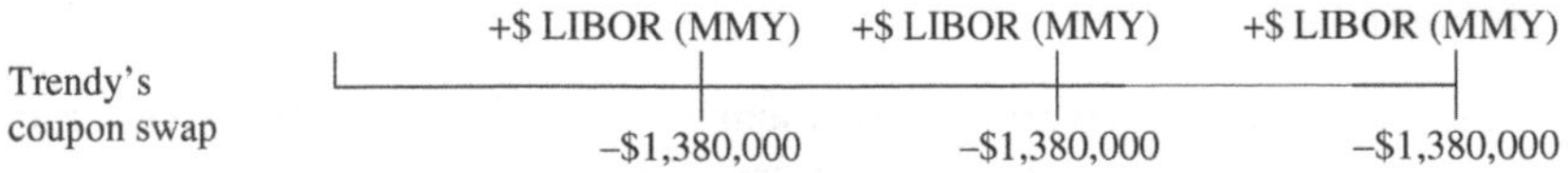


Trendy's net cash flows after the coupon swap are as follows:

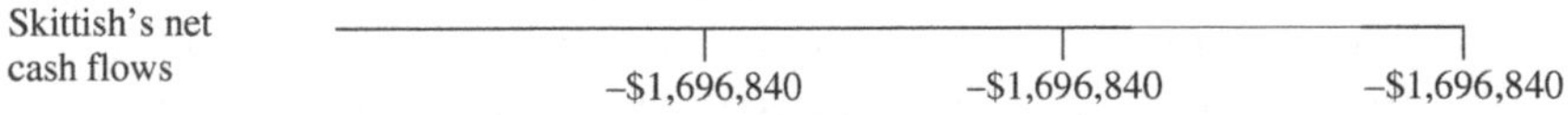


Trendy's all-in cost of fixed rate funds is thus ($1,696,840)/($50,000,000) = 0.03393681, or 3.394 percent per six months, or 6.79 percent in BEY with semiannually compounding. This confirms the interest rate calculation above. The effective annual rate is $(1 + (0.06787361/2))^2 - 1 = 0.06902532$, or about 6.9 percent per year.

**The Swap Bank's Gains** From Citigroup's perspective, the interest rate swap with Trendy offsets the interest rate swap with Skittish. On the fixed rate side, Citigroup receives 60 bps while paying only 33 bps over the Treasury note rate, for a spread of 27 bps. Citigroup earns $135,000 = ($50 million)(60bps–33bps) per year in semiannually compounded BEY on the notional principal of $50 million. Because each of the fixed rate contracts pays semiannual interest payments over five years, Citigroup is fully hedged on the fixed rate side. The floating rate side of each swap is against 6-month LIBOR flat, so Citigroup also is hedged on the floating rate side.

### Combinations of Currency and Interest Rate Swaps

Interest rate and currency swaps can be combined to form new financial products. For example, a currency coupon swap in which the domestic rate is fixed and the foreign rate is floating can be combined with an interest rate swap in the foreign currency to create a *fixed-for-fixed currency swap*. If the fixed rate side of a currency coupon swap is combined with the fixed rate side of a fixed-for-floating interest rate swap in the domestic currency, the result is a *floating-for-floating currency swap*. Floating-for-floating swaps that pair two different interest rate indexes in the same currency, such as 6-month Eurodollar rates with the U.S. 30-day T-bill rate, are called *basis swaps*. Interest rate and currency swaps can be combined in this way to transform the nature of the firm's currency and interest rate exposures quickly, effectively, and at low cost.

## 7.5 OTHER TYPES OF SWAPS

Financial price risk refers to the risk of unexpected change in a financial price, such as a currency value, interest rate, or commodity price. Swaps are traded on each of these financial prices. Swap contracts can be traded, in principle, on any asset or liability. Although there is some standardization of contracts in the most liquid segments of the currency and interest rate swap markets, customized swap contracts are written on a wide variety of other assets and in a wide variety of combinations.

### Credit Derivatives

A ***credit derivative*** is a derivative instrument that synthetically transfers credit risk from one party to another. Credit derivatives allow financial institutions, investment funds, and corporations to manage their credit risks. The most common credit derivative is a ***CDS*** in which a protection buyer pays a protection seller a periodic fee for a specified contract life for assuming the credit exposure of an underlying asset called the reference entity. The protection seller makes no payments unless a specified credit event occurs. If a credit event occurs, then the protection seller pays the protection buyer a payment that is linked to the decline in the market value of the reference entity from the credit event. The reference entity can be almost any asset or index, but is usually a corporate bond. Credit events are defined in the CDS contract and typically include bankruptcy, a material default, or a debt restructuring of the reference entity.[4] In this way CDSs act as a form of insurance against credit risk for the protection buyer.

Another common variation of the credit derivative is a ***total return swap*** in which one party makes payments based upon the total return (interest plus capital gains or losses) of a reference entity and the other party makes (fixed or floating) interest payments that are unrelated to the reference asset, much like in a coupon swap or a currency coupon swap. The difference between a CDS and a total return swap is that the CDS provides protection only against specific credit events, whereas the total return swap protects against all credit events, including changing credit spreads from changes in investor sentiment.

### Equity Swaps

Swap contracts also can be written on asset portfolios. Consider portfolio managers Bull and Bear. Bear has $100 million invested in a portfolio of stocks that is highly correlated with the Standard & Poor (S&P) 500, and wants to get into 10-year T-bonds for one year. Bull has a $100 million portfolio of 10-year T-bonds and wishes to obtain an equity exposure for one year. Unfortunately for Bull and Bear, it is expensive to sell an entire portfolio and then reinvest the proceeds in a new asset class.

In this circumstance, opposites attract. Bull and Bear could form a ***debt-for-equity swap*** in which Bear pays Bull the S&P 500 return on a $100 million notional principal and Bull pays Bear the returns from his $100 million portfolio of 10-year T-bonds. This swap could be engineered with a 1-year term. With a single swap transaction, Bull and Bear can replicate the payoffs of their desired positions and avoid the transaction costs of buying and selling individual assets. Bankers Trust introduced this type of debt-for-equity swap in 1989.[5]

A number of combinations and variations of this debt-for-equity swap are possible. A plain vanilla fixed-for-S&P 500 equity swap could be combined with a fixed-for-floating interest rate swap to create a floating-for-S&P 500 swap. The T-bond position could be swapped against the Nikkei 225 on the Japanese market rather than the S&P 500. An S&P 500 position could be swapped for another equity portfolio, such as the Nikkei 225 or a small-capitalization index on the U.S. market. These swaps allow large investors such as mutual funds and pension funds the luxury of changing their asset allocation decisions without suffering the transaction costs of buying and selling individual assets.

### Commodity Swaps

Just as swaps are traded on currencies and interest rates, ***commodity swaps*** are traded against a variety of commodities, including oil, gold, and pork bellies. The first commodity swap was a fixed-for-floating oil price swap engineered by Chase Manhattan Bank in 1986.

Commodity swaps can be based either on two different commodities or on the same commodity. Indeed, the currency swap can be thought of as a subset of the commodity swap in which the commodities underlying each contract are currencies. When the commodities are the same, commodity swaps typically take the form of a fixed-for-floating swap in which one party makes periodic payments at a fixed per-unit price for a given quantity of some commodity, while the other party makes periodic payments at a floating rate pegged to the spot commodity price. In this case, the principal is notional and is not exchanged. Commodity swaps across two different commodities can be structured as fixed-for-fixed, fixed-for-floating, or floating-for-floating swaps. In this case, the commodities could be exchanged but the difference in spot prices usually is settled in cash. This minimizes the transaction costs associated with the swap.

### Swaptions

One last note deserves mention. Swaps sometimes have an option giving one side or the other the option to enter into or modify a swap. These options-on-swaps are called ***swaptions.*** The fixed rate side of a swaption usually has the option and the floating rate side the obligation because the floating rate side (e.g., LIBOR) adjusts to changing market conditions and has less need for an option. The most common forms of swaptions include ***mirror-image swaptions*** (the fixed rate receiver has the option to cancel), ***right-to-terminate swaptions*** (the fixed rate payer has the option to cancel), and ***extendible swaptions*** (the fixed rate side has the option to extend the contract life). The option component of each of these swaps is like an option on the underlying fixed rate bond and is priced accordingly.

## 7.6 HEDGING THE SWAP BANK'S EXPOSURE TO FINANCIAL PRICE RISK

Swap pricing schedules are updated regularly to reflect changes in market pricing and to correct imbalances in the bank's swap portfolio, or ***swap book.*** Swap banks hedge their net swap positions in their swap books either internally within the bank or externally in the spot, forward, futures, options, swaps, or Eurocurrency markets. Once the swap bank finds an offsetting position, as Citigroup was able to do in the currency and interest rate swap examples, it can offset its positions on the two sides of the swap. The swap bank is then hedged against the financial price risk underlying the swap.

Mismatches in the bank's swap book can arise across a number of dimensions including in commodities or currencies, maturities, and money market instruments. For example, if the bank is paying funds on swaps pegged to 6-month LIBOR and receiving funds on swaps pegged to 1-month T-bills, the swap bank has a maturity mismatch as well as basis risk between LIBOR and T-bill rates. Swap banks also face credit and counterparty risks, some of which can be managed with credit derivatives (e.g., CDSs or total return swaps). By continually monitoring and then rebalancing the swap bank's net position at all forward dates, management can ensure that the bank is not caught by surprise by large changes in financial prices.

## 7.7 SUMMARY

Swaps provide corporations with flexibility in their financing choices by allowing corporations to transform the nature of their obligations at very low cost and without having to repurchase and then reissue those obligations. They also allow the corporation to separate the form of debt offered to the market from the form of debt preferred by the corporation and ultimately paid to the market.

> *Swaps provide financial flexibility.*

Currency swaps are patterned after parallel loan agreements in which two firms borrow in their home markets and then loan the funds to each other's foreign subsidiaries. Parallel loans allow parent firms with foreign subsidiaries to indirectly obtain foreign currency debt financing for their foreign subsidiaries at low-cost foreign rates despite facing higher borrowing costs in foreign markets.

Parallel loans had three drawbacks: (1) It was difficult to settle disputes, (2) parallel loans were capitalized, inflating debt-to-equity ratios, and (3) there were high search costs in finding matching firms. Packaging the parallel loans into a single currency swap contract remedied these problems.

Currency swaps are subject to default risk because they are in essence a bundle of forward contracts of different maturities. Although the consequences of default are greater than in a comparable futures contract, they are less than for a straight debt instrument because if one side defaults the other side is released from its obligations as well. The exchange of (possibly notional) principals further reduces the counterparties' exposures to credit risk.

## KEY TERMS

*all-in cost*
*bond equivalent yield (BEY)*
*commodity swap*
*coupon swap*
*currency coupon swap*
*currency swap*
*day count*
*debt-for-equity swap*

*difference check*
*financial engineering*
*financial price risk*
*interest rate swap*
*money market yield (MMY)*
*notional principal*
*swap book*
*swap contract*
*swap pricing schedule*
*swaption*

## CONCEPTUAL QUESTIONS

7.1 How are swaps related to forward contracts?

7.2 What is a currency coupon swap?

7.3 What is a fully covered currency coupon swap?

7.4 What is a coupon swap?

7.5 What is the difference between a BEY and a MMY?

## PROBLEMS

7.1 Little Prince Co. (LP) has $100 million of 2-year fixed rate debt with a BEY of 8.25 percent compounded semiannually. LP would prefer to have floating rate debt. The market is asking LIBOR + 100 bps. How could an investment banker help LP achieve its objective with a swap?

7.2 A swap bank quotes the following pricing schedule for Polish zloty coupon swaps.

Coupon Swap Pricing Schedule (Polish zloty)

| Maturity | Bank Pays Fixed Rate | Bank Receives Fixed Rate | Current TN Rate |
|---|---|---|---|
| 4 years | 4 yr TN sa + 24bps | 4 yr TN sa + 78bps | 7.98% |

This schedule assumes nonamortizing debt and semiannual rates (sa).
Quotes are against 6-month LIBOR Polish zloty flat.
TN = Polish Treasury note rate.

a. Ford Motor Company has 4-year floating rate zloty debt at 6-month LIBOR plus 45 bps. Ford wants to swap into fixed rate zloty debt. Describe Ford's floating-for-fixed zloty coupon swap.
b. Polish Motors (PM) has 4-year fixed rate zloty debt at 9.83 percent (BEY). PM wants to swap into floating rate zlotys. Describe PM's fixed-for-floating zloty coupon swap.
c. What does the swap bank gain from these transactions?

7.3 Consider the following swap pricing schedule for currency coupon swaps of yen and pounds:

| Currency Coupon Swap Pricing Schedule (¥/£) | Maturity | Midrate (in £) |
|---|---|---|
| | 3 years | 4.12% sa |

Deduct 5 bps if the bank is paying a fixed rate. Add 5 bps if the bank is receiving a fixed rate.
All quotes are against 6-month LIBOR yen flat.

The spot rate is ¥240.00/£. Yield curves are flat and the pound is selling at a 6-month forward discount of 58 bps. Bonds in Japan and the United Kingdom are quoted as a BEY.

a. What is the yen interest rate that corresponds to the 3-year pound swap mid-rate? Note that interest rates are compounded semiannually.
b. Japan, Inc. (JI) has ¥2.4 billion of 3-year yen debt at a floating rate of 6-month (¥) LIBOR + 105 bps (MMY), or 52.5 bps each six months. JI wants to swap this into fixed rate pound debt to fund its U.K. operations using a fully covered currency coupon swap. What is the all-in cost of JI's yen-for-pound currency coupon swap?
c. British Dog (BD) has 3-year fixed rate pound debt at 7.45 percent (BEY). BD wants floating rate yen debt to fund its expansion into Japan. What is the all-in cost of BD's fully covered yen-for-pound swap?
d. What does the swap bank gain from these transactions?

7.4 As VP Finance (Europe) at GE Capital, you manage GE's European exposures to currency risk. GE's light bulb plant in Poland generates Polish zloty (Z) after-tax operating cash inflows of Z10 million per year. Your treasury management team decides to hedge one-half of the expected future cash flow from operations (i.e., 5 million zlotys per year) for each of the next five years. Goldman Sachs quotes the following pricing schedule for currency coupon swaps of zlotys and dollars.

| Currency Coupon Swap Pricing Schedule (£/$) | Maturity | Midrate (in £) |
|---|---|---|
| | 5 years | 7.90% sa |

Deduct 20 bps if the bank is paying a fixed rate. Add 20 bps if the bank is receiving a fixed rate.
All quotes are against 1-year LIBOR Eurodollar flat.

The spot rate of exchange is Z2.80/$. The dollar and zloty yield curves are flat, with the dollar selling at a forward premium of 3.8 percent per year. Assume bonds in Poland are quoted as a 365-day bond equivalent yield with annual compounding.

To assist in your calculations, here are present value factors for 5-year annuities at various interest rates. (Note: You won't need all of these present value factors. Only use what you need.)

$$\text{PVIFA}(5\text{–years at } 8.100000\%) = 3.98220886$$

$$\text{PVIFA}(5\text{–years at } 7.900000\%) = 4.00325549$$

$$\text{PVIFA}(5\text{-years at } 7.700000\%) = 4.02448018$$

$$\text{PVIFA}(5\text{-years at } 3.949904\%) = 4.45809446$$

a. GE has 5-year floating rate dollar debt at a rate of 1-year LIBOR + 32 bps. Describe a fully covered dollar-for-zloty swap using the quotes in the swap pricing schedule. Calculate the all-in cost of GE's floating rate zloty financing.
b. Solidarity Partners (SP) has Z19,811,044 of 5-year zloty debt at 10.24 percent compounded annually. SP wants floating rate dollar debt—with interest payments reset annually—to fund its U.S. operations. Calculate the all-in cost of SP's fully covered zloty-for-dollar swap.
c. What does the swap bank gain from these transactions?

**Advanced**

7.5 Consider Problem 7.3.

a. Verify JI's all-in cost by identifying the incremental cash flows of JI's fully covered swap and then calculating the internal rate of return on these cash flows.
b. Verify BD's all-in cost by identifying the incremental cash flows of BD's fully covered swap and then calculating the internal rate of return on these cash flows.

7.6 Consider Problem 7.4.

a. Verify GE's all-in cost by identifying the incremental cash flows of GE's fully covered swap and then calculating the internal rate of return on these cash flows.
b. Verify SP's all-in cost by identifying the incremental cash flows of SP's fully covered swap and then calculating the internal rate of return on these cash flows.

## SUGGESTED READINGS

### Currency and interest rate swaps are discussed in

Robert H. Litzenberger, "Swaps: Plain and Fanciful," *Journal of Finance* 47 (July 1992), pp. 831–850.

Bernadette A. Minton, "An Empirical Examination of Basic Valuation Models for Plain Vanilla U.S. Interest Rate Swaps," *Journal of Financial Economics* 44 (May 1997), 251–277.

### Counterparty risks and credit default swaps are discussed in

Robert A. Jarrow and Fan Yu, "Counterparty Risk and the Pricing of Defaultable Securities," *Journal of Finance* 55 (October 2001), 1765–1799.

Philippe Jorion and Gaiyan Zhang, "Good and Bad Credit Contagion: Evidence from Credit Default Swaps," *Journal of Financial Economics* 84 (June 2007), 860–883.

PART

# Three

# Managing the Risks of Multinational Operations

*The blunders are all there on the board, waiting to be made.*

—Tartakover

CHAPTER 8

# Multinational Treasury Management

*When I look back on all these worries I remember the story of the old man who said on his deathbed that he had had a lot of trouble in his life, most of which never happened.*

—Winston Churchill

As a corporation grows beyond its domestic market and becomes multinational in scope, it must develop a financial system capable of managing the international transactions and currency risk exposures of its operating units and of the corporation as a whole. The treasury of the multinational corporation (MNC) fulfills this role, serving as a *corporate bank* that manages cash flows within the corporation and between the corporation and its external partners.

The modern treasury performs several functions pertinent to its international operations.

- Determine the MNC's overall financial goals and strategies
- Manage domestic and international trade
- Finance domestic and international trade
- Consolidate and manage the financial flows of the firm
- Identify, measure, and manage the firm's exposures to currency risks

Treasury management has both an internal and an external dimension. Internally, treasury must set policies and establish procedures for how the operating divisions of the firm are to interact with one another. Externally, treasury must coordinate the firm's interaction with its customers, suppliers, investors, and host governments.

This chapter covers the multinational dimensions of the first four functions of the modern corporate treasury. The last function—currency risk management—warrants a more detailed coverage over the next three chapters.

## 8.1 DETERMINING FINANCIAL GOALS AND STRATEGIES

The highly competitive global marketplace demands that MNC create and continually reassess their strategic business plan and financial strategy.

## The Multinational Corporation's Strategic Business Plan

The process of creating and implementing a strategic business plan includes the following four steps:

1. Identify the firm's core competencies and potential growth opportunities
2. Evaluate the business environment within which the firm operates
3. Formulate a strategic plan for turning the firm's core competencies into sustainable competitive advantages
4. Develop robust processes for implementing the strategic business plan

The strategic plan should incorporate all of the corporation's existing businesses, as well as plan for potential new lines of business. It should promote the refinement of existing core competencies and the development of new ones. It should be flexible enough to adapt to the exigencies of the global marketplace. Finally, the plan should be continuously updated and revised so that it is a dynamic, living guide rather than a static anchor for the firm.[1]

## Financial Strategy as a Complement to the Business Plan

Financial strategy should not stand as an island apart from other operations. Instead, financial strategy should complement the overall strategic business plan. A properly conceived financial plan integrates and promotes the core operations of the firm and furthers the goals and objectives of its individual business units. The financial plan should be formulated at the highest levels of management and faithfully implemented on an ongoing basis to meet the firm's changing needs.

*Financial strategy should complement the business plan.*

The way that the firm deals with its risk exposures is a key element of financial policy. Failure to set risk management guidelines and monitor risk management activities can expose the firm to financial loss or even ruin. For example, management must decide whether currency exposures will be managed, how actively they will be managed, and the extent to which the firm is willing to take speculative positions in the pursuit of its business and financial objectives. Failure to take action in hedging currency risk is a de facto decision to take a speculative position in foreign exchange. Yet the firm may choose to go well beyond a passive posture in the management of its exposures to currency risk.

Some hedge funds and investment banks include currency speculation among their core competencies. For manufacturing and service firms, treasury is better used as a complement to other business activities. Speculative profits from the treasury's financial market operations are more often due to chance than to any enduring expertise in anticipating market movements. Even more important, other business units are unlikely to operate at peak effectiveness if speculative activity in the treasury is distracting top management from operating the firm's core businesses. A financial strategy of taking speculative positions that are independent of the firm's operating cash flows is, in the long run, likely to destroy rather than enhance shareholder wealth.

This is not to say that the treasury should avoid speculative positions. Treasury may choose to leave an exposure unhedged if it believes that a forward price will not yield as much value as the future spot price. But choosing to leave an operating cash flow unhedged is vastly different from taking outright speculative positions for speculation's sake. Consciously deciding to leave a forward position unhedged is also a far cry from ignoring currency risks entirely. In any case, treasury's activity should complement and not compete with the firm's other business operations.

## 8.2 MANAGING THE CORPORATION'S INTERNATIONAL TRADE

International trade can be riskier than domestic trade because of the greater geographic and cultural distances between buyers and sellers. Exporters must take extra precautions to ensure payment from faraway customers. Importers must protect themselves against late shipments, or delivery of goods or services of inferior quality. When disputes arise, claimants often must pursue their grievances through foreign legal systems and on the home turf of their trading partners. This section describes how the MNC can manage the costs and risks of cross-border trade and protect itself against trade and legal disputes.

> ***Cross-border trade must overcome divergence in legal systems.***

### The Legal Environment

A major barrier to international trade is that each nation has jurisdiction over business transactions within its national borders and imposes its own laws on these transactions. Disagreements between international trade partners are difficult to settle because the legal issues span two or more legal jurisdictions. Moreover, there is no single doctrine that defines international commercial law. It is not surprising that cross-border shipments are more difficult to execute than domestic shipments.

Most of the nations in continental Europe and South America use a *civil law* system in which laws are codified as a set of rules. The United Kingdom and most of its former colonies use a *common law* system that relies heavily on the decisions of judges in previous court cases. Civil and common law systems are offshoots of ancient Roman law, differing in their emphasis on legal rules or specific case examples. Most Muslim nations follow a form of *Sharia law* based on the Quran and other holy scriptures that combines elements of civil law and common law. China is evolving from a state-based communist/socialist system into its own version of a market-based capitalist system that has recognized private property rights since 2007. International trade is handicapped by this wide divergence in national legal systems.

A majority of international trade is conducted under the terms of the United Nations Convention on Contracts for the International Sale of Goods (CISG). The CISG was created in 1980 by the United Nations Commission on International Trade Law (www.uncitral.org) to harmonize and codify the legal rules for international sales and shipments. Seventy-six countries accounting for more than 90 percent of world trade had ratified the treaty by 2011.

## Managing the Costs and Risks of International Shipping

Cross-border shipments conform to Murphy's Law: "If something can go wrong, it will." For this reason, it is advisable to clearly specify the terms of trade in writing, including who is responsible for insurance coverage, who bears the risk of loss during shipping, who pays for transportation and loading/unloading of the goods, and who is responsible for export/import clearance. For this reason, cross-border shipments are accompanied by a bewildering array of documents.

> *If something can go wrong, it will.*

- Invoice—describes the merchandise and specifies delivery and payment terms
- Packing list—an itemization of the contents of a shipment
- Certificate of origin—a document certifying the country of origin, required by some nations
- Export license—permissions required by some governments before goods can be exported
- Inspection certificate—a third-party certification that goods meet certain specifications
- Insurance certificate—proof of insurance against loss or damage
- Bill of lading—a document issued by a carrier to a shipper acknowledging receipt of goods
- Dock receipt—indicates goods have been delivered to a dock for transportation by a carrier
- Warehouse receipt—indicates the goods have been delivered from a carrier to a warehouse

For small shipments, international package delivery services such as *Federal Express* and *United Parcel Service* dominate the market with safe, timely, and convenient shipments. For large shipments, ***freight forwarders*** coordinate the transfer of goods and the logistics of trade. These agents select the best mode of transportation and arrange for a particular carrier to handle the shipment of goods. Many commercial banks maintain their own in-house freight forwarder to facilitate communication among importers, exporters, banks, insurers, and carriers.

## Managing the Costs and Risks of International Payments

The biggest risks faced by an exporter are that the buyer will default on payment, attempt to renegotiate the terms of trade, pay too little, or pay too late. Exporters must have assurance they will receive timely payment for the goods that they deliver. There are four common ways that exporters can arrange for payment.

- Cash in advance
- Letter of credit (L/C)
- Draft (either a sight draft or a time draft)
- Open account

| | Time of payment | Goods available to buyer | Risk to the exporter | Risk to the importer |
|---|---|---|---|---|
| **Cash in advance** | Before shipment | After payment | None, unless legal action is taken by the buyer for delivery of inferior goods or services | Seller still must ship the goods |
| **Sight draft** | When buyer presents the draft | Immediately | Buyer might not pay when presented with documents; goods must then be returned to seller or sold under duress | Seller still must ship the goods; can take time to arrange |
| **Time draft** | On maturity of the draft | Before payment | Relies on buyer to pay the draft; otherwise, same as sight draft | Same as above |
| **L/C** | Once shipped | After payment | Low risk if seller meets terms of an issued or confirmed L/C | Same as above |
| **Open account** | After shipment | Immediately | Buyer might not pay as agreed | None |

**FIGURE 8.1** Methods of Payment in International Trade.

Which terms are adopted in a particular circumstance depends on industry conventions, the bargaining positions of the buyer and the seller, and the probability and consequences of default. These payment methods differ in the protection and convenience provided to the buyer and seller, as shown in Figures 8.1 and 8.2.

**Open Account** Most domestic sales are made on ***open account***. Under this arrangement, a seller delivers goods to the buyer and then bills the buyer for the goods under payment terms such as "net 30" (payment is due in 30 days) or "1/10, net 60" (1 percent discount if paid in 10 days; otherwise the net amount is due in 60 days). An open account is most convenient for the buyer.

> ***Most domestic trade is on open account.***

Although sales on open account might attract business, they are otherwise an unattractive payment mechanism for exporters. First, an open account provides no financing for the exporter as manufacturing expenses must be paid before the product is sold to its customer. Second, the buyer may default on payment. An open account is appropriate only when the buyer and seller have established a long-term relationship and the buyer's credit record is good.

| Seller's Perspective | Payment Mechanism | Buyer's Perspective |
|---|---|---|
| Highest risk trade terms | Open account | Most advantageous trade terms |
| ⇑ | Draft (sight or time draft) or L/C | ⇓ |
| Lowest risk trade terms | Cash in advance | Least advantageous trade terms |

**FIGURE 8.2** The Risks of International Payment Methods.

**Draft** Commercial banks are in the business of assuming credit and collection risks. Commercial banks are also in the business of facilitating trade, including international trade. The total costs of international transactions can be reduced by bringing one or more commercial banks into the transaction to assist in financing, shipment, and collections.

The draft is the instrument most frequently used as an international payment mechanism. With this instrument, the seller draws a ***draft*** that instructs the *drawee* (the buyer or its bank) to pay the seller according to the terms of the draft. Drafts are also sometimes called trade bills or bills of exchange. A ***sight draft*** is payable on demand, whereas a ***time draft*** is payable at a specified future time. The drawee is liable to the seller if the drawee accepts the draft by signing it. A time draft that is drawn on and accepted by the buyer is called a ***trade acceptance***. A time draft that is drawn on and accepted by a commercial bank is called a ***banker's acceptance***.

*Most cross-border trade is paid with drafts.*

The draft and the trade documents are then presented to a commercial bank. If the buyer and seller cannot agree on a single bank to serve as intermediary, they each can retain a bank to represent their individual interests. The trade documents giving control over the goods are released to the buyer only when the buyer or its commercial bank pays the draft or accepts the draft for payment.

Bankers' acceptances are useful because they substitute the credit risk of the accepting bank for that of the buyer. An exporter holding a banker's acceptance can sell the acceptance at a discount from face value and turn this receivable into cash. The discount depends on the time value of money and the reputation of the accepting bank. The outstanding balance of bankers' acceptances is several hundred billion dollars and finances a large proportion of international trade.

*A banker's acceptance ensures the seller of payment.*

A banker's acceptance may be sold to a third party only if it is ***negotiable***. To be negotiable, a banker's acceptance must satisfy five criteria: (1) It must be in writing, (2) it must be signed by a representative of the bank, (3) it must contain an unconditional payment guarantee payable upon satisfactory receipt of the trade documents, (4) it must be payable on demand (a sight draft) or at a specified time (a time draft), and (5) it must be payable to either order or bearer.

Figure 8.3 illustrates how trade is accomplished through a banker's acceptance. After negotiating the terms of trade (A), the exporter sends an invoice to the importer (B). The importer writes a time draft drawn on its bank (C). The bank accepts the draft forwards it to the exporter (D). The exporter initiates shipment of the goods (E). Upon receipt of the goods, the warehouse signs the trade documents indicating that the shipment meets the specified terms of trade (F). The trade documents are then sent to the importer's bank by the exporter (G). Upon receipt of the trade

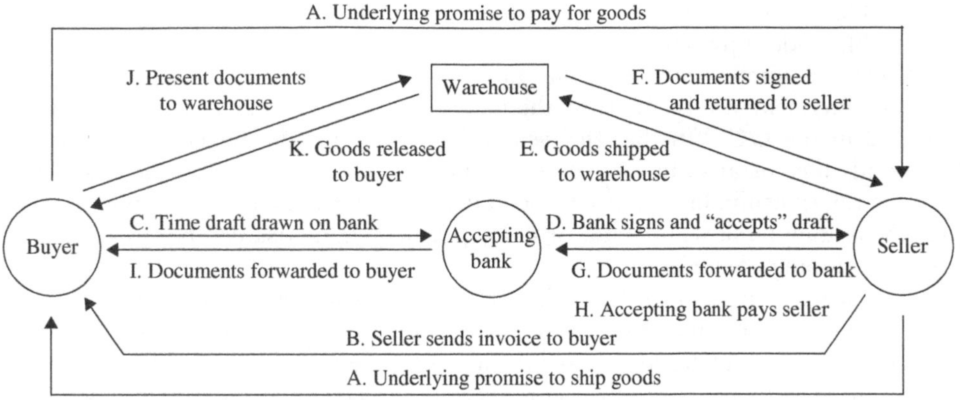


**FIGURE 8.3** Payment through a Banker's Acceptance.

documents, the bank is obligated to honor its promise to pay the exporter at the specified future date (H). The trade documents are forwarded to the importer (I). Finally, the importer presents the trade documents to the warehouse (J) and collects the goods (K). The timing of the payment from the importer to the bank depends on the importer's cash flow needs, its credit standing, and its relationship with the bank. The purpose of this elaborate series of transactions is to ensure that all parties fulfill their responsibilities according to the terms of trade.

**Letter of Credit** The exporter's credit risks can be mitigated by having the importer's bank issue a *L/C* that guarantees payment upon presentation of the trade documents identified in the L/C. A L/C protects the exporter because payment is guaranteed by a bank rather than the importer.

*An L/C ensures the seller of payment.*

The *International Chamber of Commerce* (www.iccwbo.org) describes two legal principles surrounding the international L/C.

- *Independence principle.* The L/C is independent of the sales transaction.
- *Strict compliance principle.* The issuing bank must honor the L/C upon receipt of the documents specified in the L/C.

These principles protect the right of the exporter to receive payment under the terms of the L/C. This substitutes the credit standing of the issuing bank for that of the buyer.[2]

A L/C is *irrevocable* if payment is conditional upon receipt of the trade documents identified in the L/C. The L/C is *revocable* if it stipulates conditions under which the buyer or the issuing bank can declare the L/C invalid. Nearly all L/Cs are irrevocable. In fact, if the L/C says nothing about revocability, it is assumed to be irrevocable under international law.

Under an *unconfirmed L/C*, the buyer instructs its bank to issue a L/C that promises payment will be made by the issuing bank upon receipt of the documents specified in the L/C. Whether the issuing bank requires the buyer to pay for the L/C in advance or at some later date depends on the buyer's creditworthiness and banking relationship. In an unconfirmed L/C, the exporter is still exposed to the risk that the issuing bank will default or delay payment. This risk can be substantial in some developing countries.

One way to mitigate the default risk of the issuing bank is for the L/C to be *confirmed* by an advisory bank selected by the exporter. The advisory bank confirms the terms of trade, required documents, and L/C are in order and that the issuing bank is in good financial health. Upon confirming that this is the case, the advisory bank promises payment to the exporter regardless of whether the issuing bank honors its obligation. The L/C is then called a *confirmed L/C*. Payment terms depend primarily on the default risk of the bank originally issuing the L/C. The sequence of events is similar to payment through a banker's acceptance. In this way, the exporter is assured that payment will be made.

**Cash in Advance** *Cash in advance* requires the buyer to pay for goods prior to shipment. This limits the seller's exposure to credit risk, although the cost of this protection may be a reduced sales price or lower sales. Cash in advance is the least convenient payment method for the buyer, who must trust the seller to deliver the goods in a timely manner and in good condition. Cash in advance is used when the buyer has a poor credit history or where demand far outstrips supply. It is seldom used when the buyer and seller have a long and satisfactory relationship.

## Countertrade

*Countertrade* (also called reciprocal trade) refers to barter-like techniques used to exchange goods or services without the use of cash. Barter is easiest to arrange when the values of the goods being exchanged are the same and the shipments take place at the same time. Well-known examples of countertrade include PepsiCo's exchange of Pepsi syrup for Russian Stolichnaya vodka, and Coca-Cola's exchange of Coke syrup for Russian Lada automobiles.

> *Countertrade is a noncash exchange of goods or services.*

The two most common forms of countertrade are counterpurchases and offsets.

- *Counterpurchase*. A barter arrangement in which one sales contract is conditional upon fulfillment of another ("I'll give you my lunch tomorrow if you give me your desert today.")
- *Offset*. Countertrade required as a condition of trade; common in sales of military aircraft

Companies from developed countries use countertrade to gain footholds in developing markets that lack hard currency reserves. Countries that lack hard currency use countertrade to promote international trade and attract key industries. Countertrade is difficult to negotiate and execute, but sometimes it is the only way for countries without hard currency to pay for manufactured goods or for MNCs to gain access to these markets.

It is difficult to determine the magnitude of countertrade activity because in many countries countertrade is reported as a transformation of assets rather than as business income. Estimates of the importance of countertrade to international commerce vary widely, typically falling in a range from 10 to 40 percent of all cross-border trade. The World Trade Organization (www.wto.org) has estimated that about 15 percent of international trade is conducted on a noncash basis, almost entirely through reciprocal trade companies. Countertrade is best suited to large firms with diversified markets and products and experience in international markets. These companies are better able to assume and manage the costs and risks of countertrade. Numerous clearinghouses specialize in reselling goods obtained through countertrade.[3] Countertrade is likely to continue to be useful to companies operating in countries that lack hard currencies.

## 8.3 FINANCING THE CORPORATION'S INTERNATIONAL TRADE

Money is not free, so someone must finance a sale of goods between the time an order is made and the time the goods are received by the buyer. When a sale is paid for in advance, the buyer is providing financing for the seller. When a sale is made on open account, the seller is providing financing for the buyer. Some international payment methods, such as bankers' acceptances and L/C, allow someone other than the buyer or seller to provide financing for international trade. These financing alternatives are described here and summarized in Figure 8.4.

### The Exporter's Perspective

The corporation's sources and uses of cash can be categorized as follows:

- Sources of cash—a decrease in an asset account or an increase in a liability account
- Uses of cash—an increase in an asset account or a decrease in a liability account

As an exporter manufactures goods, inventories of work-in-process and finished goods increase. An increase in inventory is an increase in an asset account and therefore a use of cash. This investment in inventory is financed by drawing down cash or increasing accounts payable to pay for raw materials. Each of these is a source of cash to the firm. When a sale is booked on open account, the asset is transferred out of inventory (a source of cash) and into accounts receivable (an offsetting use of cash). If sale is made through a trade or banker's acceptance, the acceptance is a negotiable instrument and therefore a marketable security. Whether the sale resides in accounts receivable or in marketable securities, the exporter is now in a position to recoup its investment in inventory and capture a gain on the sale.

| | Exporter's Perspective | Importer's Perspective |
|---|---|---|
| **Cash in advance** | Financing is provided by buyer | Because the transaction is not secured, financing usually must come from some other source |
| **Open account** | Accounts receivable can be sold to a factor or discounted to the bank; long-term receivables can be sold to a forfaiter | Financing is provided by seller |
| **Trade acceptance** | Trade acceptances can be sold at a discount to face value, with or without recourse | In an accepted time draft, the seller extends credit to the buyer |
| **Banker's acceptance** | Bankers' acceptances are negotiable and can be sold at a discount to face value | Buyer's bank charges a fee in the form of a compensating balance, a required line of credit, or an outright fee |
| **L/C** | In the United States, exporters do not borrow against or discount L/Cs; L/Cs can be discounted or used as collateral in some other countries | L/Cs tie up the buyer's borrowing capacity; bank fees for unconfirmed L/Cs range from 0.125% to 0.5% of the face amount; confirmed L/Cs can add another 0.05% to 0.5% |

**FIGURE 8.4** Methods of Payment and the Financing of International Trade.

In the rest of this section, we'll examine how each of the following international payment methods creates a source of financing (i.e., cash) for the firm.

- A decrease in a current asset account
  - Sell short-term accounts receivable at a discount to face value
  - Sell medium-term or long-term accounts receivable at a discount to face value
  - Sell a marketable security (e.g., a trade or banker's acceptance) at a discount
- An increase in a current liability account
  - Borrow against an asset, such as accounts receivable or inventory

Each of these sources of financing has an opportunity cost. As with other financial transactions, the exporter must shop around for the best value. The least cost financing method in any particular circumstance depends on competitive conditions in the exporter's goods and financial markets, and the exporter's borrowing capacity and banking relationships.

### Sell a Current Asset

> *Factoring refers to discounted sale of a receivable.*

Credit risks can be high on export sales, and collections can be costly. For this reason, many exporters are unwilling or unable to support an in-house credit and collections department. One alternative is for the exporter to ***factor*** or sell receivables at a discount to face value to a third party (typically a commercial bank) that is better able to bear the costs and risks of credit assessments and collections.

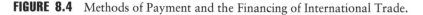

Most factoring is done on a nonrecourse basis, although the factor may insist on recourse when credit risks are high.

Factors can have an advantage over in-house credit departments in bearing international credit and collection risks. Because of the volume of trade they service, factors can maintain greater access to credit information on foreign customers and can diversify credit and collection risks over a broader customer base. Factors' comparative advantage in credit assessments and collections is greatest over small firms with a high proportion of export sales and geographically dispersed customers.

***Forfaiting*** resembles factoring but involves medium- to long-term receivables with maturities of six months or longer. In a typical forfaiting arrangement, a forfaiter (often a commercial bank) purchases a medium-term receivable with a 1- to 7-year maturity from an exporter at a discount and without recourse. The forfaiter provides the financing and assumes the credit and collection risks for the exporter. The receivable typically is denominated in an actively traded currency such as the U.S. dollar or the euro, and usually is backed by a payment guarantee such as a letter of credit that reduces the collection risk of the forfaiter.

Forfaiting is used by European Union banks to finance export sales to companies from developing countries that have difficulty obtaining financing from local sources. Political risks are high in many of these countries, and importers can be poor commercial risks as well. In these circumstances, neither importers nor exporters are well positioned to assume the risks of international trade. Through long years of experience in these markets, European banks have developed expertise in estimating and managing these commercial and political risks.

Commercial banks are willing to purchase trade and bankers' acceptances at a discount to face value, where the discount depends on the terms of the receivable and the credit risk of the borrower. This factoring process is known as ***discounting,*** and allows exporters to sell or accelerate their receipt of cash to provide financing for continuing operations. Discounting may be done with or without recourse. Acceptances discounted with recourse require the seller to pay the bank the face value of the draft should the buyer fail to pay the bill when due. Acceptances discounted without recourse release the seller from this responsibility. The bank assumes the credit risk on acceptances discounted without recourse, so bank fees and interest rates on discounts without recourse are higher than on similar acceptances discounted with recourse. L/C can be discounted in some countries (e.g., China), but not in others (e.g., the United States).

Discounting is the discounted sale of an acceptance

Discount rates on prime bankers' acceptances are near the discount rates on prime commercial paper. For large firms with access to the commercial paper market, the cost of commercial paper (including placement fees and back-up lines of credit) is frequently lower than the cost of a banker's acceptance. Small and medium-sized firms without access to the commercial paper market are more likely to use bankers' acceptances to finance their international trade.

The costs and risks of a trade or banker's acceptance or a letter of credit can be reduced by insuring it against commercial and political risks through national or international trade insurance agencies, such as the World Bank's Multilateral Investment Guarantee Agency (www.miga.org) or the United States' Export-Import Bank (www.exim.gov). These agencies provide guarantees and insurance against credit and political risks for companies engaged in international trade.

**Borrow against a Current Asset** An exporter can lower its financing costs by using current assets as collateral. Accounts receivable and inventory balances are often used as collateral to reduce the interest cost on bank lines of credit and short-term loans. Similarly, marketable securities and bank demand deposits can be used as compensating balances to reduce the risk of nonpayment to the bank on short-term borrowings. L/Cs also are sometimes used as collateral, although this convention varies by country. The use of compensating balances or collateral provides insurance to the bank and thereby reduces the fees charged by the bank.

### The Importer's Perspective

The most convenient method of payment for the importer is for the exporter to extend credit on an open account. The least convenient method of payment for the importer is cash in advance. This requires that the buyer obtain a source of cash prior to purchase, either by reducing an asset account or increasing a liability account. Payment of cash in advance may be undesirable or even impossible for some importers, in which case other sources of financing are required.

In a trade or banker's acceptance, the seller extends credit to the buyer. This credit does not come free of charge. The seller will try to cover shipping, credit, and collection costs in the payment terms offered to the buyer. The terms of a banker's acceptance include these costs, as well as any fees, lines of credit, or compensating balance requirements that the bank demands for accepting the draft. Bank fees on unconfirmed L/Cs range from 0.125 to 0.5 percent of the face amount of the credit. Another 0.05 to 0.5 percent is charged if the L/C is confirmed by a bank in the seller's country. Whether the buyer or seller bears the shipping and financing costs is determined by their respective bargaining positions and abilities.

### The All-In Cost of Export Financing

The *all-in cost* of export financing, such as a discounted draft, includes the draft's discount along with any bank fees and insurance premiums. To identify the all-in cost, simply identify all cash flows associated with the transaction and then calculate the internal rate of return (IRR).

> *All-in cost is the IRR based on financial cash flows.*

As an example, suppose a 1 percent acceptance fee is charged on a 6-month banker's acceptance with a face value of $1 million. The fee of (0.01)($1,000,000) = $10,000 is taken out of the face value at maturity. This acceptance fee may well be worth paying, because it greatly reduces the credit risk of the receivable to the exporter. The holder of the acceptance receives $990,000 at maturity.

An exporter can convert this banker's acceptance into cash by selling it on a discount basis, much like a U.S. Treasury bill. If the current discount rate on prime banker's acceptances is 8 percent compounded semiannually (or 4 percent per six months), then the exporter will receive ($990,000)/(1.04) = $951,923 immediately.

The all-in cost of trade financing includes the acceptance fee on the banker's acceptance. Without this fee, the exporter is promised the \$1 million face value of the receivable. If the exporter incurs the 1 percent acceptance fee on the banker's acceptance and then sells the acceptance for \$951,923 (with its 4 percent semiannual opportunity cost), it forgoes the \$1 million face value of the receivable. Hence, the incremental cash flows of this transaction from the exporter's perspective look like this.

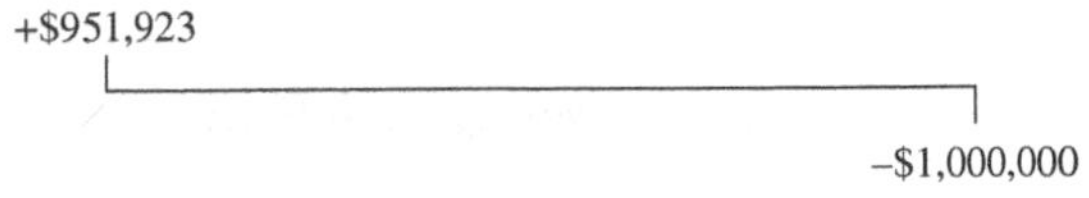


The all-in cost of this acceptance to the exporter is

$$(V_1/V_0) - 1 = (\$1{,}000{,}000/\$951{,}923) - 1 = 0.0505$$

or 5.05 percent per six months. The effective annual cost is $(1.0505)^2 - 1 = 0.1036$, or 10.36 percent. This includes the 1 percent semiannual cost of obtaining the acceptance from the bank and the 4 percent semiannual cost of discounting the acceptance with the bank. The all-in cost of other export financing methods can be found in a similar manner.

An exporter's receivables may have a fair amount of credit risk, depending on its customers' creditworthiness. Suppose the exporter's borrowing cost using accounts receivable as collateral is 12 percent compounded semiannually, or 6 percent per six months. This exceeds the 5.05 percent all-in cost of the banker's acceptance over six months, so the banker's acceptance is the lower cost alternative in this example.

## 8.4 MANAGING THE MULTINATIONAL CORPORATION'S CASH FLOWS

Management of the firm's cash flow has both an internal and an external dimension, and includes

- Cash management—including multinational netting and forecasting funds needs
- Managing relations between the operating divisions of the firm and with external investors, partners, suppliers, and customers
    - Setting or negotiating transfer prices between the firm's operating divisions
    - Determining the required return (or hurdle rate) on new investments
    - Credit assessment and approval

Individual business units transact with other business units within the firm as products are moved through the corporate value chain. Treasury serves as a central clearinghouse for the transfer payments associated with these transactions, and treasury is sometimes involved in setting or negotiating internal transfer prices on these intrafirm transactions. Consolidating all of these operations in a central clearinghouse allows the treasury to monitor and forecast the company's need for funds, minimize transaction costs, manage exposures to operating and financial risks, and take advantage of financial market opportunities as they arise.

## Cash Management

**Multinational Netting** To effectively manage its financial resources, the MNC's treasury must implement a cash management system that tracks cash receipts and disbursements within the company and with the company's external partners. The treasury has several cash management tools at its disposal. Chief among these tools is a process called ***multinational netting*** in which intrafirm transfers are minimized by "netting" offsetting cash flows in various currencies.[4]

> *Multinational netting eliminates offsetting cash flows.*

**Forecasting Cash Flows and the Need for Funds** By tracking cash flows to and from the firm's external suppliers and customers and serving as a central clearinghouse for intrafirm transactions, the MNC's treasury is in an excellent position to forecast the funding needs of the corporation. With accurate forecasts of cash requirements, the treasury can ensure that each operating division has sufficient funds to run its operations. When cash is in short supply, the treasury can use its banking relationships to draw upon its lines of credit. When there is temporarily excess cash in the system, the treasury can pay down obligations or invest in money market instruments in the currencies of its choice. By forecasting cash flows, the treasury can use multinational netting both across operating divisions and over time to minimize the number and size of transactions with the external financial markets. By consolidating intrafirm transactions and serving as a single source of funds, the treasury can obtain funds from the source that minimizes the firm's overall cost of capital.

## Managing Internal and External Relations

Relationship management is a key function of the multinational treasury.

**Credit Management** Managing international credit relations is harder than managing domestic credit relations because of cross-border differences in laws, business and accounting conventions, banking relations, and political systems. The risks of multinational credits can be managed through the payment mechanisms and trade finance vehicles described earlier in this chapter.

**Transfer Pricing** In most countries, transfer prices on intrafirm transactions are required to be set at market value.[5] When market prices are not available—such as on transfers of intermediate goods or services—the corporate treasury has some latitude in setting transfer prices. All else constant, the MNC has a tax incentive to shift revenues toward low-tax jurisdictions and shift expenses toward high-tax jurisdictions.

Transfer pricing decisions should be made to benefit the firm as a whole. Nevertheless, individual units are subject to performance standards and have incentives to maximize their sales prices and minimize costs. This can create disputes within the MNC if headquarters determines transfer prices purely for tax reasons and not according to the value added at each stage of production. Treasury must ensure that the managers of the individual business units are not unjustly penalized or rewarded by transfer prices that diverge from market prices.

**Identifying Divisional Costs of Capital** Disputes also arise among operating divisions over hurdle rates on new investments. Finance theory states that in order to maximize shareholder wealth, managers should use a discount rate that reflects the market's opportunity cost of capital. However, managers are often more interested in maximizing the corporate resources over which they have control. This can result in the adoption of artificially low divisional hurdle rates, as managers try to justify new investments in their divisions. The chief financial officer must insist that market-based hurdle rates are used within the company in the evaluation of new investment proposals. Treasury is in contact with capital markets on a continuing basis, and so is in a good position to identify required returns on new investments. Treasury can be an independent arbiter of transfer prices and hurdle rates, as it is somewhat detached from the managerial fiefdoms of the operating divisions.

## 8.5 CURRENCY RISK MANAGEMENT IN THE MULTINATIONAL CORPORATION

Risk management is a central responsibility of the multinational treasury. Some risks are faced by any corporation—domestic or multinational. These risk exposures include potential loss of income or assets due to natural or manmade disasters, labor strikes, and occupational health and safety hazards. Businesses protect themselves from these risks with a variety of strategies and products, including fire and property/casualty insurance.

Other risks are unique to corporations with multinational operations, particularly currency and foreign political risks. Whereas political risk affects all of the major disciplines of business, currency risk is distinctly financial in nature.

### Exposure to Currency Risk

There is a difference between currency risk and currency risk exposure. ***Risk*** exists when the future is unknown; that is, when actual outcomes can deviate from expected outcomes. With regard to foreign exchange rates, an expected devaluation of a currency by a foreign government does not constitute risk. Risk exists if and only if the actual devaluation can differ from the expectation.

Businesses or individuals have an ***exposure*** to currency risk when the value of their assets or liabilities can change with unexpected changes in currency values. Exposure to currency risk depends on how much is at risk. If a U.S. resident has €150,000 on deposit in a German bank, then the *amount* of this exposure to unexpected change in the dollar-per-euro spot rate is €150,000. Note that it is natural to denominate foreign currency exposure in the foreign currency. If the €150,000 is converted into $150,000, then the dollar value of this amount is no longer exposed to unexpected changes in the exchange rate.

*Exposure depends on how much is at risk.*

| Market value balance sheet | | |
|---|---|---|
| | Monetary assets | Monetary liabilities |
| | Real assets | Common equity |

| | |
|---|---|
| • Economic exposure | Potential change in the value of future cash flows due to unexpected forex (FX) changes |
| – Transaction exposure | Potential change in the value of *contractual* cash flows (i.e., monetary assets & liabilities) due to unexpected FX changes |
| – Operating exposure | Potential change in the value of *noncontractual* (nonmonetary) future cash flows due to unexpected FX changes |
| • Translation exposure | Potential change in financial accounting statements due to unexpected FX changes (also called accounting exposure) |

**FIGURE 8.5** A Taxonomy of Exposures to Currency Risk.

**Contractual versus Noncontractual Exposures** A useful way to categorize assets and liabilities is according to whether they are monetary (contractual) or nonmonetary (noncontractual) in nature. Consider the market value balance sheet in Figure 8.5. ***Monetary assets and liabilities*** have contractual payoffs, so that the size and timing of promised cash flows are known in advance. The firm's monetary assets include cash and marketable securities, accounts receivable, bank deposits, and the cash inflow side of forwards, futures, options, and swaps. Monetary liabilities include wages and accounts payable, domestic and Eurocurrency debt, and the cash outflow side of currency forwards, futures, options, and swaps.[6] These monetary contracts may be denominated in the domestic currency or a foreign currency.

***Nonmonetary (real) assets and liabilities*** are assets and liabilities that are not monetary or contractual in nature. Real assets include the firm's productive technologies and capacities, whether these assets are tangible (such as a manufacturing plant) or intangible (such as a patent or copyright). Inventory is considered a real asset, unless payment has been contractually promised in some way. Returns on real assets are noncontractual and hence uncertain. Real assets can be exposed to currency risk regardless of where they are located. For example, a domestic manufacturing plant is exposed to currency risk if export sales depend on foreign exchange rates.

As the residual owner of the firm, common equity is a nonmonetary liability. The cash flows that accrue to equity depend on the noncontractual (operating) cash flows of the firm's real assets, as well as the contractual cash flows of the firm's monetary assets and liabilities. Although each of these asset and liability categories can be exposed to currency risk, the nature of the risk exposure varies depending on whether the account is contractual or noncontractual in nature.

**Cash Flow Exposures** ***Economic exposure*** refers to potential changes in all—monetary or nonmonetary—future cash flows due to unexpected changes in exchange rates. Managing economic exposure is an important long-term goal of the multinational financial manager. Economic exposure can be divided into the transaction exposure of the firm's monetary assets and liabilities and the operating exposure of the firm's real assets. As the residual owner of the firm, equity is exposed to currency risk through the operating exposure of real assets and the transaction exposure of monetary assets and liabilities.

***Transaction exposure*** refers to changes in the value of monetary cash flows as a result of unexpected changes in currency values. Monetary contracts denominated in a foreign currency are fully exposed to changes in the value of that currency, so transaction exposure is an important short-term concern of the multinational financial manager. Domestic monetary contracts are not directly exposed to currency risk,[7] although they are exposed to domestic inflation risk. The exposure of ***net monetary assets*** (monetary assets less monetary liabilities) depends on whether the exposures of monetary assets and liabilities are offsetting. Because monetary assets and liabilities involve contractual cash flows, transaction exposure can be effectively hedged with financial market instruments such as currency forwards, futures, options, or swaps.

*Transaction exposures are contractual exposures.*

***Operating exposure*** refers to potential changes in the value of real (nonmonetary) assets or operating cash flows as a result of unexpected changes in exchange rates. Although firms can partially hedge against operating exposures to currency risk with financial derivatives (forwards, futures, options, or swaps), the contractual cash flows of a financial derivative is not very effective at hedging the uncertain cash flows of the firm's real assets. Operating exposures are more effectively hedged through management of the firm's location, production, sourcing, distribution, and marketing decisions. Whereas financial hedges are easy to create and reverse, operational hedges are difficult to achieve and involve high entry and exit costs.

*Operating exposure is the exposure of nonmonetary assets.*

Figure 8.6 illustrates the evolution of currency exposures from nonmonetary to monetary. Suppose U.S.-based GTE has invested in a cellular phone system in India consisting of a country-wide network of microwave relay stations and switching equipment. At the time of investment, future proceeds from the investment can be estimated but are not known for certain. GTE's real assets—the microwave relay stations and switching equipment—have an operating exposure to currency risk because the dollar value of the proceeds from this investment depends on the dollar value of the rupee. As GTE's advertising campaign attracts customers, some of these uncertain future proceeds become sales contracts. This creates rupee-denominated receivables for the subsidiary in India. These receivables have transaction exposure for GTE because their dollar value depends on the exchange rate. GTE has no exposure to currency risk on these payments once they are repatriated. Its economic

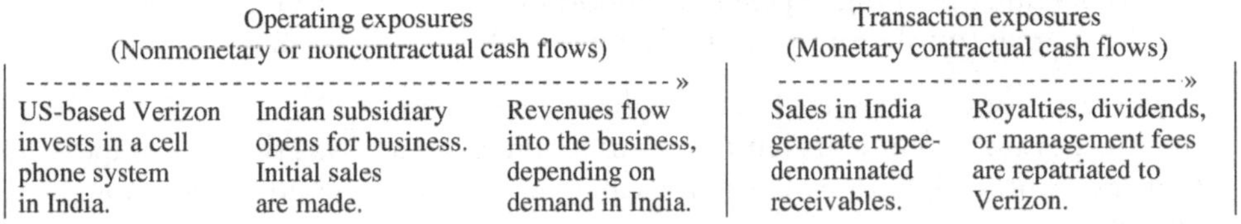
Operating exposures
(Nonmonetary or noncontractual cash flows)
Transaction exposures
(Monetary contractual cash flows)
US-based Verizon invests in a cell phone system in India.
Indian subsidiary opens for business. Initial sales are made.
Revenues flow into the business, depending on demand in India.
Sales in India generate rupee-denominated receivables.
Royalties, dividends, or management fees are repatriated to Verizon.

**FIGURE 8.6** Verizon's Exposures to Currency Risk in India.

exposure to currency risk remains, however, through the operating exposure of its subsidiary in India.

**Translation Exposures** *Translation* (or *accounting*) *exposure* refers to potential changes in financial accounting statements as a result of changes in currency values. Translation exposure arises as the parent firm translates the financial accounting statements of its foreign subsidiaries back into its domestic currency using the generally accepted accounting principles of the parent country. Translation exposure may or may not reflect changes in the value of the firm's assets or liabilities, and hence may or may not be related to the economic exposure of the firm.

*Translation exposure may or may not be related to cash flow or firm value.*

Although translation exposure may not be of direct concern to debt and equity stakeholders, it is vitally important to the managers of the firm. Performance evaluations and compensation often are tied to accounting performance, so managers have a strong incentive to minimize their translation exposures. To the extent that managers change their actions based on translation exposure, debt and equity investors also should be concerned because it affects the value of the firm indirectly through the actions of the managers.

### A Forward Hedge of a Currency Exposure

*Financial price risk* arises from the possibility that a financial price—such as a currency value, an interest rate, or a commodity price—will differ from its expectation. Currency risk is a particular form of financial price risk. Here is an example of a transaction exposure to currency risk that can be hedged with a forward contract.

#### MARKET UPDATE Corporate Views on Currency Risk Exposures

Jesswein, Kwok, and Folks surveyed corporate treasurers and chief financial officers of U.S. firms concerning their views on the relative importance of these types of exposures to currency risk. These financial managers were asked whether they (1) strongly agreed, (2) agreed, (3) were neutral, (4) disagreed, or (5) strongly disagreed with each of the following statements:

| | Mean level of agreement |
|---|---|
| Managing transaction exposure is important. | 1.4 |
| Managing operating exposure is important. | 1.8 |
| Managing translation exposure is important. | 2.4 |

Mean responses are reported to the right of each question.

Corporate respondents felt that transaction exposure was the most important exposure. Operating exposure came in a close second, even though operating exposure is the more important long-term exposure. Transaction exposures to currency risk are one-for-one in that a percentage change in the value of a foreign currency causes the same percentage change in the domestic currency value of exposed cash flows. This makes transaction exposures easy to identify and to hedge with currency derivatives. The exposures of operating cash flows are more difficult to estimate and hedge. Translation (accounting) exposure came in a distant third in importance in this survey.

Monetary assets and liabilities involve cash flows that are contractual in nominal terms, and so are directly exposed to changes in nominal exchange rates. Real assets, on the other hand, are primarily exposed to changes in real exchange rates. Real exchange rates measure changes in the relative purchasing power of two currencies by adjusting for inflation differences between the two currencies. Real exchange rates are an important concept in international finance and are discussed in Chapter 4.

*Source:* Jesswein, Kwok, and Folks, "Adoption of Innovative Products in Currency Risk Management: Effects of Management Orientations and Product Characteristics," *Journal of Applied Corporate Finance* (1995).

**An Example of Exposure to Currency Risk** You live in Canada and have booked a vacation to Copenhagen, Denmark. When you booked the trip six months ago, you promised to pay expenses of DKK25,000 including DKK20,000 for food and lodging, and another DKK5,000 for a quick side trip to visit a classmate who lives in Odense. The spot rate was C$0.20/DKK when you booked the trip, so your expected Canadian dollar cost was (DKK25,000)(C$0.20/DKK) = C$5,000. At this point, you have a short position in Danish kroner.

As you pack for your trip, you discover to your dismay that the kroner has appreciated by 25 percent from C$0.20/DKK to C$0.25/DKK. The Canadian dollar cost of your kroner obligation has thus increased from (DKK25,000)(C$0.20/DKK) = C$5,000 to (DKK25,000)(C$0.25/DKK) = C$6,250. The 25 percent appreciation of the kroner has increased the Canadian dollar value of your kroner obligation by 25 percent, or C$1,250. Perhaps you'll have to cancel your side trip.

A ***risk profile*** (or payoff profile) is a graph of the value of a particular position against an underlying source of risk. Here is a risk profile for your underlying short kroner position:

**Risk profile of a short DKK position**

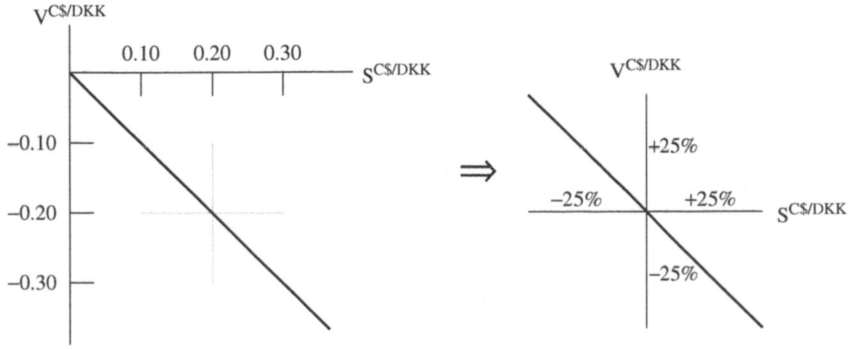

The risk profile on the left shows the Canadian dollar value of the kroner $V^{C\$/DKK}$ as a function of the spot exchange rate $S^{C\$/DKK}$. The relationship between $V^{C\$/DKK}$ and $S^{C\$/DKK}$ is one-for-one, so the risk profile is a 45-degree line. As the kroner rises in value, it costs you more in Canadian dollars to pay for your kroner obligations, and vice versa.

Recall that lowercase symbols refer to changes in value. The right-hand graph displays changes in the value of the underlying position $V^{C\$/DKK}$ as a function of changes in the spot rate $S^{C\$/DKK}$ after centering the graph on the expected spot rate of C\$0.20/DKK. You are short the kroner, so a 25 percent kroner appreciation results in a 25 percent increase in the Canadian dollar value of your kroner obligation.

**The Exposure of a Forward Hedge** Six months ago, you could have hedged your short kroner position by buying the kroner and selling the Canadian dollar forward. Suppose the 6-month forward rate at that time was $F^{C\$/DKK}$ = C\$0.20/DKK. At that rate, you could have purchased DKK25,000 and ensured that your Canadian dollar obligation would have been C\$5,000 irrespective of the actual spot exchange rate.

> *Currency forwards can reduce exposure to FX risk.*

The following graph shows the risk profile of a long kroner forward contract. If the actual spot rate is equal to the forward rate of C\$0.20/DKK, then there is no gain or loss on the forward (aside from the transaction cost built into the bid-ask spread). The DKK25,000 receipt equals the C\$5,000 cost of the forward at the C\$0.20/DKK spot rate. If the kroner appreciates to C\$0.25/DKK, then the forward contract allows (indeed, requires) you to exchange C\$5,000 for DKK25,000 at the C\$0.20/DKK forward rate. This would have cost C\$6,250 in the spot market, resulting in a C\$1,250 gain over the market rate of exchange.

**Risk profile of a long DKr hedge**

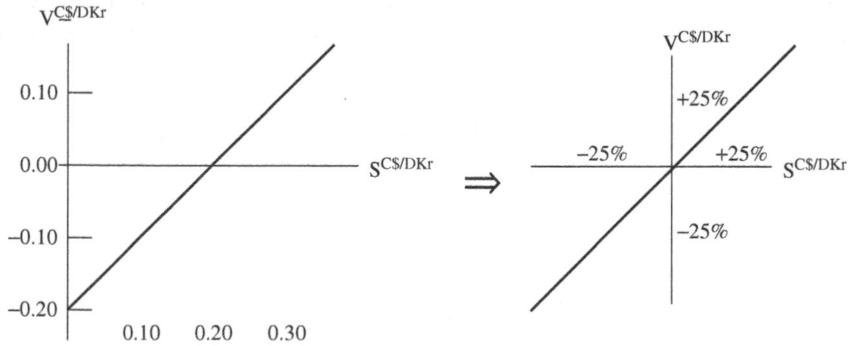


Of course, if the spot rate had fallen to C\$0.15/DKK, you still would have had to pay C\$5,000 for DKK25,000 according to the terms of the forward contract. Purchase of DKK25,000 in the spot market at C\$0.15/DKK would have cost only C\$3,750. Your opportunity cost on the long kroner forward contract would then have been C\$1,250, or C\$0.05/DKK.

The long kroner forward hedge intersects the y-axis at −C\$0.20/DKK, because if the spot rate falls to C\$0/DKK in value you'll still have an obligation to pay

C$0.20/DKK. The risk profile intersects the x-axis at C$0.20/DKK, because if the spot rate closes at C$0.20/DKK then your obligation to pay C$0.20/DKK has zero net value.

Here is a convenient way to relate the slope of the risk profile to the sign of the underlying long (+) or short (−) position.

> Identifying the *sign* of an exposure to currency risk
>
> If the currency of reference is in the *denominator* of the exchange rate, then the slope of the risk profile has the same sign as the underlying cash flow.

In this example, the underlying short kroner exposure loses from an appreciation and gains from a depreciation of the kroner. Conversely, a long kroner position as in the forward hedge gains from an appreciation and loses from a depreciation of the kroner. As long as the currency of reference is in the denominator of all foreign exchange quotes, the slope of the risk profile has the same sign as the underlying exposure.

**The Exposure of the Hedged Position** The short kroner underlying position and the long kroner forward hedge have offsetting exposures to the spot exchange rate. This can be illustrated with time lines.

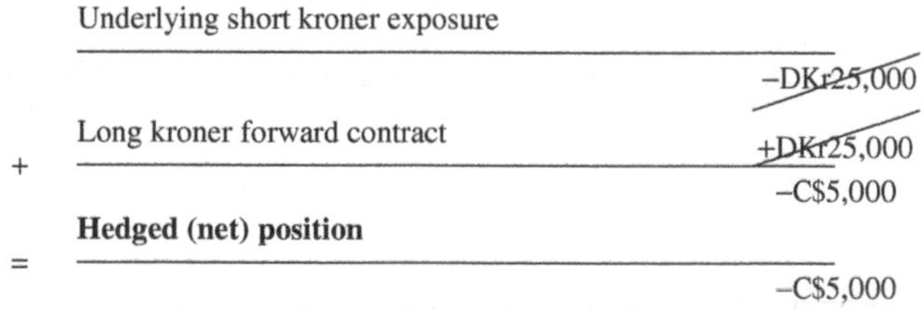


In the hedged position, the underlying short position is offset by the long forward contract. The net result is an obligation of C$5,000 regardless of what happens to the C$-per-kroner rate.

Similarly, the two risk profiles can be combined to illustrate that the payoff to the hedged position is independent of the exchange rate.

**The hedged position**

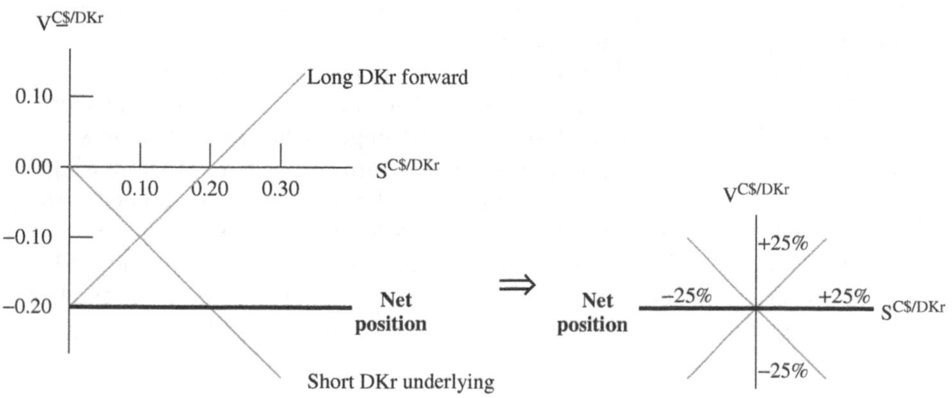

The hedged position is the sum of the two exposures. If the spot rate rises, the gain on the forward hedge exactly offsets the loss on the underlying position. Conversely, if the spot rate falls, the loss on the forward hedge exactly offsets the gain on the underlying position. You will be able to exchange your C$5,000 for DKK25,000 regardless of what happens to the exchange rate, and can be assured of an enjoyable affair in Odense.

### The Five Steps of a Currency Risk Management Program

Currency risk management begins with a forecast of future exchange rates and volatilities. Given these forecasts, the impact of potential exchange rate changes on operating cash flows is estimated from past and expected future exchange rate sensitivities. The procedure is as follows:

1. *Identify exposures.* Identify those currencies to which the firm is exposed, as well as the distribution of possible future exchange rates for each of these currencies.
2. *Estimate sensitivities.* Estimate the firm's sensitivities to changes in these currency values.
3. *To hedge or not.* Determine the desirability of hedging, given the firm's estimated risk exposures and risk management objectives.
4. *Evaluate hedging alternatives.* Evaluate the performance of each alternative, given the forecasted distributions and exposures, in order to select and implement a hedging strategy.
5. *Monitor performance.* Monitor the evolving exposures and revisit these steps as necessary.

#### MARKET UPDATE Barings Bank (In for a Penny—In for a Pound)

As one of the world's more venerable merchant banks, London's Barings Bank frequently had been involved in affairs of state during its distinguished 233-year history. It had bankrolled kings, wars, business magnates, and the Louisiana Purchase for the U.S. government. Its owners and top management boasted five hereditary peerages, and the company had accumulated nearly half a billion dollars in owners' equity.

Despite this long and distinguished history, Barings unexpectedly collapsed over the weekend of February 23–24, 1995. Nick Leeson, a 28-year-old Barings trader based in Singapore, had accumulated huge positions in Nikkei stock index futures on the Singapore and Osaka futures exchanges on Barings' behalf. When the market moved against him, Leeson doubled his bets in the futures markets and added index options to his position in the hopes of a market turnaround. On February 25, Barings announced that it had lost $1.4 billion on these contracts—more than three times Barings' book equity. The Bank of England then placed Barings into bankruptcy proceedings.

Industry practice is to closely monitor market exposures and isolate the trading and bookkeeping functions. Contrary to industry practice, Barings had placed Leeson in charge of both trading and bookkeeping in the Singapore office and had then failed to monitor Leeson's trading activities. This recipe for disaster allowed Leeson to hide the size of Barings' Nikkei exposures from top management in London, even though the size of Barings' exposure was common knowledge on the Osaka and Singapore exchanges.

Had Leeson acted properly as an agent of Barings Bank, he would have promptly disclosed his initial losses to headquarters. He probably would have lost his job in the process, but Barings could have recognized the initial losses and then continued in business. Instead, Leeson gambled everything on an unlikely market turnaround. For his role in Barings' collapse, Leeson received a six-and-one-half-year sentence from a Singapore court of justice.

The principal–agent relationship is prone to trouble during financial distress. The fact that Leeson was speculating rather than hedging reinforced the chasm between the incentives of the agent (Leeson) and the principal (Barings' owners). Without proper monitoring, Leeson was free to run amok and lead Barings to ruin.

Management of currency risk should not be a one-time affair. Exposure to currency risk changes over time with changes in exchange rates and the geographic and product mix of the firm. Managers should monitor and periodically reassess the firm's risk management policies, strategies, and positions in light of changing market, industry, and company conditions.

Estimates of exposure can be based on the income statement or on the balance sheet. Estimates of the operating exposures can help the financial manager understand the components of the firm's overall exposure to currency risk. In combination with the net exposure of monetary assets and liabilities, cash flow-based estimates of exposure can assist the financial manager in formulating a plan that manages exposures and can react to changing conditions.

Estimates of exposure based on the past relationship between operating cash flows and exchange rates are appropriate only if the historical relationship is expected to persist into the future. Estimates based on past outcomes will not work for evolving businesses or newly acquired business units. These situations call for a heavier-than-usual dose of managerial judgment.

***Managers should be proactive rather than reactive.***

To be proactive rather than reactive, managers should try to answer these questions.

- What is likely to happen to exchange rates and to our business in the future?
- How has the relationship between exchange rates and operating cash flows changed?
- How might our competitors respond to a change in exchange rates?

Several *decision support tools* are useful in answering these questions, including scenario analysis, Monte Carlo simulation, and decision trees.

- *Scenario analysis*. Scenario analysis asks, "What if?" In the context of currency risk, scenario analysis consists of asking, "What if exchange rates change?" Scenario analysis answers this by evaluating the impact of a few representative exchange rate scenarios on the firm. This is by far the most commonly used financial risk management tool for nonfinancial companies.[8]
- *Monte Carlo simulation*. Monte Carlo simulation is similar to scenario analysis, but uses the entire distribution of exchange rates rather than just a few representative scenarios.[9]
- *Decision trees*. Decision trees are graphical representations of sequential decisions that allow managers to assess possible competitive responses to new conditions and ask questions such as, "What if exchange rates appreciate and our competitors respond in this way?"

These decision support tools allow managers to stress-test the firm's exposures and hedges, and quantify their impact on the firm's position under adverse conditions. They encourage managers to anticipate possible future events rather than simply react to circumstances after the fact, and thus help in establishing proactive strategies for dealing with an uncertain future.

### Formulating a Risk Management Policy: To Hedge or Not to Hedge

To ensure that the corporate treasury's hedging and risk management strategies are consistent with the overall goals of the corporation, top management must be actively involved in formulating risk management policy and monitoring its implementation. This sounds obvious, but most derivative-related losses result from a failure to follow this simple rule. A framework for characterizing the corporation's risk management policy appears in Figure 8.7.

The MNC first must decide whether it will take a passive or an active approach to hedging its exposures to currency risk. *Passive management* does not try to anticipate currency movements, assuming instead that financial markets are informationally efficient. Passive policies often apply the same hedging rule to each exposure. For example, if corporate policy is to hedge 50 percent of net yen exposures at each maturity, then this rule can be uniformly applied regardless of market or company conditions or the value of the yen.

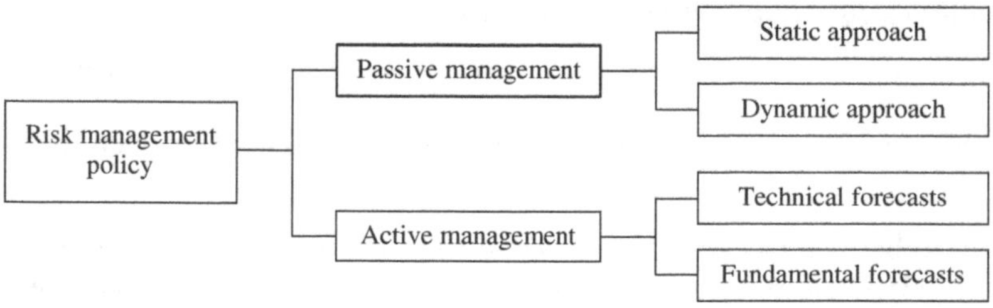


**FIGURE 8.7** Risk Management Policy.

Passive hedging strategies can be applied in either a static or a dynamic manner. A *static approach* hedges exposures as they are incurred and then leaves these hedges in place until maturity. A static approach is appropriate only for companies with infrequent and easily identifiable transaction exposures. More effective but time-consuming is a *dynamic approach* that periodically reviews underlying exposures and hedges and revises these positions as appropriate. Dynamic strategies that follow a passive approach can adapt to changing market or company conditions, but nevertheless are applied with little managerial discretion under the firm's risk management policy.

Surveys find that financial managers believe they possess information that provides them with an advantage in anticipating financial price movements, and that they incorporate these views into their risk management decisions.[10] *Active management* selectively hedges currency exposures depending on these beliefs, so actual positions can diverge from the MNC's average or benchmark position. Active positions give rise to the risk that hedged return will differ from the benchmark return. For example, corporate policy might call for a benchmark position in a forward contract of 50 percent of any net yen exposures. Active management might diverge from this benchmark, in which case actual performance is likely to diverge from the benchmark.

Two forecasting approaches are available to managers who think they possess the expertise and risk tolerance to actively manage foreign exchange exposures. ***Technical analysis*** uses recent exchange rate movements to predict the direction of future exchange rate movements. Technical models have achieved some success in forecasting near-term exchange rates. ***Fundamental analysis*** uses macroeconomic data (such as money supply or gross national product (GNP) growth) to forecast long-term exchange rates. Although technical and fundamental forecasts sometimes have difficulty beating market-based forecasts such as forward exchange rates as predictors of long-horizon spot rates, they are nevertheless popular with practitioners.

## Hedging and the Market Value of the Firm

There is a fair amount of empirical support for the notion that risk management can increase the values of MNCs.[11] However, the nature of an MNC's assets often determines where and when risk management can create value. Consider the following two studies.

Allayannis and Weston (2001) examined a sample of large multinationals and found a positive relation between currency derivative usage and market values.[12] Moreover, MNCs that instituted a hedging policy experienced an increase in value relative to firms that did not hedge, and firms that stopped hedging saw a decrease in value relative to firms that continued to hedge.

In contrast, Jin and Jorion (2006) studied a sample of oil and gas producers and found no difference between the values of firms that hedged and firms that did not hedge their exposures to commodity price risk.[13] The absence of a hedging premium for oil and gas producers suggests that these firms are somehow different from other nonfinancial firms, perhaps in the types of risks to which they are exposed.

The currency risk exposures of MNCs are difficult to identify from outside the firm, and so are not easily hedged with currency derivatives. Indeed, multinationals often have operating exposures that are best managed with operating—rather than financial—hedges. In contrast, oil and gas producers have commodity price exposures that are both easy to identify from published financial statements and easy to hedge using exchange-traded derivatives such as oil price futures.

## APPLICATION Financial Risk Management at Ford Motor Company

Divisional managers have an incentive to hedge against currency risk in order to reduce the variability of their divisional performance. But hedges are not costless, and one division's exposures may be offset by exposures elsewhere in the company. By "netting" exposures within the company, treasury can take an integrated approach to financial risk management so that duplicate or offsetting hedges are avoided and financing costs minimized. Operational flexibility is one of the principal advantages of a globally diversified firm over a "classic" exporter relying solely on domestic production, but global operations increase the challenges of treasury management.

Globally diversified Ford Motor Company has consolidated its automotive operations into four geographic regions: North America, South America, Europe, and Asia/Pacific/Africa. Manufacturing operations in each region are used to support sales in that region. This provides a natural operating hedge as both revenues and expenses are drawn from the same region. These regional organizations are supported by several global platforms including treasury and product development to leverage the firm's global assets across the regions.

Ford separates its financial reporting into two sectors—automotive (Ford and Lincoln) and financial services (Ford Credit, reported on a global basis). Here are some of Ford Motor Company's key performance measures (in millions of U.S.$) and derivatives positions at the end of fiscal year 2010.

| | Sales and revenues | Income before taxes |
|---|---|---|
| **Automotive sector** | $119,280 | $4,146 |
| **Financial Services sector** | 9,674 | 3,003 |
| Total | $128,954 | $7,149 |

| | | Fair (market) value of | |
|---|---|---|---|
| **Automotive sector** | **Notionals** | **Assets** | **Liabilities** |
| Cash flow hedges (foreign exchange contracts) | 664 | 8 | 15 |
| Derivatives not designated as hedging instruments | | | |
| Foreign exchange contracts—operating exposures | 2,434 | 50 | 78 |
| Commodity contracts | 846 | 69 | 6 |
| Other—interest rate contracts and warrants | 12 | 2 | – |
| Total automotive sector derivative instruments | 3,956 | 132 | 99 |

| Financial Services sector | Notionals | Fair (market) value of Assets | Liabilities |
|---|---|---|---|
| Fair value hedges—interest rate contracts | 8,826 | 503 | 7 |
| Derivatives not designated as hedging instruments | | | |
| Interest rate contracts | 52,999 | 709 | 322 |
| Foreign exchange contracts | 3,835 | 24 | 73 |
| Cross currency interest rate swap contracts | 1,472 | 25 | 189 |
| Total financial services sector derivative instruments | 67,132 | 1,261 | 591 |

By consolidating its treasury operations, Ford can match and net currency exposures internally across the geographic regions, as well as across the automotive and financial services sectors of the business. After matching exposures internally, treasury then manages Ford's net transaction exposure in the financial markets. By offsetting exposures internally before going to the financial markets, Ford minimizes its external hedging costs and maximizes the effectiveness of its hedging strategies.

Ford hedges all three forms of financial price risk. Ford is exposed to commodity price risk on the inputs (steel, glass, and energy) to its automotive production. Interest rate risk exposures arise primarily in the financial services sector, where Ford finances car purchases through loan and lease contracts. Transaction and operating exposures to currency risk arise through the global automotive production and sales activities.

In the hedges shown above, Ford explicitly offsets some of its hedges against their underlying exposures using the hedge accounting rules of Financial Accounting Standard (FAS) #133 "Accounting for Derivative Instruments and Hedging Activities" (see Chapter 11). Ford chooses to not use the hedge accounting rules for other hedges, which are reported as "Derivatives not designated as hedging instruments."

*Source:* Ford Motor Company, 2010 Annual Report.

Hedging policy can increase firm value only when it can either increase the firm's expected future cash flows or decrease the discount rate in a way that cannot be replicated by investors. A possible explanation why oil and gas producers do not see their market values increase when they hedge is that investors can already identify and hedge these exposures for themselves with commodity derivatives. This does not explain why oil and gas producers that hedged do not benefit from reductions in expected costs of financial distress, tax liabilities, or agency costs. Cost savings from these sources can be captured only by the firm, and not by outside investors through homemade hedging. At the very least, Jin and Jorion's findings indicate that the hedging premium depends on the types of risks to which the firm is exposed.

## 8.6 SUMMARY

The goal of multinational treasury management is to allow the core business activities of the MNC to attain their potentials. To add to corporate value, the officers of the multinational treasury must

- Determine the firm's overall financial goals
- Manage the corporation's international transactions
- Arrange financing for the corporation's international transactions
- Consolidate and manage the financial flows of the firm
- Identify, measure, and manage the firm's exposures to currency risks

The first four of these are discussed in this chapter. The last function—currency risk management—is important enough to warrant separate treatment and is covered in the next three chapters.

In order to introduce the topic of currency risk management, we classified the MNC's exposure to currency risk as follows:

- Economic exposure: change in value due to unexpected changes in exchange rates
  - Transaction exposure refers to change in the value of contractual future cash flows (i.e., cash flows from monetary assets and liabilities) due to unexpected changes in exchange rates
  - Operating exposure refers to change in the value of noncontractual future cash flows (i.e., operating cash flows from nonmonetary assets and liabilities) due to unexpected changes in exchange rates
- Translation (accounting) exposure: change in financial accounting statements due to unexpected changes in exchange rates

Monetary contracts denominated in a foreign currency are fully exposed to currency risk, and yet are fairly easy to hedge with financial market instruments such as currency forward contracts. Real assets, such as a manufacturing plant, can be exposed to currency risk regardless of where they are located if the uncertain cash flows of the real asset depend on exchange rates.

## KEY TERMS

*all-in cost*
*banker's or trade acceptance*
*cash in advance*
*countertrade*
*discounting*
*draft (trade bill, bill of exchange)*
*economic exposure*
*factoring and forfaiting*
*financial price risk*
*freight shippers (freight forwarders)*
*fundamental or technical analysis*
*letter of credit (L/C)*
*monetary assets and liabilities*
*multinational netting*
*negotiable acceptance*
*net monetary assets*
*nonmonetary (real) assets and liabilities*
*open account*

*operating exposure*
*risk (payoff) profile*
*risk versus risk exposure*
*sight or time draft*
*transaction exposure*
*translation (accounting) exposure*

## CONCEPTUAL QUESTIONS

8.1 What is multinational treasury management?

8.2 What function does a firm's strategic business plan perform?

8.3 Why is international trade more difficult than domestic trade?

8.4 Why use a freight shipper?

8.5 Describe four methods of payment on international sales.

8.6 What is a banker's acceptance, and how is it used in international trade?

8.7 What is discounting, and how is it used in international trade?

8.8 How is factoring different from forfaiting?

8.9 What is countertrade? When is it most likely to be used?

8.10 What is multinational netting?

8.11 How can treasury assist in managing relations among the operating units of the MNC?

8.12 What are the five steps in a currency risk management program?

8.13 What is the difference between passive and active currency risk management?

8.14 What is the difference between technical and fundamental analysis?

8.15 Are small, medium-sized, or large firms most likely to use derivatives to hedge currency risk? How do firms benchmark their hedges?

## PROBLEMS

8.1 Fruit of the Loom has a banker's acceptance drawn on Banque Paribas with a face value of $10 million due in 90 days. Paribas will withhold an acceptance fee of $10,000 at maturity. Fruit of the Loom's bank is willing to buy the acceptance at a discount rate of 6 percent compounded quarterly.

a. How much will Fruit of the Loom receive if it sells the banker's acceptance?
b. What is the all-in cost of the acceptance, including Paribas' acceptance fee?

8.2 Fruit of the Loom, Inc. sells $10 million in accounts receivable to a factor. The receivables are due in 90 days. The factor charges a 2 percent per month factoring fee, as well as the face amount, for purchasing the accounts receivable from Fruit of the Loom on a nonrecourse basis.

a. How much will Fruit of the Loom receive for its receivables?
b. What is the all-in cost of the acceptance?

8.3 Savvy Fare has a banker's acceptance drawn on Credit Lyonnais with a face value of \$1 million due in six months. Credit Lyonnais receives an acceptance fee of \$2,000 at maturity. A U.S. bank is willing to buy the acceptance at a discount rate of 5% compounded quarterly.

a. How much will Savvy Fare receive if it sells the banker's acceptance?
b. What is the all-in cost of the acceptance, including the acceptance fee?

8.4 Suppose Savvy Fare sells a \$1 million receivable to a factor. The receivable is due in six months. The factor charges an upfront fee of 4 percent for purchasing the receivable on a nonrecourse basis, and a factoring fee of 1 percent per month for every month the receivable is outstanding. The 1 percent per month factoring fee is paid at the time the receivables are sold to the factor.

a. How much will Savvy Fare receive for its receivables?
b. What is the all-in cost of the acceptance to Savvy Fare?

8.5 Hippity Hops will deliver €1 million to the Czech brewer Pilsner Urquel in one year. The spot and 1-year forward rates between the Czech koruna and the euro are $S_0^{CZK/€} = F_1^{CZK/€} =$ CZK40/€. The sale is invoiced in korunas. Pilsner Urquel promises to pay Hippity Hops CZK40 million in one year.

a. Identify Hippity Hops' expected cash flow in Czech korunas on a time line.
b. Draw a risk profile for Hippity Hops in terms of euros per koruna.
c. If the actual spot rate in one year is CZK25/€ (or €0.04/CZK), how much gain or loss will Hippity Hops have if it does not hedge its currency exposure? (Use the current spot exchange rate as the starting point in calculating the gain or loss.)
d. Form a forward market hedge based on the forward price $F_1^{CZK/€} =$ CZK40/€. Indicate how the hedge eliminates foreign exchange exposure by identifying the forward contract's cash inflows and outflows on a time line. Construct a payoff profile that combines the exposures of the underlying position and the forward contract.

## SUGGESTED READINGS

### Currency risk hedging policies and practices are described in

George Allayannis and James P. Weston, "The Use of Foreign Currency Derivatives and Firm Value," *Review of Financial Studies* 14 (Spring 2001), 243–276.

Gordon M. Bodnar, Gregory S. Hayt, and Richard C. Marston, "1998 Wharton Survey of Financial Risk Management by U.S. Non-Financial Firms," *Financial Management* 27 (Winter 1998), 70–91.

Christopher C. Géczy, Bernadette A. Minton, and Catherine M. Schrand, "Taking a View: Corporate Speculation, Governance, and Compensation," *Journal of Finance* 62, No. 5 (2007), 2405–2443.

Kurt Jesswein, Chuck C.Y. Kwok, and William R. Folks, Jr., "What New Currency Risk Products Are Companies Using, and Why?" *Journal of Applied Corporate Finance* 8 (Fall 1995), 115–124.

Yanbo Jin and Philippe Jorion, "Firm Value and Hedging: Evidence from U.S. Oil and Gas Producers," *Journal of Finance* 61 (April 2006), 893–919.

Judy C. Lewent and A. John Kearney, "Identifying, Measuring, and Hedging Currency Risk at Merck," *Journal of Applied Corporate Finance* 2, No. 4 (1990), 19–28.
Henri Servaes, Ane Tamayo, and Peter Tufano, "The Theory and Practice of Corporate Risk Management," *Journal of Applied Corporate Finance* 21, No. 4, (2009), 60–78.
Charles Smithson and Betty J. Simkins, "Does Risk Management Add Value? A Survey of the Evidence," *Journal of Applied Corporate Finance* 17 (Summer 2005), 8–17.
René M. Stulz, "Risk Management Failures: What Are They and When Do They Happen?" *Journal of Applied Corporate Finance* 20, No. 4 (2008), 39–48.

## APPENDIX 8A: THE RATIONALE FOR HEDGING CURRENCY RISK

Why should the MNC bother to hedge its exposures to currency risk? On the surface, the answer seems obvious. Hedging creates value by reducing the risk of assets exposed to currency fluctuations. However, the conditions under which hedging can add value are not as obvious as one might think. What if currency risk is entirely diversifiable and does not matter to investors? In this case, hedging can reduce cash flow variability, but cannot change investors' required returns or the corporation's cost of capital. Where, then, is the value in hedging?

Firm value can be viewed as the present value of expected future cash flows discounted at a rate that reflects the systematic risk of those cash flows.

$$V = \Sigma_t[E[CF_t]/(1+i)^t] \quad (8A.1)$$

If hedging is to add value to the firm, then it must affect cash flows or the cost of capital in a way that cannot be replicated by investors. The issue of whether currency risk affects the discount rate is discussed in the chapter on international asset pricing. This appendix shows how hedging exposure to currency risk can increase expected cash flows in the *numerator* of Equation 8A.1.

Hedging can add value to the firm when market imperfections make it costly or impossible for individual investors to capture the same benefits from hedging as the firm can capture. The most important imperfections in the context of the firm's hedging and risk management decisions are costs of financial distress including agency conflicts in distress.[14] These imperfections create incentives to hedge on the part of one or more of the firm's principal stakeholders (i.e., stockholders, bondholders, or management). MNCs are well positioned to take advantage of imperfections in financial markets, just as they are well positioned to take advantage of imperfections in markets for real goods and services. The value that can be added to the firm by hedging currency risk in any particular circumstance depends on the characteristics of the firm, stakeholders' preferences, and the extent of the financial market imperfections.

### Costs of Financial Distress

Costs of financial distress are by far the most important consideration in the MNC's hedging decision. These costs can be either direct or indirect. ***Direct costs*** are expenses such as legal fees that occur during bankruptcy, liquidation, or reorganization. More difficult to measure are ***indirect costs*** of financial distress that arise prior to bankruptcy, including lost credibility in the marketplace and various forms of stakeholder gamesmanship that accompany financial distress.

**Equity as a Call Option on Firm Value** The impact of financial distress on financial policy is easiest to understand by viewing equity as a call option on firm value. A ***call option*** is an option to buy an asset at a predetermined exercise price and on a predetermined expiration date. Suppose debt is given a claim on the assets of the firm. In an option context, the promised payment to debt is the exercise price of the option and the due date on the debt is the expiration date of the option. Equity holds a claim on any residual value after the debt has been paid its promised claim. In bankruptcy, the firm's assets go first to debt. Any remaining value then goes to equity.

> *Equity owns a call option on firm value.*

The positions of debt and equity are shown in Figure 8A.1 in the absence of costs of financial distress. If the firm's assets are worth more than the promised payment to debt, then equity will exercise its option to buy the assets of the firm from the debt at the exercise price of the option. If firm assets are worth less than debt's claim, then equity will not exercise its option and debt receives all of the firm's remaining asset value, less the direct costs of financial distress.

Suppose the firm has promised to pay the debt \$1,000 in one period and that the assets of the firm will be worth either \$750 or \$1,750 at that time, depending on the value of an exchange rate to which the firm is exposed. If these outcomes are equally likely, the firm's expected value is

$$E[V_{Firm}] = (1/2)(\$750) + (1/2)(\$1,750) = \$1,250$$

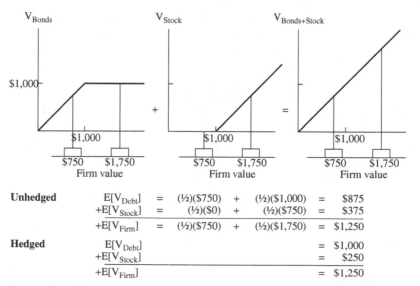

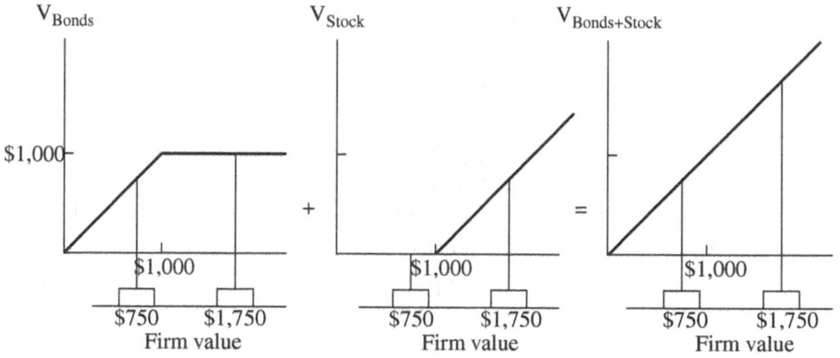


| | | | | | | | |
|---|---|---|---|---|---|---|---|
| **Unhedged** | $E[V_{Debt}]$ | = | (½)(\$750) | + | (½)(\$1,000) | = | \$875 |
| | $+E[V_{Stock}]$ | = | (½)(\$0) | + | (½)(\$750) | = | \$375 |
| | $+E[V_{Firm}]$ | = | (½)(\$750) | + | (½)(\$1,750) | = | \$1,250 |
| **Hedged** | $E[V_{Debt}]$ | | | | | = | \$1,000 |
| | $+E[V_{Stock}]$ | | | | | = | \$250 |
| | $+E[V_{Firm}]$ | | | | | = | \$1,250 |

**Assumptions**: There are no costs of financial distress. Debt has been promised a payment of \$1,000 in one period. Equity has the option of repurchasing the firm from debt for \$1,000 at that time. In the absence of hedging, firm value is either \$750 or \$1,750 with equal probability. Hedging results in firm value of \$1,250 with certainty.

**FIGURE 8A.1** The Equity Call Option on Firm Value.

In one year, the assets of the firm will be split between debt and equity according to their respective claims. If assets are worth \$750, equity will not exercise its option to buy back the firm for \$1,000. In this case, equity receives nothing and debt receives \$750 rather than its promised claim of \$1,000. If assets are worth \$1,750, equity will exercise its call option and pay debt its promised claim of \$1,000. Equity retains the residual \$750 value after paying the debt its \$1,000 claim. The \$1,250 expected value of the firm is split between debt and equity according to

$$E[V_{Debt}] = (1/2)(\$750) + (1/2)(\$1{,}000) = \$875$$

$$E[V_{Stock}] = (1/2)(\$0) + (1/2)(\$750) = \$375$$

Alternatively, the firm's expected value is $E[V_{Firm}] = E[V_{Debt}] + E[V_{Stock}] = \$875 + \$375 = \$1{,}250$.

Suppose hedging can completely eliminate the firm's exposure to currency risk and lock in a firm value of $(1/2)(\$750) + (1/2)(\$1{,}750) = \$1{,}250$. The value of assets has not changed; there is still \$1,250 available to debt and equity. The distribution of this value does change; debt is certain to receive its promised payment of \$1,000, and equity is certain to receive the residual of \$250. Equity is in fact worth \$125 less (\$250 versus \$375) when cash flows are hedged than when they are unhedged. Debt value increases by a corresponding amount—from \$875 to \$1,000—when the exposure is hedged. The net effect of hedging is to transfer \$125 of value from equity to debt.

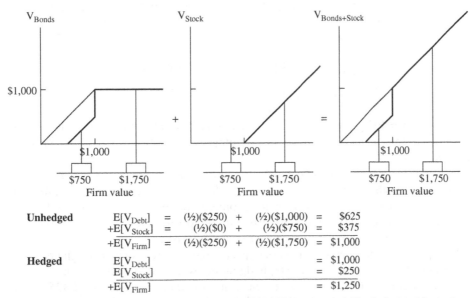

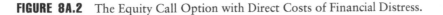

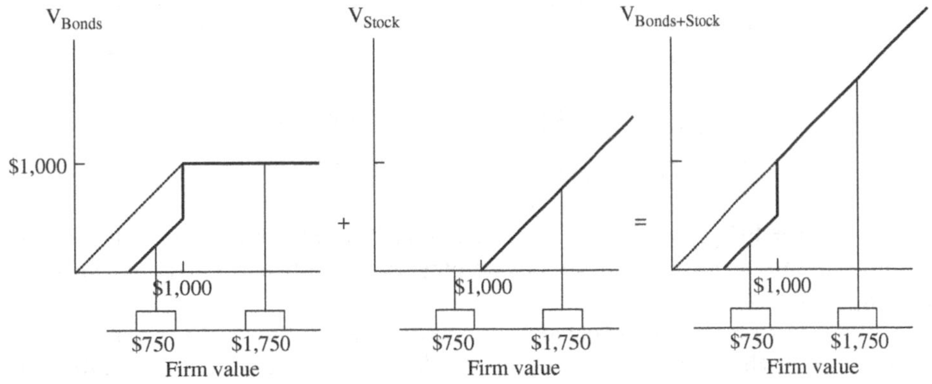


| | | | | | | | |
|---|---|---|---|---|---|---|---|
| **Unhedged** | $E[V_{Debt}]$ | = | (½)(\$250) | + | (½)(\$1,000) | = | \$625 |
| | $+E[V_{Stock}]$ | = | (½)(\$0) | + | (½)(\$750) | = | \$375 |
| | $+E[V_{Firm}]$ | = | (½)(\$250) | + | (½)(\$1,750) | = | \$1,000 |
| **Hedged** | $E[V_{Debt}]$ | | | | | = | \$1,000 |
| | $E[V_{Stock}]$ | | | | | = | \$250 |
| | $+E[V_{Firm}]$ | | | | | = | \$1,250 |

**Assumptions**: Debt has been promised a payment of \$1,000 in one period. If end-of-period firm value is less than this, direct bankruptcy costs of \$500 are incurred. Equity has the option of repurchasing the firm from debt for \$1,000 in one period. Firm value is \$750 or \$1,750 with equal probability without hedging. Firm value is \$1,250 with hedging.

**FIGURE 8A.2** The Equity Call Option with Direct Costs of Financial Distress.

This example illustrates an important property of options.[15]

A decrease in the variability of firm value is good news for debt and bad news for the equity call option, other things held constant. What debt gains, equity must lose. With no costs of financial distress, the net effect of hedging in this example is a \$125 transfer of wealth from equity to debt. Equity has a disincentive to hedge unless hedging can create value for the firm in some other way, such as through a reduction in expected costs of financial distress.

*Option values increase as the volatility of the underlying asset increases.*

### Direct Costs of Financial Distress

*Direct costs occur at bankruptcy.*

Suppose direct costs of \$500 are incurred if the company defaults on its debt (see Figure 8A.2). If the firm's assets are worth \$750, then debt receives the remaining \$250. If the assets are worth \$1,750, then no direct bankruptcy costs are incurred. In this case, debt receives its promised payment of \$1,000 and equity receives the remaining \$750. The expected value of the firm net of bankruptcy costs is $E[V_{Firm}] = (1/2)(\$250) + (1/2)(\$1,750) = \$1,000$. This expected firm value is split between debt and equity according to

$$E[V_{Debt}] = (1/2)(\$250) + (1/2)(\$1,000) = \$625$$

$$E[V_{Stock}] = (1/2)(\$0) + (1/2)(\$750) = \$375$$

Thus, $E[V_{Firm}] = E[V_{Debt}] + E[V_{Stock}] = \$625 + \$375 = \$1,000$. The $(1/2)(\$500) + (1/2)(\$0) = \$250$ expected cost of bankruptcy is a deadweight loss to the debt and equity stakeholders.

The firm can reduce its expected bankruptcy costs by hedging its exposure to currency risk. In this example, if hedging can lock in a firm value of \$1,250 with certainty, then debt always receives its promised payment of \$1,000 and stock receives the \$250 residual value. The firm can avoid the potential of a \$500 direct bankruptcy cost by hedging its exposure to currency risk.

Who benefits from this reduction in expected bankruptcy costs through hedging? Because debt has first claim on assets, hedging helps debt first and may or may not add value to equity. In our example, the value of debt increased by \$375 (from \$625 to \$1,000). In contrast, the \$250 value of the equity in the hedged alternative is \$125 less than the \$375 value of the equity in the unhedged alternative. The \$375 increase in debt value comes from two sources: a \$250 reduction in expected bankruptcy costs and a \$125 transfer in value from the equity to the debt.

Option values are positively related to both the level and the variability of the asset value underlying the option. The \$250 increase in the value of firm assets net of bankruptcy costs is good news for both debt and equity. The decrease in the variability of the firm's asset value is good news for debt, but bad news for equity. In this example, the net effect is a $375 increase in the value of debt and a $125 decrease in the value of the equity call option.

Does this mean that it is not in the best interests of equity to hedge? Not necessarily. It is useful to look at the costs and benefits of hedging in two ways: (1) at the time debt is issued (i.e., during the *opening moves*) and (2) after debt has been issued (we'll call this the *endgame*).

**Opening Moves: Reducing the Cost of Debt with a Hedging Policy** A risk management policy can benefit equity in its initial negotiations with debt. Both debt and equity claims on the firm are based on their expectations of firm value, the probability of bankruptcy, and the direct and indirect costs associated with bankruptcy. As expected costs of financial distress rise, debt requires higher returns to compensate for the additional risks. If the variability of firm value can be reduced through hedging, then debt can be raised at a lower cost and with fewer restrictions. With lower and less restrictive financing costs, more value can be left for the equity. Whether equity ultimately wins or loses through hedging depends on whether equity captures enough of the savings in expected financial distress costs to compensate for the transfer of value to debt from lower volatility in the firm's operating cash flows. In this way, a properly conceived and executed hedging policy can increase the value of equity by capturing some of the gain from lower expected costs of financial distress.

**The Endgame: Reducing Bankruptcy Costs with a Pre-Packaged Bankruptcy** There are other circumstances in which equity can gain through hedging, even when the firm is already in distress. In our example of direct bankruptcy costs, there is a 50 percent probability of bankruptcy if the firm does not hedge. Shareholders want to avoid hedging, because hedging reduces the value of the equity call option. In contrast, debt prefers that the firm hedge.

In order to avoid the direct costs of bankruptcy, the firm's stakeholders may negotiate a "pre-packaged bankruptcy" prior to formal bankruptcy proceedings. Direct bankruptcy costs can be avoided entirely in this example if debt is willing to accept less than its promised $1,000 payment in exchange for equity's promise to hedge the firm's exposure to currency risk. Debt gains if it can capture more than the $625 expected payoff when the firm does not hedge. Equity gains if they can capture more than their $375 expected payoff in the unhedged case.

Suppose debt and equity agree to split the $250 reduction in expected bankruptcy costs achieved through hedging. In exchange for equity's promise to hedge, debt could accept a certain payoff of $750. This is a $125 increase from debt's expected unhedged payoff of $625. If debt is paid $750, equity receives a certain payoff of $450: $125 more than equity's expected unhedged payoff of $325. By negotiating prior to formal bankruptcy, both debt and equity can gain.[16]

**Indirect Costs of Financial Distress** Indirect costs of financial distress are far more important to corporate hedging decisions than are direct costs, but also are less obvious. Financial distress affects all of the firm's stakeholders, including customers, suppliers, and employees, as well as debtholders, shareholders, and managers.

Indirect costs of financial distress influence these stakeholders not just in bankruptcy, but prior to bankruptcy as well. Financial distress can affect operations through diminished credibility and through stakeholder gamesmanship.

**The Costs of Lost Credibility** Firms find it more difficult to sell their products amid rumors of financial distress, especially for products that rely on quality or after-sale service. Customers are reluctant to buy from a company in the midst of a bankruptcy sale because of the possible low quality of the firm's remaining products. Moreover, there may be no recourse for dissatisfied customers if the firm goes out of business.

> *Firms in distress find it expensive to operate.*

Foreign customers are especially sensitive to rumors of distress because distressed firms often service their home market first. Firms in distress also can find it more difficult to acquire labor, materials, and capital to run their business. Offsetting this increased sensitivity to distress is the fact that foreign customers may not be as informed as domestic customers about the company's financial situation. Suppliers tend to put more effort into serving repeat customers, so a firm in distress also can find itself receiving other firms' rejected goods or inferior services.

Suppliers are especially sensitive to the financial situation of foreign partners, because of poor recourse in foreign courts. Suppliers that ordinarily sell on credit terms might demand that firms in financial distress pay their bills "cash on delivery" or finance their sales through bank L/Cs that guarantee payment to the supplier. Employees also may demand their compensation in cash or be less willing to work toward the long-term betterment of the firm.

**Conflicts of Interest between Debt and Equity** It is during difficult times that the struggle for the firm's scarce assets is most contentious. During financial distress, stakeholders shift their focus from firm value maximization to endgame strategies that maximize the value of their claim over the firm's diminishing assets. Debt wants to preserve the value of its claim, whereas equity wants to increase the value of its call option on the firm's assets even if this is at the expense of the debt. In particular, equity has the following incentives during financial distress[17]:

> *Debt and equity vie for scarce resources in financial distress.*

- An incentive to under-invest in new projects
- An incentive to take large risks

Under-investment occurs when equity refuses to provide additional capital for positive-net present value (NPV) investments during periods of financial distress. Why should equity invest more funds if debt gets the first claim on any value generated by the investment? On the contrary, equity has an incentive to withdraw any funds that it can before liquidation, perhaps as an extra cash dividend. This is when protective covenants (in particular, a limitation on liquidating dividends) can be important to the debt. Through covenants, debt can reduce the ability of other stakeholders to play games with the funds that they have loaned to the firm.

In financial distress, equity also has an incentive to promote risky ventures that *increase* the variability of investment outcomes. This increases the value of equity's call option on firm value. In some cases, equity may even want to take on negative-NPV projects if equity value increases because of more variable outcomes, despite the decrease in value from the investment. In this case, debt bears the brunt of both the negative-NPV project and the value transfer to the equity call option from increased volatility in the value of the firm's assets. Protective debt covenants are specifically written to prevent this sort of gamesmanship.

**An Example of the Equity Call Option with Both Direct and Indirect Costs of Financial Distress** Suppose indirect costs of financial distress cause a $250 decrease across the entire distribution of firm value, so that the value of the firm's assets will be either $500 or $1,500 with equal probability. If direct bankruptcy costs are still $500, then the positions of debt and equity are as in Figure 8A.3. Without hedging, the expected value of the firm is $E[V_{Firm}] = (1/2)(\$500 - \$500) + (1/2)(\$1{,}500) = \$750$. This is split between debt and equity according to

$$E[V_{Debt}] = (1/2)(\$0) + (1/2)(\$1{,}000) = \$500$$

$$E[V_{Stock}] = (1/2)(\$0) + (1/2)(\$500) = \$250$$

In this example, both debt and equity suffer from the costs of financial distress.

If the firm hedges its exposure to currency risk and locks in a value of $1,000, direct costs of financial distress can be avoided and debt receives its promised payment of $1,000 with certainty. Stockholders would receive nothing. This is similar to the situation with direct costs, except that firm value has been shifted to the left by the $250 indirect cost of financial distress.

Suppose the firm can avoid indirect financial distress costs through its risk management policies, perhaps because hedging reduces the perceived risk of the firm and improves its credibility in the marketplace. If indirect costs can be eliminated entirely, then the distribution of firm value reverts to its original position of either $750 or $1,750 with equal probability. In the hedged case, this results in firm value of $1,250 with certainty as in the original example. Debt receives its promised payment of $1,000 and equity receives $250 with certainty. Debt is now unambiguously better off than in the unhedged situation. Although the expected value of equity is unchanged, equity receives a certain $250 rather than a [$0, $500] gamble.

As in the situation with direct costs alone, this reduction in expected costs of financial distress through hedging can create value for both debt and equity. As debt negotiates the initial contract with the firm, they should be willing to accept a smaller promised return in the hedged firm than in the unhedged firm because of the unhedged firm's lower risk. And, in the endgame, firms in distress can find that hedging allows negotiation of a pre-packaged bankruptcy that can benefit both debt and equity. The objective of a pre-packaged bankruptcy is to create a "win-win" situation for the firm's stakeholders, possibly including management.

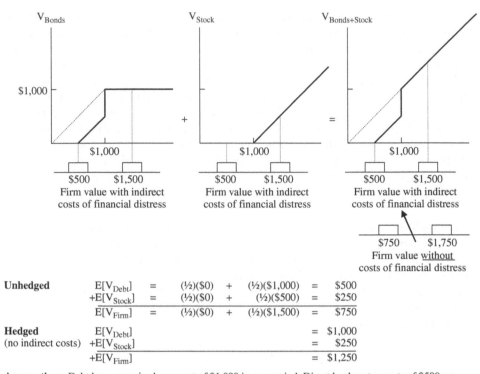

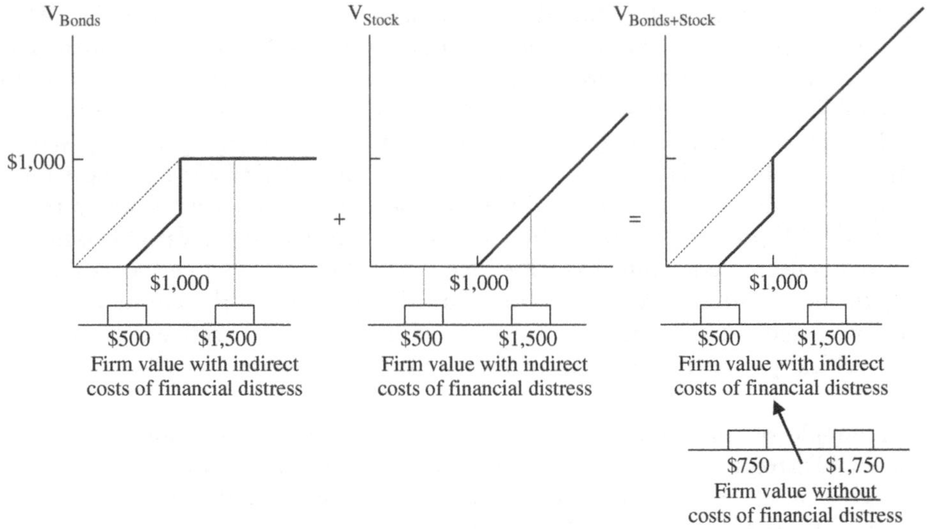


| | | | | | | | |
|---|---|---|---|---|---|---|---|
| **Unhedged** | $E[V_{Debt}]$ | = | (½)($0) | + | (½)($1,000) | = | $500 |
| | $+E[V_{Stock}]$ | = | (½)($0) | + | (½)($500) | = | $250 |
| | $E[V_{Firm}]$ | = | (½)($0) | + | (½)($1,500) | = | $750 |
| **Hedged** | $E[V_{Debt}]$ | | | | | = | $1,000 |
| (no indirect costs) | $+E[V_{Stock}]$ | | | | | = | $250 |
| | $+E[V_{Firm}]$ | | | | | = | $1,250 |

**Assumptions**: Debt has a promised payment of $1,000 in one period. Direct bankruptcy costs of $500 are incurred if end-of-period asset value is less than this amount. Equity has the option of repurchasing the firm from debt for $1,000 in one period. Firm value is either $750 or $1,750 with equal probability before indirect costs of financial distress. If the firm does not hedge, indirect costs of financial distress drain $250 from each of these values. Hedging eliminates direct and indirect costs of financial distress and results in firm value of $1,250 with certainty.

**FIGURE 8A.3** The Equity Call Option with Direct and Indirect Costs of Financial Distress.

**The Value of Distress-Related Incentives to Hedge** In summary, viewing equity as a call option on firm value yields the following conclusions in the presence of financial distress costs:

- Hedging can increase firm value and the expected cash flows available to debt and equity by reducing the direct and indirect costs of financial distress.
- Hedging increases the value of debt by reducing the variability of operating cash flows.
- Equity may or may not benefit from hedging, depending on whether the increase in firm value is more or less than the transfer of value to the debt from the reduction in risk.

In addition to a reduction in the expected costs of financial distress, hedging can further benefit the firm if it results in additional debt capacity. Graham and Rogers estimate that the tax benefits associated with this hedging-induced increase in debt capacity averages 1.1 percent of firm value for U.S. firms with assets greater than $150 million.[18]

> *Hedging increases debt capacity.*

### agency costs

Managers are hired to run the firm, but their objectives differ from those of other stakeholders. This leads to agency conflicts as managers act nominally as agents for the firm's stakeholders, but in actuality in their own interests. As in the conflict between debt and equity, conflicts between managers and other stakeholders are especially prevalent when financial distress threatens the corporation. Agency conflicts give rise to ***agency costs*** as other stakeholders try to ensure that managers do not act against their interests.

> *Agency costs are costs of ensuring that managers act in the interests of other stakeholders.*

**Managers' Incentives to Hedge** Divisional managers have an incentive to hedge their unit's exposure to currency risk because their performance evaluations and compensation are based on unit performance. This is true even if the corporation as a whole is hedged against currency risk. Consider a U.S.-based firm with an export and an import division. The export division buys jewelry in Santa Fe, New Mexico, and sells it in Paris, France. Contracts are denominated in euros and payable in one month. This month's euro sales transactions are as follows:

| t = 0 | t = 1 |
|---|---|
| | + €1million |

The import division of the company buys fashions in Paris and sells these items to tourists in Santa Fe. Again, sales are invoiced in euros and payable in one month. This month's euro expenses in this division are as follows:

| t = 0 | t = 1 |
|---|---|
| | – €1million |

These two transactions net to zero, so the firm and its investors have no need to hedge these exposures to the euro-per-dollar exchange rate.

Nevertheless, each divisional manager has an incentive to reduce the variability of divisional performance. If both managers hedge their exposure, there is neither a gain in expected cash flow nor a reduction in risk for the firm. The cost of the offsetting hedges is a deadweight loss to other stakeholders. If only one manager hedges, there is a loss from the cost of the hedge, as well as a new and—from the firm's point of view—undesirable exposure to currency risk from the hedge.

**Hedging and the Shareholder–Manager Relationship** Shareholders and management are in a classic ***principal–agent relationship*** in which shareholders hire managers to run the firm on their behalf. In a world of incomplete and asymmetric information, it is costly or even impossible to fully observe management's performance on behalf of the shareholders. Even if a manager's performance could be fully observed, judging the value of that performance is problematic. Successful managers could be merely lucky, and unsuccessful managers merely unlucky.

Equity's challenge is to ensure that managers have appropriate incentives so that they act in shareholders' best interests. If a contract could be designed that aligned the objectives of managers and shareholders, managers would have no need to hedge divisional performance on their own behalf. In the absence of such an optimal contract, management usually has an incentive to hedge. If hedging also reduces the costs of agency conflicts between managers and shareholders, then it actually may *increase* equity value by aligning managers' incentives with shareholders' preferences.

There can be a downside to allowing managers to hedge. Capital markets value the expected returns and risks of the firm's investment and financing choices and pronounce a verdict in the form of a share price. New external financing imposes financial discipline on managers by forcing them to raise new money at market prices. Managers have an incentive to hedge if, by reducing cash flow variability, they can finance projects internally and avoid the discipline of external financial markets. To the extent that managers use hedging to reduce their need for new external financing, hedging might *decrease* shareholder wealth.[19]

Stock options further complicate the issue, because managers that own options on their own company's stock have little incentive to hedge. Indeed, stock options may encourage managers to actively pursue riskier investments in order to maximize the value of their options. However, stock options are only one part of a compensation contract and may be more or less important than other elements of the contract such as salary or job security.

It is not surprising that there is little empirical evidence regarding how the shareholder–manager relationship affects managers' incentives to hedge. Intuition and a great deal of scholarship suggest that the principal-agent relationship is important in determining managers' risk management behaviors. Yet, which effect dominates is situation-dependent, and so it is difficult to make unequivocal statements about the impact of agency costs on managers' hedging incentives.

## Market Imperfections and the Hedging Decision

The decision of whether and how much to hedge must be made on a case-by-case basis. Although the need to hedge is greater for smaller, less-diversified, and riskier firms, the costs of hedging also are greater for these firms. For example, there are large economies of scale in direct bankruptcy costs, so small firms experience larger direct costs as a percent of assets than large firms do.[20] Unfortunately for small firms, there are also large economies of scale in the costs of most financial hedges. Bid-ask spreads on currency forward, option, and swap contracts traded through commercial or investment banks are smaller for larger transactions, so firms attempting to hedge small exposures can face relatively large percentage costs from their bankers. Similarly, large firms receive volume discounts and smaller percentage fees when hedging with currency derivatives. These tradeoffs are examined in depth in the next several chapters.

## KEY TERMS

*agency costs*
*call option*
*direct costs of financial distress*
*indirect costs of financial distress*
*principal—agent relationship*

## CONCEPTUAL QUESTIONS

8.1 Define financial distress. Give examples of direct and indirect costs of financial distress.

8.2 What is an agency conflict? How can agency costs be reduced?

## PROBLEMS

### Direct costs of financial distress

8A.1 Gidget International is domiciled in the Land of Make Believe. The local currency is called the Goodwill (abbreviated G). Gidget will own assets worth either G6,000 or G16,000 this year (with equal probability), depending on the value of the local currency on world currency markets. Gidget has a promised payment to debt of G10,000 due in one year. Although there are no taxes in the Land of Make Believe, there are lawyers (this isn't a perfect world, after all). If Gidget cannot meet its debt obligations, legal fees will impose direct bankruptcy costs of G2,000 as the firm is divided among its creditors.

a. How much will the debt and equity owners receive at asset values of G16,000 and of G6,000?
b. Draw the value of debt and of equity as a function of the value of firm assets as in Figure 8A.2.
c. How can hedging increase the value of Gidget International in the presence of direct bankruptcy costs? Who wins—debt, equity, or both?

### Direct and indirect costs of financial distress

8A.2 Refer to Problem 8A.1. Suppose that, in the absence of risk hedging, the indirect costs of financial distress shift sales downward and result in an asset value of either G14,000 or G4,000 with equal probability.

a. Draw the value of debt and of equity as a function of firm value, as in Figure 8A.3.
b. Calculate the expected payoffs to debt, stock, and the overall firm for the unhedged and for the hedged case.
c. Can hedging (and perhaps some creative financial contracting between debt and equity) increase the value of Gidget International in the presence of direct and indirect financial distress costs? Who wins—debt, equity, or both?

8A.3 Suppose that a firm has promised to pay the debt £10,000 in one period and that, depending on the value of the pound, the firm will be worth either £9,000 or £19,000 with equal probability at that time. The assets of the firm will be worth £14,000 if it hedges against currency risk.

a. Identify the value of debt and of equity under both unhedged and hedged scenarios, assuming there are no costs of financial distress.
b. Suppose the firm will incur direct costs of £1,000 in bankruptcy. Identify the value of debt and of equity under both unhedged and hedged scenarios.
c. In addition to the £1,000 direct bankruptcy cost, suppose indirect costs reduce the asset value of the firm to either £6,000 or £18,000 (before the £1,000 direct bankruptcy cost) with equal probability. Hedging can eliminate both direct and indirect bankruptcy costs, resulting in firm value of £14,000 with certainty. Identify the value of debt and of equity under both unhedged and hedged scenarios.

## SUGGESTED READINGS

### Imperfections that contribute to the incentive of stakeholders to hedge currency risk are discussed in

Henk Berkman and Michael L. Bradbury, "Empirical Evidence on the Corporate Use of Derivatives," *Financial Management* 25 (Summer 1996), 5–13.

Arturo Bris, Ivo Welch, and Ning Zhu, "The Costs of Bankruptcy: Chapter 7 Liquidation versus Chapter 11 Reorganization," *Journal of Finance* 61 (June 2006), 1253–1303.

Assaf Eisdorfer, "Empirical Evidence of Risk Shifting in Financially Distressed Firms," *Journal of Finance* 63 (April 2008), 609–637.

John R. Graham and Daniel A. Rogers, "Do Firms Hedge in Response to Tax Incentives?" *Journal of Finance* 57 (April 2002), 815–839.

John R. Graham and Clifford W. Smith, Jr., "Tax Incentives to Hedge," *Journal of Finance* 54 (December 1999), 2241–2262.

Deanna R. Nance, Clifford W. Smith, Jr., and Charles W. Smithson, "On the Determinants of Corporate Hedging," *Journal of Finance* 48 (March 1993), 267–284.

Peter Tufano, "Agency Costs of Corporate Risk Management," *Financial Management* 27 (Spring 1998), 67–77.

### Pre-packaged bankruptcies are discussed in

Stuart C. Gilson, "Managing Default: Some Evidence on How Firms Choose Between Workouts and Chapter 11," *Journal of Applied Corporate Finance* 4 (Summer 1991), 62–70.

John J. McConnell and Henri Servaes, "The Economics of Pre-Packaged Bankruptcy," *Journal of Applied Corporate Finance* 4 (Summer 1991), 93–97.

CHAPTER 9

# Managing Transaction Exposure to Currency Risk

*He who multiplies riches multiplies cares.*

—Benjamin Franklin

***Transaction exposure*** to currency risk is defined as change in the value of monetary (contractual) cash flows due to an unexpected change in exchange rates. Nearly every foreign currency transaction is exposed to this risk at some time. The good news is that transaction exposures are relatively easy to identify and manage, either by offsetting transactions within the firm or through external financial market hedges. This chapter covers the basics of transaction exposure management.[1]

## 9.1 AN EXAMPLE OF TRANSACTION EXPOSURE TO CURRENCY RISK

Rupert Taylor hadn't always been a successful tycoon. Growing up in Australia, his early passion was for Australian-rules football. Rupert was born with size and speed, and through athletic competition he developed daring and an indomitable will to succeed. He was particularly adept at running from one point to another and picking up a ball or knocking someone down (preferably both). After a coach from Ohio State University witnessed his domination of a national all-star game, he was offered a scholarship to play American-rules football in the United States.

Rupert attacked this new sport with his customary enthusiasm. Perhaps too enthusiastically, for within days of his arrival he had antagonized most of his teammates with his aggressive play. Frustrated with his inability to play within the rules, he became belligerent with teammates and coaches alike. A part of Rupert's frustration was simply in understanding the rules of American football. As he told his mates back home, "Nobody understands American football." In the end, he was thrown off the team when he attacked and seriously injured a teammate during an intrasquad scrimmage. Rupert's claim that it was "just part of the game" was a poor defense.

Rupert returned to Australia to work in his father's beer distributorship in Melbourne. Although his athletic career was at an end, the lessons learned from a life of competition remained. He set about expanding his father's business through a series of bold business deals, ruthlessly forcing out his competitors. In the coup d'grace, Rupert obtained the exclusive right to import and distribute Anheuser-Busch products in Melbourne.

Rupert's problems are now the problems of success. He has an accounts payable balance of \$10 million with Anheuser-Busch that is invoiced in U.S. dollars and due in three months. The cash flow associated with this transaction is shown here.

**Rupert's underlying exposure**

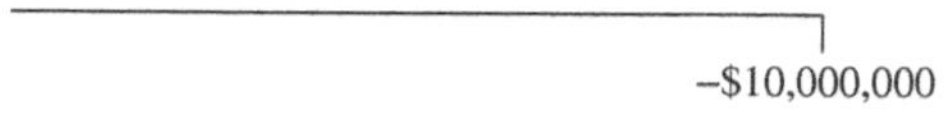


The value of Rupert's obligation in Australian dollars rises and falls with the value of the U.S. dollar. If the spot rate stays at the current level of $S_0^{A\$/\$}$ = A\$1.60/\$, Rupert will owe A\$16 million = (\$10 million)(A\$1.60/\$). If the U.S. dollar rises to A\$1.70/\$, he will owe A\$17 million. If the U.S. dollar falls to A\$1.50/\$, he will owe A\$15 million. Rupert doesn't mind a bit of risk, but this exposure to the value of the U.S. dollar is one that he would just as soon avoid.

Rupert's exposure can be represented as a ***risk profile*** (or payoff profile) of the A\$ value of his U.S. dollar obligation ($V^{A\$/\$}$) as a function of the spot rate $S^{A\$/\$}$, as shown below on the left.

**Rupert's risk profile in levels**

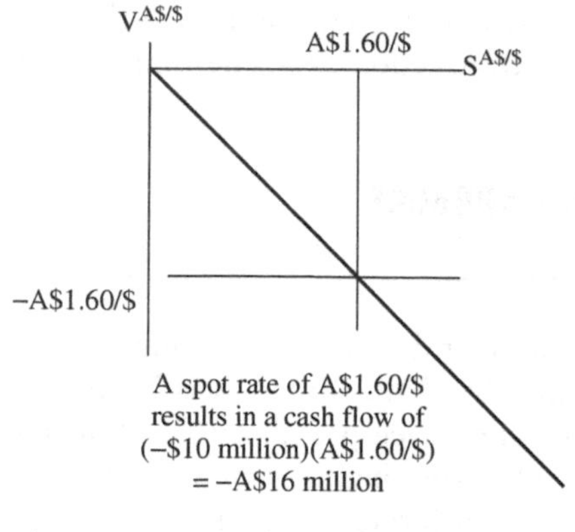


**Rupert's risk profile in percentage changes**

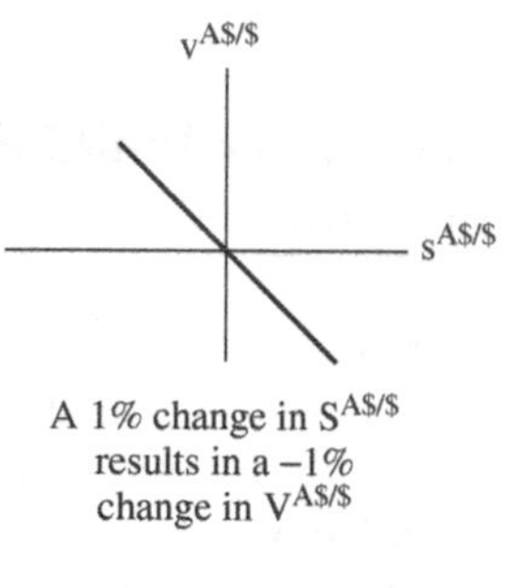


Alternatively, Rupert's risk profile is shown on the right as the percentage change in the Australian dollar value of his obligation, $v^{A\$/\$} = \Delta V^{A\$/\$}/V^{A\$/\$}$, as a function of the percentage change in the spot rate $s^{A\$/\$} = \Delta S^{A\$/\$}/S^{A\$/\$}$. This is the same as the risk profile in levels, except that the origin is centered on the point ($s^{A\$/\$}$,$v^{A\$/\$}$) = (0,0) rather than ($S^{A\$/\$}$,$V^{A\$/\$}$) = (A\$1.60/\$, –A\$1.60/\$). In either representation, the A\$ value of Rupert's obligation rises and falls inversely (indeed, one-for-one) to the value of the U.S. dollar in the denominator of the exchange rate.

## 9.2 MANAGING TRANSACTION EXPOSURES INTERNALLY

Geographically diversified operations provide a natural hedge of the multinational corporation's (MNC's) exposures to currency risk. Consider General Electric (GE), a U.S.-based MNC. GE's exposure to any single currency is reduced because of the diversity of currencies in which it operates. Moreover, inflows and outflows within GE often offset one another. GE's treasury can manage currency risk exposures internally through multinational netting and through leading and lagging.

### Multinational Netting

Currency risk management in a MNC begins with this process of ***multinational netting*** in which currency transactions from within the firm are offset and then netted against one another. The multinational treasury can identify the exposure of the corporation as a whole by consolidating and netting the exposures of the firm's operating units.

> ***Intrafirm exposures sometimes cancel out.***

**An Example** Consider GE's intracompany transactions depicted in Figure 9.1. These transactions are denominated in U.S. dollars, H.K. dollars, Japanese yen, and British pounds sterling in the top of the figure. The values of these transactions are restated in U.S. dollars (GE's currency of reference) in the middle of the figure using the cross-exchange rates. Gross transfers of value to and from each division after this translation to the U.S. dollar are as follows:

- The U.S. parent receives \$140,000 and pays \$110,000, for a net cash inflow of \$30,000
- The U.K. affiliate receives \$120,000 and pays \$180,000, for a net cash outflow of \$60,000
- The H.K. affiliate receives \$80,000 and pays \$70,000, for a net cash inflow of \$10,000
- The Japanese affiliate receives \$100,000 and pays \$80,000, for a net inflow of \$20,000

Treasury can minimize its transaction costs by coordinating the cash flows of its operating units. In the bottom figure, transfers are reduced from \$440,000 to \$60,000 by eliminating redundant transfers. In this way, intrafirm transactions are periodically reconciled and internal debits and credits allocated across the operating units according to the net amount due each unit. The periodicity of this reconciliation (daily, weekly, or monthly) depends on the size and frequency of the transactions. Large commercial banks and active treasuries such as GE's net these cash flows at a minimum of once per day; smaller firms net their multinational cash flows on a less frequent basis. Actual payments can be transferred in whatever currencies the operating units prefer, with the corporate treasury acting as an internal bank to minimize the firm's internal and external market transactions.

In contrast to diversified MNCs such as GE, importers and exporters usually cannot offset their exposures internally. For example, to hedge internally Rupert Taylor would need a U.S. dollar cash inflow to offset his U.S. dollar obligation. Rupert could begin exporting Foster's beer to the United States to create a U.S. dollar

**Cross-exchange rates**

| | H.K. | Japan | U.K. | U.S. |
|---|---|---|---|---|
| H.K. dollar | | 10.0 | 0.067 | 0.10 |
| Japanese yen | 0.10 | | 0.007 | 0.01 |
| U.K. pound | 15.0 | 150 | | 1.50 |
| U.S. dollar | 10.0 | 100 | 0.667 | |

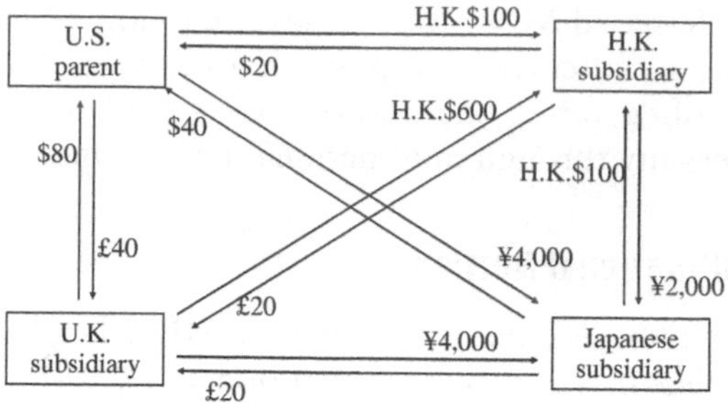


**Cash flows translated into U.S. dollars**

| In- | Outflow | | | | Total |
|---|---|---|---|---|---|
| flow | U.S. | U.K. | H.K. | Japan | receipts |
| U.S. | $0 | $80 | $20 | $40 | $140 |
| U.K. | $60 | $0 | $30 | $30 | $120 |
| H.K. | $10 | $60 | $0 | $10 | $80 |
| Japan | $40 | $40 | $20 | $0 | $100 |

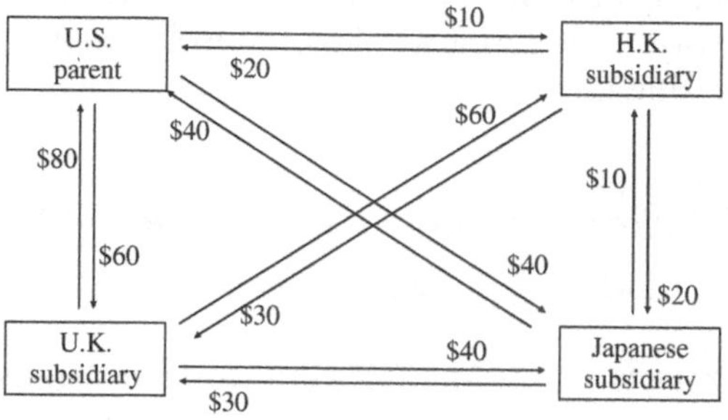


**Cash flows after multinational netting**

| | Gross cash flows | | Net cash flows | |
|---|---|---|---|---|
| Entity | Inflow | Outflow | Inflow | Outflow |
| U.S. | $140 | $110 | $30 | $0 |
| U.K. | $120 | $180 | $0 | $60 |
| H.K. | $80 | $70 | $10 | $0 |
| Japan | $100 | $80 | $20 | $0 |

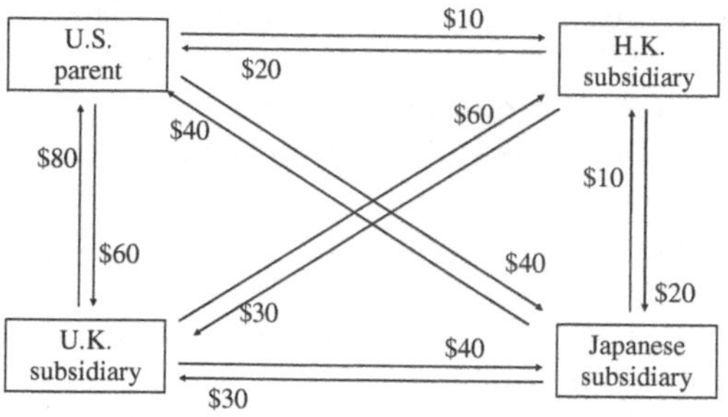


**FIGURE 9.1** Multinational Netting (Currency values in thousands).

receivable, but creating an export business merely to hedge an import business is putting the cart before the horse. Rupert can hedge his U.S. dollar exposure much more easily through the financial markets, without the considerable risks of starting up a new business venture.

**Internal Hedges of Transaction Exposure** Hedging decisions are centralized in the corporate treasury to minimize the firm's overall risk exposures and hedging costs. Nevertheless, managers of individual operating units often wish to stabilize their accounting income or cash flow through hedging. In these cases, treasury can continue to write internal hedging contracts (e.g., currency forwards or options) for the individual operating units. Treasury can minimize its external financial market transactions by netting offsetting exposures within the firm and writing internal hedging contracts when necessary. Consolidating and netting exposures rather than hedging each individual exposure allows managers of individual units to hedge as needed, while avoiding the costs (commissions and bid-ask spreads) of hedging in external markets. Treasury needs to consider hedging only the firm's net exposures.

Treasury should charge *market prices* to the individual operating units for hedging within the firm. For example, a request from an operating unit for a long 3-month forward contract on the U.S. dollar should be quoted at the market's bid rate for a transaction of comparable size. The dollar bid rate is used because the treasury is buying and the operating division is selling the dollar forward, just like in a transaction with a commercial bank. Treasury has access to these prices through its commercial and investment banking relations. Market prices allow treasury to benchmark internal hedges to transactions that could be realized in the financial market, and hence reflect the true cost of hedging.

This places the corporate treasury at the center of the firm's cash flow and risk management activities. Centralized treasury management promotes operational efficiency and reduces the risk that a divisional manager will put the entire company at risk with an ill-advised or redundant financial market hedge that could go awry.

> *Charge market prices for internal hedges.*

### Leading and Lagging

In some cases, altering the timing of cash flows can reduce transaction exposure. This process is known as ***leading and lagging***. For example, if a U.S. parent is short euros, euro repatriations from foreign subsidiaries to the parent can be accelerated. This is known as *leading*. Similarly, the U.S. parent can delay or *lag* euro payments to its foreign subsidiaries. Of course, the euro balances and risk exposures of the parent's subsidiaries will change accordingly. Like multinational netting, leading and lagging works best when the currency needs of individual units within the MNC offset one another.

**An External Market Example** In principle, altering the timing of internal cash flows is no different from altering the timing of external cash flows. External market transactions provide a performance benchmark for internal treasury transactions that is both reliable and relevant.

Suppose Rupert pays Anheuser-Busch $10 million every January, April, July, and October. Rupert also has cash inflows of $7.5 million every February, May, August, and November from an export sales contract with a partner in New York. Although he has denominated this contract in U.S. dollars to offset his dollar payables, Rupert has a mismatch in the timing of his dollar cash inflows and outflows. The timing of Rupert's cash flows is shown in Figure 9.2.

Rupert can synchronize his inflows and outflows if he can accelerate or *lead* his receivables by one month. This can be done in several ways.

- Factor: Sell receivables to the bank at a discount to the $7.5 million face value
- Borrow: Borrow $7.5 million for one month using receivables as collateral
- Renegotiate: Negotiate with his customer to receive payment one month earlier

In each alternative, Rupert will be giving up $7.5 million in one month for a lesser amount today. Rupert needs to calculate the ***all-in cost*** of each alternative

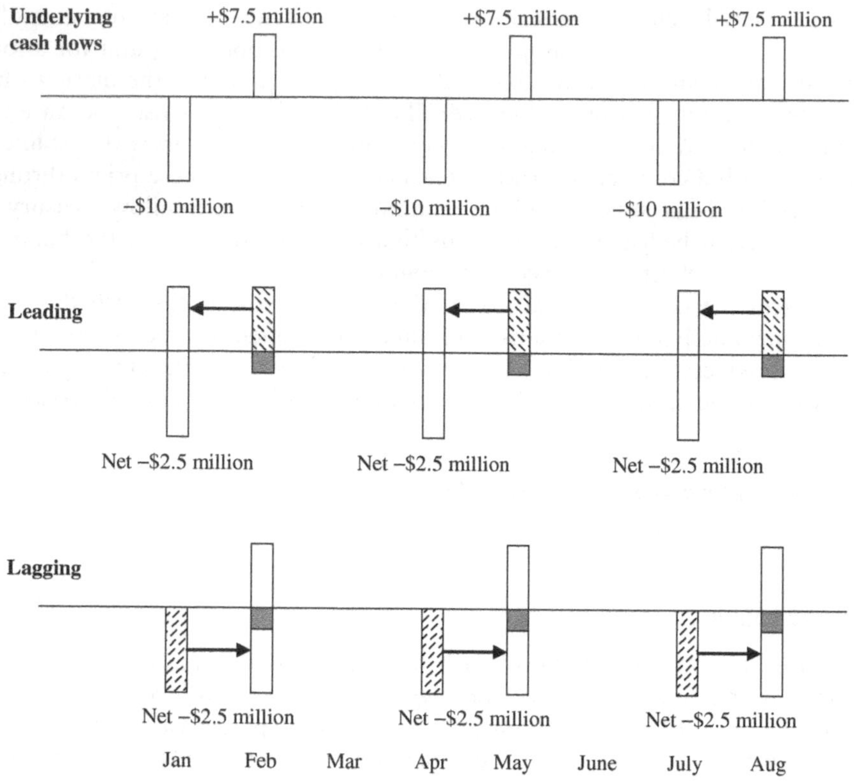


**Key:** Gross cash inflows and outflows appear in white. Net cash flows are shown in grey beside the gross cash flows.

**FIGURE 9.2** Leading and Lagging.

including any bank fees. All-in cost is the interest rate implied by size and timing of the cash flows, as shown here.

+$??? **All-in cost**

–$7,500,000

Suppose the cost of each alternative is as follows:

- Factor: The bank will buy the receivables for $7.48 million
- Borrow: The bank charges a monthly rate of 0.25 percent on a secured line of credit
- Renegotiate: The New York customer is willing to pay $7.46 one month early

The all-in cost of each alternative is then:

- Factor: ($7.5000/$7.4800) – 1 = 0.002674, or 0.2674 percent per month
- Borrow: ($7.5000/$7.4813) – 1 = 0.002500, or 0.2500 percent per month
- Renegotiate: ($7.5000/$7.4600) – 1 = 0.005362, or 0.5362 percent per month

Rupert's least cost alternative appears to be a bank loan at a monthly cost of 0.25 percent using accounts receivable as collateral. He'll receive ($7,500,000/1.0025) = $7,481,300 in cash today at the 0.25 percent per month discount rate. However, note that Rupert is exposed to the credit risk of his customer in this alternative. If the customer has significant credit risk, Rupert might prefer to sell his receivables to the bank without recourse (i.e., the bank accepts the credit risk of this receivable) for $7.48 million. If the factoring bank insists on recourse to Rupert in the case of a bad debt, then borrowing is the preferred alternative.

Alternatively, Rupert can negotiate with Anheuser-Busch to delay or *lag* his $10 million payable by one month. He'd then owe $2.5 million plus one month's interest on the lagged payable of $7.5 million every February, May, August, and November. Rupert will prefer this alternative if Anheuser-Busch's all-in cost of a late payment is less than Rupert's borrowing cost of 0.25 percent per month.

> *All-in cost is based on* all *cash flows associated with a transaction.*

This is an example of cash management with external partners. Treasury usually has even more control over the timing of internal transactions. With control over the timing of transfer payments within the MNC, treasury can smooth its cash flow streams in each currency and ensure that funds are available for each operating unit as needed.

**Internal Cash Management Systems** Although leading and lagging can be beneficial to the corporation as a whole, it can distort the rates of return earned by the various operating units. In essence, leading or lagging creates a loan from one unit of the firm to another. This calls for an internal recognition of the distortion caused by leading or lagging. The best alternative for solving the incentive problems created by leading or lagging is for treasury to recognize the cash flows of the operating units as they occur. Once the cash flows are paid or received, the onus of managing the timing of the cash flows can then be on treasury and not on the operating units.

> *Apply market interest rates when leading or lagging.*

Treasury should apply *market interest rates* whenever it alters the timing of intracompany cash flows. The market rate of interest depends on the time value of money and the riskiness of the cash flow. Selling a receivable to treasury is similar to factoring, in that the interest rate should reflect the credit risk of the cash flow. If a bank is willing to purchase 1-month receivables at an effective rate of 0.2674 percent per month as in the previous example, then the same rate should be applied to an operating unit when accelerating this cash flow internally. The unit that is selling its receivable to treasury (or to another unit) should be credited with $7.48 million today for a $7.5 million forgone receivable in one month. This benchmarks the cash flows to interest rates actually charged in the market on similar transactions.

Many national governments place limits on corporate leading and lagging. For example, Japan places a 360-day limit on leading and lagging. Most Latin American countries and many Asian countries place even more restrictive limits on leading and lagging and, in some cases, on multinational netting as well. There are no limits on leading and lagging activities in the United States, the United Kingdom, Canada, or Mexico. Managers should check local regulations before getting too aggressive with this cash management tool.

**Corporate Treasuries and Commercial Banks** Corporate treasuries manage cash flows in much the same way that commercial banks manage cash flows. Although large banks have higher transaction volumes than most corporations, treasury's cash management process is essentially the same as a bank's. Each tries to balance the size and timing of its cash flows to minimize external market transactions and risk exposures. Banks earn a profit on their bid-ask spreads. Corporate treasuries try to minimize the cost of funds while ensuring that cash is available for operations.

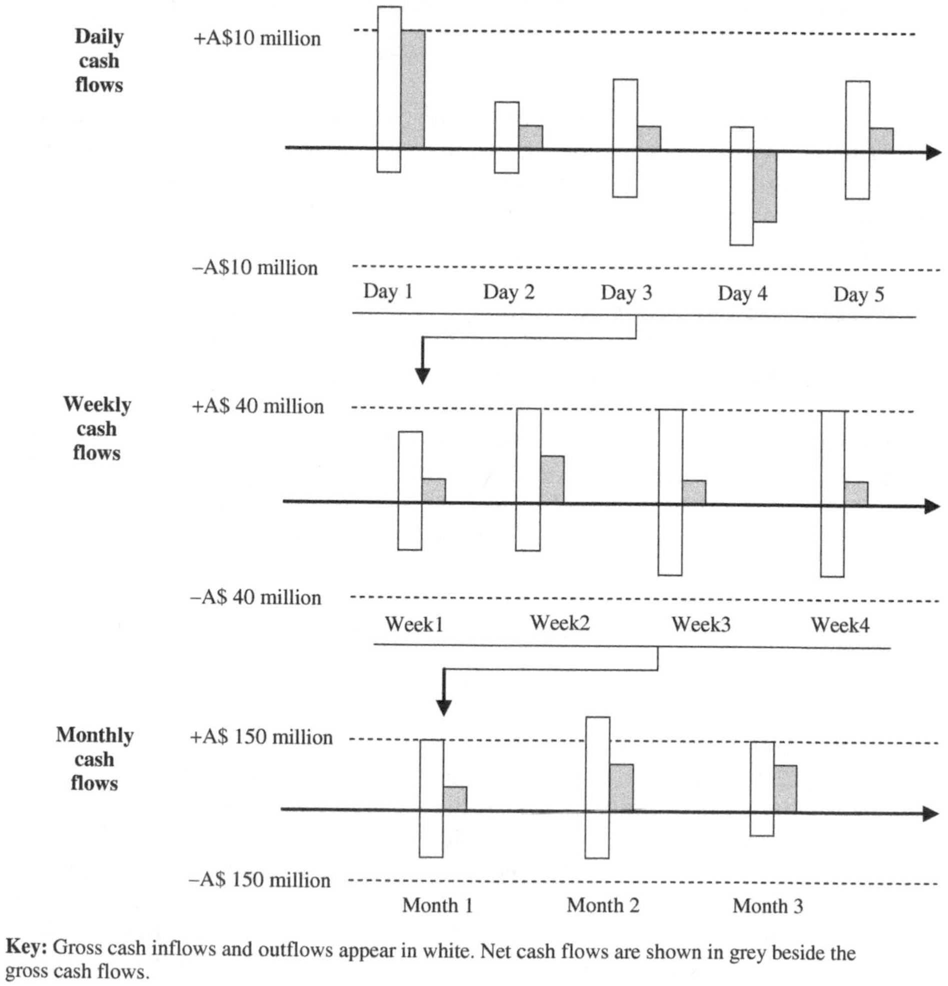


**FIGURE 9.3** A U.S. Bank's Exposures to the Australian Dollar.

Consider a U.S. bank's Australian dollar exposures as shown in Figure 9.3. In the top of the figure, the bank faces cash inflows of A$12 million and outflows of A$2 million on day 1 for a net cash inflow of +A$10 million. On day 2, inflows and outflows net to +A$2 million. During the first week, the bank expects to receive a total of A$30 million and pay A$20 million for a net inflow of A$10 million. The bank's expected daily cash flows are aggregated into expected weekly cash flows in the middle figure. During the first month, the bank expects to receive a total of A$150 million and pay A$100 million for an expected net monthly inflow of A$50 million, as shown in the bottom figure. Although this bank is negatively exposed to the Australian dollar over some periods (such as day 4), on balance this bank is positively exposed to the Australian dollar during the next several months.

Commercial banks make markets in interest rate and currency contracts—buying low and selling high—and make a profit on the difference. To minimize currency risk, they keep their net exposures to a minimum in each currency and at each forward date. To this end, banks keep track of their expected exposures on a daily basis out several months. Beyond that time, they track their exposures on a less frequent (e.g., weekly or monthly) basis. If the bank begins to accumulate an unbalanced position at a particular maturity in a foreign currency, it can hedge or lay off this exposure through the financial markets. For example, the U.S. bank in Figure 9.3 might reduce its exposure to currency risk by selling Australian dollars forward in weekly maturities for up to one month ahead and in monthly maturities beyond one month. The task facing the corporate treasury is in many ways the same as the task facing a large commercial bank, just on a smaller scale.

## 9.3 MANAGING TRANSACTION EXPOSURE IN FINANCIAL MARKETS

When the MNC's transaction exposures to currency risk do not offset internally, treasury must consider hedging its exposures in the financial markets. Financial market hedges are appropriate for hedging transaction exposures because the contractual payoffs of the financial market hedges can be matched to those of the underlying foreign currency transactions. The exposure of a foreign currency contract to an unexpected change in the value of that foreign currency is one-to-one, so identification and management of transaction exposure is relatively straightforward.

> *Financial hedges work well for transaction exposures.*

Figure 9.4 reviews the features of the financial market hedging instruments, which include currency forwards, currency futures, money market hedges, currency swaps, and currency options. More detailed discussions of currency futures, options, and swaps appear in the chapters dedicated to these derivative securities.

| Instrument | Advantages | Disadvantages |
|---|---|---|
| Currency forwards | Provide exact hedges of transactions of known date and amount (near-term or long-term) | Bid-ask spreads can be large, especially for small transactions, long maturities, and infrequently traded currencies |
| Currency futures | Provide an effective and low-cost hedge if the amount and maturity match the underlying exposure; a low-risk hedge because of daily marking-to-market and settlement by the futures exchange | Exchange-traded futures come in a limited number of currencies and maturities; daily marking-to-market sometimes can cause a cash flow mismatch with the underlying exposure |
| Money market hedges | Forward positions can be synthetically constructed in currencies for which there are no forward markets | A relatively expensive hedge because it entails at least one interest rate contract; might not be possible if there are constraints on foreign currency borrowing or lending |
| Currency swaps | Provides a low-cost switch into other currencies or payoff structures (e.g., fixed vs floating) | Innovative swaps are costly and difficult to value; not the best choice for one-time or near-term exposures |
| Currency options | "Disaster hedge" insures against unfavorable currency movements | Option premiums reflect option payoffs, so currency options can be costly |

**FIGURE 9.4** Financial Market Hedges of Transaction Exposures.

## APPLICATION Foreign Exchange Losses at Japan Air Lines

In 1985, Japan Air Lines (JAL) entered into a ten-year forward agreement to buy \$3.6 billion for ¥666 billion at a price of ¥666bn/\$3.6bn $\approx$ ¥185/\$. At the time of the forward agreement, the spot exchange rate was ¥240/\$. By October 1994, the dollar had fallen to ¥100/\$. If the contract had been settled in October 1994, Japan's national airline would have had to pay ¥666 billion for dollars worth only (\$3.6 billion)(¥100/\$) = ¥360 billion, which would have resulted in a ¥306 billion (or \$3.06 billion) forward exchange loss.

Since entering into this agreement, JAL had charged some of the foreign exchange losses against operating profits. However, as of October 1994 the extent of the losses had not been fully reported. In late 1994, the Japanese Ministry of Finance required exchange-listed Japanese companies to disclose unrealized gains or losses from forward currency trading. JAL had a ¥45 billion (\$450 million) unrealized loss at that time. JAL had been spending about ¥80 billion (\$800 million) each year on new airplanes, so its total loss on the forward contract was about half its annual budget for new airplanes.

There is good news for JAL, however. Although the falling dollar resulted in yen losses on JAL's short dollar forward contract, it also resulted in lower yen costs on airplanes that JAL was buying from U.S. manufacturers. Sensationalist news reports emphasized JAL's forex (FX) losses on the forward hedge, and usually neglected to mention the corresponding gains on the underlying exposure.

> Currency risk management can be a "damned if you do and damned if you don't" proposition for a financial manager. If exposures are left unhedged, exchange rates will move adversely about half the time and the manager will be open to criticism. If exposures are hedged, the financial manager can be criticized if exchange rates move in favor of the underlying exposure and against the hedge, as in the JAL case. The financial manager's best defense is to make sure that hedges are clearly associated with an underlying exposure and executed in a manner that is consistent with the firm's overall financial policies.

## Hedging with Currency Forwards

Currency forward contracts are simple and yet powerful instruments for hedging exposures to currency risk. Consider Rupert Taylor's U.S. dollar forward obligation.

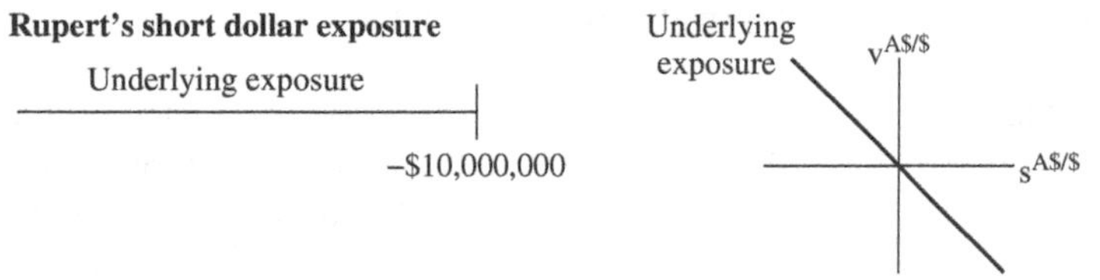


Rupert can hedge his forward obligation with a ***currency forward*** contract of $10 million. In the forward contract, a long forward position of $10 million is offset by a short forward position of A$16 million at the 3-month forward rate of $F_1^{A\$/\$}$ = A$1.60/$. The combination of Rupert's underlying exposure with the forward market hedge results in no net U.S. dollar exposure.

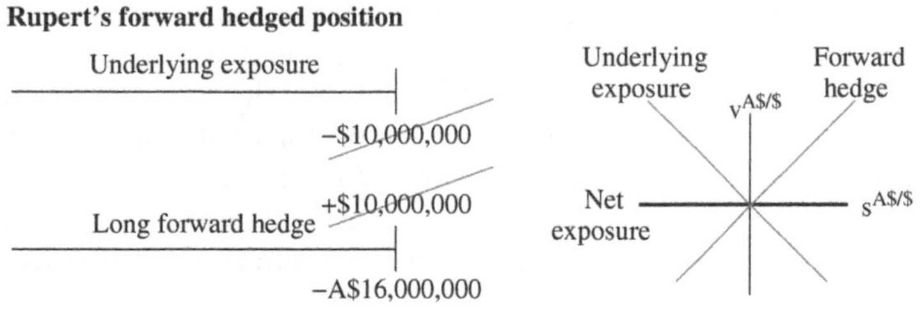


Regardless of the spot rate, Rupert will have locked in a payment of A$16 million for his beer. He will make an operating profit if he can sell the beer in Australia for more than A$16 million.

**Partial Hedges** Many MNCs choose to hedge only a fraction of their exposures. Rupert might choose a partial hedge if he anticipates a depreciation of the U.S. dollar. Suppose Rupert decides to hedge 50 cents of every dollar of underlying exposure. This partial hedge can be accomplished with a $5 million long forward position. Here is Rupert's resulting net exposure:

**Rupert's forward hedged position (50 percent cover)**

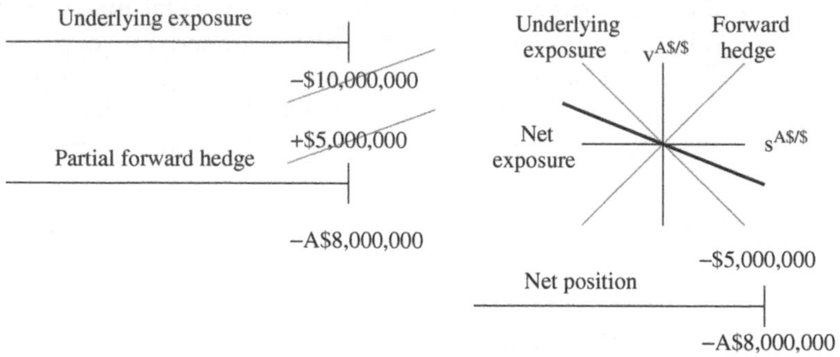


A survey by Bodnar, Hayt, and Marston found that U.S. firms typically hedge about 50 percent of near-term transaction exposures, such as Rupert's 3-month dollar obligation.[2] Only a third of U.S. firms hedged more than 75 percent of their total near-term transaction exposures to currency risk.

**Currency Speculation** If Rupert anticipates an appreciation of the U.S. dollar, he might be tempted to buy more than $10 million forward. However, this would tilt the nature of his business away from beer distribution and toward currency speculation. The value of this particular transaction might then depend more on the exchange rate and less on his beer sales within Australia. Unless Rupert feels he has some special skill in forecasting exchange rates, he is probably better off sticking to what he knows best.

### Hedging with Currency Futures

Hedging with a currency futures contract is similar to hedging with a currency forward contract. Exchange-traded ***currency futures*** contracts come in standard currencies, amounts, and settlement dates. Over-the-counter futures contracts offered by commercial and investment banks can be tailored to the size, timing, and currency needs of the customer. Whereas gains or losses on forward contracts are settled at maturity, futures contracts are settled or *marked-to-market* based on daily changes in exchange rates. Aside from this difference, a currency futures position can be used to hedge foreign exchange exposure in the same way as a currency forward contract.

> *Futures are like forwards with daily marking-to-market.*

If a forward or futures hedge is expensive or simply unavailable in a particular currency, a ***currency cross hedge*** can be formed using a related currency. Suppose Rupert is importing beer from Canada and wants to hedge his Canadian dollar obligation due in three months. Bid-ask spreads on C$ forwards are much wider than on U.S. dollar forwards because of lower trading volume in Canadian dollars, especially on small transactions such as Rupert's. If Canadian dollar futures are unavailable, then Rupert needs an alternative way to hedge his obligation.

The value of the Canadian dollar is highly correlated with the U.S. dollar, so a cross hedge using actively traded U.S. dollar forward or futures contracts can eliminate most of Rupert's exposure to the Canadian dollar. A cross hedge using a related currency sometimes can cost less than a hedge in a thinly traded currency and can be nearly as effective, depending on the correlation between the exposed and the cross-hedged currencies.

## Money Market Hedges

Forward or futures contracts are sometimes unavailable or prohibitively expensive for distant expiration dates in thinly traded currencies. In these circumstances, it is sometimes possible to form a ***money market hedge*** that replicates the forward exchange rate through the spot currency and Eurocurrency markets. A money market hedge is a form of *synthetic* or *homemade* forward contract constructed from other financial instruments.

***Money market hedges can replicate forward hedges.***

As an example, Rupert can replicate a long dollar forward contract and hedge his dollar obligation due in three months by: (1) borrowing Australian dollars from his local bank for three months, (2) converting Australian dollars to U.S. dollars in the spot market, and (3) investing the resulting U.S. dollars in a 3-month Eurodollar interest rate contract.

**Rupert's money market hedge**

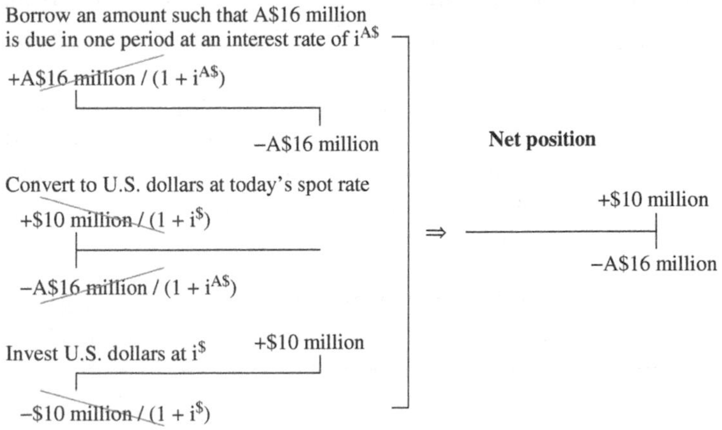


Each of the time lines on the left represents a quarterly contract in the interest rate parity relation, $S_0^{A\$/\$}[(1 + i^{A\$})/(1 + i^{\$})] = F_1^{A\$/\$}$. In combination, the three contracts on the left replicate the payoff on a long U.S. dollar forward contract on the right of the equation.

In practice, the last two legs of this hedge are sufficient to eliminate the foreign exchange risk of Rupert's underlying dollar obligation. An *uncovered money market hedge* results from omitting the first of the three transactions.

**Rupert's uncovered money market hedge**

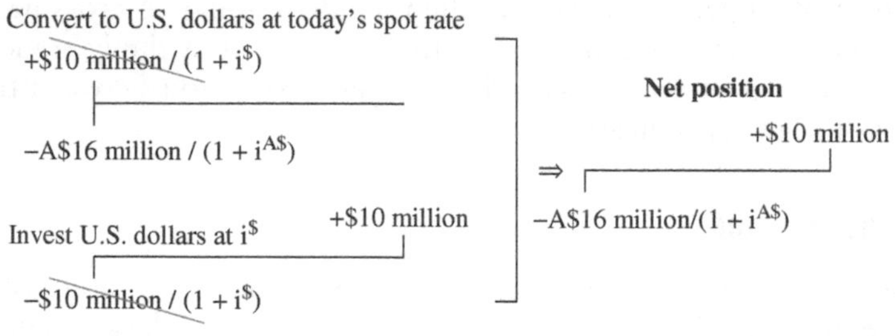


This reduces Rupert's transaction costs on the hedge, while ensuring him of a $10 million cash inflow in three months. This forward cash inflow exactly offsets his underlying U.S. dollar exposure. The uncovered position differs from the money market hedge only in the timing of Rupert's A$ obligation; rather than paying A$16 million in three months, Rupert would pay the present value of A$16 million today.

## Hedging with Currency Swaps

Forwards, futures, and money market hedges can hedge a single foreign currency cash flow. The exposure of a contract that calls for periodic cash flows in a foreign currency can be hedged with a portfolio of forwards or futures of varying maturities. Alternatively, long-term contracts with periodic foreign cash flows can be hedged with a single contract—a ***currency swap***—in which two counterparties agree to swap currencies on a periodic basis for a fixed period of time.

> *A currency swap is an agreement to trade interest payments in two currencies.*

Suppose Anheuser-Busch holds a contract with a distributor in Taiwan calling for quarterly payments of 340 million in new Taiwan dollars (T$) over the next five years. This contract is denominated in new Taiwan dollars, rather than U.S. dollars as in Anheuser-Busch's Australian contract. Promised cash flows from this contract expose Anheuser-Busch to the $S^{\$/T\$}$ spot rate.

**Underlying Taiwan dollar exposures**

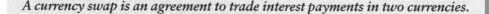

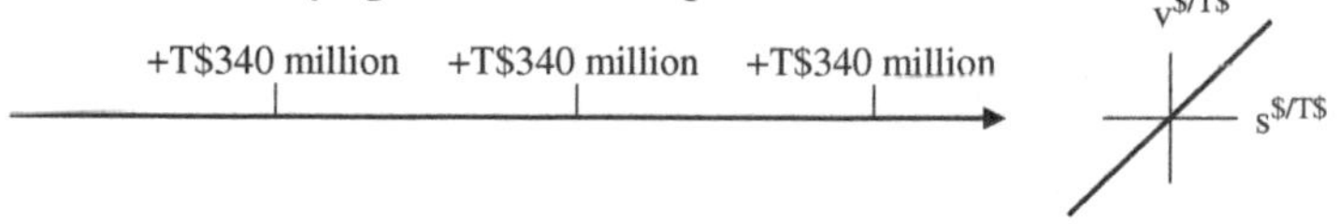


Anheuser-Busch could agree to make quarterly payments of T$340 million over five years to a swap bank (a commercial or investment bank making a market in currency swaps) in exchange for quarterly payments of $10 million from the swap bank. Anheuser-Busch's cash flows on this swap transaction would look like this.

**Currency swap hedge**

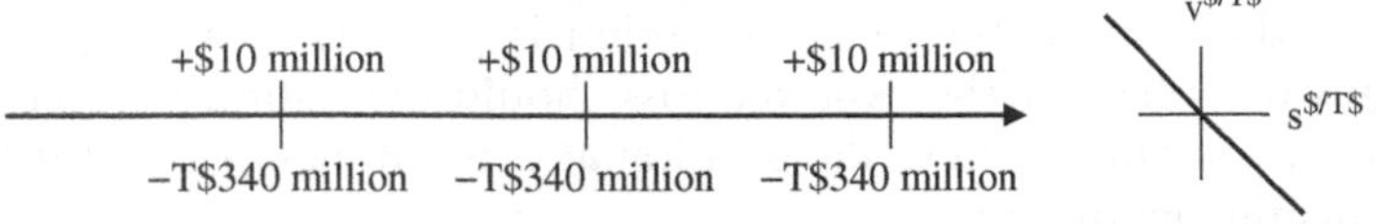


When combined with Anheuser-Busch's underlying exposure to the Taiwan dollar, the net result is a stream of $10 million payments every three months for the next five years.

**Hedged position**

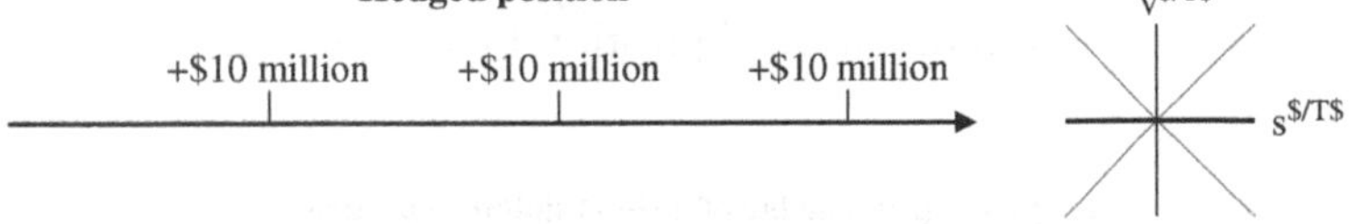


Currency swaps such as this can quickly and inexpensively change a foreign currency liability into a domestic currency liability, or vice versa. Commercial and investment banks maintain an active international market in interest rate and currency swaps.

## Hedging with Currency Options

Gains and losses on currency forwards, futures, swaps, and money market hedges are symmetric around the forward exchange rate, and so these financial market hedges often are used to minimize the variability of a hedged position. ***Currency options*** have a somewhat different role to play. A ***currency call option*** gives the buyer (or holder) of the option the right but not the obligation to *buy* an underlying currency at a contractually determined ***exercise price*** or exchange rate on (or perhaps before) a contractually determined ***expiration date.*** The seller (or writer) of the option has the obligation to deliver the specified currency at the exercise price. Conversely, a ***currency put option*** gives the buyer the right to *sell* an underlying currency at the exercise price. The option writer then has the obligation to buy the currency at the exercise price.

> *Currency options can insure against adverse currency moves.*

This asymmetry between the buyer's option and the seller's obligation results in the following payoff profile at the expiration of a dollar call with an exercise price of A$1.60/$[3]:

**A long call option on the U.S. dollar**

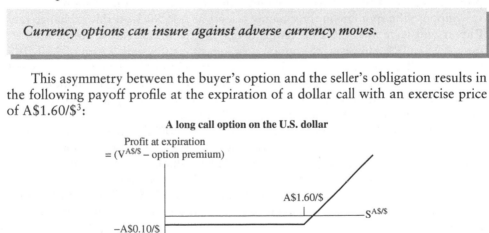

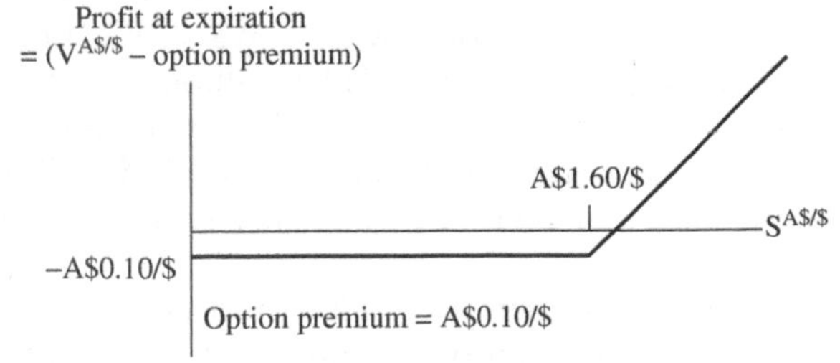

The ***option premium*** of A$0.10/$ is the price of the option and is paid by the buyer to the seller at the time the option is purchased. The option premium compensates the seller for the expected loss should the option be exercised by the buyer. The y-axis is the profit of the position at expiration, equal to the value of the option minus the option premium.

Because of their asymmetric payoffs, currency options can be used as an insurance policy against an adverse movement in a foreign currency value. For example, Rupert can hedge his short exposure to the U.S. dollar at a 3-month maturity with a 3-month call option on the U.S. dollar. If the exercise price at which currencies are exchanged is set equal to the expected future spot rate of $E[S_1^{A\$/\$}] = F_1^{A\$/\$}$ = A$1.60/$, the resulting hedged position looks like this.

**A long call option hedge of a short dollar exposure**

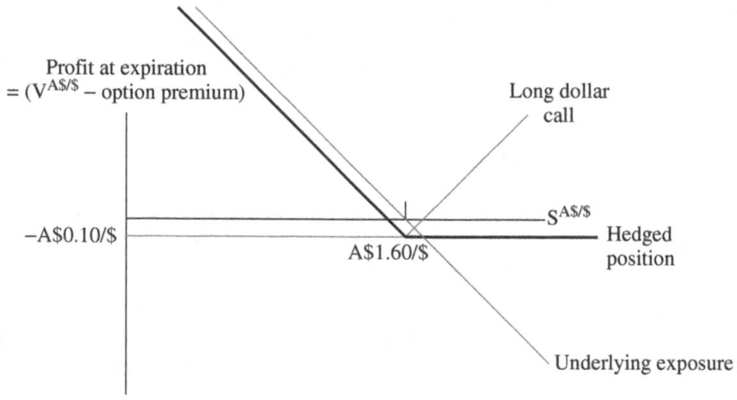


If the U.S. dollar rises above A$1.60/$ in three months, Rupert has an option to buy $10 million at the exercise price of A$1.60/$. Any loss on the underlying position is then offset by a corresponding gain on the call option position.

Suppose the spot rate in three months closes at A$1.80/$. At this exchange rate, Rupert will have lost A$0.20/$ on his underlying position relative to the forward rate of A$1.60/$. However, the option position offsets this with a gain of A$0.20/$, because he'll own an option to buy dollars at A$1.60/$ when they are worth A$1.80/$ in the market. Rupert's total A$ obligation is then A$17 million: A$16 million for the underlying $10 million obligation at A$1.60/$, plus (A$0.10/$)($10 million) = A$1 million for the U.S. dollar call option.

On the other hand, if the spot rate closes at A$1.40/$ in three months, Rupert's A$ obligation on his $10 million exposure will be (A$1.40/$)($10 million) = A$14 million. He also will have paid (A$0.10/$)($10 million) = $1 million for a call option that has no value (i.e., an option to buy dollars at A$1.60/$ when the market price is only A$1.40/$). His total obligation is thus A$15 million: A$14 million for the underlying obligation at A$1.40/$, plus A$1 million for the call option at A$0.10/$.

The bottom line is this: If Rupert hedges his short dollar exposure with a long dollar call option, he'll be paying an option premium for insurance or protection against a rise in the value of the dollar.

## 9.4 TREASURY MANAGEMENT IN PRACTICE

This section discusses best practices in treasury management of currency risk.

### Derivatives Usage by Nonfinancial Corporations

Corporations use derivatives primarily for hedging rather than for speculation. Recent research suggests that derivatives used in this way can reduce a firm's sensitivity to financial price risks and perhaps increase firm value as well.[4] But what types of firms use derivatives to hedge? And what types of hedges do they use?

Bartram, Brown and Fehle examined risk management practices in more than 7,000 nonfinancial firms from 50 countries and accounting for 80 percent of global market capitalization.[5] Not surprisingly, these authors found that firms were much more likely to use derivatives if they resided in a country with easy access to derivatives markets. Firms from less developed economies were less likely to use derivatives to hedge their exposures to financial price risks.

Bartram et al. also found that currency derivatives were the most frequently used derivative product, particularly in less developed markets. Figure 9.5 compares derivatives usage of firms from developed countries that are members of the OECD with derivatives usage of firms from non-OECD countries. About 64 percent of firms from OECD member countries used derivatives, whereas only 40 percent of firms in non-OECD countries used derivatives. Firms from non-OECD countries also placed a heavier reliance on currency derivatives than on interest rate derivatives, whereas interest rate derivatives were used nearly as much as currency derivatives in developed economies. Derivatives users also tended to be larger and more profitable firms.

*Derivatives users tend to be large firms.*

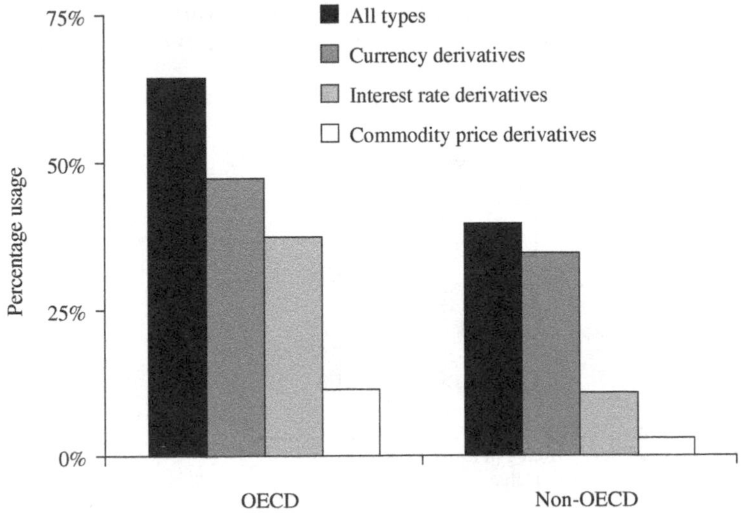


**FIGURE 9.5** Derivatives Usage by Nonfinancial Corporations.
Source: Bartram, Brown, and Fehle, "International Evidence on Financial Derivatives Usage," *Financial Management* (2009). OECD stands for the Organisation for Economic Co-operation and Development (www.oecd.org).

Bodnar, Hayt, and Marston surveyed U.S. corporations and found similar evidence that derivatives usage is strongly related to firm size. These authors report the following usage rates[6]:

- Large firms (83 percent)
- Medium-sized firms (45 percent)
- Small firms (12 percent)

Among those firms using derivatives, usage rates depended on the type of risk exposure. Currency risk again was the most commonly hedged risk, closely followed by interest rate risk.

- Currency risk (83 percent)
- Interest rate risk (76 percent)
- Commodity price risk (56 percent)

Firms tended to hedge their transaction exposures to currency risk before their operating or translation exposures, because transaction exposures are easier to identify and to hedge with derivatives. Firms tended not to hedge the full amount of their exposures. The average amount hedged was less than 50 percent for all types of currency risk exposures, including transaction exposure (40–49 percent), operating exposure (7 percent), and translation exposure (12 percent). A large majority of derivatives users (89 percent) centralized their currency risk management activities.

*Most firms centralize their risk management activities.*

## Active Management of Currency Risk

It is difficult to consistently outperform the market's exchange rate expectations. Nevertheless, most financial managers incorporate their view of the market into

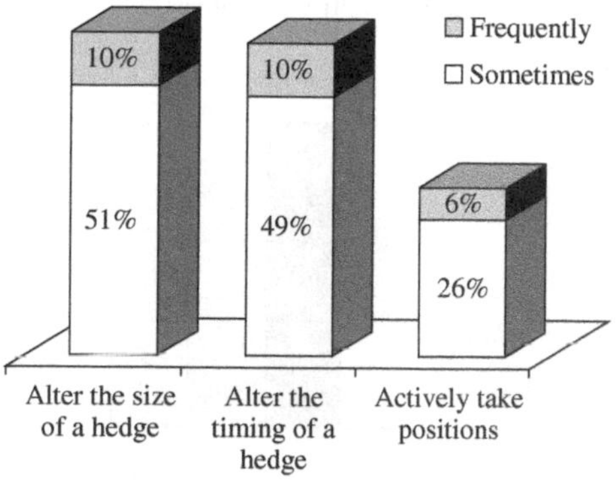


**FIGURE 9.6** Active Currency Risk Management.
Source: Bodnar, Hayt, and Marston, "1998 Wharton Survey of Financial Risk Management by U.S. Non-Financial Firms," *Financial Management* (1998).

their risk management decisions. Figure 9.6 presents Bodnar, Hayt, and Marston's findings on the extent of active management among corporate users of financial derivatives.

About 10 percent of U.S. derivatives users report that they "frequently" alter the size or timing of their financial hedges based on their market expectations. Many more firms "sometimes" alter the size (51 percent) or timing (49 percent) of their hedges based on their market view. Nearly a third of respondents stated they "actively take positions," although the survey did not ask whether these positions were risk-reducing or speculative in nature. A large proportion of U.S. firms actively manage their FX exposures. Active FX risk management is the norm in other countries as well.[7]

> *Most firms actively manage FX exposures*

**Benchmarking the Performance of an Actively Managed Hedge** Firms that actively manage their exposures need to evaluate their performance against a benchmark. As shown in Figure 9.7, 42 percent of firms benchmarked their hedges against forward rates. Forward rates are a simple and appropriate benchmark, as they reflect the market's view of future spot rates through forward parity, and the opportunity costs of capital in the foreign and domestic currencies through interest rate parity. Another 17 percent of firms benchmarked their performance against a baseline that was less than 100 percent of the amount exposed. Still another 17 percent used some other form of benchmark, such as an unhedged position or an option hedge.

Curiously, 24 percent of firms that benchmarked used the beginning-of-period spot rate to evaluate their hedging performance. The random nature of exchange rate movements makes this appropriate only for short-term exposures. Forward rates are generally preferable as benchmarks, because they reflect market prices for future exchange as well as the relative opportunity costs of capital. Using the current

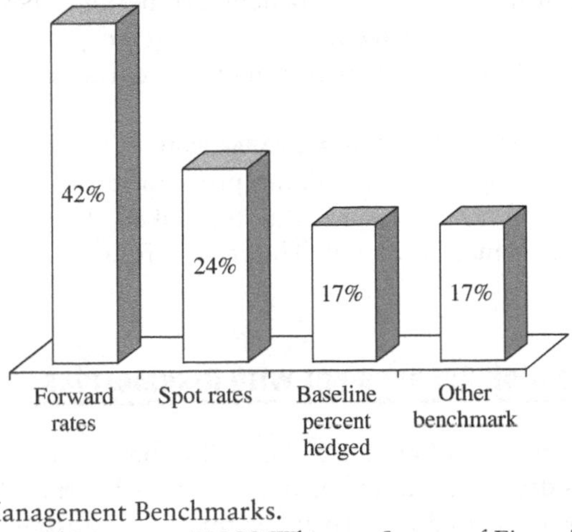


**FIGURE 9.7** Risk Management Benchmarks.
Source: Bodnar, Hayt, and Marston, "1998 Wharton Survey of Financial Risk Management by U.S. Non-Financial Firms," *Financial Management* (1998).

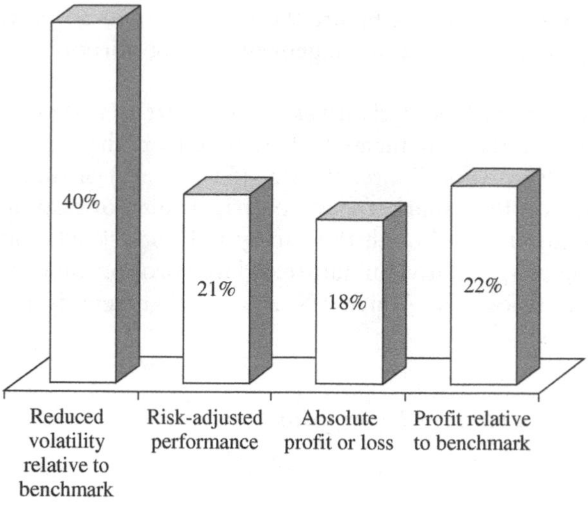


**FIGURE 9.8** Evaluation of Risk Management Performance.
Source: Bodnar, Hayt, and Marston, ibid.

spot rate as the benchmark fails to reflect the market's expectations of future spot rates, inflation differences, or the relative opportunity costs of capital.

*Forward rates are a simple and appropriate benchmark.*

About 40 percent of respondents in the survey managed their currency risk exposures in a passive manner. Correspondingly, about 44 percent of firms in the survey indicated that they did not benchmark their hedging performance. One can only hope that these firms choose not to benchmark because they have decided, after a thorough review by top management, that a passive hedging approach to currency risk management is sufficient for their risk management needs.

**Evaluating the Performance of Active Risk Management** Once a benchmark is selected, the performance of a hedge or of a hedging program must be evaluated according to some criterion. Bodnar, Hayt, and Marston asked derivatives users how they evaluate the risk management function. The results are reported in Figure 9.8.

**MARKET UPDATE Risk Assessment with RiskMetrics**

Growth in derivatives trading since the 1980s has been truly phenomenal. Unfortunately, as derivatives have become a standard part of the financial manager's toolkit, losses related to derivatives trading correspondingly increased. The early 1990s saw a rising call by industry watchdogs and policymakers for risk management standards, and consistency and transparency in measuring and reporting risks related to derivative transactions.

In 1994, investment banker J.P. Morgan began providing free access to a central component of its internal *RiskMetrics* system for measuring financial risks. This product proved to be hugely popular, and *RiskMetrics* was spun off from J.P. Morgan in 1998, listed on the NYSE in 2005, and then acquired by MSCI (www.msci.com) in 2010. *RiskMetrics* now provides users with up-to-date data on several hundred financial prices, including interest rates, exchange rates, commodities, and equity market indices. The system estimates time-varying volatilities and correlations between indices, and is designed to assist users in assessing their exposures to financial price risks. *RiskMetrics*' objective in providing access to the system is to promote greater transparency, so that financial managers can concentrate on developing informed risk management strategies. For a fee, *RiskMetrics* will fine-tune the system to a particular user's needs.

Computers and statistical analysis are central to measurement, management, and control of the risks that come with derivative use. Yet statistical analysis cannot replace good judgment. As the *Introduction to RiskMetrics* states in bold print on page 1:

> "*We remind our readers that no amount of sophisticated analytics will replace experience and professional judgment in managing risks.*"

"Risk reduction relative to a benchmark" was the performance criterion in 40 percent of the firms. These firms believe that risk reduction was the overriding objective in their risk management operations. However, a majority of firms included some measure of profit or loss in their performance criteria. The objective "risk-adjusted performance" (profits or savings adjusted for volatility), "absolute profit or loss," or "increased profits (or reduced costs) relative to a benchmark" was used in more than 60 percent of firms. The latter two criteria are strictly profit-based and were used in 40 percent of firms. This is a surprising result, as a profit-based performance criterion can encourage financial managers to actively take positions in the currency markets, rather than use the markets to reduce the risk exposures of the firm's operating units. Evaluating managers based on the profitability of their positions relative to a benchmark can encourage them to seek, rather than avoid, risk.

Géczy, Minton, and Schrand extend the Wharton survey to investigate the characteristics of managers and firms that use derivatives to "take a view" on interest rate or currency movements.[8] Managers that actively take positions believe they possess informational or cost advantages that provide them with a competitive advantage in anticipating financial price movements. Firms encourage managers to take positions through compensation contracts that align the objectives of managers with those of the firm, and use derivatives-specific controls such as performance benchmarks to manage potential abuses. Managers' ability to take positions also tends to be closely monitored and controlled by top management. Firms that actively manage their derivatives positions tend to be large firms with centralized risk management, use sophisticated valuation methodologies such as value-at-risk for managing their risk exposures, and frequently (often daily) mark their derivatives positions to market. These are active corporate treasuries that specialize in interest rate or currency risk management, depending on the firm's underlying economic exposures.

*Active managers tend to be closely monitored.*

## 9.5 SUMMARY

Transaction exposure to currency risk is defined as change in the value of a contractual cash flow due to an unexpected change in an exchange rate. Transaction exposure is hard to ignore because the value of a monetary asset denominated in a foreign currency moves one-for-one with a change in the foreign exchange rate. For this reason, financial managers rank transaction exposure as the MNC's most important exposure to currency risk.

Transaction exposures first should be offset within the firm. Once this is done, the financial manager must choose which of the firm's net transaction exposures to hedge and how much of each net exposure to hedge. Financial market hedges include

- Currency forwards (the basic building block of derivative instruments)
- Currency futures (like forwards, but marked-to-market daily)
- Money market hedges (synthetic forwards)
- Currency options (insurance against extreme currency movements)
- Currency swaps (used for repeated, long-term exposures)

It is imperative that top management be involved in establishing and administering the firm's risk management policies. Managerial oversight is necessary to ensure that risk management is implemented in a way that supports, rather than competes with, the firm's core businesses.

Corporations that use derivatives to manage their currency exposures tend to be large MNCs with geographically diversified operations. These large MNCs usually centralize their treasury activities to allow them to most effectively manage their cross-currency cash flows. Many of these firms actively manage their exposures and their hedges, with careful oversight of managers involved in the hedging function. Others take a more passive approach to currency risk management. For both active and passive hedgers, it is important to identify a benchmark hedging strategy against which to compare treasury's hedging performance.

## KEY TERMS

*all-in cost*
*currency cross hedge*
*currency forwards*
*currency futures*
*currency options (calls and puts)*
*currency swaps*
*exercise price*
*expiration date*
*leading and lagging*
*money market hedge*
*multinational netting*
*option premium*
*risk (payoff) profile*
*transaction exposure*

## CONCEPTUAL QUESTIONS

9.1 What is transaction exposure to currency risk?

9.2 What is a risk profile?

9.3 In what ways can diversified multinational operations provide a natural hedge of transaction exposure to currency risk?

9.4 What is multinational netting? Why is it used by MNCs?

9.5 What is leading and lagging? Why is it used by MNCs?

9.6 Define or give an example of each of the following: (a) currency forwards, (b) currency futures, (c) currency options, (d) currency swaps, and (e) money market hedges.

9.7 What is a currency cross hedge? Why might it be used?

9.8 Do a majority of firms actively manage their currency risk exposures?

## PROBLEMS

9.1 Refer to the following set of transactions. Identify cash flows after netting of internal transactions.

| | Paying affiliate | | | | Total | Net | Net |
|---|---|---|---|---|---|---|---|
| Receiving affiliate | U.S. | Can. | Mex. | P.R. | receipt | receipt | payments |
| United States | 0 | $300 | $500 | $600 | _____ | _____ | _____ |
| Canada | $500 | 0 | $400 | $200 | _____ | _____ | _____ |
| Mexico | $400 | $700 | 0 | $200 | _____ | _____ | _____ |
| Puerto Rico | $400 | $900 | $400 | $0 | _____ | _____ | _____ |
| Total payments | _____ | | | | _____ | _____ | _____ |

9.2 Refer to the set of transactions in the graph that follows. Identify the net transactions within this system by filling in the following table. Draw a new set of transactions to identify which division pays funds and which division receives funds after multinational netting of transactions.

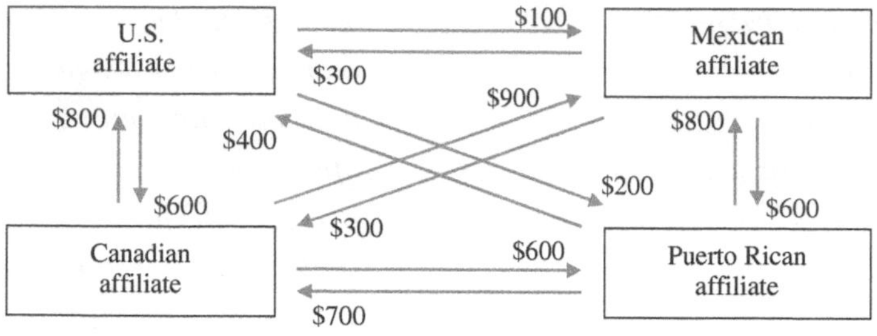


| | Paying affiliate | | | | Total | Net | Net |
|---|---|---|---|---|---|---|---|
| Receiving affiliate | U.S. | Can. | Mex. | P.R. | receipt | receipt | payments |
| United States | | | | | _____ | _____ | _____ |
| Canada | | | | | _____ | _____ | _____ |
| Mexico | | | | | _____ | _____ | _____ |
| Puerto Rico | | | | | _____ | _____ | _____ |
| Total payments | | | | | _____ | _____ | _____ |

9.3 You have recently graduated from college and accepted a position in the receivables division of Ex-Im-Age Corporation, a software company located in California and specializing in language-independent, icon-based software. Ex-Im-Age has just made a large sale to Germany and has a euro-denominated accounts receivable balance of €1,000,000 that is expected to be received in six months.

a. Represent Ex-Im-Age's euro exposure as a risk profile showing: (i) the dollar value of the euro receivable ($V^{\$/€}$) as a function of the dollar value of the euro ($S^{\$/€}$), and (ii) change in the dollar value of the euro receivable ($\Delta V^{\$/€}$) as a function of change in the dollar value of the euro ($\Delta S^{\$/€}$).
b. Using risk profiles, show how Ex-Im-Age's euro exposure can be hedged with each of the following: (i) a currency forward contract, (ii) a currency futures contract, (iii) a money market hedge, and (iv) a currency option contract.

9.4 It is February 14, and Rupert Taylor has an obligation to pay Anheuser-Busch $5 million on May 13. Rupert's bank quotes "A$1.6010/$ Bid and A$1.6020/$ Ask" in the spot market and "A$1.6025/$ Bid and A$1.6035/$ Ask" for forward exchange on May 13. Rupert must pay the bank's ask price if he wants to buy dollars from the bank. Evaluate each of the following statements:

a. The dollar is selling at a forward premium, so Rupert is better off buying dollars in the spot market rather than in the forward market.
b. If Rupert expects the dollar to close below the forward ask price of A$1.6035/$, he should hedge his entire $5 million exposure by purchasing dollars forward.

c. If Rupert expects the dollar to close above A$1.6035/$, he should hedge his entire $5 million exposure by purchasing dollars forward.
d. If Rupert expects the dollar to close above the forward ask price of A$1.6035/$, he should buy even more than $5 million in the forward market in the expectation of making a profit on the difference between the actual spot exchange rate in three months and his forward exchange rate from the bank.
e. Within the next month, Rupert anticipates incurring an additional $5 million obligation that also will be payable on May 13. Rupert should not hedge more than his original $5 million exposure even if he expects the dollar to close above the bank's forward asking price of A$1.6035/$.

9.5 Given the same information as in Problem 9.4, answer the following questions:

a. How can Rupert hedge his dollar exposure with a currency futures contract? What is the difference between a futures contract and a forward contract? Does the currency futures contract need to be traded on an Australian exchange?
b. How can Rupert replicate a long forward position with a money market hedge? What is the likely cost of such a hedge compared with a currency forward hedge?
c. How can Rupert hedge his dollar exposure with a currency option?
d. Suppose Rupert expects a dollar exposure of about $5 million every three months until his distribution contract with Anheuser-Busch expires in five years. How can Rupert hedge his dollar exposure with a currency swap?

9.6 Suppose $S_0^{\$/£} = \$1.25/£$, $F_1^{\$/£} = \$1.2/£$, $i^{£} = 11.56\%$, and $i^{\$} = 9.82\%$. You are to receive £100,000 on a shipment of Madonna albums in one year. You want to fix the amount you must pay in dollars to avoid foreign exchange risk.

a. Form a forward market hedge. Identify which currency you are buying and which currency you are selling forward. When will currency actually change hands—today or in one year?
b. Form a money market hedge that replicates the payoff on the forward contract by using the spot currency and Eurocurrency markets. Identify each contract in the hedge. Does this hedge eliminate your exposure to foreign exchange risk?
c. Are these currency and Eurocurrency markets in equilibrium? How would you arbitrage the difference from the parity condition? (Refer to interest rate parity in Chapter 4.)

## SUGGESTED READINGS

### Studies of firms' hedging policies and practices appear in

Söhnke M. Bartram, Gregory W. Brown, and Frank R. Fehle, "International Evidence on Financial Derivatives Usage," *Financial Management* 38 (Spring 2009), 185–206.

Gordon M. Bodnar and Gunther Gebhardt, "Derivatives Usage in Risk Management by U.S. and German Non-Financial Firms: A Comparative Survey," *Journal of International Financial Management & Accounting* 10 (Autumn 1999), 153–187.

Gordon M. Bodnar, Gregory S. Hayt, and Richard C. Marston, "1998 Wharton Survey of Financial Risk Management by U.S. Non-Financial Firms," *Financial Management* 27 (Winter 1998), 70–91.

Christopher C. Géczy, Bernadette A. Minton, and Catherine M. Schrand, "Taking a View: Corporate Speculation, Governance, and Compensation," *Journal of Finance* 62 (October 2007), 2405–2443.

Peter MacKay and Sara B. Moeller, "The Value of Corporate Risk Management," *Journal of Finance* 62 (June 2007), 1379–1419.

CHAPTER 10

# Managing Operating Exposure to Currency Risk

*To get anywhere, or even to live a long time, a man has to guess, and guess right, over and over again, without enough data for a logical answer.*
—Robert Heinlein, *Time Enough for Love*

Transaction exposure is the most visible currency risk exposure and commands the most attention from financial managers. Operating exposure is less visible than transaction exposure, but is often the more important long-term exposure. Operating exposure to currency risk is defined as change in the value of *nonmonetary* cash flows (that is, the noncontractual cash flows of the firm's real assets) due to unexpected changes in exchange rates. Although operating exposure is more difficult to measure and manage than transaction exposure, it is the more important long-term exposure because it involves the firm's core business activities.

## 10.1 OPERATING EXPOSURES TO CURRENCY RISK

*Operating exposure refers to operating cash flow sensitivity to forex (FX) rates.*

Operating exposure refers to changes in the value of operating cash flows generated by the firm's real assets due to unexpected changes in one or more foreign currency values. Real assets include physical assets, such as plant and equipment. Real assets also include human assets, such as key managerial and technical personnel and the organizational structure that binds them together.

### Operating Exposure and the Competitive Environment

Operating exposures depend on the firm's operating environment and on those of its competitors.

**Market Segmentation versus Integration** Operating exposure to currency risk depends on the extent of market segmentation or integration for the firm's inputs and outputs. In an ***integrated market***, purchasing power parity (PPP) holds so that equivalent assets trade for the same price regardless of where they are traded. If PPP does not hold across two markets, then the markets are at least partially ***segmented***. This integration/segmentation continuum also exists in markets for financial assets and liabilities. Common causes of market segmentation in markets for goods and services include transportation costs, information costs or barriers, legal or institutional frictions, governmental intervention in the form of taxes or tariffs, and other barriers to the free flow of goods or labor.

> ***Prices in segmented markets are isolated from other markets.***

Prices in globally integrated markets are determined by worldwide supply and demand. Domestic prices in an integrated market fluctuate with exchange rates, such that PPP is maintained across international markets. In contrast, when markets are completely segmented from other markets, prices are determined entirely in the local market. Real-world prices typically fall somewhere between these two extremes. For example, labor costs tend to be determined by local supply and demand, whereas the prices of actively traded financial assets (currencies, interest rates, and financial claims on oil or gold) are determined by supply and demand in global markets.

**Market Integration/Segmentation and Price Determination** Figure 10.1 classifies firms according to whether revenues and expenses are determined locally or in a competitive global marketplace. The degree of market integration determines the extent to which the values of the firm's real assets move with foreign exchange rates. The foreign currency exposures that characterize domestic firms, importers, exporters, and globally competitive firms are indicated in parentheses in the quadrants of Figure 10.1.

Domestic firms with revenues and operating expenses that are locally determined (upper-left quadrant of the figure) are the least sensitive to currency movements. This is the case when local factor and product markets are segmented from foreign markets. For example, service industries that rely heavily on local labor are relatively insensitive to currency fluctuations. When labor is relatively immobile across national

| | | Revenues | |
|---|---|---|---|
| | | Local | Global |
| Operating expenses | Local | Domestic firms (zero exposure to $s^{d/f}$) | Exporters (positively exposed to $s^{d/f}$) |
| | Global | Importers (negatively exposed to $s^{d/f}$) | Global multinational corporations (MNCs) and importers or exporters of globally priced good (exposure could be +, –, or 0) |

**FIGURE 10.1** A Taxonomy of Exposure to Foreign Currency Risk.

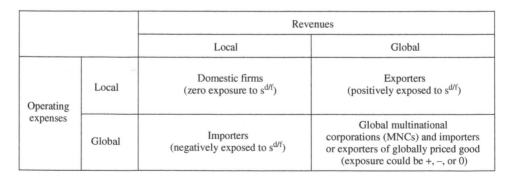

borders, wages move with domestic supply-demand forces and local inflation rather than with international factors. Local labor costs in such industries tend to be less dependent on foreign currency values than most other factor inputs. Local service companies also tend to compete with other local companies and not with global companies, so both revenues and expenses depend more on the local economy than on foreign currency values.

The "classic importer" is an MNC with international involvement through its operating expenses, buying goods in competitive world markets and selling them in local markets. If the local market is segmented from other markets (shown in the lower-left quadrant of Figure 10.1), the importer has a negative exposure to foreign currency values. If the importer competes in goods such as oil or electronics for which there is a competitive global market (lower-right quadrant), then local prices move with foreign currency values. In this case, both revenues and costs are exposed to currency risk.

*Operating exposure depends on the firm's business.*

Exporters face an exposure that is opposite that of importers. The "classic exporter" is an MNC with international involvement through its revenue stream. The exporter manufactures goods in a local economy and sells in competitive global markets. If the local market is segmented from other markets (upper-right quadrant), the exporter is positively exposed to foreign currency values. If the exporter's goods are sold in competitive global markets (lower-right quadrant), both costs and revenues move with foreign currency values.

The nature of a MNC's exposure to currency risk depends on the particular products and markets in which it competes. For the truly global corporation operating in global markets, both revenues and operating expenses are likely to be sensitive to exchange rates. Seldom are revenues matched one-for-one with operating expenses, so currency risk management is usually an important function of the multinational financial manager.

## Measuring the Exposure of Operating Cash Flows

***Exposure*** to currency risk refers to the *sensitivity* of an asset or liability to changes in an exchange rate. Currency risk exposure can be measured as the percentage change in the domestic currency value of an asset or a liability, $v^d = \Delta V^d / V^d$, resulting from a percentage change in the spot exchange rate, $s^{d/f} = \Delta S^{d/f} / S^{d/f}$.

$$\text{Exposure} = v^d / s^{d/f} \tag{10.1}$$

In some contexts, we'll replace $v^d$ with $r^d$ to indicate a percentage return $r^d$ (e.g., the percentage return on a share of stock) rather than the percentage change $v^d$ in the value of an arbitrary asset or liability. This is the nomenclature used in the chapters on international portfolio diversification (Chapter 19) and international asset pricing (Chapter 20).

In the sections of the book covering derivatives (Chapters 5–7), the measure of exposure in Equation 10.1 is translated into $v^{d/f}/s^{d/f}$ because many foreign currency derivatives are priced in d-per-f currency units, such as a dollar-per-euro currency option contract on the Chicago Mercantile Exchange (CME). The relations $v^d/s^{d/f}$ and $v^{d/f}/s^{d/f}$ are equivalent for a contractual value that is denominated in a foreign currency. For example, a 10 percent increase in the dollar-per-euro ($/€) price of a €125,000 CME option contract corresponds to a 10 percent increase in the dollar value of this €125,000 contract.

For a monetary (contractual) cash flow denominated in a foreign currency, it is also useful to consider the change in value in the domestic currency, $\Delta V^d$, arising from an exposure to currency risk. The exposure of a contractual cash inflow to the spot rate $s^{d/f}$ is $(v^d/s^{d/f}) = 1$, and the exposure of a contractual cash outflow is $(v^d/s^{d/f}) = -1$. For a foreign currency contract in a (positive or negative) amount $V^f$, change in the domestic currency value $\Delta V^d$ is given by[1]

$$\Delta V^d = V^f\,(\Delta S^{d/f}) \tag{10.2}$$

Equation 10.2 states that change in the domestic currency value of a contractual foreign currency asset or liability is equal to the product of the amount exposed ($V^f$) and the change in the spot rate ($\Delta S^{d/f}$). For example, if General Electric (GE) has a £1 million liability due in one month, then a $0.10/£ increase in the dollar value of the pound will change GE's dollar value by $\Delta V^{\$} = (V^{£})(\Delta S^{\$/£}) = (-£1\text{ million})(\$0.10/£) = -\$100{,}000$. The one-for-one exposure of contractual foreign currency amounts is reflected in the lines of slope +1 (for assets denominated in a foreign currency) and −1 (for liabilities denominated in a foreign currency) in Figure 10.2.

In contrast to monetary assets and liabilities, the value of a real asset can change more or less than one-for-one with changes in currency values because the operating cash flows generated by the firm's real assets are uncertain. Even if a 1 percent increase in a foreign currency value is accompanied, on average, by a 1 percent increase in firm value, the actual change is likely to be more or less than 1 percent because of uncertainty over future revenues and operating costs. The amount of the foreign currency exposure $V^f$ in Equation 10.2 can be difficult to estimate for operating cash flows or for assets (or liabilities) with operating exposures to currency risk because $V^f$ is not set by contract. Indeed, the value $V^f$ itself may be sensitive

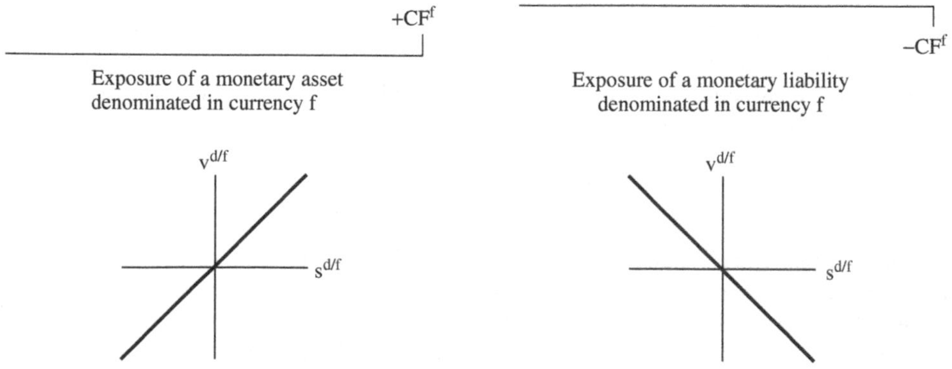


**FIGURE 10.2** The Exposures of Monetary Assets and Liabilities.

to exchange rate changes. Thus, Equation 10.2 holds for transaction exposures, but not necessarily for operating exposures. We'll return to this notion in Section 10.5.

*Real asset exposures are seldom one-for-one.*

Another difference between transaction and operating exposure is that operating exposure is to real (rather than nominal) changes in exchange rates. For example, a real appreciation of a foreign currency raises the price of foreign goods relative to domestic goods. This improves the competitive position of exporters and undermines that of importers. In contrast, nominal exchange rate changes that merely reflect differences in inflation have no real impact on the firm's competitive position.

*Real asset exposures are to real FX rates.*

## 10.2 THE EXPOSURE OF SHAREHOLDERS' EQUITY

Shareholders' equity has a residual claim on the assets of the firm after all the financial obligations of the firm have been satisfied. As such, equity absorbs the transaction exposure of monetary assets and liabilities, as well as the operating exposure of real assets. ***Net monetary assets*** are defined as monetary assets less monetary liabilities. Similarly, "net monetary assets exposed to currency risk" is equal to exposed monetary assets less exposed monetary liabilities. Shareholders' exposure to currency risk thus is the sum of the transaction exposure of net monetary assets exposed to currency risk plus the operating exposure of the firm's real assets.

### An Illustration of an Exporter's Exposures

*Equity is exposed to the net of all other assets and liabilities.*

Consider the common size balance sheet of the domestic exporter shown in Figure 10.3. For simplicity, this exporter's balance sheet is presented in cents based on a one-dollar unit of the firm. Forty cents of every dollar (or 40 percent of the firm) are invested in monetary assets denominated in a foreign currency. Twenty cents of every dollar are in monetary liabilities denominated in the foreign currency. This leaves net monetary assets of 20 cents with a transaction exposure to currency risk.

Suppose the foreign currency unexpectedly appreciates by 10 percent, resulting in a 10 percent appreciation in both nominal and real terms. As the nominal value of the foreign currency appreciates, foreign monetary assets rise by 4 cents and foreign monetary liabilities rise by 2 cents in value. This is a $(20¢)(0.10) = 2¢$ increase in

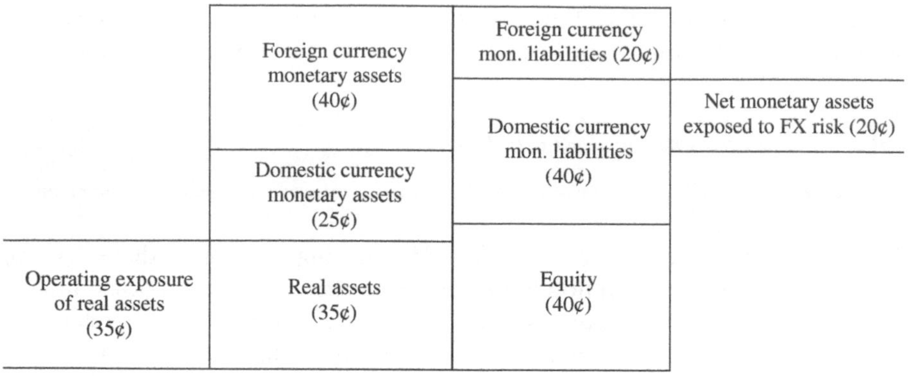


**FIGURE 10.3** The Exposure of Shareholders' Equity.

firm value in the domestic currency. As the residual owner of the firm, equity gains the net 2 cents in value from the foreign currency appreciation.

This exporter has invested 35 cents of every dollar in real assets. The real assets of a classic exporter are positively exposed to foreign currency values. The magnitude of this operating exposure may be more or less than one-for-one.[2] As the foreign currency appreciates in real terms, the purchasing power of foreign customers increases. If the exporter retains its sales price in the foreign currency, then (assuming other exporters do not change their prices) its contribution margin will increase on the same sales volume. Alternatively, if the exporter retains its existing sales price and contribution margin in the domestic currency, then a foreign currency appreciation results in a drop in the foreign currency price and export volume will rise. In either case, the value of the exporter in its domestic currency should rise.

Suppose this exporter's real assets are exposed "0.8-to-1.0" to the value of the foreign currency; that is, exposure $= v^d/s^{d/f} = 0.8$. In this case, a 10 percent appreciation of the foreign currency results, on average, in an 8 percent increase in the value of real assets. This is an increase of 2.8 cents per dollar, based on real assets of 35 cents. When combined with the increase in firm value of 2 cents from the net monetary assets exposed to currency risk, a 10 percent appreciation of the foreign currency is likely to increase the value of shareholders' equity by 4.8 cents. The actual change in value will be more or less than this amount because the change in the value of real assets is uncertain.

Two perspectives can be taken in estimating the exposure of shareholders' equity to currency risk. The first perspective views the firm from outside and measures the impact of exchange rate changes on the value of the firm's equity in the financial markets. The second approach attempts to separately identify the exposures of revenues and operating expenses generated by the firm's real assets. These elements of operating exposure are then combined with the transaction exposures of the firm's monetary assets and liabilities. This managerial or insider's view of currency risk exposure is useful for anticipating the impact of, and formulating a competitive response to, changes in exchange rates. Estimates of these exposures are more easily done by management than by external analysts because management has greater access to information on the firm's operating cash flows, risk exposures, and business strategies.

## Market-Based Measures of the Exposure of Shareholders' Equity

Shareholders' equity is exposed to currency risk to the extent that equity value changes in response to exchange rate changes.

**Exposure as a Regression Coefficient** Viewed from outside the firm, the exposure of equity to currency risk can be estimated by the slope coefficient in a regression of stock returns on changes in the spot exchange rate.

$$r_t^d = \alpha^d + \beta^f s_t^{d/f} + \varepsilon_t^d \tag{10.3}$$

where

$r_t^d$ = equity return in the domestic currency d in period t
$s_t^{d/f}$ = percentage change in the spot exchange rate during period t

This measure of exposure is similar to the measure of exposure in Equations 10.1 and 10.2. In each equation, exposure measures the *sensitivity* of an asset's (or a liability's) value to changes in exchange rates. In Equation 10.3, the exposed asset is the equity share in the domestic currency.

Equation 10.3 decomposes the change in firm value into two parts: a part that is exposed to currency risk ($\beta^f s_t^{d/f}$) and a part that is independent of currency risk ($\alpha^d + \varepsilon_t^d$). The regression coefficient $\beta^f$ is equal to

$$\beta^f = \rho_{r,s}(\sigma_r/\sigma_s) \tag{10.4}$$

where $\sigma_r$ is the standard deviation of equity returns $r_t^d$, $\sigma_s$ is the standard deviation of percentage changes in the spot exchange rate $s_t^{d/f}$, and $\rho_{r,s}$ is the correlation between equity returns $r_t^d$ and currency returns $s_t^{d/f}$. The intercept term $\alpha^d$ is the expected equity return in the domestic currency when $s^{d/f} = 0$, such that $E[r^d | s^{d/f} = 0] = \alpha^d$. The $\beta^f$ coefficient itself is unit-less; the superscript merely reminds us that this is the asset's sensitivity to changes in the value of currency f. The error term $\varepsilon_t^d$ usually is assumed to be normally distributed with a standard deviation of $\sigma_e$ and an expected value of zero.[3]

If the regression in Equation 10.3 yields a slope coefficient of $\beta^f = 0$, then share price is not exposed to changes in the value of the foreign currency. Changes in the exchange rate then have no power to explain changes in domestic equity value. The slope coefficient in Equation 10.3 is nonzero if there is a (positive or negative) relation between domestic equity values and foreign currency values. The greater the equity exposure, the greater is the magnitude of $\beta^f$. This conceptualization of currency risk exposure as a regression coefficient is illustrated in Figure 10.4.

*Exposure can be measured as a slope coefficient.*

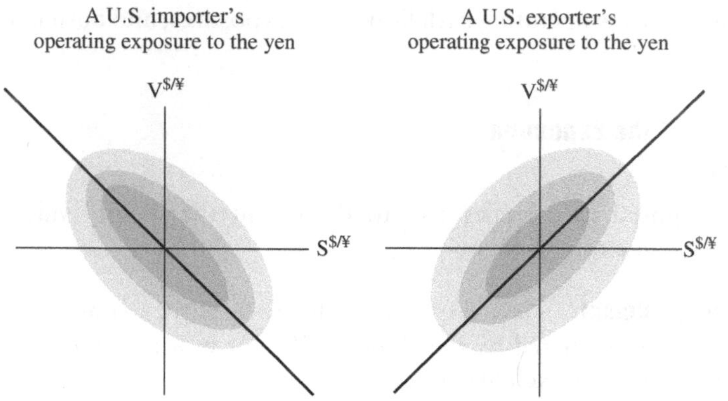

**FIGURE 10.4** The Operating Exposure of Real Assets.

Variability around the regression line is measured by ***r-square*** (also called the *coefficient of determination* or $r^2$). R-square is equal to the square of the correlation coefficient, $(\rho_{r,s})^2$, and measures the percent of the variation in $r_t^d$ that is "explained" in a statistical sense by variation in $s_t^{d/f}$. If the correlation between $r^d$ and $s^{d/f}$ is zero, then r-square is zero and equity return is not exposed to exchange rate changes. If the correlation between $r^d$ and $s^{d/f}$ is 0.2, then r-square is $(0.2)^2 = 0.04$ and 4 percent of the variation in equity value comes from variability in the exchange rate.

Note that risk-free contractual cash inflows and outflows denominated in a foreign currency have exposures of $\beta^f = +1$ and $\beta^f = -1$, respectively. In this case, the correlation $\rho_{r,s}$ between $r^d$ and $s^{d/f}$ is either $+1$ or $-1$ and r-square is $r^2 = (\pm 1)^2 = 1$. All observations lie on the regression line so that $\sigma_e = 0$, and variability in $s^{d/f}$ explains 100 percent of the variability in return $r^d$. All of the transaction exposures in Chapter 9 were of this type.

**An Example** Consider Philips NV, one of the world's largest electronics companies with 2010 revenues of €25 billion and 119,000 employees. Philips is incorporated in the Netherlands and has its principal listing in Amsterdam. Philips exports worldwide from its manufacturing base in the Netherlands. For a European exporter such as Philips, a real appreciation of the euro raises operating costs relative to Philips' competitors from outside the Eurozone. Conversely, a euro real depreciation lowers Philips' operating costs relative to its non-euro competitors.

Suppose the sensitivity of Philips' euro share price to changes in the value of the U.S. dollar is estimated as $\beta^\$ = 0.1$ in the following regression:

$$r_t^{€} = \alpha^{€} + \beta^{\$} s_t^{€/\$} + \varepsilon_t^{€} \tag{10.5}$$

According to this measure of exposure, a 10 percent dollar appreciation is associated with a 1 percent increase in the euro value of Philips shares, on average. Conversely, a 10 percent depreciation of the dollar is associated with a 1 percent decrease in Philips' euro share price. Because there is not a perfect correlation between Philips' euro share price and the spot rate, actual changes in the share price are likely to vary more or less than expected with changes in the euro-per-dollar spot rate. Indeed, the r-square is only $(0.1)^2 = 0.01$, so exchange rate changes explain only 1 percent of the variation in Philips' equity returns.

Philips is exposed to a variety of currencies besides the dollar, including to the euro value of pounds sterling and Chinese new yuan (CNY) through its sales and operations in the United Kingdom and China. Philips is indirectly exposed to the Japanese yen through the exposures of its Japanese competitors, such as Sony and Toshiba. Even if the euro doesn't change in value against the dollar, pound, or yuan, Philips' competitive position is diminished if its Japanese competitors benefit from a depreciation of the yen.

> *MNCs can be exposed to more than one foreign currency.*

A more inclusive measure of Philips' currency exposures can be estimated with the following multiple regression:

$$r_t^{€} = \alpha^{€} + \beta^{£} s_t^{€/£} + \beta^{\$} s_t^{€/\$} + \beta^{CNY} s_t^{€/CNY} + \beta^{¥} s_t^{€/¥} + \cdots + \varepsilon_t^{€} \qquad (10.6)$$

where the coefficients $\beta^{£}, \beta^{\$}, \beta^{CNY}$, and $\beta^{¥}$ represent the sensitivity of Philips' euro share price to changes in the value of each currency. This multiple regression approach reminds us that an MNC such as Philips has exposure not just to a single currency but to any number of currencies, depending on the nature and geographic scope of its operations and on those of its competitors.

A word of caution. Multiple regressions such as Equation 10.6 suffer from multicollinearity when the independent variables are correlated (that is, move together). In the presence of multicollinearity, slope coefficients have large standard errors and hence are imprecise measures of exposure. Multicollinearity is a concern in Equation 10.6 because the spot rates are related through their common dependence on the euro. Using either Equation 10.5 or Equation 10.6, the firm is considered to be exposed to a particular currency if the slope coefficient is statistically significant at a given (e.g., 5 percent) level of significance. Multicollinearity won't make an insignificant coefficient appear significant in Equation 10.6, but it can make one or more important exposures appear statistically insignificant through its effect on the standard errors of the slope coefficients. Equation 10.6 can be used in conjunction with a set of single regressions as in Equation 10.5 to identify and estimate the firm's principal exposures to currency risk.

## APPLICATION Daimler's Sell-Off of Chrysler

In 2007, DaimlerChrysler announced the sale of its Chrysler unit to private equity firm Cerberus Capital Management. Prior to the sale, DaimlerChrysler had significant manufacturing capacity in the United States to counterbalance its U.S. sales. The mix of dollar-denominated revenues and expenses dramatically changed after the sale, so the historical relation of Daimler's share price to the U.S. dollar no longer held. (This is actually good news for students of finance. After all, someone's gotta come up with those revised estimates of currency risk exposures.)

Regressions based on historical relationships can be unsatisfactory indicators of current and future exposures to currency risk. Regressions are necessarily backward looking. Because the competitive environment and the firm's mix of international sales and expenses change over time, regressions based on historical data can provide inaccurate measures of the firm's current exposures. Regression coefficients based on historical performance also do not allow the financial manager to perform "what if" analyses of proposed changes in the firm's operations. This creates a need for a more flexible, forward-looking measure of operating exposure. This is the topic of the next section.

### An Insider's View of Operating Exposure

Managers can develop a better sense of the sensitivity of the firm's operating cash flows to currency risk by unbundling the revenues and expenses of the firm and examining the sensitivity of each to changes in exchange rates. Using data from internal operations, managers can estimate the following for each major business unit:

$$\text{rev}_t{}^d = \alpha_{rev}{}^d + \beta_{rev}{}^f s_t{}^{d/f} + \varepsilon_t{}^d \tag{10.7}$$

$$\text{exp}_t{}^d = \alpha_{exp}{}^d + \beta_{exp}{}^f s_t{}^{d/f} + \varepsilon_t{}^d \tag{10.8}$$

where $\text{rev}_t{}^d$ and $\text{exp}_t{}^d$ represent percentage changes in the domestic currency values of revenues and expenses, respectively. Separating these two components of operating cash flow allows managers to estimate to what extent revenues and expenses from different business units are exposed to currency risk. Armed with estimates of the past sensitivities of revenues and expenses, managers then are in a better position to assess the exposure of future operating cash flows to currency risk as well as competitors' responses to exchange rate changes. The operating exposure of the firm's real assets can then be combined with the net transaction exposure of the firm's monetary assets and liabilities to estimate the exposure of shareholders' equity. As a reality check, this managerial estimate of the exposure of equity to currency risk can be compared with an estimate from Equation 10.3 using appropriate market-based data.

*The FX exposures of revenues and costs can be identified separately.*

## 10.3 MANAGING OPERATING EXPOSURE IN THE FINANCIAL MARKETS

Financial market hedges are attractive because they are zero-net present value (NPV) transactions. However, they might not be effective in hedging operating exposures to currency risk.

### Financial Market Hedging Alternatives

Transaction exposures are mostly short term in nature. In contrast, operating exposures typically have a very long time horizon. Financial market hedges of operating exposures should be long-lived—or at least renewable—to match the maturities of the underlying exposures.

> *Operating exposures are usually long-term exposures.*

**An Exporter's Financial Market Hedging Alternatives** Exporters typically have operating cash inflows denominated in one or more foreign currencies. These foreign currency inflows can be at least partially hedged by securing foreign currency cash outflows through the financial markets. Here are some alternatives for hedging in the financial markets:

- Sell the foreign currency with long-dated forward contracts.
- Finance a foreign project with foreign debt.
- Use currency swaps to acquire financial liabilities in the foreign currency, such as with a swap of existing domestic currency debt for foreign currency debt.
- Use a rolling hedge (a series of consecutive short-term forward or futures contracts) to repeatedly sell the foreign currency.

Each of these financial alternatives locks in contractual cash outflows that are in the same currency as the firm's operating cash inflows. This reduces the exposure of both the foreign subsidiary and the parent corporation to foreign currency fluctuations.

**An Importer's Financial Market Hedging Alternatives** Conversely, importers buy their goods from foreign suppliers and have obligations in foreign currencies. An importer has the following alternatives for hedging foreign currency outflows through the financial markets:

- Buy the foreign currency with long-dated forward contracts.
- Invest in long-dated foreign bonds.
- Use currency swaps to acquire financial assets in the foreign currency, such as with a swap of existing foreign currency debt for domestic currency debt.
- Use a rolling hedge to repeatedly buy the foreign currency with a series of consecutive short-term forward or futures contracts.

These financial alternatives lock in contractual cash inflows in the foreign currency that hopefully offset the importer's noncontractual foreign currency cash outflows.

### Advantages and Disadvantages of Financial Market Hedges

The main advantage of a financial market hedge is that the costs of buying or selling financial instruments are low compared with the costs of changing operations or investing/disinvesting in real assets. In isolation, financial market transactions also are likely to be zero-NPV transactions. In contrast, changes in the firm's operations by their nature are usually not zero-NPV transactions.

The main disadvantage of a financial market hedge is that the contractual cash flows of a financial instrument cannot fully hedge the uncertain operating cash flows of the firm's real assets. Hedging operating exposure with a financial market hedge does not reduce the operating exposure itself. Rather, it offsets this operating exposure with a financial hedge that has a roughly opposite exposure to currency risk. Thus, it changes the transaction exposure of the firm in a way that hopefully offsets the operating exposure of the firm. Because of this mismatch of the exposure and the hedge, a financial hedge is almost certain to over- or under-hedge the exposure.

***Financial market hedges cannot completely hedge operating exposures.***

Consider Duracell's exports of batteries from the United States to Japan. There are two sources of variability to dollar cash flows from Duracell's Japanese sales: (1) variability in yen revenues, and (2) variability in the dollar value of the yen. Suppose Duracell expects revenues of ¥100 million next year from Japan, but actual revenues can be as little as ¥50 million or as much as ¥150 million according to the following distribution:

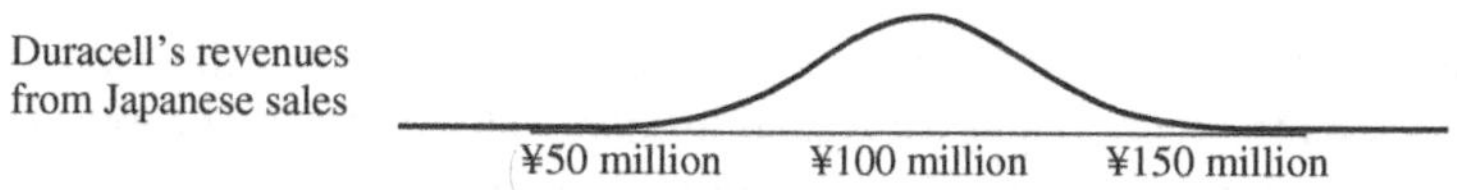


Given the level of yen revenues, the dollar value of Duracell's sales depends on the spot rate of exchange. At a forward and expected future spot rate of $F_1^{\$/¥} = E[S_1^{\$/¥}] = \$0.01/¥$, the resulting expected dollar inflow is (¥100 million)($0.01/¥) = $1 million. As a classic exporter, Duracell is positively exposed to the value of the yen. Change in the dollar value of Duracell's yen cash flow ($v^{\$/¥}$) with respect to a change in the spot rate ($s^{\$/¥}$) is shown as a positively sloped 45-degree line, indicating a one-for-one exposure to the yen.

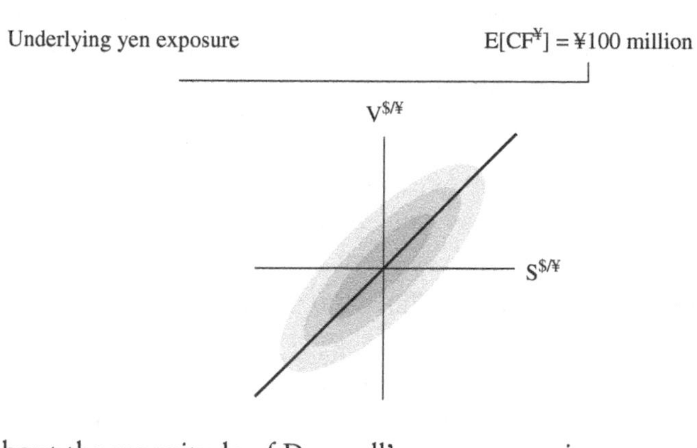


Uncertainty about the magnitude of Duracell's yen revenue is represented in the risk profile as a fuzzy area around the 45-degree line.

Duracell can hedge the expected cash inflow of ¥100 million by selling ¥100 million forward, thus securing an expected cash inflow of $1 million.

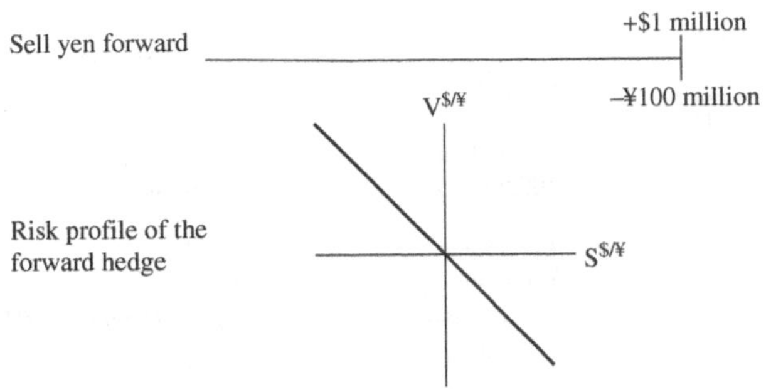


There is no uncertainty about the terms of this forward contract, so the risk profile is represented by a negatively sloped 45-degree line. In terms of Equation 10.3, $r^2 = 1$ and $\sigma_e = 0$. The resulting combination of the underlying yen exposure and the forward market hedge looks like this.

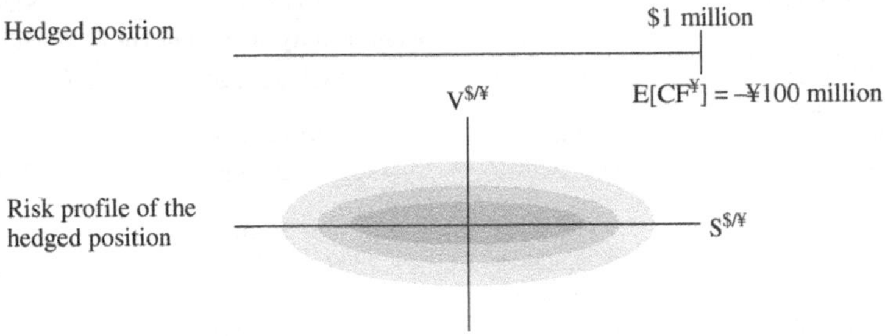


The *expected* payoff of the yen side of this hedged position is zero, but the actual payoff will depend on yen revenues and the value of the yen.

To focus on the variability of yen revenues, suppose the actual spot rate equals its expectation of \$0.01/¥ as in the top panel of Figure 10.5. Variability in the hedged cash flows is shown as a function of the level of yen revenues. In general, the net exposure of the hedged position depends on sales as well as the exchange rate. Duracell is perfectly hedged only when yen revenues are exactly ¥100 million. If yen revenues are any other amount, Duracell has a mismatch between the size of its underlying exposure and the size of its forward hedge.

If yen revenues are only ¥50 million, the ¥100 million forward contract over-hedges by ¥50 million. Duracell receives \$1 million on the long dollar forward position, but must pay ¥100 million on the short side of the forward contract against only ¥50 million in sales. The net result is a \$1 million cash inflow and a ¥50 million cash outflow. The ¥50 million cash outflow costs \$500,000 at the \$0.01/¥ spot rate, for net revenues in dollars of \$500,000. Conversely, when Japanese sales are ¥150 million, the ¥100 million forward contract under-hedges by ¥50 million. In this case, Duracell receives \$1 million on the long dollar forward but must pay ¥100 million on the short yen side against ¥150 million in revenues. This results in cash flows of \$1 million and ¥50 million, or a total value of \$1.5 million at the \$0.01/¥ spot rate.

Duracell's hedged position remains exposed to currency risk because of uncertainty in the magnitude of its yen revenues. Consider the case when Japanese sales are ¥50 million, as shown in the middle panel of Figure 10.5. The forward hedge

| | Uncertain yen revenues | | |
|---|---|---|---|
| Underlying revenues in yen | +¥50 million | +¥100 million | +¥150 million |
| Cash flows of the forward hedge | | | |
| long dollars | +$1 million | +$1 million | +$1 million |
| short yen | −¥100 million | −¥100 million | −¥100 million |
| Net position | | | |
| in dollars | +$1 million | +$1 million | +$1 million |
| in yen | −¥50 million | ¥0 million | +¥50 million |
| | **Exchange rate uncertainty at revenues of ¥50 million** | | |
| Underlying revenues in yen | +¥50 million | +¥50 million | +¥50 million |
| Cash flows of the forward hedge | | | |
| long dollars | +$1 million | +$1 million | +$1 million |
| short yen | −¥100 million | −¥100 million | −¥100 million |
| Net position | | | |
| in dollars | +$1 million | +$1 million | +$1 million |
| in yen | −¥50 million | −¥50 million | −¥50 million |
| Actual exchange rate | $0.005/¥ | $0.010/¥ | $0.015/¥ |
| Actual revenues in dollars | +$750,000 | +$500,000 | +$250,000 |
| | **Exchange rate uncertainty at revenues of ¥150 million** | | |
| Underlying revenues in yen | +¥150 million | +¥150 million | +¥150 million |
| Cash flows of the forward hedge | | | |
| long dollars | +$1 million | +$1 million | +$1 million |
| short yen | −¥100 million | −¥100 million | −¥100 million |
| Net position | | | |
| in dollars | +$1 million | +$1 million | +$1 million |
| in yen | +¥50 million | +¥50 million | +¥50 million |
| Actual exchange rate | $0.005/¥ | $0.010/¥ | $0.015/¥ |
| Actual revenues in dollars | +$1,250,000 | +$1,500,000 | +$1,750,000 |

**FIGURE 10.5** Duracell's Operating Exposure to the Yen.

results in a yen position of −¥50 million from the operating shortfall, plus the long $1 million position from the forward contract. If the yen appreciates to $0.015/¥ as in the right column, this short yen position costs $750,000. The net cash flow in dollars falls to $1,000,000 − $750,000 = $250,000. If the yen depreciates to $0.005/¥ as in the left column, the ¥50 million short position costs $250,000 and dollar revenues are $1,000,000 − $250,000 = $750,000. In this way, exchange rate variability causes the value of the net position to vary from $250,000 to $750,000.

Conversely, if Japanese sales are ¥150 million as in the bottom panel, then the forward hedge results in a long position of ¥50 million plus the $1 million from the forward contract, as shown in the bottom panel of Figure 10.5. At an exchange rate of $0.015/¥, Duracell's net cash flow is $1,000,000 + $750,000 = $1,750,000. If the yen depreciates to $0.005/¥, the net cash flow is $1,000,000 + $250,000 = $1,250,000. With underlying revenues of ¥150 million, exchange rate variability causes the value of the net position to vary between $1,250,000 and $1,750,000.

## Assessing the Effectiveness of a Financial Market Hedge

Because of the mismatch between the certain cash flows of a financial market hedge and the uncertain cash flows of an underlying operating exposure, it is important for managers to undertake an analysis of the likely performance of financial market hedges.[4] Managers should assess the performance of financial market hedges of operating exposures in the following ways:

- Vary pro forma operating performance within reasonable limits.
- Vary the exchange rate and assess the resulting competitive position of the firm.
- Assess the interaction of operating performance with exchange rate changes.

The effectiveness of various financial market hedges can then be investigated in the following ways[5]:

- Vary the type of hedge (e.g., forwards, futures, options, or swaps).
- Vary the amount of the hedge.
- Vary the term or maturity of the hedge.

In many cases, management will choose to hedge less than the expected cash flow. For example, Duracell may choose to sell only ¥50 million forward rather than the full ¥100 million expected operating cash flow. This partially reduces the sensitivity of operating performance to the exchange rate while avoiding the risk of over-hedging.

## 10.4 MANAGING OPERATING EXPOSURE THROUGH OPERATIONS

Trying to hedge an operating exposure with a financial market hedge is like trying to cure cancer with pain killers. A financial hedge can reduce the discomfort of an operating exposure, but cannot cure the underlying cause. Consequently, many MNCs with geographically diversified operations choose to hedge their operating exposures with operating hedges, rather than by trying to reduce their exposure with financial market hedges.[6] Indeed, the use of financial hedges by large nonfinancial firms often is small relative to the size and overall risk profiles of these firms.[7]

This section discusses how the MNC can reduce operating exposure to currency risk and possibly increase operating cash flow by adjusting its operations. Because they treat the underlying cause, operating hedges usually are more effective than financial hedges in reducing the MNC's net exposures to currency risk. However, they also fundamentally change the operations of the MNC and should be undertaken only after due consideration.

> *Operational hedges are seldom zero-NPV*

By themselves, financial market hedges are zero-NPV transactions. Financial hedges create value by combining with an underlying risk exposure to reduce the firm's expected taxes, financial distress costs or agency costs, or cost of capital. A firm that is contemplating an operational hedge cannot assume that proposed changes in operations are zero-NPV. Although some operational changes might be good for stakeholders, others are likely to destroy value. A capital budgeting analysis should be performed (discussed in Chapter 13) to fully evaluate any proposed change in operations.

### Types of Operational Hedges

Whether any of the operational hedges that follow are viable in a particular circumstance depends on competitive conditions in the MNC's host countries and markets. Each relies on geographic dispersion to reduce the MNC's operating exposure to currency risk.

**Plant Location** The MNC can gain an advantage over domestic rivals by securing low-cost labor, capital, or resources through its plant location decisions. These decisions must consider a number of local factors, including labor costs, labor and capital productivities, taxes and tariffs, and legal, institutional, and social infrastructures.

**Product Sourcing** Importers and MNCs with a global manufacturing base or established networks of foreign suppliers can respond more quickly than domestic competitors to real changes in currency values. As local real costs or exchange rates change, MNCs can shift production toward locations with the lowest real costs. Diversifying production across countries also hedges against exposures to political risks, such as expropriation or changes in tariffs.

**Market Selection and Promotion** When local markets are segmented from global competition, local prices and costs are slow to adjust to real changes in exchange rates. In these circumstances, a real appreciation of a foreign currency benefits exporters by increasing the purchasing power of foreign customers. In the presence of real exchange rate changes, globally diversified MNCs can shift their marketing efforts toward countries with overvalued currencies and thus create a spectrum of favorable pricing alternatives. These alternatives are developed in Section 10.5.

### Combining Operational and Financial Hedges

Although the world's markets for goods and services are becoming increasingly integrated, it remains difficult to establish reliable cross-border business relations. Compared with domestic trade, the costs and risks of international shipments and payments are high. Domestic firms without an established network of foreign suppliers or customers must overcome these trade barriers if they hope to take advantage of differential prices in foreign markets.

Multinational corporations have a natural advantage over domestic firms in responding to changes in real exchange rates. A real exchange rate change results in a change in one currency's purchasing power relative to another. This, in turn, can lead to a currency appearing overvalued or undervalued relative to another. Prices of goods and services are slow to react to changes in real exchange rates, and PPP can take several years to be restored. In the meantime, MNCs can take advantage of cross-border price differences in labor or materials.

*MNCs can flexibly respond to changes in real FX rates.*

Nevertheless, geographic diversification alone may not be enough to reduce foreign exchange exposure. Allayannis, Ihrig, and Weston study the impact of operating and financial hedges on the exchange rate exposures and firm values of a set of large U.S. firms. These authors find that geographic diversification across countries does not, by itself, reduce exposure to currency risk.[8] In contrast, these authors find that financial hedging strategies *are* related to lower exposures to currency risk. Moreover, firms that used operational hedges in combination with financial market hedges tend to have higher market values than other firms, all else constant. These results suggest that a judicious combination of operating and financial hedges can help maximize the value of the firm.

## 10.5 PRICING STRATEGY AND THE FIRM'S COMPETITIVE ENVIRONMENT

The effectiveness of pricing strategy as a hedge against operating exposure to currency risk depends on the competitive environment of the firm.

### An Example of an Exporter's Operating Exposure to Currency Risk

The MNC's pricing decisions are an important component of overall business and financial strategy. Pricing decisions also affect the firm's operating exposure to currency risk. An example of an exporter's exposure will illustrate the main effects.

Imagine a hair growth product that is so strong it can grow hair on a bowling ball. Now, imagine how much bald men and women around the world would pay for this product. Let's call our product GroMane, manufactured by Tao Corporation of Singapore for sale in the United States. Tao's income statement is shown in U.S. and Singapore dollars as the "base case" in the leftmost columns of Figure 10.6.

Tao Corporation manufactures GroMane in Singapore at a price of S\$20 per bottle. The S\$20 price is equivalent to \$10 at the current exchange rate of $S_0^{S\$/\$}$ = S\$2.00/\$. Inflation is the same in Singapore and the United States, and expected future exchange rates are expected to remain constant at $E[S_t^{S\$/\$}]$ = S\$2.00/\$. Labor expense is Tao's only cost of goods sold (COGS) and is S\$10 per bottle. Tao's labor force is local, and labor costs are contractually fixed in Singapore dollars. The production costs of Tao's international competitors are similarly fixed in their own local currencies. The corporate income tax rate in Singapore is assumed to be 50 percent in this problem.

Tao expects to sell 2,000 bottles per year in perpetuity for an annual after-tax cash flow of $E[CF^{\$}]$ = \$5,000, or $E[CF^{S\$}]$ = S\$10,000 at the current exchange rate. The after-tax hurdle rate on investments in this risk class is $i^{\$} = i^{S\$} = 10$ percent in each country. With perpetual cash flows, the value of Tao Corporation is $V^{S\$}$ = (S\$10,000)/(0.1) = S\$100,000.[9] This is equivalent to $V^{\$}$ = (\$5,000)/(0.1) = \$50,000 at the S\$2.00/\$ exchange rate.

| | Base case S$2.00/$ | | 25 percent U.S. dollar appreciation from S$2.00/$ to S$2.50/$ | | | | | |
|---|---|---|---|---|---|---|---|---|
| | | | Maintain $10 price | | Maintain S$20 price | | | |
| | | | Sales volume remains constant | | Elastic demand Sell 50% more | | Inelastic demand Sell 10% more | |
| Income statement | $ | S$ | $ | S$ | $ | S$ | $ | S$ |
| Price per bottle | $10 | S$20 | $10 | S$25 | $8 | S$20 | $8 | S$20 |
| Cost per bottle | $5 | S$10 | $4 | S$10 | $4 | S$10 | $4 | S$10 |
| Bottles sold | 2,000 | 2,000 | 2,000 | 2,000 | 3,000 | 3,000 | 2,200 | 2,200 |
| Revenues | $20,000 | S$40,000 | $20,000 | S$50,000 | $24,000 | S$60,000 | $17,600 | S$44,000 |
| - COGS | −10,000 | −20,000 | −8,000 | −20,000 | −12,000 | −30,000 | −8,800 | −22,000 |
| Before-tax profit | 10,000 | 20,000 | 12,000 | 30,000 | 12,000 | 30,000 | 8,800 | 22,000 |
| - Tax (at 50%) | −5,000 | −10,000 | −6,000 | −15,000 | −6,000 | −15,000 | −4,400 | −11,000 |
| Net cash flow | 5,000 | 10,000 | 6,000 | 15,000 | 6,000 | 15,000 | 4,400 | 11,000 |
| Value of Tao at $i^{\$} = i^{S\$} = 10\%$ | $50,000 | S$100,000 | $60,000 | S$150,000 | $60,000 | S$150,000 | $44,000 | S$110,000 |
| Percentage change in firm value | | | 20% | 50% | 20% | 50% | −12% | +10% |

**FIGURE 10.6** Tao Corporation's Pricing Strategies.

## Alternative Pricing Strategies

Suppose the U.S. dollar unexpectedly appreciates by 25 percent, from S$2.00/$ to S$2.50/$, and is expected to remain at this new level indefinitely. This is a 20 percent depreciation of the Singapore dollar, from $0.25/S$ to $0.20/S$. Suppose further that the U.S. dollar retains its value against other currencies, so that the Singapore dollar depreciates by 20 percent against all other currencies. What is the value of Tao Corporation after this Singapore dollar depreciation?

Tao's situation with respect to the exchange rate is that of a classic exporter. Tao's COGS is fixed in Singapore dollars and is unlikely to change as the Singapore dollar changes in value against other currencies. In contrast, the price that Tao receives for GroMane is determined in the U.S. market. In this situation, a depreciation of the Singapore dollar enhances Tao's competitive position relative to its competition from other countries. Pricing strategies that Tao can pursue in response to a U.S. dollar appreciation include the following:

- *Constant foreign price.* Hold the U.S. dollar price constant at $10 per bottle (or S$25 per bottle at the S$2.50/$ exchange rate) and try to sell the same quantity in the United States.
- *Constant domestic price.* Hold the Singapore price constant at S$20 per bottle ($8/btl at S$2.50/$) and try to increase volume in the United States.

**Constant Foreign Currency Price** If Tao holds its dollar price constant at $10 per bottle, it receives S$25 per bottle at the S$2.50/$ spot rate as shown in the "Maintain $10 price" column of Figure 10.6. Because the dollar price is unchanged, Tao's annual sales of 2,000 bottles should remain unchanged assuming no change in the position of Tao's competitors in the U.S. market. The S$25 per bottle price increases Tao's contribution margin to S$15 per bottle, or S$7.50 per bottle after corporate income taxes. After-tax cash flow is (S$7.50/bottle)(2,000 bottles) = S$15,000 per year, which is worth S$150,000 at the 10 percent after-tax discount rate. The value of Tao in Singapore dollars should increase if it does nothing more than maintain its U.S. dollar price for GroMane.

The dollar value of Tao may or may not increase depending on which effect dominates: the increase in contribution margin at the higher Singapore dollar sales price or the decrease in the value of the Singapore dollar. In this example, the increase in contribution margin dominates, and Tao's U.S. dollar value increases to \$60,000 at the S\$2.50/\$ exchange rate.

**Constant Domestic Currency Price** What will happen to Tao's value if it holds the Singapore dollar price constant at S\$20? Tao's contribution margin remains S\$10 per bottle, but the lower U.S. dollar price of \$8 per bottle should increase sales in the United States. All else equal, the value of Tao in Singapore dollars should go up. As before, the U.S. dollar value may go up or down, depending on whether the increase in sales volume is enough to overcome the 25 percent appreciation in the U.S. dollar. The actual change in value will depend on the price elasticity of demand for GroMane.

### Pricing Strategy and the Price Elasticity of Demand

The exporter's optimal pricing strategy depends on the competitive structure of the firm's industry, the price elasticity of demand for its products, and its marginal costs.[10] ***Price elasticity of demand*** is defined as minus the percentage change in quantity demanded ($q = \Delta Q/Q$) for a given percentage change in price ($p = \Delta P/P$).

$$\begin{aligned}\text{Price elasticity of demand} &= -(\Delta Q/Q)/(\Delta P/P)\\ &= -q/p \qquad (10.9)\end{aligned}$$

*Optimal pricing depends on the price elasticity of demand.*

If percentage changes in quantity sold are equal to percentage changes in price, then the product has *unit elasticity*. This is a useful starting point, because goods with unit elasticity will see no change in total revenue (Rev = PQ) with a change in price. What is lost (or gained) in price is exactly offset by a gain (or loss) in quantity sold. Price elasticities greater than one are said to be *elastic* and result in a decrease (increase) in revenue with an increase (decrease) in price. Elasticities less than one are said to be *inelastic* and result in an increase in revenue with an increase in price, or a decrease in revenue with a decrease in price.

Strictly speaking, this measure of elasticity holds only for infinitesimally small changes in price and quantity. Larger changes are multiplicative rather than additive. For example, if price decreases by 20 percent, then quantity sold must increase by 25 percent to leave revenue unchanged. Algebraically, this is given by $Rev_1^{\$} = P_1^{\$}Q_1 = [(0.80)P_0^{\$}][(1.25)Q_0] = P_0^{\$}Q_0 = Rev_0^{\$}$. For this reason, price elasticity measures the sensitivity of sales volume to infinitesimally small changes in price.

Suppose the beneficial effects of GroMane on hair retention are quickly lost and difficult to recover once treatment is suspended. Whether GroMane is price elastic or inelastic will depend on whether GroMane customers have other sources of supply in the U.S. market. In the absence of substitutes, some users of GroMane are likely to do almost anything to replenish their supply. If Tao owns a patent on GroMane and can control supply, demand is likely to be price inelastic. On the other hand, demand is likely to be price elastic if there are generic substitutes in a competitive U.S. marketplace.

### The Consequences of Alternative Pricing Strategies

If Tao keeps the Singapore dollar price of GroMane unchanged at S$20 per bottle, as shown in the right half of Figure 10.6, this reduces the U.S. dollar price of GroMane to $8 per bottle at the S$2.50/$ spot rate of exchange. This reduction in the U.S. dollar price of GroMane should increase Tao's sales in the United States. The amount of the sales increase depends on the price elasticity of demand.

For most goods, quantity demanded is a decreasing function of price.[11] The quantity demanded for a good or service is usually inelastic up to a certain point, and then elastic at higher prices. The optimal price point for a particular good or service is the price that yields the highest value of after-tax cash flow. This is often at a point of the demand curve where demand is near unit elasticity.

**Price Elastic Demand** Suppose the 20 percent decrease in the U.S. dollar price of GroMane increases sales volume by 50 percent, to 3,000 bottles. This increases revenues to (3,000 bottles)(S$20/bottle) = S$60,000, but also increases costs to (3,000 bottles)(S$10/bottle) = S$30,000. The net result is a S$15,000 annual after-tax cash flow and a S$150,000 value for Tao. Tao is (again) worth $60,000 at the S$2.50/$ spot exchange rate. The dollar value of Tao increases to $60,000 (from $50,000 in the base case) because the additional cash flow on a 50 percent increase in sales volume more than offsets the 20 percent depreciation of the Singapore dollar.

If the price elasticity of demand is greater than one, then Tao probably should have decreased its U.S. dollar sales price regardless of the change in the spot rate. In particular, if Tao can decrease price by 20 percent and create a 50 percent increase in quantity demanded, then it probably should have already made this price adjustment. This would have increased its U.S. revenues to $Rev_1^{\$} = P_1^{\$}Q_1 = [(0.80)P_0^{\$}][(1.50)Q_0] = (1.20)P_0^{\$}Q_0 = (1.20)Rev_0^{\$}$, or by 20 percent. Nevertheless, this example does illustrate the relation between price elasticity of demand and operating exposure to currency risk.

**Price Inelastic Demand** The columns at the right of Figure 10.6 show what can happen when demand is price inelastic. If Tao holds its Singapore dollar price fixed at S$20 per bottle (or $8 per bottle) in this example, the increase in sales volume is not sufficient to offset the decrease in contribution margin. Sales volume increases by only 10 percent on a 20 percent fall in price. If price is set at S$20 per bottle rather than the S$25 price from the "maintain dollar price" strategy, revenues fall by 12 percent according to $Rev_1^{\$} = P_1^{\$}Q_1 = [(0.80)P_0^{\$}][(1.10)Q_0] = (0.88)Rev_0^{\$}$. Faced with inelastic demand, Tao is better off holding its dollar price fixed at $10 per bottle (or S$25 per bottle) and reaping the benefits of the higher S$ contribution margin.

As in the case of price elastic demand, Tao didn't need to wait for a change in the exchange rate to adjust its price. If quantity demanded truly is price inelastic at $10, Tao should have considered raising the price regardless of the change in the spot rate. The relatively small decrease in quantity sold means that revenues and profits are likely to increase on lower volume.

### Reprise

This section illustrates how currency risk exposure interacts with the firm's pricing strategies through the price elasticity of demand for the firm's goods or services. A history of price changes can be used to estimate a product's price elasticity of demand. History also provides a record of how the firm's competitors have responded to price changes and other competitive pressures. The international marketing director of the MNC must combine this knowledge and experience with current market conditions in formulating her pricing strategies. The multinational financial manager must be aware of the competitive structure of the firm's industries and the consequences of the firm's pricing decisions, because the price elasticity of demand for the firm's goods or services affects the firm's operating exposure to currency risk.[12]

## 10.6 SUMMARY

This chapter deals with the operating exposure of real assets to currency risk and with equity's exposure to currency risk. Operating exposure to currency risk is more difficult to measure and manage than transaction exposure because it involves *uncertain* rather than contractual cash flows.

As the residual owner of the firm, the exposure of shareholders' equity is determined by the net transaction exposures of monetary assets and liabilities and the operating exposure of the firm's real assets. Whereas monetary assets and liabilities are exposed to changes in nominal exchange rates, operating cash flows are exposed to changes in real exchange rates. Thus, equity is exposed to both real and nominal changes in currency values.

The classic importer buys its goods in foreign markets at prices that are determined in the foreign markets and sells these goods to domestic customers at prices that are determined in the domestic market. Thus, importers tend to gain (lose) from a real appreciation (depreciation) of the domestic currency. Conversely, the classic exporter tends to gain (lose) from a real depreciation (appreciation) of the domestic currency. How much the firm wins or loses in value depends on the firm's pricing policies and the price elasticity of demand for its products.

Operating strategies for reducing the firm's sensitivity to unexpected changes in real exchange rates include marketing, production, and distribution strategies that allow the MNC to take advantage of the benefits of international diversification while (hopefully) enhancing revenues and reducing operating costs. Financial hedges of operating exposure also can reduce the impact of exchange rate changes on the firm's cash flows, real asset values, and share price. The key difference between financial and operating hedges of currency risk is that changes in operations directly affect the value of the corporation, whereas financial market hedges are essentially side-bets that do not directly affect the firm's operations.

## KEY TERMS

*integrated versus segmented markets*
*net monetary assets*
*operating exposure*
*price elasticity of demand*
*r-square*
*transaction exposure*

## CONCEPTUAL QUESTIONS

10.1 What is operating exposure to currency risk, and why is it important?

10.2 In a discounted cash flow framework, in what ways can operating risk affect the value of the MNC?

10.3 What is an integrated market? A segmented market? Why is this distinction important in multinational financial management?

10.4 State how each of the following companies are affected by a real depreciation of the domestic currency: (a) an exporter, (b) an importer, and (c) a diversified MNC competing in globally competitive goods and financial markets.

10.5 What is meant by the statement, "Exposure is a regression coefficient"?

10.6 Suppose the correlation of a share of stock with a foreign currency value is +0.10. Calculate r-square. What does it tell you?

10.7 Define net monetary assets. Define the net exposure of monetary assets and liabilities to currency risk. Why are these measures important?

10.8 List several financial market alternatives for hedging operating exposure to currency risk. How effective are these in hedging the nonmonetary cash flows of real assets? Why might firms hedge through the financial markets rather than through changes in operations?

10.9 List several operating strategies for hedging operating risk. What are the advantages and disadvantages of these hedges compared with financial market hedges?

10.10 What is the price elasticity of demand, and why is it important?

10.11 What five steps are involved in estimating the impact of exchange rate changes on the value of the firm's real assets or on the value of equity?

## PROBLEMS

10.1 Why is operating exposure to currency risk more difficult to manage than transaction exposure?

10.2 Sterling & Company is a silverware manufacturer based in the town of Sevenoaks in the United Kingdom. Although Sterling exports to companies around the world, its biggest customers are in the United States. Accounts that are denominated in dollars are indicated with "($)" in the following balance sheet. The exchange rate is currently \$1.50/£.

| | Value in local currency | Value in £s | | Value in local currency | Value in £s |
|---|---|---|---|---|---|
| Cash (\$) | \$30,000 | £20,000 | Payables (\$) | \$45,000 | £30,000 |
| Cash (£) | | £20,000 | Payables (£) | | £10,000 |
| Receivables (£) | | £30,000 | | | |
| Inventory (£) | | £10,000 | | | |
| Current assets | | £80,000 | Current liabilities | | £40,000 |
| | | | Long-term debt (\$) | \$90,000 | £60,000 |
| | | | Long-term debt (£) | | £20,000 |
| Real assets | | £80,000 | Net worth | | £40,000 |
| Total assets | | £160,000 | Total liabilities | | £160,000 |

a. What is the value of monetary assets and of monetary liabilities that are exposed to the dollar? What is the value of net monetary assets with a dollar exposure?
b. If the dollar appreciates by 10 percent, by how much will monetary assets change in value? By how much will monetary liabilities change in value? What are the r-squares of these relations?
c. Suppose inventory is not exposed to the dollar and that the exposure of real assets is $\beta^{\$} = \rho_{r,s}(\sigma_r/\sigma_s)$, where $\rho_{r,s} = 0.10$, $\sigma_r = 0.20$, and $\sigma_s = 0.10$. If the dollar rises in value by 10 percent, by how much are Sterling & Company's real assets likely to change in value? What is the r-square of this relation? Do you have much confidence in this estimate of the change in value? Why or why not?
d. Given your results in parts b and c, by how much is Sterling & Company's equity likely to change in value with a 10 percent appreciation of the dollar?
e. Sterling has a relatively large amount of dollar debt. Is this reasonable given its operating exposure from part c? Relate your answer to the r-square of the exposure coefficient in part c.
f. Sterling is considering opening a manufacturing plant in the United States to hedge its dollar exposure. Discuss the advantages and disadvantages of this operating hedge of Sterling's dollar exposure.

10.3 Consider the balance sheet of a U.S. firm exporting to Europe. Euro-denominated accounts have been translated into U.S. dollars at the current exchange rate.

| | | | |
|---|---|---|---|
| Cash (in \$s) | \$40,000 | Wages payable (in \$s) | \$40,000 |
| Accts receivable (in \$s) | \$30,000 | Accts payable (in \$s) | \$70,000 |
| Accts receivable (in €s) | \$60,000 | Bank note due (in €s) | \$10,000 |
| Inventory (in \$s) | \$20,000 | Total current liabilities | \$120,000 |
| Total current assets | \$150,000 | Bank note (in €s) | \$50,000 |
| Plant and equipment | \$50,000 | Common equity | \$30,000 |
| Total assets | \$200,000 | Total liabilities & equity | \$200,000 |

This firm considers inventory to be a real, rather than a monetary, asset.

a. What is the dollar value of the firm's monetary assets? What is the dollar value of the firm's monetary liabilities? What is the dollar value of net monetary assets?
b. What is the dollar value of the firm's monetary assets exposed to currency risk? Exposed monetary liabilities? Net exposed monetary assets (exposed monetary assets less exposed monetary liabilities)?
c. This firm has a bank note denominated in euros. Does this foreign currency liability increase or reduce the firm's net monetary exposure to currency risk? Explain.
d. Is the operating performance of a U.S. exporter such as this likely to be improved or worsened by a real appreciation of the euro? Explain.

10.4 Studies have found that corporations based in the United States typically have low exposures to other currencies. In contrast, studies have found that a much higher percentage of firms in other countries (including Canada, Germany, and Japan) are exposed to the dollar. Why might this be? What does it suggest about currency risk management in these countries relative to currency risk management in the United States?

10.5 Use a spreadsheet to reconstruct Figure 10.5 assuming Duracell uses a ¥50 million forward contract rather than the ¥100 million forward hedge in the figure.

10.6 Dow of the United States makes bungee cords for sale in the United Kingdom. Dow charges $6 per cord, or £4 at the $1.50/£ spot rate. At this price, Dow expects annual sales of 20,000 cords in perpetuity. Variable costs are $3 per cord in the United States. The discount rate is 10 percent in each currency. Dow is considering its price response to a 20 percent pound depreciation from $1.50/£ to $1.20/£ (corresponding to a 25 percent dollar appreciation from £0.6667/$ to £0.8333/$). Reconstruct Figure 10.6 as follows:

a. Estimate Dow's value (in pounds and dollars) assuming it maintains the £4 U.K. price and sales volume in the United Kingdom does not change.
b. Estimate Dow's value (in pounds and dollars) assuming Dow maintains the $6 U.S. price (or, a £5 price) and U.K. sales volume falls by 50 percent. What is Dow's optimal pricing strategy if demand is price elastic in this way?
c. Estimate Dow's value (in pounds and dollars) assuming Dow maintains the $6 U.S. price (or, a £5 price) and U.K. sales volume falls by 10 percent. What is Dow's optimal pricing strategy if demand is price inelastic in this way?

## SUGGESTED READINGS

### Merck's use of computer modeling for corporate hedging decisions is described in

Judy C. Lewent and A. John Kearney, "Identifying, Measuring, and Hedging Currency Risk at Merck," *Journal of Applied Corporate Finance* 2, No. 4 (1990), 19–28.

### The effect of financial and operating hedges on firm value is investigated in

George Allayannis, Jane Ihrig, and James P. Weston, "Exchange-Rate Hedging: Financial Versus Operational Strategies," *American Economic Review* 91 (May 2001), 391–395.

Gordon M. Bodnar, Bernard Dumas, and Richard C. Marston, "Pass-Through and Exposure," *Journal of Finance* 57 (February 2002), 199–231.

Wayne R. Guay and S.P. Kothari, "How Much Do Firms Hedge with Derivatives?" *Journal of Financial Economics* 70 (December 2003), 423–461.

Young Sang Kim, Ike Mathur, and Jouahn Nam, "Is Operational Hedging a Substitute for or a Complement to Financial Hedging?" *Journal of Corporate Finance* 12 (September 2006), 834–853.

CHAPTER 11

# Managing Translation Exposure and Accounting for Financial Transactions

*Evolution has her own accounting system and that's the only one that matters.*

—R. Buckminster Fuller

In its consolidated financial statements, a parent company with foreign operations must translate the assets and liabilities of its foreign subsidiaries into its reporting currency. ***Translation*** (or ***accounting***) ***exposure*** refers to the impact of exchange rate changes on the parent firm's consolidated financial statements arising from this translation.

This chapter describes the foreign currency translation method used in the United States, Financial Accounting Standard No. 52 (FAS #52) "Foreign Currency Translation" of the Financial Accounting Standards Board (FASB). This method is very similar to the translation accounting method recommended by the International Financial Reporting Standards (IFRS) of the International Accounting Standards Board (IASB). Reasons for and against hedging the firm's translation exposure to currency risk are then discussed. Hedge accounting for derivative transactions concludes the chapter.

## 11.1 THE CURRENT RATE METHOD OF FINANCIAL ACCOUNTING STANDARD NO. 52

Translation (or accounting) exposure refers to the impact of exchange rates on a parent firm as it consolidates the financial statements of its foreign subsidiaries. The key issue for standard setters in translation accounting is whether to translate foreign accounts at current or at historical exchange rates. The FASB in the United States translates foreign accounts using the ***current rate method*** of FAS #52 "Foreign Currency Translation" introduced in 1982. This standard is summarized below and in Figure 11.1.

1. All assets and liabilities except common equity are translated at the current exchange rate.
2. Common equity is translated at historical exchange rates.

| | | Are market values observable? |
|---|---|---|
| Assets | | |
| Short-term monetary assets | Translated at current exchange rate | Yes |
| Long-term monetary assets | Translated at current exchange rate | Yes |
| Real assets | Translated at current exchange rate | **Seldom** |
| Liabilities and owners' equity | | |
| Short-term monetary liabilities | Translated at current exchange rate | Yes |
| Long-term monetary liabilities | Translated at current exchange rate | Yes |
| Net worth (common equity) | Translated at historical exchange rates | **Seldom** |
| Translation gains or losses | Translation gains/losses from balance sheet accounts are not reported on the income statement. Instead, they are put in a cumulative translation adjustment (CTA) account under net worth on the balance sheet. | |

**FIGURE 11.1** Summary of FAS #52 "Foreign Currency Translation".

3. Income statement items are translated at a current exchange rate.
4. Any imbalance between the book value of assets and liabilities is recorded as a separate equity account on the balance sheet called the *CTA*.

> *Forex (FX) rates' effect on financial statements is called translation exposure.*

The current exchange rate is the rate prevailing on the date of a financial statement. Historical exchange rates are those that prevailed when items were first entered into the accounts. Under FAS #52, firms are given a choice of translating income statement items at the average exchange rate for the reporting period, the exchange rates prevailing on the dates that income statement items were entered on the company's books, or a weighted average exchange rate for the period.

> *FAS #52 places translation gains or losses into an equity account.*

A key measure of translation accounting exposure is ***net exposed assets***, defined as the book value of assets exposed to currency risk less the book value of liabilities exposed to currency risk. Under FAS #52, all assets are exposed to exchange rate changes because they are translated at current exchange rates. All liabilities *except owners' equity* also are exposed. Under FAS #52, net exposed assets thus equal the net worth of the foreign subsidiary; that is, total assets minus monetary (contractual) liabilities.

Figure 11.2 illustrates translation exposure accounting under FAS #52. In the example, net exposed assets equal the net worth of the foreign subsidiary; or (€15,000 − €10,000) = €5,000. A 20 percent depreciation in the value of the euro results in a 20 percent decrease (−$1,000) in the book value of the foreign subsidiary. This translation loss of $1,000 is absorbed by the CTA account in the owners' equity section of the balance sheet. Reported earnings thus reflect only operations during that reporting period, and not any changes in balance sheet accounts.

| Assets | Value in euros | Dec '12 value at \$1.00/€ | Dec '13 value at \$0.80/€ | | Translation gains or losses | |
|---|---|---|---|---|---|---|
| Cash & marketable securities | €2,500 | \$2,500 | \$2,000 | Exposed assets | –\$500 | |
| Accounts receivable | €2,500 | \$2,500 | \$2,000 | | –\$500 | |
| Inventory | €2,500 | \$2,500 | \$2,000 | | –\$500 | |
| Plant and equipment | €7,500 | \$7,500 | \$6,000 | | –\$1,500 | |
| Total assets | €15,000 | \$15,000 | \$12,000 | | –\$3,000 | |
| Liabilities | | | | | | |
| Accounts payable | €2,500 | \$2,500 | \$2,000 | Exposed liabilities | –\$500 | |
| Short-term debt | €2,500 | \$2,500 | \$2,000 | | –\$500 | |
| Long-term debt | €5,000 | \$5,000 | \$4,000 | | \$0 | |
| Net worth | | | | | | |
| Common equity | €5,000 | \$5,000 | \$5,000 | | \$0 | Net exposure |
| CTA | – | \$0 | –\$1,000 | | –\$1,000 | |
| Total liabilities and net worth | €15,000 | \$15,000 | \$12,000 | | –\$3,000 | |

**FIGURE 11.2** An Example of the Current Rate Method.

Consider the balance sheet in Figure 11.1. Monetary (contractual) assets and liabilities with observable prices have a transaction exposure to currency risk and should be valued at their market values in the foreign currency ($P^f$) and at prevailing exchange rates ($S^{d/f}$) according to $P^d = P^f S^{d/f}$. In contrast, real assets often do not have observable market values and are instead kept on the foreign subsidiary's books at historical costs in the foreign currency. The key issue in translation accounting is the operating exposure of these real assets; that is, whether the value of these real assets varies with the exchange rate. Along with the net exposure of monetary assets and liabilities, the exposure of the subsidiary's real assets then determines the effect of exchange rates on the value of owners' equity.

Valuing the subsidiary at historical exchange rates is appropriate if the real assets of the subsidiary are unaffected by exchange rates. This would occur if the operating exposures of revenues and operating expenses are offsetting, leaving no net exposure. A special case would be if the subsidiary is operating in a purely local market, with both revenues and operating expenses unexposed to exchange rates and hence no net exposure to exchange rates. In contrast, valuation at current exchange rates assumes real assets have a one-to-one exposure to exchange rates.

For most firms, the truth is somewhere between these two positions. The most obvious effect of a foreign currency depreciation is a decrease in the domestic currency value of foreign assets according to $P^d = P^f S^{d/f}$. However, foreign currency depreciations also tend to increase the competitiveness of foreign assets and their value in the foreign currency. This increase ($\Delta P^f > 0$) in the foreign currency value of the asset may or may not be enough to offset the decrease ($\Delta S^{d/f} < 0$) in the value of the foreign currency itself. Consequently, each of these translation accounting methods is a simplified view of the true operating exposure of a foreign subsidiary's real assets. No simple translation accounting convention can hope to accommodate the variety of operating exposures observed in practice.

Under FAS #52, gains or losses caused by translation adjustments are not included in the calculation of net income. Rather, they are placed into a cumulative translation adjustment account in the equity section of the balance sheet. The CTA account allows balance sheet gains or losses to be isolated from reported income, rather than flowed through income into retained earnings. This relieves managers of the burden of explaining to shareholders poor earnings outcomes arising from balance sheet translation effects. The IFRS of the IASB recommend a similar treatment of translation gains and losses.

## 11.2 CORPORATE HEDGING OF TRANSLATION EXPOSURE

Finance theory states that the firm should consider only hedging risk exposures that are related to firm value. Hedging has value when it can reduce the variability of firm value and thereby reduce expected taxes, costs of financial distress, or agency costs.[1] There is no value in hedging noncash transactions that do not cost or risk cash.

*Only risk exposures that are related to firm value should be hedged.*

Translation exposure involves income statement and balance sheet accounts. It may or may not involve cash flows. Consider an inventory of crude oil held by a foreign subsidiary of a U.S. parent. Oil prices rise and fall with the dollar, so an appreciation (or depreciation) of a currency against the dollar typically decreases (increases) the price of oil in that currency. If oil inventory is carried at historical cost on the foreign subsidiary's balance sheet and translated back to the parent's financial statements at the current exchange rate, then the U.S. parent has a translation exposure to currency risk without a corresponding economic (transaction or operating) exposure. Hedging this foreign currency translation exposure with a financial market transaction is unlikely to increase shareholder value. To the extent that hedging a noncash translation exposure increases risk or costs cash, hedging actually may decrease the value of the firm.

Conversely, suppose the U.S. subsidiary of a foreign-based parent has an inventory of oil. The price of oil is associated with the dollar, so the foreign parent has an economic exposure to the dollar. If inventory is translated back to the parent at historical exchange rates, then the parent corporation has an economic but not a translation exposure to currency risk. Even though it has no translation exposure to the value of the dollar, the parent's economic exposure to the dollar—or perhaps to oil prices—might be worth hedging.

### Information-Based Reasons for Hedging Translation Exposure

In a perfect financial market, the firm's borrowing capacity and required return on investment are determined in the marketplace by rational, informed investors. Managing translation exposures that do not involve cash flows will not add to the value of the firm.

**MARKET UPDATE International Accounting Standards**

The International Accounting Standards Committee (IASC) was formed in 1973 with the goal of harmonizing accounting standards around the world. To this end, the IASC developed a series of International Accounting Standards (IAS) that could apply to both emerging and developed economies. In 2001, the IASB replaced the IASC and focused on harmonizing the accounting standards of developed economies. The board has six trustees from the Asia/Oceanic, European, and North America regions, as well as one trustee from Africa and one from South America. Two trustees are at large. The board also has a number of nonvoting participants from national standard setters and other interested parties including the European Commission, the International Organization of Securities Commissioners, and other national and international standard-setting bodies. The pronouncements of the IASB are now called IFRS. The IAS and the more recently issued IFRS are a significant force in global accounting and financial reporting.

Harmonized standards are important to international investors, because they make it easier to compare companies from different countries. Many MNCs use the IFRS to report their financial performance to international investors. International accounting standards also ease the reporting requirements of MNCs and facilitate the international flow of capital.

In the real world of imperfect markets, there are situations in which translation exposure to currency risk can have valuation-relevant consequences above and beyond the firm's economic exposures. Management of translation exposure may be justifiable in these circumstances. In particular, hedging may improve the quality of earnings by reducing uncertainty regarding the firm's operating performance. Higher quality accounting earnings allow investors to more accurately assess managerial performance and the value of the firm's assets and liabilities.

***Hedging translation exposure can create value if it improves earnings quality.***

Here are three practical reasons for hedging translation exposure to currency risk.[2]

- *Satisfying loan covenants.* Loan covenants often require that a firm maintain certain performance levels in operating profit or interest coverage. Violation of a loan covenant can lead to a reduction in borrowing capacity. In these circumstances, a hedge of translation exposure can ensure that the firm retains access to funds. The perfect market view is that the firm's borrowing capacity is determined in the marketplace and not through artifices such as loan covenants. In the real world, accounting constraints can have a profound effect on borrowing capacity and firm value.

- *Meeting profit forecasts.* The perfect market view is that investors see through accounting profits to cash flows and the firm's intrinsic value. In a less-than-perfect market, a firm that has announced a profit forecast might wish to retain its credibility with analysts and investors by hedging against a translation loss. Management's credibility might be worth protecting, even if it means hedging a noncash translation exposure with a financial market hedge that costs and risks cash.
- *Retaining a credit rating.* Managers have an incentive to hedge translation exposure if the firm's credit rating depends on profits and not on its cash flows. Although investors in a perfect market would see through to the firm's underlying cash flows and intrinsic value, information is imperfect and costly to acquire in the real world. To the extent that hedging translation exposure can avoid a downgrade in a credit rating, hedging can preserve value by maintaining the firm's access to funds.

Note that each justification relies on costly or restricted access to information on the part of investors or information providers.

### Cross-Country Differences in Hedging of Translation Exposure

Several studies have documented higher derivatives usage and a greater willingness to hedge translation exposure to currency risk in non-U.S. than in U.S. companies.

> *Non-U.S. firms may be more willing than U.S. firms to hedge translation exposure.*

- Belk and Glaum reported that companies in the United Kingdom are more likely to hedge translation exposure than their counterparts in the United States.[3]
- Hakkarainen et al. found that companies in Finland are more likely than U.S. firms to hedge translation exposure, perhaps because of the foreign currency translation rules specified in the Finnish Accounting Act of 1993.[4]
- In a sample of U.S. and German companies matched on size and industry, Bodnar and Gebhardt found derivatives usage by 78 percent of German firms and only 57 percent of comparable U.S. firms.[5] Bodnar and Gebhardt also documented national differences in (1) the goal of hedging, (2) the choice of hedging instruments, and (3) the influence of managers' market view when taking derivatives positions.

Reasons for these cross-country differences in hedging policies appear to be related to differences in national financial reporting standards, the relative importance of financial accounting statements, and corporate policies controlling derivatives usage.

There is evidence that MNCs adapt their translation hedging activities to the prevailing generally accepted accounting principles (GAAP) regarding foreign currency translation. For example, prior to FAS #52 the United States followed a translation accounting standard called FAS #8 in which translation gains or losses were reflected in earnings on the income statement and then flowed into retained earnings on the balance sheet. As a consequence, translation restatements of balance sheet accounts sometimes overwhelmed operating performance and reported earnings. Houston and Mueller found that U.S. MNCs were less inclined to hedge translation exposure after FAS #52 isolated balance sheet translation gains or losses from reported income.[6] Godfrey and Yee found that Australian mining companies increased their hedging activities after changes in Australian GAAP increased their translation exposures.[7] These results suggest that managers are sensitive to their translation exposure to currency risk.

## Aligning Managerial Incentives with Shareholder Objectives

Managerial performance evaluations should be tied to financial performance—to underlying cash flows and values—and not merely to accounting profits. Nevertheless, managers often are evaluated based on accounting performance simply because it is easier to measure accounting flows than financial performance. If risk-averse managers are not allowed to hedge, they may forgo value-creating investments that would expose them to additional risk. Allowing managers to hedge against translation exposure to currency risk can reduce ***agency costs*** (i.e., the costs of ensuring that managers act in the best interests of shareholders) and thereby more closely align managerial incentives with shareholder objectives.[8]

> *Hedging can align managers' incentives with share-holder objectives.*

The multinational treasury can facilitate this process by providing internal hedges to managers of individual operating units. For example, if a division manager wants to hedge divisional accounting performance against a drop in a currency value, treasury can quote prices on currency forward or option contracts that allow the manager to lock in an accounting profit for performance evaluation purposes. The internal cost of this hedge to the operating division should be based on market prices, such as forward rates or option premiums. Benchmarking divisional performance to a hedged position reduces the dependence of divisional performance measures on exchange rates, and can add value to the firm to the extent that it helps align managers' incentives with shareholder preferences.

Even though it has provided a hedge to an internal operating division of the firm, treasury does not have to actually execute this hedge in the external financial markets. Instead, treasury should make its own assessment of the desirability of hedging based on cash flow (rather than accounting profit) considerations after netting exposures across the individual operating divisions.

Value-based incentive plans based on economic value added (EVA) are another way to align managerial incentives with shareholder objectives. ***EVA*** is a method of financial performance evaluation that adjusts accounting performance for a charge reflecting investors' required return on investment.[9] Alternatively, divisional performance can be benchmarked to the performance of other divisions or to firms with similar exposures to currency risk. Each of these methods of performance evaluation is an attempt to align managerial incentives with shareholder objectives.

### To Hedge or Not to Hedge: Policy Recommendations

The decision of whether to hedge translation exposure to currency risk depends on the company, its owners and managers, and the markets in which its securities are traded. It therefore must be made on a case-by-case basis. Nevertheless, here are some general recommendations.

> *Hedge only exposures that cost or risk cash.*

1. As a general rule, do not hedge translation exposures in the financial markets unless the purpose of the hedge is to reduce transaction or operating exposure to currency risk. Exceptions can occur in the following circumstances:
   a. Investors have restricted access to information about the firm.
   b. Corporate access to funds depends on accounting performance measures.
2. Foreign affiliates should use local sources of debt or equity capital to the extent permitted by the corporation's overall financial plan. This can offset the translation and, more importantly, the economic exposures of foreign operations.
3. Managerial performance evaluation and compensation should be structured so that managers are insulated from unexpected changes in exchange rates.
   a. Benchmark divisional performance to the performance of other divisions or firms with similar exposures to currency risk.
   b. Allow managers to hedge their exposures internally through the corporate treasury.
4. If hedging of an individual unit's translation exposure is deemed necessary to align managerial incentives with shareholder objectives, the corporate treasury should quote market prices to the individual units.
   a. If individual units have noncash exposures, treasury should hedge internally.
   b. External financial market hedges should be used only for hedging the firm's net transaction or operating exposures to currency risk.

Providing a way for managers to reduce uncertainty should ultimately benefit shareholders and other corporate stakeholders.

## 11.3 ACCOUNTING FOR FINANCIAL MARKET TRANSACTIONS

The growth of derivatives trading during the 1980s and 1990s created a need for accounting standards to recognize and report on derivatives usage. Derivatives-related failures in the early 1990s lent urgency to this need, and the prominent derivatives-related losses during the global financial crisis of 2008 added an emphatic exclamation point.

**MARKET UPDATE Some (In)Famous Derivatives-Related Losses**

With the increasing use of derivative instruments for corporate risk hedging and investment purposes, losses are bound to occur. Many of the biggest losses were from credit default swaps during the 2008 crisis.

| Loss ($bil) | Company | Derivative product(s) | Year |
|---|---|---|---|
| $18.0 | AIG Financial Products (U.S.) | Credit default swaps | 2008 |
| $9.0 | Morgan Stanley (U.S.) | Credit default swaps | 2008 |
| $7.2 | Société Générale (France) | Stock index futures | 2008 |
| $6.5 | Amaranth Advisors (U.S.) | Natural gas futures | 2006 |
| $4.6 | LTCM Long-Term Cap Mgmt (U.S.) | Interest rate, FX, equity derivatives | 1998 |
| $2.6 | Sumitomo Corporation (Japan) | Copper futures | 1996 |
| $2.5 | Aracruz (Brazil) | FX options | 2008 |
| $1.9 | Citic Pacific (Hong Kong, China) | FX derivatives | 2008 |
| $1.3 | Barings Bank (U.K.) | Equity futures and options | 1995 |
| $1.3 | Metallgesellschaft Corp (Germany) | Crude oil futures | 1993 |

Financial contracts are two-sided bets; for every loser, there is a winner on the other side of the contract.
Of course, the winners are less likely to make the headlines.

In the United States, the FASB introduced FAS #133 "Accounting for Derivative Instruments and Hedging Activities" in 1999. This standard has four key elements.

1. Derivatives are assets and liabilities that should be reported in financial statements, and not hidden from the public.
2. Fair (market) value is the most relevant measure of value.
3. Only assets and liabilities should be reported as such. Income and expenses should be reported on the income statement.
4. Special accounting rules should be limited to qualifying hedge transactions.

Under FAS #133, derivatives are included on the balance sheet at fair (market) value and derivative gains or losses are immediately recognized in earnings. If certain conditions are met, derivative instruments can be designated as a hedge to offset the risk of another asset, liability, or anticipated transaction. Special accounting rules apply to qualifying hedge transactions.

*FAS #133 values derivatives at market.*

FAS #133 was widely hailed by investors, regulators, and academicians as promoting transparency in financial accounts. It was not well received by investment bankers and securities traders, who felt that the complexity of the new standard would deter users from trading in derivatives. The standard requires substantially more effort on the part of financial managers and their accountants to comply with the new and complex rules, especially on qualifying hedge transactions. Commercial banks also objected to the standard, because it does not apply market value accounting consistently across the balance sheet. In particular, long-term assets and liabilities are accounted for differently depending on whether they are a part of a qualified hedge. Similar standards for financial market transactions have been adopted by most national and international standard-setting bodies. The rest of this section describes the four key elements of FAS #133.

## Derivatives Should Be Reported

Standard setters around the world responded to derivatives-related failures by requiring increased disclosure of off-balance-sheet derivative transactions, such as currency or interest rate forwards, futures, options, and swaps. Off-balance-sheet derivative transactions can be effective risk management tools, but they expose companies to financial price risks that might not be apparent to investors. These lessons were re-emphasized during the global financial crisis of 2008.

In the United States, disclosure of derivative transactions is required by FAS #119, "Disclosures about Derivative Financial Instruments." The IASB requires similar standards in its IFRS #7 "Financial Instruments: Disclosures" and IFRS #9 "Financial Instruments." Many national standard setters are either adopting or converging to IFRS, including Argentina, Australia, Brazil, Canada, China, the European Union, India, Indonesia, Japan, Mexico, Korea, Russia, Saudi Arabia, South Africa, and Turkey. The intent of these standards is to promote transparency in reported financial statements.

## Fair (or Market) Value Accounting

Two desirable characteristics of FASs are ***reliability*** and ***relevance***. The FASB defines these in "Statement of Financial Accounting Concepts No. 2" as follows:

- *Reliability.* The quality of information that assures that information is reasonably free from error and bias and faithfully represents what it purports to represent.
- *Relevance.* The capacity of information to make a difference in a decision by helping users to form predictions about outcomes of past, present, and future events or to confirm or correct prior expectations.

Reliability is a function of the estimation process, whereas relevance is a function of the economic environment. An ideal accounting standard would be reliable in that two different accountants examining the same situation would reach the same accounting valuation. An ideal standard also would be relevant to decision makers in that the assigned valuation would be timely and accurate, reflect the economic reality of the situation, and have predictive value for decision makers. Unfortunately, it can be difficult to achieve both of these objectives concurrently.

The international trend in financial accounting has been toward fair (or market) value accounting. Market values have high relevance to the extent that market prices reflect economic reality. Even when market values are not directly observable, such as for privately placed debt, they can be inferred from the debt's payoff structure and the yield on similar publicly traded debt.

> ***Real assets often do not have observable market values.***

Unfortunately, many assets and liabilities do not have readily observable market values. Examples include real assets such as plant and equipment, and privately held debt or equity for which no market value is observable. In these situations, market value accounting lacks reliability. Historical costs are reliable, in that everyone can agree on the book value of an asset or a liability that is entered into financial statements at historical cost. But historical costs seldom reflect economic reality, and so lack relevance.

Market value accounting standards have been proposed by accounting standard setters in the United States, the United Kingdom, Canada, Australia, and the European Union, as well as by the IASB. In the United States, FAS #133 requires market value accounting for short-term financial assets and liabilities and derivative securities that are held for trading or hedging purposes. Investment or financing positions intended to be held for the long term or to maturity are valued on a historical cost basis.

### Assets and Liabilities Should Appear on the Balance Sheet

As the values of financial assets and liabilities change, so too does the value of the firm. Hence, it is important for the firm to recognize gains and losses on financial assets and liabilities as they occur. According to FAS #133, financial assets and liabilities such as derivative transactions are measured on the balance sheet at market value, even if they have offsetting cash flows that result in no net cost, as in a currency forward or swap contract. Changes in value from marking-to-market are reported in earnings. Under this rule, gains or losses from currency speculation are immediately recognized in the firm's financial statements.

> ***Derivatives should appear on the balance sheet, unless they are a hedge.***

The only exception to this rule is for derivative transactions used to hedge an underlying risk exposure. Rather than recognizing gains or losses immediately as financial assets and liabilities are marked-to-market, gains or losses from hedges are recognized as the hedge and its underlying exposure mature. In this case, special hedge accounting rules apply.

### Accounting for Hedge Transactions

According to FAS #133 and other national and IASs, accounting for gains or losses associated with derivative transactions depends on the use of the derivative. The reason for these special hedge accounting rules is that financial market transactions distort the balance sheet when they are used as hedges. Hedge accounting rules recognize hedges that reduce risk by offsetting a gain or loss on an underlying exposure.

**Derivatives and the Balance Sheet** To illustrate the impact of including derivative hedges on the balance sheet, consider the balance sheet of U.S.-based Brothers and Sons, Inc.

**Brothers and Sons, Inc.**

| **Assets** | | **Liabilities and owners' equity** | |
|---|---|---|---|
| Accts receivable (long £1,500) | $2,500 | Accts payable | $1,000 |
| Plant and equipment | $2,500 | Owners' equity | $4,000 |
| Total assets | $5,000 | Liabilities and owners' equity | $5,000 |

Brothers has a market value debt ratio of ($1,000/$5,000) = 0.20, or 20 percent. Brothers' accounts receivable balance is a £1,500 receivable denominated in pounds sterling, due in three months, and carried on Brothers' books at the current spot rate of £0.60/$.

To hedge this exposure, suppose Brothers sells £1,500 at a forward exchange rate of £0.60/$. This transaction creates an asset ($2,500) and an offsetting liability (£1,500), each with a maturity of three months. If Brothers places the forward contract on the balance sheet by recognizing a dollar receivable of $2,500 with an offsetting pound payable worth $2,500 at the forward rate of £0.60/$, the balance sheet will look like this.

**Brothers and Sons, Inc.**

| **Assets** | | **Liabilities and owners' equity** | |
|---|---|---|---|
| Accts receivable (long £1,500) | $2,500 | Accts payable | $1,000 |
| Forward asset (long $2,500) | $2,500 | Forward liability (short £1,500) | $2,500 |
| Plant and equipment | $2,500 | Owners' equity | $4,000 |
| Total assets | $7,500 | Liabilities and owners' equity | $7,500 |

These offsetting entries inflate Brothers' apparent debt ratio to ($3,500/$7,500) ≈ 0.48, or 48 percent. Yet Brothers is no more highly levered after the hedge transaction than before. If anything, Brothers is less risky after the hedge than before.

Currency forwards, futures, options, and swaps inflate reported debt ratios when they are capitalized on the balance sheet because they increase both assets and liabilities by the same amount. This is despite the fact that they usually are used to reduce risk, such as in Brothers' hedge of its pound sterling exposure. To avoid capitalizing hedges on the balance sheet, FAS #133 allows special accounting rules for qualifying hedge transactions.

### Hedging versus Speculation

> *Hedging and speculation are points on a spectrum.*

In a survey on derivatives usage, financial managers at large U.S. corporations were asked, "Do you speculate?" Respondents were nearly unanimous in answering "No!"[10] In a follow-up survey, executives were asked, "Does your view of the markets cause you to alter the timing of your hedge? The size of your hedge? To actively take positions?"[11] This question elicited quite a different response. With regard to foreign exchange transactions, 72 percent said they sometimes altered the timing of their hedges, 60 percent said they altered the sizes of their hedges, and 39 percent said they actively took positions in foreign currency without any underlying exposure. These were the same executives who, just one year earlier, claimed they did not speculate. Apparently, these executives believe there is a difference between outright speculation and active foreign exchange management.[12]

Accounting for derivatives is troublesome because it is difficult to distinguish between a hedge and a speculative position. Suppose you are a U.S.-based MNC with a receivable of ¥1 billion, which is worth \$10 million at the forward exchange rate of $F_1^{¥/\$} = ¥100/\$$.

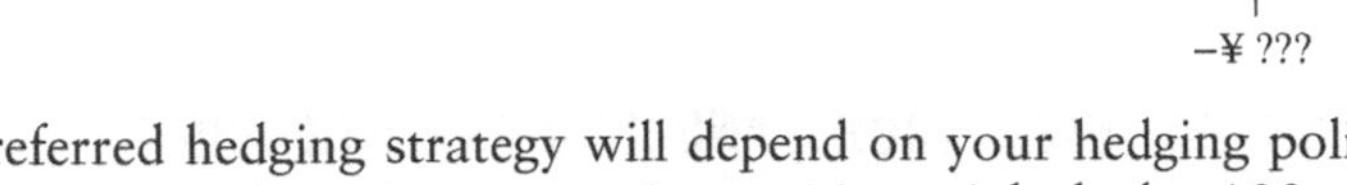


This position gains (loses) in value with a yen appreciation (depreciation). To hedge your position, you can sell yen at the forward exchange rate. How many yen should you sell?

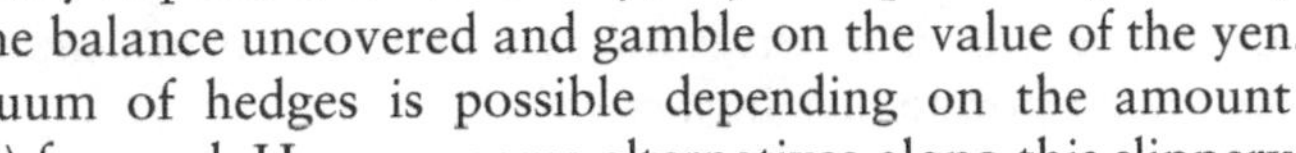


Your preferred hedging strategy will depend on your hedging policy and your exchange rate expectations. A conservative position might hedge 100 percent of the forward currency exposure. Alternatively, if you expect the yen to appreciate, you might leave the balance uncovered and gamble on the value of the yen.

A continuum of hedges is possible depending on the amount of yen sold (or purchased) forward. Here are some alternatives along this slippery slope.

1. Sell ¥1,000 million forward to eliminate your exposure to the yen.
2. Sell ¥500 million forward to cut your exposure to the yen in half.
3. Do not hedge and accept the future spot exchange rate.

4. Sell ¥1,500 million forward to take advantage of an expected depreciation of the yen.
5. Buy ¥500 million forward to take advantage of an expected appreciation of the yen.

Most people would say that strategies 1 and 2 are conservative and that 4 and 5 are speculative. Yet these are really just points along a continuum. If leaving a forward position uncovered as in strategy 3 is a form of currency speculation, then is selling a single yen forward a hedge? Speculation? Both? Is a position taken in anticipation of a possible future transaction a hedge or speculation? Accounting standards for hedge transactions must deal with these difficult issues.

**Qualifying a Hedge** To qualify for hedge accounting treatment under FAS #133 (and under the standards of Australia, the United Kingdom, the European Union, and the IASB), a hedge must be clearly defined, measurable, and effective. This requires that financial managers document their reasons for entering into or modifying a hedge. This documentation process can be complex and time-consuming.

> *Derivatives used as hedges qualify for special accounting rules.*

FAS #133 allows hedge accounting where there is a clearly identifiable exposure that is offset with a clearly identifiable hedge transaction. This makes it relatively easy to qualify a hedge of a transaction exposure. An example is a foreign currency receivable due in 90 days that is hedged with a 90-day forward contract. Another example would be a rolling hedge in which a long-term transaction exposure is hedged with successive short-term forward contracts or a currency swap contract. It is more difficult to qualify a hedge when there is not a clearly defined underlying exposure.[13] This is the case for most operating exposures, as well as for net transaction exposures.

FAS #133 recognizes derivative gains or losses immediately in earnings, along with the offsetting losses or gains on the underlying exposure. For hedges of anticipated foreign currency transactions, FAS #133 recognizes gains or losses in a balance sheet reserve account and then flows these into earnings when the underlying exposure is recognized and capitalized on the balance sheet. This allows both sides of the hedged position to be recognized at the same time.

## 11.4 ACCOUNTING, DISCLOSURE, AND CORPORATE HEDGING ACTIVITIES

The accounting treatment of derivatives interacts with the firm's information environment to influence corporate hedging activities.

### Accounting Disclosure and Adverse Selection

When there is inadequate accounting disclosure, informational asymmetries among investors can create ***adverse selection costs*** as uninformed investors attempt to protect themselves against trading with informed investors. Adverse selection costs inflate the bid-ask spread and impair liquidity in the firm's shares. To overcome investors' reluctance to buy shares in illiquid markets, firms must issue capital at lower prices, resulting in a higher cost of capital and lower firm value. Increased accounting disclosure can reduce information asymmetries between corporate insiders and outsiders, resulting in lower adverse selection costs, smaller bid-ask spreads, greater liquidity, lower costs of capital, and higher firm values.

*Adverse selection costs lead to lower liquidity and a higher cost of capital.*

The diversity of accounting conventions around the world creates even more asymmetry between informed and uninformed investors, despite the efforts of the IASB to internationalize accounting standards. Without detailed information about future prospects, investor uncertainty and diversity of opinion can lead to higher share price volatility and lower trading volume. If the costs of becoming an expert on national and IASs could be overcome, increased accounting disclosure should increase (1) the quality of earnings, (2) trading volume, and (3) share price sensitivity to underlying risk exposures. Increased disclosure also should decrease (1) share price volatility, (2) bid-ask spreads, and (3) the equity cost of capital.

## The Value-Relevance of Derivatives Disclosures

When U.S. firms issue securities to the public, they are required to file a 10-K statement with the Securities and Exchange Commission (SEC) that discloses information about the firms' securities. The SEC requires that 10-K statements include information about corporate exposures to interest rate, exchange rate, or commodity price risks. These forward-looking, quantitative risk assessments must be disclosed as (1) tables of fair values and contract terms sufficient to identify the expected maturity dates and cash flows of financial price risks, (2) sensitivity analyses of the likely effect on earnings, cash flows, and market values of possible changes in financial prices, or (3) value-at-risk measures expressing estimates of potential loss with a certain level of confidence and over a certain horizon due to adverse movements in financial prices. Studies have found that increased disclosures about financial price risks have the following share price effects:

- Increased share price sensitivity to changes in underlying financial prices[14]
- Lower trading volume sensitivity to changes in underlying financial prices[15]

These results are consistent with increased accounting disclosure increasing the consensus among investors, reducing investor uncertainty, and increasing the quality of information.

Additional evidence on the value of accounting disclosure to international investors comes from Germany. Disclosure requirements under German accounting standards were relatively few until the European Union adopted IASB disclosure standards in 2005. Before that time, several German firms voluntarily adopted U.S. FASB or international IASB standards to attract international investors, which substantially increased their disclosure requirements. Increased disclosure should lower adverse selection costs and result in lower bid-ask spreads and higher trading volume. Consistent with theory, Leuz and Verrecchia found that this commitment to increased disclosure resulted in lower bid-ask spreads and higher trading volume, other things being equal.[16]

*Derivatives disclosures are value-relevant.*

The economic value of increased disclosure has been corroborated in other studies. Wang, Alam, and Makar study the disclosures of U.S. commercial banks and find that the derivatives disclosures required by FAS #119 and #133 provide value-relevant information to the market.[17] Bailey, Karolyi, and Salva examine non-U.S. firms that cross-list in the United States and conclude that the additional responsiveness of the market to earnings announcements by these firms is due to increased disclosure, rather than to changes in market liquidity, ownership, or trading venue.[18]

### The Impact of FAS #133 on Corporate Hedging Activities

Bodnar, Hayt, and Marston surveyed U.S. firms on the impact of FAS #133 on corporate hedging activities and derivatives usage.[19] As shown in Figure 11.3, 37 percent of derivatives users expressed high concern over the accounting treatment of derivatives. High concern over derivatives' market risks (i.e., unexpected changes in market values) was expressed by 31 percent of derivatives users. Monitoring and evaluating hedge performance was of high concern to 29 percent of users. Credit risk was fourth in importance on the list with 25 percent of respondents expressing high concern, even though in the 1995 Wharton survey it caused the most concern among derivatives users.[20] Respondents thought the remaining three issues were of relatively low concern. The accounting treatment of derivatives is clearly managers' #1 concern, and continues to be a point of contention between accounting standard setters and business managers.

*Managers worry about derivatives accounting.*

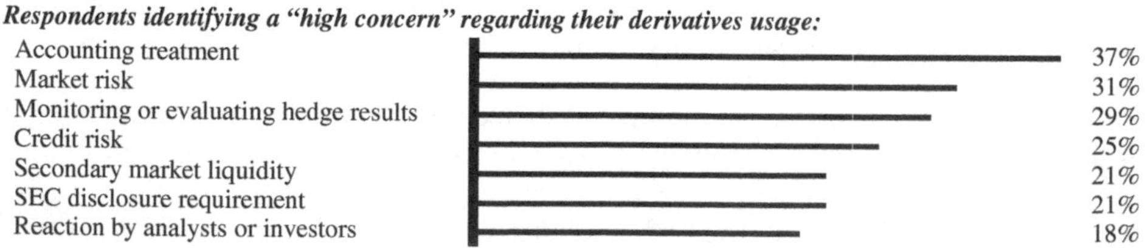


**FIGURE 11.3** Managers' Concerns Regarding Derivatives.
Source: Bodnar, Hayt, and Marston, "1998 Wharton Survey of Financial Risk Management by U.S. Non-Financial Firms," *Financial Management* 27 (Winter 1998).

## 11.5 SUMMARY

Translation (or accounting) exposure refers to the impact of changes in currency values on a firm's consolidated financial statements. Differences between translation methods arise when some accounts are translated at current exchange rates and other accounts are translated at historical exchange rates. The key issues in translation accounting for a foreign subsidiary are: (1) the operating exposure of real assets; and (2) how to treat gains or losses from foreign currency translations of balance sheet accounts.

In the United States, FAS #52 "Foreign Currency Translation" translates *all* assets and liabilities except equity at the current exchange rate. Equity is translated at historical exchange rates. This method correctly values monetary assets and liabilities, and implicitly assumes that real assets are exposed one-for-one to exchange rate changes. Translation gains or losses from changes in balance sheet accounts do not appear in reported earnings. Instead, they are recorded as a CTA in the equity portion of the balance sheet.

According to most finance theory, only exposures that are related to cash flow should be hedged. Translation exposure can have indirect cash flow consequences above and beyond the firm's transaction and operating exposures when the following conditions hold:

- Loan covenants are tied to measures of accounting income.
- Meeting profit forecasts retains management's credibility in the marketplace.
- Credit ratings are tied to accounting performance rather than cash flow.

Whether for legitimate or for self-serving reasons, many managers prefer to hedge translation exposure to currency risk. Allowing managers to hedge against currency risk can be valuable when it helps to align managerial incentives with shareholder objectives.

Finally, we discussed accounting for financial market transactions, including derivative instruments such as forwards, futures, options, and swaps. This is a difficult area of accounting because the effect of a financial market transaction depends on how it is used—as an investment, to fund operations, as a hedge, or for speculative purposes. In the United States, FAS #133 applies the following rules to derivative transactions:

- Derivatives are assets and liabilities that should be reported in financial statements.
- Fair (market) value is the most relevant measure of value.
- Changes in the values of assets and liabilities should be reported on the balance sheet rather than on the income statement.
- Special rules for hedge accounting are limited to qualifying hedge transactions.

Financial managers must document and justify their hedges in order to qualify for the hedge accounting rules and keep derivatives off the balance sheet.

## KEY TERMS

*adverse selection costs*
*agency costs*
*cumulative translation adjustment (CTA)*
*current rate method of FAS #52*
*economic value added (EVA)*
*monetary/nonmonetary translation method*
*net exposed assets*
*reliability and relevance (accounting definitions)*
*translation (accounting) exposure*

## CONCEPTUAL QUESTIONS

11.1 List the translation accounting rules of the U.S. standard FAS #52 "Foreign Currency Translation."

11.2 For which accounts does FAS #52 do a good job? For which accounts is it less reliable?

11.3 According to theory, what determines whether an exposure to currency risk should be hedged?

11.4 List three information-based reasons for hedging a translation exposure to currency risk.

11.5 How can corporate hedging of translation exposure reduce the agency conflict between managers and other stakeholders? In what other ways can agency conflicts be reduced?

11.6 Identify several cross-border differences in corporate hedging of translation exposure. What might account for these differences?

11.7 Recommend general policies for deciding whether to hedge a translation exposure to currency risk.

11.8 Describe the rules of FAS #133 "Accounting for Derivative Instruments and Hedging Activities."

11.9 What are the advantages and disadvantages of valuing assets and liabilities at historical cost? At market value?

11.10 How did accounting standard-setters react to the derivatives-related failures of the 1990s?

11.11 What is the IASB? Over which national accounting organizations does it have jurisdiction?

11.12 What is a hedge? Why is it difficult to distinguish a hedge from a speculative position? How does a hedge qualify for the hedge accounting rules under FAS #133?

## PROBLEMS

11.1 Finlandiva, a furniture manufacturer based in Finland, is owned by U.S.-based Couch Potato, Inc.. Finlandiva's balance sheet at the current exchange rate of $1.00/€ is shown in the following table:

| Assets | Value in euros | Value at $1.00/€ | Value at $0.80/€ | Translation gains or losses |
|---|---|---|---|---|
| Cash & marketable securities | €50,000 | $50,000 | | |
| Accounts receivable | €30,000 | $30,000 | | |
| Inventory | €20,000 | $20,000 | | |
| Plant and equipment | €900,000 | $900,000 | | |
| **Total assets** | **€1,000,000** | **$1,000,000** | | |
| **Liabilities** | | | | |
| Accounts payable | €125,000 | $125,000 | | |
| Short-term debt | €75,000 | $75,000 | | |
| Long-term debt | €750,000 | $750,000 | | |
| Net worth | €50,000 | $50,000 | | |
| **Total liabilities & net worth** | **€1,000,000** | **$1,000,000** | | |

a. Identify Couch Potato's exposed assets, exposed liabilities, and net exposed assets under FAS #52.
b. Identify the impact of a 20 percent depreciation of the euro on Couch Potato's consolidated balance sheet.

11.2 Vincent's Folly, a yo-yo manufacturer based in Canada, is owned by YoBeta, Inc., of the United States. Vincent's balance sheet at the current exchange rate of C$1.60/$ is shown as follows:

| Assets | Value in C$ | Value at C$1.60/$ | Value at C$1.50/$ | Translation gains or losses |
|---|---|---|---|---|
| Cash & marketable securities | C$320,000 | $200,000 | | |
| Accounts receivable | C$160,000 | $100,000 | | |
| Inventory | C$640,000 | $400,000 | | |
| Plant and equipment | C$480,000 | $300,000 | | |
| **Total assets** | **C$1,600,000** | **$1,000,000** | | |
| **Liabilities** | | | | |
| Accounts payable | C$320,000 | $200,000 | | |
| Wages payable | C$160,000 | $100,000 | | |
| Net worth | C$1,120,000 | $700,000 | | |
| **Total liabilities & net worth** | **C$1,600,000** | **$1,000,000** | | |

a. Identify YoBeta's exposed assets, liabilities, and net exposed assets under FAS #52.
b. Identify the impact of a depreciation of the U.S. dollar from C$1.60/$ to C$1.50/$ on YoBeta's consolidated balance sheet.

11.3 Silver Saddle Motel of Santa Fe, New Mexico, has the following balance sheet:

| Assets | | Liabilities and owners' equity | |
|---|---|---|---|
| **Current assets** | | **Current liabilities** | |
| Accounts receivable (€60,000 at \$1.00/€) | \$60,000 | Accounts payable (MXN300,000 at MXN0.10/\$) | \$30,000 |
| **Fixed assets** | | **Long-term liabilities & owners' equity** | |
| Furnishings (beds & blankets) | \$30,000 | Long-term debt | \$170,000 |
| Property and buildings | \$910,000 | Owners' equity | \$800,000 |
| Total assets | \$1,000,000 | Total liabilities & owners' equity | \$1,000,000 |

Silver Saddle's accounts payable balance is a 300,000 Mexican peso (MXN) purchase of authentic Mexican rugs and blankets for use in the motel. The purchase is denominated in Mexican pesos (MXN) and was placed on the books at an exchange rate of \$0.10/MXN. The balance is due in six months and is payable in Mexican pesos. To hedge this peso exposure, Silver Saddle decides to buy MXN 300,000 six months forward at a forward rate of \$0.10/MXN.

a. What are Silver Saddle's accounts if this forward transaction is capitalized on the balance sheet as a forward asset of MXN 300,000 (worth \$30,000 at the \$0.10/MXN forward exchange rate) and an offsetting forward liability of \$30,000?
b. Calculate Silver Saddle's current ratio (current assets divided by current liabilities) and debt-to-assets ratio (including all liabilities except owners' equity in the numerator of the debt-to-assets ratio) before and after the forward contract is capitalized. Is Silver Saddle's financial risk higher or lower after the Mexican peso liability is hedged? How do you reconcile this conclusion with the apparent deterioration in Silver Saddle's debt-to-assets (leverage) and current (liquidity) ratios? Explain.
c. Can Silver Saddle qualify this hedge under the FAS #133 rules? What will Silver Saddle's balance sheet look like if the forward currency transaction is accounted for as a hedge?

11.4 Consider Problem 11.3. The accounts receivable balance is an anticipated receipt of €60,000 in six months from a German tourist agency. The tourist agency insists on paying in euros. Silver Saddle can hedge its euro exposure at a forward rate of \$1.00/€, which also happens to be the current spot rate of exchange. Repeat parts a through c of Problem 11.3 for this forward hedge. In what ways is this hedge of an anticipated future receipt different from the hedge of a future obligation in Problem 11.3?

11.5 Consider Problem 11.3. The owner often has Canadian visitors that prefer to pay in Canadian dollars. Her intuition tells her that the Canadian dollar will close above the \$1.10/C\$ 6-month forward price. She buys C\$20,000 six months forward at this price. Repeat parts a through c of Problem 11.3 for this transaction. In what ways is this position different from the underlying exposure and hedge in Problem 11.3?

11.6 The spot exchange rate between won and dollars is $S_0^{W/\$} = W1000/\$$. Interest rates are the same in the United States and S. Korea, so $F_1^{W/\$} = S_0^{W/\$} = W1000/\$$ through interest rate parity. The Korean subsidiary of a U.S. parent purchases an asset worth $1 million and capitalizes this asset in its financial statements at $BV_0^W = (P_0^\$)(S_0^{W/\$}) = (\$1\text{million})(W1000/\$) = W1$ billion. Suppose the spot rate is $S_1^{W/\$} = W1250/\$$ in one year, and that the dollar value of the Korean asset remains $1 million.

a. The parent firm consolidates its financial statements at the end of the year. Translate the book value of the Korean asset back into dollars at the current spot rate and the historical cost of W1 billion.
b. How large is the translation gain/loss on this asset from the perspective of the U.S. parent? Is this translation loss to the U.S. parent also an economic loss?
c. Suppose the parent hedges against the translation loss by selling W1 billion forward one year. What is the consequence of this forward hedge for the net translation exposure of the firm? Compare the consequence of this forward hedge for the translation and economic exposures of the firm.
d. Is this forward hedge likely to qualify as a hedge under FASB #133?

## SUGGESTED READINGS

### The effect of accounting disclosures on the firm's information environment is discussed in


Warren B. Bailey, George Andrew Karolyi, and Carolina Salva, "The Economic Consequences of Increased Disclosure: Evidence from International Cross-Listings," *Journal of Financial Economics* 81 (July 2006), 175–213.

P.A. Belk and M. Glaum, "The Management of Foreign Exchange Risk in U.K. Multinationals: An Empirical Investigation," *Accounting and Business Research* 21 (Winter 1990), 3–14.

Peter M. DeMarzo and Darrell Duffie, "Corporate Incentives for Hedging and Hedge Accounting," *Review of Financial Studies* (Fall 1995), 743–771.

Yuan Ding, Ole-Kristian Hope, Thomas Jeanjean, and Hervé Stolowy, "Differences between Domestic Accounting Standards and IAS: Measurement, Determinants and Implications," *Journal of Accounting and Public Policy* 26 (January–February 2007), 1–38.

Thomas J. Linsmeier, Daniel B. Thornton, Mohan Venkatachalam, and Michael Welker, "The Effect of Mandated Market Risk Disclosures on Trading Volume Sensitivity to Interest Rate, Exchange Rate, and Commodity Price Movements," *Accounting Review* (April 2002), 343–377.

Christian Leuz and Robert E Verrecchia, "The Economic Consequences of Increased Disclosure," *Journal of Accounting Research* 38 (Supplement 2000) 91–124.

Shivaram Rajgopal, "Early Evidence on the Informativeness of the SEC's Market Risk Disclosures: The Case of Commodity Price Risk Exposure of Oil and Gas Producers," *Accounting Review* 74 (July 2002), 251–280.

Li Wang, Pervaiz Alam, and Stephen Makar, "The Value-Relevance of Derivative Disclosures by Commercial Banks: A Comprehensive Study of Information Content under SFAS Nos. 119 and 133," *Review of Quantitative Finance and Accounting* 25 (December 2005), 413–427.

### Managers' responses to translation exposure to currency risk are discussed in

Raj Aggarwal, "Management of Accounting Exposure to Currency Changes: Role and Evidence of Agency Costs," *Managerial Finance* 17, No. 4 (1991), 10–22.

Gordon M. Bodnar and Gunther Gebhardt, "Derivatives Usage in Risk Management by U.S. and German Non-Financial Firms: A Comparative Survey," *Journal of International Financial Management & Accounting* 10 (Autumn 1999), 153–187.

Gordon M. Bodnar, Gregory S. Hayt, and Richard C. Marston, "1995 Wharton Survey of Derivatives Usage by US Non-Financial Firms," *Financial Management* 25 (Winter 1996), 113–133.

Gordon M. Bodnar, Gregory S. Hayt, and Richard C. Marston, "1998 Wharton Survey of Financial Risk Management by U.S. Non-Financial Firms," *Financial Management* 27 (Winter 1998), 70–91.

Gordon M. Bodnar, Gregory S. Hayt, Richard C. Marston, and Charles W. Smithson, "Wharton Survey of Derivatives Usage by U.S. Non-Financial Firms," *Financial Management* 24 (Summer 1995), 104–114.

Jayne M. Godfrey and Benita Yee, "Mining Sector Currency Risk Management Strategies: Responses to Foreign Currency Accounting Regulation," *The Accounting Review* 26 (Summer 1996), 200–214.

Antti Hakkarainen, Nathan Joseph, Eero Kasanen, and Vesa Puttonen, "The Foreign Exchange Exposure Management Practices of Finnish Industrial Firms," *Journal of International Financial Management & Accounting* 9, No. 1 (1998), 34–57.

Carol Olson Houston and Gerhard G. Mueller, "Foreign Exchange Rate Hedging and SFAS No. 52—Relatives or Strangers?" *Accounting Horizons* 2 (December 1988), 50–57.

Laurent L. Jacque and Paul M. Vaaler, "The International Control Conundrum with Exchange Risk: An EVA Framework," *Journal of International Business Studies* 32, No. 4 (2001), 813–832.

### Issues involved in qualifying a hedge under FAS #133 are discussed in

Ira G. Kawaller, "What Analysts Need to Know about Accounting for Derivatives," *Financial Analysts Journal* 60 (March/April 2004), 24–30.

Ira G. Kawaller, "Interest Rate Swaps: Accounting vs. Economics," *Financial Analysts Journal* 63 (March/April 2007), 15–19.

# PART Four

# Valuation and the Structure of Multinational Operations

*Opportunities always look bigger going than coming.*

—Anonymous

# CHAPTER 12

# Foreign Market Entry and Country Risk Management

*Listen up, my Cossack brethren.*
*We'll ride into the valley like the wind, the thunder of our horses*
*and the lightning of our steel striking fear in the hearts of our enemies!*
*...And remember—stay out of Mrs. Caldwell's garden.*

—Gary Larsen, *The Far Side*

This chapter introduces several modes of entry into international markets. It then describes sources of country risk and their cash flow consequences for international investors and the multinational corporation (MNC). Strategies for reducing exposures to country risk—preferably while maximizing the expected return on investment—are then examined.

The chapter begins with a description of alternative entry modes into foreign markets including exporting, international contracting, and investment-based foreign market entry. Many important issues regarding the choice of market entry mode are addressed. For example, why are some manufactured goods and services successfully exported while other products and services sell only in local markets? Why do some MNCs prefer to export while others build overseas manufacturing facilities and invest directly in the foreign market? When are franchising and licensing preferred to exporting or foreign direct investment as a means of market entry? An understanding of the sources of the MNC's competitive advantage can provide insight into how multinationals create and preserve value through their foreign operations. This understanding can, in turn, guide the multinational financial manager's search for positive-net present value (NPV) investments and help the manager sustain these advantages despite the costs and risks of operating in unfamiliar business environments.

One of the most important risks facing the multinational enterprise is ***country risk***—the risk that the business environment in a host country will change unexpectedly. A corporation is exposed to country risk to the extent that its value changes with unexpected events in that country. Exposure to country risk results in more-uncertain investment and financial outcomes for the MNC.

The two most important sources of country risk are political risk and financial risk. ***Political risk*** is the risk that a sovereign host government will unexpectedly change the rules of the game under which businesses operate. Political risks arise because of unexpected changes in the political environment within a host country or in the relationship of a host country to other countries. ***Financial risk*** refers to unexpected events in a country's financial or economic situation. Financial risk is determined by a host of financial and economic factors, many of which are interrelated with political risk.

*Country risks include political and financial risks.*

Country risk indices usually have a political and a financial component. International lenders use these indices to judge the risks of lending to a particular country. As any loan officer knows, a creditworthy borrower must have both the *ability* and the *willingness* to repay a loan. In a sense, financial risk indices reflect a country's *ability* to repay its loans, whereas political risk indices reflect a country's *willingness* to repay its loans. Country risk indices are used by MNCs in much the same way that they are used by international lenders—to judge the risks of investing in a particular country. Country risk can affect the value of a MNC through changes in expected future cash flows or through changes in investors' required returns.

## 12.1 STRATEGIC ENTRY INTO INTERNATIONAL MARKETS

Figure 12.1 displays the risks of multinational operations as a function of the MNC's knowledge of, or experience with, a foreign market. Unfamiliarity with a market is the biggest obstacle to entry, so companies tend to first enter countries that are culturally close. These markets are more easily understood and offer more familiar operating environments than culturally distant ones. Knowledge of foreign markets increases with experience. As an MNC's knowledge of a foreign market grows, the real and perceived risks of dealing with the market usually decrease. With this increasing familiarity comes an increasing ability and willingness to take a more direct role in cross-border operations.

In the product life cycle, goods and services often are introduced in the home market and then marketed in foreign lands as the domestic market matures. The pace of this evolution varies in different countries. New products tend to be distributed first in advanced countries and only later in less developed countries.

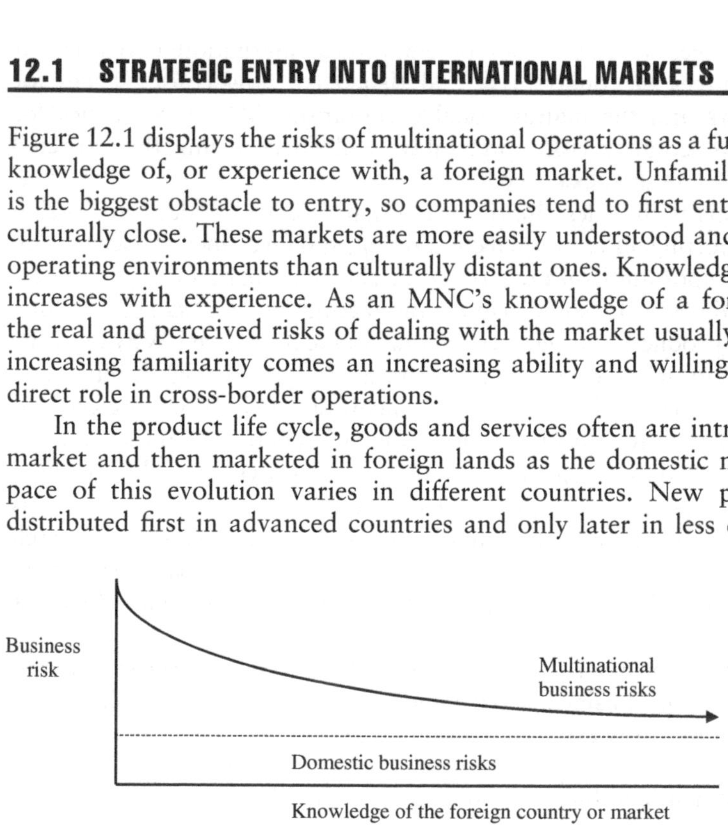


**FIGURE 12.1** The Risks of Foreign Operations as a Learning Curve.

Product evolution also proceeds at a different pace in different product markets. For example, new products tend to be introduced more quickly in technology-intensive industries than in consumer durables because of technology's shorter product cycle.

Products that have reached maturity in their home markets may be ripe for sale elsewhere. But what is the best way to enter a foreign market? There are several modes of entry, although the optimal form of entry depends on many country- and asset-specific characteristics. These forms of entry include

- Exporting
- Importing
- Contract-based entry (e.g., license agreements)
- Investment-based entry (including international joint ventures)
- Strategic alliance

The choice of entry mode is one of the most important strategic decisions made by the firm expanding into international markets. Once made, this choice cannot be easily reversed.

An important difference among these foreign market entry modes is the resource commitment of the parent firm. In exporting and licensing, production remains in the home country, and few resources need be committed to international operations. In investment-based entry, production is transferred to the host country and controlled by the parent company. This requires a substantially larger commitment of corporate resources including capital and management time. Required investment and ownership in a joint venture or strategic alliance are negotiated between the partners and hence vary across business deals.

Another important difference between these entry modes is whether the parent maintains control of the production process. In exporting, the parent transfers the final good or service from the domestic to the foreign market while maintaining domestic production. In contract-based entry, the rights to the production process usually are transferred from the domestic owner to a foreign licensee for an agreed-on length of time. In investment entry, the parent preserves an ownership stake in the foreign assets and may transfer control of the production process to the foreign market. In an investment-based joint venture, two or more partners share the benefits, costs, and risks by pooling their real, financial, or human resources.

## Export-Based Foreign Market Entry

*Exporting* relies on domestic production and foreign sales. Exporters cannot rely on the sympathy of host governments, so import barriers and foreign political risks can be high. On the other side of the coin, exporters do not have to worry about barriers to investment in the foreign market, and production technology is safely kept at home. The growth of worldwide package delivery services has made this form of market entry easier today than it was just two decades ago.

As the potential of a foreign market becomes apparent, producers need to consider the best way to gain entry to the market. Two effective approaches to market entry are through (1) a sales agent or distributor, or (2) a foreign sales branch or subsidiary.

**Agents or Distributors** A relatively low-risk mode of export entry is to use a *sales agent* or distributor to handle marketing and distribution in the foreign market. Hiring an agent requires little commitment in time or capital on the part of the exporter. With little investment at risk, the exporter is relatively insulated from the risks of foreign sales. The producer retains control of production, ensuring that quality standards are maintained and that production technology stays at home. A disadvantage is that the exporter cedes control of marketing and distribution channels to the agent, which prevents the exporter from gaining experience in foreign markets.

*Sales agents provide an easy way to enter foreign markets.*

Sales agents can be based in the domestic or the foreign market. Although exporters without international experience often are more comfortable dealing with domestic export agents, domestic agents are not as familiar as a local agent with the preferences and peculiarities of the foreign market. Domestic sales agents do have the advantage of being more aware of the exporter's goals and preferences.

Key to the relationship between the exporter and the sales agent is the termination or cancellation clause in the sales contract. The termination clause is a double-edged sword. With a strong termination clause, the exporter can exercise more control over the agent, terminate the contract if the contractual performance criteria are not met, or even exit the market. However, to fully commit to the sales arrangement, the sales agent must have some assurance of a continuing relation with the exporter. To avoid cross-border legal disputes, the contract must be legally binding in both countries and should identify the jurisdiction in which disputes are to be settled.

**Foreign Sales Branches or Subsidiaries** As they become more familiar with foreign markets, exporters often take a more active role in marketing and distribution through a ***foreign branch or foreign subsidiary***. Foreign subsidiaries are incorporated in the host country, whereas foreign branches are treated as a part of the parent rather than as a separate legal entity in the host country. Because of this difference, the choice between a foreign sales branch and a foreign sales subsidiary is driven by liability and tax considerations.

This mode of entry can offer greater potential sales than a sales agent. Establishing a sales branch or subsidiary in the foreign market allows exporters to manage the marketing and distribution channels, and thereby reduce the agency costs involved in hiring a sales agent. Having a foreign branch also allows the manufacturer to be more aware of, and responsive to, changing conditions in the foreign market.

On the other hand, establishing a foreign sales branch comes with bigger risks because of the greater resource commitment. With an increased commitment, the exporter can find itself facing more business and political risk in its foreign operations. Moreover, if the exporter is unfamiliar with the culture of the foreign market, establishing a foreign branch can lead to unexpected delays and costs as the exporter deals with unfamiliar business conditions or governmental regulations.

These costs and risks must be weighed against the higher sales potential when considering this mode of foreign market entry.

### Import-Based Foreign Market Entry

***Importing***, the flip side of exporting, relies on foreign production and domestic sales. Importers buy goods from other countries because similar goods are more costly, of poorer quality, or simply unavailable in the domestic market.

Successful importers sometimes extend their business models through other market entry modes. For example, U.S.-based Nike Corporation has become a MNC by exporting its brand name and business model to countries outside the United States. Nike was founded in 1980 as an importer of footwear, apparel, and sporting equipment from factories in Asia. Nike is now a multinational company with sales throughout the world, although its suppliers are still from Asia. In 2011, the United States accounted for only 36 percent ($7.5 billion) of Nike's $20.9 million in revenue. Nike's biggest sales growth was from emerging markets. Nike's footwear was primarily sourced from hundreds of suppliers in China, Vietnam, Indonesia, and Thailand. These countries are suppliers to Nike and other importers because of their abundant and low-cost labor.

Rapid globalization and the quest for low-cost production have fostered poor working conditions in many developing countries, and importers such as Nike are often criticized for their overseas labor practices. Children in developing countries often work in conditions that would not be tolerated in developed countries. The United Nation's International Labor Organization (www.ilo.org) estimates that one out of six children in the world is employed and more than half work in hazardous conditions, often in agriculture. This is a difficult social issue, as refusing to employ children merely sends them out into the streets and even more difficult social and economic circumstances. In response to activist protests and media exposés, many MNCs have developed factory-monitoring programs to ensure compliance with international labor standards. Nike has an entire division devoted to its contractor compliance program.

### Contract-Based Foreign Market Entry

In an international ***license agreement***, a domestic company (the licensor) contracts with a foreign company (the licensee) to market the licensor's products in a foreign country in return for royalties, fees, or other compensation. The foreign licensee assumes the responsibility of producing, marketing, and distributing goods or services in the foreign market. The international licensing agreement is designed to ensure that a standardized product or service is delivered to the foreign market, to protect the licensor's reputation in both the domestic and foreign markets. International license agreements come in many forms, including franchise agreements (McDonald's or Hilton Hotels), reciprocal market agreements (common in the pharmaceutical industry), and management contracts (Disney's theme parks in France, Japan, and Hong Kong).

Licensing has several advantages for the MNC. It provides rapid and relatively painless entry into foreign markets without a large resource commitment. Licensed products and services are produced in the host country, so import quotas or tariffs are not a hindrance and political risk is low. Although the resource commitment of the licensor is small, returns can be limited as well. For example, host governments sometimes impose a limit (such as 5 percent of revenues) on the royalties that can be repatriated to the parent through an international license agreement.

### Investment-Based Foreign Market Entry

Manufacturing firms typically use exports for their initial entry into international markets. Exporting is a low-risk way to acquire knowledge of foreign markets. Unless the MNC already has experience exporting to a particular market, investment-based entry typically comes later in the product life cycle, usually when the product is in the mature stage in its domestic market. That is when the manufacturer begins to look for ways to extend the product life by penetrating new markets or reducing operating costs.

> *Investing requires a high resource commitment.*

Investment-based entry into foreign markets can be accomplished in several ways.

- Foreign direct investment
- International mergers and acquisitions
- International joint ventures

Investment-based market entry differs from exporting in that production typically is shifted to the foreign country while ownership and control are retained by the parent corporation. Because this requires a large resource commitment, great care must be taken before using one of these entry modes. The manufacturer must be far enough down the learning curve of Figure 12.1 to ensure that it can avoid the more obvious pitfalls in its international management, marketing, production, and distribution functions.

> *Market entry methods include foreign direct investment (FDI), mergers and acquisitions (M&A), and joint ventures (JV).*

**Foreign Direct Investment** Building productive capacity directly in a foreign country is called *FDI*. An important advantage of market entry through FDI is that it can provide a more sustainable foothold in the foreign market. The principal disadvantage is the higher resource commitment of the parent.

Although FDI is evaluated in much the same way as domestic investment, it is exposed to additional risks that may or may not be offset by higher revenues or lower costs. Because they entail substantial investments in capital and time, these investments should be analyzed with great care. The consequences of failure for managers and other stakeholders can be high.

> *M&A is the most popular cross-border investment vehicle.*

**Cross-Border Mergers and Acquisitions** Cross-border mergers or acquisitions are by far the most popular methods of obtaining control over assets in another country. In a cross-border merger or acquisition, a domestic parent acquires the use of a productive asset in a foreign country through one of three ways.

- Cross-border acquisition of assets
- Cross-border acquisition of stock
- Cross-border merger

An ***acquisition of assets*** is the most straightforward way to acquire productive capacity because only the asset is acquired. None of the liabilities supporting that asset are transferred to the purchaser. A major consideration in an asset acquisition is the purchase price. In particular, the cost of buying an existing manufacturing plant in a foreign country should be compared with the cost of building a similar plant through FDI.

In an ***acquisition of stock***, an MNC buys an equity interest in a foreign company. This is easiest to accomplish in countries with active public equity markets. The purchaser can make either a friendly offer to management or a (possibly hostile) offer directly to stockholders through the financial markets.

In a ***merger***, two firms pool their assets and liabilities to form a new company. Stockholders trade their shares in the original firms for shares in the new company according to a negotiated exchange ratio. For example, DaimlerChrysler was formed in the 1998 merger of Daimler-Benz and Chrysler Corporation.

Cross-border mergers can be difficult to consummate. Not only must a large proportion of stockholders in each company approve the merger (the proportion varies by company and by country), but the merger also must be approved by governments in each country. Mergers often have antitrust implications, and government agencies in different countries can have widely divergent views on what is in the public interest.

**International Joint Venture** An international *JV* is an investment-based agreement in which two or more companies pool their resources in order to execute a well-defined mission. A new company usually is created to accomplish the mission. Resource commitments, responsibilities, and earnings are contractually shared. JV are useful when companies in a single industry or in complementary industries want to share the risk of a large venture, such as development of a new product or market.

In an international JV, the incentive to act opportunistically and violate the terms of the agreement can be great once a foreign partner has acquired the technology necessary for production. The partner can become a competitor, sometimes even in the parent's home market. Because of this threat, an MNC using a JV must find the right partner and then structure the deal to their (mutual) advantage. Companies in technology-intensive industries, such as pharmaceuticals, electronics, and biotechnology, must maintain control of their patents, trademarks, and production technologies. When the risk of technology loss is high, another mode of market entry might be preferred.

### Foreign Market Entry through a Strategic Alliance

Although these entry modes have been presented as distinct categories, many cross-border alliances have elements of more than one entry mode. A ***strategic alliance*** is any collaborative agreement that is designed to achieve some strategic goal. Strategic alliances are used to reduce the costs and risks of product development in industries with heavy research and development (R&D) requirements, and to penetrate foreign markets in which domestic firms have little expertise or experience. Firms that master the intricacies of partnering can reap the benefits of access to new products and technologies without having to develop their entire product line from scratch.

Strategic alliances have been elevated to perhaps their highest form in the Japanese keiretsu system. A keiretsu is a collaborative group of firms that are integrated either horizontally in a conglomerate structure or vertically along a supply chain. Firms within a keiretsu have extensive relationships through share cross-holdings, employee exchanges, and cooperative business planning. Non-Japanese firms trying to enter the Japanese market have discovered that the keiretsu structure can be difficult to penetrate. For this reason, Japanese keiretsu are often criticized for excluding foreign companies from Japanese markets and creating barriers to foreign investment in Japan. Indeed, there are only a handful of U.S. parts suppliers operating in Japan because most Japanese automakers are members of a vertical keiretsu. On the other hand, there are more than a thousand Japanese parts suppliers operating in the United States.

## 12.2 COUNTRY RISK ASSESSMENT

Like other sources of risk, country risk is based on *unexpected* change in the business environment of a host country. If an MNC knows with certainty that a foreign income tax rate is to be increased from 10 percent to 30 percent, then this is not a source of risk. The higher tax rate will reduce future profitability, but by knowing the new tax rules in advance the firm can incorporate these rules into its investment, financial, and tax-planning decisions. The MNC faces country risk from the possibility that an *unexpected* change in that country's business environment will affect the value of the firm.

> *Country risk indices track the risks of investing in a single country.*

An entire industry is devoted to providing assessments of country risk. Figure 12.2 lists some of the providers of country risk rating services. Many of these services combine political risk assessment with an overall assessment of the business or financial climate in a country. For example, the Coface Group (see Figure 12.3) assigns an overall ranking similar to Moody's or Standard and Poor's (S&P's) bond

**Country risk ranking providers**

| | |
|---|---|
| Aon Risk Services–Political risk assessment (e.g., terrorism) | www.aon.com |
| Bank of America–Ability to pay, trade performance, indebtness | www.bankofamerica.com |
| Business Environment Risk Intelligence–Political, operational, repatriation | www.beri.com |
| Coface Group–Country, political & financial risk | www.coface-usa.com/ |
| Dun & Bradstreet–Political, economic, commercial | www.dnb.com |
| Economist Intelligence Unit–Political, policy, lending & trade | www.eiu.com |
| Euromoney / Risk Assessment Index–Political, financial, economic | www.euromoney.com |
| Institutional Investor–Country credit ratings | www.iimagazine.com |
| Moody's Investor Services–Sovereign debt ratings | www.moodys.com |
| Organization for Economic Co-Operation & Development–Economic surveys | www.oecd.org |
| Political Risk Services | www.prsgroup.com |
| International Country Risk Guide–Political, financial, economic | |
| Coplin-O'Leary Rating System–Financial transfer, direct investment, exports | |
| Standard and Poor's Ratings Group–Sovereign debt ratings | www.standardandpoors.com/home/en/us |

**Organizations that study global and regional risks**

| | |
|---|---|
| United Nations | www.un.org/en/ |
| World Bank | www.worldbank.org |
| World Economic Forum | www.weforum.org |

**FIGURE 12.2** Political and Country Risk Rating Services.

ratings to summarize a country's average credit risk. Predictably, the lowest risks are found in the developed countries of Europe, North America, Asia, and the Middle East. The highest risks are found in the developing countries of Africa, Southeast Asia, Central Europe, and South America.

In similar fashion, Political Risk Services' ICRG produces a composite index that is a weighted average of political (50 percent), financial (25 percent), and economic (25 percent) risk factors. The ICRG political risk index is based on qualitative characteristics that encompass a country's political leadership, the extent of government corruption, and internal and external political tensions. The ICRG economic risk index is based on a variety of quantitative elements, including a country's inflation rate, current account balance, and foreign trade collection experience. The ICRG financial risk index has both qualitative and quantitative components, including the country's history of losses from currency controls, asset expropriations, contract renegotiations, payment delays, and loan restructurings or cancellations.

Not surprisingly, country risk rankings from various sources are positively correlated. Erb, Harvey, and Viskanta calculated a cross-country correlation of 0.35 between the ICRG composite risk index and Institutional Investor's credit risk index and concluded that these indices reflect the same underlying economic phenomena.[1]

> ***Macro risks affect all firms in a host country, whereas micro risks are asset-specific.***

Companies that rate country risk typically provide macro assessments of country credit risk. ***Macro risks*** affect all firms in a host country. Examples of macro country risks include unexpected changes in a host country's monetary or fiscal policies,

| | Africa | Asia | Europe | Middle-East | Americas |
|---|---|---|---|---|---|
| A1 | | Australia, Hong Kong, Japan, New Zealand, Singapore, Taiwan | Luxembourg, Norway, Sweden, Switzerland | | Canada |
| A2 | | Malaysia, South Korea | Austria, Czech Rep., Belgium, Denmark, Finland, France, Germany, Malta, Netherlands, | Kuwait, Qatar | Chile, United States |
| A3 | Mauritius, Namibia, South Africa | China, India, Thailand | Estonia, Poland, Slovakia, Slovenia, United Kingdom | Israel, Oman, UAE | Brazil, Trinidad & Tobago |
| A4 | Algeria, Botswana, Morocco, Tunisia | | Iceland, Ireland, Italy, Lithuania, Spain, Turkey | Bahrain, Saudi Arabia | Colombia, Costa Rica, Mexico, Panama, Peru, Uruguay |
| B | Benin, Cape Verde, Gabon, Ghana, Senegal, Tanzania | Indonesia, Papua New Guinea, Philippines | Bulgaria, Croatia, Cyprus, Hungary, Kazakhstan, Latvia, Portugal, Romania, Russian Fed. | Jordan | Dominican Rep., El Salvador, Guatemala |
| C | Angola, Burkina Faso, Cameroon, Congo, Djibouti, Ethiopia, Kenya, Madagascar, Mauritania, Mozambique, Niger, Sao Tome, Sierra Leone, Togo, Uganda, Zambia | Bangladesh, Mongolia, Sri Lanka, Timor-Leste, Vietnam | Albania, Armenia, Azerbaijan, Georgia, Greece, Macedonia, Montenegro, Serbia | Egypt, Lebanon | Argentina, Bolivia, Ecuador, Honduras, Jamaica, Paraguay, Venezuela |
| D | Burundi, Chad, Central African Rep., Dem. Rep. of Congo, Eritrea, Guinea, Equatorial Guinea, Ivory Coast, Liberia, Malawi, Mali, Nigeria, Rwanda, Sudan, Zimbabwe | Afghanistan, Cambodia, Laos, Myanmar, Nepal, Pakistan | Belarus, Bosnia & Herzegovina Kyrgyzstan, Moldova, Tajikistan, Turkmenistan, Ukraine, Uzbekistan | Iran, Iraq, Libya, Syria, Yemen | Cuba, Haiti, Nicaragua |

Not ranked: Gambia, Seychelles, Somalia, Swaziland, North Korea

**FIGURE 12.3** Coface Country Risk Ratings.
Source: The Coface Group, August 2011, www.coface-usa.com. Ratings measure average default risk on corporate payments and reflect local business, financial, and political outlooks. See the Coface website for current ratings.

banking system, tax rates, capital controls, exchange rates, or bankruptcy and ownership laws. Changes in any of these policy variables affect MNCs doing business in the country. Companies that rate country risk supplement their ratings with written analyses of the factors that contribute to country risk.

For a fee, these companies provide assessments of ***micro risks*** that are specific to an industry, company, or project. Changes in immigration laws are an example

## MARKET UPDATE Political Risk and "21st-Century Socialism" in Venezuela

Although asset expropriation has a low probability of occurrence in most foreign countries, the value of assets lost to a foreign government can be high. For this reason, the expected loss (the probability of a loss times the value of the loss) can be large. Venezuela's recent history serves as a cautionary tale for investors.

Venezuelan President Hugo Chavez's philosophy of "21st-century socialism" favors state ownership and control of key national industries and resources. Since his election as President in 1998, Chavez has moved to consolidate power and nationalize assets in oil (which accounts for more than 90 percent of Venezuela's exports), banking, and agriculture. MNCs that have had their assets expropriated or threatened with expropriation include Cargill, Coca-Cola, ExxonMobil, Haagen-Dazs, McDonald's, and Verizon. Venezuela has offered partial compensation, but many cases of expropriation have gone to arbitration before the World Bank International Centre for the Settlement of Investment Disputes (ICSID). Preserving asset value also is difficult for investors that remain in Venezuela, as the government limits repatriations from Venezuela to foreign multinationals. Even officially sanctioned repatriations can be politically difficult, as Transparency International's (www.transparency.org) "2010 Corruption Perceptions Index" ranks Venezuela 164th out of 178 countries. *Forbes* magazine ("Obama, Chavez and the American Shareholder," by Richard Miniter, January 12, 2011) quotes one investor as saying:

> *"You never know what Venezuelan President Hugo Chávez will say, but whatever it is, it will cost you money."*

of a political risk that differentially impacts some assets within a country. Most governments keep tight controls on foreign labor within their borders. Employers attempting to bring labor into a host country must demonstrate that imported laborers are not displacing domestic workers. Changes in immigration policies can adversely affect the competitive position of an MNC relative to local and global competitors if the MNC uses imported labor, such as expatriate managers from the home office.

### Political Risk

Political risk is the risk of an unexpected change in the political, legal, or regulatory environment. Political risks arise because of unexpected changes in the political environment within a host country or the relationship of a host country to other countries.

*Political risks are due to the political environment.*

Political risk is related to instability in a government or its policies. Stable governments tend to follow stable policies. Unstable governments are more likely to change policies and create political risks for the MNC. Policy instability is most pronounced when there is a factional change in government; that is, when a government changes hands. The bigger the factional change, the more likely is a policy change. In addition to the stability of government policies, the MNC must consider whether a change in policy is likely to be to its benefit or detriment. It is the adverse consequences of political risk that detract from firm value and most concern managers and other stakeholders.

Policy stability is greatest when power resides in a single political party. In democratic countries, governmental policies change through elections, referendums, and the normal legislative process. Changes tend to be small when the incumbent party retains power. Similarly, the policies of communist and socialist countries are likely to change only incrementally when the ruling party retains control. Political stability is somewhat less when control of the government passes from one group to another, such as between Democrats and Republicans in the United States, factions of the Liberal Democratic Party (LDP) in Japan, or factions of the Communist Party in Russia.

Policy stability is least when factional change is the result of an armed conflict, such as a war, revolution, insurrection, or coup. For example, after the Shah of Iran was deposed during the Iranian revolution of 1979, Iran expropriated (that is, seized) from foreign-based MNCs Iranian assets worth several billion dollars. The biggest losers were U.S. oil companies with investments in Iran. In response, the United States froze Iranian assets in the United States. It took the U.S.-Iran Claims Tribunal (an international tribunal based in the Netherlands) more than ten years to settle the resulting disputes. The largest settlement went to Amoco Corporation for $600 million. This settlement was only a fraction of Amoco's losses during the revolution and its aftermath.

MNCs are exposed to political risk at least in part because their objectives differ from those of host governments. A government's primary responsibility is to its citizens, and then to its society as a whole. Corporations are responsible to stockholders, bondholders and other creditors, employees, suppliers, and customers. Quite often, these stakeholders are concentrated in the MNC's home country and not in the host countries in which the corporation conducts its foreign operations. Even if corporate and governmental constituencies were one and the same, political leaders are responsible for the public good, and corporate leaders are responsible for the private welfare of their stakeholders. It is not surprising that governments and MNCs come into conflict.

Companies and organizations that specialize in political risk assessment base their analyses on an intimate knowledge of the local political environment, experience, and guesswork. Although these companies summarize their analyses into quantifiable measures of political risk, these political risk ratings largely depend on qualitative factors. The written analyses that accompany a political risk rating are at least as important as the rating itself.

## Financial Risk

In addition to political risk, country risk assessments usually include an assessment of a country's financial or economic risk. Financial risk factors include quantitative macroeconomic factors as well as qualitative factors that reflect a nation's financial or economic health. Quantitative macroeconomic factors include the following:

- Currency risk
- Interest rate risk
- Inflation risk
- The current account balance
- The balance of trade

***Financial risk measures are qualitative or quantitative.***

These macroeconomic factors are influenced by a government's monetary, fiscal, and trade policies, as well as many domestic and international events that are outside governmental control.

Many qualitative factors influence the financial environment. Like the quantitative factors, many of these qualitative factors have a political dimension. Political Risk Services' *ICRG* includes assessments of the following factors in their financial risk indices:

- Loan defaults or loan restructurings
- Payment delays
- Cancellations of contracts by a host government
- Losses from exchange controls
- Expropriation of private investments

Other companies that rank country risks include assessments of the extent of restrictive trade practices, tariffs, or trade regulations and the state of private ownership and bankruptcy laws. Political risk itself sometimes is included as a separate qualitative factor in determining a country's financial risk. Risk rating agencies summarize these factors into one or a few indices that reflect the local financial environment.

### Specific Types of Country Risk

This section discusses several specific sources of political risk that can affect the MNC's value, and hence are of concern to the multinational financial manager. Some of these political risks are categorized in Figure 12.4.

**Expropriation** Mao Zedong wrote: "Political power grows out of the barrel of a gun." Indeed, the most extreme form of political risk is ***expropriation***, in which a company's physical or financial assets are seized or confiscated by a foreign government. This most often occurs after an insurrection or a revolution, such as Iran's 1979 revolution, as the new regime attempts to throw out the foreign infidels and make a fresh start. Some form of expropriation is a possibility whenever extraordinary events take place. For example, the United States froze Osama bin Laden's U.S. assets (at least those that could be identified) after the Saudi millionaire and terrorist was implicated in the 1998 bombings of U.S. embassies in Kenya and

| | | |
|---|---|---|
| **Political risks** | | |
| Business environment factors | – | Taxes and tariffs |
| | – | Local content and labor regulations |
| | – | Protection of intellectual property rights |
| | – | Protectionism |
| | – | Tradition of law and order |
| Political environment factors | – | Civil war |
| | – | Corruption |
| | – | Military or religion in politics |
| | – | Racial or ethnic tensions |
| | – | Terrorism |
| **Financial risks** | | |
| Macro (economic) factors | – | Currency risk |
| | – | Inflation risk |
| | – | Interest rate risk |
| | – | The current account |
| | – | The balance of trade |
| Micro (asset-specific) factors | – | Cancellation of contracts by a host government |
| | – | Capital controls on investment, repatriation, or forex (FX) |
| | – | Involuntary loan defaults or restructurings |
| | – | Payment delays |
| | – | Expropriation |

**FIGURE 12.4** An Overview of Country Risks.

Tanzania. This is a common governmental response to real or perceived injuries by foreign parties.

*Expropriation can occur after war or revolution.*

From a conceptual standpoint, expropriation risk is relatively easy to handle. Nobody appreciates having assets confiscated, but you can plan ahead if you know that this is a possibility. The valuation methodology in Chapter 13 incorporates expropriation risk by assuming expropriation is diversifiable and hence does not affect the required return on investment, and then adjusting expected future cash flows for the probability of expropriation. In practice, expropriation is a messy affair that involves disruptions in operations in the short term, negotiations with the host government and affiliated parties in the intermediate term, and litigation through international courts in the long term.

**Disruptions in Operations** Expropriation is the most extreme form of political risk. However, political risk comes in many more-subtle forms that can disrupt the local and even worldwide operations of the MNC. Although the consequences for the MNC are not as catastrophic as outright expropriation, disruptions in operations are far more prevalent than disruptions in ownership.

*Political risks often disrupt operations.*

Governments impose burdens on MNCs through tariffs, local content regulations that require a certain percentage of the final product to be manufactured locally, foreign exchange controls, limitations on the use of expatriate workers, and taxes and regulations within the host country. In the absence of change in the business environment, each of these burdens is merely a cost of foreign operations. Occasionally host governments also provide incentives for foreign direct investment in the form of subsidized financing, import subsidies, or privileged access to restricted markets. If the magnitude of costs or incentives can change unexpectedly for political reasons, then this uncertainty creates a political source of risk in the host country.

Although political risk is relatively low in the United States, both foreign and domestic companies doing business in the United States are exposed to a variety of political risks. The U.S. Congress periodically tinkers with the U.S. tax code, and both foreign and domestic firms are subjected to periodic changes in the U.S. regulatory environment as well. Firms face political risk as these regulations evolve. Disruptions in the MNC's operations are bound to occur as governments implement their fiscal, monetary, and social agendas.

**Protectionism** Foreign firms often must overcome distrust and resentment in host countries. Although some products (such as Parisian fashions and U.S. cigarettes) command a certain romantic cachet among select foreign clienteles, local residents usually have a strong preference for homegrown products and services. Foreign firms exporting to the United States face "buy American" sentiment from individuals, government officials, labor unions, and special interest groups. Similarly, Germans prefer German beer, the French prefer French wine, and the Japanese prefer Japanese rice. This economic manifestation of nationalism is called ***protectionism*** when it is codified in a nation's business laws, regulations, or tax code.

> ***Protectionism is found in most countries.***

Governments routinely impose regulations to protect some segments of the domestic economy from foreign competition. For example, many governments impose "local content" rules that specify the percentage of goods that must be manufactured locally. Protectionism is particularly prevalent in manufacturing and agriculture.

It can be difficult to gain entry to foreign markets, even when the local government does not expressly restrict competition. For example, investment securities historically have been sold to individuals in Japan through networks of local agents visiting investors in their homes. This institutional structure began to change during the Japanese financial difficulties of the 1990s, as Japan began liberalizing its financial markets to allow greater access by foreign brokers, investors, and investment bankers. Nevertheless, a non-Japanese securities firm trying to establish a distribution network in Japan still faces formidable entry costs. The considerable uncertainty over the course and pace of reform are a significant political source of risk in Japanese financial markets.

**Blocked Funds** Funds generated by foreign investment that cannot be immediately remitted to the parent company are called ***blocked funds***. Blocked funds arise from repatriation restrictions placed by a host government on remittances to the parent company. An extreme form of restriction occurs when a host government does not allow its currency to be freely converted or exchanged into other currencies. This currency inconvertibility effectively locks cash flows from foreign sources in the foreign economy.

*Blocked funds can't easily be sent home.*

Blocked funds may or may not earn a rate of return in the foreign market that exceeds their cost of capital. If the host government has imposed both capital inflow and outflow restrictions, local rates of return can exceed comparable rates of return elsewhere in the world. More commonly, the host government places restrictions only on capital outflows to prevent capital flight and retain currency in a struggling local economy. In this circumstance, local rates of return are likely to be below rates of return available elsewhere.

In the absence of unexpected change in repatriation restrictions or currency convertibility, blocked funds are simply a cost of foreign operations.[2] Blocked funds become a political source of risk only when unexpected changes arising from political events affect the MNC's ability to remit funds from its foreign operations.

**Loss of Intellectual Property Rights** Another example of a political source of risk lies in the MNC's potential loss of intellectual property rights to competitors or former business partners through a government's actions or inactions. ***Intellectual property rights*** are patents, copyrights, trademarks, or proprietary technologies or processes (i.e., trade secrets) that are the basis of the MNC's competitive advantage in local and global markets. Corporations protect their intellectual property by restricting access to products, technologies, or processes. To the extent that a host government allows one or more local firms to steal or otherwise misappropriate the intellectual property rights of another company, that company is exposed to a political source of risk.

***Intellectual property rights could be a patent, copyright, trade secret, or trademark.***

MNCs must be especially careful to minimize their exposure to this political source of risk in developing countries. Developing countries are usually more interested in obtaining technology to promote economic growth than in protecting the intellectual property rights of foreign individuals or companies. If the MNC does not exercise vigilance in the management, control, and transfer of its intellectual property rights, it can find itself competing against former partners in foreign markets or even in its own domestic market.

## 12.3 STRATEGIES FOR MANAGING COUNTRY RISK

The magazine *Sports Illustrated* asked the following question during the 1992 Olympic Games in Barcelona: "How do you avoid being an ugly American in Barcelona?" The answer was "Don't go." Staying home—that is, not investing—is always an option for the MNC. According to discounted cash flow valuation methodology, the MNC should forgo any project with a negative NPV. It is especially important that the MNC consider all of the real options that come with foreign investment, as well as any opportunity costs of investing.[3]

With a little forethought, the MNC can take steps to maximize the expected return and minimize the damage of any negative political or financial events that might take place in a foreign country. Once an investment decision has been made, the MNC has four options for increasing the returns and decreasing the risks of foreign investment.

- Negotiate the environment with the host country.
- Obtain political risk insurance.
- Structure operations to minimize the MNC's risk exposure and maximize return.
- Plan for disaster recovery.

These strategies are discussed below.

### Negotiating the Environment

When a MNC invests in a foreign asset, it enters a relationship with a foreign host government. Some elements of this relationship are explicit, such as the laws of the host country that govern the corporation's behavior. Other elements are

#### MARKET UPDATE Political Risk in Indonesia

President Suharto assumed power in Indonesia in 1967 and ruled for more than 30 years. During this time, Indonesian law prohibited foreign investors from holding majority stakes in Indonesian firms. MNCs doing business in Indonesia routinely formed alliances with members of the Suharto family. When President Suharto was deposed during the currency and stock market crisis of 1998, there were massive public demonstrations and riots against the government amid charges of nepotism and corruption.

Although the transfer of power to Suharto's successor, B.J. Habibie, went fairly smoothly, companies doing business with the Suharto family were exposed to significant new political risks. For example, the Indonesian Attorney General's Office reviewed nearly $100 billion worth of deals that had been personally approved by former President Suharto. Many contracts with foreign MNCs were canceled or renegotiated on less favorable terms. These renegotiated contracts were a form of expropriation by the Indonesian government.

implicit, such as an expectation on the part of the MNC that the host government will not impose punitive tariffs or regulations after the firm has invested. As in any relationship, FDI involves give-and-take between the MNC and the host government.

Before investment, the MNC must negotiate with the host government to create an environment that maximizes its expected return on investment while minimizing exposure to political and financial risks. This negotiation often culminates in an ***investment agreement*** that spells out the rights and responsibilities of the MNC and the host government. In colonial times, these agreements were called *concessions* because they gave the multinational firm privileged or monopoly access to the resources of the host country, sometimes with little compensation to the host country. In today's more competitive international business environment, investment agreements are less likely to be concessions and more likely to benefit both the MNC and the local economy.

*Investment agreements specify each party's rights and responsibilities.*

The investment agreement should specify the rights and responsibilities of each party with regard to the investment and financial environments. The investment agreement also should specify remedies in case the relationship turns sour. In particular, it should specify a venue and identify jurisdiction for the international arbitration of disputes. The beauty of a well-conceived and carefully written investment agreement is that it allows both parties to act with dignity.

**The Investment Environment** These items in the investment environment should be negotiated.

- Tax rates, taxable bases, tariffs, and tax holidays
- Concessions that grant the MNC privileged access to restricted markets (e.g., an agreement that restricts the entry of competing firms)
- Obligations to undertake tie-in projects (e.g., negative-NPV infrastructure projects such as airports, ship yards, rail yards, schools, or hospitals)
- Rights or restrictions on imports from, or exports to, other markets (e.g., requirements on local sourcing of labor or materials or host-country quotas on local production)
- Provisions for planned divestiture of the investment (e.g., build-operate-transfer project financing transfers ownership to the host government after a prespecified period of time)
- Allowable uses of expatriate managers or technicians to run local operations
- Assurances of performance on the part of the MNC and the host government
  - Remedies against expropriation, renegotiation, or delay
  - Provisions and venues for the international arbitration of disputes

Each of these items in the investment environment affects cash flows from the project.

**The Financial Environment** These financial items should be negotiated.

- Rules governing remittance of cash flows from affiliates to the parent corporation
  - Transfer prices
  - Management fees
  - Royalties
  - Loan repayments
  - Dividends
- Access to capital markets in the host country
- The possibility of subsidized financing from the host government
- The corporate governance environment
  - Host-country restrictions on ownership of the local subsidiary
  - Remedies in the case of nonperformance or default by either party
  - Provisions and venues for the international arbitration of disputes

By negotiating with the host government prior to investment, the MNC can avoid adverse outcomes and more easily manage its affairs.

## Political Risk Insurance

Insurance contracts, such as insurance against political risk, are a form of put option. A put option is an option to sell an underlying asset at a specified exercise price on or before a specified date. Put options are used to protect against a drop in the value of the underlying asset. Insurance contracts are out-of-the-money put options in that they insure against negative outcomes but are left unexercised if the outcome is neutral or positive.

Many political risks can be mitigated through political risk insurance. A corporation's need for insurance depends on the extent of its geographic diversification and its exposure to political sources of risk. MNCs that have geographically diversified operations and cash flows in a large number of countries and currencies are, in essence, self-insuring. Less-diversified companies, especially those with a major proportion of their operations located in a single foreign country, have a much greater need for political risk insurance.

**Insurable Risks** An insurable political risk ideally would possess the following four conditions:

1. The loss is identifiable in time, place, cause, and amount.
2. A large number of individuals or businesses are exposed to the risk, ideally in an independently and identically distributed manner.
3. The expected loss over the life of the contract is estimable, so that the insurer can set reasonable premiums.
4. The loss is outside the influence of the insured.

The first condition is necessary to write an enforceable insurance contract based on a specific risk and a specific insured amount.

The second condition allows an insurer to spread losses across a large pool of insured parties. The relevant risk to the insurer is then the risk of the portfolio, rather than that of any single insurance contract in isolation. In this respect, micro political risks are better candidates for insurance than macro political risks because the insured events are more likely to be independent within any single country. Insurers must spread their macro political risks across a number of countries, ideally with independent political risk outcomes.

The third condition allows the insurer to set reasonable premiums based on the insurer's exposures to political risks. Private insurers will insist that premiums cover expected losses from political risk insurance. Governmental agencies sometimes set premiums below those of private insurance to promote trade with particular countries. Although governments are able to capture some societal benefits that private insurers cannot (such as increased or more stable employment in the domestic economy), in most instances the costs of below-market political risk insurance premiums are borne by the taxpayers of the sponsoring country.

The last condition rules out ***moral hazard***; that is, the risk that the existence of a contract will change the behaviors of parties to the contract. In the present context, the last condition precludes the insured parties from influencing the outcome or consequences of a political source of risk. This is a necessary condition, as insurance coverage reduces the incentives of insured parties to avoid losses or reduce the amounts lost in the event of adverse outcomes. For example, automobile owners are less concerned with protecting their vehicles when they are insured than when they are not insured.

**Insurable Political Risks** Exposed assets can be insured against the following political risks.

- Expropriation due to:
  - War
  - Revolution
  - Insurrection
  - Civil disturbance
  - Terrorism
- Repatriation restrictions
- Currency inconvertibility

As with any insurance policy, premiums rise as coverage is expanded to include more risks, as the insured amount increases, or as the likelihood of an adverse outcome increases.

**Political Risk Insurers** Political risk insurance is available from international agencies, government export credit agencies, and private insurers. Here are the major players.

- International agencies
  - The World Bank—Multilateral Investment Guarantee Agency (MIGA)

- Government export credit agencies
  - Canada—Export Development Corporation
  - France—Compagnie Francaise d'Assurances pour le Commerce Exterieur
  - Germany—Hermes Kreditversicherung
  - Hong Kong—Export Credit Insurance Corporation
  - Italy—Sezione Speciale per l'Assicurazione del Credito all'Esportazione
  - Japan—Ministry of International Trade and Industry
  - Netherlands—Nederlandsche Credietverzekering Maatschappij NV
  - United Kingdom—Export Credits Guarantee Department
  - United States—Overseas Private Investment Corporation (OPIC)
- Private insurers
  - Lloyd's of London
  - London-based Nelson Hurst PLC
  - U.S.-based American International Group (AIG)
  - U.S.-based Chubb Corporation
  - U.S.-based Reliance National Insurance Company
  - Bermuda-based Exporters Insurance Company
  - Bermuda-based Sovereign Risk Insurance Ltd.

By diversifying across countries and industries, these insurers spread political sources of risk from individual countries across their entire portfolio.

The World Bank created the MIGA in 1990 to promote international trade. MIGA's importance has grown with the growth of international trade. In 2010, MIGA issued $2.1 billion in guarantees and held an insured portfolio of several billion dollars. Companies based in the United States can obtain political risk insurance through a U.S. government agency called the OPIC, as well as through private insurers such as Lloyd's of London and AIG. OPIC is the largest national political risk insurer, with annual guarantees of more than $10 billion and coverage of up to $250 million per project for up to 20 years. Many other countries offer political risk insurance through government agencies.

Prior to the 1990s, government agencies such as OPIC were the primary underwriters of political risk insurance. Private insurers were not as active in insuring trade or investment risks. Political risk coverage typically was available only up to about $10 million and for terms of only about three years. During the 1990s, private insurers emerged as significant players in the market for political risk insurance. These private insurers have provided much-needed liquidity, increased insurable amounts to more than $100 million, and extended terms to as long as 20 years. They also established a reinsurance market that allows insurers to lay off their political risks onto other insurers or private investors.

***Private insurers provide liquidity to the market for political risk insurance.***

Growth in the private market for political risk insurance was driven by the increase in project finance during the 1990s. ***Project finance*** is a way to raise nonrecourse financing for a specific project. The project is established as a separate legal entity in the host country and relies heavily on debt financing with payments contractually linked to the cash flow generated by the project. Project finance has become a popular way to fund infrastructure projects in developing economies, especially power generation capacity and transportation (roads, rail, or airport) projects. Investors such as financial institutions rely on political risk insurance to mitigate the political risks of investment in these economies.

The costs of political risk insurance depend on the risks. Annual insurance premiums through private insurers can be as high as 10 percent of the amount of the investment in high-risk countries. OPIC insurance premiums are generally less than those of private insurers. The premiums of private insurers vary widely, so it makes sense to shop around.

## Political Risk and the Structure of Foreign Operations

The MNC's investment decisions are made through its capital budgeting process. Although this process culminates in a "go/no go" choice, the process should consider alternatives that determine how the investment is structured. These choices influence the project's marketing, production, distribution, human resource, and financial and operating leverage decisions. Careful choices in these areas can reduce the MNC's exposure to the consequences of harmful actions on the part of hostile or opportunistic host governments.

> *The MNC can limit its exposures to political risks.*

**Limit the Scope of Technology Transfer to Foreign Affiliates** Assets that reside in a foreign country are at risk of expropriation. This is as true for intellectual property rights, such as proprietary technologies and production processes, as it is for physical assets such as a research facility or a manufacturing plant. The MNC can reduce its exposure to expropriation by limiting the scope of any technology transfer to include only nonessential steps of the production process.

**Limit Dependence on Any Single Partner** A host government has more to gain through expropriation when an entire production process is housed in a single location. By maintaining relationships with more than one host government, the MNC can reduce its exposure to any single government and thereby reduce the risk of expropriation. For example, an automaker can source engines from one country, drivetrains from another country, and the chassis from a third country.

Similarly, maintaining more than one source for each component limits the MNC's exposure to political risk. A loss of capacity in one location can then be filled by other international sources. This also reduces the MNC's exposure to other sources of business risk, such as a labor strike in a foreign country or in the domestic country. Of course, the benefits of diversification must be balanced against the costs of maintaining relations with more than one partner.

**Enlist Local Partners** Local partners can reduce the MNC's exposure to political risk. For example, raising local debt and equity funds reduces the amount of money that the MNC has at risk in the local economy. Enlisting local employees or managers to run the business also helps insulate the MNC from adverse changes in the political environment. The likelihood and consequences of adverse outcomes are reduced when local stakeholders can represent the MNC in local affairs.

**Use More Stringent Investment Criteria** Discounted cash flow is the most commonly used capital budgeting criterion. According to this methodology, expected cash flows from investment are discounted at a rate that reflects investors' opportunity cost of capital to form an estimate of the NPV of a project. All incremental cash flows are to be included, and the discount rate should depend on the systematic risk of the asset.

MNCs sometimes modify this methodology when investing in uncertain environments. The two most common modifications to capital budgeting theory on investment in locations with high country risk are use of a short-term investment horizon and use of an inflated hurdle rate. The motivation for using a short-term horizon for investments in risky countries is to capture a return on investment before the situation in the host country can change. For example, the ***discounted payback period***—the length of time needed to recoup the present value of an investment—can be used to favor projects with a rapid return on investment.

Another common variation of NPV is to use an inflated or above-market hurdle rate on investments exposed to high country risk. Use of an inflated hurdle rate can be justified when it is difficult to value managerial flexibility in the face of uncertain investment environments. In particular, it can be difficult to value managerial options to expand, contract, or abandon a project with discounted cash flow methods. An inflated hurdle rate builds in a margin of safety for managers, and perhaps also for debt and equity stakeholders.[4]

Truncated investment horizons and inflated hurdle rates are, at best, ad hoc adjustments for high country risk. A better approach for capital-intensive projects is to try to identify possible future states of the world and anticipate how the MNC might respond to each state. In this way, the MNC can be proactive in an uncertain world and proceed with its investment decisions in the most informed way.

## Planning for Disaster Recovery

Once invested, the firm must work with its foreign partners in business and government to minimize the adverse consequences of political or financial events. If a worst-case scenario occurs, the corporation must take action to minimize its losses with an eye toward leveraging its experiences into new growth opportunities. Ideally, disaster recovery strategies are planned in advance. Advance planning can greatly increase the speed and effectiveness of the MNC's response to adverse outcomes.

> ***Disaster recovery strategies should be planned in advance.***

**MARKET UPDATE Creating and Maintaining Competitive Advantage at Apple**

In 2011, Apple topped *Fortune*'s list of the "World's Most Admired Companies" for the fourth consecutive year based on its run of successful product introductions of the iPod, iPad, and iPhone. These products were technical successes, yet it was Apple's canny marketing of these products that snared new buyers and ensured customer loyalty. Still, uneasy lies the head that wears a crown. Apple is in a fierce competition for telecom market share with Google and other service providers.

In sports, you're only as good as your last game. Similarly, businesses cannot rest on their past successes. Time will tell whether Apple can stay at the top of the charts. Let the games begin...

Consider the Iraqi invasion of Kuwait in 1990. Iraqi troops took just 12 hours to occupy the tiny, oil-rich country. In addition to threatening world peace, this invasion created a number of new risks for oil companies with Middle East operations. Assets were jeopardized, personnel were endangered, shipments and procurement became riskier and more difficult, and oil price volatility increased. Even before the U.N.-led counterattack against Iraq in January 1991, Kuwait officials had hired U.S.-based Bechtel Corporation as project manager to restore Kuwait's damaged oil capacity. Bechtel engineers entered Kuwait in March 1991, just days after Iraqi troops were ousted from the desert kingdom. Bechtel mobilized an international workforce of more than 16,000 specialists from more than 40 countries to put out more than 600 wellhead fires, assess the economic and environmental damage, and coordinate operations, procurement, logistics, and reconstruction of Kuwait's oil production capacity. After the last fires were extinguished in November 1991, Bechtel sent more than 200 engineers to rebuild Kuwait's infrastructure to its prewar production capacity of two million barrels per day. Although Bechtel's operations were by far the most extensive, other oil companies with assets in the region mounted similar disaster recovery operations. By being prepared with a disaster recovery plan, the MNC can minimize its losses and retain its foothold in foreign markets.

## 12.4 PROTECTING THE MULTINATIONAL'S COMPETITIVE ADVANTAGES

A key competitive advantage of MNCs is their ownership of intellectual property rights—patents, copyrights, trademarks, and trade secrets—and their ability to leverage these assets across national markets. Protection of these assets is a key strategic imperative.

### Intellectual Property Rights

Intellectual property rights are at the root of the MNC's competitive advantage. In order to encourage innovation, most governments allow protection of specific intellectual property rights for a fixed length of time after their creation. These protections provide a temporary monopoly to the inventor or creator.

> ***Protect your intellectual property rights.***

A ***patent*** is a government-approved right to make, use, or sell an invention for a period of time. The patent application process is an important competitive weapon in protecting and extending the MNC's global reach. Most countries follow some version of a *first-to-file* system in which patents are awarded to the first to file a patent application. This system encourages aggressive patent applications in order to protect both current and potential future innovations. The United States adopted a *first-to-file* system in 2011 (effective March 2013), replacing a *first-to-invent* system that had been at odds with international standards. Patent protection often lasts for 20 years counted from the filing date, following the World Trade Organisation's (WTO's) "Agreement on Trade-Related Aspects of Intellectual Property Rights" (TRIPs Agreement).

A ***copyright*** prohibits the unauthorized reproduction of creative works, including books, magazines, drawings, paintings, musical compositions, and sound and video recordings. Copyright protection in the United States lasts for the life of the creator, plus an additional 70 years. Computer software is an example of a creative work for which copyright laws vary greatly from country to country. Although the United States and most other developed countries extend copyright protection to computer software, many developing countries do not.

A ***trademark*** is a distinctive name, word, symbol, or device used to distinguish a company's goods or services from those of its competitors. Trademark protection varies from country to country. Trademarks in the United States are protected as long as they are in active use. The United States follows a first-to-invent policy by granting trademark protection to the first company to commercially establish a trademark in the marketplace. Most other countries follow a first-to-file policy, whether or not that individual or corporation has established the trademark in the marketplace. For this reason, MNCs can find their trademarks legally copied and used by competitors in foreign markets. If a local company already has trademark protection, the multinational can find itself competing against its own trademark. Registering a trademark in all possible future markets is a good idea for the MNC with a distinctive trademark or trade name.

A ***trade secret*** is an idea, a process, a formula, a technique, a device, or information that a company uses to its advantage. In the United States, protection of trade secrets is extended as long as the owner takes reasonable steps to maintain secrecy. This category includes a wide range of ideas and processes that may or may not be patentable. Whether to patent a trade secret is an important decision. Had Coca-Cola patented its formula for Coke when it was created in 1914, the company would have lost its patent protection just prior to World War I. By keeping it a trade secret, Coca-Cola has squeezed a full century of life out of the formula.

## Loss of Competitive Advantage

The MNC's intellectual property rights can be lost in any of three ways. First, these competitive advantages naturally dissipate as new products and technologies erode the value of old innovations. Managers must continually strive to leverage their core competencies into new products and new markets. Second, competitors can steal intellectual property rights. Third, the company's intellectual property rights can be transferred, either intentionally or unintentionally, to licensees and joint venture partners. This transfer can come with or without the knowledge and consent of the MNC. The rest of this section discusses the last two of these threats.

**Theft of Intellectual Property Rights** Theft of intellectual property rights is a growing problem, especially for MNCs from developed countries. Developing countries are desperate for technologies that will improve their standards of living, and they often pay less attention to intellectual property rights than more developed countries do. The governments of less developed countries often allow their local companies

### MARKET UPDATE The Modern Pirates of the High Seas

Developed countries such as the United States and Japan fight a fierce cross-border battle with developing countries over protection of intellectual property rights. Computer software companies such as Microsoft face rampant copyright infringement, even in those countries that do extend copyright protection to computer software. A 2010 study by the Business Software Alliance (www.bsa.org) estimated a worldwide software piracy rate of 42 percent that cost software companies $59 billion. Regional piracy rates were as follows:

- 64 percent in Central and Eastern Europe
- 64 percent in Latin America
- 58 percent in the Middle East/Africa
- 60 percent in Asia-Pacific region
- 33 percent in Western Europe
- 21 percent in North America

China has been one of the worst offenders. The Business Software Alliance estimates that 78 percent of the installed software in China is illegal. Attempts by the Chinese government to crack down on copyright infringement have met with limited success. When piracy operations are shut down in Shanghai, they often move to Hong Kong, Macao, or China's vast interior and continue operations. Indeed, pirated software was called "patriotic software" during China's emergence into international commerce because of its ability to speed the country's modernization efforts. Since its 2001 entry into the WTO, the Chinese government has been trying to develop a climate that protects intellectual property rights. There is clearly still a long way to go.

to acquire "by hook or by crook" any technology they can in fields such as pharmaceuticals, electronics, computer software, and publishing. Mechanisms for the protection of intellectual property rights are lax or nonexistent in many of these countries. Licensees sometimes steal technology with the implicit or even explicit cooperation of the host government. Intellectual property rights are vulnerable even in some developed and developing countries, including Hong Kong, Italy, South Korea, and Taiwan. To make matters worse, patent and trademark rights are conferred by individual nations, so contractual restrictions on where and when the licensee can sell a product may not have force in other countries. When patent protection is suspect, the risk of losing production technology makes cross-border collaboration less attractive.

**Sleeping with the Enemy** The MNC can extend its expertise into new markets or technologies by participating in strategic alliances and JVs. As Prahalad and Hamel observed, "Unlike physical assets, [core] competencies do not deteriorate as they are applied and shared. They grow."[5] However, in the dynamic give-and-take of a strategic alliance lies the MNC's biggest threat—the threat of an ally looting the company of its competitive advantages and then competing head-to-head with its former partner. How does the MNC allow its core competencies to grow through a strategic alliance without losing its competitive edge? Critical elements in a successful partnership include finding the right partner and appropriately structuring the deal.

### Finding the Right Partner and Managing the Relationship

The first and most important element in a successful partnership is in choosing the right partner.[6] In a successful partnership, neither party gains at the other party's expense. The partners share a common goal and agree on the means for attaining this goal. This seems like an obvious point, but good communication is truly the single most important element of any partnership.

> *Good partners are essential.*

Management must exercise patience in structuring the deal so that the goals of the alliance and the means of obtaining these goals are clearly defined. The more complicated the deal, the more patience is required. Once a partnership is formed, it is important for key executives from both companies to participate in the development and management of the partnership. Opportunism is most likely to raise its ugly head when the partners lose the need or the will to work together. Companies that can master these steps can gain access to new products and technologies, extend the life of their existing products, and reap the benefits of an increasingly integrated global village.

In addition to finding the right partner and working hard (and smart) to nurture the relationship, there are several more explicit ways in which the MNC can limit its exposure to technology loss through international alliances such as license agreements or joint ventures.[7]

- Limiting the scope of technology transfer to include only nonessential parts of the process
- Limiting the transferability of the technology by contract
- Limiting dependence on any single partner
- Using only assets near the end of their product life cycle
- Using only assets with limited growth options
- Trading one technology for another
- Removing the threat by acquiring the stock or assets of the foreign partner

These remedies limit the ability and willingness of the foreign partner to behave opportunistically and become a competitor rather than a partner.

## 12.5 SUMMARY

An initial entry into international markets often begins with importing or exporting, but is likely to evolve into international contracting or investment-based entry as international operations expand. These international operations bring additional sources of country risk; that is, the risk that the business environment in a host country will unexpectedly change. Country risk includes political and financial risks. Political risk is the risk of unexpected change in the political environment of a host country, whereas financial risk refers more generally to unexpected change in the financial, economic, or business environment of a host country.

A variety of national and supranational agencies and private companies provide country risk assessments. Macro assessments of a country's overall business climate are often supplemented with a micro assessment of the risk exposures of particular industries or companies.

The MNC's exposures to country risks can be managed in several ways. First, the investment and financial environments should be negotiated with the host government prior to investment to ensure that agreement is reached on each party's rights and responsibilities. This negotiation can take the form of an investment agreement between the host government and the MNC. A formal investment agreement can greatly reduce the risks involved in cross-border investment, allowing the host government and the MNC to strike a deal in which both parties benefit.

Political risk insurance can be used to cover the risks of repatriation restrictions, currency inconvertibility, and expropriation due to war or revolution. Political risk insurers are able to price these risks (and set premiums accordingly) because losses from these events are tied to an identifiable action by the host government. Country risks also are usually diversifiable in a global portfolio, allowing insurers to pool these risks across countries.

The MNC's competitive advantages are based on its intellectual property rights, which include patents, copyrights, trademarks, and trade secrets. The MNC protects and renews its intellectual property rights through investment in its existing core competencies and development of new core competencies. Strategic alliances are one way to obtain access to new core competencies, but they come with the risk of losing control of existing assets.

## KEY TERMS

*acquisition of assets or stock*
*blocked funds*
*copyright*
*country risk (financial risk or political risk)*
*discounted payback period*
*exporting*
*expropriation*
*foreign branch*
*foreign direct investment (FDI)*
*foreign subsidiary*
*importing*
*intellectual property right*
*investment agreement*
*joint venture (JV)*
*license agreement*
*macro and micro country risks*
*merger*
*moral hazard*
*patent*
*project finance*
*protectionism*
*sales agent*
*strategic alliance*
*trademark*
*trade secret*

## CONCEPTUAL QUESTIONS

12.1 Describe five modes of entry into international markets. Which of these modes requires the largest resource commitment on the part of the MNC? Which has the greatest risks? Which offers the greatest growth potential?

12.2 What are the relative advantages and disadvantages of FDI, international acquisitions and mergers, and international JVs?

12.3 Define country, political, and financial risks. Give an example of each different type of risk.

12.4 What factors contribute to risk in a country according to the ICRG country risk rating system?

12.5 What is the difference between a macro and a micro country risk? Give an example of each.

12.6 How is expropriation included in a discounted cash flow analysis of a proposed foreign investment? Does expropriation affect expected future cash flows? From a discounted cash flow perspective, is it likely to affect the discount rate on foreign investment?

12.7 What is protectionism, and how can it affect the MNC?

12.8 What are blocked funds? How might they arise?

12.9 What are intellectual property rights? How are they at risk when the MNC has foreign operations?

12.10 What is an investment agreement? What conditions might it include?

12.11 What constitutes an insurable risk? List several insurable political risks.

12.12 What operational strategies does the MNC have to protect itself against political risk?

12.13 How can the MNC protect its competitive advantages in the international marketplace?

## PROBLEMS

12.1 Russia suffered a currency and stock market crisis in 1998 that drove the dollar value of Russian stocks down to 10 percent of their pre-crash value. The crash caught investors by surprise, including hedge fund managers specializing in emerging markets. One hedge fund manager was quoted in the *Financial Times* ("Funds Suffer 'Confiscated' Russian Assets," by Eaglesham and Martinson, August 28, 1998, p. 22) as saying:

> *"If Russia had taken over a plant belonging to General Motors, the government would have done something about it.... Essentially, the Russian government has confiscated Western capital, and nobody is doing anything about it."*

Is the risk of a market crash in an emerging economy a political risk or a financial risk? Explain.

12.2 Expropriation occurs when a host government confiscates the assets of a corporation doing business in that country. Can expropriation occur in other ways? Explain.

12.3 Suppose the systematic risk of a domestic investment is $\beta_i = \rho_{iW}\ (\sigma_i/\sigma_W)$, where $\rho_{iW} = 0.4$ is the correlation between domestic asset returns and world market returns, $\sigma_i = 0.2$ is the standard deviation of returns to the domestic asset, and $\sigma_W = 0.10$ is the standard deviation of the world market return. A comparable foreign asset has $\rho_{i'W} = 0.3$ and $\sigma_{i'} = 0.3$.

a. Is the total risk of the foreign asset more or less than that of the domestic asset?
b. Is the systematic risk of the foreign asset more or less than that of the domestic asset?

12.4 Select a country (e.g., Brazil) of interest to you. Perform a search of popular and academic articles using as keywords: "*Brazil* AND *risk*." If you find too many entries under this search criterion, try more restrictive keywords such as credit risk, country risk, expropriation, copyright, patent, investment agreement, or protectionism. What types of country risks can you document for MNCs doing business in your chosen country?

## SUGGESTED READINGS

### The effect of political risk on required returns and the cost of capital on foreign investment is discussed in

Claude Erb, Campbell Harvey, and Tadas Viskanta, "Political Risk, Financial Risk and Economic Risk," *Financial Analysts Journal* 52 (November/December 1996), 28–46.

### Articles that address protection of intellectual property rights in the context of corporate strategy include

Gary Hamel, Yves L. Doz, and C. K. Prahalad, "Collaborate with Your Competitors—and Win," *Harvard Business Review* 67, (January–February 1989), 133–139.

C.K. Prahalad and Gary Hamel, "The Core Competence of the Corporation," *Harvard Business Review* 68 (May–June 1990), 79–91.

# CHAPTER 13

# Multinational Capital Budgeting

*There is nothing more difficult to take in hand, more perilous to conduct, or more uncertain in its success, than to take the lead in the introduction of a new order of things.*

—Machiavelli, *The Prince*

In principle, there is little difference between domestic and multinational capital budgeting. From the perspective of the parent firm, project value is still the discounted present value of expected cash flows from the investment discounted at an appropriate risk-adjusted cost of capital. Projects should be undertaken only if the present value of the expected future cash flows from investment exceeds the cost of the investment.

Although the principle is the same, in practice multinational investment decisions are more complex than their domestic counterparts. First and foremost, cross-border projects usually involve one or more foreign currencies. If the international parity conditions do not hold (and they usually do not), then the project will have a different value to foreign than to domestic investors. Cross-border projects also are more likely than domestic projects to involve special circumstances or side effects including capital flow restrictions that block funds in a host country, project-specific subsidies such as tax holidays or subsidized financing provided by host governments, or project-specific penalties such as tariffs or possible asset seizures by a host government. This chapter shows how to apply the discounted cash flow (DCF) framework to each of these multinational investment problems.

To simplify the analysis, we'll assume that the foreign project is 100 percent equity financed. This avoids the difficult issue of how the financing of a foreign project affects its value. We'll also assume that tax treatments in the foreign and domestic countries are the same. In practice, cross-border differences in taxes can have a large impact on project value. These topics are left to later chapters in order to focus on the identification and valuation of the expected future cash flows from a cross-border investment project.

## 13.1 THE ALGEBRA OF MULTINATIONAL CAPITAL BUDGETING

We'll begin our development of multinational capital budgeting from the capital budgeting recipe that you learned in your first course in finance.

## The Domestic Capital Budgeting Recipe

In your first course in finance, you learned to value assets using the *DCF* method. Consider a domestic company evaluating an investment proposal in its domestic currency. According to the DCF valuation method, the net present value (NPV) of a domestic project is calculated according to the following recipe:

1. Identify the expected future cash flows $E[CF_t^{\,d}]$ generated over the life of the investment, as well as the initial cost of investment $CF_0^{\,d}$.
2. Identify the discount rate $i^d$ appropriate for the risk of the cash flows.
3. Discount the expected future cash flows at the risk-adjusted discount rate.

For a project that lasts T periods, NPV is given by

$$V_0^{\,d} = \sum_{t=0}^{T} [E[CF_t^{\,d}]/(1+i^d)^t] \tag{13.1}$$

According to the DCF approach, projects should be undertaken if and only if their NPV is greater than zero.

In this approach, expected future cash flows are estimated according to two rules.

- Include only incremental cash flows.
- Include all opportunity costs.

The first rule says to *include only incremental cash flows* that are associated with the project in the capital budgeting analysis. Sunk costs that have already been spent, for instance, should not be included in the analysis. The second rule says to *include all opportunity costs* in the analysis. If building a manufacturing plant in Malaysia reduces sales from your Indonesian plant, then the cash flows associated with the reduction in sales from the Indonesian plant should be incorporated into the decision to invest in Malaysia. Lost sales from the Indonesian plant are an opportunity cost of opening the Malaysian plant.

*Discount rates should reflect the risk of the cash flows.*

Note that the discount rate depends on the nature of the cash flows. This is a more general and pervasive rule than you might think. In particular, you should

- Discount cash flows in a particular currency at a discount rate in that currency.
- Discount nominal (real) cash flows at a nominal (real) discount rate.
- Discount cash flows to equity (debt) at the cost of equity (debt).
- Discount cash flows to debt and equity at a weighted average cost of capital.

For example, discounting U.S. dollar cash flows at an Australian dollar discount rate is inappropriate. Similarly, discounting nominal cash flows at a real discount rate makes no sense. Follow these rules and your valuations will be, if not accurate, at least internally consistent. Violate any one of these rules, and your valuations are guaranteed to miss the mark.

## The International Parity Conditions and Project Valuation

There are two complementary approaches to the valuation of a foreign project. The first approach values the project in the foreign (or local) currency and then translates this foreign currency value into the parent's domestic currency at the spot rate of exchange. This is algebraically expressed as

$$V_0^{d}|i^{f} = S_0^{d/f}\left[\sum_{t=0}^{T} E[CF_t^{f}]/(1+i^{f})^{t}\right]$$

$$\text{or} \quad V_0^{d}|i^{f} = S_0^{d/f}V_0^{f} \qquad (13.2)$$

where $V_0^{f}$ is the value of the project in the foreign currency. This approach captures the domestic currency value of foreign cash flows *provided discounting is done in the foreign currency*, $V_0^{d}|i^{f}$.

***Projects can be valued from the parent's or from the project's perspective.***

The second approach takes the perspective of the parent corporation and discounts expected cash flows in the parent's domestic currency at the required return in that currency. This approach usually is conducted under the assumption that the international parity relations hold, so that

$$\begin{aligned} F_t^{d/f}/S_0^{d/f} &= [(1+i^{d})/(1+i^{f})]^{t} \\ &= [(1+E[p^{d}])/(1+E[p^{f}])]^{t} \\ &= E[S_t^{d/f}]/S_0^{d/f} \end{aligned}$$

These four ratios are in fact determined by the differential in expected inflation $(1+E[p^{d}])/(1+E[p^{f}])$, assuming equal real required returns. Expected cash flows from the project are then translated into the domestic currency at expected future rates of exchange as $E[CF_t^{d}] = E[CF_t^{f}]E[S_t^{d/f}]$.[1] Project value is the discounted present value of this cash flow stream over the life of the project.

$$V_0^{d}|i^{d} = \sum_{t=0}^{T} [E[CF_t^{f}]E[S_t^{d/f}]/(1+i^{d})^{t}] \qquad (13.3)$$

**Recipe 1 Project Valuation from the Foreign (or Local) Perspective**

**Discount – then convert:** $V_0^d|i^f = S_0^{d/f} [ \sum_{t=0}^{T} E[CF_t^f] / (1+i^f)^t ] = S_0^{d/f} V_0^f$

1. Estimate expected future cash flows $E[CF_t^f]$ in the foreign currency
2. Identify the appropriate risk-adjusted discount rate in the foreign currency $i^f$
3. Discount the foreign currency cash flows at the foreign currencydiscount rate to find its local value $V_0^f$
4. Convert the project's foreign value $V_0^f$ to the domestic currency at the spot rate $S_0^{d/f}$ to find $V_0^d|i^f$

**Recipe 2 Project Valuation from the Parent's (Domestic) Perspective**

**Convert – then discount:** $V_0^d|i^d = \sum_{t=0}^{T} [E[CF_t^d] / (1+i^d)^t]$ where $E[CF_t^d] = E[CF_t^f] F_t^{d/f}$

1. Estimate expected future cash flows $E[CF_t^f]$ in the foreign currency
2. Convert these foreign currency cash flows to the domestic currency at the forward exchange rates $F_t^{d/f}$
3. Identify the appropriate risk-adjusted discount rate in the domestic currency $i^d$
4. Discount domestic currency cash flows at the domestic discount rate to find $V_0^d|i^d$

**These two NPVs are the same <u>if</u> the international parity conditions hold.**

**FIGURE 13.1** Cross-Border Capital Budgeting Recipes.

where $V_0{}^d|i^d$ is the domestic currency value of the foreign project *provided discounting is done in the domestic currency.* Forward rates often are substituted as unbiased predictors of spot rates, in which case valuation from the parent's perspective is

$$V_0{}^d|i^d = \sum_{t=0}^{T} [E[CF_t{}^f]F_t{}^{d/f}/(1+i^d)^t] \tag{13.4}$$

These valuation equations are equivalent in that they value expected cash flows at an appropriate risk-adjusted discount rate—either in the foreign currency as in Equation 13.2 or in the parent's domestic currency in Equations 13.3 and 13.4. These approaches are summarized in Figure 13.1.

The good news is that these methods give the same result when the international parity conditions hold.[2] The bad news, of course, is that financial and (especially) goods markets are far from perfect and the parity conditions are a poor description of currency and Eurocurrency prices. Before we move on to these issues, let's set the stage by illustrating these approaches in a world in which there are no financial market imperfections and the international parity conditions hold.

## 13.2 AN EXAMPLE: WENDY'S RESTAURANT IN NEVERLAND

Wendy lives in London and is considering opening a restaurant in Neverland, an imaginary world in which markets are perfect and the international parity conditions hold.[3] Neverland is governed by the dread pirate Captain Hook, a vindictive tyrant with a consuming jealousy of Wendy and her friend Peter. We'll deal with Hook's influence on project value in Section 13.4 on special circumstances. For now, let's consider Wendy's investment proposal in its most basic form.

The details of Wendy's Neverland project appear in Figure 13.2. Wendy will purchase one of Captain Hook's ships and convert it into a fast-food restaurant to

- The project lasts four years, at which time Wendy grows up. (Only Peter stays young forever.)
- An initial investment of £10,000 (Cr40,000) will purchase Captain Hook's ship.
- An additional £6,000 (Cr24,000) will be needed for inventory at that time. Increases in other current asset accounts are offset by increases in current liabilities, so the increase in net working capital (current assets minus current liabilities) is also £6,000.
- Expected annual sales are Cr30,000, Cr60,000, Cr90,000, and Cr60,000 in nominal terms.
- Variable operating costs (wages to Lost Boys) are 20 percent of sales.
- Fixed maintenance costs on the ship are Cr2,000 at the end of the first year and are expected to increase at the rate of inflation thereafter.
- The ship will be owned by the foreign subsidiary. Neverland's tax code calls for the ship to be depreciated on a straight-line basis over four years to a zero salvage value.
- The inventory will be sold at the end of the project and is expected to retain its Cr24,000 real value.
- The ship is expected to retain its Cr40,000 real value.
- Income taxes are 50 percent in both the United Kingdom and Neverland. Capital gains on the sale of the ship and inventory at the end of the project are also taxed at 50 percent.
- All cash flows except the initial investment occur at the end of the year.

**FIGURE 13.2** Details of Wendy's Neverland Restaurant Project.

satisfy the appetites of the many pirates on the island. The ship is ship-shape and Wendy (with a little help from Peter) can have the galley ready for business at time $t = 0$. Wendy will invest the necessary equity capital. Peter will serve as the local manager of the restaurant, and the local Lost Boys will provide the labor.

Market rates are shown in Figure 13.3. The parity conditions are known to hold (this is an imaginary land), so the real required return on risk-free government bills should be the same in both British pounds sterling (Wendy's currency) and Neverland crocs (the foreign currency). Real required return is $\text{R}_F = 1$ percent per year in Figure 13.3.

According to the Fisher equation, the 20 percent nominal required return on comparable investments in the United Kingdom includes expected inflation and a real required return on restaurant projects according to $(1 + i^{£}) = (1 + E[p^{£}])(1 + \text{R}^{£}) = (1.0891)(1.1018) = 1.20$, or $i^{£} = 20$ percent.[4] Because the parity conditions hold, the real required return of $\text{R}^{£} = 10.18$ percent on restaurant projects in the United Kingdom must equal the real required return of $\text{R}^{Cr} = 10.18$ on restaurant projects in Neverland. With expected croc inflation of 36.14 percent, the nominal required return in crocs is given by $(1 + i^{Cr}) = (1 + E[p^{Cr}])(1 + \text{R}^{Cr}) = (1.3614)(1.1018) = 1.50$, or $i^{Cr} = 50$ percent. The international Fisher relation ensures the difference between nominal returns in Neverland and the United Kingdom is driven entirely by the difference in inflation between the two currencies. With the pound in the denominator of the international Fisher relation, nominal interest rates as well as the expected inflation rate are 25 percent higher in Neverland crocs than in pounds.

$$(1 + i^{Cr})/(1 + i^{£}) = (1 + i_F{}^{Cr})/(1 + i_F{}^{£}) = (1 + E[p^{Cr}])/(1 + E[p^{£}])$$
$$= (1.5000)/(1.2000) = (1.3750)/(1.1000) = (1.3614)/(1.0891) = 1.25$$

| | | |
|---|---|---|
| Expected annual inflation over the next four years | $E[p^{£}] \approx 8.91\%$ | $E[p^{Cr}] \approx 36.14\%$ |
| Nominal risk-free government T-bill rate | $i_F{}^{£} = 10.00\%$ | $i_F{}^{Cr} = 37.50\%$ |
| Nominal required return on risky restaurant projects | $i^{£} = 20.00\%$ | $i^{Cr} = 50.00\%$ |
| Real required return on T-bills | $R_F{}^{£} = 1.00\%$ | $R_F{}^{Cr} = 1.00\%$ |
| Real required return on risky restaurant projects | $R^{£} \approx 10.18\%$ | $R^{Cr} \approx 10.18\%$ |

**FIGURE 13.3** Interest and Inflation Rates in Neverland.

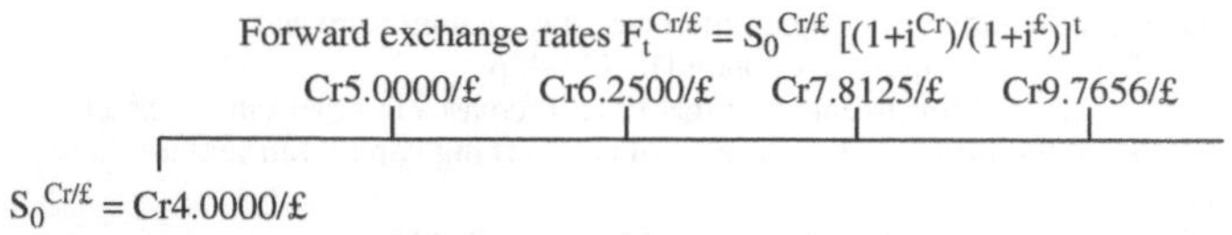


**FIGURE 13.4** Croc-per-Pound Exchange Rates.

This implies the forward premium on the pound and the expected change in the spot rate are 25 percent per year, so the pound (in the denominator) is expected to appreciate 25 percent per year.

$$E[S_t^{Cr/£}]/S_0^{Cr/£} = F_t^{Cr/£}/S_0^{Cr/£} = (1.25)^t$$

The current spot rate of exchange between the croc and the pound is Cr4.00/£. Forward prices at the 25 percent annual forward premium are shown in Figure 13.4.

### Recipe #1: Discounting in the Foreign Currency

Figure 13.5 displays the project's cash flows. As in a domestic capital budgeting problem, the task is made simpler if we view the cash flow stream as being composed of three parts: (1) the initial investment cash flow, (2) operating cash flows during the life of the project, and (3) end-of-project cash flows. The investment cash flows include the Cr40,000 cost of the ship and the Cr24,000 investment in net working

| **Discounting in crocs** | t=0 | 1 | 2 | 3 | 4 |
|---|---|---|---|---|---|
| Purchase ship | –Cr40,000 | | | | |
| Purchase inventory | –24,000 | | | | |
| Revenues | | Cr30,000 | Cr60,000 | Cr90,000 | Cr60,000 |
| – Variable operating costs | | –6,000 | –12,000 | –18,000 | –12,000 |
| – Fixed maintenance cost | | –2,000 | –2,723 | –3,707 | –5,046 |
| – Depreciation | | –10,000 | –10,000 | –10,000 | –10,000 |
| Taxable income | | 12,000 | 35,277 | 58,293 | 32,954 |
| – Taxes | | –6,000 | –71,639 | –29,147 | –16,477 |
| Net income | | 6,000 | 17,639 | 29,147 | 16,477 |
| + Depreciation | | 10,000 | 10,000 | 10,000 | 10,000 |
| Net CF from operations | | 16,000 | 27,639 | 39,147 | 26,477 |
| Sale of ship | | | | | 137,400 [a] |
| – Tax on sale of ship | | | | | –68,700 [b] |
| Sale of inventory | | | | | 82,440 [c] |
| – Tax on sale of inventory | | | | | –29,220 [d] |
| $E[CF_t^{Cr}]$ | $-^{Cr}64{,}000$ | $^{Cr}16{,}000$ | $^{Cr}27{,}639$ | $^{Cr}39{,}147$ | $^{Cr}148{,}397$ |
| $V_0^{Cr}$ at $i^{Cr} = 50\%$ | $-^{Cr}137$ | | | | |
| **Discounting in pounds** | t=0 | 1 | 2 | 3 | 4 |
| Expected spot $E[S_t^{Cr/£}]$ | 4.0000 | 5.0000 | 6.2500 | 7.8125 | 9.7656 Cr/£ |
| $E[CF_t^{£}]$ | –£16,000 | £3,200 | £4,422 | £5,011 | £15,196 |
| $V_0^{£}$ at $i^{£} = 20\%$ | –£34.25 | | | | |

**Key:** [a] $(^{Cr}40{,}000)(1.3614)^4 = {}^{Cr}137{,}400$ [b] $(^{Cr}137{,}400)(0.5) = {}^{Cr}68{,}700$
[c] $(^{Cr}24{,}000)(1.3614)^4 = {}^{Cr}82{,}440$ [d] $(^{Cr}82{,}440 - {}^{Cr}24{,}000)(0.5) = {}^{Cr}29{,}220$

**FIGURE 13.5** Valuation of the Neverland Project's Cash Flow.

capital. After-tax cash flows from operations in this example are straightforward, and can be computed from either of the following equivalent equations:

$$\begin{aligned} CF &= \text{After-tax operating income} + \text{Depreciation tax shield} \\ &= [(\text{Revenues} - \text{Expenses})(1 - T)] + [(\text{Depreciation})(T)] \\ \text{or} \quad CF &= \text{Net income} + \text{Depreciation} \\ &= [(\text{Revenues} - \text{Expenses} - \text{Depreciation})(1 - T)] + \text{Depreciation} \end{aligned}$$

where the corporate income tax rate T is assumed to be the same in both countries.[5] Croc cash flows from these equations are shown as "Net cash flow from operations" in Figure 13.5.

Wendy must recognize the after-tax value of the ship and inventory at the end of the project. The ship is expected to grow in value at the croc inflation rate to $(Cr40{,}000)(1.3614)^4 = Cr137{,}400$ at $t = 4$. The ship is being depreciated to zero over the life of the project, so the entire amount is a capital gain. Capital gains taxes are 50 percent in Neverland, so a payment of Cr68,700 is expected to be made to Hook's treasury at the end of the project. Inventory also is expected to grow in value at the croc inflation rate, so recovery of net working capital is expected to yield $(Cr24{,}000)(1.3614)^4 = Cr82{,}440$ after four years. If inventory is still carried on the books at its historical cost of Cr24,000, Wendy will have an expected taxable gain of $(Cr82{,}440 - Cr24{,}000) = Cr58{,}440$, and an expected capital gains tax liability of Cr29,220.

The resulting stream of nominal cash flows from the Neverland project is

| t = 0 | t = 1 | t = 2 | t = 3 | t = 4 |
|---|---|---|---|---|
| –Cr64,000 | Cr16,000 | Cr27,639 | Cr39,147 | Cr148,397 |

Wendy's investment is worth $V_0^{Cr} = -Cr137$ at the risk-adjusted croc discount rate of 50 percent. This is worth $V_0^{£}|i^{Cr} = S_0^{Cr/£}V_0^{Cr} = -£34.25$ to Wendy at the Cr4/£ spot exchange rate. Relative to the £16,000 (Cr64,000) investment, this is pretty close to a zero-NPV opportunity for Wendy.

### Recipe #2: Discounting in the Domestic Currency

Expected pound cash flows from the parent's perspective are shown at the bottom of Figure 13.5 after converting at the forward exchange rates. The NPV of Wendy's restaurant project is –£34.25, whether the cash flows are discounted in crocs or pounds.

NPVs from the croc and pound perspectives are equal in this example because the international parity conditions are assumed to hold. Compare this situation with one in which the required croc return on comparable projects is 60 percent rather than 50 percent. In that case, NPV depends on whether discounting is done in crocs or pounds. Tax differences and the size, timing, and form (dividends, interest, royalties, or fees) of cash flows back to the parent corporation can further distort the picture.

The remainder of this chapter develops a variety of real-world complications that can alter the simple logic underlying valuation of this cross-border investment.

Section 13.3 introduces violations of the international parity conditions and discusses their implications for the investment and financing decisions of the multinational corporation (MNC). In Section 13.4, Captain Hook causes a number of investment and financing nightmares for Wendy, as well as some business opportunities. These special circumstances are common in cross-border investments.

## 13.3 INTERNATIONAL PARITY DISEQUILIBRIA

The two capital budgeting recipes $V_0^d|i^f$ and $V_0^d|i^d$ yield consistent values when the international parity conditions hold. They can give conflicting results when international parity does not hold, such as when there are cross-currency differences in real required returns or risk premiums. They also give conflicting results when managers have an *exchange rate view* that differs from market expectations.

This section shows how the relative magnitudes of $V_0^d|i^f$ and $V_0^d|i^d$ can provide us with information on how to structure a cross-border investment when parity disequilibria or managers' expectations result in different values from the two perspectives. In particular, comparing the two project values can help us decide when to hedge a foreign project's cash flows, and when to leave the currency exposures unhedged and hope for the best.

### The Parent's and Project's Perspectives on Valuation

*The project view considers only local cash flows.*

**Project Valuation from the Local Perspective** A local perspective on project valuation is shown in Figure 13.6 for U.S.-based 3M Corporation's investment in China.

**3M's Chinese perspective**

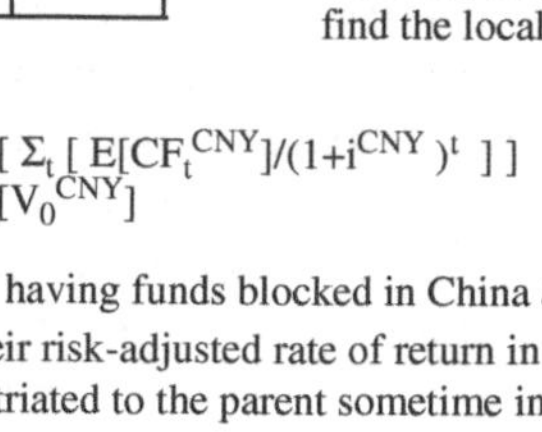


$CF_1^{CNY}$ $CF_2^{CNY}$ $CF_3^{CNY}$

$CF_0^{CNY}$

Discount CNY cash flows at $i^{CNY}$ to find the local currency value $V_0^{CNY}$

$$V_0^{\$}|i^{CNY} = S_0^{\$/CNY}\,[\,\Sigma_t\,[\,E[CF_t^{CNY}]/(1+i^{CNY})^t\,]\,] = S_0^{\$/CNY}\,[V_0^{CNY}]$$

The parent should not mind having funds blocked in China as long as:

(1) funds can earn their risk-adjusted rate of return in the local currency

and (2) funds can be repatriated to the parent sometime in the future

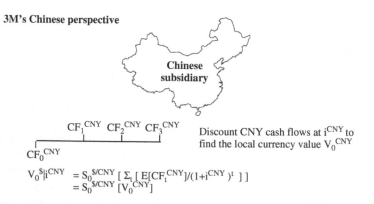

**FIGURE 13.6** Recipe #1: The Local Perspective on Project Valuation ($V_0^d|i^f$).

3M began as a sandpaper company, and its core competency remains applying coverings to backing materials. Its current product line is focused on storage media, including photographic films, digital displays, identification cards, and its ubiquitous Post-it notes.

3M's first foray into China was a sales office in Beijing opened in the early 1990s. The company did not expect to immediately recover this investment. Rather, by gaining a foothold in this huge market of more than one billion people, 3M hoped to earn a real (inflation-adjusted) return on its investment that exceeded what could be earned elsewhere on projects of similar risk. At the time of 3M's investment, Chinese repatriation restrictions prevented the firm from withdrawing its funds from China. However, if cash flows earned in China could be reinvested in other positive-NPV projects within China, then, as repatriation restrictions were eased and convertibility of the yuan improved, the hope was that eventually these assets would have a large dollar value.

It is useful to value projects relative to local alternatives in order to judge their relative merit in the local market. This is especially useful when the local government places repatriation restrictions on the return of capital to the parent. Repatriation restrictions come in many forms, including withholding taxes, royalty charges for patents or trademarks owned by a foreign parent, transfer pricing restrictions, and currency inconvertibility. Although most developed countries have liberalized their repatriation restrictions, many developing countries still limit repatriations.

**Project Valuation from the Parent's Perspective** 3M's investment in China is viewed from a U.S. perspective in Figure 13.7. A parent corporation's *functional currency* is usually its domestic currency because most of its functions are conducted in that currency. The relevant cash flows from the parent's perspective are those that are remitted to the parent in its functional currency, because these are the cash flows that are valued by domestic stakeholders.

> *Parents want cash in their functional currency*

**3M's U.S. perspective**

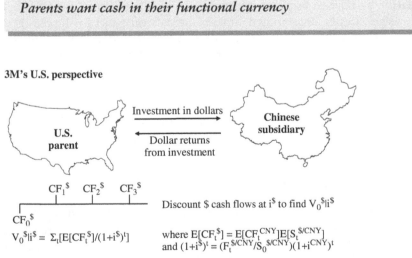

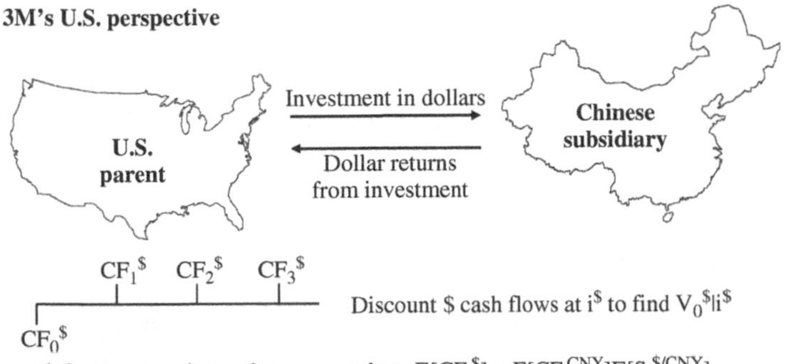


$V_0^{\$}|i^{\$} = \Sigma_t[E[CF_t^{\$}]/(1+i^{\$})^t]$ where $E[CF_t^{\$}] = E[CF_t^{CNY}]E[S_t^{\$/CNY}]$ and $(1+i^{\$})^t = (F_t^{\$/CNY}/S_0^{\$/CNY})(1+i^{CNY})^t$

The parent ultimately wants cash flows in its functional currency

**FIGURE 13.7** Recipe #2: The Parent's Perspective on Project Valuation ($V_0^d|i^d$).

Ultimately, foreign cash flows must be convertible into the MNC's functional currency in order to have any value to the parent's stakeholders. If cash flows from foreign investment cannot somehow be retrieved from the foreign country or converted into something of value to the firm's stakeholders, then foreign investment has no value to the firm's stakeholders and there is no incentive for the parent to undertake the foreign project.

MNCs sometimes do not have a single functional currency. These MNCs conduct operations and issue debt and equity claims in a variety of countries and currencies. 3M is an example of such a company, with assets that span the globe and a globally diversified investor base. 3M is nevertheless incorporated in the United States and considers the dollar to be its functional currency.

**Parity Disequilibria and Valuation Differences** We know that interest rate parity holds for *risk-free* interest rates and exchange rates.

$$F_t^{d/f} = S_0^{d/f}[(1+i_F^{\,d})/(1+i_F^{\,f})]^t \tag{13.5}$$

The international parity relations also suggest that expected future spot rates are related to nominal required returns according to

$$E[S_t^{d/f}] = S_0^{d/f}[(1+i^d)/(1+i^f)]^t \tag{13.6}$$

Disequilibria in the international parity conditions arise when there are cross-currency differences in real required returns or risk premiums in Equations 13.5 or 13.6.

The law of one price says that equivalent assets should have the same real required return and risk premium. Nominal required returns can be decomposed into expected inflation and a real required return: $(1+i) = (1+E[p])(1+\text{R})$. Nominal required returns also can be decomposed into a risk-free return and a risk premium: $(1+i) = (1+i_F)(1+rp)$. This latter characterization often is stated in arithmetic form as $i = i_F + rp$, as in the capital asset pricing model (see Chapters 14 and 20). Cross-currency differences in real required returns or risk premiums create a disconnect between Equations 13.5 and 13.6, such that $(1+i_F^{\,d})/(1+i_F^{\,f}) \neq (1+i^d)/(1+i^f)$. Managers also might have exchange rate expectations that disagree with the market's expectations. The consequences of such disagreements for project valuation are discussed below.

## How to Handle Valuation Differences

Consider the classification scheme in Figure 13.8. If both $V_0^d|i^f$ and $V_0^d|i^d$ are less than zero as in the top left cell, then the project clearly should be rejected. Conversely, if both $V_0^d|i^f$ and $V_0^d|i^d$ are greater than zero as in the bottom right cell, then the project clearly should be accepted. Ambiguous situations occur in the off-diagonal cells $V_0^d|i^d > 0 > V_0^d|i^f$ and $V_0^d|i^f > 0 > V_0^d|i^d$. The rest of this section provides guidance on what to do in the "ambiguous" and "accept" situations.

| | | Parent's perspective in the domestic currency | |
|---|---|---|---|
| | | $V_0^d\|i^d < 0$ | $V_0^d\|i^d > 0$ |
| Project's perspective in the foreign (or local) currency | $V_0^d\|i^f < 0$ Local value is negative | **Reject** This is a loser anyway you look at it | **Reject, but keep looking** Favorable forex (FX) rates suggest you keep looking for good investments in the foreign currency |
| | $V_0^d\|i^f > 0$ Local value is positive | **Accept and then structure the deal** Lock in the positive local currency value; e.g., through FX hedging or foreign currency financing | **Accept and then structure the deal** If $V_0^d\|i^d > V_0^d\|i^f$, hedging yields lower risk & lower expected return If $V_0^d\|i^d < V_0^d\|i^f$, hedging yields lower risk & higher expected return |

**FIGURE 13.8** The Parent's Perspective on Project Valuation.

**Positive-NPV for the Parent But Negative-NPV for the Project** If $V_0^d|i^d > 0 > V_0^d|i^f$ as in the top right cell, the project looks attractive from the parent's perspective but unattractive from the project's local perspective. In this case, the positive NPV from the parent's perspective is due to disequilibria in financial markets and owes nothing to the project itself. Indeed, the project is expected to lose value in the local currency.

*Reject any project for which* $V_0^d|i^d > 0 > V_0^d|i^f$.

A project can fall into the upper right cell of Figure 13.8 if spot rate expectations $E[S_t^{d/f}]$ are large relative to $F_t^{d/f}$, such that they turn a negative-NPV project valued at forward rates into a positive-NPV project valued at the expected spot rates $E[S_t^{d/f}]$ from Equation 13.6. Accepting a project solely to take advantage of parity disequilibria is a form of currency speculation, which need not rely on a risky foreign project that is negative-NPV when hedged. A more straightforward—and zero-NPV—bet would be to simply buy the foreign currency forward.

A project also might fall into the upper right cell when a manager has an optimistic exchange rate view relative to forward exchange rates. However, studies find that it is difficult to improve upon forward rates at long horizons. Accepting a project solely to take advantage of an optimistic exchange rate forecast is a form of currency speculation. Again, a manager need not rely on a risky foreign project that has a negative NPV when hedged in order to place a bet on exchange rates. Rather than accept a project that likely has a negative NPV from the project's local (or foreign) perspective, managers should continue to seek positive-NPV projects that don't rely on an exchange rate view for their value.

Rewards or penalties for currency speculation—either an outright position in the currency markets or via a cross-border investment project—depend on the firm's performance evaluation, employee compensation, risk tolerance, and risk management policies. Managers that choose to accept projects in the upper right cell of Figure 13.8 need to be confident of their exchange rate forecasts and stand ready to defend those forecasts if they differ from market-based forecasts such as the forward exchange rates.

**Positive-NPV for the Project But Negative-NPV for the Parent** If $V_0^d|i^f > 0 > V_0^d|i^d$ as in the lower left quadrant, the project is attractive from the local perspective but not from the parent's perspective. In this case, the project is worth more in the local or foreign currency than it is worth in the parent's domestic currency. The parent firm should try to realize the value of the project in the foreign currency and capture its value $V_0^d|i^f > 0$ today. This expected value can then be transferred to the parent corporation at today's spot rate of exchange.

*If $V_0^d|i^f > 0 > V_0^d|i^d$, then try to capture $V_0^d|i^f$.*

A negative expected value from the parent's perspective can arise from a disproportionately high (low) real required return or risk premium in the foreign (domestic) currency in Equation 13.6. Alternatively, a negative expected value from the parent's perspective can arise from a manager's pessimistic exchange rate forecast relative to forward rates. In either case, the manager can avoid the expected exchange rate loss by hedging the project's operating cash flows—or otherwise locking in the local currency or hedged value of the project.

Figure 13.9 lists several alternatives for locking in a positive expected value from the project's perspective. Perhaps the project could be sold to a local investor for whom the project has a positive NPV. If the project can be sold for its expected value $V_0^f$ in the foreign currency, the parent firm can then capture this value in its domestic (functional) currency today. Alternatively, the parent could form a joint venture partnership or sell a partial ownership position in the project to a local investor. The project is attractive in the local currency, so a local partner might be willing to form a joint venture partnership on terms that are advantageous to the parent corporation. Each of these asset-market alternatives is a way of locking in the positive-NPV value in the foreign (local) currency, while reducing the parent firm's exposure to currency risk over the life of the project.

**In the asset markets**

- Sell the project to a local investor
- Bring in a joint venture partner from the local market

**In the financial markets**

- Hedge the cash flows from the project against currency risk
    - Sell the foreign currency in the forward market
    - Pay foreign currency interest payments (and receive domestic currency interest payments) using a currency swap contract
    - Finance the project with local currency debt or equity

**FIGURE 13.9** Alternatives for Capturing the NPV of a Foreign Project.

In the real world, buying or selling foreign projects entails sunk costs that may be difficult to recover.[6] Actively managing the firm's real assets (e.g., by selling assets and then repurchasing them when exchange rates turn favorable) is much more costly than managing currency risk exposure through the financial markets. Moreover, active real asset management can put the MNC's intellectual property rights at risk. Selling a manufacturing plant to a local investor or sharing production processes with a local joint venture partner can create a future competitor in the parent firm's other worldwide markets.

A more realistic alternative for many parent firms is to use a financial market instrument that pays foreign currency—and receives domestic currency. These hedging alternatives include currency forwards, futures, and swaps, as well as foreign currency debt. Each of these contracts locks in foreign cash outflows that can at least partially offset expected operating cash inflows. Financial market hedges have the advantage that they are, by themselves, zero-NPV transactions. They also can be executed quickly and at low cost. The disadvantage of a financial market hedge is that the project's operating exposure to currency risk remains. A financial hedge does not change the variability of a project's underlying operating cash flows.

Currency options have a somewhat different role in hedging from that of currency forwards and forward-like instruments (i.e., futures, swaps, and foreign currency debt). Currency options lock in foreign outflows, but the nature of those outflows is asymmetric around the exercise price of the option. Because of the asymmetric nature of their payoffs, currency option hedges provide a "disaster hedge" or insurance against adverse exchange rate movements. For this reason, currency option hedges cannot be directly compared with forward-like hedges.

Whether it is best to hedge with a forward-like instrument (forwards, futures, or swaps) or with foreign currency debt depends on the relation of forward exchange rates $F_t^{d/f}$ to the firm's relative domestic and foreign borrowing costs $i_B^{\,d}$ and $i_B^{\,f}$.

$$S_0^{d/f}[(1+i_F^{\,d})/(1+i_F^{\,f})]^t = F_t^{d/f} \gtrless E[S_t^{d/f}] = S_0^{d/f}[(1+i_B^{\,d})/(1+i_B^{\,f})]^t \qquad (13.7)$$

If $F_t^{d/f} > S_0^{d/f}[(1+i_B^{\,d})/(1+i_B^{\,f})]^t$, then the firm should hedge the project's operating cash inflows with currency forwards to maximize the domestic currency value $E[CF_t^{\,d}] = E[CF_t^{\,f}]F_t^{d/f}$ of foreign cash flows. Conversely, if $F_t^{d/f} < S_0^{d/f}[(1+i_B^{\,d})/(1+i_B^{\,f})]^t$, then the foreign currency borrowing rate $i_B^{\,f}$ is a bargain relative to equilibrium and the project might be best financed with foreign debt.

> ***Hedge with FX forwards when*** $F_t^{d/f} > E[S_t^{d/f}]$.

This comparison sets the standard whenever the form of a hedge is being considered. If project cash flows are to be hedged, then the rule is to choose the hedging instrument that yields the lowest cost of foreign currency obligations and the highest expected value for the project.

**Positive-NPV for Both the Project and the Parent** When both NPVs are positive, a comparison of the two values can provide guidance on how to structure the deal.

***If $V_0^d|i^f > V_0^d|i^d > 0$, then the firm should hedge.***

When $V_0^d|i^f > V_0^d|i^d > 0$, the corporation should invest in the project. It should then hedge its exposure to currency risk or otherwise try to capture the value of the project in the foreign currency. The value of the project in the foreign currency can then be realized today and passed back to the parent in its domestic (functional) currency. In this case, hedging against currency risk has a double payoff. Hedging maximizes the expected return on the foreign project, while minimizing the corporation's exposure to currency risk. The choice of hedge follows the discussion around Equation 13.7 above.

When $V_0^d|i^d > V_0^d|i^f > 0$, the firm should invest in the foreign project. Depending on the corporation's tolerance for currency risk, financial managers may consider leaving the foreign investment unhedged to take advantage of the expected real appreciation of the foreign currency and the higher value $V_0^d|i^d$. This is a risky strategy, however, and the corporation and its financial officers must be prepared to accept the consequences of their exchange rate bet.

### Financial Market Hedges of Operating Exposures

Studies usually find that currency risk management through operating and financial hedges adds value to MNCs that are exposed to currency risk.[7] Although operating hedges are more effective in managing the underlying cause of an exposure to currency risk, they also involve fundamental changes in operations and are more of an investment decision than a currency risk management decision. Operating hedges should be pursued only after a thorough analysis of the business rationale for a proposed foreign project. Financial market hedges, on the other hand, can take advantage of market disequilibria or managers' exchange rate views without changing a project's operating cash flows.

## 13.4 SPECIAL CIRCUMSTANCES IN CROSS-BORDER INVESTMENTS

Many project-specific circumstances make application of Recipes #1 and #2 difficult even if the international parity conditions hold. For example, if cash flows cannot be freely remitted to the parent, then the equivalence of discounting in either currency may not hold. The act of remitting cash flows to the parent firm is called ***repatriation***, and repatriation restrictions can alter the value of foreign projects from the parent's perspective. Other special circumstances include tax holidays and subsidized financing provided by a host government, negative-NPV tie-in projects required by a host government, and country-specific political risks such as the risk of expropriation.

Each of these can be treated as a ***side effect*** and valued separately from the project.

$$V_{\text{PROJECT WITH SIDE EFFECT}} = V_{\text{PROJECT WITHOUT SIDE EFFECT}} + V_{\text{SIDE EFFECT}} \quad (13.8)$$

> *Special circumstances can be valued as side effects.*

Decomposing the value of a project into its component parts can help in identifying the project's key value drivers. This in turn can inform the parent firm's negotiations with the host government prior to investment. For example, knowing that a tax holiday is the major source of value in a foreign venture, a MNC can structure the investment in order to minimize the parent's exposure to the risk of a change in the tax rules. This may mean taking profits in the early years of the project before the tax privilege can be revoked. Local debt and equity partners also might be employed, because they are likely to be more effective in lobbying the host government to keep the tax holiday in place. This section uses the Neverland example as a starting point and examines the effect of several special circumstances encountered in cross-border investments.

## Blocked Funds

***Blocked funds*** are cash flows generated by a foreign project that cannot be immediately repatriated to the parent firm because of capital flow restrictions. If the expected after-tax return on blocked funds is less than the parent could earn on a similar-risk investment in the financial markets, then there is an opportunity cost to blocked funds. If after-tax returns in the local market are equal to or greater than the parent's next-best alternative in the financial market, then a blockage of funds would not change the MNC's investment plans so long as the parent expects to realize the value of its foreign investment at some point in the future. In this case, blocked funds do not impose a burden on the firm.

> ***Blocked funds cannot be immediately repatriated.***

Suppose that under Neverland law, 50 percent of the cash flows earned by a foreign investor such as Wendy must be retained within Neverland until the end of the project. Blocked funds must be placed in Captain Hook's treasure chest and earn zero interest. Captain Hook promises to return any blocked funds at the end of the project in four years. Funds not blocked by Hook can be remitted in the year they are earned.

Let's assume you are certain of retrieving funds from Hook's treasury.[8] The required return on this "investment" should be the after-tax market rate of interest on a comparable (in this case, risk-free) croc investment. Consequently, the appropriate after-tax discount rate for after-tax blocked funds is $i_F^{Cr}(1 - T) = (37.5\%)(1 - 0.5) = 18.75$ percent.

Wendy's inability to earn a market rate of return on funds blocked in Hook's treasury results in a loss to Wendy and a corresponding gain to Hook. The value of this opportunity cost can be calculated in a fairly straightforward manner, as described ahead and shown in Figure 13.10.

**Step 1: Calculate after-tax value of blocked funds assuming they are not blocked**

Blocked funds earning the market interest rate

$V_0^{Cr}$ = Cr8,000/(1.1875)$^1$+Cr13,820/(1.1875)$^2$ +Cr19,574/(1.1875)$^3$
= Cr28,226 at $i_F^{Cr}(1-T)$ = 18.75%

**Step 2: Calculate the after-tax value of blocked funds assuming they are blocked**

Release of blocked funds assuming they earn 0% in Hook's treasure chest

$V_0^{Cr}$ = Cr41,393/(1.1875)$^4$ = Cr20,816 at $i_F^{Cr}(1-T)$ = 18.75%

**Step 3: Calculate the opportunity cost of blocked funds as the difference in value**

Net foregone value of blocked funds = (actual value – expected value)
= (Cr20,816 – Cr28,226) = –Cr7,410

**FIGURE 13.10** The Forgone Value of Blocked Funds.

**Valuation of Blocked Funds** Wendy's forgone value can be found in three steps: (1) calculate the value of blocked funds assuming they are not blocked, (2) calculate the value of blocked funds assuming they are blocked, and (3) calculate the opportunity cost of blocked funds as the difference between their actual and their market value.

- *Step 1: Calculate the after-tax value of blocked funds assuming they are* not *blocked.* Funds are blocked in Neverland in the first three years of the project and can be remitted to Wendy at the end of the project. If blocked funds had been invested at the risk-free, after-tax croc rate of (37.5%)(1−0.50) = 18.75 percent, they would have grown to an after-tax value of (Cr8,000)(1.1875)$^3$ + (Cr13,820)(1.1875)$^2$ + (Cr19,574)(1.1875)$^1$ ≈ Cr56,128 at time four. This is worth Cr28,226 in present value at the after-tax discount rate of 18.75 percent.

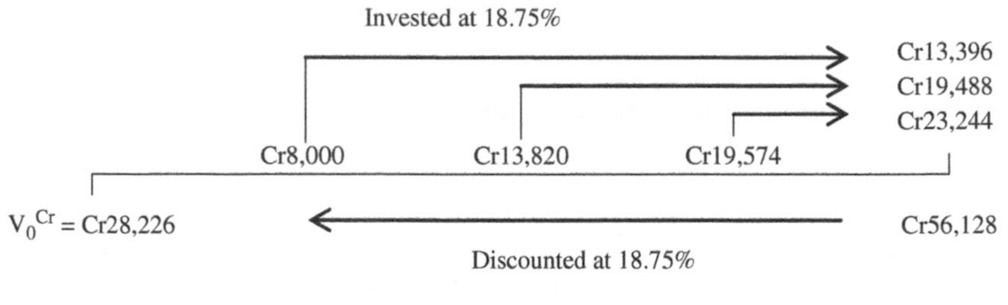


Moving values into the future and then back again at the same interest rate does not change present value, so a shortcut method is to simply discount the after-tax blocked funds at the after-tax market rate of interest: (Cr8,000)/(1.1875) + (Cr13,820)/(1.1875)$^2$ + (Cr19,574)/(1.1875)$^3$ ≈ Cr28,226.

- *Step 2: Calculate the after-tax value of blocked funds assuming they* are *blocked.* An investment in Hook's treasury is assumed to be risk-free, so the required return on blocked funds is the market rate of interest on a risk-free croc investment. The actual return is 0 percent, because payments into Hook's treasure chest earn no interest. With blocked funds, the accumulated balance as of time t = 4 is only (Cr8,000 + Cr13,820 + Cr19,574) = +Cr41,393. This has a present value of Cr20,816 at the after-tax croc discount rate of 18.75 percent.

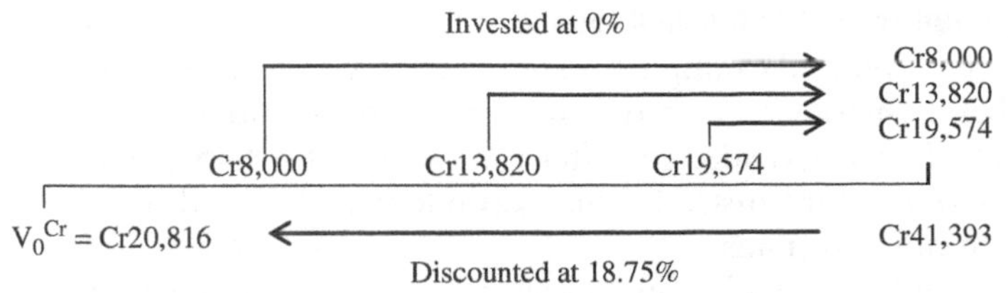


- *Step 3: Calculate the opportunity cost of blocked funds.* There is an opportunity cost to earning zero interest in Hook's treasury rather than the after-tax market rate of 18.75 percent. The incremental value of this "investment" is the difference in value from steps 1 and 2. With a Cr20,816 actual value and a Cr28,226 market value, the value of blocked funds is (Cr20,816 − Cr28,226) ≈ −Cr7,410. This investment in Hook's treasury is a negative-NPV investment for Wendy.

In the original example, the Neverland project was worth −Cr137 in the absence of blocked funds. The opportunity cost of the blocked funds is −Cr7,410. Combining these two values, the value of the project with the blocked funds is then

$$\begin{aligned} V_{\text{PROJECT WITH SIDE EFFECT}} &= V_{\text{PROJECT WITHOUT SIDE EFFECT}} + V_{\text{SIDE EFFECT}} \\ &= -\text{Cr}137 - \text{Cr}7{,}410 \\ &= -\text{Cr}7{,}547 \end{aligned}$$

Blocked funds make this an even worse investment for Wendy. It might be time for her to walk away (fly away?) from the project.

**Choice of the Discount Rate for Blocked Funds** In a capital budgeting analysis, after-tax cash flows are discounted at an after-tax discount rate to yield the NPV of a project. Why not discount the blocked funds at Neverland's 50 percent after-tax required return on restaurant projects rather than at the 18.75 percent after-tax, risk-free croc rate of interest? The answer lies in a fundamental principle of finance.

> ***The discount rate depends on where funds are going, not from where they came.***

Project value without the blocked funds reflects the 50 percent required return on restaurant projects in Neverland. Once cash flows from the restaurant project are earned, however, the appropriate discount rate on the next use of the funds (i.e., in Hook's treasure chest) depends on where they are invested and not from where they came. Because investments in Captain Hook's treasure chest are assumed to be risk-free, the croc risk-free rate should be used to value the blocked funds. If blocked funds had been invested in another restaurant project in Neverland rather than in Hook's treasure chest, then the appropriate discount rate would be the 50 percent required return on risky Neverland restaurant projects.

**When Is There an Opportunity Cost to Blocked Funds?** There was an opportunity cost to blocked funds in the Neverland example because Wendy was forced to invest the blocked funds at a below-market rate of return. A risk-free investment in Hook's treasury ordinarily would have yielded an after-tax return of 18.75 percent, but Wendy was earning a zero return instead. This example was designed to illustrate the opportunity cost of blocked funds.

Suppose Wendy's funds are blocked in Neverland, but there are no restrictions on where she can invest within Neverland. Then, there is only an opportunity cost to the blocked funds if investment alternatives within Neverland are not as attractive as elsewhere. If there are plenty of positive-NPV investments within Neverland—and Wendy ultimately can capture the value of these investments back in London—then there is no opportunity cost to the blocked funds.

This was the case in China during the late 1990s. The ability of foreign corporations to repatriate funds from their Chinese investments was restricted by rules on currency convertibility, withholding taxes on dividend and interest payments to nonresidents, and limits on royalty payments. Nevertheless, investment opportunities in China were so attractive that foreign corporate investors had little desire to pull their money out of China. Although repatriation restrictions caused a loss of liquidity for some capital-constrained firms, most corporate investors in China were more interested in growing their Chinese operations than in sending cash back home. In this setting, there was little to no opportunity cost to funds blocked within China. In other countries and at other times, there is likely to be an opportunity cost to blocked funds.

## Subsidized Financing

Governments are sometimes willing to provide loans at subsidized rates in order to stimulate foreign direct investment in key industries. In addition, international agencies charged with promoting cross-border trade occasionally offer financing at below-market rates. As a domestic U.S. parallel, the municipal (or "muni") bond market was born in the United States when the U.S. government allowed tax-free status for municipal debt in order to stimulate inner-city investment.

*Host countries sometimes provide subsidized financing.*

***Subsidized financing*** is the mirror image of blocked funds that earn below-market rates of return. In the case of subsidized financing, the MNC pays rather than receives the below-market rate. Suppose that as an investment incentive Captain Hook will provide Wendy with a Cr40,000 nonamortizing loan at a rate of 37.5 percent in Neverland crocs, even though corporate debt yields 40 percent. Interest payments on Cr40,000 at the 40 percent market rate would have been (Cr40,000)(0.40) = Cr16,000 per year. Hook requires interest payments of only (Cr40,000)(0.375) = Cr15,000 on the subsidized debt. This is a pretax savings of Cr1,000 per year, or (Cr1,000)(1 − 0.5) = Cr500 in after-tax annual interest savings. Discounted at the $i^{Cr}(1 - T) = 40\%(1 - 0.5) = 20\%$ *after-tax market cost of debt*, this interest subsidy has a value of Cr1,294.

| | | | |
|---|---|---|---|
| Cr500 | Cr500 | Cr500 | Cr500 |

$V_0^{Cr}$ = Cr1,294 Discounted at $i^{Cr}(1 - T) = 20\%$

This value is a net gain to Wendy and a net loss to Hook and the taxpayers of Neverland.

An important question for Wendy is whether this interest subsidy is separable from the Neverland project; that is, can it be obtained from Hook regardless of whether the project is accepted? In this example, Hook is likely to require that Wendy invest in the project in order to obtain the subsidy. When the subsidized loan is inseparable from the project, the value of the loan should be added to that of the project in making the investment decision.

When subsidized financing is separable from a project, the value of subsidized financing should not be allocated to the project. In this case, the manager's decision is simple: Take the subsidized loan so long as there are no other strings (such as repatriation restrictions) attached. If the firm can invest the proceeds at a higher rate in a comparable-risk investment, then borrowing at the subsidized rate and investing at a higher market rate is a positive-NPV strategy.

### Negative-NPV Tie-in Projects

Developing countries often require that foreign companies take on additional negative-NPV development or infrastructure projects in order to gain access to positive-NPV investments elsewhere in the economy. By tying approval of a project with a positive NPV to an otherwise unattractive investment in the local economy, these governments hope to capture at least some of the gain on the lucrative project. In this case, the value of the ***negative-NPV tie-in project*** should be subtracted from the value of the underlying project when making the investment decision.

### Political Risk

***Political risk*** is the possibility that political events in a host country or relationships with a host country will affect the value of corporate assets. The most extreme form of political risk is ***expropriation*** in which a host government seizes a company's assets. Expropriation risk is usually a country-specific risk that is diversifiable in a global portfolio. Hence, it affects expected future cash flows but not the discount rate.

*Expropriation is an extreme form of political risk.*

Suppose Wendy estimates that there is an 80 percent chance Hook will seize the ship at the end of the project. Actual and expected cash flows are then

| Incremental cash flows from expropriation | Actual | Expected |
|---|---|---|
| Ship | Cr0 | +Cr137,400 |
| Tax on sale of ship | Cr0 | −Cr68,700 |
| Total | +Cr0 | +Cr68,700 |

If the ship is expropriated, Wendy no longer has to pay the capital gains tax. Wendy's incremental after-tax cash flow from expropriation is then (actual—expected) = (Cr0 − Cr68,700) = −Cr68,700. With an 80 percent probability of expropriation, Wendy's expected loss from expropriation is (0.8)(−Cr68,700) = −Cr54,960.

If the international parity conditions hold, then the present value of the expected after-tax loss from expropriation can be found by discounting at the appropriate after-tax (croc or pound) rate.

Recipe #1: Discount in crocs and then convert to pounds

Present value of E[loss from expropriation] $= [E[CF_4^{Cr}]/(1+i^{Cr})^4]/S_0^{Cr/£}$

$= [Cr54{,}960/(1.50)^4]/(Cr4.00/£)$

$= £2{,}714$

Recipe #2: Convert to pounds and then discount in pounds

Present value of E[loss from expropriation] $= [\,E[CF_4^{Cr}]/E[S_4^{Cr/£}]]/(1+i^{£})^4$

$= [Cr54{,}960/(Cr9.7656/£)]/(1.20)^4$

$= £2{,}714$

This expropriation risk reduces the value of the Neverland project by £2,714.

## Tax Holidays

Developing countries are often willing to offer tax holidays to promote investment. A ***tax holiday*** usually comes in the form of a reduced tax rate for a period of time on corporate income from a project. As with other subsidies, the project should be valued both with and without the reduced tax rate. Tax holidays are negotiable, and knowing how much the tax holiday is worth is valuable when the corporation negotiates the environment of the project with the host government.

> ***Tax holidays can stimulate investment.***

For long-term projects that take a while before they begin to return positive cash flow, a tax holiday in the project's early years is not worth much. Indeed, if taxable income is expected to be negative for several years and tax losses can be carried forward, a tax holiday can rob the firm of valuable tax-loss carryforwards. The firm might prefer to be subjected to a high tax rate during the early loss-making (and tax-credit-creating) years of a project. Calculating project value both with and without the tax holiday will help you uncover situations such as this.

### The Value of Knowing the Value of a Project's Side Effects

Knowing the value of any side effects of a project can be important when negotiating the environment with the host government prior to investment. Suppose the value of a project without blocked funds is Cr6,000 and that Hook's blocked funds requirement results in a −Cr8,000 side effect. The value of the project with the side effect would then be

$$V_{\text{PROJECT WITH SIDE EFFECT}} = V_{\text{PROJECT WITHOUT SIDE EFFECT}} + V_{\text{SIDE EFFECT}}$$
$$= +\text{Cr}6{,}000 - \text{Cr}8{,}000$$
$$= -\text{Cr}2{,}000$$

Rather than giving up on this negative-NPV project, Wendy should continue to negotiate with Captain Hook. Separating the side effect from the project will prove useful to Wendy in her negotiations, as she tries to structure the deal with the host government (in particular, Hook's blocked funds requirement) so that both parties can benefit. Knowing the value of the project without the blocked funds establishes Wendy's ***reservation price***—the price below which she is unwilling to go. This is still a positive-NPV project for Wendy so long as the loss in value from blocked funds is less than Cr6,000. Wendy may be able to exert some local political pressure on Captain Hook, because employment among Neverland's Lost Boys will increase if this project is approved. Remember, everything is negotiable.[9]

## 13.5 SUMMARY

The presentation in this chapter simplified several aspects of cross-border investment and financial analysis. In particular, it developed a DCF approach to cross-border capital budgeting. In this framework, we know that

- If the international parity conditions hold, then value is the same regardless of the currency in which cash flows are discounted.
- If the international parity conditions do not hold, then value depends on your perspective. The multinational firm sometimes can take advantage of market disequilibria to enhance the value of its foreign investments.
- The DCF framework can handle many special circumstances commonly found in cross-border investment analysis. These include blocked funds, subsidized financing, negative-NPV tie-in projects, expropriation risk, and tax holidays.

The presentation in this chapter has neglected several important aspects of cross-border investment and financial management. In particular,

- We did not discuss the impact of capital structure on the cost of capital and project value.
- The impact of taxes on cross-border capital budgeting was only superficially covered.

- The DCF framework does not deal well with dynamic issues such as managerial flexibility in expanding or contracting a project.
- We did not discuss corporate governance or the international market for corporate control. This market can be used to acquire the stock or assets of companies in other countries, and provides an alternative to foreign direct investment.

Each of these issues is addressed in the chapters that follow.

## KEY TERMS

*blocked funds*
*discounted cash flow (DCF)*
*expropriation risk*
*negative-NPV tie-in projects*
*political risk*
*repatriation*
*reservation price*
*side effect*
*subsidized financing*
*tax holiday*

## CONCEPTUAL QUESTIONS

13.1 Describe the two recipes for discounting foreign currency cash flows. Under what conditions are these recipes equivalent?

13.2 Discuss each cell in Figure 13.8. What should (or shouldn't) a firm do when faced with a foreign project that fits the description in each cell?

13.3 Why is it important to separately identify the value of any side effects that accompany foreign investment projects?

## PROBLEMS

**Cross-border capital budgeting when the international parity conditions hold.**

13.1 You work for an Israeli company that is considering an investment in China's Sichuan province. The investment yields expected after-tax Chinese new yuan cash flows (in millions) as follows:

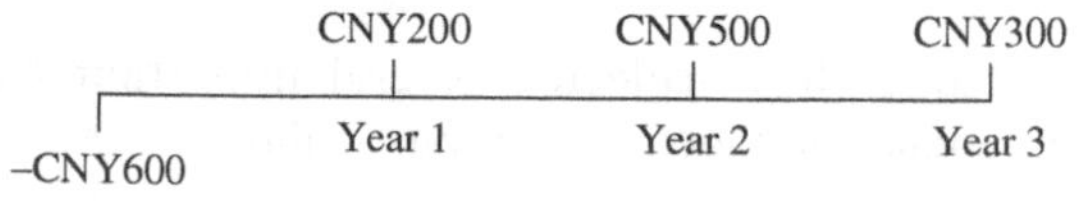


Expected inflation is 6 percent in shekels and 3 percent in yuan. Required returns for this risk class are $i^{ILS}$ = 15 percent in Israeli shekels and 11.745 percent in yuan. The spot exchange rate is $S_0^{ILS/CNY}$ = ILS 0.5526/CNY. Assume the international parity conditions hold.

a. Calculate $V_0^{ILS}|i^{CNY}$ by discounting at the appropriate risk-adjusted yuan rate $i^{CNY}$ and then converting into shekels at the current spot rate.
b. Calculate $V_0^{ILS}|i^{ILS}$ by converting yuan into shekels at expected future spot rates and then discounting at the appropriate rate in shekels.

13.2 The following project-specific information is known about investment in a beer brewery in a Western European country that uses the euro:

- The project will last two years. Operating cash flows are received at year-end.
- The euro inflation rate is 10 percent per year.
- All cash flows share the same nominal discount rate of 20 percent per year.
- An investment of €100,000 will purchase the land for the brewery. The land is to be sold after two years. The real value of the land is expected to remain constant at €100,000.
- Constructing the brewery costs €50,000, payable at the start of the project. The brewery will be owned by the foreign subsidiary and depreciated on a straight-line basis over two years to a zero salvage value. The brewery is expected to be sold for its market value of €25,000 after two years.
- An investment in working capital of €50,000 is necessary. No additional investment in working capital is necessary, but the value of this investment is expected to grow at the rate of inflation.
- Annual sales are expected to be 5,000 barrels/year.
- Beer sells for €100 per barrel. The price of beer is expected to rise at the euro rate of inflation.
- Variable operating costs are 20 percent of sales.
- Fixed operating costs are €20,000 per year and are expected to rise at the rate of inflation.
- Local tax rates on income and capital gains are 40 percent.

a. Identify expected future euro cash flows and value them at the appropriate euro discount rate.
b. Suppose the current spot exchange rate is $S_0^{\$/€}$ = \$10/€. The nominal discount rate on brewery projects in the United States is also 20 percent. Assuming the international parity conditions hold, calculate the dollar value of the brewery project from the parent's perspective as in Equation 13.4. Value the project again using the project's perspective in Equation 13.2. Are these values the same?

13.3 You currently live in Land-of-Leisure (currency is the leisure-unit L), and you are considering investment in a diploma-printing shop in a foreign country called Land-of-Work (currency is the work-unit W). Financial markets are perfect and the international parity conditions hold in these two countries. The print-shop investment will be financed with 100 percent equity. Interest and inflation rates are as follows:

| | Leisure | Work |
|---|---|---|
| Nominal risk-free government T-bill rate | $i_F^L = 0\%$ | $i_F^W = 50\%$ |
| Real required return on T-bills | $R_F^L = 0\%$ | $R_F^W = 0\%$ |
| Expected future inflation | $p^L = 0\%$ | $p^W = 50\%$ |
| Real required return on print-shop project | $R^L = 10\%$ | $R^W = 10\%$ |

The spot exchange rate is W100/L and the following information is known.

- The project will last two years.
- A W200,000 investment purchases the land for the print shop. The real value of the land will remain constant throughout the life of the project. The land will be sold at the end of the project.
- Constructing the shop and purchasing the printing press will cost W200,000, payable at the start of the project. The shop and printing press will be owned by the foreign subsidiary and depreciated on a straight-line basis over two years to a zero salvage value. The shop and printing press are expected to have zero market value at the end of two years.
- Just-in-time inventory control will be used. No investment in working capital is necessary.
- Diplomas sell for W200 in Land-of-Work. The price is expected to remain constant in real terms. Annual sales are expected to be 2,000 diplomas per year in each of the next two years.
- Variable operating costs are 20 percent of sales.
- Fixed operating costs are W45,000 in the first year and will grow at the inflation rate thereafter.
- Income and capital gain taxes are 50 percent in each country.
- Assume all operating cash flows occur at the end of the year.

a. What is the nominal required return on print-shop projects in L? in W?
b. Identify expected future exchange rates $E[S_t^{W/L}]$ for each of the next two years.
c. Identify expected future cash flows $E[CF_t^W]$ on this foreign investment project. Discount these cash flows at the work-unit discount rate from part a to find $V_0^L|i^W$.
d. Translate the work-unit cash flows to leisure-units at the expected future spot rates from part b. Discount these cash flows at the leisure-unit discount rate from part a to find $V_0^L|i^L$. Is the answer the same as in part c? Why?

13.4 Chofu Fukuhara is the production manager of Asahi Chemicals, a Japanese chemical manufacturer operating throughout Southeast Asia. Fukuhara-san is considering building a chemical plant in Thailand to service the growing Southeast Asian market. The attractiveness of the project depends on the following:

- The exchange rate is currently $S_0^{Bt/¥} = Bt0.2500/¥$.
- The manufacturing plant will cost Bt4 million and will take one year to construct. Assume the Bt4 million cost will be paid in full at the end of one year.

- The real value of the manufacturing plant is expected to remain at Bt4 million (in time t = 1 baht) throughout the life of the project. The plant will be sold at project end.
- Production begins in one year (at time 1) with annual revenues of Bt100 million per year (in nominal terms) over the 4-year life of the project. Fixed expenses are contractually fixed in nominal terms at Bt5 million each year over the 4-year life of the project. The last year of production is year 5. Variable costs are 90 percent of gross revenues. Assume end-of-year cash flows.
- The plant will be owned by a subsidiary in Thailand. Annual depreciation will be one million baht in years 2 through 5.
- Taxes are 40 percent in Thailand and Japan.
- Annual inflation is expected to be 10 percent in Thailand and 5 percent in Japan.
- The nominal required return on similar projects in Thailand is $i^{Bt} = 20$ percent.
- Assume that the international parity conditions hold.

a. Calculate the value of this investment proposal from the local (Thai baht) perspective.
b. What is the nominal required return on similar projects in Japan?
c. Identify the expected future spot exchange rates for each cash flow.
d. Calculate the yen value of the project using capital budgeting recipes #1 and #2. Are the answers equivalent? Why?

**Cross-border capital budgeting and hedging when the international parity conditions do not hold.**

13.5 Consider the investment cash flows in Problem 13.1. The spot rate is $S_0^{ILS/CNY}$ = ILS 0.5526/CNY. Risk-free bond yields of $i_F^{ILS} = 8.12$ percent and $i_F^{CNY} = 5.06$ percent mirror the expected inflation differential: $(1 + i_F^{ILS})/(1 + i_F^{CNY}) = (1.0812/1.0506) = (1 + E[p^{ILS}])/(1 + E[p_F^{CNY}]) = (1.06/1.03) \approx 1.029$. However, real (inflation-adjusted) required returns on the risky project of $i^{ILS} = 15$ percent and $i^{CNY} = 13$ percent are lower in Israel than in China: $(1 + i^{ILS})/(1 + i^{CNY}) = (1.15/1.13) \approx 1.018 < 1.029$.

a. Use interest rate parity $F_t^{ILS/CNY} = S_0^{ILS/CNY}[(1 + i_F^{ILS})/(1 + i_F^{CNY})]^t$ to find forward exchange rates. What is the value of the hedged investment from the parent's perspective using these forward exchange rates to translate the expected yuan project cash flows into shekels?
b. What are expected spot rates based on required returns on the risky project and relative purchasing power parity $E[S_t^{ILS/CNY}] = S_0^{ILS/CNY}[(1 + i^{ILS})/(1 + i^{CNY})]^t$? What is the value of the unhedged investment from the parent's perspective using these expected future spot rates?
c. Should the firm hedge?
d. The Israeli parent corporation wants to finance a portion of the project with debt and faces borrowing costs of $i_B^{ILS} = 9$ percent and $i_B^{CNY} = 7$ percent. In which currency would it make more sense to borrow? If the parent decides to hedge the project's operating cash flows, should the

hedge be done with currency forwards or foreign currency debt, all else constant?

13.6 a. Repeat part c of Problem 13.5 assuming real required returns on the risky project are $i^{ILS} = 16$ percent and $i^{CNY} = 12$ percent.

b. Repeat part d of Problem 13.5 assuming real required returns on corporate debt are $i_B{}^{ILS} = 10$ percent and $i_B{}^{CNY} = 6$ percent.

13.7 Consider the investment in China from Problem 13.1.

a. Suppose that a manager expects the following future exchange rates:

$$E[S_1{}^{ILS/CNY}] = \text{ILS } 0.5801/\text{CNY}$$

$$E[S_2{}^{ILS/CNY}] = \text{ILS } 0.6089/\text{CNY}$$

$$E[S_3{}^{ILS/CNY}] = \text{ILS } 0.6392/\text{CNY}$$

Using a yuan discount rate of 11.745 percent and the shekel discount rate of 15 percent, calculate NPV from the parent and project perspectives. Should the manager invest in the project? Should the manager hedge the project's currency risk exposure?

b. Repeat part a using the following expected future spot rates of exchange:

$$E[S_1{}^{ILS/CNY}] = \text{ILS } 0.5575/\text{CNY}$$

$$E[S_2{}^{ILS/CNY}] = \text{ILS } 0.5625/\text{CNY}$$

$$E[S_3{}^{ILS/CNY}] = \text{ILS } 0.5676/\text{CNY}$$

Should the manager invest? Should the manager hedge the project's currency risk exposure?

**Cross-border capital budgeting when there is an investment or financial side effect.**

13.8 Consider the investment in China from Problem 13.1. Suppose each cash flow generated by the project must be loaned to the China Construction Bank for one year at a zero percent interest rate. China Construction Bank bonds have a yield of 6.09 percent in yuan. China's corporate income tax rate is 25 percent. At what yuan rate should you discount the opportunity cost of these blocked funds? What is the opportunity cost of blocked funds in yuan?

13.9 Consider the investment in China from Problem 13.1. China Construction Bank is willing to provide you with a nonamortizing loan of CNY600 million at its borrowing rate of 6.09 percent per annum payable over three years. If you were to finance the project locally in China, your yuan borrowing rate would be 8.15 percent per annum. What is the yuan value of this subsidized loan? China's corporate income tax rate is 25 percent.

13.10 Consider the investment in Problem 13.1. The Chinese government insists that you build an airport near this project at a cost of CNY100 million. Should you still accept the project?

13.11 Consider the investment in China from Problem 13.1. Suppose that in any given year there is a 10 percent chance that the Chinese government will expropriate your assets. If your assets are expropriated in a particular year, then you will not receive that year's or any later year's cash flow from your investment. This risk is diversifiable and hence does not change the discount rate. What is the NPV of this asset in shekels, assuming the international parity conditions hold and the required returns $i^{ILS} = 1.5$ percent and $i^{CNY} = 11.745$ percent are after-tax discount rates?

13.12 Consider the example of blocked funds in the chapter's Neverland project. Again, assume blocked funds (50 percent of operating cash flow) earn zero interest in Hook's treasure chest. Suppose an investment in Hook's treasure chest is not risk-free and that the market's required return on Neverland bonds from Hook's treasury is 40 percent rather than 37.5 percent. What is the opportunity cost of the blocked funds, assuming the international parity conditions hold? What is the value of the project with the blocked funds?

## SUGGESTED READINGS

Charles Smithson Betty J. Simkins, "Does Risk Management Add Value? A Survey of the Evidence," *Journal of Applied Corporate Finance*17 (Summer 2005), 8–17.

CHAPTER 14

# Multinational Capital Structure and Cost of Capital

*A "sound" banker, alas, is not one who foresees danger and avoids it, but one who, when he is ruined, is ruined in a conventional and orthodox way along with his fellows, so that no one can really blame him.*

—John Maynard Keynes

***Capital structure*** refers to the proportions and forms of long-term capital used to finance the assets of the firm. Management must choose the amount of debt, its currency of denomination, maturity, seniority, fixed or floating interest payments, convertibility or callability options, and indenture provisions. Capital structure is an important determinant of the firm's overall ***cost of capital;*** that is, investors' required return on long-term debt and equity capital. Through judicious capital structure choices, the firm can minimize the cost of capital and maximize the value of operating cash flows.

*Capital structure refers to the proportions and forms of long-term capital.*

The opportunities as well as the complexities of financial strategy are many times greater for the multinational corporation (MNC) than for the domestic firm. In particular, the MNC has flexibility in choosing the markets and currencies in which it raises funds. By accessing unsatisfied demand in international capital markets, the MNC sometimes can lower its overall cost of capital and thereby increase its value. This chapter describes the MNC's choice of capital structure and its impact on project valuation and the cost of capital.

## 14.1 CAPITAL STRUCTURE AND THE COST OF CAPITAL

This section discusses factors that impact capital structure and the cost of capital, including the tax deductibility of interest, costs of financial distress, and agency costs.

## Capital Structure Theory and Practice

Before discussing how capital structure is related to the value of the firm, it is useful to first identify conditions under which capital structure—or financial policy more generally—does *not* matter. Real-world effects can then be discussed from this simple starting point.

**Capital Structure in a Perfect World** Franco Modigliani and Merton Miller (hereafter MM) were the first to identify conditions under which financial policy is irrelevant.[1] MM began with an assumption of ***perfect markets.***

- *Frictionless markets.* There are no transaction costs, taxes, government intervention, costs of financial distress, or agency costs.
- *Equal access to market prices.* Everyone is a price taker in a barrier-free market.
- *Rational investors.* Return is good and risk is bad.
- *Equal access to costless information.* Everyone has instantaneous and costless access to all public information.

To these, they added three more assumptions.

- *Homogeneous business risk classes.* There exist perfect substitutes for every asset.
- *Homogeneous investor expectations.* Everyone has the same expectations.
- *Perpetual cash flows.* Value equals periodic cash flow divided by the discount rate: $V = CF/i$.

Equivalent assets will sell for the same price, so the law of one price holds in MM's world.

With equal access to perfect markets, individual investors in MM's world can replicate any financial action that the firm can take. The firm's financial policies and strategies then cannot affect the value of the firm's assets. This leads to MM's famous ***irrelevance proposition.***

### Modigliani and Miller's Irrelevance Proposition

If financial markets are perfect, then corporate financial policy is irrelevant.

The value of an asset is then determined solely by the value of expected future investment cash flows, and not by the way in which an investment is financed.

**Capital Structure in the Real World** The assumption of perfect financial markets is a far cry from reality. Yet this assumption provides us with a starting point in understanding the workings of our imperfect and vastly more complex real world. In particular, the contraposition of MM's irrelevance proposition is that one or more of the perfect market assumptions cannot hold if financial policy is to matter. That is, to have value, financial policy must affect either operating cash flows or the risk of these cash flows.

**The Implication of Modigliani and Miller's Irrelevance Proposition**

If financial policy is to increase firm value, then it must either increase the firm's expected future cash flows or decrease the discount rate in a way that cannot be replicated by individual investors.

MM later added corporate taxes to their basic model to illustrate how this imperfection affects the firm's capital structure decision.[2] In particular, financial leverage can add value by reducing taxes through the interest tax shield. Because taxes are assessed at the corporate level, this reduction in corporate taxes cannot be replicated by individual investors.

The MM assumptions can be further relaxed to allow costs of financial distress, as well as other financial market imperfections.[3] ***Costs of financial distress*** include *direct costs*, such as court costs and attorney fees incurred during bankruptcy or liquidation, and *indirect costs* incurred prior to formal bankruptcy or liquidation. Indirect costs include lower sales and higher operating and financial expenses as managers spend their time and energy on the side effects of financial distress rather than on operating the business. Indirect costs also include the agency costs that arise from conflicts of interest between managers and other stakeholders. Each of these costs rise in financial distress, as stakeholders contend for the firm's scarce resources.

*Financial policy should minimize the cost of capital.*

Costs of financial distress affect expected cash flows to debt and equity investors, as well as the required returns of these investors. As capital costs begin to rise at higher levels of debt, costs of financial distress begin to dominate the interest tax shields from additional debt. The optimal capital structure includes an amount of debt that minimizes the overall cost of capital and thereby maximizes the value of the firm, given the nature and scale of the firm's investments.

**The Capital Structure of Foreign Affiliates** The capital structure of foreign affiliates should be subordinate to the corporation's overall financial goals. Financing should be done with the goal of minimizing the corporation's overall cost of capital, given its assets. To achieve this goal, the parent corporation can shift its financing sources toward those subsidiaries and currencies with relatively low real after-tax borrowing costs.

As a part of maximizing firm value, financial managers must pay attention to how they finance individual foreign projects. Although reducing the overall cost of capital is a primary objective, the weight given to local factors is much greater on foreign than on domestic projects. One of these factors is the risk of expropriation, through either direct government intervention or more subtle means such as suasion by local businesses or the government. Expropriation risk is greatest when the MNC fails to tie its foreign projects into local communities.

One response is to finance foreign projects with local debt and equity. This reduces the *consequences* of expropriation, because less of the corporation's own money is at risk. It also reduces the *probability* of expropriation, because locally financed projects belong not just to the foreign subsidiary but to local investors as well.

Foreign currency debt has the additional advantage of providing a *natural hedge* against the currency risk exposures of foreign operations. Offsetting a foreign subsidiary's operating cash flow with local interest expenses reduces the MNC's exposure to currency risk. In a survey of U.S. chief financial officers (CFOs), Graham and Harvey report more than 85 percent believe foreign currency debt provides an important natural hedge against currency risk.[4]

## Cost of Capital Theory and Practice

The cost of capital depends on the risk of an investment and on how it is financed.

**The Cost of Capital in an Integrated Capital Market** The perfect market assumptions applied to international capital markets are sufficient to ensure that markets are integrated. International capital markets are ***integrated*** when real required returns on assets of equivalent risk are the same everywhere.[5] Because the law of one price holds, in an integrated market the MNC cannot raise funds more cheaply in one location or currency than in another.

> *In an integrated market, prices on comparable assets are equal.*

In terms of the international parity conditions, an integrated market ensures that *uncovered interest parity* holds on any particular asset.

$$E[S_t^{d/f}]/S_0^{d/f} = (1 + i^d)^t/(1 + i^f)^t$$

The expected spot rate change is equal to the interest differential because of their joint relation to differences in expected inflation. In equilibrium, this relation reflects the fact that expected and required *real* returns on equivalent assets are equal across currencies (i.e., $R^d = R^f$).

**Capital Costs in Segmented Capital Markets** At the other end of the continuum from capital market integration is complete capital market segmentation. A market is ***segmented*** from other markets if the required rate of return in that market is independent of the required return on assets of equivalent risk in other markets. Like complete market integration, complete segmentation is not found in practice. Regardless of the ruthlessness with which governments attempt to segment national financial markets, there are invariably some cross-border price leakages. The law of one price is a powerful force, and people eventually will find a way to profit from price disparities.

Factors contributing to capital market segmentation include informational barriers, transaction costs, differing legal and political systems, regulatory interference, differential taxes, and home asset bias (investors' tendency to favor local assets). The extent of national market segmentation depends on the importance of each of these imperfections to cross-border capital flows. Although fewer barriers exist in financial markets than in markets for real goods or services, capital flow barriers nevertheless can influence the MNC's financing decisions.

***Domestic and foreign investors may prefer different assets.***

Capital market segmentation can lead to financial opportunities for the MNC if investors in foreign countries are willing to pay a higher price than domestic investors for securities that provide them with additional investment opportunities or diversification benefits. In these circumstances, MNCs with established reputations in foreign markets can gain access to debt or equity financing at rates of return that are below those available to their domestic competitors. If other companies cannot gain access to the higher prices paid by foreign investors for the firm's securities, then MNCs with access to these markets can obtain a cost of capital advantage.

Figure 14.1 depicts a situation in which the MNC's cost of capital is below that available domestically. An MNC with a cost of capital advantage over its domestic competitors can squeeze additional value from its existing projects, and even invest in positive-net present value (NPV) projects that its competitors would reject. The MNC in Figure 14.1 earns a return over its cost of capital of about (12% − 4%) = 8 cents on the first dollar of investment, whereas its domestic counterpart earns only (12% − 6%) = 6 cents on the first dollar of investment.

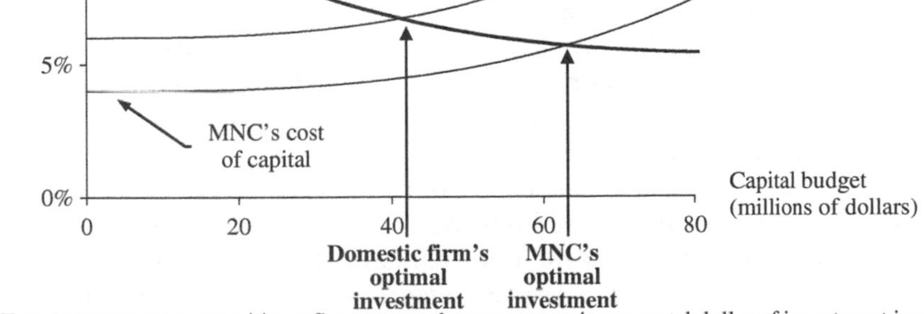


**Key**: Investment opportunities reflect expected returns on an incremental dollar of investment in a typical asset of the firm. Capital costs reflect investors' required returns on a given dollar of financing used to fund that investment.

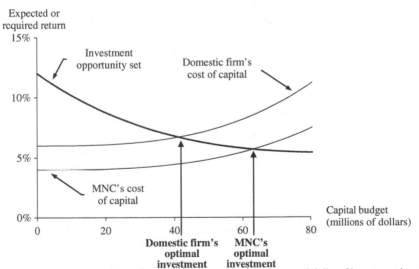

**FIGURE 14.1** The MNC's Cost of Capital.

## 14.2 PROJECT VALUATION AND THE COST OF CAPITAL

An important input into the capital budgeting decision is the required return or hurdle rate on investment. A project's required return depends on the project's systematic business risk and target capital structure. Systematic business risk refers to the systematic risk of the project's operating cash flows. The project's optimal or target capital structure is also important, as higher financial leverage leads to higher required returns on debt and equity capital.

*Systematic business risk refers to operating cash flows.*

When valuing any real or financial asset, follow one fundamental valuation rule in determining the required return on investment.

**The return on investment**

Use an asset-specific discount rate that reflects the project's opportunity cost of capital.

For consistency, the discount rate must match the characteristics of the project's cash flows.

- Domestic currency cash flows should be discounted at a domestic discount rate, and foreign currency cash flows should be discounted at a foreign currency discount rate.
- Nominal cash flows should be discounted at a nominal discount rate, and real cash flows should be discounted at a real discount rate.

The two most popular discounted cash flow valuation methodologies are the weighted average cost of capital (WACC) and adjusted present value (APV). These two approaches deal with the debt capacity of a project in different but complementary ways. The WACC approach discounts after-tax cash flows to debt and equity at a weighted average of the after-tax required returns of debt and equity. The APV approach separately values operating cash flows and financing side effects. In each method, the discount rate reflects the risk of the cash flows.

It is worthwhile evaluating investment proposals under both methods, as each brings a unique perspective. If the methods yield similar values, you will have confidence that your estimates are in the right ballpark. If the two methods yield vastly different values, you will have less confidence in your estimates. The two methods complement one another, as managers usually prefer to arrive at an approximately correct estimate of project value, rather than a single estimate that is likely to be exactly wrong.

### The WACC Approach to Project Valuation

The most popular valuation methodology is the *WACC* approach. According to this approach, expected after-tax cash flows $E[CF_t]$ to debt and equity are discounted at a rate $i_{WACC}$ that reflects the after-tax cost of the project's debt and equity capital.

$$NPV = \sum_{t=0}^{T} [E[CF_t]/(1 + i_{WACC})^t] \qquad (14.1)$$

***WACC is the most popular methodology for project valuation.***

The firm's optimal or target debt capacity is the point at which the WACC is minimized, as shown in Figure 14.2. The WACC is calculated according to

$$i_{WACC} = (B/V_L)i_B(1 - T) + (S/V_L)i_S \qquad (14.2)$$

where B = the market value of bonds (or debt) in the project's target debt/equity mix

S = the market value of common stock (or equity) in the project's target debt/equity mix

$V_L$ = B + S = the B + S = the market value of the "levered" project

$i_B$ = the required return on bonds in the project's target debt/equity mix

$i_S$ = the required return on stock (or equity) in the project's target debt/equity mix

T = the marginal corporate income tax rate

The target mix of debt and equity can be measured by a project's target debt-to-value ratio ($B/V_L$) as in Equation 14.2. In a survey of U.S. CFOs, Graham and

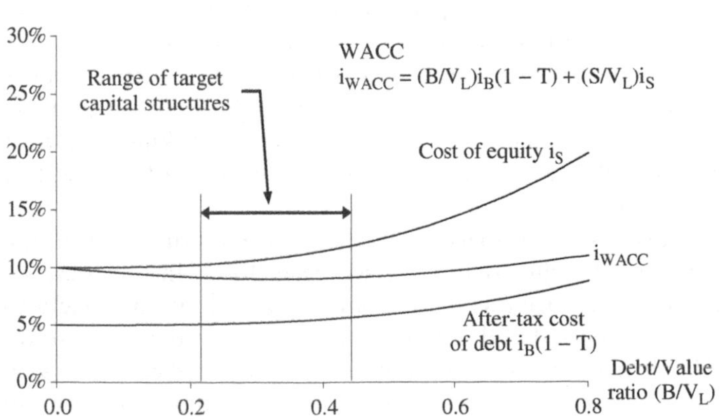


**FIGURE 14.2** The MNC's Cost of Capital.

Harvey report 80 percent of firms have a target capital structure.[6] Whereas most large firms have a fairly narrow target capital structure, only one-third of small firms have a narrow target.

> *Cost of capital is minimized at the target debt capacity.*

The discount rate $i_{WACC}$ in Equation 14.2 should reflect the project's target capital structure and not the mix of debt and equity that actually is raised to finance a particular project. The target debt capacity of a project is the amount of debt that the firm would choose to borrow if the project were financed as a stand-alone entity. Firms do not issue debt or equity on a project-by-project basis, so the proportion of debt that actually is used to finance a project can differ from the debt capacity of the project.

For example, if an MNC borrows £50 million to finance a project in the United Kingdom, the debt capacity of this project is not necessarily £50 million. The treasurer might have used this opportunity to tap the sterling debt market for capital to support other projects within the firm. Firms often accumulate several projects under one large securities issue to take advantage of the substantial economies of scale in the transaction costs that accompany debt and equity issues.

**The Cost of Debt** The *yield to maturity* is the discount rate that equates the present value of promised future interest payments to the market value of debt. For a bond issue with maturity T and promised cash flows $CF_t$, yield to maturity is the rate $i_B$ that satisfies the equality

$$B = \sum_t [CF_t/(1 + i_B)^t] \tag{14.3}$$

> *The cost of debt is estimated by the yield to maturity of similar-risk bonds.*

If the systematic business risk and debt capacity of a project are similar to other assets of the firm, the yield to maturity on existing debt in a particular currency can be used as a first approximation to the project's cost of debt. If the firm's debt is not publicly traded, yield to maturity can be estimated from the yield on publicly traded debt with characteristics (i.e., currency of denomination, riskiness or debt rating, maturity, seniority, callability, and convertibility) like those of the debt in the project's target debt structure.

There is one hazard in using yield to maturity as the required return, in that the calculation is based on promised rather than expected cash flows. In the presence of default risk, expected cash flows are less than promised cash flows, and yield to maturity overstates investors' expected and required return. This, in turn, overstates the firm's cost of debt. The difference between promised and expected cash flows on high-quality debt is small. On low-quality debt, the promised yield to maturity can significantly overstate required return.

International bond issuers sometimes pay Standard & Poor's or Moody's a fee for rating their bonds. These issuers have the option of not publishing their bond ratings. MNCs that do publish their ratings tend to have high-quality debt. Low-quality issuers often do not have their bonds rated or do not publish their ratings. For these issues, investors must estimate the risks and expected returns themselves.

*Market model betas measure market risk.*

**The Cost of Equity** Graham and Harvey find that large firms in Canada and the United States overwhelmingly rely on discounted cash flow techniques using cost of capital estimates from the ***capital asset pricing model (CAPM)***. Using this method, the systematic risk of equity is estimated by regressing a company's stock returns $r_i$ on a stock market index $r_M$ in a ***market model regression***

$$r_i = \alpha_i + \beta_i r_M + e_i \tag{14.4}$$

where $\alpha_i$ and $\beta_i$ are regression coefficients, and $e_i$ represents random error around the regression line. An asset's systematic (market-related) risk or ***beta*** $\beta_i$ is estimated by

$$\beta_i = \rho_{i,M}(\sigma_i/\sigma_M) \tag{14.5}$$

where $\sigma_i$ and $\sigma_M$ represent the standard deviations of returns on the stock and the relevant market index, and $\rho_{iM}$ is the correlation of the stock with the market.

*Pure-plays should match the project's systematic risk.*

The regression estimate of equity beta $\beta_i$ is then plugged into the ***security market line (SML)*** to arrive at an estimate of the cost of equity capital $i_S$ or equity required return $r_i$

$$r_i = r_F + \beta_i(E[r_M] - r_F) \tag{14.6}$$

where $r_F$ is the risk-free rate of interest and $(E[r_M] - r_F)$ is the market risk premium over the risk-free rate $r_F$. Beta represents the sensitivity of equity value to changes in the market portfolio. If a project-specific beta is needed to value a project that differs from other assets of the firm, an estimate can be obtained from the beta of a publicly traded ***pure-play*** firm that has the same systematic business risk and debt capacity as the project.

**The Market Portfolio** Equation 14.6 requires selection of the relevant market portfolio, and this in turn depends on how investors invest their funds. In an integrated financial market, "the market" is a globally diversified portfolio of securities weighted according to their market values. In the context of the CAPM, the relevant risk in determining the appropriate discount rate on a foreign or domestic project is the project's beta relative to the world market index. The only role of national market indices in the pricing of systematic risk is through their contribution to the return on a globally diversified portfolio. In contrast, in a completely segmented national market, an asset's risk and required return should depend on its beta relative to the local market.

*In an integrated market, CAPM beta is measured against the world.*

Koedijk et al. tested whether domestic and global versions of the market model led to different cost of capital estimates for firms from nine developed countries.[7] For the global model, additional terms were added to capture firms' exposures to currency risks.[8] Koedijk et al. found that firms were significantly exposed to global market returns, and that nearly half of the firms also were exposed to currency risks. However, exposures to both the global market and the exchange rates became insignificant when the domestic market was included in the regression. The domestic market dominated the global market and foreign currency factors for these firms. Most important, cost of capital estimates differed in only 5 percent of the firms when the global model was compared with the domestic model. The authors concluded that the domestic and global models lead to similar cost of capital estimates for firms in developed capital markets.

What does this mean for the choice of the market portfolio for firms in developed markets? As a practical matter, it might not matter which index is chosen. Many firms choose a domestic market index to represent the market portfolio, because many of their investors have a domestic perspective. Corporations and institutional investors in the United States often use a U.S. equity index such as the NYSE Composite. Similarly, a Japanese index such as the Nikkei 225 is commonly used in Japan. With economic and monetary integration and the introduction of the euro, European MNCs have largely switched from national to pan-European indices. Globally diversified MNCs that are cross-listed on several stock exchanges often employ a global market index in their cost of capital estimation. (Cost of capital estimation for assets or firms in emerging markets is more problematic, as we shall see in Section 14.3.)

**The Equity Premium** The equity risk premium—or *equity premium*—is the expected return on the stock market relative to the return on a benchmark. For currencies in which the local government has low default risk, the benchmark can be measured as the yield on risk-free, short-term, or long-term government securities. For example, the equity premium in the United States can be measured against the yield on short-term T-bills or on long-term T-bonds. When no risk-free benchmark is available (say, as in Myanmar), the equity premium often is stated as a real (or inflation-adjusted) rate of return. The benchmark in this case is the local inflation rate. The equity premium is an important input into cost of capital estimates, so scholars have spent a great deal of effort measuring past equity premiums and trying to estimate future equity premiums.[9]

*The equity premium is equity's expected return over the risk-free rate.*

| | Arithmetic mean real return to | | | Arithmetic mean equity premium vs | | Geometric mean real return to equity | Geometric mean equity premium vs | |
|---|---|---|---|---|---|---|---|---|
| | T-bill | T-bond | Equity | T-bill | T-bond | | T-bill | T-bond |
| Australia | 0.8 | 1.3 | 9.1 | 8.3 | 7.8 | 7.4 | 6.7 | 5.9 |
| Belgium | −0.4 | 0.2 | 5.1 | 5.5 | 4.9 | 2.5 | 2.9 | 2.6 |
| Canada | 1.7 | 2.0 | 7.3 | 5.6 | 5.3 | 5.9 | 4.2 | 3.7 |
| Denmark | 2.3 | 3.5 | 6.9 | 4.6 | 3.4 | 5.1 | 2.8 | 2.0 |
| France | −3.0 | 0.1 | 5.7 | 8.7 | 5.6 | 3.1 | 6.0 | 3.2 |
| Germany | −1.7 | −0.7 | 8.1 | 9.8 | 8.8 | 3.1 | 5.9 | 5.4 |
| Ireland | 1.1 | 1.5 | 6.4 | 5.3 | 4.9 | 3.8 | 3.0 | 2.9 |
| Italy | −3.7 | −1.1 | 6.1 | 9.8 | 7.2 | 2.0 | 5.8 | 3.7 |
| Japan | −0.5 | −0.6 | 8.5 | 9.0 | 9.1 | 3.8 | 5.9 | 5.0 |
| Netherlands | 0.6 | 1.3 | 7.1 | 6.5 | 5.8 | 5.0 | 4.2 | 3.5 |
| Norway | 1.3 | 1.7 | 7.2 | 5.9 | 5.5 | 4.2 | 3.0 | 2.5 |
| South Africa | 1.2 | 2.3 | 9.5 | 8.3 | 7.2 | 7.3 | 6.2 | 5.5 |
| Spain | 0.4 | 1.5 | 5.8 | 5.4 | 4.3 | 3.6 | 3.2 | 2.3 |
| Sweden | 2.1 | 2.6 | 8.7 | 6.6 | 6.1 | 6.3 | 4.3 | 3.8 |
| Switzerland | 1.0 | 2.5 | 6.1 | 5.1 | 3.6 | 4.2 | 3.4 | 2.1 |
| United Kingdom | 1.2 | 2.0 | 7.2 | 6.0 | 5.2 | 5.3 | 4.3 | 3.9 |
| United States | 1.1 | 1.9 | 8.3 | 7.2 | 6.4 | 6.3 | 5.3 | 4.4 |
| World ($) | 1.1 | 1.8 | 7.0 | 5.9 | 5.2 | 5.5 | 4.5 | 3.9 |

**FIGURE 14.3** Real Returns and Risk Premiums in Selected Global Markets.
*Source:* Dimson, Marsh, and Staunton, "Equity Premia Around the World" (2012). Real returns are from the Fisher equation: $(1+R = (1+i)/(1+p)$. Equity premiums omit German returns during 1922–1923.

With that as preamble, what equity premium over the short-term, risk-free rate would you expect for a country that, over the course of two centuries, arose from a backwater nation of little consequence to a position at the forefront of the world's economy? Clearly, the question is directed toward the equity premium in the United States. Siegel reconstructed U.S. debt and equity returns over 180 years and found that the mean annual U.S. equity premium over T-bills has been 6 percent, as well as about 6 percent during each 60-year subperiod.[10]

It is dangerous to estimate the global equity premium solely by U.S. stock returns precisely because of the success of the U.S. economy. Dimson, Marsh, and Staunton estimated local-currency real returns to the world stock market portfolio and 17 national markets from 1900–2010 to bring a global perspective to the problem.[11] Real returns are calculated from $(1+R) = (1+i)/(1+p)$ for a nominal return i and inflation p in a particular currency. Figure 14.3 presents their findings, which are summarized here for the world market index in U.S. dollars.

| Local currency real return | Mean | Premium versus short-term treasuries |
|---|---|---|
| Short-term treasuries | 1.1% | – |
| Long-term treasuries | 1.8% | 0.7% term premium |
| Stock market premium | 7.0% | 5.9% equity premium |

The arithmetic mean returns along the left of Figure 14.3 are the averages of 1-year returns in the respective currencies. The arithmetic mean global return to short-term treasuries was 1.1 percent, so local investors received on average a 1.1 percent return above inflation on an investment in a short-term treasury. An investment in a long-term treasury netted 1.8 percent in real terms, so the term premium between short- and long-term government bonds also was about 0.7 percent. The equity premium over T-bills was 5.9%, or about 6 percent as in the Siegel study.

The arithmetic mean is the return that you can expect in a single year assuming the future will, on average, be like the past. This is different from the geometric holding period return that one might earn in an asset over time. Consider an investment in a stock index that doubles in value in year one ($r_1 = 100\%$)and falls by half in year two ($r_2 = -50\%$). The geometric mean return over the two years is zero according to $\dot{r} = [(1 + r_1)(1 + r_2)]^{0.5} - 1 = [(1 + 1)(1 - 0.5)]^{0.5} - 1 = 0$, whereas the arithmetic mean return is $\dot{r} = (r_1 + r_2)/2 = (1 - 0.5)/2 = 0.25$ or 25 percent. Geometric mean returns are always less than arithmetic mean returns so long as the returns vary over time. Figure 14.3 includes geometric mean real returns in the local currencies in the rightmost columns for comparison. The equity premium was 4.74 percent when calculated as a geometric mean return.

Another risk is that a stock market will lose most or all of its value because of financial or political unrest. Jorion and Goetzmann examined stock markets in 33 countries during the 1900s and found that seven of the 33 countries had a reporting gap of several years resulting from political or financial crises, wars, or nationalizations.[12] Several national stock markets lost nearly 100 percent of their value at some point, including Germany (twice), Japan, and Portugal.

To assess practitioners' views of the equity premium, Graham and Harvey surveyed U.S. CFOs each quarter from June 2000 through June 2010.[13] Average estimates are displayed over time in Figure 14.4, along with a measure of disagreement (±1 standard deviation). CFO estimates of the equity premium peaked after the 2000 dot-com and 2008 financial crises. Disagreement among the CFOs also increased after 2008.

Where does this leave us with regard to our estimate of the equity premium? A range of 3 to 6 percent seems reasonable in that it is consistent with historical returns

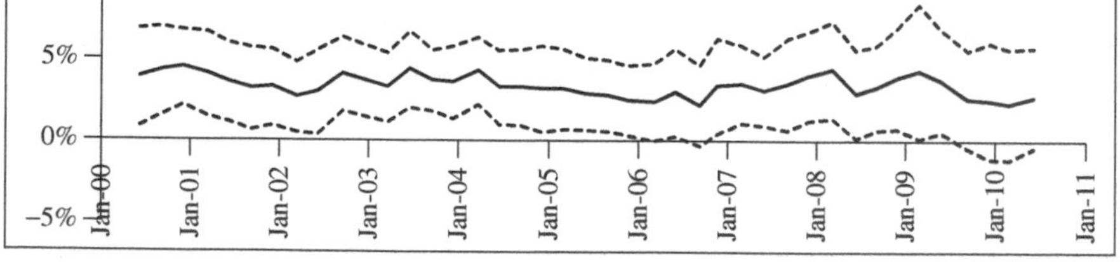


**FIGURE 14.4** A Survey of CFO Estimates of the Equity Premium.
*Source:* John R. Graham and Campbell R. Harvey, "The Equity Risk Premium in 2010" (2010). The black line is the average CFO estimate of the equity premium relative to the 10-year T-bond yield. The dotted lines are plus or minus one standard deviation of the distribution of CFO estimates. The survey is available at www.ssrn.com.

around the world and reflects estimates of the equity premium used in practice. The wide variation in national stock market returns and in practitioners' forecasts of the premium should caution us against excessive confidence in our estimates.

> *An equity premium of 3 percent to 6 percent often is used in practice.*

## APPLICATION Project Valuation Using the WACC at Philips NV

The debt of Philips NV has a market value of €5 billion and a before-tax yield of $i_B^€ = 4$ percent. The 250 million outstanding shares have a share price of €60 on Amsterdam's Euronext Stock Exchange and a beta of 1.20. The risk-free yield on long-term government treasuries is 3 percent in euros, and the equity premium over this rate is estimated to be 3 percent per year. The tax rate in the Netherlands is 40 percent. A project costs €800 million, generates annual cash flows of €100 million in perpetuity, and has the same systematic risk and debt capacity as Philips' average asset.

Philips' equity required return from the SML is

$$r_i^€ = r_F^€ + \beta_i(E[r_M^€] - r_F^€) = 0.03 + 1.20(0.03) = 0.066, \text{ or } 6.6 \text{ percent}$$

The market value of equity is (€60 per share)(250 million shares) = €15 billion, resulting in a debt-to-value ratio of (€5 billion)/(€5 billion + €15 billion) = 0.25, or 25 percent. The WACC is then

$$\begin{aligned} i_{WACC}^€ &= (B/V_L)i_B^€(1 - T) + (S/V_L)i_S^€ \\ &= (€5 \text{ billion}/€20 \text{ billion})(0.04)(1 - 0.4) \\ &\quad + (€15 \text{ billion}/€20 \text{ billion})(0.066) \\ &= 0.0555, \text{ or } 5.55 \text{ percent} \end{aligned}$$

The after-tax cost of debt is only (0.04)(1 – 0.4) = 0.024 or 2.4 percent, because every euro of interest expense reduces corporate taxes by 0.4 euros. In the Netherlands, as in most countries, the after-tax cost of equity is the same as the before-tax cost because the firm's dividend payments, unlike interest, are not tax deductible.

The value of the project net of the initial investment is then

$$\begin{aligned} V_0^€ &= V_{PROJECT} - \text{Initial investment} \\ &= (€100 \text{ million})/(0.0555) - €800 \text{ million} \\ &\approx €1{,}802 \text{ million} - €800 \text{ million} = €1{,}002 \text{ million} \end{aligned}$$

### The Adjusted Present Value Approach to Project Valuation

APV is an alternative approach to project valuation that separately values the unlevered project and its financing side effects.

**Adjusted Present Value** It is useful to have an idea of how much of the value of a project is from the investment itself and how much is from the way that it is financed. The ***APV*** approach to project valuation attempts to separate the NPV of a project into three parts: (1) the value of an unlevered project $V_U$, (2) the value of any financing side effects, and (3) the initial investment.

$$APV = V_U + PV(\text{financing side effects}) - \text{Initial investment} \qquad (14.7)$$

Unlevered project value $V_U$ is simply the present value of after-tax operating cash flows from an unlevered project discounted at the unlevered cost of equity. The most important financial side effects are the interest tax shields and costs of financial distress that accompany debt. The APV approach can be used for valuation of individual projects or for the firm itself.

*The value of an investment depends on its financing.*

**The Unlevered Cost of Equity and Unlevered Project Value** The APV approach begins with an estimate of the value of a project as an all-equity investment. This, in turn, requires an estimate of the unlevered cost of equity.

***Business risk*** is the risk of the firm's operating cash flows, measured by the standard deviation of earnings before interest and taxes ($\sigma_{EBIT}$). ***Systematic business risk*** is the systematic or nondiversifiable portion of business risk; that is, the portion of $\sigma_{EBIT}$ that is related to movements in the market portfolio. Systematic business risk also is referred to as the firm's ***unlevered beta,*** $\beta_U$, and represents the beta of an unlevered or all-equity project such that $\beta_U = \beta_{EBIT} = \rho_{EBIT,M}(\sigma_{EBIT}/\sigma_M)$.

If a publicly traded pure-play firm can be found with similar systematic business risk and no debt in its capital structure, then the beta of this unlevered pure-play can be used as a proxy for the unlevered beta of the project.[14] Using the unlevered pure-play beta in the SML of Equation 14.6 yields an estimate of the unlevered cost of equity. As with levered beta, estimation of unlevered beta in Equation 14.6 requires identifying the relevant market portfolio.

**The Value of Financing Side Effects** In a perfect capital market with no taxes or costs of financial distress, there are no financing side effects and the value of the levered firm is equal to the value of the unlevered firm. Financial market imperfections introduce a number of financing side effects. In particular, higher levels of debt generate greater interest tax shields, but also greater direct and indirect costs of financial distress.

The financial manager's objective is to determine the debt level at which the increase in value from interest tax shields is offset by the decrease in value from costs of financial distress. This optimal capital structure can be difficult to determine, because expected future costs of financial distress are not directly observable.[15] Because the optimal debt capacity cannot be precisely determined, many financial managers try to maintain their capital structure within a target range.

**Project Valuation and Other Side Effects** Chapter 13 identifies several side effects associated with cross-border investments including blocked funds, subsidized financing, negative-NPV tie-in projects, expropriation risk, and tax holidays. Some of these side effects are investment-based while others are financial in nature. The approach to project valuation in Chapter 13 separated the value of the side effect from the value of the underlying project.

$$V_{\text{PROJECT WITH SIDE EFFECT}} = V_{\text{PROJECT WITHOUT SIDE EFFECT}} + V_{\text{SIDE EFFECT}} \tag{14.8}$$

Both APV and this valuation equation decompose project value. Whereas APV aggregates all financial side effects into a single term and adds this value to the value of the unlevered project, the approach in Chapter 13 isolates a single side effect from the rest of project. Although this side effect could be *all* financial side effects as in Equation 14.7, it also could be a single financial side effect, or even an investment side effect such as the threat of expropriation.

## APPLICATION Project Valuation Using APV at Philips NV

A project at Philips NV (Netherland) costs €800 million, generates annual cash flows of €100 million in perpetuity, and has the same systematic risk and debt capacity as Philips' average asset. The required return on unlevered Philips equity based on Equation 14.6 and Philips' unlevered beta is $r_U = 0.05$, or 5 percent. The value of financing side effects (the present value of expected future tax shields minus the costs of financial distress) is €198 million.

The value of the unlevered project and the APV of the project are

$$V_U = (\text{€}100 \text{ million})/0.05 = \text{€}2{,}000 \text{ million}$$

$$\begin{aligned} \text{and} \quad \text{APV} &= V_U + \text{PV(financing side effects)} - \text{Initial investment} \\ &= \text{€}2{,}000 \text{ million} + \text{€}198 \text{ million} - \text{€}800 \text{ million} \\ &= \text{€}1{,}002 \text{ million} \end{aligned}$$

The NPV of the unlevered project is the difference between the value of the unlevered project $V_U$ and the cost of the initial investment: $NPV_U = (V_U - \text{initial investment}) = (\text{€}500 \text{ million} - \text{€}400 \text{ million}) = \text{€}100 \text{ million}$.

**MARKET UPDATE The Risk-Free Rate in the New World Order**

The 2008 financial crisis had an interesting consequence for financial managers in that it cast doubt on whether U.S. treasury securities truly are free of default risk. Indeed, Standard & Poor's downgraded U.S. government debt from AAA to AA+ in 2011 as the nation increased its debt ceiling to $14.3 trillion. Other governments have default risk as well and often are not the least risky borrower in their own local currency. Although default risk is not yet a big concern for U.S. treasury debt, the default risk of the local government is a concern in many other currencies.

This raises an interesting problem for investors and financial managers. Risk-free rates of interest are necessary to estimate a project's cost of capital in the CAPM. If local treasury securities in a particular currency are not risk-free, then yields on these securities cannot be used as the baseline for cost of capital estimation. There sometimes is an easy solution to this problem: If the local government has bonds that sell in dollars alongside U.S. treasuries, then the local currency risk-free rate can be estimated by subtracting the sovereign yield spread over U.S. treasuries. Identifying a risk-free rate is more difficult when no such securities are available.

## 14.3 THE COST OF CAPITAL ON MULTINATIONAL OPERATIONS

An important issue in multinational capital budgeting is whether the additional risks of cross-border operations result in a higher or a lower systematic risk and cost of capital on a foreign project. This section discusses factors that influence the cost of capital on foreign projects relative to comparable domestic projects.

### Total versus Systematic Risk

The *total* operating risks of foreign investment are greater than on similar domestic investments because of exposures to cultural, political, and financial risks in the foreign market. These risks increase the variability of outcomes on foreign investment, often to the detriment of the MNC. Whether higher total risk translates into higher *systematic* risk, $\beta_i = \rho_{iM}(\sigma_i/\sigma_M)$, depends on the total risk of foreign investment $(\sigma_i)$ and the correlation of foreign returns with investors' relevant market portfolio $(\rho_{iM})$. International markets are never completely synchronous with the world market or with the MNC's home market. Consequently, an increase in total risk on foreign investment may or may not be offset by a decrease in the correlation of investment returns with market returns.

*Diversifiable risks should not affect the cost of capital.*

The diversifiability of country-specific risks, in turn, depends on the extent of capital market segmentation and on whether the firm's investors are locally or globally diversified. To investors diversified only within a local economy, country-specific risks are systematic and cannot be diversified away. This would be the case in markets that are partially segmented from other capital markets. In contrast, globally diversified investors in an integrated capital market can eliminate many country-specific risks that are nondiversifiable and hence systematic to a local investor.

Consider a local political event that is country-specific and unrelated to events outside the local economy. Local political risks increase the total variability of returns on foreign investment. However, from the perspective of a globally diversified investor, increased risk would not affect required returns as they would be exactly offset by a decrease in the correlation of local and global returns. On the other hand, from the perspective of investors that confine themselves to the local market, local political risks are not diversifiable and will affect local required returns.

Similarly, currency risks that are specific to a particular country are diversifiable to a global investor, but may not be diversifiable to investors that hold only local assets. The diversifiability of currency risks within a local portfolio depends on the diversity of a country's industries. In economies with only a few industries, the value of local stocks can be strongly related to the value of the local currency. In more diversified economies with many importers and exporters, the value of the local stock market could be unrelated to the value of the local currency. This can be true in aggregate, even though the fortunes of individual importers or exporters might be highly sensitive to the value of the local currency.

### Returns and Risks in Emerging Markets

Investments in emerging markets can offer higher expected returns than in developed markets, but these returns typically come with higher operating risks. Supplier and employee relations, bankruptcy and private ownership laws, distribution channels, and business conventions are less developed and standardized in emerging than in developed markets. High political uncertainty and the lack of business and legal conventions can lead to unpredictable returns. If emerging market investments have more total risk than developed market investments, then international investors might both expect and demand higher returns from these investments. On the other hand, if all of the additional risks are diversifiable, then the required return of international investors might be the same as in developed markets.

MNCs are faced with a wide variety of foreign projects. Each project brings its own unique set of risks and potential returns. The preferred alternative for estimating a hurdle rate of a foreign project is to identify the systematic risk and required return of a publicly traded pure-play asset or firm with similar investment and financial characteristics. Often, this is the parent firm itself. When the systematic risk of the project differs from that of the parent, another pure-play must be identified—preferably a pure-play from the foreign market. In these cases, the project-specific required return and cost of capital can be determined by comparison to the pure-play.

Emerging capital markets vary in their informational efficiency and their integration with other capital markets. Emerging capital markets evolve over time as well.[16] Perhaps for these reasons, no single asset pricing model has proven to be suitable for all markets or been able to successfully explain stock market returns in all situations.

A plausible candidate model is the international version of the CAPM. In this model, an asset's systematic risk (market model beta) is measured relative to a world stock market index. This is appropriate in a world in which capital markets are fully integrated. The cost of capital on a project is then calculated from the SML with the local risk-free rate (if one exists) and a global market risk premium. Many international asset pricing models augment the global market factor with currency risk factors. Unfortunately for this model, emerging capital markets are not fully integrated into global capital markets. Market model betas measured against world market indices often have no power to predict returns in emerging markets, and the international CAPM has found little or no empirical support in emerging markets.[17] Similarly, other factors that work well in developed markets (including the value and firm size factors discussed in Chapter 20 on international asset pricing) often fail to predict emerging market returns.

Erb, Harvey, and Viskanta provide some insight into the possible determinants of required return in international markets.[18] These authors found that country risk measures—particularly financial risk measures—are correlated with future equity market returns and risks. In particular,

- A decrease in country risk tends to be followed by an increase in equity returns in that country, and vice versa.
- Countries with high (low) country risk tend to have more (less) volatile returns.
- Countries with high (low) country risk tend to have lower (higher) betas.

The first two findings are intuitive. The last finding is somewhat less obvious. Consider market model beta, $\beta_i = \rho_{i,M}(\sigma_i/\sigma_M)$, measured against a globally diversified stock index. In the context of the international CAPM, Erb et al.'s findings suggest that the low correlations of emerging markets with the world market portfolio tend to overcome the high volatilities of emerging markets, resulting in lower systematic risks or betas in emerging markets than on comparable assets in developed markets. This unfortunately conflicts with the intuition of investors and financial managers that higher risks in emerging markets should be accompanied by higher—not lower—required returns and costs of capital.

Cost of capital models for emerging markets often apply one or more country-specific risk adjustments as an alternative to market model betas versus global or domestic market factors.

- *Total risk*—a premium based on the volatility of local stock market returns relative to the volatility of developed stock market returns or of bond market returns
- *Idiosyncratic risk*—a premium based on the volatility of residual returns (actual minus expected returns) from an asset pricing model such as the CAPM[19]
- *Sovereign yield spreads*—a default risk premium based on the difference in yield between local government debt and risk-free debt (e.g., U.S. treasuries)
- *Country credit ratings*—a premium reflecting political, economic, and financial risks[20]

However, risk premiums in many of these models are ad hoc, and the models seldom allow adjustments for the systematic risks of individual projects.

In the absence of a consensus best practice in international cost of capital estimation in emerging markets, practitioners select a model that fits their particular needs and circumstances. A domestic or an international CAPM might be chosen for a project in a developed market. One of the competing models might be chosen for a project in an emerging market, perhaps augmented with a domestic or global market factor or currency factors.

*There is no consensus cost of capital model for emerging markets.*

Practitioners sometimes use more than one model to obtain a range of estimates. If the estimates from the various models coincide, then managers can proceed with some confidence that the cost of capital estimate is in the right ballpark. If the estimates substantially diverge, valuation necessarily must be conducted with less confidence.

## Liberalizations of Emerging Capital Markets

A *liberalization* of a capital market is a decision by a government to allow foreigners to purchase local assets. Capital market liberalizations affect the cost of capital, both for local firms and for local subsidiaries of foreign-based MNCs. Bekaert and Harvey found that financial market liberalizations have the following consequences for stock market returns[21]:

- Increase the correlation of emerging stock markets with world stock markets
- Have little impact on the volatility of emerging stock market returns
- Increase local stock prices, causing a decrease in local firms' costs of capital

*Emerging markets become more integrated as they are liberalized.*

As emerging capital markets are liberalized, they tend to become more integrated with other markets. Local stocks tend to move more closely with global stocks as international investors enter the market. This integration typically is accomplished without an increase in local market volatility. At the same time, the premium that international investors pay to capture the diversification benefits of emerging markets results in a decrease in the equity cost of capital for emerging market firms. Bekaert and Harvey estimate this decrease in the cost of capital at somewhere between 5 and 75 basis points.[22]

Capital market liberalizations can improve a country's growth opportunities, as some previously negative-NPV projects become positive-NPV at the lower cost of capital. Bekaert, Harvey, and Lundblad found that equity market liberalizations in a sample of 95 countries led to an average increase in real per capital GDP of about one percent.[23] Real economic growth was highest in countries with more-developed capital markets, and better legal and corporate governance systems. If a country has the proper legal and institutional infrastructures, a liberalization of the local equity market can be good for business.

## 14.4 SOURCES OF FUNDS FOR MULTINATIONAL OPERATIONS

Graham and Harvey surveyed U.S. CFOs and found that executives rely on informal rules when choosing their capital structure, with the firm's financial flexibility and credit rating as the overriding concerns.[24] This suggests that identification of the optimal capital structure, like cost of capital estimation, is at best an inexact science.

Corporations often follow a ***pecking order*** as they raise funds.

1. Internally generated funds from domestic or international operations are the preferred source. External funds tend to be accessed only after internally generated funds have been exhausted.
2. External debt is the preferred external funding source.
3. New external equity is used only as a last resort.

Figure 14.5 displays the relative importance of each funding source for U.S. multinationals.[25] Internally generated funds—mostly from retained earnings—accounted for 36 percent of U.S. foreign investment. External foreign debt (46 percent) and equity (16 percent) constituted the rest.

### Internal Sources of Funds

*Managers prefer internal sources of funds.*

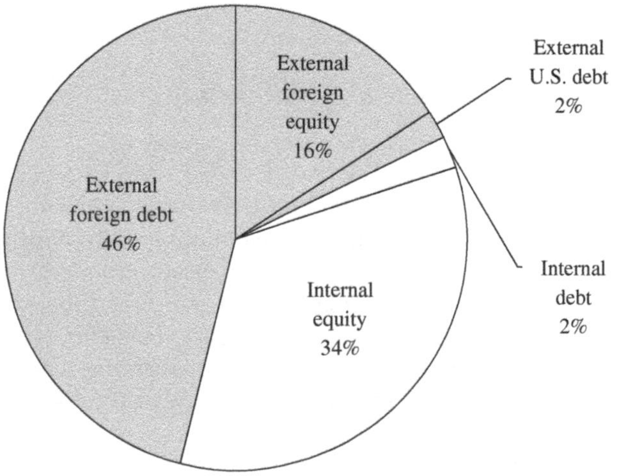


**FIGURE 14.5** Sources of Funds for Foreign Operations.
Source: Adapted from Feldstein, "The Effects of Outbound Foreign Direct Investment on the Domestic Capital Stock," in *The Effects of Taxation on Multinational Corporations*, edited by Feldstein, Hines, and Hubbard (Chicago: University of Chicago Press, 1995).

The preferred source of financing for both domestic and foreign investment is cash flow from operations, including tax shields from noncash expenses such as depreciation. Internally generated funds can come from existing operations in the parent's home country or from foreign host countries.

Internally generated funds are preferred because they are ***free cash flows***; that is, cash flows in excess of those needed to finance the firm's positive-NPV activities. Managers prefer internal funds because they allow the firm to avoid the discipline of the financial markets, as well as the transaction costs of external issues.

Vehicles for repatriating internal funds from a foreign affiliate to the parent include

- Transfer prices on intracompany sales
- Interest or lease payments to the parent on loans or lease agreements
- Royalties, management fees, or dividends paid to the parent

The MNC faces a transfer pricing problem on these repatriation vehicles.[26] If the parent wants to withdraw funds from the foreign subsidiary, it can set high transfer prices on intracompany sales to the subsidiary or low prices on purchases from the subsidiary. Similarly, rates of return must be set on management fees, royalties, interest, and lease payments. The parent can withdraw funds from the foreign subsidiary through high payments to any of these financial contracts.

To reduce abuses of the tax code, most countries specify that transfer prices be set at arm's-length or market prices. Whether the MNC has flexibility in setting transfer prices depends on applicable tax laws and whether market prices are observable. It is difficult to defend aggressive pricing on debt or lease contracts, because market prices are readily observable. The MNC has slightly more discretion in the rates that it sets on royalties and management fees, because market prices are seldom observable for the intellectual property rights that generate these fees. Partly for this reason, many countries place a limit of 5 percent of sales on royalty payments to the parent.

### External Sources of Funds

Firms without internal sources of funds must tap external sources to fund their operations. MNCs have access to international as well as domestic sources of debt and equity capital. In partially segmented markets, the firm's debt or equity securities can be more attractive to foreign than to domestic investors. In this circumstance, the corporation can reduce its cost of capital by appealing to international investors.

An international investor base can lead to several potential benefits.

- Enhanced visibility in foreign markets
- Reduced political risk (greater support from investors in their local markets)
- Greater liquidity for the MNC's debt and equity securities
- Greater access to local companies and assets
- A lower cost of capital

The costs and risks of international sources of funds include

- Language differences and other information barriers
- Capital flow restrictions in some countries

## MARKET UPDATE Novo Industri's International Sources of Funds

The impact on the firm's capital costs of moving from domestic to international sources of capital depends on the extent of capital market segmentation. The emergence of the Danish pharmaceutical and biotechnology firm Novo Industri during the late 1970s provides an illustration. Novo had already internationalized its sales and assets by the late 1970s, with 97 percent of sales outside Denmark and worldwide production and distribution. Despite the international nature of its assets, Novo's debt and equity capital came entirely from Danish sources. Its 1977 rights offering of DKK56 million ($9.8 million) consumed 25 percent of the Danish new issue market.[27] As Novo's financing needs outgrew the capacity of the local Danish capital market, Novo implemented a strategy that allowed it to gain access to international sources of funds.

Novo entered international financial markets in 1978 with a $20 million Eurodollar bond convertible into Novo shares at a 10 percent premium to Novo's DKK230 share price. Investors from the United States and the United Kingdom purchased these bonds to diversify their biotech and pharmaceutical holdings. These Eurodollar bonds were converted into common stock during 1980 as Novo's share price rose to DKK300. By the end of 1980, about one-half of Novo's shares were owned by foreign investors. During this period, Novo had been promoting itself to North American and European investors through a series of investment seminars, company visits, and press releases. After establishing foreign demand for Novo shares through its convertible Eurobond, Novo appealed directly to U.S. equity investors in the spring of 1981 with a DKK500 million ($65 million) issue of American depository receipts (ADR). These sold at a price of $36/ADR, or about DKK1,390/share at the prevailing exchange rate. This represented a 3-year increase in Novo's share price of more than 500 percent. In this way, Novo was able to escape the confines of the local Danish capital market and ensure its access to capital.

*Source:* Oxelheim et al., *Corporate Strategies to Internationalise the Cost of Capital* (1998).

- Greater disclosure requirements on some international exchanges
- Filing and listing fees
- Differences in legal systems, and exposure to judicial processes in foreign markets
- Dilution of domestic ownership and control

It is difficult for small firms that lack visibility in foreign markets to overcome high information and transaction costs on foreign issues. Percentage issue costs diminish with issue size, so firms with small capital needs are at a disadvantage in both domestic and international markets. Firms with recognizable brand names or copyrights sometimes can leverage their visibility into greater access to international financial markets.

**International Bonds** The usual progression of a domestic firm into international capital markets begins with an issuance of international debt. Information costs are higher on equity issues, so equity issues usually must wait until the firm has established a foothold in international markets through a debt issue. Although offerings can be privately placed with financial institutions, the ultimate goal is usually to obtain access to the liquidity provided by public capital markets.

***International bonds*** are traded outside the country of the issuer and can be categorized into two types. A ***foreign bond*** is an international bond issued by a domestic borrower in the internal market of a foreign country and denominated in the currency of that country. A ***Eurobond*** is traded in a market outside the borders of the country in which the bond is denominated. A Eurobond is called a ***global bond*** when it trades in one or more internal (foreign or domestic) bond markets as well as in the external Eurobond market.

*Firms use bonds to enter international markets.*

An advantage of a foreign bond is that it ties the MNC into the local community and reduces the MNC's exposure to foreign political risk. A disadvantage is that the bond is regulated and taxed by authorities in the foreign market. In contrast, Eurobonds trade outside the jurisdiction of any single nation and are largely exempt from local regulation and taxation.

Eurobonds are issued as fixed rate bonds or as floating rate bonds at a spread over a floating rate index such as London Interbank Offer Rate (LIBOR). Eurobonds are usually bearer bonds with detachable coupons that allow collection of an annual interest payment. There are many variations, such as dual currency Eurobonds that pay interest in one currency and principal in another. Many Eurobonds also involve options, including

- Equity-linked Eurobonds (convertibles or warrants)
- Eurobonds with call or put options, granted to the issuer or bondholder to buy or sell the bonds at a fixed exercise price
- Currency option Eurobonds (a form of dual currency bond) that give the bondholder or the issuer the option to select the currency of payment at each coupon date

***Convertible bonds*** can be traded for a fixed number of shares of stock at the option of the bondholder, allowing participation in a firm's good fortune while providing a minimum promised return from the bond component. Institutional investors that are prohibited from owning equity sometimes use convertible Eurobonds as an indirect way to participate in the equity market.

***Warrants*** are detachable options that allow the purchase of additional shares of stock at a fixed exercise price. This allows the debt and equity components of an offering to appeal to different clienteles. For example, prior to 1998 the Japanese Ministry of Finance did not allow stock options to be traded on Japanese exchanges. Many Japanese firms issued Eurobonds with detachable warrants that were then purchased by Japanese investors as an indirect way to hold options on Japanese stocks.

*Eurobonds often are convertible or have warrants.*

**Global Equity Issues** Corporations increasingly appeal to investors by offering equity securities directly in foreign markets. Equity issues that are offered directly to investors in international markets are called ***global equity*** issues.

*Global equity issues are sold into global markets.*

Most securities in the United States are issued in registered form. The convention in most Western European securities markets is to issue securities in bearer form. To allow U.S. corporations to compete for capital in international markets, the Tax Reform Act of 1986 (TRA) allowed U.S. corporations to issue securities in bearer form directly to foreign investors.[28] To reduce the costs of overseas financing, the U.S. Treasury Department exempted ***targeted registered offerings*** to foreign financial institutions from the information-reporting and tax-withholding requirements of the 1986 TRA. Four requirements must be satisfied to qualify as a targeted registered offering.

1. The registered owner must be a financial institution in another country.
2. Interest coupons or dividends must be paid to this registered financial institution.
3. The issuer must certify it has no knowledge that a U.S. taxpayer owns the security.
4. The issuer and the foreign institutions must follow Securities and Exchange Commission (SEC) certification procedures.

The foreign institution then maintains an over-the-counter secondary market in the securities.

Foreign corporations seeking access to the U.S. stock market typically use foreign shares or depository receipts. ***Foreign shares*** are shares of a foreign corporation issued directly to domestic investors, usually through an investment bank acting as a transfer agent. Foreign shares are denominated in the currency of the issuing company, so dividends and capital gains are paid to investors in the issuer's currency. The shares of foreign companies that sell directly on U.S. exchanges are called ***American shares*** and are issued through a transfer agent in accordance with SEC regulations. American shares pay dividends in the currency of the MNC's home country.

***Depository receipts*** are derivative securities backed by a pool of foreign shares held in trust by an investment banker. Depository receipts sold in the United States are called ***ADRs***. ADRs pay dollar dividends and trade on U.S. exchanges just as other U.S. equities, but their prices move with the U.S. dollar value of the company's shares in the foreign market. Similarly, U.S. MNCs use depository receipts to appeal to investors in foreign markets.

Part of the reason that external equity is last in the financial pecking order is that domestic markets tend to react negatively to equity issues in the long term. Although initial public offerings (IPOs) typically are underpriced and have positive returns at the time of issue, both IPOs and seasoned equity offerings (SEOs) underperform comparable nonissuing firms in the years following an issue. Loughran and Ritter report negative mean returns of nearly 3 percent upon the announcement of a SEO, and average annual returns of 7 to 8 percent less than nonissuing companies over the five years following an equity issue.[29] The usual explanation for this negative reaction is that equity issues signal managers' beliefs that equity is overvalued.

> ***First-time issuers of global equity tend to gain in share price.***

Global equity offerings do not appear to suffer the same degree of post-issuance underperformance as domestic issues. Foerster and Karolyi examine returns to non-U.S. firms when they first cross-list their shares on U.S. exchanges as ADRs.[30] Cross-listing is associated with positive returns of over 20 percent in the year prior to and including the listing week. These same firms average a 14 percent drop in share price during the year after listing. The net result is an increase in share price, rather than the decrease associated with domestic offerings. Results for U.S. firms listing on non-U.S. exchanges are qualitatively similar.[31] However, there is evidence that gains in share price from international cross-listings are not permanent.[32]

**Project Finance** *Project finance* allows a project sponsor to raise external funds for a specific project. Three characteristics distinguish project finance from other forms of financing.

- The project is a separate legal entity and relies heavily on debt financing.
- The debt is contractually linked to the cash flow generated by the project.
- Governments participate through infrastructure support, operating or financial guarantees, rights-of-way, or assurances against political risk.

The hallmark of project finance is that claims on the project are contractually tied to the cash flows of the project. When a corporation finances an investment project using internal funds, cash flows from the project are commingled with those of other projects. Project finance unbundles the project from other assets, allowing the market to value the project as a stand-alone entity. Debt and equity have a claim on project cash flows, but not on the assets or cash flows of the corporation sponsoring the project.

> ***In project finance, claims are contractually tied to the cash flows of the project.***

Examples of developments funded by project finance include the Channel Tunnel between England and France, the EuroDisney theme park outside Paris and Hong Kong Disneyland in China, the Orange County (California) and Cuernavaca-Acapulco (Mexico) toll roads, and oil exploration and development in the Forties Field in the North Sea off the coast of England.

## MARKET UPDATE Project Finance through the Ages

Suppose you live in Devon, England, and have discovered a rich vein of silver on your property. England is in a recession, and London's bankers are unwilling to lend you money to mine the silver. Desperate for funds, you arrange for an Italian bank to finance the construction of the silver mine in return for the mine's entire revenue stream for a period of one year. Both parties can benefit from this arrangement. The bank is assured of a good return on its investment through its contractual claim on project cash flows. You get your silver mine after one year, minus a few tons of ore. This example of project finance actually took place—in the year 1299.

Project finance was a popular way to fund international ventures throughout the Middle Ages and Renaissance. Oceanic voyages to America and the Far East were financed by governments and merchant banks, with the proceeds distributed to the project sponsor at journey's end. Christopher Columbus's voyage to the New World was financed in this way by the Queen of Spain. As international trade flourished, fleets of ships eventually were brought under one corporate banner, and the need to fund journeys on a trip-by-trip basis declined.

*Source:* Kensinger and Martin, "Project Finance: Raising Money the Old-Fashioned Way," *Journal of Applied Corporate Finance* (1988).

Project finance works best for finite-lived, tangible assets that offer stable cash flows that are capable of supporting high debt levels. Ownership of the project is transferred at the end of the project to the sponsor or host government. In a *build-operate-own* (BOO) contract, ownership is transferred to the project sponsor. In a *build-operate-transfer* (BOT) contract, ownership is transferred to the host government.

Natural resource developments, toll roads, bridges, and telecom and power generation projects are attractive candidates for project finance because cash flows are stable and tied to a particular location. Stable cash flows permit the project to borrow against future revenues, which sometimes are guaranteed by selling the output prior to construction. This allows cash flows to be contractually allocated to those investors most willing and able to bear the risks of the project.

Quite often, commitments are made by the project sponsor or by supporting governments, suppliers, or customers to ensure that cash flow projections and debt payments are met. Government contributions increase the expected return and reduce the risk to other project participants, although these assurances are not always honored. For example, weeks before the planned opening of a project-financed toll road around Bangkok, the Thai government seized control of the highway in violation of the project's 30-year, BOT agreement and reduced the toll by a third. Because of the country-specific risks of project finance, lenders seek to protect themselves with political risk insurance against expropriation and the imposition of currency or repatriation controls.

## 14.5 THE INTERNATIONAL EVIDENCE ON CAPITAL STRUCTURE

Identifying the determinants of capital structure in an international setting is somewhat more difficult than in a domestic setting. Financial and accounting data is difficult to obtain in many countries and, when available, is subject to widely divergent accounting conventions. There is also great heterogeneity among national tax and bankruptcy codes, legal systems, corporate governance conventions, and markets for corporate control. Although variability in these business environments limits the inferences that can be drawn from cross-border studies of capital structure, these studies also are potentially more revealing of the underlying determinants of capital structure because of the heterogeneity in national capital structure norms. This section examines the empirical evidence on the determinants of capital structure choice by domestic and MNCs.

### Evidence from Developed Capital Markets

> *Leverage is positively related to asset tangibility and firm size.*

Rajan and Zingales studied financial leverage in the G-7 countries of Canada, France, Germany, Italy, Japan, the United Kingdom, and the United States.[33] Adjustments were made for accounting differences, and the average debt-to-equity ratio was calculated for each country. Rajan and Zingales then examined the relation of leverage to firm characteristics and found the following.

- *Asset tangibility.* The ratio of fixed to total assets is a measure of asset tangibility. Tangible assets can lower the cost of debt by serving as collateral. Secured debt also is less susceptible to agency problems that can plague unsecured issues. For example, unsecured debt loses value when a firm shifts into riskier assets. Firms can partially ensure debt against opportunistic behaviors by managers or equity shareholders by securing debt with tangible assets. All else being equal, reductions in agency costs result in increased firm value. The relation between leverage and asset tangibility was positive and significant in six of the seven countries.
- *Firm size.* Large firms tend to be more diversified than small firms. Diversification reduces the variability of cash flows and firm value, and can lead to a reduction in costs of financial distress. Consequently, large diversified firms have greater debt capacity, all else constant. The relation between firm size and leverage was generally positive and statistically significant.
- *Growth opportunities.* Asset market-to-book ratios are a measure of a firm's growth opportunities. Asset market-to-book ratios were negatively related to leverage in each country and were statistically significant in five countries. This result was driven by firms with high market-to-book ratios within each country. The relation was weak or absent in firms with low market-to-book ratios and few growth opportunities. Rajan and Zingales concluded that firms issue stock when they have investment opportunities (growth options) that result in high share prices relative to earnings or book values.

*Leverage is negatively related to growth opportunities and profitability.*

- ***Profitability.*** The theoretical relation between profitability and leverage is ambiguous. On the one hand, profitable firms can avoid external capital markets and so should have less leverage than unprofitable firms.[34] On the other hand, the larger cash flows of profitable firms can support more debt and generate higher tax shields. Thus, higher debt levels should be forced on managers in countries with efficient markets for corporate control.[35] Rajan and Zingales found that the relation between profitability and leverage was negative and significant in a majority of the G-7 countries.

### Evidence from Emerging Capital Markets

Booth et al. analyzed the capital structure choices of firms in 10 emerging markets.[36] They concluded that capital structure decisions are affected by many of the same variables as in developed markets.

- The influences of asset tangibility, firm size, growth opportunities, and profitability are similar in developed and emerging capital markets.
- The strongest result is that profitable firms use less debt in emerging markets.

These findings hold despite profound cross-country differences in institutional factors such as the relative magnitude of corporate and personal tax rates, regulations governing bankruptcy and reorganization, financial disclosure requirements, and the availability of different forms of financing provided by developed capital markets.

*Profitable firms use less debt in emerging markets.*

Despite these similarities with developed markets, country-specific factors play an important role in emerging markets. In particular, the influences of the various factors are highly variable across the sample countries. Booth et al. concluded that the country of origin is usually at least as important as firm-specific factors (such as profitability) in explaining capital structures in emerging markets.

## 14.6 SUMMARY

In an integrated financial market, real rates of return are equal on equivalent assets. In such a world, MNCs would not enjoy financing advantages over domestic firms. In the real world of partially segmented markets, corporations with access to alternative sources of capital can lower their cost of capital through judicious financing choices.

We began with a description of the two most popular approaches to project valuation.

- The WACC method discounts expected after-tax cash flows to debt and equity at a rate that reflects the after-tax required returns on debt and equity capital.
- The APV approach separately values the unlevered project and the financing side effects.

A critical input into each of these valuation approaches is a project's systematic risk, and hence required return and cost of capital. This in turn depends on the extent of capital market segmentation. In the context of the CAPM:

- In integrated markets, systematic risk should be measured against the world market portfolio.
- In segmented markets, systematic risk should be measured against a local stock market index.
- In partially segmented markets, systematic risk can depend on a mix of global and local factors.

There is no consensus best practice for cost of capital estimation in segmented markets. Judgment must be used to form an estimate that is at least in the right ballpark.

We then moved on to sources of funds for multinational operations. Internal sources of funds are preferred by managers and include free cash flow (cash flow in excess of the firm's investment needs) from domestic and foreign sources. External sources of funds include internal and external market issues of debt and equity, including domestic and foreign bonds, Eurobonds, global bonds, and domestic and global equity issues. Project finance—relying heavily on debt financing—also can be a funding source for projects that generate a clearly identifiable and stable cash flow stream.

Finally, we reviewed the international evidence on capital structure. In most countries, firms that are large or have tangible assets tend to use debt as a source of funds. In contrast, firms with growth opportunities or high profitability tend to avoid debt. High-growth firms prefer to fund their growth through external equity issues, and profitable firms are able to fund their operations through internal sources of funds. Country-specific factors appear to be at least as important as company-specific factors in emerging markets.

## KEY TERMS

*adjusted present value (APV)*
*American depository receipt (ADR)*
*American shares*
*beta (a measure of systematic risk)*
*business risks*
*capital asset pricing model (CAPM)*
*capital structure*
*convertible bond*
*cost of capital*
*costs of financial distress*

*depository receipt*
*equity premium*
*Eurobond*
*foreign bond*
*foreign shares*
*free cash flow*
*global bonds and global equity*
*integrated versus segmented capital markets*
*international bond*
*irrelevance proposition*
*liberalization*
*market model regression*
*pecking order*
*perfect markets*
*project finance*
*pure-play*
*security market line (SML)*
*systematic business risk or unlevered beta*
*tangible assets*
*targeted registered offering*
*warrant*
*weighted average cost of capital (WACC)*
*yield to maturity*

## CONCEPTUAL QUESTIONS

14.1 Does corporate financial policy matter in a perfect financial market?

14.2 What distinguishes an integrated from a segmented capital market?

14.3 What factors could lead to capital market segmentation?

14.4 Does the required return on a project depend on who is investing the money or on where the money is being invested?

14.5 Does the value of a foreign project depend on the way it is financed?

14.6 An important input into the required return on equity in the SML is the market risk premium. How large is the market risk premium?

14.7 When is the APV approach to project valuation most useful?

14.8 What is the usual consequence of an increase in country risk on a national stock market? Do stock markets in high-risk countries have higher or lower volatility than other markets? Do they have higher or lower betas relative to a world stock market index?

14.9 What is a stock market liberalization? What are the effects of liberalizations on (a) emerging market correlations with the world stock returns, (b) local market volatility, and (c) the local cost of capital?

14.10 What is a targeted registered offering, and why is it useful to the corporation?

14.11 What is project finance, and when is it an appropriate source of funds?

14.12 What evidence is there on the international determinants of corporate capital structure? How is the international evidence similar to the domestic U.S. evidence?

## PROBLEMS

14.1 The systematic risk (beta) of France's Oilily Corporation is 1.2 when measured against a world stock market index and 1.4 against a French stock index. The annual risk-free rate in France is 5 percent.

a. If the required return on the world market index is 12 percent, what is the required return on Oilily stock in an integrated financial market?
b. Suppose the French financial market is segmented from the rest of the world. If the required return on the French market is 11 percent, what is the required return on Oilily stock?

14.2 The systematic risk (beta) of Grand Pet is 0.8 when measured against the Morgan Stanley Capital International (MSCI) world market index and 1.2 against the London Financial Times 100 (or FTSE 100) stock index. The annual risk-free rate in the United Kingdom is 5 percent.

a. If the required return on the MSCI world market index is 10 percent, what is the required return on Grand Pet stock in an integrated financial market?
b. Suppose the U.K. financial markets are segmented from the rest of the world. If the required return on the FTSE 100 is 10 percent, what is the required return on Grand Pet stock?

14.3 Find Oilily's WACC under each of the following scenarios:

a. Oilily has a market value debt-to-value ratio of 40 percent. Oilily's pretax borrowing cost on new long-term debt in France is 7 percent. Oilily's beta relative to the French stock market is 1.4. The risk-free rate in France is 5 percent and the market risk premium over the risk-free rate is 6 percent. Interest is deductible in France at the marginal corporate income tax rate of 33 percent. What is Oilily's WACC in the French market?
b. Oilily can borrow in the Europound market at a pretax cost of 6 percent. International investors will tolerate a 50 percent debt-to-value mix. With a 50 percent debt-to-value ratio, the beta of Oilily is 1.2 against the MSCI world index. The required return on the world market portfolio is 12 percent. What is Oilily's WACC under these circumstances?
c. Suppose Oilily is expected to generate after-tax operating cash flow of $CF_1$ = €10 million in the coming year and that this is expected to grow at 4 percent in perpetuity. The valuation equation $V_0 = CF_1/(i - g)$ can value Oilily's cash flow stream given $CF_1$ is the coming year's cash flow, i is the WACC, and g is the growth rate of annual cash flow. Find the value of Oilily using the WACCs from the scenarios in parts a and b.

14.4 Find Grand Pet's WACC under each of the following scenarios:

a. *Domestic financing*: Grand Pet has a market value debt-to-equity ratio of 33 percent if funds are raised within the United Kingdom. Grand Pet's pretax borrowing cost on long-term debt in the U.K. is 6 percent. Grand Pet's beta relative to the FTSE 100 is 1.2. The risk-free rate in pounds sterling is 5 percent. The market risk premium over the risk-free rate within the U.K. is 10 percent. Interest is deductible in the U.K. at the marginal corporate income tax rate of 33 percent. What is Grand Pet's WACC within the U.K. market?

b. *Global financing*: International investors are willing to tolerate a 50 percent debt-to-equity mix for Grand Pet at the 6 percent cost of debt in pounds sterling. At this debt-equity mix, Grand Pet's equity beta is 1.1 relative to the MSCI world index. The market risk premium in pounds sterling is 10 percent and the risk-free rate is 5 percent. What is Grand Pet's WACC in international capital markets?

c. *The valuation consequence*: Grand Pet is expected to generate after-tax cash flow to debt and equity of £1 million in the coming year. This cash flow is expected to grow at g = 3 percent in perpetuity. The valuation equation $V_0 = CF_1/(i - g)$ values Grand Pet's cash flow stream, given $CF_1$ is the coming year's cash flow, i is the WACC, and g is the growth rate of annual cash flow. Find the value of Grand Pet using the WACCs from the scenarios in parts a and b.

14.5 Suppose Oilily uses an APV approach to project valuation.

a. Oilily's latest investment proposal is for a chain of retail stores in the United Kingdom. Initial investment will be €100 million and will produce a single after-tax cash flow of €12 million after one year. The chain is expected to be sold to a U.K. company for €100 million (after tax) at the end of the year. Oilily has an all-equity discount rate of 10 percent. What is the value of Oilily's project as an all-equity investment?

b. Suppose the project can support up to €50 million in debt at a pretax cost of 6 percent. Principal and interest (as well as the interest tax shield) are due in one year. Oilily's corporate tax rate is 33 percent. What is the value of the tax shield from the use of debt? Ignoring other financial side effects (i.e., costs of financial distress), what is the value of Oilily's project as a levered investment?

c. Suppose Oilily's project produces after-tax cash flow of €12 million per year in perpetuity. What are the unlevered and levered APVs from parts a and b? Assume perpetual debt at an interest rate of 6 percent.

14.6 Suppose Grand Pet uses an APV approach to project valuation.

a. Another Grand Pet investment proposal is to produce nonalcoholic beer for dogs in the United States. Initial investment will be £100 million and will produce a single after-tax cash flow of £8 million after one year. The brewery will be sold for £100 million at the end of the year. Assume there are no tax effects on sale of the brewery. An all-equity company that produces a similar brand of doggy beer trades on the London Stock Exchange and has an all-equity discount rate of 8 percent. What is the value of Grand Pet's project as an all-equity investment?

b. Suppose the project can support up to £25 million in debt at a pretax cost of debt of 6 percent. Principal and interest on the debt (as well as the interest tax shield) are due in one year. Grand Pet's corporate tax rate is 33 percent. What is the value of the tax shield from the use of debt? Ignoring other financial side effects (i.e., costs of financial distress), what is the value of Grand Pet's project as a levered investment?

c. Suppose Grand Pet's project produces after-tax cash flow of £8 million per year in perpetuity. What are the unlevered and levered APVs from parts a and b? Assume perpetual debt at an interest rate of 6 percent.

14.7 As the People's Republic of China evolves toward a market economy, capital markets are likely to replace the government as the firm's primary source of funds for investment. Nevertheless, the Chinese government remains the principal owner of many Chinese firms. Some of these firms use the government's borrowing cost (such as the rate on certificates of deposit from the Industrial Bank of China) as their required return or hurdle rate on new investment.

a. Is it appropriate to use the government's borrowing cost as a required return on investment if a firm is 100 percent owned by the government?
b. Are investments based on this criterion likely to be value-creating or value-destroying from a capital markets perspective? What consequence will the use of this hurdle rate have for the risk of the firm's and the government's asset portfolios? Explain.
c. A Chinese manager is considering an investment of 1.5 million Chinese new yuan (CNY) in a coal mine that generates an expected return of 100,000CNY per year in perpetuity. The government's borrowing rate is 5 percent. The project has a beta of 1.0 and a risk-adjusted required return of 10 percent. What is the NPV of this investment using the government's borrowing cost of 5 percent? What is the NPV of this investment using a risk-adjusted return of 10 percent?
d. The Chinese manager expects her division to be privatized in one year. Further, suppose the government does not monitor returns on its investments once they have been made. What will be the likely consequence of accepting the project in part c on the market value of her division after privatization? Does the manager have an incentive to extract as much capital from the government as possible prior to privatization, even at the cost of accepting negative-NPV projects? (Hint: Think of the agency conflict between managers and other stakeholders.)

14.8 United Kingdom's Vodafone Group needs a cost of capital estimate to evaluate an investment in Brazil's mobile phone market. Vodafone's experience investing in mobile phone infrastructure in emerging markets suggests that the systematic risk of the investment from the perspective of a U.K. investor is about the same as the average systematic risk of the emerging market. The U.K. risk-free rate is $r_F{}^{£} = 3$ percent. The world market risk premium is estimated to be $(E[r_W] - r_F) = 5$ percent. Calculate expected or required returns in pounds on a typical Brazilian investment based on each of the following models:

a. International CAPM: $E[r] = r_F + \beta(E[r_W] - r_F)$. Vodafone estimates $\beta = 1.2$ based on a regression of Brazilian stock market returns on world market returns.

b. Global and regional market factors: $E[r] = r_F + \beta(E[r_W] - r_F) + \delta(E[r_{Region}] - E[r_W])$, where $\delta$ is Brazil's systematic risk relative to Latin American regional risk that is not included in the world market return. Vodafone estimates $\beta = 1.2$, $\delta = 1.5$, and $(E[r_{Region}] - E[r_W]) = 4\%$.
c. Country credit risk model: $E[r] = E[r_W] + CR$, where CR is an adjustment for credit risk in Brazil. Vodafone estimates $CR = 4\%$.
d. Country spread model: $E[r] = E[r_W] + S$, where S is the 1-year Brazilian government bond yield minus the 1-year Eurocurrency yield. Currently, this sovereign yield spread is $S = 2\%$.
e. Modified country spread model: $E[r] = r_F + S(\sigma_{Br\text{-}stocks}/\sigma_{Br\text{-}bonds})$, where $\sigma_{Br\text{-}stocks} = 30\%$ is the annual volatility on Brazilian stocks and $\sigma_{Br\text{-}bonds} = 10\%$ is the annual volatility on Brazilian bonds.

## SUGGESTED READINGS

### Capital structure and cost of capital are developed and tested in

Isik Inselbag and Howard Kaufold, "Two DCF Approaches for Valuing Companies Under Alternative Financing Strategies," *Journal of Applied Corporate Finance* 10, No. 1 (1997), 114–122.

Franco Modigliani and Merton Miller, "The Cost of Capital, Corporation Finance and the Theory of Investment," *American Economic Review* 48 (June 1958), 261–297.

Franco Modigliani and Merton Miller, "Corporate Income Taxes and the Cost of Capital: A Correction," *American Economic Review* 53 (June 1963), 433–442.

### Articles on the multinational corporation's cost of capital include

Claude B. Erb, Campbell R. Harvey, and Tadas E. Viskanta, "Expected Returns and Volatility in 135 Countries," *Journal of Portfolio Management* 22 (Spring 1996), 46–58.

Claude B. Erb, Campbell R. Harvey, and Tadas E. Viskanta, "Political Risk, Financial Risk and Economic Risk," *Financial Analysts Journal* 52 (November/December 1996), 29–46.

John R. Graham and Campbell R. Harvey, "The Theory and Practice of Corporate Finance: Evidence from the Field," *Journal of Financial Economics* 61 (2001), 187–243.

Kees G. Koedijk, Clemens J.M. Kool, Peter C. Schotman, and Mathijs A. van Dijk, "The Cost of Capital in International Financial Markets: Local or Global?" *Journal of International Money and Finance* 21 (2002), 905–929.

### The equity risk premium is investigated in

Elroy Dimson, Paul Marsh, and Mike Staunton, "Equity Premia Around the World," presented at the 2012 AFA Annual Conference (available at www.ssrn.com). See also Elroy Dimson, Paul Marsh, and Mike Staunton, *Triumph of the Optimists* (Princeton, NJ: Princeton University Press, 2002).

John R. Graham and Campbell R. Harvey, "The Equity Risk Premium in 2010," working paper available at www.ssrn.com (2010).

Philippe Jorion and William N. Goetzmann, "Global Stock Markets in the Twentieth Century," *Journal of Finance* 53 (June 1999), 953–980.

Jeremy Siegel, "The Equity Premium: Stock and Bond Returns Since 1802," *Financial Analysts Journal* 48 (January/February 1992), 28–38.

## The impact of international financing is investigated in

Susan Chaplinsky and Latha Ramchand, "The Impact of Global Equity Offerings," *Journal of Finance* 55 (December 2000), 2767–2789.
Martin Feldstein, "The Effects of Outbound Foreign Direct Investment on the Domestic Capital Stock," in *The Effects of Taxation on Multinational Corporations*, edited by Martin Feldstein, James R. Hines, Jr., and R. Glenn Hubbard, (Chicago: University of Chicago Press, 1995).
Stephen R. Foerster and G. Andrew Karolyi, "The Effects of Market Segmentation and Investor Recognition on Asset Prices: Evidence from Foreign Stocks Listing in the United States," *Journal of Finance* 54 (June 1999), 981–1013.
John W. Kensinger and John D. Martin, "Project Finance: Raising Money the Old-Fashioned Way," *Journal of Applied Corporate Finance* 1 (Fall 1988), 69–81.
Sergei Sarkissian and Michael J. Schill, "Are There Permanent Valuation Gains to Overseas Listing?" *Review of Financial Studies* 22 (January 2009), 371–412.

## Attempts to document the international determinants of capital structure include

Laurence Booth, Varouj Aivazian, Asli Demirguc-Kunt, and Vojislav Maksimovic, "Capital Structures in Developing Countries," *Journal of Finance* 56 (February 2001), 87–130.
Raghuram G. Rajan and Luigi Zingales, "What Do We Know About Capital Structure? Some Evidence from International Data," *Journal of Finance* 50 (December 1995), 1421–1460.

## Agency costs are discussed in

Michael C. Jensen, "Agency Costs of Free Cash Flow, Corporate Financing, and Takeovers," *American Economic Review* 76, No. 2 (1986), 323–339.
Timothy Loughran and Jay R. Ritter, "The New Issues Puzzle," *Journal of Finance* 50 (March 1995), 23–52.
Stewart C. Myers and Nicholas S. Majluf, "Corporate Financing and Investment Decisions When Firms Have Information That Investors Do Not Have," *Journal of Financial Economics* 13, No. 2 (1984), 127–221.

## The impact of market segmentation on investment and the cost of capital are examined in

Andrew Ang, Robert J. Hodrick, Yuhang Xing, and iaoyan Zhang, "High Idiosyncratic Volatility and Low Returns: International and Further U.S. Evidence," *Journal of Financial Economics* 91 (January 2009), 1–23.
Geert Bekaert and Campbell Harvey, "Foreign Speculators and Emerging Equity Markets," *Journal of Finance* 55 (April 2000), 565–613.
Geert Bekaert, Campbell R. Harvey, and Christian Lundblad, "Does Financial Liberalization Spur Growth?" *Journal of Financial Economics* 77 (July 2005), 3–56.
Geert Bekaert, Campbell R. Harvey, Christian Lundblad, and Stephan Siegel, "Global Growth Opportunities and Market Integration," *Journal of Finance* 62 (June 2007), 1081–1137.
Geert Bekaert, Campbell R. Harvey, Christian T. Lundblad, and Stephan Siegel, "What Segments Equity Markets?" *Review of Financial Studies* 24 (December 2011), 3841–3890.
Campbell Harvey, "Predictable Risk and Returns in Emerging Markets," *Review of Financial Studies* 8 (Fall 1995), 773–816.
Frank de Jong and Frans de Roon, "Time-Varying Market Integration and Expected Returns in Emerging Markets," *Journal of Financial Economics* 78 (December 2005), 583–613.
Lars Oxelheim, Arthur Stonehill, Trond Randøy, Kaisa Vikkula, Kåre Dullum, and Karl-Markus Modén, *Corporate Strategies to Internationalise the Cost of Capital* (Copenhagen: Copenhagen Business School Press, 1998).

# CHAPTER 15

# Taxes and Multinational Corporate Strategy

*The income tax has made more liars out of the American people than golf has.*

—Will Rogers

This chapter shows how governments tax corporate income from foreign sources, such as foreign corporations or branch offices. Tax planning can be a major source of value for the multinational corporation (MNC) because of national differences in tax systems and tax rates. Careful planning can lessen the corporation's tax liability and thereby increase the value of the firm.

Here is a word of caution before we begin. This chapter is not intended to be your sole reference on international taxation and tax planning. International taxation is an exceedingly complex area that requires a detailed knowledge of the domestic tax code, as well as knowledge of foreign tax systems and bilateral tax treaties. The chapter uses the U.S. tax code to illustrate issues in international taxation, such as how a system of foreign tax credits (FTCs) reduces the threat of double taxation of foreign-source income. Nevertheless, for brevity the chapter ignores many subtleties and exceptions in the U.S. tax code. If the advice "Consult with your tax accountant" applies to domestic business, it applies tenfold to international business.

## 15.1 THE OBJECTIVES OF NATIONAL TAX POLICY

We often hear that the only sure things in life are death and taxes. Taxes are collected to pay for public services, including police and fire protection, roads and infrastructure, social programs, and national defense. ***National tax policy*** refers to the way in which a nation chooses to allocate the tax burden across its residents.

> *A neutral tax does not divert capital flows.*

## Tax Neutrality: A Level Playing Field

A useful starting point in our discussion of national tax policy is the concept of ***tax neutrality***. A neutral tax is one that does not divert the natural flow of capital from its most productive uses. Taxes are a form of market friction. As long as taxes fall neutrally on all business activities, they are merely a drain on cash flows and do not divert capital from its natural destinations.

There are two forms of tax neutrality for MNCs.

- ***Domestic tax neutrality*** is a situation in which incomes arising from the foreign and domestic operations of a domestically based MNC are taxed similarly by the domestic government. For example, domestic tax neutrality holds if GM's U.S. and European operations are taxed at the same rate.
- ***Foreign tax neutrality*** is a situation in which taxes imposed on the foreign operations of domestic companies are similar to those facing local competitors in the foreign countries. For example, foreign tax neutrality holds if BMW's U.S. operations are taxed in the same way by the U.S. government as GM's U.S. operations are taxed.

Tax neutrality preserves equality by ensuring that an undue tax burden is not differentially imposed on foreign or domestic operations. Although U.S. tax law has emphasized domestic neutrality in recent years, the balance between domestic and foreign tax neutrality is the subject of continuing debate.[1]

## Violations of Tax Neutrality

In practice, tax neutrality is almost impossible to achieve because of cross-border differences in tax rates and systems. For example, if corporate income tax rates are 30 percent in the United Kingdom and 35 percent in the United States, then tax rates on the U.K. and U.S. income of a U.S.-based MNC can be consistent either with U.S. or U.K. taxes, but not both. Similarly, tax rates on British Petroleum's U.S. operations can be consistent either with U.S. or U.K. taxes, but not both.

*Taxes are seldom neutral.*

MNCs with operations that span two or more tax jurisdictions are well positioned to take advantage of cross-border differences in tax rates and systems through their tax planning operations. Differential taxes influence a number of corporate decisions, including the firm's choices of asset classes, financing instruments, and organizational forms.

- *Different tax jurisdictions.* Income received from different tax jurisdictions often is taxed at different rates. Some countries, such as Sweden, impose relatively high taxes to finance ambitious social welfare programs. Others, such as Ireland, choose relatively low corporate tax rates to attract foreign investment. Cross-border differences in tax rates and tax codes are important considerations in market entry and exit decisions, and in how the MNC repatriates income from its foreign operations.

- *Different asset classes*. Income received from different types of assets in the same tax jurisdiction, such as active business income versus passive investment income, often is taxed at different rates or at different times. In the United States, losses on active (general limitation) income cannot be used to offset gains on passive income, and vice versa. Many countries make a distinction between different forms of income for tax purposes.
- *Different financing instruments*. Returns on financial securities are taxed differently depending on whether the security is debt, equity, a debt-equity hybrid (such as preferred stock), or an equity-linked security (such as a stock option or warrant). On the other side of the contract, the tax treatment of financial expenses is different for payments to different classes of creditors, such as interest to debt or dividends to equity. For example, interest expense is tax deductible in most countries, whereas dividend payments usually are not. Different corporate and personal tax treatments on interest and dividend payments mean that different capital structures might be preferred in different tax jurisdictions.
- *Different organizational forms*. Income received from different legal organizational forms often is taxed at different rates or in different ways. For example, different tax rates apply to corporate and partnership income in the United States and other countries. Different tax rules also apply to the foreign branches and foreign subsidiaries of domestic corporations. Foreign branches are legally a part of the parent, whereas foreign subsidiaries are incorporated in a foreign country. Many countries (including the U.S.) tax foreign branch income as it is received, but delay taxes on foreign subsidiaries until income is repatriated to the parent. Because of cross-border differences in tax systems, an MNC must consider the tax consequences of its choice of organizational form when operating in foreign countries.

National tax policies thus influence the types and locations of assets held by a multinational, the way in which these assets are financed, and the organizational forms chosen for its operations.

## 15.2 TYPES OF TAXATION

### National Taxes on Foreign-Source Income

The major issues in international taxation revolve around the fact that ***foreign-source income*** (i.e., income earned from foreign operations) falls into two or more tax jurisdictions. Countries apply one of two tax regimes to income earned by firms incorporated within their borders.

- In a ***worldwide tax system***, foreign-source income is taxed by the home country as it is repatriated to the parent. Income from foreign subsidiaries usually is not taxed until it is repatriated, as long as it is reinvested in an active business outside of the home country. FTCs for income taxes paid to foreign governments prevent double taxation of foreign-source income. This tax regime is used for the income of domestic firms in a majority of developed countries, including the United States, the United Kingdom, and Japan.

- A ***territorial tax system*** imposes a tax only on income that is earned within the borders of the country, regardless of the location of the taxpayer's incorporation or operations. Territorial tax systems for resident incomes are found in Hong Kong, France, Belgium, and the Netherlands. More than half of organization for economic cooperation and development (OECD) countries have a territorial system for nonresidents, either by statute or by treaties with other countries.

Many countries follow a worldwide system for residents and a territorial system for nonresidents. The intent of each system is to avoid double taxation of foreign-source income.

*Tax treaties avoid double taxation.*

Although the details of national income tax systems vary, bilateral tax treaties ensure some consistency in the tax treatment of foreign-source income. Many of these tax treaties follow the *Model Tax Convention of the Organization for Economic Cooperation and Development.* Tax treaties are intended to ensure foreign tax neutrality; that is, that the foreign operations of each nation's MNCs are not disadvantaged relative to local competitors in the foreign country. Bilateral treaties also reduce the threat of double taxation of foreign-source income.

## Explicit versus Implicit Taxes

**Explicit Taxes** National governments impose many different kinds of ***explicit taxes.*** Figure 15.1 lists several countries' overall tax burden as a percent of gross domestic product (GDP), as well as corporate and personal income and value-added tax (VAT) rates. Explicit taxes include the following:

- Corporate and personal income taxes
- Withholding taxes on dividends, interest, and royalties
- Sales taxes and VAT
- Property and asset taxes
- Tariffs on cross-border trade

The costs of doing business in a foreign country depend in large part on the types and levels of taxes imposed by host governments.

Local taxes sometimes can be important as well. For example, most of the political and taxing power in Switzerland resides in 26 cantons or provinces—each of which has a different tax rate. Municipalities add another small tax. Figure 15.1 lists a corporate tax rate of 21.2 percent for Switzerland, but effective corporate tax rates range from 11.6 percent in the canton of Schwyz to 24.4 percent in the canton of Geneva.

| Country | Tax as % of GDP | Highest rate Corp | Personal | VAT | Country | Tax as % of GDP | Highest rate Corp | Personal | VAT |
|---|---|---|---|---|---|---|---|---|---|
| Argentina | - | 35.0 | 35.0 | 21.0 | Italy | 43.2 | 31.4 | 43.0 | 20.0 |
| Australia | 30.8 | 30.0 | 45.0 | 10.0* | Japan | 28.3 | 40.7 | 50.0 | 5.0* |
| Austria | 42.9 | 25.0 | 50.0 | 20.0 | Korea | 26.6 | 24.2 | 35.0 | 10.0 |
| Belgium | 44.3 | 34.0 | 50.0 | 21.0 | Mexico | 21.1 | 30.0 | 30.0 | 16.0 |
| Brazil | - | 34.0 | 27.5 | 25.0 | Netherlands | 37.5 | 25.0 | 52.0 | 19.0* |
| Canada | 32.2 | 28.3 | 46.4 | 5.0 | New Zealand | 34.5 | 28.0 | 33.0 | 15.0 |
| China | - | 25.0 | 45.0 | 17.0 | Norway | 42.1 | 28.0 | 47.8 | 25.0 |
| Czech Rep | 36.6 | 19.0 | 15.0 | 20.0 | Poland | 34.9 | 19.0 | 32.0 | 23.0 |
| Denmark | 48.3 | 25.0 | 55.4 | 25.0 | Portugal | 36.5 | 25.0 | 46.5 | 23.0 |
| Finland | 42.8 | 26.0 | 49.2 | 23.0 | Russia | - | 20.0 | 13.0 | 18.0 |
| France | 43.1 | 33.3 | 41.0 | 19.6 | Spain | 33.0 | 30.0 | 45.0 | 18.0 |
| Germany | 36.4 | 29.4 | 45.0 | 19.0 | Sweden | 47.1 | 26.3 | 56.6 | 25.0 |
| Greece | 31.3 | 20.0 | 45.0 | 23.0 | Switzerland | 29.4 | 21.2 | 40.0 | 8.0 |
| Hungary | 40.1 | 19.0 | 16.0 | 25.0 | Turkey | 23.5 | 20.0 | 35.0 | 18.0 |
| Ireland | 28.3 | 12.5 | 48.0 | 21.0 | United Kingdom | 35.7 | 28.0 | 50.0 | 20.0 |
| Israel | - | 24.0 | 45.0 | 16.0 | United States | 26.9 | 40.0 | 35.0 | 0.0 |

**FIGURE 15.1** National Tax Rates.
*Source:* Total taxes as a percent of GDP are from *OECD Factbook 2010* (www.oecd.org). Maximum corporate and personal tax rates are from KPMG 2011 surveys (www.kpmg.com). Corporate taxes include an estimate of local taxes. Individual taxes include social security taxes. VAT rates are from www.worldwide-tax.com.
*VAT is called a consumption tax in Japan and a goods and services tax (GST) in Australia, Canada & New Zealand. The U.S. government does not charge a tax on the sale of goods or services, although most U.S. states do.

As might be expected, there is little consistency in the national definitions of taxable income. Countries following a territorial tax system typically do not tax foreign-source income. Countries following a worldwide tax system usually tax foreign-source income as it is repatriated to the parent company, using a system of credits for foreign taxes paid. Regardless of whether countries follow worldwide or territorial tax systems, the net effect of most bilateral tax treaties is to make foreign-source income taxable at the higher of the two national corporate income tax rates.

Withholding taxes are intended to ensure that residents' taxable income is reported to the tax authorities in the host country. For distributions to nonresidents, withholding taxes also compensate the host government for lost tax revenues from forgone personal income taxes in the host country.

Withholding taxes on dividend distributions are the norm, especially for dividend payments to nonresidents. The dividend withholding tax rate is most frequently 5 percent between countries with bilateral tax treaties, but it varies from 0 percent on cross-border dividend distributions from Hong Kong and the United Kingdom to 30 percent on some dividend distributions from the United States to nonresidents. Many national governments also impose withholding taxes on interest or royalty payments.

As an example of why governments impose withholding taxes, the West German tax court (Bundesrechnungshof) estimated in the 1980s that 65 to 70 percent of all interest income received by individuals in Germany went unreported. Germany instituted several tax law changes in the early 1990s in an effort to increase reporting compliance. First, the level at which interest income became taxable was raised to several thousand marks in order to help break the tradition of noncompliance. Second, a withholding tax on interest payments by corporations and banks was instituted and administered through the banking system. Withholding taxes can be partially recovered by those declaring their interest income to the government. Finally, penalties for noncompliance were increased. Prior to these tax law changes, most violations went undiscovered until death or divorce brought them to the attention of the tax court.

Most countries around the world use a ***VAT*** that is collected at each stage of production in proportion to the value added during that stage. Each of the countries in the European Union uses a VAT. In contrast, the United States uses a ***sales tax*** on the final sale to the consumer. Although the merits of VATs are periodically debated in the United States, proposals to institute a VAT have met strong resistance in the U.S. Congress.

Tax policy is a competitive tool that governments can use to attract businesses that otherwise might not locate in a particular tax jurisdiction. Developing economies can use tax holidays to attract foreign investment and promote development in key regions and industries. Countries that actively employ tax policy to attract investment include Hong Kong, Hungary, and Ireland. Low taxes or tax subsidies in the form of tax relief or tax holidays allow some locations to overcome the handicaps that may make them less desirable than competing locations.

## Implicit Taxes

The law of one price requires that equivalent assets sell for the same price. The law of one price can be restated on an after-tax basis as follows:

> The law of one price requires that equivalent assets sell to yield the same *after-tax* real rate of return.

Not all taxes are neutral. Higher before-tax required returns are demanded in high-tax jurisdictions to compensate for the additional tax burden. Lower expected returns on assets subject to lower tax rates are a form of ***implicit tax.***

Suppose an MNC can invest \$100,000 in Country H to yield \$112,500 for a pretax return of $i_H = 12.5\%$. If corporate income in Country H is taxed at a relatively high rate of $t_H = 60\%$, then after-tax return in Country H is $i_H(1-t_H) = (0.125)(1-0.60) = 0.05$, or 5 percent. Alternatively, the corporation can invest \$100,000 in Country L and face a lower corporate tax rate of $t_L = 40\%$. If a pretax return of $i_L = 12.5\%$ can be earned in this country, then \$100,000 can be turned into \$107,500 after taxes for an after-tax return of $i_L(1-t_L) = (0.125)(1-0.40) = 0.075$, or 7.5 percent.

> ***There is an implicit tax on returns in low-tax countries.***

This situation cannot persist. Investors will move their investments toward the low-tax country and away from the high-tax country in pursuit of the highest after-tax return. This activity will continue until, in equilibrium, expected after-tax rates of return are equal.

$$i_H(1 - t_H) = i_L(1 - t_L) i_H/i_L = (1 - t_L)/(1 - t_H) \quad (15.1)$$

In this example, this means that $i_H/i_L = (1 - t_L)/(1 - t_H) = (1 - 0.40)/(1 - 0.60) = 1.50$. In equilibrium, pretax returns in H will be 50 percent higher than pretax returns in L to compensate for the higher income tax in H. For example, if prices are bid up in the low-tax country until before-tax returns fall to $i_L = 10\%$, then prices in Country H will fall and before-tax expected rates of return will rise until $i_H = 15\%$ in equilibrium. After-tax return is then 6% in each country. The higher prices and lower expected returns in Country L are a form of implicit tax on earnings in that country.

## 15.3 U.S. TAXATION OF FOREIGN-SOURCE INCOME

The U.S. Internal Revenue Service (IRS) is responsible for collecting taxes and ensuring compliance with the U.S. tax code. The foreign-source income of U.S. taxpayers is categorized by the U.S. tax code into one of two income baskets.

- *Passive income.* Passive income is income, such as investment income, that does not come from an active business. Income that is not specifically included in passive income is classified as general limitation income.
- *General limitation income.* General limitation income is earned from participation in an active business, such as dividends or interest received from a more-than-50-percent-owned or -controlled foreign corporation (CFC), and income from foreign branches.

The treatment of foreign-source income depends on how foreign operations are organized and controlled.

- *Income from foreign corporations.* A ***foreign corporation*** is any business entity that is not created or organized under U.S. laws. Income from a foreign corporation is treated in one of three ways, depending on the U.S. parent's level of ownership.
- *Ownership of less than 10 percent.* Income such as a dividend from a foreign corporation in which the U.S. parent owns less than 10 percent of the market value and voting power is placed into the passive income basket as it is repatriated to the parent, reflecting the U.S. parent's passive stake in the corporation.
- *Ownership of between 10 and 50 percent.* A dividend from a foreign corporation owned 10 percent or more but less than or equal to 50 percent in terms of market value or voting power is treated as passive income and taxed as it is repatriated to the parent corporation. Foreign corporations in this category sometimes are referred to as "10/50 corporations." Many joint ventures fall into this category.

- *Ownership of more than 50 percent.* If a U.S. parent owns more than 50 percent of a foreign corporation in terms of market value or voting power, the foreign company is called a *CFC.* Income from a CFC is taxed as general limitation income as funds are repatriated to the U.S. parent in the form of dividends, interest, rents, royalties, or management fees.

> *Income from a CFC is taxed as it is repatriated.*

- *Income from foreign branches.* The U.S. tax code treats foreign branches as a part of the U.S. parent, rather than as a separate legal entity in the foreign country. Income earned from a foreign branch is treated as general limitation income and taxed as it is earned.

### Foreign Corporations and Check-the-Box Regulations

Multinational tax management for U.S.-based MNCs is made simpler by ***check-the-box regulations*** that allow a U.S. parent to choose whether a foreign corporation is treated as a corporation or as a flow-through entity for U.S. tax purposes. A ***flow-through entity*** does not pay its own separate U.S. tax. Instead, its income "flows through" to the U.S. parent, which can then consolidate this income with other foreign and domestic sources and pay a single U.S. tax, depending on whether the income falls into the passive or general limitation income basket. This avoids double taxation of foreign-source income. It also has a profound effect on the structure of the domestic and foreign operations of MNCs.

Consider the example in Figure 15.2. The U.S. parent owns 100 percent of the Swiss Holding Company, which in turn owns 100 percent of each of its subsidiaries. In the absence of check-the-box regulations, the U.S. parent must account for income from each of its CFCs. If the U.S. parent "checks the box" for each subsidiary, then all of the transactions below the Swiss Holding Company flow through to the Swiss Holding Company and otherwise are ignored for U.S. tax purposes. All of the foreign income is then deferred from U.S. taxation until it is repatriated to the U.S. parent because it is treated as earned by the Swiss Holding Company, which is a CFC of the U.S. parent. This greatly simplifies U.S. taxation of foreign-source income.

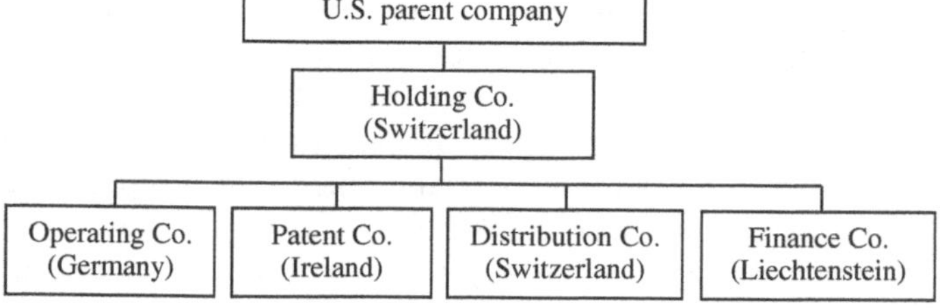


**FIGURE 15.2** A Foreign Holding Company Structure.

## Foreign Tax Credits and the Overall Foreign Tax Credit Limitation

**Foreign Tax Credits for a Single Foreign Subsidiary** The United States allows a *FTC* against domestic U.S. income taxes up to the amount of foreign taxes paid on foreign-source income from a CFC. The amount of the FTC applied to the U.S. parent's tax liability depends on the amount and form of taxes paid to the foreign government. Foreign taxes used in the computation of the FTC include foreign income taxes, as well as foreign withholding taxes on dividend, interest, or royalty distributions to the parent.

> *FTCs avoid double taxation of foreign-source income.*

Consider the CFCs—located in Norway and Russia—of two different U.S. MNCs, as shown in Figure 15.3. Suppose that each is the only foreign subsidiary of its U.S. parent, so that we do not have to bother for now with limitations on foreign-source income pooled across several foreign subsidiaries. (The overall FTC limitation on general limitation income will be discussed shortly.) After translating foreign-source incomes into dollars, each subsidiary has $1,000 of taxable income (line d). Corporate income tax rates are 28 percent in Norway and 20 percent in Russia. Withholding taxes on dividend distributions to the U.S. parent of each

| Tax statements as single foreign subsidiaries | | Norway | Russia |
|---|---|---|---|
| a | Dividend payout ratio | 100% | 100% |
| b | Foreign dividend withholding tax rate | 25% | 15% |
| c | Foreign tax rate | 28% | 20% |
| d | Foreign income before tax | 1000 | 1000 |
| e | Foreign income tax (d×c) | 280 | 200 |
| f | After-tax foreign earnings (d–e) | 720 | 800 |
| g | Declared as dividends (f×a) | 720 | 800 |
| h | Foreign dividend withholding tax (g×b) | 180 | 120 |
| i | Total foreign tax (e+h) | 460 | 320 |
| j | Dividend to U.S. parent (d-i) | 540 | 680 |
| k | Gross foreign income before tax (line d) | 1000 | 1000 |
| l | Tentative U.S. income tax (k×35%) | 350 | 350 |
| m | FTC (i) | 460 | 320 |
| n | Net U.S. taxes payable [max(l–m,0)] | 0 | 30 |
| o | Total taxes paid (i+n) | 460 | 350 |
| p | Net amount to U.S. parent (k–o) | 540 | 650 |
| q | Total taxes as separate subsidiaries ($\Sigma_o$) | 810 | |
| **Consolidated tax statement as subsidiaries of a single U.S. parent** | | | |
| r | Overall FTC limitation ($\Sigma_k$×35%) | 700 | |
| s | Total FTCs on a consolidated basis ($\Sigma_i$) | 780 | |
| t | Additional U.S. taxes due [max(0, r–s)] | 0 | |
| u | Excess tax credits [max(0, s–r)] (carried back 1 year or forward 10 years) | 80 | |

**Note**: Foreign currency amounts are in U.S. dollar equivalents. Local taxes are ignored for simplicity in this example.

**FIGURE 15.3** Repatriation of Foreign-Source Income.

foreign subsidiary (not shown in Figure 15.1) are 25 percent in Norway and 15 percent in Russia. The highest corporate income tax rate in the U.S. is 35 percent.

In Figure 15.3, the parents' foreign and domestic income tax liabilities assume that 100 percent of after-tax earnings are repatriated as a dividend from each subsidiary. The rules are slightly more complicated when the foreign corporation repatriates less than 100 percent of earnings. The foreign-source income of each CFC is taxed as it is earned in the foreign country (line e). An additional tax on the dividend distribution to the U.S. parent is withheld by each foreign country (line h). The declared dividend net of the dividend withholding tax is available to the U.S. parent (line j). Total foreign tax (line i) is the sum of the foreign income tax (line e) and the foreign dividend withholding tax (line h).

With a 100 percent dividend distribution, 100 percent of foreign-source income is taxed as it is received in the United States (line k). The tentative U.S. income tax on each subsidiary is then $350 (35 percent of $1,000 on line l). This is the amount of tax that would have been due had the income been earned in the United States. With a 100 percent dividend distribution, each subsidiary provides a tax credit equal to total foreign taxes paid (line m). If the tentative U.S. tax is larger than the FTC, as is the case for the subsidiary in Russia, then the U.S. parent must pay the difference (line n) between the tentative U.S. tax and the FTC. If the FTC is larger than the tentative U.S. tax, as is the case for the subsidiary in Norway, then no additional tax is due in the United States. If these subsidiaries are the sole foreign operations of their respective parents, then the total (foreign and domestic) taxes paid by these two foreign subsidiaries is $810.

**Multiple Foreign Subsidiaries and the Overall Foreign Tax Credit Limitation** The previous example assumed that these were the sole foreign operations of their respective U.S. parents. In this setting, the FTC limitation is simple to apply. The allowable FTC in any year is the minimum of foreign taxes paid and the U.S. tax that would have been paid if the income was earned in the United States. The net effect is that the U.S. parent pays current-year taxes at the higher of the two rates.

MNCs owning more than one foreign subsidiary face an ***overall FTC limitation*** that limits the total FTC on earnings from foreign businesses to the amount of U.S. tax attributable to foreign-source income. Total foreign income is pooled or consolidated across all foreign subsidiaries in each income basket, so that losses in some countries are offset by gains in other countries. When an MNC's domestic income has already placed it in the highest U.S. tax bracket (35 percent), the overall FTC limitation is calculated as

$$\text{Overall FTC limitation} = (\text{Taxable foreign-source income}) \times (\text{U.S. tax rate}) \tag{15.2}$$

*The overall FTC limitation applies to consolidated income.*

In Figure 15.3, total foreign-source income from the two subsidiaries is $2,000. At the 35 percent U.S. tax rate, the overall FTC limitation is ($2,000)(0.35) = $700 (line r). The $780 sum of the FTCs is greater than the tentative U.S. tax of $700, so an MNC owning these two foreign subsidiaries has excess FTCs of $780 – $700 = $80 (line u). Excess FTCs can be carried back one year or forward ten years in the United States.

### Other Limitations on Foreign Tax Credits

The U.S. tax code places other limitations on FTCs, including the following.

**Income Baskets** Categorization of foreign-source income as either passive or general limitation income limits the use of FTCs, because losses in one income basket cannot be used to offset gains in the other income basket. For example, passive gains on currency transactions cannot be used to offset losses from an active foreign investment, such as a foreign branch.

**Allocation-of-Income Rules** Another limitation on the usefulness of FTCs comes in the form of ***allocation-of-income rules.*** When not all profits are repatriated to the parent, the U.S. tax code applies the allocation-of-income rules to determine what portion of earnings are taxable and how interest and other expenses are to be allocated between foreign-source and domestic-source income. The general rule is that income and any related expenses should be allocated to the tax jurisdiction in which the income is earned. These rules are important because of the different tax rates that can apply to income from different foreign and domestic tax jurisdictions.

*Allocation-of-income rules limit the value of FTCs.*

### MARKET UPDATE La Mordida—"The Little Bite"

One of the categories of income recognized by the 1962 Revenue Act was illegal foreign bribes. Bribery is relatively uncommon in the United States and is illegal in any case, so this category seems strange from a U.S. perspective. In many other countries, it is quite common for government bureaucrats and the managers of private businesses to use bribes or kickbacks as they conduct their daily business.

Suppose you are a sales representative for IBM in the process of negotiating a contract to supply personal computers to the Mexican government. Competitors from Shanghai are offering to pay the local official in charge of computer acquisitions a modest sum in an effort to secure the contract. If you stick to your (U.S.) principles and refuse to pay la mordida ("the little bite"), you'll probably lose the contract. On the other hand, you are fairly sure that you can secure the contract if you offer a small "commission." What should you do?

A 1999 OECD convention on bribery signed by 35 countries states that "enterprises should not, directly or indirectly, offer, promise, give, or demand a bribe or other undue advantage to obtain or retain business." Although this sounds sensible, few countries have passed anti-bribery legislation. In the United States, the 1977 Foreign Corrupt Practices Act outlaws bribery as a way to promote the interests of U.S. corporations or their foreign affiliates. This act requires that U.S. multinationals compete with local firms in foreign markets according to U.S. rules. This can put U.S. firms at a disadvantage in countries where bribery is commonplace.

Despite good intentions, enforcement of the U.S. Foreign Corrupt Practices Act has been lax. Defense contractor Titan Corporation was fined $28.5 million in 2005 after admitting it had bribed foreign officials in six African countries and filed false tax returns in cases dating to 1998. The previous record was held by Lockheed Corporation, which was fined $24.8 million in 1995 after admitting it bribed an Egyptian official to arrange the sale of aircraft in 1988. Aside from these two prominent cases, very few fines have been imposed and most have been under $1 million. Further, it is difficult to tell the difference between a bribe and a "facilitation payment" to a local official to expedite a contract. In 2001, British Petroleum testified to the British parliament that it made facilitation payments but would "never offer, solicit or accept a bribe in any form." This is a very slippery slope.

- *Allocation of interest expense to general limitation income.* As a general rule, interest expense is allocated according to the proportion of foreign and domestic assets on the firm's consolidated tax return, where assets are measured either on the basis of tax book value or fair market value. Under this regulation, the proportion of interest that is allocated to foreign and domestic income depends on the firm's proportion of foreign and domestic assets and not on whether the parent or a foreign subsidiary actually issued the debt. The philosophy behind this rule is that money is fungible, in that money raised by one unit can be used by other units of the firm.

  *Example.* Mixed Blessing & Associates (MBA) uses the fair market value method to allocate interest. Assets with a market value of $2 million generated foreign-source income and assets with a market value of $8 million of domestic income during the year. MBA's $200,000 interest expense is allocated $40,000 to foreign-source general limitation income and $160,000 to domestic-source income.
- *Qualified nonrecourse financing.* There are several exceptions to the general allocation rule above. The most relevant for the financial manager is "qualified nonrecourse debt" used to support a specific physical asset or assets with a useful life of more than one year. The physical asset must be expected to generate sufficient cash flow to pay the interest and must be used as security on the debt. Interest expense under this exception is allocated to the

income from the physical asset. Project finance makes extensive use of this exception.

*Example.* MBA borrowed $1 million to purchase its $2 million foreign asset. MBA has annual interest expense of $50,000 on this debt, and the debt is secured by the asset. In this case, all of the $50,000 interest expense is allocated to the foreign-source income generated by the foreign asset.

- *Allocation of research and experimentation (R&E) expenses.* Allocation of R&E expenses depends on whether the taxpayer elects the sales method or the gross income method. Under the sales method, 50 percent of R&E expenses is allocated to domestic-source income with the remainder allocated to foreign- and domestic-source income according to the proportion of foreign sales. Under the gross income method, 25 percent of R&E expenses is allocated to domestic-source income with the remainder allocated according to the proportion of gross income from foreign sources. Expenses that do not directly arise from an income-related activity (such as general and administrative expenses of the home office) are allocated according to the proportion of sales or gross income from foreign and domestic sources.

  *Example.* MBA uses the gross income method of allocating R&E expense. MBA spent $1 million on product development. Foreign-source income constituted 40 percent of MBA's total gross income. In this case, the 25 percent rule allocates $250,000 of R&E expense to domestic-source income. An additional 60 percent of the remaining $750,000 R&E expense (or $450,000) is allocated to domestic-source income. A total of ($250,000 + $450,000) = $700,000 is thus allocated to domestic-source income. The remaining $300,000 (40 percent of $750,000) is allocated to foreign-source income.

There are a number of exceptions to these allocation-of-income rules, particularly for CFCs, so it is best to consult a tax expert about the best way to issue debt to support foreign operations.

Along with the passive and general limitation income baskets, the allocation-of-income rules limit the ability of U.S.-based MNCs to reduce their tax liabilities through international tax planning.

## 15.4 TAXES AND ORGANIZATIONAL FORM

Tax systems influence the choice of organizational form for foreign affiliates, because most nations tax income from branches and subsidiaries differently. Figure 15.4 summarizes the differences between these two organizational forms according to the U.S. tax code.

Most U.S.-based MNCs conduct their foreign operations through CFCs. These are foreign corporations owned more than 50 percent either in market value or voting power. CFCs are incorporated in the host country and are governed by the laws and tax rules of the host country. CFC income is not taxed by the IRS until it is repatriated to the parent in the form of dividends, interest, royalties, or management fees. Foreign governments usually impose a withholding tax on dividend distributions to the U.S. parent as compensation for lost tax revenues from

| | CFC | Foreign branch |
|---|---|---|
| **Legal** | Separate legal entity in the host country | Foreign branches are a part of the parent for legal purposes |
| **Tax** | U.S. tax paid as income is repatriated to the parent | U.S. taxes paid as foreign income is earned by the subsidiary |
| **Disclosure** | Disclosure limited to activities in the host country | Foreign branches might be required to disclose parent's global income |
| **Liability** | Liability limited to assets in the host country | Legal liability extends to the parent |

**FIGURE 15.4** The Organizational Form of Foreign Operations.

forgone personal income taxes in the host country. Interest withholding taxes are somewhat less common.

*Most U.S. MNCs use CFCs for foreign operations.*

Some foreign business is conducted by U.S. MNCs through foreign branches. Foreign branch income is fully taxable in the United States as it is earned. The immediate taxability of foreign branch income is often the overriding tax consideration that leads MNCs to organize foreign operations as incorporated subsidiaries rather than branches, particularly for operations located in low-tax countries. Operating as a foreign branch immediately exposes foreign-source income to the higher domestic tax rates. In contrast, CFCs can reinvest abroad without having to pay the higher domestic tax rates until funds are repatriated to the parent.

Foreign branches do have some tax advantages over foreign subsidiaries. Foreign branch income is taxed as it is earned. This creates a tax advantage for the foreign branch organizational form for start-up operations that are expected to lose money. Losses from foreign branch operations are immediately deductible against domestic income, so there is a tax incentive to establish start-up operations that are expected to suffer losses as foreign branches. The foreign branch can be incorporated once operations become profitable, although previously deducted losses must be recaptured as income. Also, there are no withholding taxes on foreign branch income because it is not a dividend distribution. Finally, transfers of property to foreign branches are not a sale to a separate legal entity and hence are usually not taxable.

There are several other reasons for incorporating in a host country. First, incorporation limits the liability of the parent company on its foreign operations. The MNC's exposure to the activities of each foreign subsidiary is limited to the assets of that subsidiary. For example, a 1984 leak of methyl isocyanate gas at Union Carbide's chemical plant in Bhopal, India, caused one of the worst industrial disasters in history with deaths in the thousands. Union Carbide was insulated from much of the litigation surrounding the leak because the subsidiary was incorporated in India and Union Carbide was a junior partner to the government of India. Courts in both India and the United States ruled that Union Carbide was not responsible for losses arising from the disaster. This limit on liability is not absolute. If plaintiffs can show that the parent company has effective control of the subsidiary despite the legal separation, then attorneys can "pierce the corporate veil" and claim that the parent is culpable for the activities of the subsidiary. There is still the difficult issue of which country has jurisdiction over disputes.

Disclosure requirements imposed by a host country also favor incorporating in the host country rather than operating as a foreign branch. Some countries require that firms operating within their borders disclose information on their worldwide operations. The worldwide operations of a foreign subsidiary are limited to those of the subsidiary, but the worldwide operations of a foreign branch include those of the parent. MNCs use incorporated foreign subsidiaries when they would be hurt by publicly disclosing sensitive information on their worldwide operations.

Tax considerations also affect the attractiveness of the international joint venture as an organizational form. The 1986 TRA required that 10/50 dividends received from each foreign corporation be treated as a separate income basket, so that excess FTCs from 10/50 dividends in high-tax countries could not be applied to income from low-tax countries. Desai and Hines found this greatly reduced the attractiveness of international joint ventures, especially with partners in low-tax countries. Indeed, U.S. participation in international joint ventures fell after 1986, particularly in low-tax countries.[2] These country-specific income baskets were repealed beginning in 2003, and dividends from international joint ventures now fall into the general limitation income basket.

## 15.5 TRANSFER PRICING AND TAX PLANNING

***Transfer prices*** on sales from one unit of a firm to another create an opportunity for tax planning when the units are located in different tax jurisdictions. Transfer prices are important both for tax planning and business management because they allocate taxable income, tax liabilities, and operating profit across business units. Indeed, a 2010 survey by Ernst & Young found that transfer pricing is the most important tax-related issue facing the MNC.[3]

*Tax codes call for arm's-length transfer prices.*

Most national tax codes require that transfer prices be set as ***arm's-length prices*** that would be negotiated between independent parties. Both Section 486 of the U.S. Internal Revenue Code and Article 9 of the OECD Model Tax Convention call for arm's-length pricing. It can be difficult to set defensible transfer prices on assets without observable market prices. The Ernst & Young survey finds the most common method for tangible assets is ***cost plus***; that is, cost plus a gross profit markup based on independent market transactions between unrelated parties. The second most common transfer pricing method is ***comparable uncontrolled price*** (market price) based on independent market transactions. Consistent application of these methods allows the MNC to defend its transfer prices to domestic and foreign tax authorities.

Transfer price management is most effective when intracompany transfers involve

- Products with high gross operating margins
- Intermediate or final products for which there are no observable market prices

Firms with intangible assets (trademarks, trade secrets, franchises, copyrights, or patents) are prime candidates for transfer price planning, because intangible assets often have high gross margins and no observable market prices. For this reason, the Ernst & Young survey found that transfer pricing is most important in high-margin industries such as pharmaceuticals, electronics, and biotech. With wide discretion in setting transfer prices, multinationals in these industries can shift expenses toward countries with high tax rates to minimize taxes and maximize firm value.

### An Example

*Income can be shifted to low-tax countries.*

Consider the example in Figure 15.5. ConAgra, Inc. is a diversified U.S.-based corporation with operations in both Australia and Japan. ConAgra's Australian subsidiary exports beef to the Japanese subsidiary. The 40 percent corporate income tax rate in Japan is more than the 30 percent rate in Australia. How can transfer prices affect ConAgra's worldwide taxes?

The key to understanding the impact of transfer pricing on ConAgra's worldwide tax liability is to recognize that shifting taxable income toward low-tax jurisdictions reduces worldwide taxes. Suppose ConAgra prices the beef at \$5,000 using the "cost-plus" method as in the left panel of Figure 15.5. The good news is that the \$5,000 in Japanese costs is far less than the \$10,000 in Japanese revenues. The bad news is that this income is taxed at the relatively high 40 percent Japanese tax rate. Relatively little taxable income is exposed to the lower 30 percent Australian tax rate. Worldwide income is effectively taxed at 38 percent under this transfer price.

| | Cost-plus transfer price | | | Market-based transfer price | | |
|---|---|---|---|---|---|---|
| | Australia | Japan | Consolidated | Australia | Japan | Consolidated |
| Income tax rate | 30% | 40% | | 30% | 40% | |
| Revenue | 5,000 | 10,000 | 10,000 | 8,000 | 10,000 | 10,000 |
| Cost of goods sold | 3,000 | 5,000 | 3,000 | 3,000 | 8,000 | 3,000 |
| Other expenses | 1,000 | 1,000 | 2,000 | 1,000 | 1,000 | 2,000 |
| Taxable income | 1,000 | 4,000 | 5,000 | 4,000 | 1,000 | 5,000 |
| Taxes | 300 | 1,600 | 1,900 | 1,200 | 400 | 1,600 |
| Net income | 700 | 2,400 | 3,100 | 2,800 | 600 | 3,400 |
| Effective tax rate (tax/taxable income) | | | 38% | | | 32% |

**FIGURE 15.5** Transfer Pricing and Tax Planning (in U.S. dollars).

Suppose comparable beef sells between unrelated parties for $8,000 in Japan. If ConAgra sets the transfer price equal to this "comparable uncontrolled price" based on market prices, it recognizes Australian revenues and Japanese expenses of $8,000. This shifts taxable income from Japan to Australia, where it is taxed at the lower 30 percent rate. Under this transfer price, the effective tax rate on worldwide operations falls from 38 percent to 32 percent.

## Transfer Price Planning

The potential for transfer price abuses by MNCs is high, so tax authorities closely monitor transfer price policies. The 2010 Ernst & Young survey reported that 68 percent of respondents in 25 countries reported an audit related to transfer prices somewhere in the organization. If a tax authority disagrees with a transfer price, it can unilaterally reassess a firm's tax liability. Appeals of transfer pricing decisions can take years to resolve, and more than one company has gone through Chapter 11 reorganization to avoid the additional tax bite.

> *Intangibles seldom have observable market prices.*

For example, Storage Technology produced disk storage devices in Puerto Rico during the 1970s to take advantage of Puerto Rico's "possessions corporation" tax status. Most of the company's revenues but none of its R&D expenses were allocated to the subsidiary. The resulting earnings were exempt from U.S. income tax. The IRS challenged Storage Technology's transfer prices and allocations of R&D expenses. Storage Technology declared bankruptcy in 1983 largely to avoid the back taxes due on earnings from its Puerto Rican manufacturing facilities.

Some transfer price planning is intended to reduce the likelihood of a dispute with tax authorities. Firms follow the IRS's allocation-of-income rules to reduce the likelihood that the IRS will disagree with their transfer prices. Nevertheless, there is room for discretion even within the IRS rules. For example, one input into the allocation rules is a product's manufacturing cost. Firms sometimes choose their investments to increase the manufacturing cost in high-tax jurisdictions and reduce the manufacturing cost in low-tax jurisdictions. This investment-based income shifting toward low-tax jurisdictions can be particularly difficult for the IRS to monitor.[4]

### MARKET UPDATE Wal-Mart's Advance Pricing Agreement with the IRS and China

MNCs can reduce the uncertainty over how the local tax authority views their transfer pricing arrangements through *advance pricing agreements* (APAs). An APA is a contract with the domestic tax authority that identifies a methodology for evaluating whether transfer prices are arm's-length prices. An APA ensures compliance with tax regulations and greatly reduces the risk of litigation or penalties from transfer pricing issues. A *bilateral APA* includes the tax authority of a foreign government to ensure that both foreign and domestic tax authorities are in agreement on the transfer pricing method. The U.S. IRS issued 69 APAs in 2010, of which 49 were bilateral agreements with another country.

In 2007, the world's largest retailer, Wal-Mart, concluded the first bilateral APA between the U. S. IRS and the People's Republic of China. The APA was initiated at the request of the IRS, and created a process for negotiating APAs with China's State Administration of Taxation that smoothed the way for subsequent APA.

*Sources:* "Announcement and Report Concerning Advance Pricing Agreements" (2011), available at www.irs.gov; "Wal-Mart Clinches First US-China APA," *International Tax Review* (February 2007).

Evidence suggests that large MNCs actively manage their transfer prices to shift income across tax jurisdictions. Collins, Kemsley, and Lang found U.S. multinationals facing foreign tax rates that exceed the U.S. rate exhibit stronger evidence of tax-motivated income shifting than other U.S. multinationals.[5] These authors estimated that U.S. multinationals in their sample shifted income worth about $4 billion per year from high-tax countries to the Unites States during 1984–1992. Evidence of income shifting was found for all sample years and for most industries in their study.

Whether it is to reduce the likelihood of a tax audit or to shift income to reduce taxes, transfer price planning is a necessary activity of the MNC.

## 15.6 TAXES AND THE LOCATION OF FOREIGN ASSETS AND LIABILITIES

National tax systems influence the location of foreign operations, as MNCs use tax planning to minimize their expected tax liabilities.

### The Effect of Shifting Operations to Low-Tax Jurisdictions

MNCs have a tax incentive to shift operations toward countries with low income tax rates. For U.S. MNCs, this is particularly true when the overall FTC limitation is binding. If the limitation is binding, unused FTCs from high-tax countries absorb the additional U.S. taxes due on foreign-source income from countries with low tax rates.

**An Example** To illustrate the effect of shifting operations toward low-tax jurisdictions, suppose sales are shifted from the Norwegian to the Russian subsidiary in Figure 15.3 such that taxable income in Norway falls to $0 while taxable income in Russia rises to $2,000. As shown in Figure 15.6, the overall FTC limitation is still 35 percent of $2,000, or $700. Once sales are shifted to Russia, total foreign

**Shift sales from Norway to Russia**

| | Tax statements as single foreign subsidiaries | Norway | Russia |
|---|---|---|---|
| a | Dividend payout ratio | 100% | 100% |
| b | Foreign dividend withholding tax rate | 25% | 15% |
| c | Foreign tax rate | 28% | 20% |
| d | Foreign income before tax | 0 | 2000 |
| e | Foreign income tax (d×c) | 0 | 400 |
| f | After-tax foreign earnings (d–e) | 0 | 1,600 |
| g | Declared as dividends (f×a) | 0 | 1,600 |
| h | Foreign dividend withholding tax (g×b) | 0 | 240 |
| i | Total foreign tax (e+h) | 0 | 640 |
| j | Dividend to U.S. parent (d–i) | 0 | 1,360 |
| k | Gross foreign income before tax (line d) | 0 | 2000 |
| l | Tentative U.S. income tax (k×35%) | 0 | 700 |
| m | FTC (i) | 0 | 640 |
| n | Net U.S. taxes payable [max(l–m,0)] | 0 | 60 |
| o | Total taxes paid (i+n) | 0 | 700 |
| p | Net amount to U.S. parent (k–o) | 0 | 1,300 |
| q | Total taxes as separate subsidiaries ($\Sigma_o$) | 700 | |
| | **Consolidated tax statement as subsidiaries of a single U.S. parent** | | |
| r | Overall FTC limitation ($\Sigma_k$×35%) | 700 | |
| s | Total FTCs on a consolidated basis ($\Sigma_i$) | 640 | |
| t | Additional U.S. taxes due [max(0, r–s)] | 60 | |
| u | Excess tax credits [max(0,s–r)] (carried back 1 year or forward 10 years) | 0 | |

**FIGURE 15.6** Effect of Shifting Sales toward Low-Tax Countries.

tax paid ($640) is $60 less than the FTC limitation of $700. This means that $60 in additional tax is due to the U.S. tax authorities. Shifting sales from Norway to Russia reduces the U.S. parent's total tax bill in the current fiscal year from $780 in Figure 15.3 to $700 in Figure 15.6. Excess FTCs in the U.S. are correspondingly reduced by $80.

> ***MNCs have an incentive to shift income toward low-tax countries.***

In the base case without shifting sales, total taxes depend on whether the $80 excess tax credit can be applied against foreign taxes paid in other years. If the overall FTC limitation is binding in other years (as is often the case for firms with excess FTCs), then the $80 excess tax credit in Figure 15.3 could not be carried backward or forward and simply would be lost to the corporation. Shifting sales to Russia would then capture an $80 reduction in current-year taxes.

**The Effect of Implicit Taxes** In this example, Russia is the tax-preferred location because of its low tax rates. However, this is not the whole story. Operations in Russia are likely to face implicit taxes as MNCs from around the world shift their operations toward Russia in pursuit of Russia's tax advantages. In equilibrium, this flow of foreign capital into Russia will squeeze profit margins, and before-tax expected and required returns will fall. Conversely, before-tax profit margins and before-tax and expected and required returns in Norway will rise to compensate for the relatively high Norwegian tax rates. This process will continue until, in equilibrium, after-tax expected returns are equal across both countries.

Explicit taxes are one of many factors to be considered in global location decisions. Implicit taxes also must be taken into account. Minimizing explicit taxes cannot be the overriding criterion in MNC site selection because of the many and subtle forms of implicit taxes faced by the MNC.

When governments offer tax incentives to attract foreign investment, it is usually because they cannot compete for capital without the incentives. Countries offering tax incentives often have poorly educated workforces, inadequate physical or legal infrastructures, poor communication systems, poor corporate governance, high corruption, or other handicaps that lead to higher operating costs or lower final goods prices or quality. MNCs must assess the after-tax, rather than before-tax, expected returns on investment. To the extent that before-tax expected returns are driven down by low explicit tax rates, MNCs may choose to locate elsewhere. The criteria determining site selection for a foreign operation thus should include, but not be dominated by, tax considerations.

### Taxes and the Location of Treasury Operations

Many corporations maintain offshore financial affiliates in tax-haven countries such as Bermuda and the Cayman Islands. ***Tax havens*** offer low tax rates on corporate income, and low withholding tax rates for dividend and interest distributions to nonresidents. Tax havens often are protective of financial information as well.

The tax-haven affiliates of MNCs often take the form of re-invoicing centers that channel funds among the multinational's foreign operations without triggering domestic taxes on repatriated dividends. Re-invoicing centers often handle cash management and other treasury functions as well, including management of financial price risks.

### Taxes and Multinational Debt Location Decisions

Differences in international tax rates and tax regimes affect MNCs' debt location decisions. Arena and Roper examined the debt location decisions of MNCs from 23 countries and found that debt tends to be issued from high-tax jurisdictions.[6] Issuing debt from high-tax jurisdictions allows these MNCs to take advantage of foreign interest deductions to reduce their foreign tax liabilities and increase after-tax cash flows to the parent.

> *MNCs issue debt in high-tax countries.*

In the United States, the debt location decision is influenced by the FTC limitation. Newberry and Dhaliwal found that U.S.-based MNCs that have reached their FTC limitation have an incentive to place qualified nonrecourse debt through foreign subsidiaries in high-tax jurisdictions because foreign interest deductions in high-tax countries are more valuable than domestic interest deductions.[7] These firms

| Tax status of U.S. buyer | Host country tax rate | |
|---|---|---|
| | Low | High |
| Excess FTCs | Neutral | Neutral |
| No excess FTCs | Unattractive | Attractive |

**FIGURE 15.7** Taxes and Cross-Border Mergers and Acquisitions.

also tend to have unused domestic tax-loss carryforwards, so additional domestic interest deductions are of no value. Issuing qualified nonrecourse debt from high-tax jurisdictions maximizes foreign interest deductions and cash flows to the parent.

Dhaliwal, Newberry, and Weaver found that the FTC limitation influences U.S. firms' use of debt for acquisitions of foreign stock.[8] Firms that have not yet reached their FTC limitation tend to use debt because they benefit from domestic interest tax shields. In contrast, firms with excess FTCs are more likely to use internal funds to finance foreign acquisitions.

## Taxes and the Location of Cross-Border Mergers and Aquisitions

The FTC limitation in the U.S. tax code also affects the foreign investment of U.S. multinationals. Figure 15.7 summarizes the interaction of FTC limitations with the tax rate of the host country. Figure 15.8 extends the example in Figure 15.3 to illustrate the impact of the FTC limitation on the parent's worldwide tax liability from an incremental investment in each country.

When a MNC has excess FTCs from operations elsewhere in the world, the effective worldwide tax on incremental foreign investment equals the tax rate in the foreign market. Consequently, there is no tax incentive to invest or disinvest internationally. The "excess FTC" panel of Figure 15.8 shows the impact of the FTC limitation on the worldwide tax liability of the U.S. parent. In this case, investments

| | | Russia | Norway |
|---|---|---|---|
| **Host country tax rate** | | | |
| FTC as percent of foreign source income | | 32% | 46% |
| **Excess FTCs** (FTC limitation already reached) | | | |
| r | Overall FTC limitation (k×35%) | $350 | $350 |
| s | Total FTCs on a consolidated basis | 320 | 460 |
| t | Additional U.S. taxes due | 0 | 0 |
| | Unused excess FTCs | 0 | 110 |
| v | Total taxes paid | 320 | 460 |
| Attractiveness of foreign investment relative to local firms | | **Neutral** | **Neutral** |
| **No excess FTCs** (FTC limitation not yet reached) | | | |
| r | Overall FTC limitation (k×35%) | 350 | 350 |
| s | Total FTCs on a consolidated basis | 320 | 460 |
| t | Additional U.S. taxes due | 30 | −110 |
| v | Total taxes paid | 350 | 350 |
| Attractiveness of foreign investment relative to local firms | | **Unattractive** | **Attractive** |

**FIGURE 15.8** Taxes and Cross-Border Mergers and Acquisitions—An Example.

in low-tax countries such as Russia consume some FTCs, and the effective tax rate on income from low-tax countries equals the low foreign tax rate. Meanwhile, excess FTCs generated on income from high-tax countries such as Norway go unused, so the effective tax rate on income from high-tax countries equals the high foreign tax rate. In either case, the MNC is in the same competitive position as foreign competitors, and there is no tax incentive or disincentive to invest in the foreign market.

An interesting result arises when a U.S.-based MNC has not yet reached its FTC limitation and there are no excess FTCs, as in the bottom panels of Figures 15.7 and 15.8. In this case, foreign-source income from a low-tax country such as Russia is effectively taxed at the higher U.S. corporate income tax rate. This provides a tax-based disincentive toward investing in low-tax countries. Conversely, foreign-source income from a high-tax country such as Norway generates excess FTCs that can be used to offset the U.S. tax liability on the multinational's existing operations in low-tax countries. This creates a tax-based incentive to invest in high-tax countries. The net result is an incentive to invest in high-tax countries and avoid low-tax countries when the MNC has not yet reached its overall FTC limitation.[9]

### Taxes and the Location of the Surviving Parent in Cross-Border Mergers and Acquisitions

Cross-border mergers and acquisitions provide an opportunity for the surviving firm to choose where to incorporate, and taxes are a factor in this decision. Huizinga and Voget studied the effect of international double taxation on cross-border takeovers.[10] Double taxation arises in a worldwide tax system when host country withholding taxes on dividend or interest distributions to nonresidents combine with domestic income taxes in the MNC's home country. Huizinga and Voget found that countries with relatively high levels of double taxation typically are not chosen to host the surviving firm after a cross-border takeover. In this way, international double taxation impacts the organizational structure of the surviving firm.

## 15.7 SUMMARY

The goal of this chapter is to provide a brief survey of national tax policies, because of international taxation's importance to multinational business strategy. Multinational tax management attempts to minimize taxes and maximize after-tax cash flows. However, tax management does not operate in a vacuum. The attractiveness of cross-border investment and financing opportunities depends on national tax policies, as well as a host of nontax factors that relegate tax management to an important but ultimately supportive role in multinational business strategy. One of these factors is the existence of implicit taxes in the form of lower pretax expected and required returns in low-tax countries.

The United States follows a worldwide tax system in which foreign-source income is taxed as it is repatriated to the parent company. Foreign branches are legally a part of the parent company, so income is taxed as it is earned in the foreign country. Income from affiliates that are incorporated in a host country is taxed as it is repatriated to the parent in the form of dividends, interest, management fees, transfer prices, or royalties. The U.S. tax code allows a FTC against domestic U.S.

income taxes up to the amount of foreign taxes paid on foreign-source income. Excess FTCs can be carried back one year or forward ten years.

Other portions of the U.S. tax code further limit the tax deductibility of business expenses. These limitations include the following:

- Separate income baskets for income from different sources (i.e., general limitation income versus passive income)
- Allocation-of-income rules that determine how income and expenses are allocated between foreign and U.S. operations

These limitations influence how the overall FTC limitation is applied to different tax jurisdictions, organizational forms, asset classes, and financing instruments.

Countries with a worldwide tax system like that in the United States use a system of FTCs to avoid double taxation of foreign-source income. In contrast, countries following a territorial tax system tax only income that is earned within that country. In some countries, both tax systems are used depending on whether there is a tax treaty with a particular foreign government.

Although international tax planning is more complicated than domestic tax planning, the opportunities for increasing the value of the firm through tax planning are correspondingly greater. The international business environment provides the MNC with a number of opportunities that are either not available to the domestic firm or available in a greatly diminished form. Because of these opportunities, tax planning is even more important for the MNC than for its domestic counterpart.

## KEY TERMS

*allocation-of-income rules*
*arm's-length pricing*
*check-the-box regulations*
*comparable uncontrolled price*
*controlled foreign corporation (CFC)*
*cost plus*
*explicit tax*
*financial services income*
*foreign corporation*
*foreign-source income*
*foreign tax credit (FTC)*
*implicit tax*
*national tax policy*
*overall FTC limitation*
*tax havens*
*tax neutrality (foreign and domestic)*
*territorial tax system*
*transfer prices*
*value-added taxes (VAT)*
*worldwide tax system*

## CONCEPTUAL QUESTIONS

15.1 What is tax neutrality? Why is it important to the MNC? Is tax neutrality an achievable objective?

15.2 What is the difference between an implicit and an explicit tax? In what way do before-tax required returns react to changes in explicit taxes?

15.3 How are foreign branches and CFCs taxed in the United States?

15.4 How does the U.S. Internal Revenue Code limit the ability of U.S.-based MNCs to reduce taxes through multinational tax planning and management?

15.5 Are taxes the most important consideration in global location decisions? What other considerations might be important?

## PROBLEMS

15.1 Costa Rica imposes a 30 percent tax rate on corporate income. Chile's corporate income tax rate is 20 percent. If pretax returns in Chile are 7 percent, how much must pretax returns be in Costa Rica for the law of one price to hold?

15.2 U.S.-based Swift Solutions, Inc. has manufacturing facilities in Poland and New Zealand. Each facility earns the equivalent of $10 million in foreign-source income before tax. From Figure 15.1, corporate income taxes are 19% in Poland and 28% in New Zealand. Dividend withholding taxes are 0% in Poland and 30 percent in New Zealand.

a. Use Figure 15.3 to calculate the overall U.S. tax liability (or excess FTC) of Swift Solutions. Assume 100 percent of foreign-source earnings from each subsidiary is paid as a dividend to the U.S. parent.
b. Suppose Swift Solutions is able to shift operations so that pretax income is $20 million in Poland and zero in New Zealand. What is the U.S. tax liability (or excess FTC) under this scenario?
c. Suppose Swift Solutions is able to shift operations so that pretax income is $20 million in New Zealand and zero in Poland. What is the U.S. tax liability (or excess FTC) under this scenario?
d. Is Swift Solutions likely to be able to earn the same pretax return in Poland as in New Zealand based on the same effort? Why or why not?

15.3 Quack Concepts produces its patented drug Metafour (a duck extract used as an antioxidant) in both Hong Kong and the United States. The effective marginal tax rate is 35 percent in the United States and 17 percent in Hong Kong. No additional taxes are due in the United States from Hong Kong sales. Quack sells Metafour to U.S. consumers for $10 per bottle and has annual sales of 100,000 bottles.

a. Because the patent is an intangible asset, Quack has wide latitude in the transfer price that it sets on sales from its Hong Kong manufacturing subsidiary back to the U.S. parent company. Quack's cost of goods sold is $1 per bottle in Hong Kong. Use Figure 15.5 to calculate the effective tax rate on Metafour sales for transfer prices of $1 and $10 per bottle.
b. Suppose the cost of goods sold is $0.50 per bottle if Metafour is manufactured at Quack's U.S. plant. Where should Quack produce Metafour, based on tax considerations alone? Conduct your analysis using a $1 per bottle transfer price on sales from Hong Kong to the U.S. parent.

## SUGGESTED READINGS

### Articles on how taxes influence the amount and form of foreign operations include

Matteo P. Arena and Andrew H. Roper, "The Effect of Taxes on Multinational Debt Location," *Journal of Corporate Finance* 16 (December 2010), 637–654.

Julie Collins, Deen Kemsley, and Mark Lang, "Cross-Jurisdictional Income Shifting and Earnings Valuation," *Journal of Accounting Research* 36 (Autumn 1998), 209–229.

Mihir Desai and James R. Hines, Jr., "Basket Cases: Tax Incentives and International Joint Venture Participation by American Multinational Firms," *Journal of Public Economics* 71 (March 1999), 379–402.

Dan Dhaliwal, Kaye J. Newberry, and Constance D. Weaver, "Corporate Taxes and Financing Methods for Taxable Acquisitions," *Contemporary Accounting Research* 22 (Spring 2005), 1–30.

Harry P. Huizinga and Johannes Voget, "International Taxation and the Direction and Volume of Cross-Border M&As," *Journal of Finance* 64 No. 3 (2009), 1217–1249.

Gil B. Manzon, Jr., David J. Sharp, and Nickoloas G. Travlos, "An Empirical Study of the Consequences of U.S. Tax Rules for International Acquisitions by U.S. Firms," *Journal of Finance* 49, No. 5 (1994), 1893–1904.

Kaye J. Newberry and Dan S. Dhaliwal, "Cross-Jurisdictional Income Shifting by U.S. Multinationals: Evidence from International Bond Offerings," *Journal of Accounting Research* 39 (December 2001), 643–662.

Michael J. Smith, "Ex Ante and Ex Post Discretion over Arm's Length Transfer Prices," *Accounting Review* 77 (January 2002), 161–184.

### An excellent resource on international taxation for U.S. companies is provided by

Michael L. Moore, Edmund Outslay, and Gary A. McGill, *U.S. Tax Aspects of Doing Business Abroad*, 7th edition (forthcoming) (New York: *American Institute of Certified Public Accountants, Inc.,* 2005).

CHAPTER 16

# Real Options and Cross-Border Investment Strategy

*The blunders are all there on the board, waiting to be made.*
—Savielly Tartakower

Chapter 13 introduced the net present value (NPV) decision rule—"invest in all positive-NPV projects"—and applied this rule to situations encountered in cross-border capital budgeting. In market-based economies, this approach to investment decision making is the overwhelming favorite among companies large and small. Yet companies employing discounted cash flow techniques occasionally make decisions that, at least on the surface, appear to violate the NPV decision rule.

These apparent violations of the NPV rule often arise when valuation models fail to consider managerial flexibility in an uncertain and ever-changing world. As it is usually applied, NPV is a static calculation that fails to consider the many options that managers have to expand, contract, abandon, renovate, accelerate, or delay a project, or respond to new information gained from a project. A real option approach to the investment decision captures managerial flexibility by viewing the investment decision as a ***real option***; that is, as an option on a real asset.[1]

Section 16.2 casts the market entry decision as a simple investment option in order to introduce the role of real options in investment strategy. Section 16.3 develops the role of uncertainty. Section 16.4 provides insight into market entry as a portfolio of real options. Section 16.5 discusses the relative merits of traditional and real option investment analyses.

## 16.1 REAL OPTIONS AND THE THEORY AND PRACTICE OF INVESTMENT

This section introduces the concept of a real option, as well as some of the terminology of the literature on real options.

### Conventional versus Real Option Approaches to the Investment Decision

According to the conventional discounted cash flow approach to project valuation, the value of an investment is determined by discounting expected cash flows at their risk-adjusted cost of capital. The NPV of an investment that has an initial cost $CF_0$ and that lasts T periods is

$$V = \Sigma_t[E[CF_t]/(1+i)^t] \qquad (16.1)$$

According to this approach, a project should be undertaken if and only if the NPV of the project is greater than zero.

Naively applying this methodology fails to incorporate ***managerial flexibility*** in the timing, scale, and scope of investment. Like financial options, real options give the firm the right but not the obligation to pursue an investment opportunity. Whereas a financial option is written on an underlying financial asset, such as a share of stock or a currency, the value of a real option depends on the cash flows generated by an underlying real asset.

Foreign operations are the lifeblood of the multinational corporation (MNC). MNCs are well-positioned to take advantage of cross-border opportunities, because of their experience in managing the uncertainties of unfamiliar business environments. Indeed, studies find that the share prices of MNCs are more responsive to changes in their foreign income than to changes in their domestic income.[2]

A real option framework is a useful valuation tool in the presence of uncertainty, as real options gain much of their value from managerial flexibility in moving both proactively and reactively in an uncertain world. With the arrival of information, managers can make more informed choices and modify investment plans to fit the circumstances. This managerial flexibility is difficult to value with traditional discounted cash flow methods. This chapter shows how the firm's cross-border opportunities can be analyzed in a real option framework.

## Types of Options

An option conveys the *right but not the obligation* to assume a position in an underlying asset at an ***exercise price*** (also called a strike price) at, or prior to, the option's ***expiration date.*** A ***call option*** is an option to buy the underlying asset, and a ***put option*** is an option to sell the underlying asset. Most financial options are contractually written as ***simple options*** on an underlying financial asset, with a single source of uncertainty and no other options attached. An option can be a ***European option*** that is exercisable only at expiration or an ***American option*** that can be exercised early.

A ***real option*** is an option on a real asset. The exercise price of a real option is the initial cost of the investment proposal. Whereas financial options have a contractual exercise price and expiration date, most real options have a noncontractual exercise price that varies over time and an expiration date that can be extended (perhaps indefinitely) into the future. This is the case when investment or abandonment of a project could occur at any time. Most real options also are American options that allow exercise any time before expiration, if the option expires at all.

In contrast to most financial options, real options invariably are compound options. A ***compound option*** is an option on an option. Exercise of a compound option leads to one or more additional options. A decision to invest in a real asset is a compound option, because the investment decision affects future investment opportunities.

Because the option to invest and the option to abandon are two sides of the same coin, they are called switching options.[3] A ***switching option*** is a sequence of options in which one option is exchanged for another upon exercise. Many investment decisions are switching options, including the invest–abandon, accelerate–delay, expand–contract, suspend–reactivate, and extend–shorten decisions. A switching option is thus a special case of a compound option.

A ***rainbow option*** is an option with more than one source of uncertainty. Real options are rainbow options that face uncertainties over future operating cash flows, the exercise price of the option or of additional call or put options, interest rates, and even the window of opportunity in which a project has value (i.e., the time to expiration). Indeed, real options are *compound American rainbow options* in which managers have flexibility in adapting the characteristics of investment to the competitive environment, evolving investment circumstances, and information.

## 16.2 MARKET ENTRY AS A SIMPLE REAL OPTION

Market entry is one of a broad class of decisions that fruitfully can be viewed as real options. This section presents market entry as a real option and discusses the sources of value in this option.

### An Option to Invest in a Natural Resource Project

Crude oil increasingly is being produced from offshore oil wells. Such wells already exist in many parts of the world, and advances in seismic exploration, drilling, and extraction technologies are opening up previously inaccessible regions of the ocean floor. The most promising deep-water prospects are located off the coasts of Angola, Brazil, Malaysia, Mexico, Namibia, the Philippines, the United Kingdom, and the United States.

Governments often lease offshore tracts of land to oil companies for fixed periods of time, such as 10 or 15 years. For our purposes, the lease contract identifies the time to expiration of the oil company's real option. The option to invest expires with the termination of the lease.

Deep-sea oil exploration and extraction entail large sunk costs.[4] The value of a well depends on expectations of oil prices in the years following investment. Oil has a very long shelf life when it is stored in the oil field itself. Investments in oil wells could be delayed indefinitely were it not for high demand, limited supply, and competition for productive capacity in the industry.

Uncertainty regarding future prices is called ***price uncertainty***. Oil prices are subject to unexpected demand shocks, such as when winter temperatures are unusually severe. Oil prices also are subject to unexpected supply shocks, for example, resulting from a natural disaster or political turmoil. Because of such uncertainties, oil exploration is undertaken only when expected returns are substantially higher than required returns. Projects with small positive NPVs relative to the initial costs typically are not undertaken. This is an apparent violation of the "invest in all positive-NPV projects" rule. In fact, the NPV rule still works if we include the opportunity cost of investing today and forgoing the option to invest at some future date. The following example illustrates the pitfall in applying the "invest in all positive-NPV projects" rule in a naive fashion.

### An Example of the Option to Invest

Suppose British Petroleum (BP) owns a lease to extract crude oil from the deep waters of the North Sea and is considering the construction of a deep-sea oil rig. Construction costs are $I_0 = \$100$ million, and these costs are expected to grow at a constant rate of $g = 10\%$ per year. The risk-free rate of interest is $i = 10\%$ as well, so the cost of the well discounted at the risk-free rate is $100,000,000 in present value terms regardless of when construction begins. The current price of oil is $P_0 = \$70$ per barrel (bbl). Once a well is set up, BP's variable production cost to extract the crude oil is $C = \$18$ per barrel in perpetuity. The well will produce $Q = 200{,}000$ barrels per year in perpetuity. All cash flows are assumed to occur at the end of the year. Production can start immediately, in which case the first cash flow occurs at the end of the first year.[5]

Organization of the Petroleum Exporting Countries (OPEC) members are involved in a heated debate that will determine oil output and prices into the foreseeable future. If OPEC members maintain their cartel, production will be limited and oil prices are expected to rise to $84/bbl in perpetuity. If the cartel breaks up, production will rise and prices will fall to $56/bbl in perpetuity. This negotiation will be settled within one year. Once the new price is established, it is expected to remain at that level (either $56/bbl or $84/bbl) in perpetuity. BP estimates that an oil price rise and an oil price fall are equally probable.

Suppose there are two investment alternatives in this example: BP can either invest today or wait one year and reconsider the investment at that time. If BP invests today, perpetual cash flows begin in one year and the valuation equation is

$$\text{Invest today: } V = [(P - C)Q/i] - I_0 \tag{16.2}$$

BP's option to invest expires in one year, and by delaying investment it can remove the uncertainty over future oil prices and make a more informed decision. If BP waits one year before making an investment, the valuation equation as of time $t = 0$ is

$$\text{Wait one year: } V = \left[\frac{(P - C)Q/i}{(1+i)}\right] - I_0(1+g)/(1+i) = \left[\frac{(P - C)Q/i}{(1+i)}\right] - I_0 \tag{16.3}$$

for $g = i = 10$ percent.

To keep things simple, suppose crude oil prices and production costs are unrelated to changes in the world market portfolio. Hence, the systematic risk of this project is zero, and future cash flows from investment should be discounted at the risk-free rate of interest.[6]

### The Value of the Option to Invest

NPV calculations are least complicated when an investment must be made immediately or lost forever. For such now-or-never projects, there is no chance to wait for more information, and value is simply the discounted value of the expected cash flows net of the initial investment.

Unless a project is a now-or-never proposition, the firm has the option to delay the investment decision so it can obtain more information about future prices, costs, risks, and volume. Because of the option to delay investment, projects must compete not only with other projects but also with variations of themselves initiated at each future date. That is, the decision to invest in a project today must be compared with the alternative of investing in the same or similar projects at some future date. By exercising its option to invest, the firm is forgoing the opportunity to invest in the future. A part of the exercise price is the opportunity cost of investing today rather than at some future date. The optimal time to invest is when the value of the forgone future investment becomes less than the value of investing immediately.

The value of a real or financial option can be divided into two distinct parts.

- The ***intrinsic value*** of the option if exercised today
- The ***time value*** of the option arising from the fact that the option need not be exercised today

These two components of option value are depicted in Figure 16.1 for BP's real option. The value of an option is determined by the five variables listed at the bottom

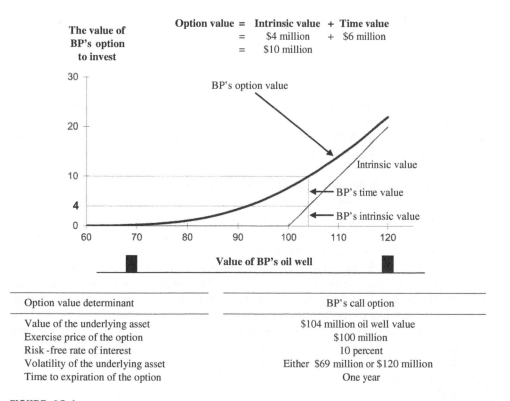

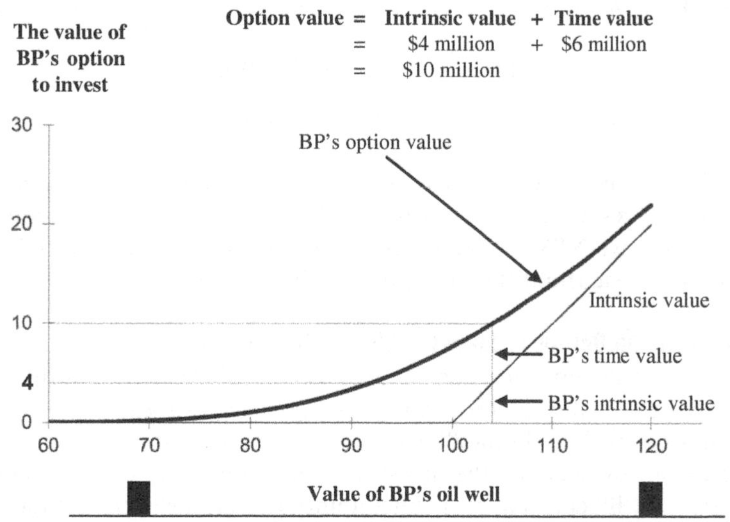


| Option value determinant | BP's call option |
|---|---|
| Value of the underlying asset | $104 million oil well value |
| Exercise price of the option | $100 million |
| Risk-free rate of interest | 10 percent |
| Volatility of the underlying asset | Either $69 million or $120 million |
| Time to expiration of the option | One year |

**FIGURE 16.1** The Value of BP's Option to Invest.

of Figure 16.1. The determinants of the value of BP's investment option are: (1) the value of the underlying asset (the oil well), (2) the required investment, (3) the risk-free rate of interest, (4) the time to expiration of the option, and (5) expected future volatility in the value of the oil well.

**The Intrinsic Value of the Option to Invest** The intrinsic value of an option depends only on the value of the underlying asset and the exercise price of the option. An ***in-the-money option*** is an option that would have value if exercised today. The intrinsic value of an in-the-money call option is the value of the underlying asset minus the exercise price. For a real option, the underlying asset is the present value of the expected cash flows from the project and the exercise price is the cost of the investment. As project value increases, the option to invest climbs further in-the-money and the investment becomes more valuable. When the value of the underlying asset is below the exercise price, a call option is ***out-of-the-money*** and has no value at expiration.

The exercise price of BP's investment option is the \$100 million initial cost of the project. The expected price level is \$70/bbl and variable costs are \$18/bbl, so the expected contribution margin is \$52/bbl in perpetuity. Expected production is 200,000 barrels per year, so expected cash flows are (\$70/bbl − \$18/bbl)(200,000 bbl) = \$10.4 million per year in perpetuity. With an initial investment of \$100 million and a 10 percent cost of capital, the value of the oil well if investment is made today is

$$\begin{aligned} V(\text{invest today}) &= \left[\frac{((\$70/\text{bbl}) - (\$18/\text{bbl}))(200{,}000\text{bbl})}{0.10}\right] - \$100{,}000{,}000 \\ &= +\$104{,}000{,}000 - \$100{,}000{,}000 \\ &= +\$4{,}000{,}000 > \$0 \Rightarrow \text{Invest today (?)} \end{aligned}$$

The expected value of the well is \$104 million. With a \$100 million exercise price, the NPV of the "invest today" alternative is \$4 million. Following the conventional "invest in all positive-NPV projects" decision rule, BP apparently should invest immediately. But what about the time value of the option to invest?

**The Time Value of the Option to Invest** Although tempting, the conclusion of the previous section is incomplete. The "invest today" alternative ignores the firm's ***timing option***—the ability of the firm to postpone investment and to reconsider investment at a future date. In the BP example, the value of the well depends on the future price of oil. By delaying the investment decision while OPEC decides on its production quotas, BP can reduce its uncertainty over future prices. Indeed, in this example BP can eliminate this price uncertainty. BP can then make a more informed investment decision based on new information. In particular, BP has an opportunity to avoid the negative outcomes of investment should oil prices fall.

Figure 16.2 shows a decision tree that captures possible future events. Our objective is to maximize the value of the oil well by following the optimal decision path. Just as in solving a maze, it is convenient to start at the end and work backward toward the beginning. The critical uncertainty facing BP is the future price of oil. Let $V|P_1$ be the NPV of investment given oil price $P_1$. If OPEC keeps production down

| | |
|---|---|
| Initial investment | $I_0$ = \$100,000,000 |
| Price of oil | $P_1$ = \$84 or \$56 with equal probability |
| Variable production cost | VC = \$18/bbl |
| Expected production | Q = 200,000 bbl/year |
| Discount rate | i = 10% |

Invest today

→ V(invest today)

= [((\$70/bbl)-(\$18/bbl))(200,000 bbl)]/(0.10) –\$100,000,000

= +\$4,000,000

→ V|($P_1$=\$84)

= [((\$84/bbl)-(\$18/bbl))(200,000 bbl)]/(0.10) ]/(1.10) –\$100,000,000

= +\$20,000,000

Wait one year

→ V|($P_1$=\$56)

= [((\$56/bbl)-(\$18/bbl))(200,000 bbl)]/(0.10) ] / (1.10) –\$100,000,000

= –\$30,909,090 < \$0

⇒ Don't invest, in which case V|($P_1$=\$56) = \$0

⇒ V(invest today) = +\$4,000,000

⇒ V(wait one year) = [Prob($P_1$=\$84)](V|$P_1$=\$84) + [Prob($P_1$=\$56)] (V|$P_1$=\$56)

= (½)(\$20,000,000) + (½)(\$0)

= +\$10,000,000

| | | | | |
|---|---|---|---|---|
| Option value | = | Intrinsic value | + | Time value |
| V(wait one year) | = | V(invest today) | + | Additional value from waiting a year |
| \$10,000,000 | = | \$4,000,000 | + | \$6,000,000 |

**FIGURE 16.2** Uncertainty and the Option to Invest.

and prices up, then the price will be \$84. If BP postpones its investment decision for one year and oil prices rise to \$84, then NPV is

$$V|P_1 = \$84) = \left[\frac{((\$84/\text{bbl}) - (\$18/\text{bbl}))(200{,}000\text{bbl})}{0.10} \Big/ (0.10)\right]$$
$$- \$100{,}000{,}000 = \$20{,}000{,}000 > \$0$$
$$\Rightarrow \text{Invest in one period if } P_1 = \$84$$

If BP postpones the decision for one year and oil prices fall to \$56/bbl, then

$$V|P_1 = \$56) = \left[\frac{((\$56/\text{bbl}) - (\$18/\text{bbl}))(200{,}000\text{bbl})}{0.10} \Big/ (1.10)\right]$$
$$- \$100{,}000{,}000$$
$$= -\$30{,}909{,}091 < \$0 \Rightarrow \text{ Do not invest in one period if } P_1 = \$56$$
$$\Rightarrow V|(P_1 = \$56) = \$0$$

By postponing the investment, BP can choose to *not invest* if oil prices fall to \$56/bbl. If BP does not invest, then the NPV of the project is \$0 along this branch of the tree.

To determine whether it is worthwhile to wait one year before making its investment decision, BP must consider the probabilities of $P_1 = \$56$ and $P_1 = \$84$. Prices rise or fall with equal probability, so $\text{Prob}(P_1 = \$56) = \text{Prob}(P_1 = \$84) = 1/2$. The expected NPV of delaying the decision for one period is an equally weighted average of the two possible outcomes.

$$\begin{aligned} V(\text{wait one year}) &= [\text{Prob}(P_1 = \$56)]\,(V|P_1 = \$56) \\ &\quad + [\text{Prob}(P_1 = \$84)]\,(V|P_1 = \$84) \\ &= 1/2(\$0) + 1/2(V|P_1 = \$84) = \$10{,}000{,}000 \end{aligned}$$

This is \$6 million greater than the value of investing today, so BP should wait until OPEC announces its production quotas before making its investment decision.

Consider the components of the value of the option to invest.

$$\begin{aligned} \text{Option Value} &= \text{Intrinsic Value} + \text{Time Value} \\ V(\text{wait one year}) &= V(\text{invest today}) + \text{Additional value from waiting one year} \\ \$10{,}000{,}000 &= \$4{,}000{,}000 + \$6{,}000{,}000 \end{aligned} \tag{16.4}$$

By investing today, BP forgoes an alternative with an expected value of \$10 million. The intrinsic value of the option to invest—the "invest today" NPV—does not include the \$6 million value of the timing option. Hence, the opportunity cost of investing today is \$6 million.

Failure to recognize the value of this timing option can result in premature investment and a failure to capture the maximum potential value of the firm's real assets. This opportunity cost can be avoided by investing at the most opportune time.

## Theory versus Practice: Some Apparent Puzzles Resolved

Managers often take actions that seem inconsistent with the NPV decision rule "accept all positive-NPV projects." In fact, these actions often can be reconciled with the NPV decision rule when they are viewed in a real option framework.

### Multinational Corporations' Use of Inflated Hurdle Rates in the Face of Political Risk

The NPV rule says to accept all positive-NPV projects, which is the same thing as saying, "Accept all projects with expected returns that exceed their required returns." Yet MNCs often impose higher hurdle rates on investments in countries with high political risks, despite the fact that country-specific political risk is diversifiable and should not matter to globally diversified investors. This use of inflated hurdle rates is an apparent violation of the NPV decision rule. Managers usually have very good reasons for the actions they take. Is the use of inflated hurdle rates in uncertain environments truly inconsistent with maximizing the expected NPV of investment?

Many times, investment is not made in an apparently positive-NPV project because the investment is expected to have an even higher NPV if initiated at some later date when the investment climate is more favorable. This is true in any circumstance in which there is uncertainty about how the business and investment climate will evolve. Even if immediate investment in an uncertain environment yields more than the opportunity cost of capital and a positive expected NPV, market entry at some future date might yield even more value.

> *The option value of waiting for additional information can lead firms to demand higher hurdle rates in uncertain environments.*

Exercising the investment option means giving up the option of investing at some future date when more information will be known about the likely payoffs of investment. Once exercised, the option to invest cannot be easily reversed. This opportunity cost of investing today can sometimes dominate the value of the option to invest.

**Multinational Corporations' Failure to Abandon Unprofitable Investments** Firms often remain in markets even though they are losing money. This frequently happens when real exchange rates move against local firms. For example, international automakers with Brazilian operations struggled to profitably export from Brazil during 2011 because the value of the Brazilian real was 40 percent higher in relative purchasing power than its long-run average. Why did foreign automakers persist in operating their Brazilian plants in these difficult circumstances? The hope, of course, was that the real would fall back to normal levels and Brazilian operations would return to profitability. The automakers had an option to abandon Brazilian production, but once abandoned it would be costly for them to re-enter the Brazilian market.

The abandonment decision can be thought of as an American call option in which the MNC can choose to pay an abandonment cost (the exercise price of the option to abandon) in order to avoid losses from a project. Similar to the investment option, the total value of the abandonment option is the sum of the intrinsic value and the time value of the abandonment option.

$$\text{Option Value} = \text{Intrinsic Value} + \text{Time Value}$$

$$\begin{aligned}\text{Value of the option}&\\ \text{to abandon today} &= \text{Value of abandoning the investment today}\\ &\quad + \text{Additional value from waiting to abandon}\end{aligned}$$

The exercise price is the cost of abandonment; that is, the intrinsic value of the option to abandon. But if the abandonment option is exercised, the MNC forgoes the ability to continue operations if conditions change for the better. Failure to consider this opportunity cost (i.e., the abandonment option's time value) can lead an MNC to premature abandonment.

Exit and abandonment decisions also come in the form of American put options.[7] For example, if an investment can be sold to a competitor, then the owner of the investment holds an American put option to sell the underlying asset at an exercise price equal to the competitor's offer price for the asset. As with American call options, the values of American put options depend on the value of the underlying asset and its volatility, the exercise price, the time to expiration of the option, and the time value of money.

The time value of the option to abandon is the flip side of the option to invest. In an uncertain environment, a firm that has control over the timing of its investments will wait until expected returns are well above required returns before it invests. This results in hurdle rates that are well above investors' required returns. Similarly, firms will delay their abandonment decisions until the expected savings from abandonment are well above the up-front costs of abandonment. This is the reason firms continue to operate under adverse conditions.

The time value of an option to invest arises from an ability to avoid negative outcomes should oil prices fall. Conversely, the time value of an abandonment option arises from an ability to participate in positive outcomes should oil prices rise. That is, real investment options gain value by avoiding bad times, whereas real abandonment options gain value by staying invested during good times. Because of the value of the timing option, firms often adopt a wait-and-see attitude before incurring sunk investment or abandonment costs.

> ***Firms continue to operate in unfavorable environments when there is a chance that prospects will improve and the sunk costs of abandonment can be avoided.***

**Investment and Disinvestment Strategies in Combination** In the presence of uncertainty, firms impose hurdle rates that are higher than investors' required returns because of the investment timing option. Similarly, once invested, a firm will not abandon investment until the gain from disinvestment is large enough to overcome the alternative of waiting for the situation to improve and thereby avoiding the sunk costs of abandonment. This is a *compound option* in which exercise of an option leads to one or more additional options.

When the investment and abandonment options are considered in combination, the firm faces two thresholds. A sufficiently high level of expected return is necessary to induce the firm to invest. Similarly, a sufficiently high level of expected loss is necessary to induce the firm to disinvest. Because of these twin thresholds, firms' investment behaviors can appear sticky. Firms can forgo investing in markets that appear attractive and, once invested, persist in operating at a loss. This behavior is called ***hysteresis*** and is characteristic of multinational firms with high entry and exit costs and high uncertainty associated with their foreign operations.

MNCs often see the value of their investments rise and fall with changing real exchange rates. An increase in a country's real exchange rate makes goods manufactured in that country relatively more expensive on world markets. A fall in the real value of a currency makes that country's output relatively inexpensive on world markets. When the real value of the dollar was at a peak in the mid-1980s, U.S. manufacturers complained that their products were too expensive relative to foreign competitors' products. Similarly, as the yen appreciated in real terms against other currencies during the mid-1990s, Japanese manufacturers complained that they were losing sales to foreign competitors. Hysteresis arises as changes in real exchange rates drive foreign investments into and then out of profitability, and then back again. The time value of the abandonment option is the reason MNCs choose to weather the storm and persist in foreign markets despite adverse exchange rate conditions.[8]

More generally, management has flexibility in "rightsizing" projects in the following ways as new information arrives:

- *Invest in or abandon a project.* Abandoning a project can spoil the MNC's relationship with the host country and force the firm into forgoing positive-NPV projects later on.
- *Expand or contract a project or extend or shorten its life.* MNCs squeeze additional value out of their products by continuing to fine-tune their marketing, production, and distribution efforts throughout the product life cycle.
- *Suspend (mothball) or reactivate a project.* Suspending or mothballing a project is often less costly than outright abandonment and retains the option to reactivate the project if and when conditions improve.

If conditions improve, the firm can exercise its option to expand the scale or scope of investment. If conditions deteriorate, the firm can exercise its option to reduce, mothball, or abandon its investment. These are compound options in that exercising one option brings with it additional flexibility and managerial options.

## 16.3 UNCERTAINTY AND THE VALUE OF THE OPTION TO INVEST

Volatility in the value of an underlying asset is a key input into the value of a real or financial option. This section discusses the effect of uncertainty on the value of a real option.

### The Determinants of Option Value

Reductions in uncertainty allow the firm to avoid making decisions that turn out to be wrong. In the BP example, the possibility of a fall in oil prices provides the incentive to delay investment. BP can avoid the 50 percent probability of a loss by delaying the investment decision one period. Consider the change in price from \$70/bbl to either \$56/bbl or \$84/bbl. Each of these is equally likely, so BP is equally exposed to both the increase and the decrease in oil price if it invests today. If the option to invest is exercised today, BP cannot benefit from new information. The "wait one year" strategy allows BP to avoid investment when oil prices fall. For this reason, the incentive to delay investment is driven entirely by *bad news*—the size and probability of unprofitable outcomes.

The value of the option to delay can be viewed as the value of managerial flexibility. By delaying the investment decision, the firm gains flexibility. In the BP example, if oil prices turn out to be lower than expected, the firm can refuse to invest and avoid the loss associated with low oil prices. In option terminology, the option is out-of-the-money, and the firm should leave its option unexercised. If oil prices rise, the firm can exercise its option and capture the NPV arising from high oil prices.

The five determinants of the value of BP's investment option are

- The value of the underlying asset (i.e., the oil well)
- The required investment (the exercise price)
- The risk-free rate of interest
- The time to expiration of the option
- Expected future volatility in the value of the oil well

These are shown at the bottom of Figure 16.1.[9] In the BP example, uncertainty affects the time value of the option through oil price volatility and the time to expiration.

In general terms, the time to expiration of the option to invest in a natural resource, such as an oil well, should correspond to the period of the lease on the natural resource. If the option to invest can be extended indefinitely into the future, then the firm has even more flexibility and the investment is likely to have even greater time value. Conversely, time to expiration is zero in a now-or-never project. An increase in the ability to delay an investment decision thus increases both time value and option value, although at a diminishing rate. Changes in option value from changes in time to expiration diminish as the time to expiration is lengthened, so the biggest gains from increases in time to expiration occur in the earliest periods of the investment horizon.

The most important determinant of time value is the degree of uncertainty in the future value of the real asset itself. Uncertainty is the major reason why firms are reluctant to jump wholeheartedly into transition economies, such as Russia after the dissolution of the Soviet Union. Holding other determinants constant, the value of a financial option increases with an increase in the volatility of the underlying asset. Equivalently, an increase in either price or cost uncertainty increases the value of a real option.

### Exogenous Uncertainty

Managers are faced with two types of uncertainty. Uncertainty is said to be ***exogenous*** when it is outside managers' control, such as in the BP example. Here, information is revealed about price or cost as time unfolds, but the firm cannot uncover new information through its investment activities.

Uncertainty is ***endogenous*** when the act of investing reveals information (e.g., about price or cost). Endogenous uncertainty can create an incentive to *speed up* investment in order to gain more information about likely future prices, costs, or quantities. Endogenous uncertainty can create an incentive to invest in exploratory projects that, when viewed in isolation, appear to be losers. The examples in the remainder of this section deal with exogenous price and cost uncertainty. We shall return to endogenous uncertainty in Section 16.4.

**Exogenous Price Uncertainty** Option values increase with an increase in the volatility of the underlying asset. Greater uncertainty over future oil prices results in a higher time value and a greater incentive to postpone investment. In the BP example, if oil price volatility increases, then BP can gain even more value from a price increase and can still avoid investing if the price falls. Suppose the current price is \$70/bbl and that oil prices will either rise to \$95/bbl or fall to \$45/bbl with equal probability. Based on information available at time t = 0, the NPV of the "invest today" alternative is the same as in the original example.

$$V(\text{invest today}) = \left[\frac{((\$70/\text{bbl}) - (\$18/\text{bbl}))(200{,}000\text{bbl})}{0.10}\right] - \$100{,}000{,}000$$

$$= +\$4{,}000{,}000 \Rightarrow \text{Invest today (?)}$$

NPV depends on the path of oil prices if BP waits a year before making its investment decision.

$$V|(P_1 = \$95) = \left[\frac{((\$95/\text{bbl}) - (\$18/\text{bbl}))(200{,}000\text{bbl})}{0.10} \Big/ (1.10)\right]$$

$$- \$100{,}000{,}000$$

$$= +\ \$40{,}000{,}000 \Rightarrow \text{Invest one period later if } P_1 = \$95$$

$$V|(P_1 = \$45) = \left[\frac{((\$45/\text{bbl}) - (\$18/\text{bbl}))(200{,}000\text{bbl})}{0.10} \Big/ (1.10)\right]$$

$$- \$100{,}000{,}000$$

$$= -\$50{,}909{,}091 \Rightarrow \text{Do not invest one period later if } P_1 = \$45$$

$$\Rightarrow V|(P_1 = \$45) = \$0$$

The NPV of the "wait one year" strategy is then

$$\begin{aligned} V(\text{wait one year}) &= [\text{Prob}(P_1 = \$45)]\ (V|P_1 = \$45) \\ &\quad + [\text{Prob}(P_1 = \$95)]\ (V|P_1 = \$95) \\ &= (1/2)(\$0) + (1/2)(\$40{,}000{,}000) \\ &= +\$20{,}000{,}000 > V(\text{invest today}) > \$0 \Rightarrow \text{Wait one period} \end{aligned}$$

The option value is the sum of the intrinsic value and the time value.

| | | | | |
|---|---|---|---|---|
| Option Value | = | Intrinsic Value | + | Time Value |
| V(wait one year) | = | V(invest today) | + | Additional value from waiting one year |
| \$20,000,000 | = | \$4,000,000 | + | \$16,000,000 |

An increase in oil price uncertainty makes the timing option even more valuable and the opportunity cost of investment today even more harmful than in the original example.

**Exogenous Cost Uncertainty** Suppose there is exogenous cost uncertainty in BP's investment option. To focus on one variable at a time, suppose oil prices will remain constant at \$70/bbl. Does cost uncertainty increase or decrease the time value of the option to invest?

As with uncertainty over output prices, the value of the option to wait increases with increases in uncertainty over future operating costs. Suppose oil sells for \$70 per barrel and that processing costs $C_1$ will rise to \$28/bbl or fall to \$8/bbl with equal probability in one year and then remain at that level indefinitely. The NPV of the now-or-never alternative is still

$$V|(\text{invest today}) = \left[\frac{((\$70/\text{bbl}) - (\$18/\text{bbl}))(200{,}000\text{bbl})}{0.10}\right] - \$100{,}000{,}000$$

$$= +\$4{,}000{,}000 \Rightarrow \text{ Invest today (?)}$$

If BP waits one year, it can resolve its uncertainty over future operating costs.

$$V|(C_1 = \$28) = \left[\frac{((\$70/\text{bbl}) - (\$28/\text{bbl}))(200{,}000\text{bbl})}{0.10} \Big/ (1.10)\right]$$

$$- \$100{,}000{,}000$$

$$= -\$23{,}636{,}364 \Rightarrow \text{ Do not invest in one period if } C_1 = \$28$$

$$\Rightarrow V|(C_1 = \$28) = \$0$$

BP will not invest if variable production costs rise to \$28 per barrel. If production costs fall to \$8 per barrel, on the other hand, the investment is attractive.

$$V|(C_1 = \$8) = \left[\frac{((\$70/\text{bbl}) - (\$8/\text{bbl}))(200{,}000\text{bbl})}{0.10} \Big/ (1.10)\right]$$

$$- \$100{,}000{,}000$$

$$= +\$12{,}727{,}273 \Rightarrow \text{ Invest in one period if } C_1 = \$8$$

The NPV of the "wait one year" strategy is then

$$\begin{aligned} V(\text{wait one year}) &= [\text{Prob}(C_1 = \$28)]\ (V|C_1 = \$28) \\ &\quad + [\text{Prob}(C_1 = \$8)]\ (V|C_1 = \$8) \\ &= (1/2)(\$0) + (1/2)(\$12{,}727{,}273) \\ &= +\$6{,}363{,}636 > \$0 \Rightarrow \text{ Wait one period} \end{aligned}$$

Option value is decomposed as follows:

$$\begin{aligned} \text{Option Value} &= \text{Intrinsic Value} &&+ \text{Time Value} \\ \text{V(wait one year)} &= \text{V(invest today)} &&+ \text{Additional value from waiting one year} \\ \$6{,}363{,}636 &= \$4{,}000{,}000 &&+ \$2{,}363{,}636 \end{aligned}$$

Exogenous cost uncertainty has the same effect as exogenous output price uncertainty. As with exogenous price uncertainty, the option's time value derives from the ability to avoid the bad (in this case, high cost) outcome. Uncertainty in either costs or prices creates uncertainty in operating cash flows and an incentive to postpone investment. By waiting for additional information regarding the level of expected future operating cash flows, the firm can choose to either invest or not invest at a later date, depending on the arrival of new information.

## 16.4 MARKET ENTRY AS A COMPOUND REAL OPTION

When uncertainty is endogenous, real options create incentives for firms to invest in projects that, at least on the surface, may look like negative-NPV projects. However, if the act of investing reveals information about the value of the option, then firms have an incentive to speed up investment in order to gain additional information. Staged investment of this kind is a form of *compound option* in that new information revealed through investing can lead to additional investment options.

### Endogenous Uncertainty and Follow-Up Projects

Consider again BP's oil well option. Suppose that the quality of oil produced by the oil field cannot be determined until production begins. If the oil is high quality, it will sell for \$84/bbl in perpetuity. If it is low quality, it will sell for \$56/bbl in perpetuity. These two outcomes are equally likely, so the expected future price is $P_1 = (\$56 + \$84)/2 = \$70 - \$4$. Variable production costs are \$22 per barrel, rather than \$18 as in the original problem. As before, suppose the present value cost of investment in the well is \$100,000,000 regardless of when the investment is made.

Viewed as a now-or-never alternative, the NPV of investing in this setting is negative.

$$\begin{aligned} \text{V(invest today)} &= \left[\frac{((\$70/\text{bbl}) - (\$22/\text{bbl}))(200{,}000\text{bbl})}{0.10}\right] - \$100{,}000{,}000 \\ &= +\$96{,}000{,}000 - \$100{,}000{,}000 = -\$4{,}000{,}000 < \$0 \\ &\Rightarrow \text{Do not invest today (?)} \end{aligned}$$

If the investment option is viewed as a now-or-never deal, BP should not invest.

Now, suppose this well is the first of ten that BP might drill. If constructed, each well will be identical to the others and produce 200,000 barrels of oil per year in perpetuity. If BP were to invest in all ten oil wells today, the expected NPV would be −$40 million (10 wells each worth −$4 million). Viewed as a now-or-never decision, this is clearly not a good investment. But what if BP invests in a single well in order to ascertain the quality of the oil, and then makes its subsequent investment decisions on the basis of the results of the first well?

Uncertainty is said to be *endogenous* when the firm's assessment of the value of a project is influenced by the act of investing. In our example, the act of investing reveals information about the quality of oil and the value of the option to invest. BP can gain information about the potential of additional wells by investing in a single exploratory well. For simplicity, assume the quality and market price of the oil will be known one year after the first well is drilled. By investing in an exploratory well, BP can make a more informed decision on the other nine wells.

If the oil is low quality and sells for $56/bbl, BP's exploratory well will not be able to recoup its investment. The NPV of this outcome is

$$\begin{aligned} V|(P_1 = \$56) &= \left[\frac{((\$56/\text{bbl}) - (\$22/\text{bbl}))(200{,}000\text{bbl})}{0.10}\right] - \$100{,}000{,}000 \\ &= +\$68{,}000{,}000 - \$100{,}000{,}000 = -\$32{,}000{,}000 \\ &\Rightarrow \text{Do not invest further if } P_1 = \$56 \\ &\Rightarrow V|(P_1 = \$56) = \$0 \end{aligned}$$

On the other hand, if the oil is of high quality, the exploratory well has a NPV of

$$\begin{aligned} V|(P_1 = \$84) &= \left[\frac{((\$84/\text{bbl}) - (\$22/\text{bbl}))(200{,}000\text{bbl})}{0.10}\right] - \$100{,}000{,}000 \\ &= +\$124{,}000{,}000 - \$100{,}000{,}000 = +\$24{,}000{,}000 \\ &\Rightarrow \text{Invest in additional wells if } P_1 = \$84 \end{aligned}$$

If $P_1 = \$84$, then BP should invest in the nine additional wells. The present value cost of investing is $100 million regardless of the timing of investment, so each additional well has value of

$$\begin{aligned} V(\text{additional well}|P_1 = \$84) &= \left[\frac{((\$84/\text{bbl}) - (\$22/\text{bbl}))(200{,}000\text{bbl})}{0.10}\Big/(1.10)\right] \\ &\quad - \$100{,}000{,}000 = +\$12{,}727{,}273 \end{aligned}$$

The expected value of the decision to drill an exploratory well is then

$$\begin{aligned} V(\text{invest today}) &= V(\text{invest an exploratory well}) + [\text{Prob}(P_1 = \$84)] \\ &\quad (9)V(\text{additional well}|P_1 = \$84) \\ &= -\$4{,}000{,}000 + (1/2)(9)(-\$12{,}727{,}273) \\ &= +\$53{,}272{,}727 > \$0 \\ &\Rightarrow \text{Invest in an exploratory well} \end{aligned}$$

Alternatively, this NPV can be calculated as

$$\begin{aligned} V(\text{invest today}) &= \text{Prob}(P_1 = \$56)(V|P_1 = \$56) \\ &\quad + \text{Prob}(P_1 = \$84)[(V|P_1 = \$84) \\ &\quad + (9)V(\text{additional well}|P_1 = \$84)] \\ &= (1/2)(-\$32{,}000{,}000) + (1/2)[(\$24{,}000{,}000) \\ &\quad + (9)(\$12{,}727{,}273)] \\ &= +\$53{,}272{,}727 > \$0 \end{aligned}$$

Investing in the exploratory well reveals information about the oil field's potential and allows BP to make a more informed decision.

In the original example of the option to invest, uncertainty was exogenous and there was always value in waiting. In this example, there is an incentive to invest early so that BP can determine the quality of the oil. Including the value of follow-up projects can be important when uncertainty is endogenous and the act of investing reveals information that otherwise would remain undiscovered.

## Another Puzzle Resolved: Entry into New or Emerging Markets

MNCs often make small investments into emerging markets or new technologies even though the expected return on investment appears to be less than the cost of capital. When a firm enters a market for the first time, the only certainty is that management's forecasts will be wrong. Managers often invest in new markets so that they can assess the market's viability and determine how to best structure subsequent investments. In these circumstances, managers often state the investment is being undertaken for "strategic" reasons. Are managers acting irrationally? Are apparently negative-NPV investments in strategic initiatives necessarily in violation of the NPV rule? Or, is the conventional application of the NPV rule incomplete? A real option framework brings a new and useful perspective to these issues.

In option pricing parlance, the firm is purchasing an out-of-the-money compound option that entitles it to make further investments if conditions improve.

> ***Firms investing in new markets or technologies are purchasing options that entitle them to purchase additional options if conditions warrant further investment.***

By acquiring information that helps it make a better assessment of future opportunities, a firm can withdraw when its experience in a new market or technology suggests a negative outcome, and it can continue and even expand investment when the outlook is positive.

Because the firm's current and future real investments are compound options, asset values are often decomposed as

$$V_{\text{ASSET}} = V_{\text{ASSETS-IN-PLACE}} + V_{\text{GROWTH OPTIONS}} \quad (16.5)$$

***Assets-in-place*** are assets in which the firm has already invested. The value of assets-in-place represents the value of operating the firm according to the existing product mix, production levels, cost structures, and marketing and distribution efforts. In this case, valuation of assets-in-place is straightforward, following the NPV rule: Discount expected future cash flows from assets-in-place at the opportunity cost of capital.

Flexibility in the management of existing and future assets can then be viewed as a separate source of value. Valuing managerial flexibility requires that we value many different kinds of options, including the options to enter new markets, exit current and possible future markets, expand or contract the scale or scope of investment, suspend or reactivate existing and possible future investments, and develop follow-up projects to the firm's existing assets. These potential future investments arise because of the firm's unique position in the markets for real goods and services, including its brand names, patents, technological know-how, and managerial culture and expertise. These intangible assets are referred to collectively as ***growth options*** because they capture the value of managerial flexibility in responding to an uncertain world.

## 16.5 THE REAL OPTION APPROACH AS A COMPLEMENT TO NET PRESENT VALUE

Option pricing models work best for simple options on financial assets such as stocks, commodities, interest rates, or currencies. International markets for these financial assets are competitive, highly liquid, and have relatively low transaction costs and other market frictions. Consequently, financial options have an expected NPV of zero.

Real options are another matter entirely. Markets for real assets are less competitive, less liquid, and have higher transaction costs than financial markets. The NPV of a real option can be positive, negative, or zero depending on the particular investment. Indeed, the whole point of performing a capital budgeting analysis is to identify positive-NPV alternatives.

Most real options are *compound rainbow options* that provide managerial flexibility and growth options in the presence of multiple sources of uncertainty. The complexity of real investment opportunities can make it difficult to develop realistic valuation models, whether they are based on discounted cash flow or option pricing methods. Although they share this shortcoming, each valuation approach encounters its own unique difficulties in practice.

### Why Net Present Value Has Difficulty Valuing Managerial Flexibility

The NPV rule says to accept all positive-NPV projects. Although the NPV rule can faithfully value assets-in-place in the absence of managerial flexibility, it has difficulty valuing the many real options that accompany the firm's real assets. In particular, NPV calculations must include all opportunity costs, including the opportunity cost of investing at a less-than-optimal time.

One of the biggest difficulties in applying discounted cash flow methods to real options lies in identifying the opportunity cost of capital.[10] Identifying the opportunity cost of capital in the capital asset pricing model (CAPM) is facilitated by the assumption of normally distributed returns. Normal distributions are completely described by their means, standard deviations, and correlations, and the CAPM takes advantage of this fact. In the CAPM, an asset's opportunity cost of capital is a linear function of its systematic risk or beta.

The appropriate discount rate for an option is ambiguous because of the peculiar characteristics of the returns to an option position.

- *Degree of option volatility*. Options are always more volatile than the assets on which they are based. Options are levered investments, and small changes in the value of the underlying asset result in larger percentage changes in option values. Consider BP's oil well investment in Section 16.2. The value of the expected cash inflows from the oil well was [($70 – $18)(200,000)]/(0.1) = $104 million. The intrinsic value of the option to invest at an exercise price of $100 million was $4 million. Suppose the value of the oil well that underlies the option doubles, to $208 million. This 100 percent increase in the value of the underlying asset increases the intrinsic value of the option from $4 million to $108 million, or by ($108m – $4m)/$4m = 26.00 = 2600 percent. This illustrates the general rule that option returns are always more volatile than returns to the underlying asset.[11]
- *Changing degree of option volatility*. The volatility of an option changes with changes in the value of the underlying asset. Suppose the value of BP's oil well rises another 100 percent, from $208 to $416 million. The intrinsic value of BP's option rises from $108 million to $316 million. This is a percentage increase of ($316 – $108m)/$108m = 1.93, or 193 percent. Although the option is still more volatile than the underlying asset, the percentage increase in option value at this higher oil price level is less than the percentage increase at the lower oil price level. This illustrates another general rule: The volatility of an option falls as the underlying asset goes deeper in-the-money, although option volatility remains higher than the level of volatility in the underlying asset. This changing degree of option volatility has a serious consequence for discounted cash flow valuation methodologies. Because option volatility depends on the value of the underlying asset, no single discount rate reflects the opportunity cost of capital as the value of the underlying asset evolves throughout the life of the option.[12]
- *Distribution of option returns*. Even if returns to the underlying asset are normally distributed, option returns are inherently non-normal. An easy way to see this is to observe that an option payoff is truncated, or cut off, at the exercise price. Only the in-the-money portion of the distribution of underlying asset value has value to an option. This means that conventional risk measures cannot fully describe the risk of an option. In particular, neither standard deviation of return nor beta captures the asymmetric nature of option risk.

In combination, these three characteristics make determining the opportunity cost of capital on a real option a messy and unrewarding affair.

## The Option Pricing Alternative

Option pricing models circumvent the problem of identifying the opportunity cost of capital by constructing a ***replicating portfolio*** that mimics the payoffs on the option.[13] The replicating portfolio is composed of a position in the underlying asset together with risk-free borrowing or lending. This portfolio must be continuously rebalanced to reflect changes in the value of the underlying asset. An assumption of costless arbitrage then ensures that the value of the option is equal to the value of the replicating portfolio. Because the combination of an option position and a short position in the corresponding replicating portfolio is risk-free, discounting is done at the risk-free rate of interest. This eliminates the need to determine a risk-adjusted discount rate for the option position.

There are two obstacles to costless arbitrage between a real option and its replicating portfolio.

- *Transaction costs.* Arbitrage can enforce the law of one price only within the bounds of transaction costs. Transaction costs are relatively low in financial markets, so arbitrage can ensure that equivalent assets sell for the same price. Transaction costs are much more prominent in real asset markets. Consequently, costless arbitrage cannot ensure the equivalence of the option position and its replicating portfolio, even if one were to exist.
- *Unobservable prices.* Financial options are contractually written on an asset whose price is readily observable in a competitive financial market. Real assets are less frequently traded and real asset markets are far less competitive than financial markets. When real asset values are unobservable, arbitrage cannot ensure the equivalence of a real option and its replicating portfolio.

In the absence of a viable replicating portfolio, real option values can diverge from their theoretical values.

## The Real Option Approach and Net Present Value as Complements

Discounted cash flow and option pricing approaches to project valuation should be viewed as complements. Each approach has its advantages and disadvantages. As it is typically implemented, the discounted cash flow capital budgeting analysis is simple and intuitive—the art comes in accurately estimating the inputs into the analysis. Yet most capital budgeting analyses make little attempt to capture the value of managerial flexibility in an uncertain world.

Option pricing methods try to capture the value of managerial flexibility, through either decision trees or option pricing methods (e.g., Black-Scholes). Constructing a decision tree of possible future scenarios can indeed assist the financial manager in formulating competitive responses to various situations. Yet a decision tree can capture only a few of the possible future states of the world. Option pricing methods similarly start with an assumption about the distribution of project values and determine the value of the option to invest from this distribution of outcomes.

Applying both discounted cash flow and option pricing valuation methods provides a second opinion regarding the value of an investment. Managers will have confidence in their valuations if the NPV and option value estimates are close. If they differ, viewing the investment as a real option can shed light on possible sources of value from managerial flexibility.

## 16.6 SUMMARY

Uncertainty is a key variable faced by every cross-border investment. Currency, political, and cultural risks are the most prominent additional risks in cross-border investment, but business risk on foreign projects also can be higher than that of domestic projects. When uncertainty is high, the MNC's investment opportunities can be fruitfully viewed as real options. Real options include

- Options to invest or abandon investment
- Options to accelerate or delay investment
- Options to expand or contract the scale or scope of investment
- Options to suspend or reactivate an investment
- Options to extend or shorten the life of an investment
- Growth options and follow-up investments

Option values can be decomposed into their value if exercised today and the value of waiting.

$$\text{Option Value} = \text{Intrinsic Value} + \text{Time Value} \quad (16.4)$$

$$\text{V(wait one year)} = \text{V(invest today)} + \text{Additional value from waiting}$$

Option pricing methods are particularly useful for assessing the time value of a real option. The forgone time value is the opportunity cost of investing today.

Conventional valuation methods are difficult to apply to real options because

- Options are inherently riskier than the underlying asset on which they are based.
- The risk of an option changes with changes in the value of the underlying asset.
- Returns to options are not normally distributed.

Despite the difficulties of valuing investments in uncertain environments, we should not let what we *do not* know about valuation get in the way of what we *do* know. Discounted cash flow techniques are useful in many circumstances. They are the valuation tool of choice when an investment decision must be made immediately or forgone entirely. When combined with decision trees or other option pricing methods, discounted cash flow techniques can be useful in formulating competitive strategy in the timing and scale of investment.

Option valuation is simplest to implement when option values are contingent on a single financial price variable. Even when project value depends on many complex and interacting variables, viewing the project as a package of real options can begin to account for managerial flexibility in the face of an uncertain world and help you to realize an asset's full potential.

## KEY TERMS

*American and European options*
*assets-in-place*
*call and put options*
*compound option*
*endogenous uncertainty*
*exercise date*
*exercise price*
*exogenous uncertainty*
*growth option*
*hysteresis*
*in-the-money and out-of-the-money options*
*intrinsic value versus time value*
*managerial flexibility*
*price uncertainty*
*rainbow option*
*real option*
*replicating portfolio*
*simple option*
*switching option*
*timing option*

## CONCEPTUAL QUESTIONS

16.1 What is a real option?

16.2 In what ways can managers' actions seem inconsistent with the "accept all positive-NPV projects" rule? Are these actions truly inconsistent with the NPV decision rule?

16.3 Are managers who do not appear to follow the NPV decision rule irrational?

16.4 Why is the timing option important in investment decisions?

16.5 What is exogenous uncertainty? What is endogenous uncertainty? What difference does the form of uncertainty make to the timing of investment?

16.6 In what ways are the investment and abandonment options similar?

16.7 What is a switching option? What is hysteresis? Is hysteresis a switching option?

16.8 What are assets-in-place? What are growth options?

16.9 Why does the NPV decision rule have difficulty in valuing managerial flexibility?

16.10 What are the shortcomings of option pricing methods for valuing real assets?

## PROBLEMS

**Exogenous uncertainty and the option to invest**

16.1 A proposed brewery in the eastern European country of Dubiety will produce a beer—the "Dubi Dubbel"—for Grolsch N.V. of the Netherlands. A number of other Western European brewers have announced plans to produce and sell beer in the Dubi market. If too many breweries open, beer prices will fall. If some of these investment plans do not materialize, prices are likely to rise. The price of beer is determined exogenously and will be known with certainty in one year. Grolsch management must decide whether to begin production today or in one year. The following facts apply:

| | |
|---|---|
| Initial investment | $I_0$ = D200,000,000; rises by 10% each year |
| Price of beer in one year | $P_1$ = either = either D25 or D75 with equal probability |
| Variable production cost | VC = D10 per bottle |
| Fixed production cost | FC = D10,000,000 per year |
| Expected production | Q = 1,000,000 bottles per year forever |
| Discount rate | i = 10% |

a. Draw a decision tree that depicts Grolsch's investment decision.
b. Calculate the NPV of investing today as if it were a now-or-never alternative.
c. Calculate the NPV (at $t = 0$) of waiting one year before making a decision.
d. Calculate the NPV of investing today, including all opportunity costs.
e. Should Grolsch invest today or wait one year before making a decision?

**Endogenous uncertainty and growth options**

16.2 The "Dubi Dubbel" investment of Problem 16.1 is one of five brewery investments that Grolsch is considering. The quality of the beer produced in Dubiety will determine the quality of beer that Grolsch can expect from the other four investments. Grolsch will not know the quality of beer or its price until production begins. The situation is similar to Problem 16.1.

| | |
|---|---|
| Initial investment | $I_0$ = D200,000,000; rises by 10% each year |
| Price of beer in one year | $P_1$ = either D25 or D75 with equal probability |
| Variable production cost | VC = D10 per bottle |
| Fixed production cost | FC = D10,000,000 per year |
| Expected production | Q = 1,000,000 bottles per year forever |
| Discount rate | i = 10% |

a. Draw a decision tree that depicts Grolsch's investment decision.
b. Calculate the NPV of investing today as if it were a now-or-never alternative.
c. Calculate the NPV of investing in an exploratory brewery and then reconsidering investment in the other breweries in one year after the price of beer is revealed by the initial investment.
d. Calculate the NPV of investing today, including all opportunity costs.
e. Should Grolsch invest today? What is different in this problem from the setting in Problem 16.1, and how does it affect Grolsch's investment decision?

16.3 A proposed automotive plant will produce automobiles in Brazil. The Brazilian currency is the real. The following facts apply:

| | |
|---|---|
| Initial investment | $I_0$ = R100,000,000; rises by 20% each year |
| Price of automobile | $P_0 = P_1$ = R18,000 per vehicle |
| Cost per vehicle | $C_1$ = either = either R12,000 or R18,000 with equal probability |
| Production | Q = 10,000 vehicles per year forever |
| Discount rate | i = 20% |

a. Suppose production costs are determined exogenously by government fiat and will be known with certainty in one year. Management must decide whether to begin production today or in one year. Calculate (1) the NPV of investing today as if it were a now-or-never alternative, (2) the NPV (at t = 0) of waiting one year before making a decision, and (3) the NPV of investing today, including all opportunity costs.

b. Suppose this investment is one of ten plants with identical characteristics that could be built. The outcome from your initial investment will provide information about the production costs that will be incurred at other sites. Calculate (1) the NPV of investing today in all ten sites as if it were a now-or-never alternative, (2) the NPV (at t = 0) of investing in one factory today and then waiting one year before making a decision on the other nine factories, and (3) the NPV of investing today, including all opportunity costs.

16.4 You have discovered a mountain of guano in Japan. Up to five guano mines could be constructed on the mountain. Each mine costs ¥600,000 and is expected to yield 150 ounces of guano in one year. The actual yield will be either 100 ounces or 200 ounces with equal probability. All of the guano will be extracted in the first year of operation and sold to the government at a guaranteed price of ¥5,000/oz. (It's high quality guano.) Variable production costs are ¥1,000 per ounce. The yen discount rate is 0% per year. The mines will be worthless after the guano is extracted. Because of the importance of guano to Japanese politics, the government has agreed to provide you with a zero tax rate on the mine. (Note that noncash depreciation or depletion allowances have no effect on cash flow when the tax rate is zero.) You can invest in an exploratory mine today and then base subsequent investment on the outcome of the first mine. Once you know the yield of the first mine, you will know the yield of the other four mines with certainty. Each additional mine costs ¥600,000 in nominal terms. Price and variable cost will remain constant at ¥5,000 and ¥1,000 per ounce, respectively.

a. Calculate the NPV of investing in all five mines as a now-or-never alternative.

b. Calculate the NPV (as of t = 0) of investing in a single mine and then waiting one year before considering investment in the other four mines.

c. Should you invest in the exploratory mine?

16.5 Solve Problem 16.4 assuming a nominal yen discount rate of 10 percent per year and a corporate tax rate of T = 30 percent. The initial cash outflow of ¥600,000 will be capitalized on the balance sheet and depleted for tax purposes during the year. At the end of the year, you will receive a depletion tax shield of ¥600,000(0.30) = ¥180,000. Note that taxes also will reduce your operating cash flow by 30 percent.

### Exogenous uncertainty and the option to abandon

16.6 Grolsch management has gone ahead with the investment in Problem 16.1. The market has grown increasingly competitive, and nearly all of the brewery investments in eastern Europe are losing money. To make matters worse, variable production costs of D20/bottle are higher than expected. According to local laws, employees cannot be laid off so long as the brewery is open, and Grolsch must either produce at capacity or close the brewery. A competitor is considering exiting the market. If this brewer does not abandon, price will remain D15/bottle. If the brewer abandons, price will rise to D35/bottle. Assume Grolsch's abandonment decision does not influence the competitor's decision, so price uncertainty is exogenous. The following facts apply to the abandonment decision:

| | |
|---|---|
| Cost of abandoning brewery | $I_0$ = D10,000,000; rises by 10% each year |
| Current price of beer | $P_0$ = D15 per bottle in perpetuity |
| Price of beer in one year | $P_1$ = either = either D15 or D35 with equal probability |
| Variable production cost | VC = D20 per bottle |
| Fixed production costs | FC = D10,000,000 per year |
| Expected production | Q = 1,000,000 bottles per year forever |
| Discount rate | i = 10% |

(Note that the cash flows of this abandonment option are similar to those of the investment option. Grolsch management can pay an exercise price today to avoid future losses. But avoiding future losses is the same thing as receiving a net cash inflow—just as in the investment option.)

a. Draw a decision tree that depicts Grolsch's investment decision.
b. Calculate the NPV of abandoning today as if it were a now-or-never alternative.
c. Calculate the NPV (as of t = 0) of waiting one year before making a decision.
d. Calculate the NPV of abandoning today, including all opportunity costs.
e. Should Grolsch abandon this losing venture today?

### A rainbow option

16.7 You own land in Kenya on which five tanzanite mines can be constructed. Each mine costs 20 million Kenyan schillings (KS) and will yield either 1,000 or 2,000 carats (ct) of tanzanite with equal probability. The tanzanite will be either medium-quality (worth KS 20,000 per carat) or high-quality (worth KS 40,000 per carat) with equal probability. The quality of tanzanite in each mine is independent of the quantity. Variable production costs are KS10,000/ct. All the tanzanite will be extracted in the first year of operation, after which the mines will be worthless. There are no exit costs. The appropriate discount rate is 0% per year. The government has agreed to a zero tax rate.

a. Calculate the NPV of investing in all five mines as a now-or-never alternative.
b. Rather than investing in all five mines today, you can invest in one mine and base subsequent investment on the outcome of that mine. The price and quantity of the four additional mines will be known with certainty once the exploratory mine is operational. Find the NPV of investing in one mine and then waiting one year before considering the other four mines.
c. Is there an opportunity cost to investing in all five mines today? If so, how much is it?

**A problem in competitive strategy**

16.8 How might Grolsch's decisions be different in Problems 16.1, 16.2, and 16.6 if Grolsch's actions influence its competitors' actions, and vice versa?

## SUGGESTED READINGS

### Readable presentations of real option analysis appear in the Spring 2005, Spring 2006, and Spring 2007 issues of the *Journal of Applied Corporate Finance*. The following article is illustrative:

Robert L. McDonald, "The Role of Real Options in Capital Budgeting: Theory and Practice," *Journal of Applied Corporate Finance* 18 (Spring 2006), 28–39.

### Useful textbook references on real options and strategy include

Martha Amram and Nalin Kulatilaka, *Real Options: Managing Strategic Investment in an Uncertain World* Financial Management Association Survey and Synthesis Series (Cambridge, MA: Harvard Business School Press, 1999).

Don M. Chance and Pamela P. Peterson, *Real Options and Investment Valuation* (Aliso Viejo, CA: AIMR, 2002).

Thomas Copeland and Vladimir Antikarov, *Real Options: A Practitioner's Guide* (New York, NY: Texere, 2003).

Avinash K. Dixit and Robert S. Pindyck, *Investment under Uncertainty* (Princeton, NJ: Princeton University Press, 1994).

Han T.J. Smit and Lenos Trigeorgis, *Strategic Investment: Real Options and Games* (Princeton, NJ: Princeton University Press, 2004).

**This chapter references the following articles on real options:**

Philip G. Berger, Eli Ofek, and Itzhak Swary, "Investor Valuation of the Abandonment Option," *Journal of Financial Economics* 42 (October 1996), 257–287.

Gordon M. Bodnar and Joseph Weintrop, "The Valuation of the Foreign Income of U.S. Multinational Firms: A Growth Opportunities Perspective," *Journal of Accounting & Economics* 24 (December 1997), 69–97.

Peter Carr, "The Valuation of Sequential Exchange Opportunities," *Journal of Finance* 43 (December 1988), 1235–1256.

Stephen E. Christophe, "Hysteresis and the Value of the U.S. Multinational Corporation," *Journal of Business* 70 (July 1997), 435–462.

Nalin Kulatilaka and Alan J. Marcus, "Project Valuation and Uncertainty: When Does DCF Fail?" *Journal of Applied Corporate Finance* 5 (Fall 1992), 92–100.

CHAPTER 17

# Corporate Governance and the International Market for Corporate Control

*O world! world! world! Thus is the poor agent despised.*
—William Shakespeare

***Corporate governance*** refers to the ways in which major ***stakeholders*** exert control over the corporation and ensure themselves a return on their investment. Each nation's laws, regulatory framework, and legal institutions and conventions determine stakeholder rights in corporate governance. These national systems influence many aspects of economic life.[1]

- Ownership and control of corporations
- The opportunities available to borrowers and investors
- The way in which capital is allocated within and between national economies

Although national legal systems share many common characteristics, they also are shaped by unique legal, political, social, and economic forces that determine the ways in which corporations are governed and perform. This in turn affects the frequency and form of cross-border mergers, acquisitions, divestitures, and reorganizations.

Each nation has its own unique corporate governance system, with varying powers being wielded by corporate stakeholders including equity shareholders, bondholders, managers, employees, suppliers, customers, founding (perhaps royal) families, business groups, and governments. The ***market-based*** corporate governance of large firms in the United Kingdom and the United States is characterized by a large proportion of public debt and equity issues, and a management team that often is relatively independent of other stakeholders. Germany's ***bank-based*** system features bank ownership of debt and equity capital, and a management team that often is closely monitored by the lead bank. In other countries, the controlling shareholders might be the state (China), prominent families (Mexico), or diversified business groups (Japanese keiretsu, Korean chaebol, or Indian business groups) that began as private family-led enterprises and are at varying stages of transition toward reliance on public capital and professional management.

*Legal systems influence corporate ownership and control.*

Disparate national systems of corporate governance result in dissimilar markets for corporate control. Corporate control contests in the United States and the United Kingdom tend to be aggressive, financially motivated deals that involve public corporations or private investors operating through the capital markets. Hostile acquisitions in these markets prompt equally forceful defensive maneuvers by the managers of target firms. In Germany, change in ownership or management often is initiated and managed by the firm's lead bank or a competing financial institution. In Japan, the corporation's main bank or business partners often manage corporate transfers of ownership and control. Corporate control in China depends on the mix of state and private-sector ownership, as China navigates the transition from a state-controlled toward a market-driven economy. Control in other countries depends on the dominant stakeholder(s) in the local economy.

This chapter discusses the characteristics of effective corporate governance systems and illustrates national differences in corporate governance using the market-based models of the United Kingdom and United States, Germany's bank-based system, Japan's keiretsu system, and China's state-dominated system. These examples illustrate the key characteristics of corporate governance systems, including the controlling shareholders and the positions and legal protections of minority investors. The international market for corporate control is then examined in the context of these national differences, with a focus on public takeovers through mergers and acquisitions (M&A). The chapter concludes with the academic evidence on factors related to M&A activity and the winners and losers in domestic and cross-border M&A.

## 17.1 CORPORATE GOVERNANCE

Many national and international regulatory bodies have made recommendations on how to ensure effective corporate governance. Most of these recommendations share the following elements:

- Transparency
- Protection of shareholders' rights
- An active and accountable supervisory board

Transparency refers to the timely and accurate disclosure of information related to the firm's financial performance and ownership structure. Transparency promotes market efficiency and reduces the opportunities for managers or controlling shareholders to pursue their own interests at the expense of other stakeholders. Legal protections of shareholders' rights are necessary to ensure an equitable treatment of all shareholders, including minority shareholders.[2] Active boards are necessary to ensure effective monitoring of managers on behalf of other stakeholders in a ***principal–agent relationship***. The promotion and implementation of these corporate governance standards depend on a nation's legal framework.

An important consideration in any corporate governance setting is whether a firm has a controlling shareholder. When there is no controlling shareholder, capital markets need to ensure that executives and directors do not act opportunistically at the expense of other stakeholders. This conflict of interest results in ***agency costs*** as stakeholders must monitor managers to ensure they do not act opportunistically. Effective governance in these situations requires transparency and managerial accountability, so a country's accounting conventions and legal systems are important. When there is no controlling shareholder, the market for corporate control must be relied upon to remove ineffective managers and improve firm performance.

*Is there a controlling shareholder?*

When there is a controlling shareholder, the central problem is opportunism by the controlling shareholder rather than opportunism by executives or directors. Of course, in many countries the controlling shareholder and the executives/directors may be one and the same. The central governance problem in this setting is to ensure that the controlling shareholder does not opportunistically expropriate the assets of other stakeholders including minority or foreign shareholders. National systems of corporate governance are again important as they define the framework within which this competition takes place.

## National Corporate Governance Systems

Control of large corporations tends to be dominated by one of the following stakeholders:

- The state (China)
- Prominent families (Mexico)
- Commercial banks (Germany), perhaps in combination with business partners (Japan)
- Capital markets (the United Kingdom, the United States, Canada, and Australia)

Figure 17.1 displays the corporate governance systems of the United States, Germany, Japan, and China in three dimensions by combining families and the state into a single dimension.

In the early history of most countries, businesses are founded by individuals and then nurtured and controlled by the founder and the founders' descendants.[3] The way that these family-run businesses grow depends on a nation's corporate governance system. In countries such as Mexico, families retain their position at the center of business life in even the largest businesses. Sometimes powerful families even control the government, such as in Saudi Arabia. At their best, these family-based systems serve as benevolent dictatorships that nurture local industries and promote the welfare of local residents. At their worst, national resources are exploited for the benefit of a few through nepotism, corruption, and crony capitalism. These family-led businesses often pass into the hands of public investors and professional managers as time passes and the founder's entrepreneurial spirit wanes, so that many

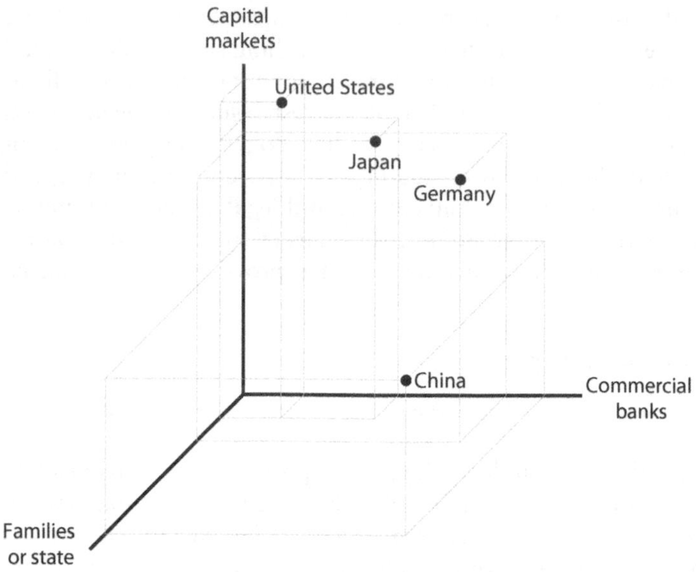


**FIGURE 17.1** National Corporate Governance Systems.

national corporate governance systems have migrated upward in Figure 17.1 toward a market-based system.

Capital markets are now the most important providers of capital to businesses in most developed countries, as well as in a growing number of developing countries. Capital market growth has reduced the influence of governments, founding families, and commercial banks in corporate boardrooms in many countries. Nevertheless, these other players continue to be controlling shareholders in many countries. Governments still dominate economic life in South America, the Middle East, and China. Families retain their controlling interests in countries such as Mexico. Commercial banks continue to be major players in continental Europe and Japan. Nevertheless, capital markets are assuming an increasing importance in these countries as they are relied upon to stimulate the creation of new businesses, allocate capital, and monitor managerial performance. Capital market growth in these countries is gradually eroding the influence of other stakeholders.

National corporate governance systems are influenced by the civil law, common law, and Sharia law traditions, as shown in Figure 17.2.[4] Common law systems were spread by the British Empire and rely on judges' interpretations of precedents set in previous court decisions. Civil law systems descend from ancient Rome and rely on a codified set of laws administered by judges trained in the application of the laws. Sharia (or Islamic) law is a code of conduct based on the Quran and other holy scriptures. Sharia law is interpreted in a wide variety of ways and sometimes coexists with another national legal system. Transition economies such as China borrow characteristics of these legal traditions, while retaining some of their own legal traditions.

A tour of the corporate governance systems in the United States, Germany, Japan, and China will demonstrate how a nation's history, culture, legal system,

| | |
|---|---|
| Civil law | Continental Europe, Latin America and Brazil, Japan, S. Korea, Taiwan, the Philippines |
| Common law | Australia, Canada, Hong Kong, India, Ireland, New Zealand, Singapore, S. Africa, United Kingdom, United States |
| Sharia law | Afghanistan, Egypt, Indonesia, Iran, Iraq, Pakistan, Palestine, Saudi Arabia |

**FIGURE 17.2** National Legal Traditions.

and regulatory environment influence its financial markets and institutions and the market for corporate control. Figure 17.3 provides an overview of the key characteristics of these four corporate governance systems.

**The Market-Based System in the United States** The composition and powers of ***supervisory boards*** that oversee management on behalf of the stakeholders vary widely across countries. In the United States, the supervisory board is called the board of directors and usually is controlled by management. The typical NYSE/AMEX firm has about 12 board members, more than half of whom are outsiders who have no other direct affiliation with the corporation.

*U.S. banks do not have a strong corporate voice.*

In contrast to many other countries, U.S. banks have little or no boardroom representation. The reason for this is historical, as a series of banking crises in the 1800s and early 1900s created a legislative and regulatory tradition that

| | Anglo-American | Germany | Japan | China[†] |
|---|---|---|---|---|
| Key stakeholder(s) | Shareholders, sometimes with a controlling interest | Shareholders, employees, & bankers | Shareholders, main bank, and business partners or keiretsu | Governments and their agencies, and state-owned banks |
| Hostile acquisitions | Common through proxy contests or tender offers | Rare; approval of lead bank and 75% of shareholders | Rare; blocked by keiretsu or business partners | Rare in state-owned enterprises (SOEs); otherwise similar to other capital markets |
| Supervisory board | Inside managers & outside directors | Outside directors, bankers, labor representatives | Inside managers, bankers, keiretsu or business partners | Two-tiered; independent board of supervisors & inside board of directors |
| Management | Managers often are relatively independent | Heavily influenced by the firm's lead bank (Hausbank) | Often collaborative with the firm's business partners | Usually controlled by the government or its agencies |
| Bank ownership of equity | No direct equity ownership | Unlimited equity ownership | Limited equity ownership (5% maximum) | Unlimited equity ownership |
| Executive turnover | Forced by the market through proxy contests or tender offers | Initiated and managed by the firm's lead bank (Hausbank) | Managed by main bank & keiretsuor business partners | Rarein SOEs with politically connected and entrenchedmanagers |

[†]Many listed firms in China are partially privatized SOEs in which the state maintains control.

**FIGURE 17.3** Characteristics of Corporate Governance Systems.

protected U.S. banks from competition while constraining the services that they could provide. The Glass-Steagall Banking Act of 1933 prohibited banks from operating as investment bankers, brokers, or equity market makers, and prevented them from owning stock except in trust for their banking clients. Later legislation (the Bank Holding Company Act of 1956) limited banks' trust activities to passive ownership in no more than 5 percent of a firm's stock. These laws effectively removed commercial banks from corporate boardrooms and prohibited banks from taking an active role in governance except when firms were in financial distress. Banks and other financial institutions are now allowed to affiliate through a holding company structure (Financial Services Modernization Act of 1999), but many restrictions remain. Banks still cannot own stock for their own account and must maintain firewalls between their commercial banking, investment banking, and brokerage activities. The U.S. banking industry lags many of its international competitors because of this history of limited bank involvement in corporate affairs.

**Germany's Universal Banking System** Commercial banks in Continental Europe have assumed a much bigger role in corporate governance than in the Anglo-American model. Germany provides an example. In Germany's system of ***universal banking,*** banks offer a full range of banking and financial services to their individual and corporate customers. This provides banks with a strong voice in corporate governance as they provide debt and equity financing, brokerage and investment banking activities, insurance underwriting, and financial consulting.

German banks influence corporate boardrooms in four ways.

- Invest directly in equity
- Supply debt capital as commercial loans to German businesses
- Actively vote the shares of their trust (pension fund) and brokerage customers
- Serve as Germany's investment bankers for debt and equity issues to the public

*German banks have an active role.*

Banks also are involved in the operation of German stock exchanges, including the largest exchange—the Deutsche Börse—in Frankfurt. Commercial banks dominate corporate governance in Germany through their control of existing capital and corporate access to new capital.

In contrast to U.S. law, German law gives banks the authority to vote on behalf of their brokerage clients. German banks obtain proxies from their brokerage customers that allow the banks to vote their shares. Banks advise the shareholders of their intentions prior to voting and, unless instructed otherwise, vote the shares on behalf of their brokerage customers. German banks also manage most of Germany's pension fund assets. This near monopoly on trust and brokerage activities provides German banks a dominant role in German corporate governance.

German corporations have a two-tiered supervisory structure with a supervisory board (Aufsichtsrat) and a separate management board (Vorstand) that reports to the supervisory board. German law stipulates the representation of various stakeholders on the supervisory board. There are 21 seats on the supervisory boards of most corporations with over €10 million in equity capitalization. Employees elect 10 seats and shareholders elect 11 seats (including the board chairman) in publicly traded corporations with at least 2,000 employees. The number of seats and the proportion held by equity and by employees vary for smaller firms and for firms in different industries. German banks control the supervisory board in large part through their dominance of the equity seats on the board. Fauver and Fuerst found that a moderate level of employee representation on the supervisory board can increase firm value in German firms, presumably by improving coordination and communication with management and reducing agency costs.[5] Nonemployee union representation on the board did not improve firm value in their study.

The control of German banks over the equity portion of the supervisory board also allows bank control of the proxy mechanism by which shares are voted. In the United States, the chief executive officer (CEO) controls the proxy mechanism, especially if the CEO serves as chairperson of the board of directors. In Germany, the CEO is prohibited from serving on the supervisory board. Without a corporate insider as the board chairperson, German managers must filter their requests to shareholders through a board that is controlled by bankers. This allows banks to control both the equity portion of the supervisory board and the proxy mechanism by which shares are voted.

Some German corporations have sought financing through the capital markets specifically to break the hegemony of banks over corporate affairs. Transaction volume on the Deutsche Börse is robust, and an active market in the equity issues of high-growth and technology companies provides capital to small and medium-sized businesses. Investment banks from other countries have captured some of the new issue market, but the market is still dominated by German banks.

**Japan's Keiretsu System** The corporate governance system in Japan owes much to its cultural and political history during the 20th century. Prior to World War II, family-controlled business groups called zaibatsu controlled one-third of Japan's banking and foreign trade, half of all shipbuilding and maritime shipping, and most heavy industry. Group members were linked through share cross-holdings organized around a family-controlled main bank. Business activity was centered on the banks, which were used to allocate funds within the zaibatsu. Zaibatsu were instrumental in the Japanese war effort, so after the war the allied powers imposed limits on Japan's banks to reduce their influence. Banks were prohibited from owning more than 5 percent of any corporation, and investment and commercial banking activities were separated. Many of these restrictions still apply today.

After the war, the traditional zaibatsu re-emerged in a Japanese institution called the ***keiretsu***. Keiretsu are collaborative groups of horizontally or vertically integrated companies, often with share cross-holdings among the group members. Each keiretsu has a small group of core members and a number of more loosely affiliated companies. About one-half of publicly traded firms in Japan are formal or informal members of a keiretsu.

> *Keiretsu are groups of interlinked firms.*

An inner circle of managers, bankers, and business partners dominates governance in Japanese firms that are a part of a keiretsu. It is rare for a member of the supervisory board to come from a group other than management, the main bank, or a business partner. Indeed, the board of a typical large corporation listed on the Tokyo Stock Exchange in the early 1990s had 23 board members but only one outsider.[6] Independent directors are gradually being introduced through changes in corporate law, but for large firms remain the exception rather than the norm.

There are two types of keiretsu. ***Vertical keiretsu*** are led by large manufacturers such as Hitachi, Sony, and Toshiba in electronics, and Honda, Nissan, and Toyota in automobiles. These industrial groups connect the manufacturers to their suppliers and customers through share cross-holdings, personnel swaps, and coordination of logistics and business strategy. These vertical keiretsu make it difficult for non-Japanese firms to gain a foothold in the Japanese market.

***Horizontal keiretsu*** often are centered on a main bank and can have between 20 and 50 primary members and several hundred more loosely affiliated members. Competition between member firms usually is avoided by having only one company in each industry. The main bank and the keiretsu partners closely monitor other keiretsu members, often exchanging employees to promote interaction among the partners. Figure 17.4 shows the members of the Mitsubishi keiretsu. Other horizontal keiretsu include Mitsui (Sony, Toshiba, Fuji Film), Sumitomo (NEC, Mazda, Asahi Breweries), Fuyo (Yamaha, Canon, Sapporo Breweries), Dai-Ichi Kangyo (Fujitsu, Isuzu), Sanwa (Sharp, Konica Minolta), and Tokai (Toyota, Suzuki).

A prolonged Japanese recession beginning in 1990 put enormous pressure on the Japanese economy and forced changes in the keiretsu system. Commercial banks found themselves with large portfolios of nonperforming loans during the recession. At the same time, the government lowered the barriers between commercial

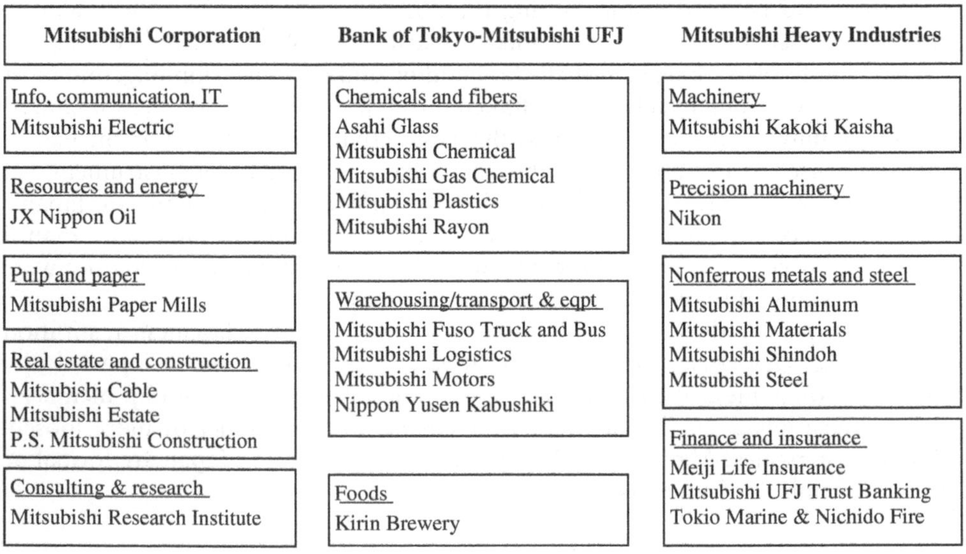
Mitsubishi Corporation
Bank of Tokyo-Mitsubishi UFJ
Mitsubishi Heavy Industries
Info. communication. IT
Mitsubishi Electric
Resources and energy
JX Nippon Oil
Pulp and paper
Mitsubishi Paper Mills
Real estate and construction
Mitsubishi Cable
Mitsubishi Estate
P.S. Mitsubishi Construction
Consulting & research
Mitsubishi Research Institute
Chemicals and fibers
Asahi Glass
Mitsubishi Chemical
Mitsubishi Gas Chemical
Mitsubishi Plastics
Mitsubishi Rayon
Warehousing/transport & eqpt
Mitsubishi Fuso Truck and Bus
Mitsubishi Logistics
Mitsubishi Motors
Nippon Yusen Kabushiki
Foods
Kirin Brewery
Machinery
Mitsubishi Kakoki Kaisha
Precision machinery
Nikon
Nonferrous metals and steel
Mitsubishi Aluminum
Mitsubishi Materials
Mitsubishi Shindoh
Mitsubishi Steel
Finance and insurance
Meiji Life Insurance
Mitsubishi UFJ Trust Banking
Tokio Marine & Nichido Fire

**FIGURE 17.4** The Mitsubishi Keiretsu.
*Source:* Mitsubishi Public Affairs Committee (www.mitsubishi.com), April 2012.

banks, investment banks, securities firms, and insurance companies. These reforms culminated in a series of mergers that produced three mega-banks.

| | |
|---|---|
| Mitsubishi UFJ Financial Group | Bank of Tokyo-Mitsubishi UFJ (including banks from the Mitsubishi, Sanwa, & Tokai keiretsu) |
| Sumitomo Mitsui Banking Corporation | Sumitomo Bank (Sumitomo keiretsu)<br>Sakura Bank (Mitsui keiretsu) |
| Mizuho Holding Financial Group | Fuji Bank (Fuyo keiretsu),<br>Dai-Ichi Kangyo Bank (Dai-Ichi Kangyo keiretsu) |

These combinations forced realignment of companies within the horizontal keiretsu, as competing firms were merged or spun off to raise capital for the survivors. Japanese share cross-holdings have fallen since the early 1990s as share realignments have weakened the traditional keiretsu ties. Although they have waned in importance since their earlier heyday, keiretsu nevertheless retain a prominent role in Japanese business life. Indeed, the Mitsubishi keiretsu has emerged largely intact and seems intent on maintaining its traditional structure.

## MARKET UPDATE Korea's Chaebol

Many prominent Korean firms belong to a *chaebol,* a family-controlled horizontally diversified group of firms that bears some resemblance to a keiretsu in Japan. The major chaebol were founded after the Korean War and rose to power through government protections and subsidies. The three major Korean chaebol, their founding families, and their most recognizable corporations are

| | | |
|---|---|---|
| Samsung | Lee | Samsung Electronics<br>The Samsung chaebol |
| Hyundai | Chung | Hyundai Kia Automotive, Hyundai Heavy Industries<br>The Hyundai chaebol was split up in 2001 following the founder's death |
| LG | Koo, Huh | LG Electronics (partial spin-off in 1999)<br>LG is pursuing joint ventures with international partners including Royal Philips Electronics (Netherlands), Nortel (Canada), and Hitachi (Japan) |

The biggest difference between a chaebol and a keiretsu is that chaebol are still largely controlled by the founding families, whereas keiretsu have passed into the hands of professional managers. The Korean chaebol also have formal organizational structures and centralized control, in contrast to the informal network of control in a Japanese keiretsu. Another difference is that Korean law prohibits a chaebol from owning a commercial bank.

The Korean government instituted reforms aimed at greater openness, competitiveness, and efficiency following the Asian crisis of 1997. Chaebol were encouraged to focus on key businesses and divest peripheral operations. Several prominent bankruptcies hastened this process, particularly in the large SK and Daewoo chaebol. The Korean economy eventually recovered from the 1997 crisis and then survived the 2008 global financial crisis in relatively good shape.

**China's Transitional System** China has enjoyed phenomenal economic growth since the late 1980s. China has three distinct business sectors.

- A "state sector" of wholly government-owned businesses
- A "listed sector" of partially privatized exchange-listed, SOEs
- A "private sector" of family- and publicly-owned firms with no government ownership

Although the government still owns and controls a large portion of the Chinese economy, much of the country's growth and prosperity also relies on the private sector. Active trade in private-sector firms and in partially privatized ***SOEs*** has created a strong equity culture, and China is rapidly evolving toward a capital market-based corporate governance system. The stock exchanges in Shanghai, Shenzhen, and Hong Kong are among the largest and most active in the world, with a combined market capitalization exceeding that of every single country except the United States.

Partially privatized SOEs include the four largest Chinese commercial banks: the Industrial and Commercial Bank of China, China Construction Bank, Bank of China, and Agricultural Bank of China. These four commercial banks collectively control nearly half of China's banking assets. The Chinese government maintains a controlling interest in each of these banks. Commercial banks are supervised and regulated by the China Banking Regulatory Commission. China's monetary policy is implemented through the People's Bank of China.

For exchange-listed firms, China has a two-tiered supervisory structure that is similar to the German system in which a board of supervisors provides oversight to a board of directors. The board of supervisors must have at least three members, with at least one member representing employees and at least one representing shareholders. The firm's managers are not allowed to serve on the supervisory board. Government bureaucrats control many exchange-listed SOEs directly through the management team and through their seats on the supervisory board. In an effort to allow market discipline to improve the performance of SOEs, independent directors that are unaffiliated with the company are now required.

## Characteristics of Corporate Governance Systems

There are national differences in who owns and controls corporations, as well as in how—and in how well—national corporate governance systems protect minority investors. This section reviews the literature on controlling shareholders and protections for minority investors.

**Controlling Shareholders** An important characteristic of a nation's corporate governance system is the concentration of equity ownership. Figure 17.5 displays the proportion of firms that are controlled by key stakeholders in several countries with disparate corporate governance systems. Large firms in the United Kingdom tend to be widely held, with no single shareholder having control. Large shareholders are more common in the United States, but often they are entrepreneurs that have retained an ownership interest.[7] Large Japanese firms seldom have a single dominant shareholder, whereas control of medium-sized firms often rests with business or keiretsu partners. South Korean firms tend to be either widely held or controlled by a founding family. Ownership of large German firms often is widely held, but is just as likely to be concentrated in the hands of the state, a financial institution, or a founding family. Nearly half of medium-sized German firms are controlled by families. Many of the largest Italian firms are state-controlled, while medium-sized firms typically are controlled by a founding family. Ownership of firms of all sizes in Hong Kong and Mexico are likely to be in the hands of a founding family.

Commercial banks are a powerful force in corporate boardrooms in many countries. Figure 17.6 compares the relative importance of the three largest banks

| Large publicly traded firms | Widely held | Family | State | Financial institution | Corporation | Other |
|---|---|---|---|---|---|---|
| United Kingdom | 100 | 0 | 0 | 0 | 0 | 0 |
| Japan | 90 | 5 | 5 | 0 | 0 | 0 |
| United States | 80 | 20 | 0 | 0 | 0 | 0 |
| South Korea | 55 | 20 | 15 | 0 | 5 | 5 |
| Germany | 50 | 10 | 25 | 15 | 0 | 0 |
| Italy | 20 | 15 | 40 | 5 | 10 | 10 |
| Hong Kong | 10 | 70 | 5 | 5 | 0 | 10 |
| Mexico | 0 | 100 | 0 | 0 | 0 | 0 |

| Medium-sized publicly traded firms | Widely held | Family | State | Financial institution | Corporation | Other |
|---|---|---|---|---|---|---|
| United States | 90 | 10 | 0 | 0 | 0 | 0 |
| United Kingdom | 60 | 40 | 0 | 0 | 0 | 0 |
| Japan | 30 | 10 | 0 | 0 | 0 | 60 |
| South Korea | 30 | 50 | 0 | 0 | 20 | 0 |
| Germany | 10 | 40 | 20 | 20 | 10 | 0 |
| Italy | 0 | 60 | 0 | 0 | 10 | 30 |
| Hong Kong | 0 | 90 | 0 | 0 | 0 | 10 |
| Mexico | 0 | 100 | 0 | 0 | 0 | 0 |

**FIGURE 17.5** Percentage of Firms with Controlling Shareholders.
*Source:* La Porta et al., "Corporate Ownership Around the World," *Journal of Finance* (1999). Figures are the percentage of firms with a single shareholder controlling 20 percent or more of the voting stock. "Widely held" indicates there is no single controlling shareholder. "Other" is a controlling interest other than one of those listed.

| | China | Germany | Japan | U.K. | U.S. |
|---|---|---|---|---|---|
| Assets of the three largest banks ($ trillions) | 5.24 | 4.07 | 6.07 | 7.06 | 6.30 |
| Gross Domestic Prodcut (GDP) (2010, U.S. $ trillions) | 10.09 | 2.94 | 4.31 | 2.17 | 14.66 |
| Ratio assets/Gross National Product (GNP) | 0.52 | 1.38 | 1.41 | 3.25 | 0.43 |
| Ratio relative to United States | 1.21 | 3.22 | 3.28 | 7.57 | 1.00 |

**FIGURE 17.6** The Importance of Firms with Controlling Shareholders.
*Source:* Bank assets at year-end 2010 from *The Banker*; GDP from www.imf.org.

in the United States, the United Kingdom, Japan, Germany, and China. Although U.S. banks are some of the world's largest, they are involved in a relatively small proportion of the U.S. economy. In 2010, the three largest U.S. banks controlled assets worth $6.30 trillion. GDP in the United States was $14.66 trillion during 2010. The three largest U.S. banks thus held a stake in assets equal to 43 percent of GDP. The ratio of bank assets to GDP was more than three times that of the United States in each of the other countries, except China. The relatively high ratio of bank involvement in the United Kingdom reflects the prominence of the largest London banks (HSBC, Barclays, and the Royal Bank of Scotland).

*Banks can help small firms to grow.*

High concentration in the banking sector may or may not be a good thing. On the one hand, a powerful bank can foster a close relationship with client firms, effectively monitor their performance, and facilitate growth. This can be important for small firms without direct access to the capital markets. Because of their informational advantage, banks also can be in a better position than capital markets to fund risky projects or projects that require staged financing. On the other hand, banks can impede growth if they become too powerful and are able to extract monopoly rents from their clients. Also, banks with a preference for conservative investments may forgo funding riskier, high-growth projects. In these situations, capital markets may be better at allocating capital and promoting growth. In an increasing number of countries, private equity and venture capital funds provide capital to high-risk (high-potential) start-ups, sometimes bypassing local capital markets in the process.

Investment funds (hedge funds, pension funds, and mutual funds) have established an important role in market-based economies. As shown in Figure 17.7, Li et al. estimate that the percentage of exchange-listed firms with at least one institutional blockholder owning more than 5 percent of shares is 33.9 percent in Germany, 49.1 percent in Japan, 72.7 percent in the United Kingdom, and 69.2 percent in the United States. Professional fund managers are common in the United Kingdom (62 percent) and the United States (56 percent). In contrast, savings and investment are conducted through financial institutions in Japan, where 39.3 percent of firms had a financial institution as a blockholder but only 5.6 percent had a professional fund manager as a blockholder. Germany is intermediate in the importance of professional fund managers.

| | Germany | Japan | U.K. | U.S. |
|---|---|---|---|---|
| Firms with institutional blockholders | 33.9% | 49.1% | 72.7% | 69.2% |
| Firms with fund managers as institutional blockholders | 12.3% | 5.6% | 62.3% | 56.4% |
| Firms with financial institutions as institutional blockholders | 9.4% | 39.3% | 2.9% | 7.8% |
| Firms with an institutional blockholder as largest shareholder | 11.3% | 19.3% | 46.4% | 43.3% |

**FIGURE 17.7** The Importance of Institutional Blockholders (in excess of 5 percent of shares).
*Source:* Li, Moshirian, Pham, and Zein, "When Financial Institutions Are Large Shareholders: The Role of Macro Corporate Governance Environments," *Journal of Finance* (2006). Institutional blockholders are defined as institutions owning more than 5 percent of shares.

*Mutual funds are prominent in market-based economies.*

**The Legal Environment and Investor Protection** National legal systems determine who exercises control over the firm's voting and cash flow rights. This sets the stage for industrial growth, new business formation, and the allocational efficiency of the nation's capital markets.

*Legal systems determine shareholder protection.*

Effective corporate governance systems have legal protections for minority investors against expropriation by managers or controlling shareholders. This is important because separation of ownership and control is difficult when there are inadequate legal safeguards to ensure minority investors a return on their investment. Legal protections influence the ways in which privately held and publicly traded firms raise capital, the concentration of equity ownership, and the turnover of top management during financial distress. Strong corporate governance systems also facilitate foreign investment by reducing information asymmetries and monitoring costs faced by foreign investors. As a consequence, foreign investors tend to avoid countries and firms with poor investor protections or disclosure requirements.[8]

Protection tends to be highest in common law countries of the United Kingdom and its former colonies. With strong legal protection of their rights, minority investors can allow their ownership claims to be separated from control of the firm. Legal protections ensure a return commensurate with their claim. These countries can afford to have a higher proportion of small, diversified investors.

Legal protections for minority investors are not as strong in civil law countries, including most countries in Europe and Latin America. Legal protections for minority shareholders have been criticized especially in Italy, where owner/managers sometimes opportunistically seize firm assets or minority investors' voting and cash flow rights. Investors avoid minority positions in these situations, and ownership tends to be concentrated in the hands of one or a few investors.

Civil law countries in the Germanic and Scandinavian spheres tend to have legal protections that are intermediate between the English and Napoleonic systems.

Studies find that firm performance in Germany is positively related to the concentration of equity ownership, particularly if a bank exercises control.[9] However, there is evidence that the gains associated with transfers of ownership accrue primarily to large stakeholders, and not to minority investors.[10] The recent growth and integration of European capital markets is changing the balance of power in European boardrooms and is likely to lead to changes in investor protections as well.

## 17.2 THE INTERNATIONAL MARKET FOR CORPORATE CONTROL

Section 17.1 reviewed the characteristics of national corporate governance systems. In this section, we turn to the issue of how equity control is transferred between shareholders.

### The Terminology of Mergers and Acquisitions

A firm can obtain control over the assets of another firm in three ways.

- Through a joint venture or strategic alliance
- Through acquisition of another firm's assets
- Through a merger or acquisition of stock

Chapter 12 discussed joint ventures and strategic alliances in the context of foreign market entry. Chapter 13 covered asset acquisitions in the context of capital budgeting decisions. This chapter focuses on M&A of stock in the market for corporate control.

In a ***merger,*** one firm absorbs another. The acquiring firm usually retains its name and legal status. All assets and liabilities of the target firm are merged into the acquiring firm. A ***consolidation*** is like a merger, except that an entirely new firm is created. When firms merge or consolidate, one firm usually serves as the dominant or acquiring firm, with the other firm as a target. The acquiring firm's managers usually retain their role in the merged firm.

In an ***acquisition of stock,*** the acquiring firm purchases some or all of the equity of another firm. A merger sometimes follows an acquisition after the acquiring firm obtains a controlling interest in the target firm. An acquisition of stock can be in any amount up to 100 percent of the acquired firm's stock. Acquisitions of stock of 50 percent or less are referred to as partial acquisitions. The target firm's management may or may not be retained.

Firms are acquired or merged in the hope that the two firms' competitive advantages can be more effectively utilized, so that the combined entity has more value than the sum of the parts. This additional value is called ***synergy*** and is measured as

$$\text{Synergy} = V_{AT} - (V_A + V_T) \tag{17.1}$$

where $V_A$ and $V_T$ are the values of the acquiring firm (A) and the target firm (T) prior to the announcement of the merger or acquisition, and $V_{AT}$ is the post-acquisition value of the combined firm. Note that synergy in Equation 17.1 is not constrained to be positive, although value-destroying combinations are not considered synergistic.

> ***Synergy is when the whole is greater than the parts.***

Synergy can come from many sources. A merged firm might enjoy greater market power and be able to extract monopoly rents, whereas the pre-merger partners were prohibited from colluding on price. A merged firm might be able to reduce operating costs through production efficiencies. A merged firm might be able to reduce financing costs via tax shields, lower financial distress costs, or better access to capital.[11] These factors can be even more important for cross-border M&A than for domestic M&A, because market frictions are greater across countries than within countries. On the other hand, cross-border M&A can be value-destroying because of physical or cultural distances between the partners, or differences in their governance environments.

The purchase price paid to the shareholders of the target firm includes the pre-acquisition value $V_T$ of the target and an acquisition premium paid to target shareholders. The difference between the purchase price and the pre-acquisition market value is the ***acquisition premium***

$$\text{Acquisition premium} = \text{Purchase price} - V_T \tag{17.2}$$

If the target is publicly traded, target shareholders will never sell for less than their pre-acquisition market value, so the acquisition premium is always positive. If the target firm is not publicly traded, the pre-acquisition value $V_T$ is not easily estimated, and target firm shareholders may end up selling for more or less than their fair market value.

Whether the acquiring firm wins or loses depends on whether the synergies created by the merger or acquisition outweigh the acquisition premium paid to the target firm. The gain (or loss) to the acquiring firm is determined as follows:

$$\begin{aligned}\text{Gain to acquiring firm} &= V_{AT} - (V_A + V_T + \text{Acquisition premium}) \\ &= \text{Synergy} - \text{Acquisition premium} \qquad (17.3)\end{aligned}$$

Acquiring shareholders win if the synergy created through the acquisition is greater than the premium paid to target shareholders. If only one or a few target firms offer the competitive advantages that are desired by acquiring firms, then the target firm's position will be enhanced as it negotiates with its suitors. The bargaining position of an acquiring firm is greatest when there are many potential targets but only a few acquiring firms in a position to make a competing offer. As we shall see in a later section, acquisitions don't always result in gains for acquiring shareholders. Firms often pay too high an acquisition premium or overestimate the synergy created in a business combination.

Cross-border M&A are conducted within the rules and conventions established by national governments and their regulatory bodies. Consequently, it is useful to describe how financial markets and institutions and the regulations that govern them affect corporate ownership and control in different countries.

| Year | Acquirer | Target | $billions | Sector |
|---|---|---|---|---|
| 2009 | Roche Holding (Switzerland) | Genentech (U.S.) | 46.7 | Pharma |
| 2009 | ABN AMRO (Netherlands) | Royal Bank of Scotland | 98.2 | Finance |
| 2008 | InBev (Belgium) | Anheuser-Busch (U.S.) | 52.2 | Beverages |
| 2007 | Royal Bank of Scotland | ABN-AMRO (Netherlands) | 99.4 | Financials |
| 2006 | AT&T (U.S.) | BellSouth (U.S.) | 89.4 | Telecom |
| 2005 | Royal Dutch (Netherlands) | Shell Transport & Trading (UK) | 74.3 | Petroleum |
| 2000 | France Telecom | Orange PLC (UK) | 46.0 | Telecom |
| 2000 | VodaphoneAirTouch (UK) | Mannesmann (Germany) | 202.8 | Telecom |
| 1999 | Vodaphone Group (UK) | AirTouch Comm (US) | 60.3 | Telecom |
| 1998 | Daimler-Benz (Germany) | Chrysler (US) | 40.5 | Auto |
| 1998 | BP Amoco (UK) | Amoco (US) | 48.2 | Oil &gas |

**FIGURE 17.8** Cross-Border M&A over $40 Billion in Value.
*Source: Mergers and Acquisitions*, various issues.

## A Brief History of Cross-Border Mergers and Acquisitions Activity

Cross-border M&A were rare as recently as 1968, when only 16 cross-border deals were completed. Cross-border deals became more common during the 1970s and 1980s, although most of these were relatively small acquisitions rather than blockbuster mega-deals. Cross-border M&A occurred with increasing frequency in the 1990s. The first deal to exceed $10 billion was in 1998. Figure 17.8 lists cross-border deals with a market value of at least $40 billion.

> *Merger waves are the long-term ups and downs in M&A activity.*

The ebbs and flows of M&A activity are referred to as ***merger waves.*** Figure 17.9 displays M&A activity involving U.S. firms since 1988. Activity in other markets generally rises and falls with U.S. M&A activity. M&A activity grew throughout the 1990s, riding on the crest of a prolonged stock market boom in Europe and North

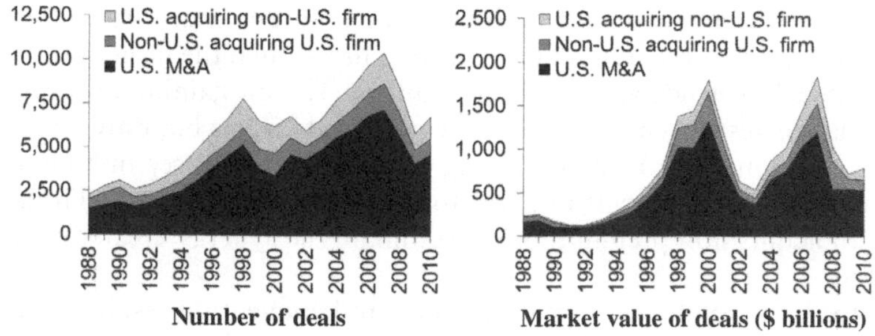

**FIGURE 17.9** Merger Waves.
*Source:* Compiled from *Mergers and Acquisitions*, various issues.

America and culminating in the 2000 Vodaphone (United Kingdom) acquisition of Mannesmann (Germany) for $202.8 billion. This merger wave crashed on the shores of the technology stock bubble in the early 2000s. M&A activity rose again from 2003–2008, and then fell after the global financial crisis of 2008. Activity has increased since the 2008 crisis and will no doubt continue until the next asset bubble or financial crisis.

### Hostile Acquisitions

> *Hostile acquisitions are common in market-based systems.*

The English common law tradition is to trust the "invisible hand" of the marketplace. In these economies, dispersed equity ownership leads to price-oriented, arm's-length transactions in a competitive marketplace. Public proxy contests are more common in countries with market-based than with bank-based governance systems. Control contests also are much more likely to be hostile in countries with market-based systems. Well-developed capital markets and dispersed equity ownership make hostile acquisitions relatively easy to accomplish in these markets.

Although there are several thousand takeovers annually in Japan, most of these are friendly acquisitions between related companies. The sums involved are usually small relative to the size of the Japanese market. Foreign acquisitions of Japanese firms are even more unusual, with fewer than 100 foreign acquisitions of Japanese companies in most years. This is a small fraction of the level of cross-border acquisition activity in other large national markets. About half of these foreign acquisitions are friendly takeovers of Japanese joint venture partners or transfers of control from one non-Japanese company to another.

Foreign takeovers of Japanese firms have been rare for two reasons.

- Share cross-holdings with one's keiretsu members or business partners
- Japan's restrictive regulations on cross-border M&A

Cross-holdings ensure that outstanding shares are in friendly hands, including a main bank. When faced with a hostile acquisition, Japanese managers rely on the shares held by their keiretsu or business partners as a source of stability. Share cross-holdings have declined since the early 1990s, making acquisitions of Japanese firms slightly more accessible for foreign investors.

> *Keiretsu make a hostile acquisition difficult.*

Until 2007, Japan had some fairly arcane restrictions on foreign acquisitions of Japanese companies. As a part of its financial deregulation, Japan enacted a new "Company Law" with M&A provisions that greatly reduced the regulatory barriers to foreign acquisitions of Japanese companies. The intent of this law is to attract foreign direct investment into Japan. Nevertheless, foreign acquisitions of Japanese companies are still the exception rather than the rule.

Hostile public takeovers in Germany are rare, but for different reasons than in Japan. The largest impediment to a hostile acquisition in Germany is the structure of the German supervisory board. Financial institutions including the corporation's Hausbank often control a majority of the voting shares in large public corporations, in which case bank cooperation is essential. Employee support is also necessary in large corporations, because employees control nearly half of the board seats. This makes it difficult for a hostile bidder to gain control of a German corporation with the intention of reducing the workforce or moving production offshore.

*A hostile public acquisition is rare in Germany.*

German law also serves to block hostile public acquisitions of stock by requiring that a supermajority of 75 percent of shareholders approve a takeover and prohibiting golden parachutes (lucrative severance packages) to management. Takeover guidelines also require that all shareholders must be paid the same price even if they previously have accepted a lower bid for their shares. For all of these reasons, hostile public takeovers are rare in Germany. Friendly takeovers account for a large proportion of M&A activity.

Of course, a "friendly" takeover can be like a "friendly" cross-country match in soccer. Ljungqvist and Jenkinson document how stakeholders with noncontrolling interests can work behind the scenes to accumulate large stakes in publicly traded German firms.[12] Aspiring shareholders can use German banks to accumulate these stakes, while at the same time avoiding public disclosure until a controlling majority can be achieved. As the Chinese military strategist Sun-tzu observed in *The Art of War*: "Keep your friends close, and your enemies closer."

## Privatization of State-Owned Enterprises

***Privatization*** of SOEs through equity sales to private investors has been a driving force toward a global equity culture. Privatizations have transformed global capital markets by establishing and sustaining equity markets in previously isolated economies. Indeed, shares of privatized companies account for more than half of the value of many non-U.S. stock markets.

*SOEs are privatized through sales to private investors.*

Changes in equity values (in the top panel of Figure 17.10) drive both domestic and cross-border M&A (in the middle panel), as well as share privatizations (bottom panel). High stock market values and an active market for corporate control allow governments to capture the most value for their SOEs. High water floats all boats in these markets.

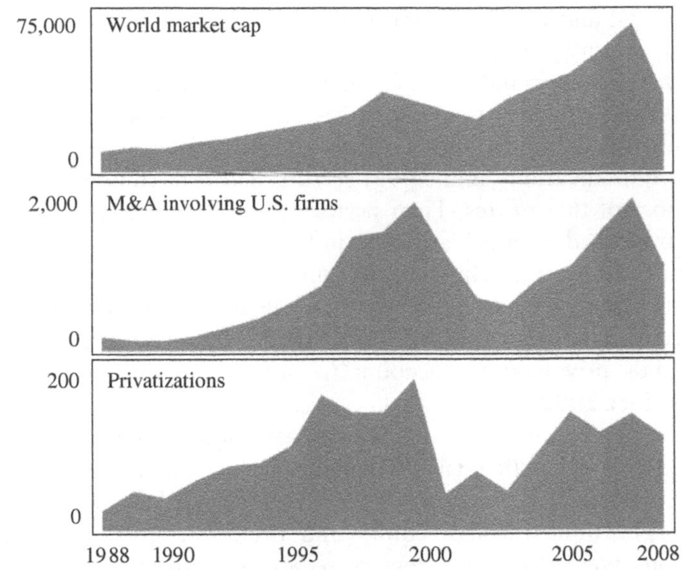


**FIGURE 17.10** Privatizations of SOEs ($ billions).
*Source:* World stock market capitalization is from the World Federation of Exchanges (www.world-exchanges.org). The total value of M&A involving U.S. firms is from *Mergers and Acquisitions*. Worldwide privatization revenues are from Megginson, "Privatization and Finance," *Annual Review of Financial Economics* (2010).

Megginson identifies three privatization waves. In the first wave from 1979–1990, governments began offering partial shares of their SOEs as a way to raise capital. The first large offering was the United Kingdom's initial public offering (IPO) of 51 percent of British Telecom to private investors in 1984. The largest offering during this period was Japan's 1988 partial privatization of the telecom giant NTT for $40 billion. This first wave of privatizations came to a halt in 1990–1991 as a recession suppressed share offerings of all kinds.

Megginson calls the 1992–2000 wave privatization's Golden Era.[13] Governments across Europe and Latin America sold partial shares in their state-owned telecoms during this period including Italy's STET (1995), Spain's Telefonica de España (1995), the Netherlands' KPN (1995), Deutsche Telekom (1996), France Telecom (1997), Brazil's Telebras (1998), and Swisscom (1998). The second wave came to a close as the technology stock bubble burst in 2000.

Privatizations in Eastern Europe (Russia, the Czech Republic, Hungary, and Poland) during this period distributed shares in entire firms to private investors, citizens, or management. This is in contrast to privatizations elsewhere in the world, which typically offered only partial ownership. These privatizations were conducted through voucher programs, management buyouts, or mass privatization programs.[14] Unfortunately, corporate governance in many of these countries did not feature enforceable contracts, minority shareholder protections, or effective monitoring of insiders. As a consequence, many of these privatizations suffered from opportunistic behaviors by corporate or political insiders including illegal takeovers, asset stripping, and outright theft and fraud. Many Eastern European business oligarchs were created during this period. Countries in Eastern Europe continue to develop their legal and regulatory infrastructures to ensure transparency and legal protections for minority shareholders.

Most privatizations in India and China have been partial privatizations in which less than a 100 percent stake is sold to investors. In response to a currency crisis in 1991, India liberalized its markets and partially privatized many of its SOEs in the utilities, telecommunications, and energy sectors. The government retains a majority position in most of these firms. Firm performance (productivity and profitability) typically has improved after privatization in India.[15]

Privatizations during the third wave from 2002–2008 have been dominated by partial privatizations of Chinese SOEs, including the $22 billion IPO of Industrial and Commercial Bank of China in 2006 and the $10 billion IPO of PetroChina in 2007. China's privatizations account for about one-third of the value of all privatizations since 2002.

We can expect yet another wave of privatization in the coming years as the world recovers from the 2008 crisis. In the aftermath of the crisis, many governments reversed their privatization efforts as they rescued troubled financial institutions and prominent corporations through equity and preferred stock investments. These capital infusions were deemed necessary to ensure liquidity, the survival of key industries, and the solvency of the international financial system. However, they also greatly increased national indebtedness. Privatizations are an attractive way for governments to recoup their investments and fund their ongoing budget deficits. Governments still have many untapped national assets, including majority stakes in telecoms and ownership of entire industries such as oil, power generation, and power distribution. Countries in South America, Africa, Europe, the Middle East, and Asia (particularly China) retain vast stakes in SOEs that would be attractive targets for international investors.

## 17.3 THE INTERNATIONAL EVIDENCE ON MERGERS AND ACQUISITIONS

The U.S. market for corporate control has been more closely studied than other national markets because of its international prominence and the fact that information is more readily available in the United States than in other countries. Although other national markets have been less extensively studied, some common themes have emerged.

### Winners, Losers, and Related Factors

> *The shareholders of acquired firms gain.*

First and foremost, shareholders of publicly traded targets capture large gains at the time of an acquisition or a merger announcement. Acquisition premiums are often in the range of 20 to 60 percent when measured from share price prior to the acquisition announcement. Returns to target firms are larger when M&A activity is high and when there are multiple bidders, suggesting that an increase in competition for target firms drives up acquisition premiums.

Returns to the shareholders of acquiring firms in domestic M&A depend on the degree of competition in the market for corporate control. In countries with highly developed capital markets such as the United States and the United Kingdom, the shareholders of acquiring firms typically either receive no gain or slightly overpay for target firms. This is consistent with a competitive market for corporate control in which acquiring firms are forced to pay nearly full value for targets.

Results are somewhat different in less competitive domestic markets for corporate control, where acquiring shareholders often benefit from public acquisitions. Alexandridis, Petmezas, and Travlos find that target shareholders in less competitive capital markets realize smaller acquisition premiums, which suggests that synergies might be more evenly split between the target and the acquiring firms.[16] Targets appear unable to capture all of the synergies created by the acquisition, because the market is less competitive and there are fewer bidders for their stock.

> *Acquirers are more likely to gain in less competitive markets.*

Often acquiring firm shareholders also gain in cross-border M&A, even those that involve a firm from a competitive takeover market such as the United States. Gains are greater when firms from countries with strong investor protections acquire firms from emerging markets or countries with weaker investor protections, and firms in countries with weak shareholders protections are less frequently the target of cross-border M&A.[17] A plausible explanation is that the capital markets value the transfer of corporate governance practices from the acquirer to the target. It might also be that synergistic gains are greater in cross-border deals, leaving more value for acquiring firm shareholders.

Factors related to acquiring firm returns include the acquirer's free cash flow, method of payment, and tax situation, as well as the relative purchasing power of the target and the acquirer.

- *Free cash flow.* Returns to acquiring firms are negatively related to the profitability of the acquiring firm. The usual interpretation is that firms with high free cash flow may engage in acquisitions that destroy rather than create value for their shareholders.
- *Method of payment.* Stock offers are associated with negative returns to acquiring firms in domestic acquisitions, whereas cash offers generate little share price movement on average. Offers of stock may signal that the managers of the acquiring firm believe their shares are overvalued, whereas offers of cash do not send a negative signal to the market.[18]
- *The tax environment.* Takeovers can generate tax advantages including realizations of tax loss carryforwards, increases in the book values of assets to fair market values and thus increases in depreciation deductions, and asset sales to change to more accelerated depreciation schedules. Cross-border differences in tax regimes also allow geographically diversified multinational corporations

(MNCs) to reduce their total tax liability through tax planning. Not surprisingly, markets respond favorably to foreign acquisitions that enhance the MNC's ability to repatriate after-tax funds and unfavorably to acquisitions that trigger additional taxes.[19]

- *The real exchange rate.* The strength of the domestic currency is positively related to the level of foreign acquisitions by domestic firms and to the gains received by domestic acquirers.[20] When the domestic currency is strong, domestic firms are more likely to acquire foreign targets, and shareholders of the acquiring firm are more likely to benefit from the acquisition.

### Firm Performance and Top Executive Turnover

An important test of a nation's corporate governance system is in how well it deals with poorly performing managers. Replacing ineffective managers should increase the value of underperforming firms.

The empirical evidence suggests that there are similarities in *when* and *why* top management is replaced for publicly traded firms in large capital markets such as in the United Kingdom, the United States, Germany, Japan, and China's private sector. In these markets, the likelihood that top management will be replaced is greater for firms reporting poor earnings performance or a recent sharp decline in share price. Further, empirical evidence indicates that firm performance tends to improve after turnover in the top management of poorly performing companies.

The major difference among these countries is in the mechanism by which top management is replaced—the *how* of top executive turnover. The likelihood of top executive turnover in poorly performing firms is positively related to the concentration of equity ownership and to the proportion of independent outsiders on the supervisory board. But the manner in which underperforming executives are replaced varies by country.

> How *executives are replaced varies by country.*

In market-based corporate governance systems, control is contested either as a proxy fight over seats on the supervisory board or through the public takeover markets. The supervisory board represents shareholders and is responsible for initiating any change in top management, so attempts by shareholders to replace top management are channeled through the board of directors. Sometimes these takeovers are led by activist funds with a large but noncontrolling interest. Takeover contests in developed capital markets receive a great deal of coverage in the popular press because they tend to be conducted in public.

In the Japanese keiretsu, the main bank or corporation takes the initiative in replacing the management of poorly performing keiretsu members.[21] Turnover in the ranks of the firm's top executives tends to be greater in bank-dominated keiretsu than in keiretsu without a main bank, perhaps because it is difficult to achieve consensus without a lead bank or corporation. Announcements of top executive turnover often increase share price, particularly following a performance decline or when the successor is appointed from outside the firm.

In Germany, the lead bank usually takes the initiative in replacing top executives. As in the United States, poor earnings or stock price performance is likely to lead to a turnover in top management and an improvement in share price and firm performance. In contrast to the United States, the gains associated with transfers of ownership often accrue only to large blockholders and not to minority investors.[22]

*Politically connected managers can become entrenched.*

In China, management turnover depends on whether the firm is a state-owned enterprise, a partially privatized SOE in the listed sector, or a publicly traded stock in the private sector. Top executive turnover is related to firm performance in China, but only for firms in the private sector. Whereas private- sector firms are likely to have entrepreneurs or professional managers at the helm and relatively independent supervisory boards, many partially privatized SOEs have current or former government bureaucrats as CEO (called a general manager) or as supervisory board members. As a consequence, the performance of many of these SOEs suffers and executives can be difficult to displace in underperforming SOEs. Fan, Wong, and Zhang studied the post-IPO performance of partially privatized SOEs and found that equity returns in politically connected firms underperformed those without political connections by 18 percent in the three years following the IPO.[23] As in other countries, market discipline is a strong force in improving managerial performance in Chinese firms.

Italy is another country that often is criticized for its poor corporate governance practices and legal protections for minority investors. Volpin studied Italian firms in which the top executive was the largest shareholder and yet had less than a 50 percent equity share.[24] In these firms, Tobin's Q (equity market-to-book) ratios are relatively low and executive turnover tends to be unrelated to performance. Each of these is an indicator of poor corporate governance and suggests that entrenched managers can pursue their own interests at the expense of other stakeholders.

## The Value of Corporate Control Benefits

The previous section suggests that there is more than one way for a corporate governance system to successfully deal with underperforming managers and to resolve the agency problems that exist between managers and other stakeholders in the firm. It also raises the possibility that not all shareholders are treated alike in corporate control contests. Indeed, minority shareholders may be at a disadvantage in *any* interaction with controlling shareholders or management.

***Tunneling*** refers to the expropriation of corporate assets from minority shareholders by controlling shareholders, management, or both. Tunneling can occur in both legal and illegal ways. Examples include self-dealing transactions such as asset sales, excessive compensation, loan guarantees, expropriation of corporate opportunities, dilutive share issues, insider trading, and other transactions that discriminate against minority shareholders. Tunneling is common in emerging markets, but also occurs in countries with effective protections of shareholders' rights.

*Tunneling is the expropriation of assets by owners or managers.*

Nenova found that legal environment variables explained 75 percent of the cross-country variation in the value of corporate control benefits.[25] The total value of votes in a control block ranged from 0 percent of firm value in Denmark to 50 percent in Mexico. Whereas Denmark has relatively strong protections for minority shareholders, Mexico is dominated by family-controlled businesses and has relatively poor protections for minority shareholders.

Foreign investors face threats to their control rights and ownership claims that are similar to those faced by minority shareholders. This deters many potential acquirers from entering countries with poor minority shareholder protections or disclosure requirements.[26] Corporate governance improvements are likely to benefit minority and foreign investors at least partly at the expense of controlling shareholders.[27]

### A Caveat

Research into the international market for corporate control is still in its infancy, and new findings surely will modify and extend the results reported here. Moreover, academic research is shooting at a moving target, as markets are becoming increasingly integrated across national borders. The factors that influence the international market for corporate control will continue to evolve. Stay tuned.

## 17.4 SUMMARY

International markets for corporate control provide the financial manager with exciting—yet challenging—opportunities to consolidate existing operations, preempt competitors from entry into existing and future markets, and protect and expand the value of current and future operations.

This chapter described national corporate governance systems and markets for corporate control with a focus on Germany, Japan, the United States, and China. Corporate governance systems share many common elements, but they have unique features as well. For example, the supervisory board represents the major stakeholders in each country. Yet the composition, powers, and responsibilities of the board vary across countries. In the U.S. market-based system, the board is elected by a diverse set of shareholders and operates relatively independently. In Germany's universal banking and Japan's keiretsu systems, banks supply both debt and equity capital. Through their equity stake in the firm, bankers in Germany and Japan maintain a prominent position on the supervisory board and closely monitor the management team. Corporate governance for large firms in China depends on whether the firm is controlled by the government (such as partially privatized SOEs). Corporate governance of public corporations is similar to the governance of publicly owned corporations in other countries, whereas government-controlled companies still pursue some of the ruling party's policy objectives.

There are important differences even within the bank-based corporate governance systems of Germany and Japan. In Germany, the lead bank supplies both debt and equity capital, and serves as investment banker and market maker for public equity offerings. Because the lead bank controls the mechanisms by which the corporation raises capital, the bank plays a very powerful role in corporate affairs. The role of commercial banks in Japan is intermediate between that in Germany and in the United States. In Japan, power is shared within the keiretsu, a network of companies linked through business partnerships that share cross-holdings and that have a major bank or corporation at the center.

The structure of these corporate governance systems influences top executive turnover and the market for corporate control. In the United States, management is much more likely to be disciplined by the public equity markets through (possibly hostile) corporate takeovers. Hostile acquisitions are much less common in Germany and are almost nonexistent in Japan because of the concentration of equity ownership in the hands of the lead bank in Germany and in other keiretsu members in Japan. A hostile acquisition is simply not possible in Germany or Japan without the cooperation of the major stakeholder or stakeholders. Top executive turnover in China is dependent on whether a firm is controlled by the government (in which case management can become entrenched) or outside the government's direct ownership and control.

## KEY TERMS

*acquisition of stock*
*acquisition premium*
*agency costs*
*chaebol*
*consolidation*
*corporate governance (family-, state-, bank-, or market-based)*
*free cash flow*
*keiretsu (horizontal or vertical)*
*merger*
*merger waves*
*method of payment*
*privatization*
*stakeholders*
*state-owned enterprise (SOE)*
*supervisory board*
*synergy*
*tunneling*
*universal banking*

## CONCEPTUAL QUESTIONS

17.1 Define corporate governance. Why is it important in international finance?

17.2 In what ways can one firm gain control over the assets of another firm?

17.3 What is synergy?

17.4 Describe several differences in the role of commercial banks in corporate governance in China, Germany, Japan, and the United States.

17.5 Describe four ways that banks can influence corporate boardrooms in countries—such as Germany—that offer universal banking?

17.6 How does the legal environment affect minority investors? Include a description of tunneling in your answer.

17.7 Why are hostile acquisitions less common in Germany and Japan than in the United Kingdom and the United States?

17.8 How is turnover in the ranks of top executives similar in China, Germany, Japan, and the United States? How is it different?

17.9 Who are the likely winners and losers in domestic M&A that involve two firms incorporated in the same country? How are the returns to acquiring firm shareholders related to the method of payment (cash versus stock) and the acquiring firm's free cash flow or profitability?

17.10 In what ways are the winners and losers in cross-border M&A different than in domestic U.S. M&A?

17.11 How are gains to bidding firms related to exchange rates?

## PROBLEMS

17.1 Connect each term to its definition or description.

| | |
|---|---|
| a. Acquisition of assets | A. Creation of an entirely new firm |
| b. Acquisition of stock | B. A combination of the assets and liabilities of two firms |
| c. Acquisition premium | C. The difference between the value of a combination and the sum of the parts |
| d. Consolidation | D. An acquisition in which one firm buys an equity interest in another |
| e. Merger | E. An acquisition in which none of the liabilities supporting an asset are transferred to the purchaser |
| f. Method of payment | F. The difference between the purchase price and the pre-acquisition value of the target firm |
| g. Synergy | G. The way in which a merger or acquisition is financed |

17.2 Suppose Agile Corporation of the United States acquires Mobile Plc of the United Kingdom. The value of Agile stock on the Nasdaq in the United States is \$3 billion. Mobile sells on the London Stock Exchange for the pound sterling equivalent of \$1 billion. Agile pays a 20 percent acquisition premium to acquire Mobile. The synergy created through the combination of Agile and Mobile adds 10 percent to the value of the combined firm. How much are Agile's shareholders likely to gain or lose through this acquisition?

17.3 You are the CEO of XO, a bulk chemical producer and processor. XO is generating quite a lot of free cash flow that cannot be profitably invested domestically. You are looking to expand XO's operations abroad through acquisition, despite having no international operations or experience. Is the existence of free cash flow a benefit or a hindrance to your international expansion plans? How might shareholders view your plans to spend free cash flow on an international investment or acquisition?

17.4 You are the chairman of Tres Equis, a family-run beverage manufacturer based in Guadalupe, Mexico. For years, you have harbored ambitions of expanding operations into other Latin American countries and perhaps even into the United States. The Mexican peso recently has risen in real terms against most foreign currencies. Is now a good time to expand internationally through acquisition? Describe the influence of exchange rates on cross-border merger and acquisition activity.

17.5 Japan's prolonged recession during the 1990s forced many changes on financial institutions and the market for corporate control within Japan. List the largest three financial institutions in Japan. Then, use your library database to see whether there has been further consolidation within the Japanese banking industry.

## SUGGESTED READINGS

### Corporate governance systems in various countries are discussed in


Lucien A. Bebchuk and Michael S. Weisbach, "The State of Corporate Governance Research," *Review of Financial Studies* 23 (March 2010), 939–961.

Larry Fauver and Michael E. Fuerst, "Does Good Corporate Governance Include Employee Representation? Evidence from German Corporate Boards," *Journal of Financial Economics* 82 (December 2006), 673–710.

Gary Gorton and Frank A. Schmid, "Universal Banking and the Performance of German Firms," *Journal of Financial Economics* 58 (October 2000), 29–80.

Nandini Gupta, "Partial Privatization and Firm Performance," *Journal of Finance* 60 (April 2005), 987–1015.

Donghui Li, Fariborz Moshirian, Peter Kien Pham, and Jason Zein, "When Financial Institutions Are Large Shareholders: The Role of Macro Corporate Governance Environments," *Journal of Finance* 61 (December 2006), 2975–3007.

Alexander Ljungqvist and Tim Jenkinson, "The Role of Hostile Stakes in German Corporate Governance," *Journal of Corporate Finance* 7 (December 2001), 397–446.

Rafael La Porta, Florencio Lopez-de-Silanes, and Andrei Shleifer, "Corporate Ownership around the World," *Journal of Finance* 54 (April 1999), 471–517.

Rafael La Porta, Florencio Lopez-de-Silanes, Andrei Shleifer, and Robert W. Vishny, "Law and Finance," *Journal of Political Economy* 106 (December 1998), 1113–1155.

Rafael La Porta, Florencio Lopez-de-Silanes, Andrei Shleifer, and Robert W. Vishny, "Investor Protection and Corporate Governance," *Journal of Financial Economics* 58 (October/November 2000), 3–27.

Paolo F. Volpin, "Governance with Poor Investor Protection: Evidence from Top Executive Turnover in Italy," *Journal of Financial Economics* 64 (April 2002), 61–90.

### The gains to shareholders in domestic and cross-border mergers and acquisitions are discussed in

Arturo Bris and Christos Cabolis, "The Value of Investor Protection: Firm Evidence from Cross-Border Mergers," *Review of Financial Studies* 21 (April 2008), 605–648.

Anusha Chari, Paige P. Ouimet, and Linda L. Tesar, "The Value of Control in Emerging Markets," *Review of Financial Studies* 23 (March 2010), 1741–1770.

John Doukas and Nickolaos G. Travlos, "The Effect of Corporate Multinationalism on Shareholders' Wealth: Evidence from International Acquisitions," *Journal of Finance* 63, No. 5 (1988), 1161–1175.

Isil Erel, Rose C. Liao, and Michael S. Weisbach, "Determinants of Cross-Border Mergers and Acquisitions," *Journal of Finance* 66, (forthcoming June 2012).

Mara Faccio and Ronald W. Masulis, "The Choice of Payment Method in European Mergers and Acquisitions," *Journal of Finance* 60 (June 2005), 1345–1388.

Mara Faccio, John J, McConnell, and David Stolin, "Returns to Acquirers of Listed and Unlisted Targets," *Journal of Financial and Quantitative Analysis* 41 (March 2006), 197–220.

Jun-Koo Kang, Jin-Mo Kim, Wei-Lin Liu, and Sangho Yi, "Post-takeover Restructuring and the Sources of Gains in Foreign Takeovers: Evidence from U.S. Targets," *Journal of Business* 79 (September 2006), 2503–2539.

### Top executive turnover as a means of restructuring poorly performing companies is discussed in

Joseph P.H. Fan, T.J. Wong, and Tianyu Zhang, "Politically Connected CEOs, Corporate Governance, and Post-IPO Performance of China's Newly Partially Privatized Firms," *Journal of Financial Economics* 84 (May 2007), 330–357.

Julian Franks and Colin Mayer, "Ownership and Control of German Corporations," *Review of Financial Studies* 14 (Winter 2001), 943–977.

Jun-Koo Kang and Anil Shivdasani, "Firm Performance, Corporate Governance, and Top Executive Turnover in Japan," *Journal of Financial Economics* 38 (May 1995), 29–58.

Jun-Koo Kang and Anil Shivdasani, "Does the Japanese Governance System Enhance Shareholder Wealth? Evidence from the Stock-Price Effects of Top Management Turnover," *Review of Financial Studies* 9 (Winter 1996), 1061–1095.

### The value of corporate control rights is assessed in

Reena Aggarwal, Isil Erel, René Stulz, and Rohan Williamson, "Differences in Governance Practices between U.S. and Foreign Firms: Measurement, Causes, and Consequences," *Review of Financial Studies* 23 (March 2010), 3245–3285.

Christian Leuz, Karl V. Lins, and Francis E. Warnock, "Do Foreigners Invest Less in Poorly Governed Firms?" *Review of Financial Studies* 23 (March 2010), 3245–3285.

Tatiana Nenova, "The Value of Corporate Votes and Control Benefits: A Cross-Country Analysis," *Journal of Financial Economics* 68 (June 2003), 325–351.

# PART Five

# International Portfolio Investment and Asset Pricing

*There are more things in heaven and earth, Horatio, Than are dreamt of in your philosophy.*

—Shakespeare, *Hamlet*

# CHAPTER 18

# International Capital Markets

*Toto, I have a feeling we're not in Kansas anymore.*

—Dorothy, in the *Wizard of Oz*

***Capital markets*** are markets for long-term assets and liabilities, with maturities greater than one year. The two most important capital markets are the markets for publicly traded stocks and bonds. Investments in internationally traded stocks and bonds are attractive for two reasons. First, international diversification results in lower portfolio risk than purely domestic diversification because of the relatively low correlations among national market returns. Second, although much of the world's wealth resides in developed markets, emerging markets are more likely to experience above-average economic growth. As information and transaction costs fall, investors in search of higher returns or lower portfolio risk increasingly are investing in international capital markets.

## 18.1 DOMESTIC AND INTERNATIONAL BOND MARKETS

Bonds can be categorized according to whether they are sold in domestic or international markets. International bonds can be further categorized as foreign bonds, Eurobonds, or global bonds.

- ***Domestic bonds*** are issued by a domestic company, traded within that country's internal market, and denominated in the functional currency of that country.
- ***International bonds*** are traded outside the country of the issuer.
  - ***Foreign bonds*** are issued in a domestic (internal) market by a foreign borrower, denominated in domestic currency, and regulated by domestic authorities.
  - ***Eurobonds*** are traded in external bond markets outside the borders of the country issuing the currency in which the bond is denominated.
  - ***Global bonds*** trade as Eurobonds, as well as in one or more domestic bond markets.

As shown in Figure 18.1, debt constitutes more than two-thirds of all publicly traded debt and equity securities in the world. Governments are the most active

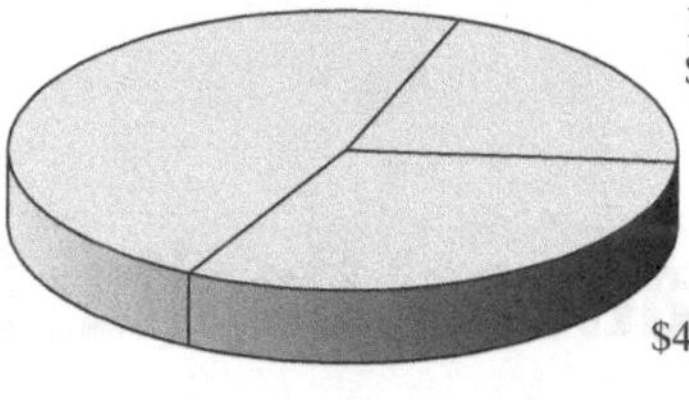

**FIGURE 18.1** Publicly Traded Debt and Equity Securities, $ trillions.
*Source:* Debt is from the BIS Quarterly Review, September 2011, Bank for International Settlements (www.bis.org). Equity value is from the World Federation of Exchanges (www.world-exchanges.org) as of September 2011.

issuers of international debt, accounting for $22.0 trillion (74 percent) of the $29.6 trillion total. Financial institutions are the most active domestic issuers, accounting for $40.0 trillion (58 percent) of the $68.7 trillion total.

Figure 18.2 displays the largest national issuers of debt securities based on data from the Bank for International Settlements. The $25.5 trillion U.S. market is the largest domestic market. Borrowers from the 17 Eurozone countries have issued $14.1 trillion in domestic debt, slightly more than in Japan's $13.6 trillion market.[1] China's $3.0 trillion domestic debt market is small relative to the size of China's economy, but is growing at a faster rate than any other market.

Borrowers in the international debt markets include multinational corporations (MNCs), governments and their agencies, and the World Bank. These well-known borrowers often find that their financing costs are lower in international markets than in domestic markets. In contrast, smaller borrowers usually find their financing costs are lower in their domestic debt market than in the international debt market because of the higher information costs faced by international investors.

| Rank | Country | Total | Domestic | Int'l | Rank | Country | Total | Domestic | Int'l |
|---|---|---|---|---|---|---|---|---|---|
| 1 | United States | 32,228 | 25,475 | 6,753 | 19 | Denmark | 772 | 613 | 159 |
| 2 | Japan | 13,754 | 13,575 | 179 | 20 | India | 738 | 711 | 26 |
| 3 | United Kingdom | 5,636 | 1,727 | 3,909 | 21 | Greece | 646 | 275 | 371 |
| 4 | France | 5,552 | 3,421 | 2,131 | 22 | Mexico | 556 | 451 | 105 |
| 5 | Germany | 5,066 | 2,815 | 2,251 | 23 | Norway | 504 | 260 | 244 |
| 6 | Italy | 4,486 | 3,236 | 1,250 | 24 | Luxembourg | 476 | 1 | 475 |
| 7 | Spain | 3,201 | 1,576 | 1,625 | 25 | Portugal | 468 | 276 | 192 |
| 8 | Netherlands | 3,186 | 1,049 | 2,137 | 26 | Switzerland | 329 | 292 | 37 |
| 9 | China | 3,075 | 3,048 | 27 | 27 | Malaysia | 306 | 278 | 28 |
| 10 | Canada | 2,245 | 1,535 | 710 | 28 | Poland | 294 | 230 | 64 |
| 11 | Australia | 1,704 | 1,085 | 619 | 29 | Turkey | 286 | 233 | 53 |
| 12 | Brazil | 1,661 | 1,528 | 133 | 30 | Chinese Taipei | 268 | 259 | 9 |
| 13 | Ireland | 1,590 | 345 | 1,245 | 31 | Finland | 264 | 85 | 179 |
| 14 | South Korea | 1,324 | 1,175 | 149 | 32 | Thailand | 236 | 228 | 8 |
| 15 | Cayman Islands | 1,152 | - | 1,152 | 33 | South Africa | 220 | 186 | 34 |
| 16 | Belgium | 943 | 576 | 367 | 34 | Singapore | 195 | 131 | 64 |
| 17 | Sweden | 867 | 445 | 422 | 35 | Russia | 154 | 81 | 73 |
| 18 | Austria | 781 | 383 | 398 | 36 | Hong Kong SAR | 147 | 65 | 83 |
| | | | | | | All countries | 98,351 | 68,717 | 29,634 |

**FIGURE 18.2** National Debt Markets by Residence of Issuer, $ billions.
*Source:* BIS Quarterly Review September 2011 (www.bis.org).

Nearly four-fifths ($23.3 trillion) of the $29.6 trillion international debt has been issued by borrowers from the United States, the United Kingdom, or one of the 17 Eurozone countries. International organizations ($1.0 trillion) such as the World Bank and issuers residing in off-shore financial centers such as the Cayman Islands ($1.2 trillion) also are active in the international market.

## Domestic Bonds—"When in Rome . . ."

> *Domestic authorities regulate domestic bonds.*

The most prominent bonds in most national markets are domestic bonds. Because they are issued and traded in the country's internal market, domestic bonds are regulated by the domestic government and are traded according to domestic conventions.

Government bonds trade over-the-counter (OTC) through commercial banks in the United States. Corporate bonds are traded OTC, as well as on the bond-trading floor of the New York Stock Exchange (NYSE). In other national markets, publicly traded corporate bonds are either exchange-listed or traded OTC by commercial and investment banks.

The "GMAC 7.25 20" bond in Figure 18.3 is a 7.25% coupon note issued by GMAC LLC, maturing in 2020, and traded in the domestic U.S. market on the NYSE bond-trading platform. The "FNMA 7.25 30" bond also trades in the domestic U.S. market, as well as in the external Eurobond market. A bond that trades as a Eurobond as well as in one or more national bond markets is called a ***global bond.*** Trade in domestic bond markets are regulated by domestic authorities (e.g., by the Securities and Exchange Commission (SEC) in the United States).

In most markets, bond prices are quoted as price-plus-accrued-interest. Bonds quoted with this convention do not necessarily fall in price on an ex-payment date, making it easier to compare prices across bonds with different coupons or payment dates. Exceptions to this convention include U.K. government bonds ("gilts") with a maturity of more than five years and some convertible and index-linked bonds. These bonds are quoted with coupons attached and fall in price on an ex-payment date in much the same way that stock prices fall on an ex-dividend date. Markets vary along several other dimensions, some of which are listed in Figure 18.4.

| | International bonds | |
|---|---|---|
| **Domestic bonds** | **Foreign bonds** | **Eurobonds** |
| GMAC 7.25 20 (NYSE) | Toronto Dominion 2.375 16 (OTC) | FNMA7.25 30 (OTC) |
| **Internal markets** | | **External markets** |

**FIGURE 18.3** Bond Market Taxonomy from a U.S. Perspective.

| Type of bond | Ownership | Coupon payments | Day count for accrued interest |
|---|---|---|---|
| Domestic & foreign bonds | | | |
| Australia | Registered | Semiannual | Actual/Actual |
| Canada | Registered | Semiannual | Actual/365 |
| Eurozone | Bearer | Semiannual or annual | Actual/Actual |
| Japan | Registered | Semiannual | Actual/365 |
| Switzerland | Bearer | Semiannual or annual | 30/360 |
| United Kingdom | Bearer | Semiannual | Actual/Actual |
| United States | Registered | Semiannual | Actual/Actual |
| Eurobonds | | | |
| Fixed rate bonds | Bearer | Annual | Actual/Actual |
| Floating rate notes | Bearer | Quarterly or semiannual | Actual/360 (same as Eurocurrencies) |

**FIGURE 18.4** Government Bond Market Conventions.

**Registered versus Bearer Issues** Bonds are issued as ***registered bonds*** in many countries, including Japan and the United States. Bond registration facilitates payment of interest and principal, but also imposes a recordkeeping burden on the bond issuer or its agent to maintain the *holders of record*. Registered bonds typically pay quarterly or semiannual interest.

The convention in European countries is to use ***bearer bonds*** rather than registered bonds. Bearer bonds are redeemed by the holder and hence retain the anonymity of the bondholder. This can be important to some investors, such as those wishing to evade the local tax authorities. The bearer is assumed to be the legal owner of the bond, so bondholders must ensure that they retain control of the bonds. Bearer bonds usually are issued with semiannual or annual coupons because it is inconvenient to present bond coupons for payment of interest.

> *Bearer bonds retain the owner's anonymity.*

**Compounding and Yield Conventions** There are many national differences in how the coupon rate and yield-to-maturity on a bond are quoted, particularly when a bond pays interest on something other than an annual basis. Fortunately, most bond dealers and financial information providers now quote an ***effective annual yield*** that assumes annual compounding. Effective annual yields allow a direct comparison of bonds with different market values or payment schedules.

Consider a 2-year bond that pays 4 percent interest every six months and sells for 97.78 percent of par. The effective semiannual yield-to-maturity on this bond is the solution to

$$97.78 = \frac{4}{(1+i)^1} + \frac{4}{(1+i)^2} + \frac{4}{(1+i)^3} + \frac{104}{(1+i)^4}$$

or $i = 4.62$ percent per six months. The effective annual yield or annual percentage rate is then

$$\text{APR} = (1+i)^n - 1 \qquad (18.1)$$

where i is the periodic interest rate and n is the number of compounding periods per year. For this bond, APR = $(1.0462)^2 - 1 = 0.0945$, or 9.45 percent per year. Effective annual yields allow a direct comparison of bond yields across national bond markets. This is important, because national markets have some rather peculiar local conventions.

For example, the convention in the United States is to assume semiannual compounding in the coupon and yield quotations. A bond that pays 4 percent interest every six months is quoted as having an 8 percent coupon. The semiannual compounding period is assumed. If the effective semiannual yield is 4.62 percent as above, the bond is quoted with a yield of $2 \times 4.62\% = 9.24$ percent. Semiannual compounding is again assumed, and the bond's yield is said to be quoted "on an annualized basis." To make matters even worse, U.S. bond prices are quoted in 32nds of a dollar, so that a price of 97.78 percent of par would be quoted as "97-25", or $97^{25}/_{32}$. Fortunately, bond prices elsewhere in the world are decimalized; that is, quoted as 1/100th of a currency unit.

*Bond quotation customs can be arcane.*

Bond quotation conventions in other countries can be equally arcane. Rather than provide examples of these "legacy" quotation conventions, we'll simply remind the reader to be aware that bond quotation conventions vary across national markets. When in doubt, it is always best to compare bond yields using the effective annual yield or APR. Most dealers and information providers quote APRs alongside the legacy quotations to facilitate comparisons.

**Day Count Conventions** Bond markets also differ in the ***day count*** convention that defines the way in which interest accrues on a bond. For example, Swiss bonds and U.S. corporate bonds are quoted as "30/360" assuming a 360-day year with 30-day months. Under this convention, no interest accrues on the 31st of a month. A U.S. corporate bond paying 10 percent interest on a semiannual basis would be quoted on February 6 assuming the bondholder is entitled to 30 days interest from January plus 5 days interest from February for $0.05(35/180) \approx 0.00972$, or 0.972 percent of the principal. Accrued interest in January would be $0.05(30/180) \approx 0.00833$, or 0.833 percent of the principal, because no interest accrues on January 31. The last day of February receives the last several days' worth of February interest; three days' interest is received on the 28th of February when this is the last day of the month. This day count convention made it easy to calculate accrued interest across months before the advent of computers, as there were always 30 days of accrued interest in each month.

*Day counts define how interest accrues.*

Prices on Canadian government bonds are quoted as "actual/365" assuming a 365-day year and interest that accrues according to the actual number of days that have passed since the most recent payment. Consider a Canadian government bond with a 10 percent coupon that pays 5 percent semiannually on June 30 and on December 31. If it is now February 6, then 36 days (January 1 through February 5) have elapsed since the last coupon interest payment. There are 181 days from January 1 to June 30 (except in leap years), so the bond price is quoted assuming the bondholder is entitled to $0.05(36/181) \approx 0.009945$, or 0.9945 percent of the principal as accrued interest. Note that there are 184 days in the period from July 1 to December 31.

## Foreign Bonds—Strangers in a Strange Land

> *Foreign bonds are issued by a foreign borrower.*

Foreign bonds are issued in an internal domestic market by a foreign borrower, denominated in domestic currency, marketed to domestic residents, and regulated by domestic authorities. Foreign bonds are priced according to domestic conventions to make the bonds attractive to domestic residents. Foreign bonds are known as *Yankee bonds* in the United States, *Bulldog bonds* in the United Kingdom, *Samurai bonds* in Japan, and *Rembrandt bonds* in the Netherlands. By far the greatest value of foreign bonds is traded in Switzerland, followed by the United States and then Japan. In Eurozone countries, foreign bonds have largely been supplanted by the euro-denominated Eurobond market.

The "Toronto Dominion 2.375 16" listed in Figure 18.3 is a dollar-denominated foreign bond issued in the domestic U.S. internal market by Canada's Toronto Dominion Bank. This Yankee bond is traded OTC through commercial and investment banks in the United States, pays a 2.375 percent semiannual coupon, and matures in 2016.

For a foreign borrower to place its debt at competitive prices, the issuer should be well known in the host country. One of the largest issuers of foreign bonds in the U.S. market is the World Bank, with a variety of maturities worth more than $35 billion. Less well-known and creditworthy borrowers receive lower prices and higher yields for their bonds.

## Eurobonds—Necessity Is the Mother of Invention

Eurobonds are issued and traded in an external market. The "FNMA 7.25 30" Eurobond in Figure 18.3 is a dollar-denominated bond issued by the Federal National Mortgage Association with a 7.25 percent annual coupon and a maturity date in 2030. This Eurobond was issued directly to non-U.S. investors (in this case, by a U.S. borrower) in an external, public debt market.

**Origins of the Eurobond Market** As with many financial innovations, the Eurobond market was born as borrowers and investors sought ways to circumvent government restrictions on cross-border capital flows. Two government-imposed barriers gave birth to the Eurobond market. The first was a U.S. tax on interest paid to U.S.

investors by foreign borrowers that negatively affected the U.S. market for foreign bonds. Rather than go directly to the U.S. market, foreign borrowers began to issue dollar-denominated bonds outside the United States. The U.S. tax lasted until 1974, but by that time the Eurodollar bond market was firmly established.

*Eurobonds trade in external markets.*

The second barrier was a U.S. interest withholding tax imposed on domestic bonds that made it expensive for foreign investors to own U.S. bonds. Eurobonds were an attractive alternative for investors wishing to own dollar-denominated bonds and avoid the interest withholding tax. When the United States dropped the withholding tax on domestic bonds in 1984, the Eurodollar bond market and the domestic U.S. bond market became close substitutes for non-U.S. investors.

Once the benefits of Eurodollar bonds became apparent, Eurobonds denominated in other currencies soon followed. Several thousand Eurobond issues now trade in the international market, usually denominated in U.S. dollars, euros, British pounds sterling, or Japanese yen.

**The Market for Euro-Denominated Eurobonds** The 12 gold stars on the European Union (EU) flag represent the 12 founding members of the European Economic Community, the predecessor of the EU (http://europa.eu/index_en.htm). Although there are now 27 EU members, only 17 had adopted the euro as of 2012. Denmark, Sweden, and the United Kingdom elected to retain their national currencies, while newer EU entrants had not yet met the convergence criteria.

*Euro issues are displacing bank loans.*

The bonds of Eurozone governments and supranational agencies converted to the euro in January 1999 according to each currency's value in the European exchange rate grid. Each nation determined the legal basis for conversion of bonds trading in its own internal market. The European Commission established rules for the conversion of external market Eurobonds.

Many European companies find that euro-denominated Eurobonds offer attractive interest rates relative to bank financing. Indeed, Eurobonds are displacing loans by commercial banks, the traditional source of capital for European businesses. A study by the Bank for International Settlements estimated that one-third of European banks' commercial loan business was diverted to public debt and equity issues by the introduction of the euro. European banks have expanded their investment banking activities as public issues displaced some of their commercial lending business. Liquidity in the market is attracting borrowers from non-Eurozone countries as well.

Eurobond dealers are members of the *International Capital Market Association* (www.icma-group.org), a self-regulated industry group based in Zurich. No commissions are charged in the Eurobond market. Instead, dealers make their profit through the bid-ask spread. Transactions in the secondary Eurobond market are settled either through the Brussels-based *Euroclear* (www.euroclear.com) system or the *Clearstream* (www.clearstream.com) system of the Deutsche Börse Group.

### Global Bonds

A *global bond* trades as a Eurobond as well as in one or more national bond markets. To appeal to a global investor base, borrowers must be large investment-grade borrowers (typically AAA-rated) and must borrow in an actively traded currency. The World Bank established this market in the late 1980s with a series of dollar-denominated issues that traded in both the domestic U.S. and the Eurodollar markets. For many years, global bonds were denominated in dollars or pounds to take advantage of high liquidity in these markets. Since the introduction of the euro in 1999, global bonds increasingly have been issued in euros.

> *Global bonds trade as Eurobonds and in one or more internal markets.*

Matsushita Electric Industrial Company was the first corporate borrower to tap the global bond market. In 1992, Matsushita issued $1 billion of 10-year, fixed rate bonds at 7.25 percent (41 basis points higher than on 10-year U.S. Treasuries). Matsushita's original allocation was 40 percent to the domestic U.S. bond market, 40 percent to Europe, and 20 percent to the Asia/Pacific region. This initial allocation did not constrain where these bonds were traded in the secondary market, so subsequent trades could occur in domestic bond markets or in the Eurobond market.

## 18.2 DOMESTIC AND INTERNATIONAL STOCK MARKETS

Figure 18.5 ranks the world's largest national stock markets by market capitalization. The United States has by far the largest equity market, with a total market capitalization of $18.0 trillion as of mid-2011. Japan was second at $4.1 trillion, and the United Kingdom was third at $3.7 trillion. China has the fastest growing national market, led by stock exchanges in Hong Kong, Shanghai, and Shenzhen. India has the second-fastest growing market, led by the Bombay Stock Exchange near Mumbai and a National Stock Exchange that links several regional exchanges.[2]

Although each national capital market retains some of its unique local character, these markets are converging in many ways. The most visible change is in the way information is processed and disseminated. Trades and prices are now tracked by computer and relayed around the globe to other markets nearly instantaneously via satellite. Telecommunications technologies have forged the segmented national markets of the 20th century into an increasingly integrated international network for the 21st century.

| Exchange | Country | Market cap | % of total |
|---|---|---|---|
| 1 NYSE Euronext/US | USA | 14,024 | 25.2 |
| 2 National Association of Securities Dealers Automated Quotation System (NASDAQ) OMX Group | USA | 3,952 | 7.1 |
| 3 Tokyo Stock Exchange (TSE) Group | Japan | 3,842 | 6.9 |
| 4 London Stock Exchange (LSE) Group | UK | 3,701 | 6.7 |
| 5 NYSE Euronext/Europe | Europe | 3,091 | 5.6 |
| 6 Shanghai Stock Exchange | China | 2,724 | 4.9 |
| 7 Hong Kong Stock Exchange | China | 2,724 | 4.9 |
| 8 Toronto Stock Exchange (TSX) Group | Canada | 2,183 | 3.9 |
| 9 BM&FBOVESPA | Brazil | 1,477 | 2.7 |
| 10 Deutsche Börse | Germany | 1,475 | 2.7 |
| 11 Bombay Stock Exchange | India | 1,437 | 2.6 |
| 12 Australian Stock Exchange (ASX) | Australia | 1,421 | 2.6 |
| 13 National Stock Exchange India | India | 1,403 | 2.5 |
| 14 BME Spanish Exchanges | Spain | 1,242 | 2.2 |
| 15 Shenzhen Stock Exchange | China | 1,233 | 2.2 |
| 16 SIX Swiss Exchange | Switzerland | 1,225 | 2.2 |
| 17 Korea Exchange (KRX) | South Korea | 1,122 | 2.0 |
| 18 NASDAQ OMX Nordic | N. Europe | 1,072 | 1.9 |
| 19 MICEX | Russia | 999 | 1.8 |
| 20 Johannesburg Stock Exchange (JSE) | South Africa | 841 | 1.5 |
| 21 Taiwan Stock Exchange (TWSE) Corp. | Taiwan | 837 | 1.5 |
| 22 Singapore Exchange (SGX) | Singapore | 647 | 1.2 |
| 23 Mexican Exchange (BMV) | Mexico | 449 | 0.8 |
| 24 Bursa Malaysia (KLSE) | Malaysia | 413 | 0.7 |
| 25 Tadawul | Saudi Arabia | 340 | 0.6 |
| 26 Indonesia Stock Exchange (IDX) | Indonesia | 333 | 0.6 |
| 27 Santiago Stock Exchange (SSE) | Chile | 320 | 0.6 |
| 28 Oslo Børs | Norway | 295 | 0.5 |
| 29 Istanbul Stock Exchange | Turkey | 283 | 0.5 |
| 30 Osaka Stock Exchange | Japan | 271 | 0.5 |
| 31 Stock Exchange of Thailand | Thailand | 254 | 0.5 |
| 32 Tel Aviv Stock Exchange | Israel | 216 | 0.4 |
| 33 Colombia Stock Exchange | Colombia | 207 | 0.4 |
| 34 Warsaw Stock Exchange | Poland | 195 | 0.3 |
| 35 Philippine Stock Exchange | Philippines | 157 | 0.3 |
| 36 Wiener Börse | Austria | 129 | 0.2 |
| 37 Lima Stock Exchange | Peru | 105 | 0.2 |
| 38 Luxembourg Stock Exchange | Luxembourg | 99 | 0.2 |
| 39 Tehran Stock Exchange | Iran | 96 | 0.2 |
| 40 Casablanca Stock Exchange | Morocco | 70 | 0.1 |
| 41 Egyptian Exchange | Egypt | 70 | 0.1 |
| 42 Athens Exchange | Greece | 69 | 0.1 |
| 43 Buenos Aires Stock Exchange | Argentina | 66 | 0.1 |
| 44 Irish Stock Exchange | Ireland | 62 | 0.1 |
| 45 Amman Stock Exchange | Jordan | 31 | 0.1 |
| 46 Budapest Stock Exchange | Hungary | 31 | 0.1 |
| 47 Colombo Stock Exchange | Sri Lanka | 21 | 0.0 |
| 48 Ljubljana Stock Exchange | Slovenia | 9 | 0.0 |
| 49 Cyprus Stock Exchange | Cyprus | 8 | 0.0 |
| 50 Mauritius Stock Exchange | Mauritius | 8 | 0.0 |
| World | | 55,606 | 100 |

**FIGURE 18.5** World's Largest Stock Exchanges (in $ billions).
*Source:* January 2011 market cap from World Federation of Exchanges (www.world-exchanges.org).

## Financial Exchanges and the Global Competition for Trading Volume

Liquidity leads to better (more informed) prices as well as lower transaction costs, so securities trade tends to migrate toward the most liquid markets. The arrival of electronic trading in the 1990s upset the old order of floor-based trade and spawned a merger wave among the world's exchanges. New alliances between these exchanges are ongoing as they seek to defend existing markets, pursue new or competing markets, and reduce settlement and clearing costs. Liquidity in global financial markets thus promotes operational, informational, and allocational efficiency.

> *Trade migrates toward liquidity.*

The NYSE is the world's largest stock exchange, with more than 2,500 U.S. listings and about 450 non-U.S. listings. The NYSE floor-trading auction system remained largely unchanged for more than 200 years after its introduction in 1792. The NYSE introduced a hybrid market in 2007 that combined elements of its traditional auction market with an electronic market. The NYSE also introduced an electronic market called *Arca* that trades more than 8,000 exchange-listed securities from around the world. The NYSE's most significant change was its 2007 merger with the pan-European exchange Euronext to form *NYSE Euronext*. This alliance trades about a third of the world's equity.

*Euronext* was formed in 2000 through a merger of the Amsterdam, Brussels, and Paris exchanges. Euronext acquired the London International Financial Futures and Options Exchange (LIFFE) in 2002 to form Euronext LIFFE, which trades financial derivatives. The Lisbon (Portugal) exchange also joined in 2002. Euronext then merged with the NYSE in 2007 to form NYSE Euronext, after rejecting offers from the Nasdaq and Deutsche Börse Group of Germany.

The *NASDAQ OMX Group* was formed in 2002 and operates 24 exchanges in the United States and northern Europe. The largest of these is the *Nasdaq*, which trades spot, futures and options contracts on a variety of financial products including equities and currencies. Nasdaq OMX operates financial markets in several other countries, including Denmark (Copenhagen), Finland (Helsinki), and Sweden (Stockholm). These exchanges compete with more than 30 other European exchanges.

The TSE is Asia's largest stock exchange, although the Osaka Stock Exchange also is quite large. The value of stocks traded in Japan actually surpassed the value of stocks traded on the NYSE in the late 1980s, but then fell behind the NYSE during the 1990–1991 crash in Japanese markets. The aftershocks of this collapse are still present in Japanese industry and politics, as well as in financial market institutions and regulations. Falling volume on the TSE after the crash prompted an exodus of foreign listings from Tokyo to exchanges in other Asian countries. Foreign listings on the TSE fell from 125 during its heyday in 1990 to only 12 at year-end 2011. The Tokyo and Osaka exchanges announced a 2013 merger (subject to the approval of the Japan Fair Trade Commission) in an attempt to retain their place in the markets.

> *The TSE is Asia's largest exchange.*

The LSE is Europe's largest exchange. London holds a special place in international finance because of the prominence of its currency and Eurocurrency markets. Not surprisingly, the LSE is the world's center for international listings, with 598 firms from more than 50 countries as of year-end 2011. The LSE owns *AIM* (Alternative Investment Market) for small companies and *EDX London* (Equity Derivatives Exchange) for derivatives, and is a majority owner of *MTS* (Mercato Telematico di Stato) for fixed-income securities.

> *The LSE is Europe's largest exchange.*

China has enjoyed rapid stock market growth in recent years. The *Shanghai Stock Exchange* is the largest exchange on the mainland. International investors have several vehicles for investing in Chinese companies, including as H-shares on the Hong Kong Stock Exchange, as N-shares on the NYSE, as L-shares on the LSE, or as B-shares on the Shanghai and Shenzhen exchanges. Chinese exchanges historically have not listed foreign shares of non-Chinese companies, although this restriction is being relaxed.

> *China is the world's fastest growing market.*

Around 7,000 companies are listed in India, although many of these are thinly traded. Market value is nearly evenly split between the *Bombay Stock Exchange* and the *National Stock Exchange*, both located in Mumbai. As in China, very few foreign shares are listed. Foreign portfolio investment was prohibited until 1992, when foreign investors were allowed to own up to 24 percent of a firm's equity. Many Indian firms took advantage of the opportunity to sell shares on exchanges outside of India. India further relaxed its investment restrictions during the 1990s.

*Deutsche Börse Group*, which owns the Frankfurt Stock Exchange, is a major competitor on the European continent. The Frankfurt Stock Exchange accounts for 75 percent of German share trading. To remain viable, smaller exchanges in Germany and elsewhere on the continent, including Hungary (Budapest), Ireland (Dublin), Austria (Vienna), and Switzerland (Zurich), are forming alliances with the Frankfurt exchange. As of late 2011, Deutsche Börse Group again was in negotiations with NYSE Euronext regarding an acquisition or a merger.

A number of other national or regional exchanges trade equities, including in Canada (TSX Group), Brazil (BM&F), Australia (ASX), Spain (BME), Switzerland (SIX), Korea (KRX), Russia (MICEX), South Africa (JSE), Taiwan (TWSE), Singapore (SGX), Mexico (BMV), Malaysia (KLSE), Saudi Arabia (Tadawul), Indonesia (IDX), and Chile (SSE). Some of these serve as hubs for the shares of firms from the region. In particular, the stock exchanges in Singapore, Mexico, and Luxembourg each list more than 250 foreign shares.

## MARKET UPDATE Share Classes in China

China's equity markets are rapidly developing under the direction of the *China Securities Regulatory Commission* (CSRC). The shares of public listed companies in China fall into the following categories.

### Shares available to domestic investors

- *State shares.* Held by the central or local government or a government-owned institution. State shares are not publicly traded, but can be transferred to another domestic institution with the approval of the CSRC.
- *Legal person shares.* Shares owned by domestic institutions. A legal person is a nonindividual legal entity. These shares are not traded, but can be transferred to other domestic institutions with the CSRC's approval.

- *Employee shares.* Offered to employees, usually at a discount to market value. Employees can sell their shares with the CSRC's approval, although top management cannot sell shares during their term of office.
- *A-shares.* Traded on Chinese exchanges and held by domestic individuals and institutions. There is no restriction on the number of shares traded, but there is a requirement that A-shares account for no less than 25 percent of total outstanding shares at the time of an initial public offering (IPO).

**Shares available to foreign investors**

- *B-shares.* Traded on Chinese stock exchanges, but available only to foreign investors and some selected domestic securities firms with the approval of the CSRC. B-shares are denominated in U.S. dollars on the Shanghai Stock Exchange, and in Hong Kong dollars on the Hong Kong and Shenzhen Stock Exchanges.
- *H-shares.* Traded on the Hong Kong Stock Exchange with the same rights and privileges as A-shares. H-shares currently cannot be traded on mainland Chinese exchanges, although this may change.
- *N-shares.* Traded on the NYSE with the same rights and privileges as A-shares. N-shares cannot be traded on domestic Chinese exchanges.

State ownership is central to management and control of Chinese firms, as the government is the largest (and often the majority) shareholder in nearly half of Chinese listed stocks.

## Institutional Differences in Stock Exchange Operations

The traditional stock exchange was a floor-trading system in a single physical location. The growth of electronic trading platforms during the 1990s transformed the way in which stocks are traded at both wholesale and retail levels.

The two most common methods for setting prices are a continuous quotation system and a periodic call auction. In a ***continuous quotation system***, buy and sell orders are matched as they arrive. The market-making function might be provided by a specialist (a single individual with a monopoly on trading in particular shares) as on the NYSE, through dealers (called "jobbers" on the LSE) competing with one another and quoting bid and ask prices, or through automated rules as on electronic trading systems. A ***periodic call auction*** sometimes is used for less actively traded shares in floor-trading systems. For example, active shares are traded continuously on the Paris Bourse while less active shares are auctioned at intervals throughout the day.

*Trading systems can be continuous or periodic.*

The most common share-trading procedure is on a spot (or cash) basis. This procedure is used on most U.S., Japanese, and German exchanges. An alternative procedure is on a forward (or futures) basis, with transactions settled on a specified future date. For example, forward trades historically have been settled biweekly in London and at the end of the month in Paris. Stock exchanges that trade on a forward basis also trade on a spot basis or provide some mechanism for customers demanding spot transactions.

> *Trades are settled on a spot or a forward basis.*

Like forward currency transactions, forward stock transactions are a form of credit instrument. Delivery is made either in cash (in a long stock trade) or in stock (in a short stock trade) on a specified future delivery date. The difference between the spot and forward price for a share of stock reflects the market rate of interest in that currency. To ensure settlement, some form of deposit usually is required on forward stock transactions.

Some markets allow margin trading—buying stock on borrowed money—as another form of stock purchase on credit. The margin account can be low risk to the broker because it is secured by shares of stock, so interest rates on margin accounts can approach the level of short-term government interest rates.

## International Differences in Securities Regulation

National differences in securities regulations create impediments to cross-border securities issues, although these barriers are lower for MNCs that frequently access international markets than for domestic companies that haven't accessed international markets.

**Securities Regulation in the United States** The Securities Exchange Act of 1933 governs new securities issues in the United States, and the Securities Exchange Act of 1934 governs U.S. secondary market activity. The Financial Services Modernization Act of 1999 deregulated the U.S. financial services industry, so that there is currently relatively open competition between commercial and investment banks, brokers, insurers, pension funds, mutual funds, and other financial companies.

> *The SEC regulates U.S. securities trading.*

Companies issuing debt or equity securities to the U.S. public in amounts greater than $1.5 million are required to file a registration statement with the *SEC* that discloses all relevant information regarding the transaction. The registration procedure applies to all securities issues with two exceptions.

- Loans maturing within nine months
- Private placements

The first exception explicitly recognizes the difference between short-term money market and long-term capital market securities. Issues with maturities of less than nine months must be accompanied by a brief ***offering statement*** rather than the full-fledged registration statement.

The second exception treats private placements differently from public securities issues. This has an enormous influence on the types of public disclosures that must be made and the type of control exerted by outside stakeholders in the firm. In the United States, ***private placements*** as defined by the Securities Exchange Act of 1933 conform to all five of the following conditions:

- Shares are sold to large and sophisticated investors
- Shares are sold to only a few investors
- Investors must have access to information like that in a registration statement
- Investors are capable of sustaining losses
- Investors purchase the securities for their own portfolios and not for resale

Securities issues satisfying these conditions presumably are placed with informed investors that are able to obtain information and judge the merits of the investment.

If an offering does not conform to these criteria, then it is a ***public securities offering*** and falls under the SEC's jurisdiction. U.S. securities laws require complete and accurate disclosure of all relevant information for public issues to ensure that investors are not fooled by exaggerated claims or outrageous promises. The securities laws do not ensure that an investment will meet its promised or expected return. Instead, the laws are designed to ensure that investors have enough information to judge the merits of a proposed investment for themselves.

**Securities Regulation in Japan** New public issues in Japan must be approved by the ***Japanese Ministry of Finance.*** The issue is priced and sold after the waiting period, as in the United States and other markets. The waiting period for new issues can be several months, which is somewhat longer than in most other markets. The Japanese government takes an active role in determining which companies are allowed to issue securities and in regulating trade in these issues.

> *Japan's Ministry of Finance regulates securities in Japan.*

Commercial banks entered the investment banking and brokerage industries in 1995 as a part of Japan's "big bang" financial deregulation, although securities activities must be kept separate from lending activities. Initially, five banks (Dai-Ichi Kangyo, Fuji, Sanwa, Sakura, and Mitsubishi) won approval to compete in the securities industry. Sumitomo Bank's proposal initially failed to win approval because the proposed name, Sumigin (a contraction of the characters for Sumitomo Bank), appeared to link Sumitomo's commercial and investment banking interests (the Japanese character for gin means "bank"). Today, all of Japan's big banks offer investment banking and brokerage services.

**Securities Regulation in the European Union** The European Union has passed a series of Directives designed to harmonize securities regulation and market operation across its member states.

*The CRD sets capital adequacy standards.*

The *Investment Securities Directive (ISD)* of 1993 provides investment firms (brokers, dealers, and securities exchanges) based in EU member states a "single passport" to operate in other EU countries if they have the approval of regulatory authorities in their home country. Firms must satisfy several conditions to qualify.

- The firm must meet the EU's capital adequacy requirements
- The firm's directors must be sufficiently experienced
- The firm must appropriately safeguard its clients' funds

The EU's *Markets in Financial Instruments Directive (MiFID)* of 2004 widens the scope of the "single passport" to trade in other financial contracts, such as commodity and credit derivatives. It also establishes the obligations of member states in regard to securities regulation. Provisions include

- *Investor protection.* The MiFID requires that member states have effective mechanisms for investigating and prosecuting violations of the rules.
- *Transparency and market integrity.* The MiFID obligates members to safeguard market integrity through transparency and reporting requirements. For example, dealers are required to disclose bid and ask prices to their clients for transactions that exceed the size of an average order.
- *Operator protection.* The MiFID establishes protections for dealers so that they can perform their market-making function without undue risk. For example, dealers cannot discriminate between retail investors by offering different quotes, but are allowed to update or withdraw their quotes.

*The MiFID widens the scope of the EU's "single passport."*

Securities regulation in the EU is not yet fully harmonized, and there remain differences in the regulations of individual member states.

The *Capital Requirements Directive (CRD)* of 2006 protects savers and investors by specifying minimum standards governing the amount of market risk a European bank or securities firm can take in relation to its capital base. Standards continue to evolve as new tools are developed for measuring exposures to credit and other risks. A series of CRD Amendments are implementing the Basel III standards on bank capital adequacy and liquidity within the EU.

In response to the 2008 financial crisis, the EU is implementing an *Alternative Investment Fund Managers Directive (AIFMD) to* regulate private investment funds, such as hedge funds, private equity funds, and real estate funds, that might have contributed to the crisis. The objective is to increase transparency and investor protections in these funds. The "single passport" is being extended to these alternative investment vehicles, allowing these funds to "passport" their services throughout the EU once they are authorized in an EU member state.

## 18.3 INTERNATIONAL INVESTMENT VEHICLES

An increasingly wide variety of international investment vehicles is becoming available as global financial markets gain in volume and liquidity.

### Investment in Individual Foreign Securities

Foreign investors can buy debt and equity directly in many national markets. The costs and benefits of this route to international diversification depend on the assets and investment vehicles chosen, and on capital flow barriers between the domestic and foreign markets.

**Direct Purchase in the Foreign Market** The most straightforward way to diversify internationally is to buy foreign securities directly in foreign markets. Unfortunately for the small investor, there are several impediments to direct purchase in foreign markets.

- Higher *information costs* on foreign assets
  - Geographic distances
  - Language and cultural differences
  - Differences in taxation, accounting measurement, and disclosure conventions
- Higher *transaction costs* on foreign assets
  - Generally higher commissions on foreign trades than on domestic transactions
  - The need to convert dividends and capital gains received in a foreign currency into investors' domestic currencies
  - Differences in tax systems and tax rates, particularly local withholding taxes on dividend or interest income from some countries

> *It can be difficult to buy shares in foreign markets.*

These imperfections can present formidable costs for small investors. They are less of a problem for professional managers with experience in international markets and executing large trades.

**Direct Purchase in the Domestic Market** A growing number of MNCs are issuing shares directly in the world's largest equity markets. Companies can list their shares on foreign exchanges as global shares or as depository receipts.

***Global shares*** represent a claim on a single class of stock issued in multiple markets around the world. Even though they trade in a domestic market, global shares are in fact ***foreign shares*** because they are fungible one-for-one with global shares trading in other markets. Global shares are called ***global registered shares*** when they are registered and regulated by local authorities; for example, by the SEC in the U.S. market. MNCs that have issued global shares on the NYSE include Deutsche Bank (DB) and Union Bank of Switzerland (UBS). These shares trade on the NYSE in the same way they are listed and traded in their home market. The emergence of common clearing and settlement systems has facilitated the market for global shares.

*Foreign firms list as global shares or depository receipts.*

***Depository receipts*** are derivative securities that represent a claim on a block of foreign stock held by a domestic trustee. Depository receipts are denominated in the domestic currency, regulated by domestic authorities, and sold through domestic brokers. A depository receipt issued in the U.S. market is called an ***American depository receipt (ADR)***. ADRs are denominated in dollars and trade just like any other U.S. share. To issue an ADR, a foreign firm enlists an investment bank to purchase a block of shares and act as the trustee. The investment bank then issues dollar-denominated stock certificates—ADRs—in the U.S. market with foreign shares as collateral. The underlying asset is a portfolio of foreign shares held by the investment bank as trustee. Dividends are converted into dollars and distributed by the trustee. A depository receipt that trades in more than one foreign market is called a ***global depository receipt (GDR)***.

The prices of global shares and depository receipts depend on the value of the foreign shares in the foreign currency and the exchange rate according to $P^d = P^f S^{d/f}$. When transaction costs and capital flow barriers are small, arbitrage ensures that the law of one price holds. If there are large transaction costs or capital flow barriers, global shares and depository receipts can sell at premiums or discounts to their foreign market value. Because the global shares and depository receipts move in price with the domestic currency value of the foreign shares, from the perspective of domestic investors these securities have the same exchange rate exposure as the underlying foreign shares.

The SEC recognizes four different classes of ADRs.

- *Level I (unlisted/OTC)*. These are offered without following U.S. generally accepted accounting principles (GAAP) or registering with the SEC. These shares cannot be listed on a U.S. exchange and must trade OTC.
- *Level II (exchange-listed)*. These follow U.S. GAAP, are regulated by the SEC, and listed on an exchange. Disclosure requirements are slightly less than for U.S. firms.
- *Level III (exchange-listed)*. These follow the same GAAP and SEC disclosure requirements as U.S. companies. Level III is required for IPOs into the U.S. market.

- *Restricted programs*. These are either private placements within the United States (SEC Rule 144A) or are offered only to off-shore, non-U.S. residents (SEC Regulation S).

Levels II and III achieve the broadest exposure to the U.S. market, but are more expensive because the issuers must conform to U.S. GAAP and the SEC's registration requirements.

J.P.Morgan (www.adr.com) reported more than 3,400 depository receipts trading worldwide in 78 countries at the beginning of 2012. In the United States, the largest number of ADRs come from firms in India (340), followed by the United Kingdom (278), Japan (258), China (253), Australia (214), and Russia (204). The majority of U.S. ADRs are traded OTC or are restricted programs; only about one-fifth are exchange-listed. Depository receipts also are common on the London, Frankfurt, Euronext, and Singapore exchanges. Well-known foreign companies with shares trading as depository receipts include Royal Dutch Shell PLC (United Kingdom/energy) and Petrobras (Brazil/energy) on the NYSE, and Gazprom (Russia/energy) on the LSE.

## Professionally Managed Funds Specializing in International Assets

Investing in professionally managed investment funds is an excellent way for individual investors to capture the benefits of international diversification with relatively low transaction costs.

**Mutual Funds** Small investors face formidable information and transaction costs in international markets. These costs can be reduced by concentrating funds from many investors in a mutual fund managed by one or a few professional portfolio managers. Mutual funds are popular investment vehicles in all of the world's developed markets. Many global, regional, and country funds are available, as are a variety of sector or industry funds. Many of the largest funds are index funds that follow a passive buy-and-hold strategy in an attempt to mimic an equity index, such as the United Kingdom's FTSE 100 or Germany's DAX index. Other international funds are actively managed, either through security selection (stock picking) or asset allocation (shifting funds across asset classes in the hope of hitting the winners).

*Mutual funds pool funds from many investors.*

In an ***open-end fund***, the amount of money under management grows (or shrinks) as investors invest in (or disinvest from) the fund. Open-end funds are known as an "open-end investment companies" in the United Kingdom and "managed funds" in Australia. Management expenses on open-end funds typically fall in the range of $1/2$ to 3 percent per year. In a ***closed-end fund***, funds under management are fixed and shares are traded in the secondary market like a depository receipt. Fund families provide a menu of global, regional, country, and sector funds. For example,

## MARKET UPDATE Mark Mobius and Templeton Investments

Mark Mobius of Franklin Templeton Investments is well known as an international stock picker. With a Ph.D. in economics and political science from MIT, Mobius travels the world in search of investment opportunities. Templeton funds have approximately $100 billion under management.

Mobius is a vocal advocate of transparent accounting and corporate governance practices. After more than 35 years of investing in emerging markets, he has seen more than his share of fraud and crony capitalism. He states:

> *"Apologists in many countries retreat to the defense of cultural differences as an excuse for not implementing good corporate governance. But it is basically about fair play, and fairness has no regional, national, cultural, or ethnic boundaries. It's best for everyone to level the playing fields and to make business dealings transparent. Only then will confidence in these markets fully return, and only then will investors benefit fully from the potential that is in global markets."*

Mobius's point is that the risks of investing in emerging markets are directly related to accounting transparency and the fairness of local legal and corporate governance systems.

*Source: Asiaweek*, London Financial Times (November 30, 2001), p. 1.

NYSE-listed Franklin Templeton Funds (www.franklintempleton.com) includes the following Templeton Funds (along with their April 2012 asset allocations):

| | |
|---|---|
| World Fund | Europe (40%) North America (39%) Asia (17%) |
| Brazil, Russia, India, China (BRIC) Fund | Brazil (32%) China (31%) Russia (17%) |
| Global Bond Fund | Europe/Africa (40%) Asia (39%) Americas (9%) |
| China World Fund | Energy (29%) Food (13%) Banks (10%) |

Closed-end funds offered by mutual fund families have a front-loaded sales charge or back-loaded charge that is due upon sale, as well as an annual charge for management expenses.

A fund's ***net asset value (NAV)*** is the sum of the individual asset values in the fund. Domestic closed-end funds usually sell at a slight discount to NAV. International closed-end funds that have been open-ended and closed-end funds of countries or regions that have no restrictions on foreign investment also tend to sell at or slightly below NAV. When there are investment restrictions, closed-end funds sometimes can sell at a premium to NAV.[3]

Closed-end funds that trade as shares on an exchange are called ***exchange-traded funds (ETFs)***. ETFs are usually index funds that try to replicate the returns on a market index. An example of an ETF family in the United States is *iShares*, which trade on the NYSE and track a variety of indices including corporate and government bonds, industrial sectors (e.g., energy), and national, regional (e.g., Europe 350), and international stocks (e.g., Global 100).

*ETFs are exchange-traded, closed-end funds.*

**Hedge Funds** *Hedge funds* are private investment funds. In many countries, they are organized as partnerships or limited liability companies with a general manager and a small number of limited partners. In the United States, a typical hedge fund pays the general partner a 2 percent management fee and 20 percent of profits. Given these lucrative compensation packages, it is not surprising that each year the top money winners on Wall Street are hedge fund managers with annual incomes that can top $1 billion. For example, hedge fund manager George Soros (Quantum Fund) earned $1.5 billion in 1995 after winning a bet against the British pound. Investors in hedge funds include large pension funds and wealthy investors that can afford the partnership fee—often a minimum investment of $1 million and a minimum investment period of several years.[4] Invested funds cannot be easily liquidated because of the partnership organization.

*Hedge funds are private partnerships.*

Hedge funds became popular in the United States during the 1950s. The first hedge funds specialized in equity short sales. Today, hedge funds employ a wide variety of strategies with risks that range from near-zero to very high. There are also "funds of funds" that diversify across hedge funds. Hedge fund managers have wide latitude in the positions they take, often using strategies such as borrowing on margin, short selling, or derivative market transactions in their pursuit of returns.

Hedge funds frequently are criticized in the popular press because of their private status, the lucrative compensation packages paid to managers, and the speculative positions taken by some of the more aggressive funds. National authorities took a renewed interest in regulating hedge funds following the 2008 financial crisis.

***Private equity*** is a type of hedge fund that specializes in private companies. Private equity strategies include buyouts and venture capital investments. An example is Cerberus Capital Management's 2007 buyout of Chrysler Corporation from Daimler-Chrysler. Other private equity strategies include ***venture capital***, which provides funds for start-up companies. Entrepreneurs receive the venture capital in exchange for a portion of their equity and sometimes power over company affairs. Many of these investments have a high expected return, but also high risk. Investments are often illiquid, and investors cannot easily exit their investment until it yields a return through an IPO, a recapitalization, or a sale to another investor.[5]

## Index Derivatives

Index derivatives provide a way to trade international stock indices. For example, the LSE trades ***stock index futures*** contracts on several national market indices, including the French CAC-40, the German DAX, the Nikkei 225, and the Standard and Poor (S&P) 500.[6] Like currency futures, stock index futures require a margin and are marked-to-market daily.

*Index derivatives provide access to foreign markets.*

***Stock index options*** are traded on many international stocks and stock indices. In the United States, exchange-listed index options trade on a variety of national market indices and global sectors. Index options have asymmetric payoffs that can be used for hedging against, or speculating on, changes in a particular national market or global sector index.

A ***stock index (equity) swap*** is possible if another party can be found that wants to swap into or out of a foreign market for a period of time. For example, a long position in a foreign market index could be swapped for a short position in a domestic (or another foreign) stock index in a stock-for-stock swap. An investor wanting to swap into a long position in the foreign market index also could construct a debt-for-equity swap with a short position in foreign bonds (perhaps hedging the foreign bonds in the currency markets), a short position in domestic bonds, or any other position that a counterparty might accept. The major disadvantage of a stock index swap is it can be difficult and costly to find a counterparty with the opposite preferences. For this reason, stock index swaps are custom-tailored deals that are arranged through an investment banker.

## 18.4 SHARE PRICES IN INTERNATIONAL MARKETS

In an integrated financial market with no market imperfections, the law of one price holds so that $P^d = P^f S^{d/f}$. In the real world, things can get a bit messy.

### The Evolution of National and International Capital Markets

Capital markets are more integrated today than in years past. Most developed markets eased their capital flow barriers in the 1980s, and many emerging markets followed in the 1980s and 1990s. With fewer barriers, market participants are able to narrow cross-market valuation differentials and enforce the law of one price. Significant barriers to full integration of international capital markets nevertheless remain. This capital market evolution has important consequences for international portfolio diversification and asset pricing, and hence for the firm's cost of capital.

Bekaert et al. (2011) construct a measure of equity market segmentation based on a country's average earnings yield (earnings divided by share price) relative to global earnings yields.[7] Earnings yield differentials are first averaged within an industry to control for industrial structure, and then averaged across industries to form a measure of that country's capital market segmentation from global markets. Relatively integrated economies such as the United States exhibited relatively low levels of segmentation, whereas emerging economies exhibited on average more than three times the U.S. level of segmentation according to this measure.

*Capital markets are not yet fully integrated.*

Bekaert et al. found that markets indeed have become increasingly integrated over time. They date the integration of developed equity markets to around 1993, but find that segmentation remains significant in many developed markets. Emerging markets are even more segmented than developed markets, but are continuing to approach the U.S. benchmark over time. Factors related to segmentation include a country's openness to cross-border capital flows, stock market development, and political risk. Global risk factors such as variations in corporate credit spreads also are related to capital market segmentation.

## Share Prices in Segmented Markets

Emerging market governments sometimes impose capital market restrictions as a way of protecting their capital markets. Capital inflow controls are intended to preserve local ownership by preventing foreign investors from investing in or controlling local assets. Capital outflow controls are intended to preserve scarce capital, but can have the perverse effect of reducing investment if foreign investors cannot freely withdraw their funds. Governments that restrict capital flows often do so through the use of closed-end country funds (CECFs) or restricted shares.

- A *CECF* is a closed-end investment fund that invests in assets—typically shares of common stock—from a single country. Emerging market governments sometimes limit access to their domestic capital market by allowing only a subset of domestic stocks to sell internationally through a CECF.

  *Example*: Korea created a closed-end "Korea Fund" in 1983 that allowed NYSE investors to own a small portion of the largest Korean firms. For a time, this CECF was the only way for foreign investors to own Korean equities. Koreans likewise were not allowed to trade in New York, so there was no way to arbitrage between the markets. With high international demand and a limited supply of Korean equities, the Korea Fund sometimes sold at a 100 percent *premium* to the fund's NAV in Korea. Selling shares to international investors at twice the Korean price reduced the firms' cost of capital, so Korean firms asked the government to increase the proportion of shares offered to foreign investors. The size of the fund soon was increased and similar funds were created on other exchanges. With increasing availability of Korean stocks in international markets, fund prices eventually converged to the underlying NAVs.
- Some countries impose capital controls by maintaining different classes of stock for domestic and foreign investors. Typically, ***restricted shares*** may be held only by domestic residents and ***unrestricted shares*** may be held by anyone.

  *Example*: Prior to 2001, the Chinese government restricted Chinese investors to local A-shares and international investors to the B-shares of Chinese companies. Although these shares had the same shareholder rights, in 2000 the internationally traded B-shares sold at an average *discount* of 72 percent to the local A-share values.[8]

These examples illustrate that restrictions can result in different prices for local and international claims on the same assets if arbitrage is unable to enforce the law of one price. In each case, markets forced local and international prices to converge as capital controls were removed.

Common explanations for this divergence in prices include: (a) an international asset pricing model with investment restrictions, (b) asymmetric information, and (c) investor sentiment.

- ***International asset pricing with investment restrictions***: A classical asset pricing framework is useful for explaining foreign share premiums such as for the Korea Fund premium in the mid-1980s.[9] In these models, rational investors with homogeneous expectations attempt to maximize the mean-variance efficiency of their portfolios subject to an investment constraint. These models suggest that international investors have lower required returns than domestic investors because they are better able to diversify their portfolios to eliminate unsystematic risk. Differential access to shares then results in different required returns for domestic and international investors, and hence different share prices for domestic and foreign versions of the same asset.
- ***Asymmetric information***: A common assumption in asset pricing models is that investors have the same expectations. Heterogeneous expectations—perhaps because of differential access to information—could conceivably result in different share prices for domestic and foreign investors. Domestic investors have a variety of informational advantages over international investors, including language and culture. Chan, Menkveld, and Yang find that measures of informational asymmetry indeed explain a significant portion of the Chinese B-share discount.[10]
- ***Investor sentiment***: Believers in investor sentiment do not assume rationality and instead take a behavioral finance approach that emphasizes heterogeneous—and possibly irrational—investor expectations. According to this view, premiums or discounts reflect differential domestic and foreign investor sentiment regarding the value of the domestic security. Changes in the relative expectations of domestic and foreign investors should then be reflected in a changing premium or discount, which suggests that these changes may be shared across international markets.[11]

Each of these explanations is likely at play in any given circumstance, but to a varying degree.

## The Effect of a Global Listing on Share Price

Studies of domestic equity issues generally document a slight decrease in share price at the time of a seasoned equity offering (SEO). A domestic issue does not increase demand, and the price pressure effect of the increase in the supply of shares tends to depress share price. Compounding this supply-side effect is the information content of a new equity issue; that is, managers are likely to issue equity rather than debt when they believe that their share prices are overvalued.

In contrast to domestic share issuance, empirical studies often find that issuing ***global shares*** in multiple national markets can be beneficial for share prices. In a study of U.S. firms cross-listing their shares in international markets, Chaplinsky and Ramchand document a 0.8 percent decrease in the adverse price reaction that typically accompanies equity issues.[12] Non-U.S. firms offering shares in U.S. markets sometimes gain even more. Foerster and Karolyi find that foreign shares cross-listed in the United States increase in value by 1.2 percent at the time of the issue.[13] Miller confirms this announcement-day effect and also finds a 3.9 percent increase in price in the 50-day period surrounding the announcement day.[14]

One might think that this increase in share price arises from the ability of cross-listings to overcome capital flow barriers. However, firms tend to cross-list in markets that are geographically, economically, and culturally close.[15] These nearby venues are the least likely to gain from international portfolio diversification. Just as MNCs tend to make their foreign direct investments in nearby or familiar markets, so too do they tend to keep their international financing issues close to home. Although international cross-listings tend to be in nearby locations, the benefits of a global listing appear to be greater for emerging market firms than for firms from developed capital markets. Emerging market firms are more likely to benefit from increased access to international capital markets.[16]

Global cross-listings also appear to improve firms' information environment. In particular, Bailey, Karolyi, and Salva find that market reactions to earnings announcements significantly increase once non-U.S. firms cross-list their shares in the United States, suggesting that the information environment of these firms changes upon cross-listing.[17] Bailey et al. attribute these changes in the information environment to changes in individual firm disclosures, rather than to changes in liquidity, ownership, or trading venue.

## The Effectiveness of Homemade International Diversification

Errunza, Hogan, and Hung have tested whether U.S. investors can achieve international diversification through securities traded in the United States.[18] These authors found that U.S. investors can replicate the diversification benefits of foreign investments by augmenting domestic stocks with U.S.-based MNCs, ADRs, and CECFs. In particular, the market values of portfolios augmented with MNCs, ADRs, and CECFs moved more closely with foreign markets than with the U.S. market. These authors also found that U.S. investors' need for direct purchases in foreign markets has diminished with the increasing U.S. availability of assets representing claims on foreign assets. These authors concluded that U.S. investors no longer need to trade abroad to achieve a portfolio that is internationally mean-variance efficient.

The benefits of direct share purchases in foreign markets are likely to be greater for investors in countries with less developed capital markets. The benefits of international diversification are greater in small countries than in large countries because small countries tend to have less diversified economies than large countries. With larger and more diversified economies, larger equity markets (e.g., the United States and the United Kingdom) offer a wider selection of assets representing claims on foreign assets than do smaller markets, including foreign shares, depository receipts, and globally oriented open-end and closed-end mutual funds. Investors without access to MNCs, depository receipts, or international ETFs or mutual funds will find it harder to achieve international diversification through assets traded solely in their domestic market.

## 18.5 ASSET ALLOCATION POLICY AND INVESTMENT STYLE

***Asset allocation policy*** refers to the target weights given to various asset classes in an investment portfolio. A mutual fund's asset allocation policy is the single most important decision made by fund management. Nobel Prize winner William Sharpe estimates that 90 percent of a portfolio's return is determined by the asset allocation decision.[19] A mutual fund's asset allocation policy also determines how it is marketed to the public.

*Targets are set for various asset classes.*

A fund's ***investment style*** or ***philosophy*** refers to the objectives pursued by the fund, including whether the fund follows an active or a passive investment approach. Individual investors tend to migrate toward either a passive buy-and-hold approach or a more active approach based on their beliefs about a market's informational efficiency or the lack thereof. Mutual funds cluster into active or passive funds to appeal to these two distinct clienteles.[20]

Mutual funds describe their investment style in the fund ***prospectus***, which identifies the asset classes in which the fund invests. The prospectus sets limits on the proportions of various assets held in the fund and states whether the fund engages in derivative transactions to take advantage of speculative opportunities or reduce exposures to financial price risks. Finally, the prospectus provides information on commission charges incurred in managing the assets of the fund.

### Passive Fund Management

The advantage of a passive buy-and-hold approach is that it is less costly to implement and less risky than an actively managed portfolio invested in similar assets, at least for the investor without above-average skill. The disadvantage of the passive approach is that returns are likely to be not much better (or worse) than returns on a benchmark portfolio of comparable risk.

*Passively managed funds often track a market index.*

The logic of passive fund management comes from the algebra of portfolio diversification and the literature on market efficiency. The efficient markets hypothesis suggests that financial markets are informationally efficient. Active fund management in such a market is futile because consistently successful market timing or security selection is not possible. If financial markets were perfect and efficient and asset returns were normally distributed, then the world market portfolio should be mean-variance efficient. An internationally diversified mutual fund that held individual assets according to their market value weight in the world market portfolio should provide better return-risk performance over the long run than actively managed portfolios.

Following this logic, passively managed funds are often diversified across countries and asset classes to exploit the ability of portfolio diversification to improve return-risk performance. Fund managers use the relatively low correlations between national markets to achieve mean-variance efficient returns, given the investment objectives of the fund. Many passively managed funds are index funds that try to hold the same proportion of stocks as a major market index. Commonly tracked global stock indices include the MSCI World Index (www.mscibarra.com) and the FTSE All-World Index (www.ftse.com). The most widely tracked global bond index is Salomon Smith Barney's World Government Bond Index (www.smithbarney.com). Each of these indices weights assets according to their market capitalization.

Many investors build diversified portfolios using index funds as building blocks. To appeal to this clientele, some index funds specialize in particular countries, regions, or industries. Individual investors may either actively or passively manage these portfolios of index funds, and the funds themselves might be actively or passively managed. Regional and national funds often are set up to track the regional or national indices published by Morgan Stanley, FTSE, or Salomon Smith Barney. Commonly tracked national indices include the NYSE Composite and the S&P 500 in the United States, Tokyo's Nikkei 225, Frankfurt's DAX, Paris's CAC 40, Hong Kong's Hang Seng, London's FTSE 30 and 100, and Shanghai's Composite stock market indices. Financial newspapers such as the *London Financial Times* and *The Wall Street Journal* publish national and international indices in the consumer products, energy, financial, industrial, materials, and technology sectors.

### Active Fund Management

Active fund management holds the promise of higher portfolio return and, by avoiding assets that fall in value, lower portfolio risk as well. For an actively managed portfolio, long-run asset allocation refers to the average proportion of each asset class in the portfolio over the long run. The extent to which a particular fund manager diverges from long-run target weights reflects the manager's investment style. Aggressively managed funds can diverge quite a bit from their long-run target weights. Less aggressive funds tilt their portfolios away from their long-run targets to a lesser degree. Passively managed funds make an explicit effort to maintain their asset allocations close to their long-run targets.

> ***Active strategies include asset allocation and security selection.***

Actively managed funds follow one or both of the following investment strategies:

- ***Active asset allocation*** (or ***market timing***) strategies, in which funds are shifted between asset classes in anticipation of market events
- ***Active security selection*** (e.g., ***stock picking***) strategies, in which funds are invested in stocks or bonds that are considered to be underpriced by the marketplace, and not invested (or sold short) in those securities that are overpriced by the marketplace

Each of these active investment strategies presumes an ability to anticipate next period's returns and shift funds accordingly. By allocating funds into the right assets at the right time, successful active strategies can increase expected return and reduce portfolio risk.

**Active Asset Allocation Strategies** National economies seldom move in phase with one another, and stock returns vary widely across national markets in both the short run and the long run. The lure of potentially higher returns and lower portfolio risk entices many investors into diverging from passive diversification into a market timing strategy of shifting among asset classes.

Evidence on the market timing performance of fund managers is mixed. Although some studies have found evidence of timing ability on the part of fund managers in the U.S. market,[21] most studies fail to find evidence of market timing ability.[22] Even if some fund managers are able to consistently outperform a buy-and-hold strategy, it may be difficult to identify these superior market timers with any degree of confidence. Even the most highly regarded market timers—such as George Soros of the hedge fund *Quantum Fund*—have achieved long-run average annual returns only slightly higher than competing benchmark portfolios, and their performance is quite variable from year to year. This is not to say that some market timers are not better than others—only that it is a difficult game to win on a consistent basis.

**Active Security Selection** Managers following an active security selection strategy attempt to identify individual securities that are mispriced relative to other securities in a market or an industry. Proponents of active security selection do not believe that assets are correctly priced in an informationally efficient market. To identify mispriced securities, these strategies require accurate and detailed information on a firm's investments and investment opportunities, new product development, and possible changes in capital structure or corporate governance. Needless to say, it is much more difficult to acquire and interpret such information from a distant market than from one's local market. Successful investing in international markets (whether through passive investing, active security selection, or market timing) also requires familiarity with the cross-border differences that exist in financial measurement and disclosure. These issues are discussed in the next section.

## 18.6 CROSS-BORDER FINANCIAL STATEMENT ANALYSIS

There are many barriers to obtaining and interpreting information on a firm from a foreign market. The most obvious barrier is language. Learning the local idiom can be a problem even for investors that share a common tongue because of differences in accounting measurement and disclosure. For example, in the United States the term *stock* refers to common equity. In the United Kingdom, the term refers to an inventory of unsold goods. In the United States, firms with large amounts of debt in their capital structures are *highly levered*. In the United Kingdom, this is referred to as *gearing*. This is enough to make you want to table the entire issue of international accounting diversity.[23]

Language barriers can be overcome with the help of an interpreter familiar with the business culture and accounting conventions of the foreign country. More difficult to overcome are cross-country differences in accounting measurement and disclosure that spring from each country's unique history, political system, cultural environment. Cross-country differences in legal, tax, and institutional structures impose further barriers to the flow of information.

*Countries have different accounting measurement and disclosure rules.*

The rest of this section examines international differences in the measurement and disclosure of financial information. This is not intended to be a comprehensive guide to cross-border financial statement analysis. It is only intended to make you aware of some of the difficulties encountered by financial analysts on their forays into the financial accounting conventions of other countries.

## Differences in Financial Accounting Measurement

Suppose you work in commercial credit for Citigroup and have just received your dream assignment: a 1-year posting to Citigroup's London office. This should be a lark, you think.

Your first assignment is to review a proposed loan to a Chelsea microbrewery called Brown Bog Brewery. Brown Bog provides you with the following current accounts:

| | | | |
|---|---|---|---|
| Cash | £20,000 | | |
| Accounts receivable | £40,000 | Wages payable | £40,000 |
| Inventory | £40,000 | Taxes payable | £20,000 |
| Total current assets | £100,000 | Total current liabilities | £60,000 |

As a seasoned loan officer, you calculate a current ratio (current assets divided by current liabilities) to measure Brown Bog's liquidity.

$$\text{Brown Bog (U.K. accounting):} \quad \text{current ratio} = \text{current assets / current liabilities}$$
$$= £100,000/£60,000 = 1.67$$

Is this current ratio high or low relative to firms in the same industry? Fortunately, you recall that you performed an analysis last year on Red Dog Brewery in the United States. Here are the U.S. microbrewer's current accounts.

| | | | |
|---|---|---|---|
| Cash | \$60,000 | Bank overdrafts | \$30,000 |
| Accounts receivable | \$60,000 | Wages payable | \$60,000 |
| Inventory | \$60,000 | Taxes payable | \$30,000 |
| Total current assets | \$180,000 | Total current liabilities | \$120,000 |

You calculate Red Dog's current ratio.

Red Dog (U.S. accounting): current ratio = current assets / current liabilities

= \$180,000/\$120,000 = 1.5

The U.K. firm is more liquid than the U.S. firm. You might as well make the loan, right?[24]

Wait a moment. By whose standards should you judge this measure of liquidity? The United Kingdom follows the *Statements of Standard Accounting Practice* of the U.K.'s Accounting Standards Board (ASB), which do not always coincide with the GAAP of the *Financial Accounting Standards* of the FASB in the United States. For example, the United States and the United Kingdom do not share a common accounting definition of cash. According to U.S. GAAP, cash is defined as cash, demand deposits, and highly liquid investments. In the United Kingdom, cash is defined as cash, demand deposits, and highly liquid investments *less bank overdrafts.*

Let's restate Red Dog's accounts after adjusting for the U.K. definition of cash.

| | | | |
|---|---|---|---|
| Cash (less overdrafts) | \$30,000 | | |
| Accounts receivable | \$60,000 | Wages payable | \$60,000 |
| Inventory | \$60,000 | Taxes payable | \$30,000 |
| Total current assets | \$150,000 | Total current liabilities | \$90,000 |

Under this convention, Red Dog's current ratio is exactly the same as Brown Bog's.

Red Dog (U.K. accounting): current ratio = current assets / current liabilities

= \$150,000/\$90,000 = 1.67

After this adjustment for the definition of cash, the current ratio of Red Dog turns out to be identical to that of Brown Bog.

If the definition of cash can make such a big difference, just think what the United Kingdom's conventions are doing to your U.S.-based notions of accounting for inflation, depreciation, and pension liabilities! Maybe this assignment won't be the lark that you had envisioned. Off you go to the pub to drown your troubles with a pint of Brown Bog ale.

### International Differences in Financial Disclosure

The MNC can respond in several ways to a demand on the part of foreign stakeholders for financial accounting information.

- *Do nothing.* Small companies that have few dealings with the outside world have neither the need nor the resources to prepare supplementary financial statements.
- *Prepare convenience translations.* Under this alternative, the firm translates the names of the financial accounts into another language but does not change the accounting conventions used in the construction of the accounts. Large U.S. MNCs seldom go beyond preparing convenience translations for foreign investors, relying instead on foreign investors to understand and interpret the financial statements according to U.S. GAAP.
- *Prepare supplementary financial statements using different accounting principles.* Many MNCs based outside the United States restate their financial statements according to U.S. GAAP or to the *International Accounting Standards* (IAS) of the International Accounting Standards Board, an international organization devoted to harmonizing accounting standards.

The response chosen by a particular firm reflects the importance of international investors and the costs of conformance with foreign or IAS.

International differences in the market for corporate control are reflected in differences in public disclosure requirements. Disclosure requirements are most common in countries with active financial markets, such as in the United States and the United Kingdom. In many developing countries, the majority of funds are still privately raised through banks, wealthy investors, or the government. There are often few public disclosure requirements in these countries.

Accounting standard setters around the world are attempting to harmonize their national conventions, often through the adoption or adaptation of U.S. or IAS standards. For example, China is promoting IAS standards for Chinese companies that want to raise capital in international markets. Japanese multinationals frequently prepare secondary financial statements according to U.S. GAAP. The EU accepts various combinations of IAS, U.S., and local standards. In the United States, the SEC requires that foreign firms follow IAS or U.S. standards. If firms use IAS standards, they must provide a statement that reconciles their use of IAS accounts with U.S. accounting standards. IAS eventually will make it easier for a firm from Milan or Shanghai, say, to cross-list on other international exchanges.

Despite this effort to harmonize accounting standards, there remain many differences between IAS and domestic standards. In particular, IAS measurement and disclosure requirements are frequently more restrictive than domestic standards. Figure 18.6 lists some of the differences between IAS and domestic standards in accounting for depreciation, lease and pension liabilities, and research and development expense. As a practical matter, U.S. and IAS standards are similar.

## 18.7 SUMMARY

This chapter began with a description of domestic and international capital markets, with an emphasis on some of the institutional differences between domestic and international markets. The chapter then described several ways to diversify into international stocks and bonds.

| | Depreciation | Lease accounting | Pension accounting | R&D expense |
|---|---|---|---|---|
| Australia | | | ✓ | ✓ |
| Canada | | | | |
| Denmark | | ✓ | | ✓ |
| Finland | ✓ | ✓ | ✓ | ✓ |
| France | ✓ | ✓ | ✓ | |
| Hong Kong | | | | ✓ |
| Japan | | ✓ | ✓ | |
| Malaysia | | | | |
| Norway | | | ✓ | |
| Singapore | | | | |
| Spain | | | ✓ | |
| Sweden | | ✓ | ✓ | |
| Switzerland | ✓ | ✓ | ✓ | ✓ |

**FIGURE 18.6** Variation in Measurement Methods of International Financial Reporting Standards (IFRS) and Domestic GAAP.
*Source:* Ashbaugh and Pincus, "Domestic Accounting Standards, International Accounting Standards, and Predictability of Earnings," *Journal of Accounting Research* 39 (December 2001). "✓" indicates that IFRS restrict accounting measurement methods relative to those under U.S. GAAP.

- Invest in MNCs based in the domestic economy
- Invest in foreign securities directly in the foreign market
- Invest in foreign assets through securities traded in the domestic market
    - Foreign shares
    - Depository receipts
    - Mutual funds
    - Hedge funds (including private equity funds)
    - Index derivatives (stock index futures, options, or swaps)

Investors with the means and inclination to invest in individual foreign stocks can purchase them directly in the foreign market or, when available, through foreign shares or depository receipts in their domestic market. Mutual funds invested in international assets provide excellent vehicles for international portfolio diversification. Hedge funds are appropriate only for wealthy investors.

We then examined the effects of capital flow barriers on share prices in international markets. In theory, the law of one price should hold and $P^d = P^f S^{d/f}$. In the real world, capital flow restrictions (e.g., through closed-end funds or restricted shares) often result in higher equity values in international markets than in local markets. Foreign investor sentiment appears to affect the international premium to local share prices, with higher premiums for large, liquid stocks in countries with low country risk. Cross-border listings appear to be beneficial for share price.

We looked at passive and active portfolio management styles and how they are implemented on a global scale. International investment opportunities can be difficult to evaluate, primarily because of barriers in obtaining and interpreting financial information on foreign companies. Individual investors and portfolio managers investing in individual companies must be aware of international differences in financial accounting measurement and disclosure.

## KEY TERMS

*active asset allocation (market timing)*
*active security selection (stock picking)*
*Alternative Investment Fund Managers Directive (AIFMD)*
*American depository receipt (ADR)*
*asset allocation policy*
*bearer versus registered bonds*
*behavioral finance*
*capital markets*
*Capital Requirements Directive (CRD)*
*closed-end versus open-end fund*
*closed-end country fund (CECF)*
*continuous quotation versus periodic call auction*
*day count*
*depository receipts*
*domestic bonds*
*effective annual yield*
*Eurobonds*
*exchange-traded fund (ETF)*
*foreign bonds*
*foreign shares*
*global bonds*
*global depository receipt (GDR)*
*global share (global equity; global registered shares)*
*hedge funds*
*international bonds*
*Investment Securities Directive (ISD)*
*investment style (investment philosophy)*
*Japanese Ministry of Finance*
*Markets in Financial Instruments Directive (MiFID)*
*net asset value (NAV)*
*offering statement*
*open-end versus closed-end mutual fund*
*private placements*
*prospectus*
*public securities offering*
*restricted versus unrestricted shares*
*Securities and Exchange Commission (SEC)*
*stock index futures, options, and swaps*

## CONCEPTUAL QUESTIONS

18.1 What are the characteristics of a domestic bond? an international bond? a foreign bond? a Eurobond? a global bond?

18.2 What are the benefits and drawbacks of offering securities in bearer form relative to registered form?

18.3 What is the difference between a continuous quotation system and a periodic call auction?

18.4 What is the difference between a spot and a forward stock market?

18.5 What is the EU's "single passport?" How can a financial market or institution qualify?

18.6 Describe the characteristics of stock index futures, options, and swaps.

18.7 List the various ways in which you might invest in foreign securities.

18.8 Do MNCs provide international portfolio diversification benefits? If so, do they provide the same diversification benefits as direct ownership of companies located in the countries in which the MNC does business?

18.9 What is the difference between a passive and an active investment philosophy?

18.10 What makes cross-border financial statement analysis difficult?

18.11 What alternatives does an MNC have when investors in a foreign country demand accounting and financial information?

## PROBLEMS

18.1 In a bond market using a "30/360" price quotation convention, how many days' worth of accrued interest would fall on July 31?

18.2 In a bond market using an "actual/365" price quotation convention, how many days' worth of accrued interest would fall on July 31 if interest payments fall on June 30 and December 31?

18.3 In a bond market using a "30/360" price quotation convention, how many days' worth of accrued interest would fall on February 29 during a leap year?

18.4 It is the year 2011 and there are exactly 30 years remaining until maturity on Daimler's dollar-denominated 8.5 percent bonds. These bonds pay a semiannual coupon of 4.25 percent for 30 years, and then the entire principal at maturity. Suppose Daimler's bonds are selling at par.

a. What is the yield to maturity using the U.S. bond equivalent yield calculation?
b. What is the yield to maturity using the German effective annual yield calculation?

18.5 Suppose Daimler's bonds in Problem 18.4 are selling at 105.66 percent of par value.

a. What is the yield to maturity using the bond equivalent yield calculation of the United States?
b. What is the yield to maturity using the German effective annual yield calculation?

18.6 Do nations with large equity markets also tend to have large bond markets? Are there notable exceptions? Refer to Figures 18.2 and 18.5 for a comparison.

18.7 You are an investor evaluating a depository receipt issued by China's Sinopec Group and selling as an N-share on the NYSE. Sinopec Group's NAV in Chinese new yuan is CNY 20 billion. The current spot exchange rate is CNY 6.25/$. Sinopec's N-shares sell for $30 per share on the NYSE. There are 100 million shares outstanding.

a. What is the NAV in U.S. dollars?
b. Is this a good investment for a U.S. investor?

18.8 There is an ongoing debate in the United States over whether hedge funds should be more closely regulated or required to report their holdings and investment performance to the public. Search your library for recent articles discussing the pros and cons of hedge fund regulation. Answer the following questions after researching this issue:

a. Do you think hedge funds should be more closely regulated?
b. Should hedge funds be required to report their holdings and investment performance to the SEC?

## SUGGESTED READINGS

### Articles that examine various investment vehicles for diversifying internationally include

Vihang Errunza, Ked Hogan, and Mao-Wei Hung, "Can the Gains from International Diversification Be Achieved Without Trading Abroad?" *Journal of Finance* 54 (December 1999), 2075–2107.

Paul Gompers and Josh Lerner, "The Venture Capital Revolution," *Journal of Economic Perspectives* 15 (Spring 2001), 145–168.

Philippe Jorion and Leonid Roisenberg, "Synthetic International Diversification: The Case for Diversifying with Stock Index Futures," *Journal of Portfolio Management* 19 (Winter 1993), 65–74.

Michael S. Rozeff, "Closed-End Fund Discounts and Premiums," *Pacific-Basin Capital Markets Research* II (1991), 503–522.

### Articles that investigate the causes of violations of purchasing power parity in share prices include

Warren Bailey, Y. Peter Chung, and Jun-Koo Kang, "Foreign Ownership Restrictions and Equity Price Premiums: What Drives the Demand for Cross-Border Investments?" *Journal of Financial and Quantitative Analysis* 34 (December 1999), 489–511.

Geert Bekaert, Campbell R. Harvey, Christian T. Lundblad, and Stephan 0Siegel, "What Segments Equity Markets?" *Review of Financial Studies* 24 (December 2011), 3841–3890.

Kalok Chan, Albert J. Menkveld, and Zhishu Yang, "Informational Asymmetry and Asset Prices: Evidence from the China Foreign Share Discount," *Journal of Finance* 63 (February 2008), 159–196.

### The impacts of global equity offerings are examined in

Warren Bailey, G. Andrew Karolyi, and Carolina Salva, "The Economic Consequences of Increased Disclosure: Evidence from International Cross-listings," *Journal of Financial Economics* 81 (July 2006), 175–213.

Susan Chaplinsky and Latha Ramchand, "The Impact of Global Equity Offerings," *Journal of Finance* 55 (December 2000), 2767–2789.

Stephen R. Foerster and G. Andrew Karolyi, "The Effects of Market Segmentation and Investor Recognition on Asset Prices: Evidence from Foreign Stocks Listing in the United States," *Journal of Finance* 54 (June 1999), 981–1013.

Karl V. Lins, Deon Strickland, and Marc Zenner, "Do Non-U.S. Firms Issue Equity on U.S. Stock Exchanges to Relax Capital Constraints?" *Journal of Financial and Quantitative Analysis* 40 (March 2005), 109–133.

Darius P. Miller, "The Market Reaction to International Cross-listings: Evidence from Depositary Receipts," *Journal of Financial Economics* 51 (January 1999), 103–123.

Sergei Sarkissian and Michael J. Schill, "The Overseas Listing Decision: New Evidence of Proximity Preference," *Review of Financial Studies* 17 (Autumn 2004), 769–809.

## Reviews of market timing and security selection across domestic and/or international markets include

Connie Becker, Wayne Ferson, David H. Myers, and Michael J. Schill, "Conditional Market Timing with Benchmark Investors," *Journal of Financial Economics* 52 (April 1999), 119–148.

Stephen J. Brown and William N. Goetzmann, "Mutual Fund Styles," *Journal of Financial Economics* 43 (March 1997), 373–399.

William N. Goetzmann, Jonathan Ingersoll, Jr., and Zoran Ivkovic, "Monthly Measurement of Daily Timers," *Journal of Financial and Quantitative Analysis* 35 (September 2000), 257–290.

Cheng-Few Lee and Shafiqur Rahman, "Market Timing, Selectivity, and Mutual Fund Performance: An Empirical Investigation," *Journal of Business* 63 (April 1990), 261–278.

William F. Sharpe, "Asset Allocation: Management Style and Performance Measurement," *Journal of Portfolio Management* 18 (Winter 1992), 7–19.

## International accounting practices and their impact on earnings predictability are investigated in

Hollis Ashbaugh and Morton Pincus, "Domestic Accounting Standards, International Accounting Standards, and Predictability of Earnings," *Journal of Accounting Research* 39 (December 2001), 417–434.

CHAPTER 19

# International Portfolio Diversification

*I have no doubt that in reality the future will be vastly more surprising than anything I can imagine. Now my own suspicion is that the universe is not only queerer than we suppose, but queerer than we can suppose.*
—J.B.S. Haldane, *Possible Worlds and Other Papers* (1927)

This chapter provides the rationale for diversifying investment portfolios across national borders. Despite the predictions of theory, investors exhibit a strong preference for assets from their home market. This home asset bias is at least partly due to the many barriers that investors face in distant and unfamiliar markets. Foremost among these are informational barriers that impede foreign investors from knowledgeably pricing and investing in local assets. Despite barriers to cross-border investment, international portfolio diversification is increasingly accessible to both fund managers and individual investors from most countries around the world.

## 19.1 THE ALGEBRA OF PORTFOLIO DIVERSIFICATION

*The risk of an asset depends on its contribution to portfolio risk.*

In 1990, Harry Markowitz and William Sharpe were awarded the Nobel Prize in economics for their work in portfolio theory and asset pricing. The insight at the heart of their work is quite simple. Markowitz and Sharpe observed that investors are concerned with the expected return and risk of their portfolio of assets, not with the return or risk of any single asset in isolation. Consequently, the characteristics of an asset that are important to investors are the asset's contributions to the expected return and risk of their portfolio. An understanding of this portfolio perspective on risk and return will allow us to appreciate the implications of this insight for asset prices in a global marketplace, as well as its limitations.

### The Mean-Variance Framework

Let's begin our analysis with two simplifying assumptions.

- Nominal returns are normally distributed.
- Investors want more nominal return and less risk in their functional currency.

The normal distribution is completely described by its mean and standard deviation (or variance) and, for multiple assets, the correlations or comovements among those assets. Faced with normally distributed returns, risk-averse investors want to maximize the expected return and minimize the standard deviation of return on their portfolio of assets.

Like the perfect market conditions, these assumptions are invoked more for convenience than for the way in which they represent the real world. Here are five violations of the assumptions that can change investor behaviors in some circumstances.

- Rational investors value after-tax real returns rather than pre-tax nominal returns.
- Investors with obligations in several currencies may want returns in those currencies.
- Most financial returns are leptokurtic or fat-tailed relative to the normal distribution.
- Asset price comovements are higher-than-normal during crisis periods.
- In some situations, investors exhibit risk-seeking rather than risk-averse behaviors.

Nevertheless, an assumption of risk-averse investors pursuing normally distributed nominal returns in a single functional currency is a convenient starting point. It greatly simplifies the algebra of portfolio diversification and captures much of what is important to investors.

## The Expected Return on a Portfolio

> *Portfolio return is a weighted average of asset returns.*

The return on a portfolio of assets is a weighted average of the returns on the individual assets in the portfolio. Algebraically, this can be expressed as $r_P = \Sigma_i x_i r_i$ where the weights $x_i$ represent the proportion of wealth devoted to asset i such that $\Sigma_i x_i = 1$. For example, the expected return on a two-asset portfolio of assets A and B is

$$E[r_P] = x_A E[r_A] + x_B E[r_B] \tag{19.1}$$

subject to $x_A + x_B = 1$. The expected return on a portfolio of N assets is a linear function of the expected returns on the individual assets in the portfolio and the weight given to each asset.

$$E[r_P] = \Sigma_i x_i E[r_i] \tag{19.2}$$

subject to $\Sigma_i x_i = 1$. If ***short selling*** is not allowed, then each weight is constrained to $0 \leq x_i \leq 1$.

Nominal returns in two currencies are not directly comparable if there are cross-currency differences in inflation. One solution is to use real (inflation-adjusted)

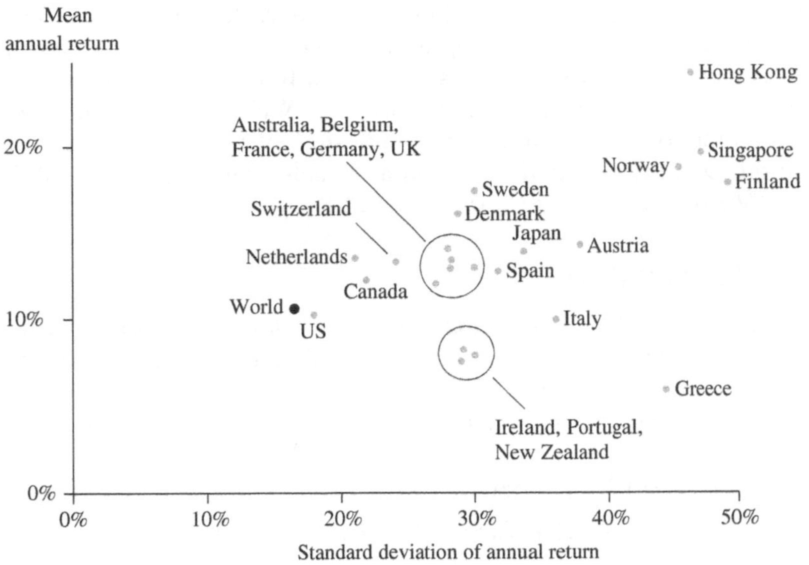


**FIGURE 19.1** Historical Performance of MSCI Stock Market Indices, in U.S. Dollars.

returns. Another solution is to calculate returns in a common currency, such as the U.S. dollar. Nominal returns can then be compared because they are stated in the same units. We'll follow the latter convention here.

Figure 19.1 graphs annual dollar returns against standard deviations for the 23 developed markets followed by Morgan Stanley Capital International from the perspective of a U.S. investor. Figure 19.2 presents return statistics for the eight largest national stock markets. As a general rule, correlations in Figure 19.2 are lower the farther markets are from one another. For example, there are relatively high correlations between the U.S. and Canadian markets, and between France, Germany, and Switzerland. Japan has the lowest correlations with other markets, followed by Australia. Each of the markets has a fairly high correlation with the world market index, and close to a zero correlation with short-term U.S. Treasuries.

| Country | $\mu$ (%) | $\sigma$ (%) | Sharpe Index | Beta | Correlation Coefficients Au | Ca | Fr | Ge | Ja | Sw | U.K. | U.S. |
|---|---|---|---|---|---|---|---|---|---|---|---|---|
| Australia | 12.0 | 27.1 | 0.22 | 1.05 | | | | | | | | |
| Canada | 12.2 | 21.9 | 0.28 | 1.01 | 0.645 | | | | | | | |
| France | 12.9 | 28.2 | 0.24 | 1.12 | 0.481 | 0.537 | | | | | | |
| Germany | 13.0 | 30.0 | 0.23 | 1.14 | 0.434 | 0.478 | 0.717 | | | | | |
| Japan | 13.9 | 33.7 | 0.23 | 1.25 | 0.359 | 0.369 | 0.431 | 0.402 | | | | |
| Switzerland | 13.3 | 24.1 | 0.30 | 0.94 | 0.467 | 0.498 | 0.664 | 0.707 | 0.450 | | | |
| United Kingdom | 13.4 | 28.3 | 0.26 | 1.13 | 0.531 | 0.562 | 0.615 | 0.523 | 0.403 | 0.607 | | |
| United States | 10.2 | 18.0 | 0.23 | 0.86 | 0.557 | 0.741 | 0.566 | 0.541 | 0.355 | 0.559 | 0.582 | |
| World | 10.4 | 18.3 | 0.23 | 1.00 | 0.643 | 0.762 | 0.725 | 0.699 | 0.677 | 0.711 | 0.728 | 0.876 |
| U.S. Treasuries | 6.1 | 3.2 | 0.00 | -0.00 | -0.071 | -0.043 | -0.013 | -0.018 | -0.006 | -0.049 | -0.005 | 0.011 |

Mean ($\mu$), standard deviation ($\sigma$), and Sharpe Index $(r_i - r_F)/\sigma_i$ are based on 1970-2011annual returns from MSCI (net of withholding taxes, see www.mscibarra.com) and Federal Reserve (www.federalreserve.gov) 1-year constant maturity Treasuries. Betas and correlations are based on monthly returns.

**FIGURE 19.2** Annual Stock Returns and Comovements, in U.S. Dollars.

Suppose investments in American (A) and British (B) stocks have return distributions as in Figure 19.2.[1] If history were to repeat itself, then the mean annual return would be 10.2 percent on American and 13.4 percent on British stocks. Of course, history is unlikely to repeat itself in precisely this way. We'll use these numbers as expected returns for convenience and not as indicators of future mean returns. Applying Equation 19.1, the expected return on an equal-weighted portfolio of A and B is $E[r_P] = ½(0.102) + ½(0.134) = 0.118$, or 11.8 percent.

## The Risk of a Two-Asset Portfolio

If an asset's returns are distributed as normal $N(\mu, \sigma^2)$, then its return distribution can be completely described by its mean $\mu$ and standard deviation $\sigma$ (or variance $\sigma^2$) of return. The variance of return on a portfolio of two assets A and B, $Var(r_P) = \sigma_P{}^2$, is found by substituting for $r_P = x_A r_A + x_B r_B$.

$$\begin{aligned} Var(r_P) &= Var(x_A r_A + x_B r_B) \\ &= Var(x_A r_A) + Var(x_B r_B) + 2Cov(x_A r_A, x_B r_B) \end{aligned}$$

where Cov(.) is a covariance term. Because the weights $x_A$ and $x_B$ are constants, they can be extracted from the variance and covariance terms.

$$\begin{aligned} Var(r_P) &= x_A{}^2 Var(r_A) + x_B{}^2 Var(r_B) + 2x_A x_B Cov(r_A, r_B) \\ &= x_A{}^2 \sigma_A{}^2 + x_B{}^2 \sigma_B{}^2 + 2x_A x_B \sigma_{AB} \end{aligned} \quad (19.3)$$

where $\sigma_{AB} = Cov(r_A, r_B)$ is the ***covariance*** of returns to assets A and B. Variance is measured as a squared percentage ($\%^2$), which doesn't have an obvious economic interpretation. It is often more convenient to use the standard deviation of return, which is in the same units (%) as expected return.

The covariance term alternatively can be stated in terms of the ***correlation*** $\rho_{AB}$ and standard deviations $\sigma_A$ and $\sigma_B$ of assets A and B.

$$\sigma_{AB} = \sigma_A \sigma_B \, \rho_{AB} \Leftrightarrow \rho_{AB} = \sigma_{AB}/\sigma_A \sigma_B \quad (19.4)$$

The correlation is simply the covariance scaled by the standard deviations of A and B. Dividing the percentage-squared units of covariance by the product of two standard deviations (each with units in percent) results in a unit-less correlation measure bounded on the interval $-1 \leq \rho_{AB} \leq +1$.

Correlation and covariance measure the extent of comovement between two assets. They are important measures because of this rule. If assets are perfectly positively correlated, then diversification is ineffective in reducing portfolio risk. If correlation is less than one, then diversification results in a standard deviation of portfolio return that is less than the average of the standard deviations of the individual assets.

***Diversification relies on low correlations.***

The extent to which risk is reduced by portfolio diversification depends on how highly the individual assets in the portfolio are correlated.

For illustration, let's calculate the standard deviation of an equally weighted portfolio of American (A) and British (B) equities using the standard deviations $\sigma_A = 18.0\%$ and $\sigma_B = 28.3\%$ from Figure 19.2. To demonstrate the impact that correlation has on portfolio risk, we'll perform this calculation under three scenarios: (1) a perfect positive correlation ($\rho_{AB} = +1$), (2) a perfect negative correlation ($\rho_{AB} = -1$), and (3) the historically observed correlation of $\rho_{AB} = 0.582$ between American and British equities from Figure 19.2. Remember, the expected return on an equal-weighted portfolio of American and British equities is $E[r_P] = \frac{1}{2}(0.102) + \frac{1}{2}(0.134) = 0.118$, or 11.8 percent regardless of the correlation of return between these assets.

**Case 1: Perfect Positive Correlation** If returns in these two markets are perfectly positively correlated ($\rho_{AB} = +1$), then the standard deviation of portfolio return is

$$\begin{aligned}\sigma_P &= (x_A{}^2\sigma_A{}^2 + x_B{}^2\sigma_B{}^2 + 2x_Ax_B\rho_{AB}\sigma_A\sigma_B)^{1/2}\\ &= (x_A{}^2\sigma_A{}^2 + x_B{}^2\sigma_B{}^2 + 2x_Ax_B\sigma_A\sigma_B)^{1/2}\\ &= [(x_A\sigma_A + x_B\sigma_B)^2]^{1/2}\\ &= x_A\sigma_A + x_B\sigma_B\end{aligned}$$

The standard deviation of an equal-weighted portfolio of American and British stocks is then

$$\sigma_P = \tfrac{1}{2}(0.180) + \tfrac{1}{2}(0.283) = 0.232, \text{ or } 23.2 \text{ percent}$$

When $\rho_{AB} = +1$, the standard deviation of a portfolio is a simple weighted average of the individual standard deviations. Combining A and B with weights that range between zero and one results in a straight line that runs between points A and B in Figure 19.3. Both the expected return and the standard deviation of the portfolio change linearly as wealth is shifted from one asset to another. In this case, there are no risk reduction benefits from portfolio diversification.

**Case 2: Perfect Negative Correlation** If returns in two markets are perfectly negatively correlated ($\rho_{AB} = -1$), then the standard deviation of portfolio return is

$$\begin{aligned}\sigma_P &= (x_A{}^2\sigma_A{}^2 + x_B{}^2\sigma_B{}^2 + 2x_Ax_B\rho_{AB}\sigma_A\sigma_B)^{1/2}\\ &= (x_A{}^2\sigma_A{}^2 + x_B{}^2\sigma_B{}^2 - 2x_Ax_B\sigma_A\sigma_B)^{1/2}\\ &= [(x_A\sigma_A - x_B\sigma_B)^2]^{1/2}\\ &= |x_A\sigma_A - x_B\sigma_B|\end{aligned}$$

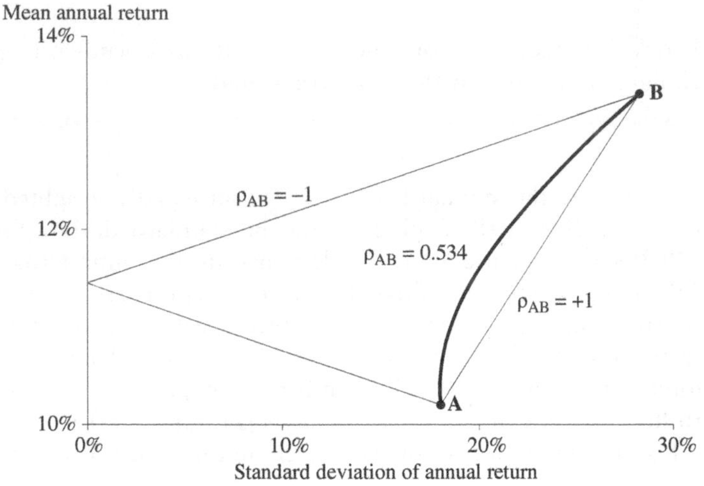


**FIGURE 19.3** Portfolio Diversification and the Correlation Coefficient.

The risk reduction benefits of portfolio diversification are at their greatest when two assets are perfectly negatively correlated. If $\rho_{AB} = -1$, then the standard deviation of an equal-weighted portfolio of American and British stocks is equal to

$$\sigma_P = |\tfrac{1}{2}(0.180) - \tfrac{1}{2}(0.283)| = 0.052, \text{ or } 5.2 \text{ percent}$$

When $\rho_{AB} = -1$, the losses on one asset can be exactly offset by gains on the other asset through a judicious choice of portfolio weights. In this example, if you pick $x_A = (0.283)/(0.180 + 0.283) \approx 0.611$ and $x_B = (1 - x_A) = 0.389$, portfolio risk falls to $\sigma_P = 0$ and losses (or gains) on A are exactly offset by gains (or losses) on B.[2] Expected return on this portfolio is $E[r_P] = (0.611)(0.102) + (0.389)(0.134) \approx 0.114$, so you can capture a riskless return of about 11.4 percent as in Figure 19.3. Progressively varying the weights on A and B defines a straight line that begins at point A, bounces off the vertical axis at the point (0, 0.114), and continues to point B.

**Case 3: Correlations Between -1 and +1** Most correlations between international stock markets range between 0.3 and 0.8. Substituting $\sigma_{AB} = \rho_{AB}\sigma_A\sigma_B$ into Equation 19.3, the equation for the standard deviation of a portfolio of assets A and B is

$$\sigma_P = (x_A{}^2\sigma_A{}^2 + x_B{}^2\sigma_B{}^2 + 2x_Ax_B\rho_{AB}\sigma_A\sigma_B)^{1/2}$$

Using the historically observed correlation of 0.582 between American and British equities in Figure 19.2, the standard deviation of an equal-weighted portfolio of assets A and B is

$$\sigma_P = [(\tfrac{1}{2})^2(0.180)^2 + (\tfrac{1}{2})^2(0.283)^2 + 2(\tfrac{1}{2})(\tfrac{1}{2})(0.582)(0.180)(0.283)]^{1/2}$$
$$= 0.207, \text{ or } 20.7 \text{ percent}$$

This is less than halfway between the standard deviation of return on American ($\sigma_A = 18.0\%$) and British ($\sigma_B = 28.3\%$) equities. By varying the proportion of wealth invested in each asset, investors can obtain any point or portfolio along the curved line from A to B in Figure 19.3. Although a correlation of $\rho_{AB} = 0.582$ does not yield the same reduction in risk as a perfect negative correlation, it does provide a noticeable improvement in portfolio risk over the straight line between A and B corresponding to $\rho_{AB} = 1$. Again, the general rule is: The lower the correlation between two assets, the greater the potential risk reduction through portfolio diversification.

*Lower correlation leads to more diversification.*

## Portfolios of Many Securities

The variance of a portfolio with N assets is a weighted average of the $N^2$ cells in the variance-covariance matrix.

$$\mathrm{Var}(r_P) = \sigma_P^2 = \Sigma_i \Sigma_j x_i x_j \sigma_{ij} = \Sigma_i x_i^2 \sigma_i^2 + \Sigma_i \Sigma_{j \; (i \neq j)} x_i x_j \sigma_{ij} \tag{19.5}$$

where the weights sum to one ($\Sigma_i x_i = 1$) across the N assets. The double summation $\Sigma_i \Sigma_j x_i x_j \sigma_{ij}$ has a total of $N^2$ terms including N variance terms ($x_i^2 \sigma_i^2$) along the diagonal of the covariance matrix and $N^2 - N$ covariance terms ($x_i x_j \sigma_{ij}$ for $i \neq j$) in the off-diagonal elements.

As an example, suppose we extract the variance-covariance matrix of a three-asset portfolio of American, British, and Japanese stocks from Figure 19.2. Each term in the variance-covariance matrix is calculated as $\sigma_{ij} = \rho_{ij}\sigma_i\sigma_j$.

| | American | British | Japanese |
|---|---|---|---|
| **American** | 0.0324 | 0.0296 | 0.0215 |
| **British** | 0.0296 | 0.0801 | 0.0384 |
| **Japanese** | 0.0215 | 0.0384 | 0.1136 |

The variance-covariance matrix for a three-asset portfolio has $N^2 = 9$ cells including $N = 3$ variances and $N^2 - N = 6$ covariances. The diagonal cells represent return variances because $\sigma_{ii} = \sigma_i^2$ for $i = j$. For example, the bottom-right cell is the variance of Japanese equity returns: $\sigma_J^2 = (0.337)^2 = 0.1136$. The off-diagonal covariances $\sigma_{ij} = \rho_{ij}\sigma_i\sigma_j$ are symmetric around the diagonal. For example, the covariance of the American and British equity markets of $\sigma_{AB} = \rho_{AB}\sigma_A\sigma_B = (0.582)(0.180)(0.283) = 0.0296$ is the same as the covariance $\sigma_{BA}$ between the British and American markets. An equal-weighted portfolio of all three indices has a return variance of

$$\begin{aligned}\sigma_P^2 &= x_A^2\sigma_A^2 + x_B^2\sigma_B^2 + x_J^2\sigma_J^2 + 2(x_A x_B \sigma_{AB} + x_A x_J \sigma_{AJ} + x_B x_J \sigma_{BJ}) \\ &= (1/3)^2[(0.0324) + (0.0801) + (0.1136)] + 2(1/3)^2[(0.0296) \\ &\quad + (0.0215) + (0.0384)] \\ &= 0.0450\end{aligned}$$

The standard deviation of return for this portfolio is $\sigma_P = (0.0450)^{1/2} = 0.212$, or 21.2 percent.

As the number of assets held in a portfolio increases, the covariance terms begin to dominate the portfolio variance calculation. The ratio of variance cells to total cells in the variance-covariance matrix is $N/N^2 = 1/N$, whereas the ratio of covariance cells to total cells is $(N^2 - N)/N^2$. For $N = 2$, there are $N = 2$ variance terms and $N^2 - N = 4 - 2 = 2$ covariance terms, so half of the cells are variances. For $N = 3$, one-third of the $N^2 = 9$ cells are variances, and two-thirds of the cells are covariances ($N^2 - N = 6$). For $N = 100$, only 1 percent of the $N^2 = 10,000$ cells in the variance-covariance matrix are variances, and 99 percent ($N^2 - N = 10,000 - 100 = 9,900$) are covariances. This observation is summarized in the following rule:

As the number of assets in a portfolio increases, portfolio variance becomes more dependent on the covariances between the assets and less dependent on the variances of the individual assets in the portfolio.

This is the large-portfolio analog of our rule from earlier in the chapter: "The extent to which risk is reduced by portfolio diversification depends on how highly the individual assets in the portfolio are correlated." In a large portfolio, variance is more dependent on the covariances between individual assets and less dependent on individual asset variances.

This rule has an interesting consequence for the risk of an asset when it is held as a part of a portfolio. If an investor is concerned with the risk of his or her total portfolio, then the characteristic of an individual asset that matters the most is the asset's return covariance with other assets in the portfolio—and not its return variance.

*The risk of an individual asset when it is held in a large portfolio depends on its return covariance with other assets in the portfolio.*

This concept is the key to understanding the benefits of portfolio diversification. It is also central to what should be included in (and excluded from) an international asset pricing model.

Of course, an investor can't pick the correlations between assets. This is determined in the capital markets. But through a judicious selection of assets with low correlations, the risk reduction benefits of international diversification can be used to maximize a portfolio's return-risk performance.

## Mean-Variance Efficiency

The popular press often claims that investor behavior is driven by "fear and greed." Portfolio theory is based on these two fundamental human motives. If asset returns are distributed as normal, then the investors' objective is to maximize the expected return and minimize the standard deviation of return in their portfolios. Investors

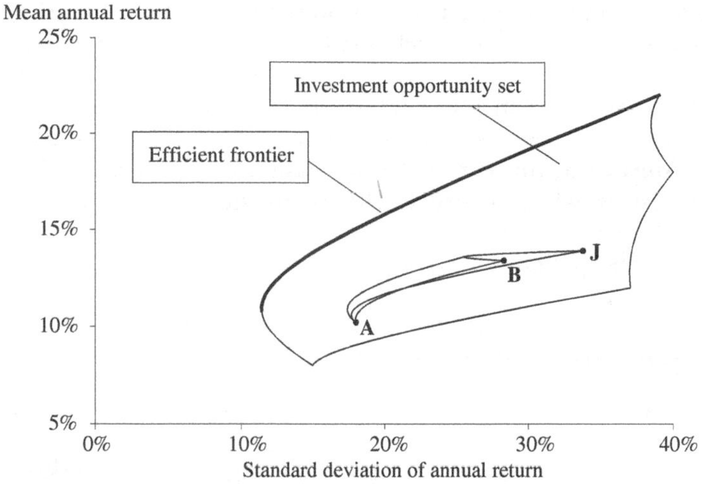


**FIGURE 19.4** The Investment Opportunity Set and the Efficient Frontier.

want to be as far up and to the left as possible in the return-risk framework in Figure 19.4. An asset is said to be ***mean-variance efficient*** when it has higher mean return than other assets at a given level of risk, or lower risk at a given level of return.[3]

*Mean-variance efficiency involves return per unit of risk.*

Consider what happens when assets are combined to form a portfolio. Let's start with the American (A) and British (B) assets in Figure 19.4. Given the correlation between A and B of $\rho_{AB} = 0.582$, an investor can reach any point along a curved line from A to B by varying the weight assigned to each asset. As additional assets are added to the set of possible investments, these new assets can be combined with A, B, or any combination of A and B.

Suppose there is an asset J (for Japan) with $E[r_J] = 13.9\%$, $\sigma_J = 33.7\%$, and correlations $\rho_{AJ} = 0.355$ and $\rho_{BJ} = 0.403$. Combining A and J in varying weights results in the curved line between points A and J in Figure 19.4. Combining B with J allows an investor to achieve any point along the curved line between B and J. The three assets also can be combined, as in the curved line that falls between point A and the B-J line.

The set of possible investments expands as more assets are added. By examining all possible asset combinations, investors can identify the ***investment opportunity set*** bounded by the outside border in Figure 19.4. As in any decision, once investors have identified the alternatives, they must choose from these alternatives based on individual preferences. This choice depends on an investor's level of risk aversion; that is, how much risk the investor is willing to accept in order to capture a given level of expected return. Investors want the most return at the least risk. These sought-after portfolios lie along the ***efficient frontier***, the upper-left border of the investment opportunity set in Figure 19.4. These portfolios are efficient in that they provide the most expected return for a given level of risk, or the least risk at a given level of expected return.

A straightforward way to measure an asset's return-risk performance is to divide the asset's excess return (return in excess of the risk-free rate $r_F$) by its standard deviation. Called the ***Sharpe index***, this performance measure is appropriate when comparing returns of investors whose entire wealth is invested in one asset or another.

$$\text{Sharpe index} = (r_i - r_F)/\sigma_i \tag{19.6}$$

*The Sharpe index measures excess return per unit of risk.*

Sharpe indices are reported in Figure 19.2 for the eight largest equity markets. These are dollar returns from a U.S. investor's perspective, so the U.S. Treasury rate is used as the risk-free rate of interest. The United States has the smallest standard deviation of all the national markets, reflecting the diversified U.S. economy and the low currency risk of domestic returns to U.S. investors. The relatively low 10.2 percent U.S. mean return and 18.0 percent standard deviation on the U.S. market index result in a Sharpe index of 0.228, or 0.228 percent in excess return (return in excess of the T-Bill rate) for every 1 percent of standard deviation.

## Systematic versus Unsystematic Risk

***Systematic risk*** is the portion of an individual asset's risk that cannot be diversified away by holding the asset in a large portfolio. Systematic risk also is called ***nondiversifiable risk*** or ***market risk*** because it is a risk that is shared by all assets in the market. Systematic risks arise through market-wide events, such as unexpected change in real economic growth, government spending, or investor sentiment regarding asset values.

The portion of an individual asset's risk that can be diversified away by holding a portfolio with many securities is called ***unsystematic risk***. Unsystematic risk also is called ***nonmarket risk*** or ***diversifiable risk***. If the asset is a share of stock, then that part of total risk that is diversifiable also is called company-specific risk. Unsystematic risks include labor strikes, changes in top management, company-specific sales fluctuations, or any other event that is unique to a single asset or company.

*Unsystematic risk can be diversified away.*

The total risk or variance of return can be decomposed into systematic and unsystematic risk.

$$\text{Total Risk} = \text{Systematic Risk} + \text{Unsystematic Risk} \tag{19.7}$$

In Chapter 20, we will see that only systematic risk matters to well-diversified investors in a perfect market. Unsystematic risk can be diversified away in a large portfolio, so it does not command a risk premium and hence is not "priced" in the marketplace.

In the return-risk framework of this chapter, the relative proportion of systematic and unsystematic risk in an individual asset's returns depends on the asset's correlations or covariances with other assets in the portfolio. If an asset's return is highly correlated with the returns on other assets, then the asset's total risk will be largely composed of systematic risk. If an asset's returns have relatively low correlations with returns on other assets in the portfolio, then the algebra of portfolio diversification results in a relatively large proportion of unsystematic risk and a smaller proportion of systematic risk.

## 19.2 RETURNS ON FOREIGN INVESTMENTS

Let the foreign currency price of a foreign asset at time t be given by $P_t^f$. The no-arbitrage condition then determines the price of the foreign asset in the domestic currency according to

$$P_t^d = P_t^f S_t^{d/f} \tag{19.8}$$

This is simply the price of the foreign asset in the foreign currency translated back into the domestic currency at the spot rate of exchange. For example, if the euro value of a French asset is €500 and the spot rate is \$1.20/€, then the value of the asset in dollars is $P_t^{\$} = P_t^{€} S_t^{\$/€} = (€500)(\$1.20/€) = \$600$.

Let the foreign and domestic currency returns on a foreign asset over period t be denoted $r^f$ and $r^d$, respectively, where the time index is dropped for notational convenience. The percentage change $s^{d/f}$ in the spot exchange rate over period t is given by

$$(1 + s^{d/f}) = (S_t^{d/f} / S_{t-1}^{d/f}) \tag{19.9}$$

The domestic currency return on the foreign asset is then

$$(1 + r^d) = (1 + r^f)(1 + s^{d/f}) = 1 + r^f + s^{d/f} + r^f s^{d/f} \tag{19.10}$$

or $r^d = r^f + s^{d/f} + r^f s^{d/f}$.[4] The domestic return on a foreign asset arises from the foreign market return $r^f$, the percentage change in the spot rate of exchange $s^{d/f}$, and the interaction of $r^f$ and $s^{d/f}$.

Suppose the Paris Bourse appreciates by 20 percent while the euro depreciates by 10 percent against the U.S. dollar. The total return to a U.S. investor in the French market is $r^{\$} = (1 + r^{€})(1 + s^{\$/€}) - 1 = (1.20)(0.90) - 1 = 0.08$, or 8 percent. The 20 percent rise in the Paris Bourse is offset by a 10 percent fall in the value of the euro, and U.S. investors will see an 8 percent rise in the dollar value of an investment in the French market.

### The Expected Return on a Foreign Asset

The expected return on a foreign asset is given by

$$E[r^d] = E[r^f] + E[s^{d/f}] + E[r^f s^{d/f}] \tag{19.11}$$

Equation 19.11 states that the expected domestic currency return on a foreign asset is composed of the expected return on the foreign asset in the foreign currency, the expected change in the value of the foreign currency, and the expectation of the cross-product.[5]

The algebra of Equations 19.10 and 19.11 is the same as that of the Fisher equation, which relates nominal interest rates i to real rates R and inflation p according to $(1 + i) = (1 + p)(1 + r)$. If the real interest rate is 1 percent and inflation is 10 percent, then the nominal rate is $i = (1 + p)(1 + r) - 1 = (1.10)(1.01) - 1 = 0.111$, or 11.1 percent. Similarly, if the foreign market goes up $r^f = 1$ percent in the foreign currency and the foreign currency value rises by $s^{d/f} = 10$ percent, then the domestic currency return on the foreign asset is $r^d = (1 + r^f)(1 + s^{d/f}) - 1 = (1.10)(1.01) - 1 = 0.111$, or 11.1 percent.

## The Variance of Return on a Foreign Asset

The general case for the variance of a random variable $r = a + b + c$ composed of (possibly random) elements a, b, and c is given by[6]

$$\text{Var}(r) = \text{Var}(a) + \text{Var}(b) + \text{Var}(c) + 2\text{Cov}(a,b) + 2\text{Cov}(b,c) + 2\text{Cov}(a,c)$$

Similarly, the variance of $r^d = r^f + s^{d/f} + r^f s^{d/f}$ is given by

$$\text{Var}(r^d) = \text{Var}(r^f) + \text{Var}(s^{d/f}) + \text{Var}(r^f s^{d/f}) + 2\text{Cov}(r^f, s^{d/f}) + 2\text{Cov}(r^f, r^f s^{d/f}) + 2\text{Cov}(s^{d/f}, r^f s^{d/f}) \qquad (19.12)$$

Let's consider riskless and then risky foreign currency cash flows in turn.

**Riskless Foreign Currency Cash Flows** Suppose a U.S.-based multinational corporation (MNC) is promised a riskless payment of 100,000 euros from the French government in six months. Spot and 6-month forward exchange rates are $S_0^{\$/€} = F_1^{\$/€} = \$1.20/€$. This unhedged cash flow is fully exposed to changes in the spot rate of exchange, as follows:

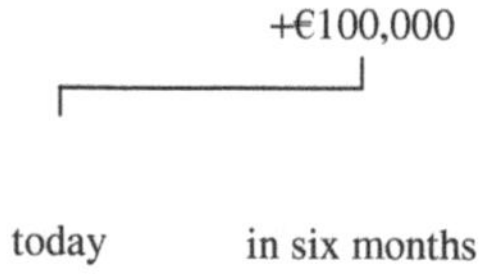


Risk profile of a long unhedged position (L)

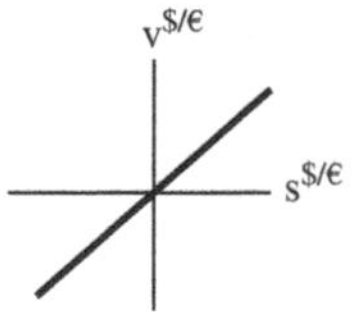


For every \$0.01/€ change in the value of the euro, there is a corresponding (\$0.01/€)(€100,000) = \$1,000 change in the value of the unhedged position. If the euro falls to $s^{\$/€} = \$1.19/€$, then €100,000 will convert to only \$119,000 rather than the \$120,000 expected value.

This is both good news and bad news for the dollar value of a riskless cash flow denominated in euros. The bad news is that the value of the cash flow in dollars depends on the exchange rate. The good news is that the dollar value of the euro cash flow depends *only* on the exchange rate. Because the euro payment is guaranteed by the French government, it has a guaranteed or certain nominal return $r_F^€$ in euros. This means that $Var(r_F^€)$ and all of the interaction terms in Equation 19.12 are equal to zero. Moreover, $Var(r_F^€ s^{\$/€}) = (r_F^€)^2 Var(s^{\$/€})$ for a constant $r_F^€$. Variability of return in dollars on this riskless euro cash flow then reduces to

$$\begin{aligned} Var(r^{\$}) &= Var(r_F^€) + Var(s^{\$/€}) + Var(r_F^€ s^{\$/€}) + \text{(covariance terms)} \\ &= 0 + Var(s^{\$/€}) + (r_F^€)^2 Var(s^{\$/€}) + 0 + 0 + 0 \\ &= [1 + (r_F^€)^2] Var(s^{\$/€}) \\ &\approx Var(s^{\$/€}) \end{aligned}$$

The euro risk-free rate $r_F^€$ is a constant, so for riskless foreign currency cash flows the only source of variability in domestic currency nominal return is exchange rate variability.

To hedge against unanticipated changes in the spot rate, the MNC should sell €100,000 for (€100,000)($1.20/€) = $120,000 at the forward exchange rate $F_1^{\$/€} = \$1.20/€$.

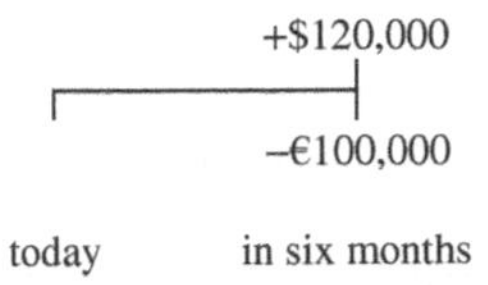


**Risk profile of a short forward hedge(S)**

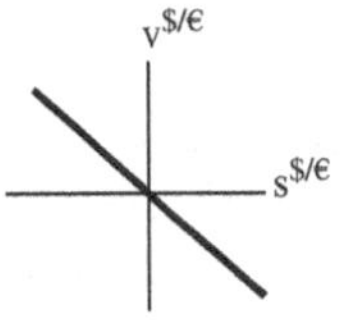


The algebra of portfolio diversification applies to all assets, including derivative securities such as currency forwards. In this example, the correlation between the long (L) underlying position and the short (S) forward hedge is $\rho_{SL} = -1$. The volatilities are identical so $\sigma_S = \sigma_L = \sigma$. If portfolio weight $x_S = x_L = ½$ is invested in each position, then the standard deviation of portfolio return is $\sigma_P = |x_S\sigma_S - x_L\sigma_L| = |½\sigma - ½\sigma| = 0$. When combined with the underlying position, the forward hedge results in a riskless net position and converts the riskless euro cash flow into a riskless dollar cash flow.

Is this dollar cash flow truly riskless? As a general rule, nominal cash flows in a domestic currency—even riskless nominal cash flows—are exposed to inflation risk. In real terms, the purchasing power of a domestic cash flow depends on domestic inflation during the period. For example, the purchasing power of a nominally riskless $120,000 cash flow may be more or less than expected depending on realized dollar inflation during the period. Hedging foreign currency risk cannot completely eliminate risk because it cannot remove domestic inflation risk.

> ***Currency hedging substitutes domestic inflation risk for currency risk.***

To hedge against domestic inflation risk, contracts must be signed in real—not nominal—terms. This means pegging all contracts to an inflation index, such as a consumer price index (CPI). This hedges against domestic purchasing power risk to the extent that changes in the CPI approximate changes in prices actually faced by the hedger. Contracts pegged to an inflation index are common in high-inflation countries. An approximation to this hedge can be obtained using contracts with rates that float according to the level of nominal interest rates. Floating rate contracts hedge against purchasing power risk to the extent that nominal interest rate changes reflect only changes in inflation and not changes in the real rate of return. In high-inflation currencies, changes in inflation tend to dominate changes in real rates of return.

**Risky Foreign Currency Cash Flows** Equation 19.12 becomes a bit messier when cash flows are uncertain. Suppose a U.S. MNC exports computers to France through a French partner. Actual sales in France will depend on the firm's pricing decisions, as well as on the product, its marketing and promotion in France, and the operational efficiency of its distribution channels.

*Risky foreign CFs are exposed to forex (FX) rates and the foreign market.*

Risky foreign currency cash flows are exposed to each of the variance terms in Equation 19.12. As with riskless cash flows, the dollar value of a euro cash flow depends on the spot rate so the exchange rate term $\text{Var}(s^{\$/€})$ contributes to dollar return variability. Because the actual return earned on the investment in euros is uncertain, the term $\text{Var}(r^{€}) > 0$ also contributes to dollar return variability.

Exchange rate changes and foreign market returns interact through the $\text{Var}(r^{€}s^{\$/€})$ and covariance terms in Equation 19.12 because the actual levels of sales and profits in France depend on the value of the euro. This is easiest to see if we consider two pricing alternatives for the French market. Pricing the computers in euros makes it easier to forecast the euro return $r^{€}$, but the dollar value of these sales will depend on the exchange rate. Pricing the computers in dollars can reduce

**MARKET UPDATE Financial Contracts in High-Inflation Countries**

The convention in many high-inflation countries is to link financial contracts to a local price index. To deal with high and volatile inflation during the 1970s and 1980s, the Brazilian government constructed a variety of consumer and producer price indices for different sectors of the economy. Brazilian financial contracts, such as bank deposits and loans, conventionally were indexed to one of these price indices. Pegging financial contracts to a representative inflation index reduces exposure to inflation risk for both borrowers and lenders.

| | | $Var(r^f)$ + | $Var(s^{\$/f})$ | + Interaction terms | = $Var(r^{\$})$ |
|---|---|---|---|---|---|
| **Stock Returns** | Australia | **77.9%** | 20.6% | 1.5% | 100.0% |
| | Canada | **88.6%** | 5.7% | 5.7% | 100.0% |
| | France | **90.0%** | 14.9% | -4.9% | 100.0% |
| | Germany | **91.7%** | 17.3% | -8.9% | 100.0% |
| | Japan | **87.9%** | 18.5% | -6.4% | 100.0% |
| | Switzerland | **93.0%** | 29.8% | -22.8% | 100.0% |
| | United Kingdom | **89.0%** | 13.8% | -2.7% | 100.0% |
| | Average | **88.3%** | 17.2% | -5.5% | 100.0% |
| **Bond Returns** | Australia | 36.6% | **90.0%** | -26.6% | 100.0% |
| | Canada | **59.1%** | 31.2% | 9.8% | 100.0% |
| | France | 26.4% | **66.4%** | 7.3% | 100.0% |
| | Germany | 20.3% | **68.1%** | 11.0% | 100.0% |
| | Japan | 23.4% | **68.6%** | 8.1% | 100.0% |
| | Switzerland | 16.7% | **73.2%** | 10.1% | 100.0% |
| | United Kingdom | 40.1% | **46.5%** | 13.4% | 100.0% |
| | Average | 31.9% | **63.4%** | 4.7% | 100.0% |

Monthly stock returns with dividends over 1971-2011 from Morgan Stanley Capital International (www.mscibarra.com). Monthly bond returns based on 10-year government bond indices from the Organisation for Economic Co-operation and Development (www.oecd.org) over 1971-2011, except Australia (1993-2011) and Japan (1989-2011).

**FIGURE 19.5** Return Variance on Foreign Investments from a U.S. Perspective Investor.

uncertainty over the exchange rate, but sales in France will fall (rise) as the value of the dollar goes up (down). This influences the euro returns $r^€$. In the typical case, foreign currency cash flows cannot be perfectly hedged against currency risk when foreign market returns are uncertain.

**Variances on Foreign Stock and Bond Investments** Figure 19.5 uses Equation 19.12 to decompose the variance of foreign stock and bond returns from the perspective of a U.S. investor. The variance of foreign stock returns arises primarily from variance in the foreign markets, $Var(r^f)$. Foreign stock market variability accounts for an average of 88 percent of total return variance across these national markets. On average, currency variability $Var(s^{\$/f})$ accounts for about 17 percent of the total variance of return. The average effect of the interaction terms is small. The dominant risk of foreign equity investments is return variability in the national stock markets themselves. Currency risk is of secondary importance for foreign equity investments.

The bottom half of Figure 19.5 performs the same decomposition for foreign government bond returns. In contrast to foreign stocks, returns to foreign bonds are dominated by currency risks. On average, exchange rate variability accounted for about 63 percent of total return variability. The average contribution of foreign market return variability was about 32 percent. The average contribution of the interaction terms was only about 5 percent of the total.

It is not surprising that bond portfolio managers spend a great deal of effort in managing their exposures to currency risks. Managers of globally diversified stock portfolios can afford to spend more of their effort on country and industry selection, and less on currency risk management.

*Bond fund managers typically hedge their FX risks.*

### The Shifting Sands of Portfolio Analysis

Time passes and things change. These two immutable truths have consequences for how we measure and manage international investment portfolios.

**The Inputs to Portfolio Analysis** Quantitative inputs to portfolio analysis include expected returns, variances, and correlations (or covariances) for global, national, and industrial-sector portfolios of stocks and bonds, and—for active security selection—individual companies.

Consider the expected return and variance of a diversified portfolio of international securities.

$$E[r_P] = \Sigma_i x_i E[r_i] \tag{19.2}$$

$$\sigma_P{}^2 = \Sigma_i x_i{}^2 \sigma_i{}^2 + \sum_{i \neq j} \Sigma_i \Sigma_j\, x_i x_j \sigma_{ij} \tag{19.5}$$

Estimates of portfolio return and risk are only as good as the inputs to these equations. Figure 19.2 provides historical measures of mean returns, standard deviations, and cross-market correlations for several national stock indices and the MSCI world index. If expected returns or standard deviations change, or if the correlations change, then historical return measures will not accurately predict the distribution of future returns. For this reason, mutual fund prospectuses prominently display the disclaimer "past returns are no guarantee of future performance."

**Time-Varying Expected Returns and Volatilities** The expected returns and volatilities of financial assets—including stocks and bonds—vary over time, and these variations are related to business cycles. Here is a summary of the evidence.

> *Expected returns and volatilities are related to business cycles.*

- Financial market volatilities vary over time.
  - Conditional volatility models can capture time-varying volatility.
- Expected returns and risk premiums also vary over time.
  - Expected returns are low (high) when economic conditions are strong (weak).

Figure 19.6 plots conditional volatilities based on *RiskMetrics*'s model as a solid line, based on local currency monthly returns to the MSCI indices for the United Kingdom and the United States.[7] Each market has seen a mix of low-and high-volatility periods, such as just before and just after the 2008 crisis.

Expected returns and risk premiums also vary over time.[8] Fama and French found that expected returns on U.S. stocks and bonds contain a default premium that is low near peaks and high near troughs of the business cycle.[9] For example, stock and bond prices were low and expected returns were high during the Great Depression in the 1930s. In contrast, prices were high and expected returns were low during the relatively strong economy of the 1950s and 1960s. Similar evidence has been found in other developed capital markets. Instability in expected returns and

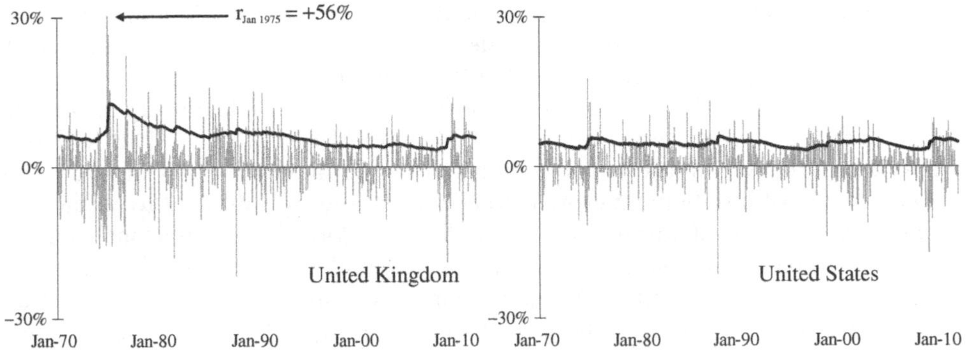


**FIGURE 19.6** Conditional Volatilities in National Stock Markets.
Source: *RiskMetrics* conditional volatility (in black) based on MSCI local currency returns (in gray) over 1970–2011.

volatilities across national indices make the portfolio manager's job more difficult, but also more interesting.

> *Estimates of future diversification benefits are imprecise.*

**Correlations between National Stock Markets: When It Rains, It Pours** Figure 19.7 plots 60-month "rolling correlations" between U.S. stocks and the national stock markets of Canada, Japan, and the United Kingdom using MSCI local-currency indices. Each point on the graph represents a correlation with the U.S. market based on returns from the previous 60 months. Canada has the highest correlation with the United States because of its geographic proximity and high level of cross-border trade. Because of their greater distance and lower levels of trade, correlations with the

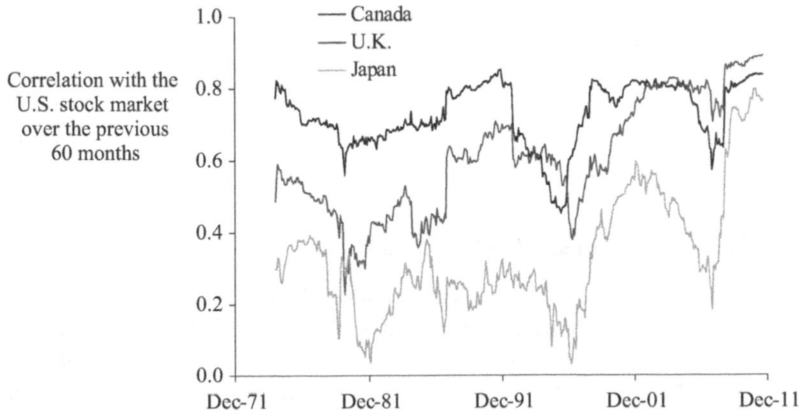


**FIGURE 19.7** 60-Month Rolling Correlations with the U.S. Stock Market.
Source: Based on monthly returns in U.S. dollars to MSCI indices.

United States tend to be lower for Japan and the United Kingdom. Although markets are increasingly integrated, there is little evidence to suggest that cross-market correlations have increased (except within Western Europe).[10]

The instability of these correlations is striking.[11] For example, the Japan–United States correlation varies from a low of 0.03 in 1997 to a high of 0.80 in 2011. Many of the largest jumps in correlation follow the financial crises of 1987 and 2008. Because of instability in cross-market correlations, it is difficult to predict the risk reduction effects of international diversification. Portfolio weights that optimize performance based on historical correlations are unlikely to deliver the same risk reduction benefits in the future. Actual benefits will be more or less than expected.

All is not lost, however. The Canadian market typically moves more closely with the U.S. market than does the Japanese or the U.K. market. Just as clearly, the Japanese stock market is likely to provide more diversification benefits than the other markets to a U.S. investor because of its lower average correlation with the U.S. market. Instability in the correlations between these national markets simply serves to caution us that the future risk reduction benefits of international portfolio diversification cannot be precisely estimated using historical data.

*Estimates of diversification benefits are imprecise.*

## 19.3 THE BENEFITS OF INTERNATIONAL PORTFOLIO DIVERSIFICATION

Domestic currency returns to a foreign asset depend on returns in the foreign market and changes in the spot exchange rate. Similarly, the risk reduction benefits of adding foreign assets to a domestic portfolio depend on the correlation of domestic assets with the foreign market and with exchange rates. International assets are attractive because both foreign markets and exchange rates have relatively low correlations with domestic assets.

Stock markets retain a distinctive national character because national economies often are dominated by a few key industries, such as oil in Persian Gulf states, auto manufacturing in Germany, and beef production in Argentina. As a consequence, local stock market returns tend to be only loosely related to stock returns in other markets. Domestic stock markets are further isolated from foreign markets by the low comovement of stock markets and exchange rates.

### Diversifying with International Equity Investments

Solnik was the first to quantify the risk reduction benefits of international diversification.[12] Figure 19.8 presents Solnik's estimate of the gain from equity diversification for a U.S. resident. The graph depicts the reduction in portfolio variance as assets are added to a portfolio. The y-axis is the ratio of portfolio variance to the variance of a typical stock. As Solnik added more stocks to a U.S. portfolio, portfolio variance fell to 27 percent of the variance of a typical U.S. stock. So, diversification within a U.S. portfolio eliminated 73 percent of the variance of a typical U.S. stock. The

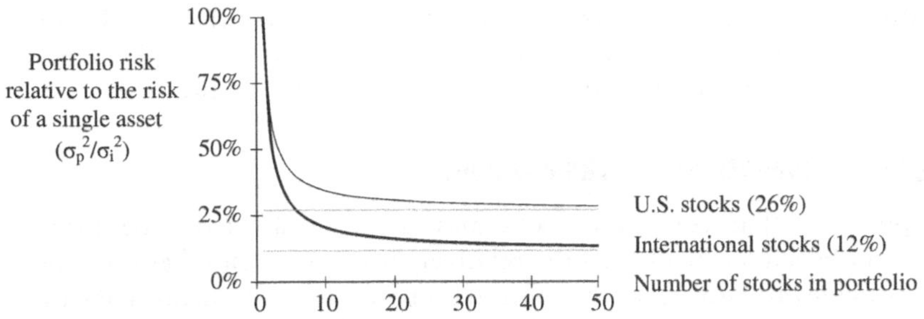


**FIGURE 19.8** Risk Reduction through Domestic and International Diversification.
Source: Adapted from "Why Not Diversify Internationally Rather Than Domestically?" by Bruno Solnik, *Financial Analysts Journal* (July/August 1974). Reprinted in 1995.

systematic risk that remained could not be eliminated through diversification within the U.S. market. As the opportunity set was expanded from domestic U.S. stocks to international equities, systematic risk fell to 12 percent of the variance of a typical stock. This was less than half of the systematic risk in a diversified domestic U.S. stock portfolio.

Solnik estimated that systematic risk constituted 35 percent of total variance for a typical stock in the United Kingdom, 33 percent in France, 44 percent in Germany, and 44 percent in Switzerland. The systematic risk component of the return to an individual stock was only 12 percent of total risk in a globally diversified portfolio, so the potential gains to international diversification are substantial in these countries. The benefits of international equity diversification are likely to be even greater for residents of countries with smaller and less diversified markets.

*Foreign investment can reduce portfolio risk.*

## Diversifying with International Bond Investments

Diversification into foreign bonds can substantially reduce the risk of a portfolio. Indeed, the potential for risk reduction through international bond diversification is even greater than with stocks.[13] For U.S. investors, dollar returns to foreign bonds have had the additional benefit of higher mean returns as well.

Bond prices are determined by nominal interest rates. Changes in nominal interest rates in turn are determined by changes in anticipated inflation and to a lesser extent by changes in real required returns. Although stock values also vary with macroeconomic factors such as expected inflation, there is a much bigger asset-specific component to stock returns than to bond returns.

Because the variability of foreign stock returns is greater than the variability of foreign bond returns, currency risk is a much larger percentage of total variance for bonds than for stocks. In Figure 19.5, exchange rate variability accounts for 63.4 percent of the variance on a typical bond portfolio and only 17.2 percent of the variance on a typical stock portfolio. Consequently, the risk reduction benefits of hedging foreign bonds against currency risk are even greater than for hedging foreign stocks. Fortunately, bonds have contractual payoffs that are simple to hedge against currency risk using currency forwards, futures, options, or swaps.

### Diversifying with International Stocks and Bonds

A domestic portfolio that combines stocks and bonds is attractive because of the diversification benefits provided by the relatively low correlation between these assets. Jorion provides an estimate of the gains to domestic stock-bond diversification from the perspective of a U.S. investor in Figure 19.9.[14] The investment opportunity set of the U.S. investor is determined by the means and standard deviations of returns to U.S. stock and bond investments, and by the relatively low stock-bond correlation (0.29 in Jorion's study).

Jorion shows that adding international assets can further improve the return-risk efficiency of a domestic portfolio. In Figure 19.9, adding foreign stocks and bonds moves the efficient frontier up and to the left as indicated by the light gray line extending down from the foreign stock investment. The gains can be substantial. For example, in Jorion's study a portfolio of internationally diversified stocks and bonds had about two-thirds the risk of U.S. stocks at the same level of expected return as for U.S. stocks.

### The Benefits of Hedging Currency Risk

Hedging the currency risk exposure of these international assets can further improve the return-risk performance of a globally diversified portfolio. There are many ways to hedge currency risks. In Figure 19.9, Jorion used a rolling 1-month forward hedge of the full amount of the stock-bond investment in each foreign currency. With a 1-month rolling hedge, the amount invested in each foreign asset is sold forward at the start of each month with a 1-month forward contract. Each hedge expires at the end of the month, and a new hedge is then established. As Figure 19.9

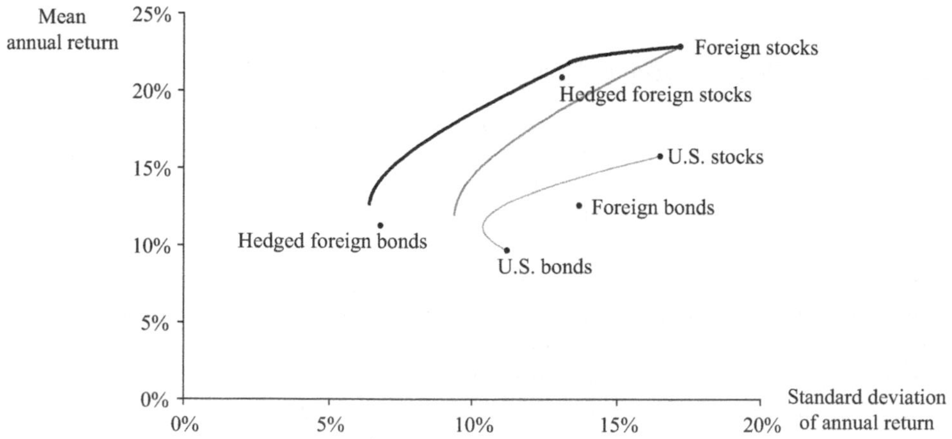


**FIGURE 19.9** Risk Reduction through International Diversification.
Source: Adapted from "Asset Allocation with Hedged and Unhedged Foreign Stocks and Bonds" by Philippe Jorion, *Journal of Portfolio Management* (Summer 1989).

shows, the potential gains in return-risk efficiency from this simple strategy for hedging exposure to currency risk can be substantial for hedged foreign stocks, and particularly for hedged foreign bonds or an internationally diversified stock-bond portfolio that has been hedged against currency risk (represented by the dark line on the left of Figure 19.9).

### Corporate Diversification and the Diversification Discount

International portfolio diversification clearly is valuable to investors. Does this mean that corporations also should attempt to diversify their products and markets in order to spread their risks and increase returns?

Corporate diversification per se should not be valuable to investors if those investors already have access to international financial markets, because investors can already capture the benefits of international diversification through their international portfolio investments. Corporate diversification into international markets cannot reduce investors' required returns or the firm's cost of capital. The MNC might be able to better employ its assets in international markets than in domestic markets, but the added value would arise from the cash flows of the investment and not from a lower cost of capital.

Indeed, corporate diversification may be detrimental to firm value. Many studies have found that both domestic and multinational conglomerates suffer a ***diversification discount***, often estimated to be about 15 percent of market value compared with portfolios of single-segment firms operating in the same industries.[15] The usual explanation is that the diversification discount is an agency cost of managers attempting to maximize their wealth and limit their risks. In particular, managers have an incentive to diversify even at shareholders' expense because it can increase their compensation through control of a larger firm, and decrease their risk through more stable business outcomes. However, it also may be that the diversification discount arises from an improper comparison to other firms, or that it is true in some lines of business and not in others. There continues to be a robust debate in the literature about the causes and even the existence of the diversification discount. The bottom line for investors is that they can already capture many of the benefits of international diversification through their portfolio investments.

> *An MNC's global reach may be offset by a diversification discount.*

## 19.4 HOME BIAS

> *Investors exhibit home bias, favoring local assets.*

Despite the compelling logic of portfolio theory, few investors fully diversify their portfolios across national borders. Instead, investors prefer assets from their

| | Market cap as % of the total | % held in domestic equities | Difference | | Market cap as % of the total | % held in domestic equities | Difference |
|---|---|---|---|---|---|---|---|
| Argentina | 0.1% | 79.7% | 79.6% | Japan | 7.4% | 82.7% | 75.3% |
| Australia | 2.6% | 80.5% | 77.8% | Korea | 1.7% | 89.3% | 87.6% |
| Austria | 0.2% | 49.3% | 49.0% | Malaysia | 0.6% | 92.6% | 92.0% |
| Brazil | 2.8% | 99.2% | 96.4% | Mexico | 0.7% | 99.3% | 98.6% |
| Canada | 3.5% | 72.8% | 69.3% | Philippines | 0.2% | 100.0% | 99.8% |
| Chile | 0.5% | 75.3% | 74.8% | Poland | 0.3% | 94.7% | 94.4% |
| China | 7.5% | data not available | | Russian Fed. | 1.5% | 99.6% | 98.1% |
| Columbia | 0.3% | 96.8% | 96.5% | Singapore | 1.0% | 70.9% | 69.9% |
| Egypt | 0.2% | 98.8% | 98.6% | South Africa | 1.7% | 88.7% | 87.0% |
| Germany | 2.7% | 47.0% | 44.3% | Spain | 3.0% | 90.9% | 87.9% |
| Greece | 0.2% | 77.3% | 77.0% | Switzerland | 2.2% | 55.5% | 53.3% |
| Hong Kong | 4.8% | 80.6% | 75.7% | Thailand | 0.4% | 97.6% | 97.2% |
| India | 5.3% | 99.9% | 94.6% | Turkey | 0.5% | 99.9% | 99.4% |
| Indonesia | 0.5% | 99.5% | 99.0% | United Kingdom | 7.2% | 66.3% | 59.1% |
| Israel | 0.4% | 83.4% | 83.0% | United States | 31.6% | 76.6% | 45.0% |

**FIGURE 19.10** Home Bias in International Equity Portfolios, 2009.
Sources: Equity market capitalization (cap) is from the World Federation of Exchanges (www.world-exchanges.org). Portfolio holdings data is from the IMF's (www.imf.org) "Coordinated Portfolio Investment Survey." Home bias is measured by subtracting the proportional market cap from the proportion of domestic equities.

own country. This tendency to invest in local assets is called ***home asset bias***, or simply ***home bias***. Home bias exists in many investable assets, including national stock, bond, and real estate markets.

Figure 19.10 presents the extent of home bias in the equity portfolios of investors from a sample of countries from year-end 2009. The difference between domestic equity holdings and the country's percentage of world market cap is provided as a measure of home bias. Investors in every country held a high percentage of their equity portfolios in domestic stocks. For example, U.S. investors held 76.6 percent of their equity portfolios in U.S. equities despite the fact that the U.S. market accounted for less than one-third of global equity value. Although investors in Western Europe have more of a tradition of international diversification, home bias is prevalent on the Continent as well. Germany accounted for only 2.7 percent of global equity value in 2009, yet Germans held 47.0 percent of their equity portfolios in German stocks. This strong home bias is evidence that national financial markets are not yet fully integrated.

Figure 19.11 compares the 2009 estimates of home bias in Figure 19.10 with estimates from 1989. The proportion of foreign equities in investors' portfolios rose in each country. For example, U.S. investors increased their proportion of foreign equities from 2.0 to 23.4 percent. German investors moved from 24.6 to 53.0 percent foreign equities. Japanese investors moved from 13.3 to 17.3 percent. Even though international equity markets are not yet fully integrated, investors' equity portfolios are more globally diversified today than just 20 years ago.

Two classes of explanations have been proposed to explain this home bias in investors' equity portfolios. One set of explanations is based on international asset pricing models, and the other set of explanations is based on capital market imperfections. International asset pricing models can argue either for or against home

| | Home bias in 1989 | | | Home bias in 2009 | | |
|---|---|---|---|---|---|---|
| | Market cap as % of the total | % held in domestic equities | Difference | Market cap as % of the total | % held in domestic equities | Difference |
| Germany | 3.2% | 75.4% | 72.2% | 2.7% | 47.0% | 44.3% |
| Japan | 43.7% | 86.7% | 43.0% | 7.4% | 82.7% | 75.3% |
| Spain | 1.1% | 94.2% | 93.1% | 3.0% | 90.9% | 87.9% |
| United Kingdom | 10.3% | 78.5% | 68.2% | 7.2% | 66.3% | 59.1% |
| United States | 36.4% | 98.0% | 61.6% | 31.6% | 76.6% | 45.0% |

**FIGURE 19.11** Home Bias in International Equity Portfolios, 1989 versus 2009.
Sources: 1989 data from Ian Cooper and Evi Kaplanis, "Home Bias in Equity Portfolios, Inflation Hedging, and International Capital Market Equilibrium," *Review of Financial Studies* 7 (Spring 1994). 2009 data from Figure 19.10.

asset bias, depending on how the asset pricing model characterizes international investment and financing opportunities. Explanations based on market imperfections generally argue for home asset bias and against international portfolio diversification. Neither explanation is wholly satisfactory; elements of each type of explanation are likely at work.

## Explanations Based on International Asset Pricing Models

International asset pricing models (see Chapter 20) send mixed signals as to whether investors should prefer local assets or an internationally diversified portfolio.

**Factors Favoring Home Bias** Investors in different countries are exposed to inflation risk in their own domestic currencies. In most models of international portfolio choice, home bias arises from the ability of domestic assets to hedge domestic inflation risk.[16]

The high levels of domestic liabilities at insurance companies and pension funds also warrant a strong home bias on the asset side of the balance sheet.[17] Insurance companies are not diversified on the liability side of the balance sheet, because it is difficult to maintain an agent base that can sell insurance products in multiple national markets. Domestic assets allow insurance companies to reduce their exposures to currency and interest rate risks by matching the currencies and maturities of their assets to those of their liabilities. This asset-liability match also reduces their exposures to domestic and foreign inflation risks.

*Home bias may serve to hedge against domestic inflation risk.*

**Factors Against Home Bias** Other portfolio-related factors suggest that investors should be more diversified internationally, not less. In particular, an individual's human capital is derived from labor income. Although an individual can borrow against his or her own income, labor income itself is a nontraded asset. Because the value of this nontraded asset is more highly correlated with domestic assets than with foreign assets, a diversified world portfolio should hold even more foreign investable assets when human capital is considered than when it is not.[18]

*Market frictions impede cross-border capital flows.*

## Explanations Based on Imperfect Markets

Market imperfections are becoming less important as more markets are opened to foreign capital. Nevertheless, many investment barriers still contribute to home bias. This section discusses real-world imperfections and the way they influence international asset prices and portfolio choice.

**Market Frictions** Market frictions impede cross-border capital flows. Frictions include

- *Government controls*. Governments sometimes try to stabilize cross-border financial flows through currency controls (such as pegged exchange rates or currency boards) or limitations on foreign ownership of domestic assets.
- *Taxes*. Taxes are imposed on two types of cross-border financial transactions: share purchases, and withholding taxes on dividend or interest distributions.
  - *Taxes on cross-border share purchases*. Some countries tax the sale or exchange of securities, and these taxes are often higher for foreign than for domestic shares. For example, Switzerland imposes a "stamp tax" of 0.15 percent of the transaction amount on transfers of domestic shares and 0.30 percent on foreign shares.
  - *Withholding taxes*. Many countries impose withholding taxes on dividend or interest paid from within their borders. Investors usually can claim withholding taxes on foreign shares as a domestic tax deduction or credit up to the amount of their domestic tax liability. Nontaxable investors, such as pension funds, typically cannot recover withholding taxes, although the size of the loss is usually small. For example, unrecoverable withholding taxes of 15 percent on a stock with a 2 percent dividend yield result in a loss of $(0.15)(0.02) = 0.003$, or 0.3 percent of share price.
- *Transaction costs*. The level of transaction costs in a market is an important measure of the market's operating efficiency and also influences the market's informational and allocational efficiency. In the United States, transaction costs can be a fraction of 0.1 percent for large transactions in actively traded stocks. In developing capital markets, direct trading costs can exceed 1 percent of the transaction amount.

These market frictions discourage international portfolio diversification by reducing the expected returns and increasing the real and perceived risks of foreign investments.

| | | | | | | | |
|---|---|---|---|---|---|---|---|
| Argentina | 52.7% | Australia | 24.8% | Brazil | 67.1% | Canada | 48.8% |
| China | 68.7% | Egypt | 40.5% | Germany | 44.7% | Hong Kong | 42.7% |
| India | 40.3% | Indonesia | 69.0% | Israel | 58.0% | Japan | 38.4% |
| Korea | 39.2% | Mexico | 26.1% | Philippines | 51.1% | Singapore | 57.1% |
| South Africa | 52.9% | Sweden | 21.0% | Switzerland | 25.7% | Taiwan | 22.3% |
| Thailand | 57.8% | Turkey | 70.9% | United Kingdom | 9.9% | U.S.A. | 7.9% |

**FIGURE 19.12** Percentage of Market Cap in Closely Held Firms (selected countries). Source: Dahlquist et al., "Corporate Governance and the Home Bias," *Journal of Financial and Quantitative Analysis* 38, Special Issue on International Corporate Governance (March 2003).

**Unequal Access to Market Prices** In perfect financial markets, large numbers of buyers and sellers ensure that no single player can influence prices. Consequently, market participants have equal access to market prices.

- *Governments and other price makers.* Equal access to prices presumes all investors are "price takers," so that no one can directly influence prices. In the real world, wealth and power are not equally distributed across market participants. The most powerful actors are governments, international cartels such as Organization of the Petroleum Exporting Countries (OPEC), investment banks, large corporations, hedge funds, and wealthy individuals.
- *The availability of shares.* Another factor to consider is that shares in many countries are likely to be controlled by a large shareholder, such as a founding family (see Figure 19.12). Dahlquist et al. estimate that 32 percent of shares worldwide are closely held.[19] Controlling shareholders usually do not trade their shares, so not all shares are available to investors. Shares that are available for trade are referred to as ***free float*** (or ***float***). Dahlquist et al. find evidence of home bias even after adjusting for free float.

**Investor Irrationality** The traditional paradigm assumes that rational investors price assets with a dispassionate eye toward expected returns and risks. Psychological factors do not enter into valuation except insofar as they affect perceived risks and returns and the cost of acquiring information. Unfortunately for this model, individuals are prone to act in irrational ways.

***Behavioral finance*** studies the impact of psychological or behavioral factors on asset prices. Behavioral finance does not presume markets are always rational, so prices can diverge from fundamental values. Here are two behaviors that can appear irrational.[20]

- *The use of heuristics.* Heuristics are rules-of-thumb or shortcuts used to simplify the decision-making process. Although heuristics can save time and simplify decisions, they also can lead to cognitive biases. In particular, people tend to place too much weight on recent, negative, or frequently received information.
- *Frame dependence.* The form in which a problem is presented can influence decisions. Here are two examples of frame dependence.
  - *Overconfidence and trading.* Individuals are often overconfident about their abilities, knowledge, and future prospects. Overconfidence can lead investors

to trade more than rational investors, even when excessive trading lowers expected returns.[21] Interestingly, trading behavior and overconfidence are gender-related, with males trading more than females while generating higher fees and lower returns.[22]

- *The desire to avoid recognizing losses*. Humans have an innate desire to avoid regret. In financial markets, regret avoidance causes investors to hold onto their losing investments and sell their winners early.[23]

*Behavioral finance does not assume rational investors.*

The cognitive biases associated with heuristics and frame dependence can result in inefficient markets; that is, in prices that deviate from fundamental values.

Behavioral finance does not yet have an agreed model of investor behavior and asset prices. Nevertheless, a behavioral approach can provide insights into why prices might not fit traditional theories. There is a robust debate in the literature between the two sides. Proponents of the traditional view strive to explain the insights of behavioral finance using a rational expectations framework. Proponents of the behavioral view dismiss the beliefs of traditionalists as frame dependent; that is, as overconfident in their beliefs and unwilling to recognize their losses. As they say in the fight game: "Let's get ready to rumble!"

**Unequal Access to Information** It can be difficult to obtain and interpret information from distant markets. It also is more difficult to monitor the actions of managers in distant locations. Here is some evidence on how familiarity and access to information contribute to home bias.

*Information is costly.*

- *Distance and portfolio choice*. Grinblatt and Keloharju found that investors in Finland are more likely to own firms that are located nearby.[24] There is increasing evidence of home bias within domestic markets as well. For example, Coval and Moskowitz found U.S. fund managers prefer local firms, especially small and highly levered firms that produce goods consumed locally.[25] Information and monitoring costs are particularly high for distant investors in these types of firms.
- *Language, culture, and portfolio choice*. Grinblatt and Keloharju also found that Finnish investors are more likely to own firms that communicate in their native language (Finnish versus Swedish) or have CEOs of the same cultural background. This suggests that language and culture influence investors' portfolio choices.

These studies conclude that investors prefer to hold local assets because of their greater access to information and the familiarity of local assets. There is conflicting evidence on whether local investors enjoy an informational advantage over more distant investors that allows them to earn higher returns on their local investments.

### The Effect of Home Bias on Prices and Required Returns

One might think that home bias on the part of domestic investors would tend to increase local equity values. However, there is both theoretical and empirical evidence that capital market imperfections that create a home bias in fact tend to decrease equity values and increase required returns. From a theoretical perspective, the reason for lower prices and higher required returns in segmented markets is that—with little international risk sharing—local investors must bear a greater proportion of firms' total risks.[26] Recent empirical evidence is consistent with this notion. Countries with greater degrees of home bias indeed have lower equity values and higher costs of capital than other countries.[27]

> *Home bias lowers equity values and increases required returns.*

## 19.5 SUMMARY

Assuming nominal returns are normally distributed, the expected return and variance of a portfolio are given by

$$E[r_P] = \Sigma_i x_i E[r_i] \tag{19.2}$$

$$\begin{aligned} \text{and} \quad Var(r_P) &= \Sigma_i \Sigma_j x_i x_j \sigma_{ij} \\ &= \Sigma_i x_i^2 \sigma_i^2 + \Sigma_i \Sigma_j{}_{\,i \neq j}\, x_i x_j \sigma_{ij} \end{aligned} \tag{19.5}$$

The variance calculation in Equation 19.5 has three implications for portfolio risk and return.

- The extent to which risk is reduced by portfolio diversification depends on how highly the individual assets in the portfolio are correlated.
- As the number of assets held in a portfolio increases, the variance of return on the portfolio becomes more dependent on the covariances between the individual securities and less dependent on the variances of the individual securities.
- The risk of an individual asset when it is held in a portfolio with a large number of securities depends on its return covariance with other securities in the portfolio and not on its return variance.

According to the algebra of portfolio theory, the total risk of an asset can be decomposed into systematic and unsystematic components. Systematic risks are related to risks in other stocks and cannot be diversified away in a large portfolio. Unsystematic risks are unrelated to risks in other stocks and are diversifiable in a large portfolio.

Returns on foreign investments are given by

$$(1 + r^d) = (1 + r^f)(1 + s^{d/f}) = 1 + r^f + s^{d/f} + r^f s^{d/f} \tag{19.10}$$

Equation 19.10 has the following consequences for the expected return of a portfolio:

$$E[r^d] = E[r^f] + E[s^{d/f}] + E[r^f s^{d/f}] \tag{19.11}$$

and the variance of return on a portfolio:

$$\begin{aligned} Var(r^d) = {} & Var(r^f) + Var(s^{d/f}) + Var(r^f s^{d/f}) + 2Cov(r^f, s^{d/f}) + 2Cov(r^f, r^f s^{d/f}) \\ & + 2Cov(s^{d/f}, r^f s^{d/f}) \end{aligned} \tag{19.12}$$

The principal determinants of return variance on a foreign asset are the variance of return in the foreign market and the variance of exchange rate changes. The cross-product terms are relatively minor contributors to portfolio risk.

International stock and bond investments differ in the relative contribution of each source of variability. The largest source of variability in international stock returns comes from return variance in the foreign market. Variability in foreign exchange rates plays a lesser role. In contrast, international bond returns are influenced both by bond price variability in the foreign markets and by exchange rate variability. Bond fund managers spend more of their time managing exchange rate exposures than do stock fund managers because of the greater importance of exchange rate variability in international bond returns.

Despite the logic of portfolio theory, few investors fully diversify their investment portfolios across national borders. Instead, investors tend to invest in local assets. This home bias exists in most investable asset markets, including stocks, bonds, and real estate.

## KEY TERMS

*behavioral finance*
*correlation and covariance*
*efficient frontier*
*free float (or float)*
*home asset bias (or home bias)*
*investment opportunity set*
*market risk (systematic risk in the Capital asset pricing model (CAPM))*
*mean-variance efficiency*
*nonmarket risk (unsystematic risk in the CAPM)*
*Sharpe index*
*short selling*
*systematic or nondiversifiable risk*
*unsystematic or diversifiable risk*

## CONCEPTUAL QUESTIONS

19.1 How is portfolio risk measured? What determines portfolio risk?

19.2 What happens to portfolio risk as the number of assets in the portfolio increases?

19.3 What happens to the relevant risk measure for an individual asset when it is held in a large portfolio rather than in isolation?

19.4 In words, what does the Sharpe index measure?

19.5 Name two synonyms for systematic risk.

19.6 Name two synonyms for unsystematic risk.

19.7 Which portfolio has the most to gain from currency hedging—a portfolio of international stocks or a portfolio of international bonds? Why?

19.8 Is international diversification effective in reducing portfolio risk? Why?

19.9 What is a perfect financial market?

19.10 Are real-world financial markets perfect? If not, in what ways are they imperfect?

19.11 Describe some of the barriers to international portfolio diversification.

19.12 What is home asset bias? What might be its cause?

19.13 What is "free float"?

## PROBLEMS

19.1 Based on the historical returns in Figure 19.2, calculate the mean and standard deviation of return in dollars for an equal-weighted portfolio of French and German stocks. Calculate the Sharpe index for this portfolio using the historical mean return on U.S. T-bills as the risk-free rate.

19.2 Based on the historical returns in Figure 19.2, calculate the mean and standard deviation of return in dollars for an equal-weighted portfolio of German and Japanese stocks. Calculate the Sharpe index for this portfolio using the historical mean return on U.S. T-bills as the risk-free rate.

19.3 The MSCI world stock market index in Figure 19.2 had a mean annual return of 10.4 percent and a standard deviation of 18.3 percent. Meanwhile, dollar returns to a globally diversified bond portfolio had a mean of 8.4 and a standard deviation of 10.8 percent. The correlation between these two indices was 0.360. Calculate the mean and standard deviation of an equal-weighted portfolio of global stocks and bonds. Also, calculate the Sharpe index for this stock-bond portfolio using the historical 6.1 percent U.S. T-bill rate.

19.4 Based on the historical returns in Figure 19.2, calculate the expected return and standard deviation of return in dollars to an equal-weighted portfolio of U.S., U.K., and Japanese stocks. Calculate the Sharpe index for this portfolio using the historical mean return on risk-free U.S. T-bills.

19.5 Suppose expected returns in the United States and Germany are 10 percent and 20 percent, respectively. Standard deviations are also 10 percent and 20 percent, respectively. Calculate the standard deviation of an equal-weighted portfolio under the following four cases: (a) perfect positive correlation, (b) perfect negative correlation, (c) zero correlation, and (d) a correlation of 0.3.

19.6 A portfolio consists of assets A, B, and C. Weights are $x_A = 20\%$, $x_B = 30\%$, and $x_C = 50\%$. Expected returns are $E[r_A] = 8\%$, $E[r_B] = 10\%$, $E[r_C] = 13\%$. What is the portfolio expected return?

19.7 Suppose you calculated a Sharpe index for every security in the world over the most recent year. Are any of these securities likely to exhibit performance (measured as excess return per unit of risk) that is superior to that of the world market portfolio? Why or why not?

19.8 Suppose that an asset, A, earns 16 percent in the United States over the period of one year. If the cost of a dollar to a resident of the European Union goes from €0.7064/$ at the beginning of the year to €0.7182/$ at the end of the year, what is the euro return on the U.S. asset?

19.9 Share prices on the Philippine Stock Exchange rise 12 percent in Philippine pesos. During the same period, the peso rises from $0.0425/peso to $0.0440/peso. By how much does the Philippine stock market rise in U.S. dollars?

19.10 What is the standard deviation of return on the Philippine stock market to a U.S. investor if the standard deviation of the local stock market is 24.8 percent, the standard deviation of the dollar-per-peso exchange rate is 32.7 percent, and the interaction terms involving local market returns and the exchange rate are negligible?

19.11 How much of the return variance on a foreign stock investment is likely to come from variation in the foreign stock market and how much from the variation in the exchange rate? What are the proportions for a foreign bond investment?

19.12 Suppose you replicate Solnik's experiment in Figure 19.9 for Greenland. What percent of the variance on a typical Greenland stock do you think would be eliminated within a portfolio of domestic stocks? What percent of the variance of a typical stock is likely to be diversifiable within a globally diversified portfolio?

19.13 You are planning for retirement and must decide on the inputs to use in your asset allocation decision. Knowing the benefits of international portfolio diversification, you want to include foreign stocks and bonds in your final portfolio. What statistics should you collect on the world's major national debt and equity markets? Can you trust that the future will be like the past?

19.14 A portfolio manager gathers monthly stock returns going back to the year 1901 and estimates mean returns, variances, and cross-market correlations for 50 countries. She identifies the efficient frontier and then invests in the portfolio that is mean-variance efficient relative to the U.S. risk-free rate. Is this fund manager's performance over the coming year likely to be similar to the historical record? Over the next five years? Over the next ten years? Explain.

## SUGGESTED READINGS

### Articles on international asset pricing with implications for the home bias observed in domestic portfolios include

Michael Adler and Bernard Dumas, "International Portfolio Choice and Corporation Finance: A Synthesis," *Journal of Finance* 38 (June 1983), 925–984.

Ines Chaieb and Vihang Errunza, "International Asset Pricing under Segmentation and PPP Deviations," *Journal of Financial Economics* 86 (November 2007), 543–578.

Kalok Chan, Vicentiu Covrig, and Lilian Ng, "Does Home Bias Affect Firm Value? Evidence from Holdings of Mutual Funds Worldwide," *Journal of International Economics* 78 (July 2009), 230–241.

Sie Ting Lau, Lilian Ng, and Bohui Zhang, "The World Price of Home Bias," *Journal of Financial Economics* 97 (August 2010), 191–217.

### Articles that make a case for international portfolio diversification include

Cliff S. Asness, Roni Israelov, and John M. Liew, "International Diversification Works (Eventually)," *Financial Analysts Journal* 67 (May/June 2011), 24–38.

Haim Levy and Zvi Lerman, "The Benefits of International Diversification in Bonds," *Financial Analysts Journal* 44 (September/October 1988), 56–64.

Philippe Jorion, "Asset Allocation with Hedged and Unhedged Foreign Stocks and Bonds," *Journal of Portfolio Management* 15 (Summer 1989), 49–54.

Bruno Solnik, "Why Not Diversify Internationally Rather Than Domestically?" *Financial Analysts Journal* 30 (July/August 1974), 48–54. Reprinted in *Financial Analysts Journal* 51 (January/February 1995), 89–94.

### The literature on time-varying expected returns, volatilities, and comovements tends to be rather technical.

Geert Bekaert, Robert J. Hodrick, and Xiaoyan Zhang, "International Stock Return Comovements," *Journal of Finance* 64 (December 2009), 2591–2626.

Eugene F. Fama and Kenneth R. French, "Business Conditions and Expected Returns on Stocks and Bonds," *Journal of Financial Economics* 25 (November 1989), 23–50.

William N. Goetzmann, Lingfeng Li, and K. Geert Rouwenhorst, "Long-Term Global Market Correlations," *Journal of Business* 78 (January 2005), 1–38.

Jonathan Lewellen, "The Time-Series Relations among Expected Return, Risk, and Book-to-Market," *Journal of Financial Economics* 54 (October 1999), 5–43.

Weng-Ling Lin, Robert F. Engle, and Takatoshi Ito, "Do Bulls and Bears Move Across Borders? International Transmission of Stock Returns and Volatility," *Review of Financial Studies* 7 (Fall 1994), 507–538.

### Home asset bias is investigated in

Marianne Baxter and Urban J. Jermann, "The International Diversification Puzzle Is Worse Than You Think," *American Economic Review* 87 (March 1997), 170–180.

Joshua D. Coval and Tobias J. Moskowitz, "Home Bias at Home: Local Equity Preference in Domestic Portfolios," *Journal of Finance* 53 (December 1999), 2045–2074.

Ian Cooper and Evi Kaplanis, "Home Bias in Equity Portfolios, Inflation Hedging, and International Capital Market Equilibrium," *Review of Financial Studies* 7, No. 1 (Spring 1994), 45–60.

Timothy M. Craft, "Home Bias Makes Sense for U.S. Pension Plans," *Journal of Portfolio Management* 32 (Spring 2006), 26–33.

Magnus Dahlquist, Lee Pinkowitz, René M. Stulz, and Rohan Williamson, "Corporate Governance and the Home Bias," *Journal of Financial and Quantitative Analysis* 38, Special Issue on International Corporate Governance (March 2003), 87–110.

Mark Grinblatt and Matti Keloharju, "How Distance, Language, and Culture Influence Stockholdings and Trades," *Journal of Finance* 56 (June 2001), 1053–1073.

### Behavioral finance is discussed in

Brad M. Barber and Terrance Odean, "Boys Will Be Boys: Gender, Overconfidence, and Common Stock Investment," *Quarterly Journal of Economics* 116 (February 2001), 261–292.

Daniel Kahneman and Amos Tversky, "Prospect Theory: An Analysis of Decision Under Risk," *Econometrica* 47 (March 1979), 263–292.

Terrance Odean, "Do Investors Trade Too Much?" *American Economic Review* 89 (December 1999), 1279–1298.

Hersh Shefrin and Meir Statman, "The Disposition to Sell Winners Too Early and Ride Losers Too Long: Theory and Evidence," *Journal of Finance* 40 (July 1985), 777–782.

### The global diversification discount is discussed in

David J. Denis, Diane K. Denis, and David Yost, "Global Diversification, Industrial Diversification, and Firm Value," *Journal of Finance* 57 (October 2002), 1951–1979.

# CHAPTER 20

# International Asset Pricing

*We dance round in a ring and suppose,*
*But the Secret sits in the middle and knows.*

—Robert Frost

This chapter develops several models for pricing international assets. We begin with the single-currency capital asset pricing model (CAPM). A few assumptions to ensure purchasing power parity then lead to an international version of the CAPM called the international asset pricing model (IAPM). The appeal of these asset pricing models is that an asset's risk is uniquely identified by its systematic risk or beta measured against a broadly diversified market portfolio.

Unfortunately for the CAPM and IAPM, betas estimated with conventional methods have almost no relation to mean returns. In the absence of a relation between mean returns and beta, finance has continued its search for models to explain returns to domestic and international assets. Recent innovations include models with macroeconomic, country/industry, value/growth, size, and currency risk factors, as well as models with time-varying coefficients, and momentum. The chapter concludes with a discussion of contemporary asset pricing models.

## 20.1 THE INTERNATIONAL CAPITAL ASSET PRICING MODEL

This section extends the familiar *CAPM* introduced in your first course in finance to a multicurrency setting.

### The Traditional Capital Asset Pricing Model

Before we develop an international version of the CAPM, we need to complete the development of the traditional, single-currency CAPM shown in Figure 20.1. Chapter 19 on international portfolio diversification invoked two assumptions.

- Perfect financial markets
  - Rational investors have equal access to information and prices in frictionless markets.

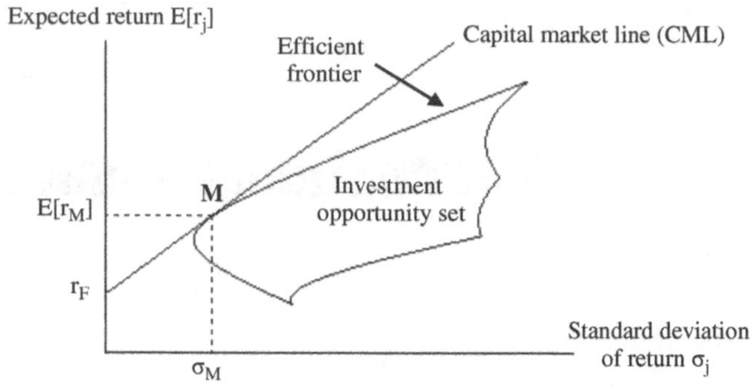


**FIGURE 20.1** The CAPM and the CML.

- Normally distributed returns
  - Only the mean and standard deviation of portfolio return matter to investors.

Two more assumptions are necessary to complete the traditional version of the CAPM.

- Investors have homogeneous expectations regarding future expected returns and risks.
- Everyone can borrow and lend at the risk-free rate of interest $r_F$.

The first of these is an assumption that all investors have the same expectations. In such a world, every investor faces the same investment opportunity set in Figure 20.1. An assumption of homogeneous expectations is out of place in a book founded on differences among the peoples of the world, but it is necessary for the traditional version of the CAPM.

The risk-free asset yields a nominal rate $r_F$ at which any party can borrow or lend. Nominal returns to this asset are certain ($\sigma_F = 0$), so the covariance or correlation of the risk-free asset with any risky asset A is zero ($\sigma_{F,A} = \rho_{F,A} = 0$). This means that a combination of the risk-free asset and any risky asset forms a straight line between the two points in E[r]-σ space.[1]

*The CML is mean-variance efficient.*

In Figure 20.1, the *CML* extends from the risk-free asset $r_F$ to point M. Along this tangency line, investors achieve the highest level of expected return per unit of risk of any combination of the risk-free and a risky asset. Point M is called the ***market portfolio*** in the CAPM and includes all assets in the investment opportunity set weighted according to their market values. There typically is a single tangency point, in which case the market portfolio is unique. Investors receive the biggest bang for the buck (or euro, or yuan) along this line.

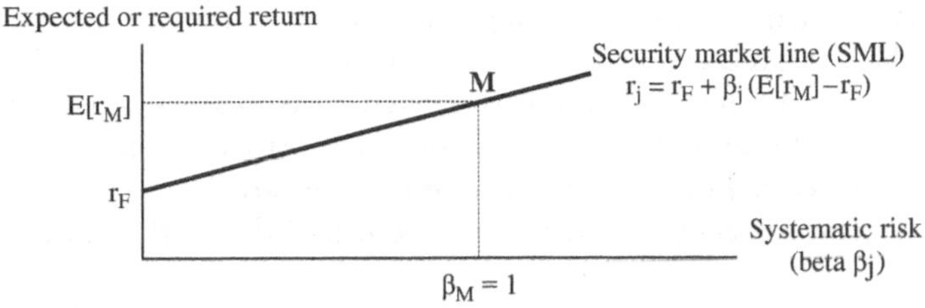


**FIGURE 20.2** The SML.

Under the assumptions of the CAPM, each investor choosing to invest in a risky asset will hold the market portfolio. The ***systematic risk*** of an individual asset (also called ***market risk*** or ***nondiversifiable risk*** in the context of the CAPM) can then be measured by how its returns covary with those of the market portfolio. This allows us to shift the focus from capital market equilibrium depicted in Figure 20.1 to the expected return and systematic risk of a single asset in the market portfolio, shown in Figure 20.2.

**Systematic (Nondiversifiable) Risk and the Security Market Line** Assets are correctly priced in efficient financial markets, so the expected net present value of any financial investment is zero. This means that an asset's expected return must equal that asset's required return. In the CAPM, expected or required return is determined by the ***SML.***

$$r_j = r_F + \beta_j(E[r_M] - r_F) \tag{20.1}$$

> *The SML describes the relation between required return and systematic risk.*

The SML is graphed in Figure 20.2. This relation states that the required return on an individual asset is equal to the risk-free rate $r_F$ plus a risk premium appropriate for the systematic risk of the asset. The risk premium is the product of the ***market risk premium*** (i.e., the risk premium $E[r_M] - r_F$ on the market portfolio) and the firm's systematic risk or beta ($\beta_j$). ***Beta*** reflects the sensitivity of an asset's price to changes in the value of the market portfolio. Systematic risks arise through market-wide events, such as unexpected changes in real economic activity or investor sentiment regarding asset values. In the CAPM, an asset's beta measured against the market portfolio is the *only* measure of systematic risk.

Risk-adjusted investment performance is measured in the CAPM by the difference between actual return and the expected return from Equation 20.1,

$$e_j = r_j - E[r_j] = r_j - [r_F + \beta_j(r_M - r_F)] \tag{20.2}$$

where $r_j$ is the observed return to asset j and $E[r_j]$ is the expected or required return from the SML. The current T-bill or T-bond yield is used as $r_F$, depending on the maturity of the firm's assets (with a corresponding adjustment to the size of the market risk premium). The observed excess return of the market portfolio over the risk-free rate is given by $(r_M - r_F)$. The residual return $e_j$ then measures risk-adjusted performance over the period. Because $E[e_j] = 0$, abnormal (positive or negative) investment performance is measured by the difference of $e_j$ from zero.[2]

Beta is estimated by regressing security return on the return of the market index.

$$r_j = \alpha_j + \beta_j r_M + e_j \tag{20.3}$$

This ***market model*** regression is depicted in Figure 20.3. The slope coefficient $\beta_j$ captures that part of the variation in an individual stock that is linearly related to the market return.

As with any regression coefficient, beta can be restated as a correlation coefficient scaled by the standard deviations of $r_j$ and $r_M$, or as the covariance $\sigma_{jM}$ divided by the market variance $\sigma_M{}^2$.

$$\beta_j = \rho_{j,M}(\sigma_j/\sigma_M) = \sigma_{jM}/\sigma_M{}^2 \tag{20.4}$$

In this way, beta measures an asset's systematic risk; that is, the asset's sensitivity to market returns. The beta of the market itself is $\beta_M = \rho_{M,M}(\sigma_M/\sigma_M) = 1$. The beta of the risk-free asset is $\beta_F = 0$. Stocks with betas greater than one have more systematic risk than the average stock. These stocks tend to perform better than average when the market is up and worse than average when the market is down. Another way of stating this is that firms with betas greater (less) than one are more (less) sensitive to changes in the market index than the average firm.

**Unsystematic (Diversifiable) Risks** The residual $e_j$ captures all variation in $r_j$ that is unrelated to the market portfolio; that is, that portion of individual security risk that can be diversified away by holding the security in a portfolio with many securities. Such risk is called ***diversifiable risk*** or ***unsystematic risk***. It also is called ***nonmarket risk*** in the context of the CAPM. If returns are normally distributed, then the residual term also is distributed as normal with zero mean ($E[e_j] = 0$), and is uncorrelated with other securities ($Cov(e_i, e_j) = \sigma_{ij} = 0$ for $i \neq j$) and with the market portfolio ($Cov(e_j, r_M) = \sigma_{jM} = 0$).

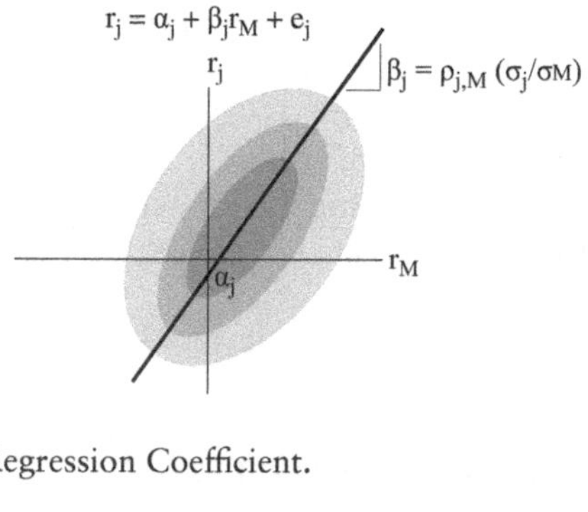


**FIGURE 20.3** Beta as a Regression Coefficient.

If the asset is a national stock market, then the portion of risk that is diversifiable also is called ***country-specific risk.*** To the extent that country-specific risks (such as country-specific political risks) can be diversified away within a globally diversified portfolio, these risks are unsystematic and hence should not be reflected in the required return from the SML. The theoretically correct way to handle country-specific risks is to incorporate them into the expected cash flows from investment, as in the treatment of expropriation risk in Chapter 13.

### The International Asset Pricing Model

**Two Additional Assumptions** In addition to the assumptions of the traditional CAPM, two more conditions are necessary to ensure that the international parity conditions hold in a world in which investors have different functional currencies.[3]

- Purchasing power parity holds, so that asset prices and real required rates within a particular asset class are the same in every country and for every individual.
- Investors have the same consumption basket, so that inflation is measured against the same benchmark in every country.

If the international parity conditions hold, then changes in exchange rates simply mirror inflation differentials. In this world, the exchange rate is nothing more than a device for translating between currencies and holds no real power over investors.

> *IAPM investors hold the market and a hedge portfolio.*

Once these conditions are imposed, extension of the CAPM to a world of many functional currencies is straightforward. The resulting model is called the ***IAPM.*** Just as in the traditional CAPM, all investors hold their funds at risk in a single, mean-variance efficient market portfolio of risky assets. In the IAPM, the market portfolio is a globally diversified portfolio comprising all risky assets weighted according to their market values at prevailing exchange rates. In the IAPM, investors also hold a currency-specific ***hedge portfolio*** that serves a role similar to that of the risk-free asset in the traditional CAPM. This hedge portfolio consists of risk-free domestic and foreign assets and is held for two reasons.

- As a store of value (like the risk-free asset in the traditional CAPM)
- To hedge the currency risk of the market portfolio

If inflation is a constant in each currency, then the hedge portfolio held by each investor reduces to the investor's home-currency, risk-free asset as in the CAPM.

**Financial Market Segmentation and Choice of the Market Portfolio** The assumptions of the IAPM are sufficient to ensure that financial markets are ***integrated,*** such that prices are simultaneously established across all markets and required returns on assets of the same risk are the same in all locations. The world market portfolio is then a fully diversified set of risky international assets that is shared by investors in every country. Risk-averse investors hold a hedge portfolio that includes risk-free domestic and foreign bills. In the IAPM, the systematic risk of an asset reflects the asset's sensitivity to changes in the value of the world market portfolio. Industry and national market indices are of importance only in that they reflect the sensitivity of the industry or national market to changes in the value of the world market portfolio.

In completely ***segmented*** national markets, the price of a particular asset or asset class is set independently in each national market. In this case, purchasing power parity will not hold across national markets even though it might hold within a national market. Without access to international markets, investors hold their own national market portfolio of risky assets. The systematic risk of an asset in a segmented national market then depends on its sensitivity to national market movements and not on its sensitivity to world market movements. The reality of present-day financial markets invariably lies somewhere between these extremes and differs across markets depending on how closely each market is integrated with other markets.[4]

**Empirical Evidence** The intuition behind the CAPM is simple—higher risks demand higher expected and required returns. This intuition suggests that there should be a relation between mean returns and betas. In fact, if returns are normally distributed and performance is measured against a market portfolio that is ex post mean-variance efficient, then the algebra of the CAPM *requires* that beta and only beta explains an asset's mean return. There is no systematic portion of return left to be explained by any other variable.

> *Tests find no relation between beta and mean return.*

Unfortunately for proponents of the CAPM, empirical tests commonly find no relation between mean returns and betas. Fama and French conclude that "the relation between market beta and average return is flat, even when beta is the only explanatory variable."[5] This is a curious and unsettling finding for the CAPM. If beta is unrelated to return, then it makes little sense to use beta in estimating the cost of capital or measuring investment performance. Thus, we need to look a little more closely for meaningful measures of systematic risk and required return.

## 20.2 FACTOR MODELS AND ARBITRAGE PRICING THEORY

The CAPM and IAPM have intuitive and practical appeal because they suggest a simple measure of systematic risk (beta) and a simple linear relation (the SML) between systematic risk and expected return. The finding that beta has little relation to ex post mean return—at least with regression-based estimates such as Equation 20.3—is a critical failure of these models.

## MARKET UPDATE The Relevance of Market Indices

Although market model betas are suspect, market indices nevertheless are useful benchmarks. Indeed, comparison of investment returns to those of an index with the same target weights is the most widely accepted criterion of investment performance. Financial newspapers such as *The Wall Street Journal* and the London *Financial Times* report global, regional, local, and industry indices on a broad range of assets. National market indices, such as the Standard and Poors 500 and London's Financial Times Stock Exchange All-Shares 750, track the performance of national markets. Regional indices track returns in regions such as the Americas, Europe, or Asia/Pacific regions. Some industry indices are local in scope, such as the Dow Jones Utilities Index. Others are transnational, such as Morgan Stanley Capital International's industry indices for aerospace, automobiles, and banking. These stock market indices provide performance benchmarks for investments in these asset classes.

Ross developed ***arbitrage pricing theory (APT)*** in response to these criticisms.[6] Like the CAPM, APT assumes a linear relation between systematic risk and expected return. Unlike the CAPM, it does not require homogeneous expectations, nor does it claim that an asset's relation to the market portfolio is the only measure of systematic risk.

The APT takes a more general view of the types of risks that might be priced. In the APT, an asset's rate of return is assumed to be a linear function of K systematic risk factors according to

$$r_j = \mu_j + \beta_{1j}F_1 + \cdots + \beta_{Kj}F_K + e_j \tag{20.5}$$

where
$r_j$ = a random, normally distributed rate of return on asset j
$\mu_j$ = the mean or expected return on asset j
$\beta_{kj}$ = the sensitivity of asset j's return to factor k for $k = 1, \ldots, K$
$F_k$ = a systematic risk factor k
$e_j$ = a normally distributed random error or noise term specific to asset j

Factor models such as Equation 20.5 are based on the idea that the actual return on an individual security can be decomposed into an expected part and an unexpected part. The expected return $E[r_j] = \mu_j$ depends on the expected risk premium associated with each factor. The unexpected part of the return contains a systematic risk component $(\Sigma_k\beta_{kj}F_k)$ and an unsystematic risk or error component $e_j$. The systematic risk factors $F_k$ are risks that affect a large number of assets. In this way, the systematic risk and, hence, the expected and required return of an individual security j depend on the K systematic risk factors and on the asset's sensitivities to those factors.

As in the CAPM, unsystematic risk $e_j$ is specific to a single asset. For a company j, company-specific risks can include unexpected management changes, research breakthroughs, labor strife, and retirement of key personnel. For a country j,

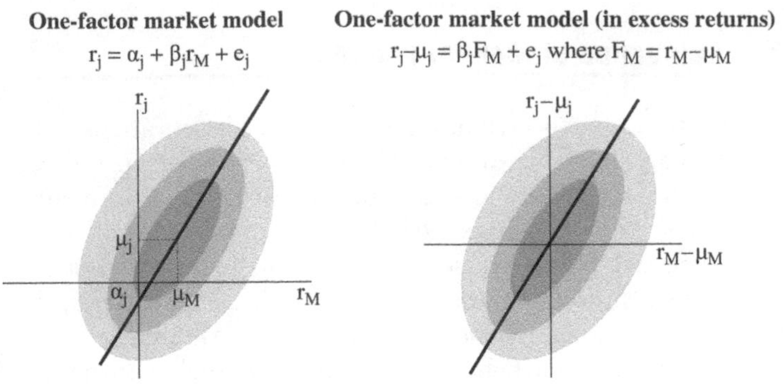


**FIGURE 20.4** The One-Factor Market Model.

country-specific risks can include unexpected changes in laws, taxes, fiscal or monetary policies, or political events. Assuming a correctly specified model, the APT's linear structure ensures that asset-specific error $e_j$ is unrelated to the systematic risk factors as well as to other firms' errors, so that $E[e_j] = Cov(e_i, e_j) = 0$ for $i \neq j$.

> *APT does not identify priced factors a priori.*

The major drawback of a factor model is that the factors that might be priced in the market are not identified a priori by the model. The major appeal of the CAPM is that there is one and only one systematic risk factor—the market return. In APT, systematic risk factors must be either empirically identified from the data (e.g., through factor analysis) or independently identified through another asset pricing model that guides the search for factors that might be priced.

A prominent special case is the one-factor market model. Figure 20.4 presents this model in graphical form. This is the same market model that was used in Equation 20.3 to estimate beta in the CAPM, although it will be developed in a little more detail here. The model is as follows:

$$r_j = \alpha_j + \beta_j r_M + e_j \tag{20.3}$$

The expectation of this equation is $E[r_j] = \alpha_j + \beta_j E[r_M]$. Substituting observed means $\mu_j$ and $\mu_M$ for the expectations and subtracting the resulting equation ($\mu_j = \alpha_j + \beta_j \mu_M$) from the one-factor market model in Equation 20.3 results in a one-factor market model in *excess return* form:

$$r_j = \mu_j + \beta_j F_M + e_j \tag{20.6}$$

The systematic risk factor in this model is the difference between the actual and the mean market index return, $F_M = r_M - \mu_M$. Equation 20.6 is the APT equivalent of the one-factor (CAPM or IAPM) market model in Equation 20.3. The measure of systematic risk, $\beta_j = \rho_{j,M}(\sigma_j/\sigma_M)$, captures the sensitivity or exposure of security return to unexpected changes in the market index.

### APPLICATION An Example of Arbitrage Pricing

Suppose there are no transaction costs, rational investors have equal access to market prices and information, and there are no short-sale restrictions. Investors in this world may care about multiple sources of risk, such as unexpected changes in asset prices, inflation, or gross domestic product growth. Investors are rational and will attempt to exploit any investment opportunities that arise. Now, suppose investors are given the following opportunity:

1. A mutual fund (M) invests in the market, sells for £100, and has an expected payoff of £110 in one year.
2. An asset (A) has the same systematic risk as M, sells for £100, and has an expected payoff of £120.

The systematic risk of assets A and M might be from their exposure to the market index. Alternatively, it might arise from their exposures to macroeconomic risk factors, such as industrial production or the term structure of interest rates. It really doesn't matter, so long as investors are able to estimate the sensitivities of assets A and M to the relevant systematic risk factors and identify their required return.

Because the assets have the same systematic risk and required return, the winning strategy is to short the market portfolio M and invest in asset A. Returns are uncertain, so the actual payoff is uncertain. The actual return on M is the expected plus the unexpected return: $r_M = E[r_M] + e_M$. Similarly, the actual return on A is $r_A = E[r_A] + e_A$. The actual return on short selling M and investing in A is $(r_A - r_M) = (E[r_A] - E[r_M]) + (e_A - e_M) = (£120 - £110) + (e_A - e_M) = £10 + (e_A - e_M)$. Although this position has a positive expected return of $E[r_A - r_M] = £10$ and no net investment, it also has unsystematic risk through the unexpected returns $e_A$ and $e_M$.

The winning strategy is not "pure" or riskless arbitrage because of this risk. Instead, it is "risk arbitrage" or "arbitrage in expectation." This is the meaning of "arbitrage" in APT.

## 20.3 FACTOR MODELS FOR INTERNATIONAL ASSETS

International asset pricing is one of the most active and interesting areas of finance, at least in part because of the failure of standard models such as the CAPM to adequately describe returns. This section rounds up some of the more prominent studies.

### Macroeconomic Factors Associated with Domestic Stock Returns

One of the first applications of APT was Chen, Roll, and Ross's study of U.S. stocks.[7] These authors identified several macroeconomic factors that ought to be sources of systematic risk based on a simple discounted cash flow model. Their factors included the following[8]:

$F_1$ = unexpected changes in inflation
$F_2$ = unexpected changes in industrial production
$F_3$ = unexpected changes in the slope of the term structure of interest rates measured by the spread between long-term and short-term government bonds
$F_4$ = unexpected changes in risk premiums measured by the spread between risky corporate bonds (rated Baa and below) and risk-free U.S. government bonds

The factor model for estimating the relation of these factors to an asset's mean return is

$$r_j = \mu_j + \beta_{1j}F_1 + \beta_{2j}F_2 + \beta_{3j}F_3 + \beta_{4j}F_4 + e_j \quad (20.7)$$

Each factor is constructed as "actual minus expected" (e.g., actual minus expected inflation), such that the expectation of each factor $E[F_k] = 0$. The mean return $\mu_j$ is subtracted from each side to obtain the excess return form.

$$r_j - \mu_j = \beta_{1j}F_1 + \beta_{2j}F_2 + \beta_{3j}F_3 + \beta_{4j}F_4 + e_j \quad (20.8)$$

This centers the regression on an asset's mean return $\mu_j$ and on the mean of each factor.

The coefficient on each factor was significant. The influence of these fundamental economic factors was especially strong for the industrial production, risk premium, and term structure indices. Moreover, when a market index was included along with the economic factors, the market factor had an insignificant coefficient, whereas the economic factors were undiminished. These authors concluded that any explanatory power of the market factor is a statistical artifact—a consequence of the fact that all stocks are exposed to economic risks that underlie returns to the market. The market factor had no power to explain movements in individual stocks or cross-sectional differences in mean returns once these fundamental economic factors were included.

## Country versus Industry Factors

Many fund managers allocate their assets across countries in the belief that the risk reduction benefits of international portfolio diversification are driven by country factors. Others allocate their assets across industries in the belief that international returns are driven by industry or sector factors. So which is it—country or industry diversification—that determines the benefits of international diversification? Although the results of factor models applied to this question are not in complete unanimity, three stylized facts have emerged.[9]

- Although there is a long-term trend toward increasing capital market integration, in most cases this increase in capital market integration has not been accompanied by an increase in correlations with other national markets. The usual explanation is that countries are differentially exposed to the factors that drive global market returns, so that cross-country correlations do not necessarily increase as markets are integrated.

- Cross-country correlations typically are lower than cross-industry correlations, so that diversification across countries usually brings greater diversification benefits than does diversification across industries.
  - There are periods where global market crashes temporarily increase the correlations between nearly all of the world's financial markets, thereby decreasing the importance of both country and industry diversification. The safest place to be during these troubled times is in an asset—such as cash—that is uncorrelated with one's portfolio of risky assets, regardless of which risky assets are held.
  - There also are periods where high volatility in selected industries—such as during the IT bubble of the late 1990s—temporarily reduces cross-industry correlations and thereby increases the importance of industry diversification.

Of course, investment strategies based on country and industry portfolios are not mutually exclusive. Many investors and investment funds pursue (active or passive) country strategies along with internationally diversified industry strategies in their quest for superior return-risk performance during both good times and bad.

## The International Value Premium

In which type of firm would you rather invest—a firm in financial distress with a track record of low earnings growth and poor stock market performance, or a firm that recently has experienced high earnings growth and stock price appreciation? Alternatively, would you rather invest in a stable large blue-chip company, or a small company with volatile earnings and uncertain return prospects?

> *A good company might not be a good stock.*

Keep in mind that a good (i.e., well-run) company does not necessarily make a good investment. If investors correctly anticipate the firm's growth prospects, then each of these firms should be properly priced in the market according to its expected cash flows and systematic risk. On the other hand, if investors fail to incorporate information into share prices, savvy investors might be able to identify bargain stocks.

**Firm Size and Relative Financial Distress Factors** Fama and French estimated a 3-factor model.[10]

$$r_j = \mu_j + \beta_j F_M + \beta_{SMBj} F_{SMB} + \beta_{HMLj} F_{HML} + e_j \tag{20.9}$$

The coefficient $\beta_j$ is stock j's sensitivity to the domestic market factor $F_M = (r_M - \mu_M)$. The coefficients $\beta_{SMBj}$ and $\beta_{HMLj}$ reflect the sensitivity of stock j to a firm size and to a relative financial distress factor, respectively. In combination, these three factors explain a significant proportion of mean returns in stocks around the world.

Fama and French model the firm size factor $F_{SML}$ as the difference in mean return between the smallest and the biggest 10 percent of firms. The acronym *SMB* stands for "small-minus-big." Small firms tend to have higher mean returns than large firms in both U.S. and non-U.S. markets. In Fama and French's study of New York Stock Exchange (NYSE) and American Stock Exchange (AMEX) stocks in the United States from 1965–1990, small firms averaged over 7 percent higher annual return than large stocks. Many developed and emerging markets exhibit a similar ***size effect***—a tendency for small firms in a national market to outperform large firms in that market.

Fama and French constructed their relative financial distress factor $F_{HML}$ as the difference in mean return between portfolios of firms with high and with low ratios of book-to-market equity, where book-to-market equity is defined as equity book value divided by equity market value. The *HML* factor is named after these "high-minus-low" book-to-market portfolios. Stocks were first ranked into deciles according to each firm's book-to-market ratio. Firms with high book-to-market ratios are called ***value stocks*** and firms with low book-to-market ratios are called ***growth stocks.*** Value stocks have depressed share prices due to low earnings growth or financial distress. Low prices result in relatively high equity book-to-market ratios, as well as high earnings-to-price, cash-flow-to-price, and dividend-to-price ratios. Conversely, growth stocks have low earnings-to-price, cash-flow-to-price, dividend-to-price, and book-to-market ratios. The relative financial distress factor is the difference in mean return between the extreme decile portfolios of value and growth stocks.

Figure 20.5 shows average annual returns to ten portfolios of U.S. companies ranked on equity book-to-market. Value stocks outperformed growth stocks by an average of 12 percent per year. According to Fama and French, this ***value premium*** reflects a systematic risk—relative financial distress—that is not captured by the traditional CAPM or one-factor market model.

*Value outperforms growth.*

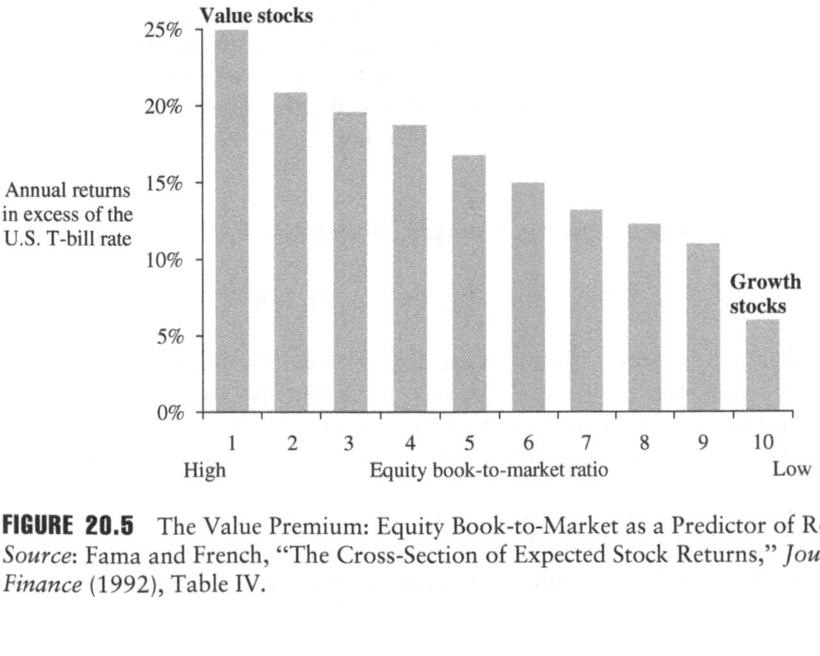


**FIGURE 20.5** The Value Premium: Equity Book-to-Market as a Predictor of Return.
*Source*: Fama and French, "The Cross-Section of Expected Stock Returns," *Journal of Finance* (1992), Table IV.

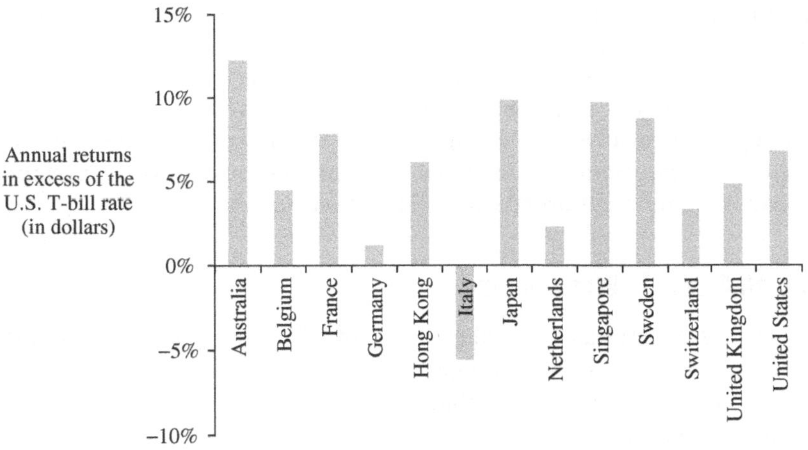


**FIGURE 20.6** Difference in Excess Returns for Value and Growth Stock Portfolios.
*Source*: Fama and French, "Value versus Growth: The International Evidence," *Journal of Finance* (1998), from Table III.

*Value premiums exist in most markets.*

**The International Evidence** Fama and French found evidence of a value premium (i.e., value stocks outperforming growth stocks) in 12 of 13 national stock markets from 1975–1995 (see Figure 20.6).[11] The value premium was statistically significant in about half of these developed markets. The difference between average annual returns on global portfolios of value and growth stocks was 7.6 percent. Fama and French found similar value premiums when international stocks were sorted on earnings-to-price, cash-flow-to-price, and dividend-to-price.

Fama and French also found evidence of a value premium in emerging stock markets. Rouwenhorst has corroborated the existence of both a value premium and a size effect in emerging markets.[12] These risk factors are negatively related to share turnover, with small firms and value stocks having lower turnover than large firms and growth stocks.

Griffin examined whether global or national factors are more useful in explaining average returns in the three-factor model of Equation 20.9.[13] Griffin estimated this equation with global and country-specific factors for stocks from the United States, the United Kingdom, Japan, and Canada. Domestic factors explained much more of the variation in returns than did global factors. Moreover, adding the global factors to the domestic model resulted in more pricing errors than the domestic model alone. Griffin's results indicate that size and relative financial distress factors should be estimated with country-specific factors, rather than with global factors.

*Size and distress appear to be country-specific factors.*

So, would you rather invest in a value stock or a growth stock? Value stocks have higher mean returns than growth stocks, but higher mean returns could reflect exposure to a systematic risk factor such as relative financial distress. If markets are efficient, then you are merely getting what you pay for. If markets are inefficient, then this might represent an investment opportunity. We'll return to the issue of whether the value premium represents rational asset pricing or irrational investor behavior after discussing momentum-based investment strategies.

## The Currency Risk Factor in Stock Returns

**Portfolio Theory and the Irrelevance of Hedging in a Perfect World** In a perfect capital market, the firm cannot do anything through diversification that investors cannot already do for themselves. Hedging a risk that is not priced by investors is a waste of managers' time and shareholders' money.

> *Hedging does not add value to the firm in a perfect capital market.*

Consider two companies, L (Long) and S (Short). Each company resides in China and uses the Chinese new yuan (¥) as its functional currency. A European customer of Company S has promised to make a payment of €100,000 to Company L in one year. Company L is long the euro (and short the yuan). Company S is short the euro (and long the yuan). Figure 20.7 shows the risk profile of each company with respect to the euro.

A well-diversified investor owning shares in each company faces no net transaction exposure to this contract. Changes in the value of Company L in response to changes in the spot rate $S^{¥/€}$ are exactly offset by changes in the value of Company S. To a well-diversified investor owning shares in each company, exposures to currency risks such as these are diversifiable and result in the risk profile (well, in this case it's a risk*less* profile) shown at the right in Figure 20.7.

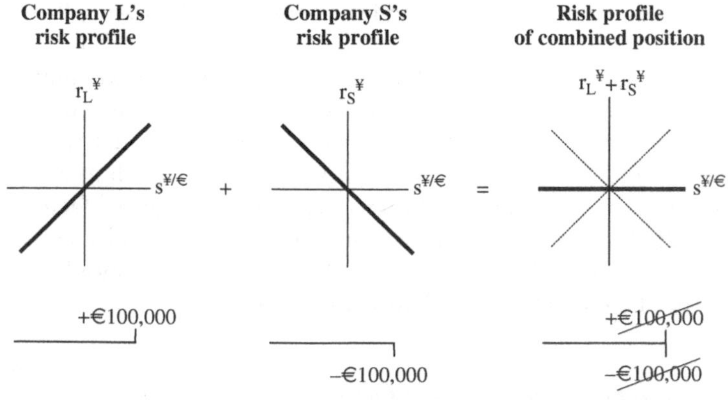


**FIGURE 20.7** The Diversifiability of Exposure to Currency Risk.

In a globally integrated capital market, currency risks such as these are diversifiable and hence should not be priced in required return. If the manager of either firm hedges these risks, hedging costs such as bank fees or bid-ask spreads are a deadweight loss to the firm with no reduction in stakeholders' systematic risk or required return.[14]

**Measuring Currency Risk Exposure** Because investors do not operate in perfect markets, the magnitude and relevance of currency risk exposure is an empirical question. Like other risk factors, exposure to currency risk can be measured in a regression framework. Continuing with our previous example, a Chinese firm's exposure to the euro can be modeled as

$$r_j^{¥} = \alpha_j^{¥} + \beta_j^{€} s^{¥/€} + e_j^{¥} \tag{20.10}$$

where $r_j^{¥} = (1 + r_j^{€})(1 + s^{¥/€}) - 1$ = yuan-denominated return on the euro-denominated asset j

$r_j^{€}$ = return on asset j in euros

$s^{¥/€}$ = percentage change in the yuan/euro spot rate $s^{¥/€}$

In its factor model form, Equation 20.10 becomes

$$r_j^{¥} = \mu_j^{¥} + \beta_j^{€}(s^{¥/€} - \mu_s) + e_j^{¥} \tag{20.11}$$

If exchange rates are a random walk, then the mean spot exchange rate change $\mu_s$ is zero and Equation 20.11 reduces to $r_j^{¥} = \mu_j^{¥} + \beta_j^{€} s^{¥/€} + e_j^{¥}$.

Equation 20.11 decomposes the variability of yuan returns into three components. The $\mu_j^{¥}$ term is shared by all assets and depends on the risk-free yuan interest rate $r_F^{¥}$ and the expected risk premium associated with the currency risk factor. The $\beta_j^{€} s^{¥/€}$ component reflects the stock's exchange rate sensitivity. The $e_j^{¥}$ component represents the random element of return that is unrelated to the other two components of return. Euro returns $r_j^{€}$ are exposed to currency risk if $\text{Cov}(r_j^{€}, s^{¥/€}) \neq 0$, so the euro exposure coefficient $\beta_j^{€}$ depends on changes in both the spot exchange rate and the value of the asset in the local currency. The error term $e_j^{¥}$ is denominated in yuan and includes all sources of variability in yuan returns that are unrelated to exchange rates, such that $\text{Cov}(e_j^{¥}, s^{¥/€}) = 0$. The expectation of the error is simply $E[e_j^{¥}] = 0$.

Hedging exposures to currency risk cannot, in general, completely eliminate exposure to risk. Hedging merely removes that part of the variation in $r_j^{¥}$ that is related to changes in the spot exchange rate $s^{¥/€}$. The remaining uncertainty is independent of the exchange rate. The firm remains exposed to other sources of risk in the local (euro) value of the foreign asset, including business risk, inflation risk, and default risk.

**Is Currency Risk Priced in International Capital Markets?** If exposure to currency risk is diversifiable, then currency risk exposures should not be reflected in expected returns. On the other hand, if currency risk exposures are systematic to a large number of stocks, then investors should incorporate this risk in share prices and in their expected and required returns.

Classic or *unconditional* asset pricing models assume that returns have constant means, variances, and covariances. These models often find that currency risk is not priced in mean returns, especially in the broadly diversified U.S. stock market. In contrast to unconditional models, *conditional* asset pricing models allow risks—such as currency and market risks—to vary over time. These models often yield different conclusions than unconditional asset pricing models. For example, the market risk factor is insignificant in most unconditional tests, but is often significant in conditional asset pricing models.

De Santis and Gérard estimated conditional and unconditional versions of the international CAPM with a sample of stocks from the United States, the United Kingdom, Japan, and Germany.[15] When the authors applied an unconditional IAPM that constrained currency and market risks to be constant over time, neither risk appeared to be priced by investors. However, these risks were significant in a conditional IAPM that allowed required returns and volatilities to vary over time. After estimating their conditional model, these authors concluded that both market and currency risks are priced in international equity markets when measured with conditional models.

National stock markets had varying exposures to these risks. Currency risk was a small fraction of total risk in the U.S. market, but a significant percentage of total risk in the United Kingdom, Japan, and Germany. Other studies similarly have found that exposure to currency risk is more important in markets outside the United States than in the U.S. market.[16] Currency risk is likely to be especially important in emerging markets with relatively undiversified economies.

**Currency Risk Exposure and Corporate Hedging Activities** Whether or not currency risk affects required returns, there is considerable cross-sectional variation in the exposures of individual firms and industries. A stylized characterization of the currency exposure of exporters and importers appears in Figure 20.8. Exporters, such as domestic mining and manufacturing firms, tend to benefit from a depreciation of the domestic currency. Importers, such as domestic textile and apparel firms, tend to benefit from an appreciation of the domestic currency.

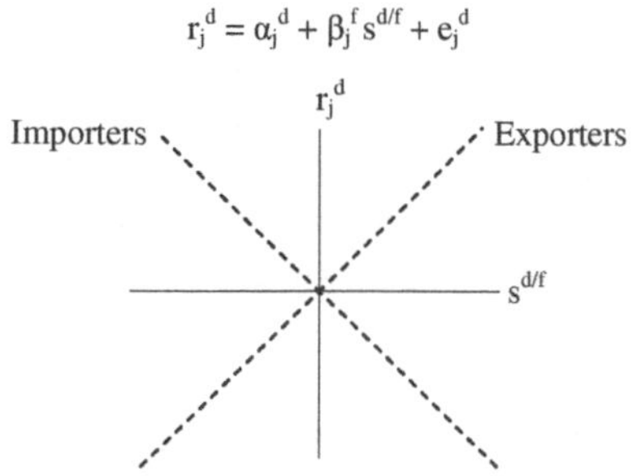


**FIGURE 20.8** The Currency Risk Exposure of Importers and Exporters.

Consider the currency exposure of General Motors (GM). GM exports a large proportion of its worldwide sales from its U.S. facilities. When the dollar appreciates in real terms against foreign currencies, GM's production costs rise relative to those of its non-U.S. competitors. Conversely, when the dollar depreciates in real terms, GM's production costs fall relative to non-U.S. automakers. A real depreciation of the dollar allows GM to either earn higher profits per car, or lower its prices and sell more cars. Hence, the value of an exporter such as GM is negatively related to the domestic currency or, as in Figure 20.8, positively related to foreign currency values.

In contrast, importers are likely to benefit from a real appreciation of the domestic currency. Consider Zappos.com, the world's largest online shoe retailer. Zappos is based in Nevada and most of its sales are to U.S. customers. Zappos benefits from a dollar appreciation because it costs fewer dollars to purchase shoes from its suppliers in Southeast Asia. Zappos can either keep U.S. dollar prices constant and reap more profits per shoe, or drop its dollar prices and try to sell more shoes. In either case, it is likely to enjoy higher profits on its U.S. sales. Conversely, as the dollar depreciates these foreign inputs cost more in dollars. For these reasons, the value of an importer such as Zappos tends to be positively related to the value of the domestic currency or, as in Figure 20.8, negatively related to foreign currency values.

Just as currency risk seems to be less of a consideration for firms in the United States, the proportion of firms with exposures to currency risk also is smaller in the U.S. than in other national markets. Jorion found that around 5 percent of a sample of U.S. MNCs had significant currency exposures.[17] At a 5 percent significance level, this is just what you'd expect from chance. In contrast, about one-quarter of Japanese firms, two-thirds of Canadian firms, and nearly all large German firms have significant exposures to currency risk.[18] The magnitude of exposure is positively related to the proportion of international operations or sales. Firms with a high proportion of international operations or sales tend to have greater exposures to currency risk.

***Managers have an incentive to hedge FX risks.***

In contrast to other stakeholders, managers have a huge incentive to hedge the firm's exposure to currency risk. A manager's livelihood depends on the health and continued existence of the company. Managers are over-invested in the firm and are unable to fully diversify their wealth. Further, the performance evaluation and compensation of divisional managers are tied to divisional performance, so that the managers of international divisions are sensitive to exchange rate fluctuations. In these circumstances, managers have an incentive to hedge against currency risk even if this risk is diversifiable from the perspective of shareholders.

Firms can change their currency exposures through operating and financial market hedges. For example, even though the operations of a U.S. exporter may be hurt by a real appreciation of the dollar, the exporter can mitigate this operating risk by hedging with currency forwards, futures, options, or swaps. Unfortunately, many corporate hedging activities are not observable by investors unless and until they are disclosed in the financial statements. Even then, only a portion of the firm's hedging activities typically are reported. The sensitivity of stock prices to foreign exchange rates reflects the market's best guess of a firm's net exposures to currency risks; that is, net of the firm's financial and operating hedges of currency risks.

## 20.4 MOMENTUM STRATEGIES

Would you rather invest in a firm that recently has risen in price or one that recently has fallen in price? In an efficient capital market, rational investors react instantaneously and without bias to information, and stocks are correctly priced at all times. Future returns will depend only on systematic risks and chance, and there will be no price or volume patterns in the data that will help you predict returns. Ex ante, it won't matter which stock you buy—you'll merely get what you pay for.

### The U.S. Evidence

*Momentum strategies* selectively buy or sell securities based on their recent performance. In a widely cited article, Jegadeesh and Titman studied momentum in U.S. stocks by categorizing firms into ten equal-sized portfolios according to observed return over the preceding six months.[19]

Stocks in the portfolio with the highest returns over a particular 6-month measurement period were called *Winners* and stocks in the portfolio with the lowest returns were called *Losers*. After forming portfolios of past Winners and Losers, returns were examined over the subsequent 36 months. The perspective was then moved forward one month and the procedure repeated.

The dark bars on the left of Figure 20.9 show the difference in monthly returns to the Winner and Loser portfolios in Jegadeesh and Titman's sample of U.S. stocks over holding periods of up to 36 months. The cumulative difference between the two portfolios is displayed as a dark line on the right of Figure 20.9. Over the first 12 months, portfolios formed on past Winners realized returns that were 10 percent

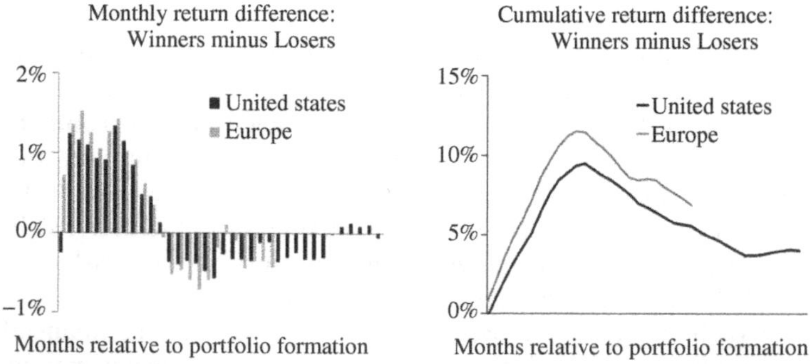


**FIGURE 20.9** Return Difference Between Winner and Loser Portfolios.
*Source:* Jegadeesh and Titman, "Returns to Buying Winners and Selling Losers," *Journal of Finance* (1993), from Table VII; and Rouwenhorst, "International Momentum Strategies," *Journal of Finance* (1998), from Table VI.

greater than returns to the Losers. This Winner-over-Loser pattern subsequently reversed itself, with the Winners giving up more than half of their accumulated gain over Losers during the next 24 months.

### The International Evidence

Rouwenhorst replicated Jegadeesh and Titman's study on 12 European markets.[20] The gray bars on the left of Figure 20.9 show the difference in monthly returns to the European Winner-minus-Loser portfolios over holding periods of up to 24 months (the maximum period reported by Rouwenhorst). Momentum was present in the United States and in each of the 12 European markets even after controlling for market risk and size. Momentum was strongest in small firms, although it was present in all size deciles. As in Jegadeesh and Titman's study, momentum profits were about 10 percent over the first year and then turned negative. Rouwenhorst also found momentum in emerging markets to be qualitatively similar to momentum in developed markets.[21]

> *There is momentum in both emerging and developed markets.*

### Is Momentum Rational Asset Pricing or a Behavioral Phenomenon?

Like religion, views on the efficiency of capital markets tend to be held as a matter of faith. If one accepts the premise that capital markets are efficient, then the profitability of investing in size, value, or momentum strategies can be explained as compensation for risk. Size, value, and momentum in this view are systematic risk factors that must be included in asset pricing models in order to correctly price risk. If a new anomaly is found that does not fit the prevailing wisdom, then a new factor must be added to capture this previously unidentified systematic risk. If one is unwilling to accept market efficiency, then anomalies such as the size effect and the value premium are prima facie evidence of asset mispricing. Like religious convictions, the truth of a particular set of beliefs becomes self-evident once you accept a particular point of view.

The challenge for a factor model explanation of momentum is the curious reversal in the Winner-minus-Loser returns that occurs in both U.S. and European stocks after about one year. If the superior return performance of Winners over Losers did not reverse itself, an omitted risk factor plausibly could have driven the return difference. For example, the Winners portfolio could have contained smaller firms, stocks with high relative financial distress, or stocks with some other omitted systematic risk factor(s). However, the subsequent reversal in return performance suggests that investors react slowly to information or that their reactions are biased.[22]

> *Return reversals are hard to reconcile with market efficiency.*

There appears to be a behavioral element to momentum returns, and this behavioral element appears to differ across countries. Chui, Titman, and Wei examined whether momentum is related to national differences in investor characteristics using Hofstede's popular "cultural distance" framework.[23] One of Hofstede's cultural dimensions is *individualism*, defined as "the degree to which individuals are integrated into groups."[24] In an individualistic society, people are expected to look after themselves and their immediate families, and are more likely to act independently. Chui et al. found individualistic cultures have higher trading volumes, return volatilities, and momentum profits, all else constant. These are similar to findings at the level of the individual investor and suggest that investor overconfidence and frame dependence influence investor behaviors.

*Individual behaviors influence momentum trading.*

## 20.5 CONTEMPORARY ASSET PRICING MODELS

Einstein stated, "It is the theory that decides what can be observed." For there to be a return surprise, there must be something in observed returns that is not in the theory or asset pricing model. As empirical anomalies are uncovered and confirmed by subsequent research, they eventually must become a part of the prevailing theory.

*Theory decides what is observable.*

The current convention for stock returns is to use Fama and French's three-factor model with market, firm size, and relative financial distress factors. The rationale for including a market factor springs directly from the CAPM. The size factor reflects the fact that small stocks have higher mean returns than large stocks, and the relative financial distress factor reflects the fact that the mean return of value stocks exceeds that of growth stocks. The Fama-French model is related to many other return anomalies, including the association of returns with sales growth, turnover, and ratios of cash flows, earnings, and dividends to price. These factors often are modeled with conditional or time-varying coefficients to reflect the fact that volatilities—as well as correlations—change over time.

The Fama-French model is unable, however, to explain stock return momentum. To recognize the existence of momentum, some asset pricing studies that require a model of expected return augment the Fama-French factors with a momentum factor modeled as the return on a portfolio of recent winners minus the return on a portfolio of recent losers.[25] In this way, the model or "theory that determines what can be observed" includes a good deal of what is known regarding stock market behaviors.

There is nevertheless still much work to be done. Recent work suggests that systematic risk factors in addition to size and value/growth are important in emerging markets, including the liquidity of a firm's shares, the firm's idiosyncratic risk (the volatility of residual return $e_t$ after other factors have been included in the pricing model), and a country's sovereign debt or credit risk rating.[26] Our efforts to identify factors that influence systematic risks and required returns bring to mind Robert Frost's line at the start of this chapter: "We dance round in a ring and suppose, but the Secret sits in the middle and knows."

## 20.6 SUMMARY

Assumptions necessary to develop the CAPM are (1) perfect financial markets (frictionless and competitive with equal access to information), (2) normally distributed nominal returns, (3) rational investors (return is good and risk is bad), (4) homogeneous expectations, and (5) equal access to the risk-free rate $r_F$. A fundamental result of this model is the SML,

$$r_j = r_F + \beta_j(E[r_M] - r_F) \tag{20.1}$$

in which the required return on an asset j is a linear combination of the expected market risk premium and the asset's sensitivity to changes in market returns. Market model beta, $\beta_j = \rho_{j,M}(\sigma_j/\sigma_M)$, is a measure of the sensitivity of security j's returns to market returns and is estimated with the regression equation

$$r_j = \alpha_j + \beta_j r_M + e_j \tag{20.3}$$

We then developed an IAPM by extending the CAPM to a multicurrency setting. Two additional assumptions were necessary: (1) purchasing power parity holds, and (2) investors in each country have the same consumption basket. This ensures that the international parity conditions hold. The market portfolio in the IAPM is a globally diversified portfolio of risky assets, and the risk-free asset is replaced by a hedge portfolio of risk-free domestic and foreign assets. Unfortunately, market model betas estimated with unconditional models against national or global stock market indices have very little relation to mean return, which casts doubt on the validity of the CAPM and the IAPM.

### APPLICATION Job Interviews

Suppose you are interviewing for a job as a securities analyst and your potential employer asks whether you believe in the informational efficiency of local, national, and global stock markets. That is, do market prices truly reflect value? As a serious student of the markets and of finance, how should you respond?

Answer an emphatic "No!" The job wouldn't exist if the employer believed in efficient markets. The concept of an efficient market is a noble benchmark, but, like perfection in any realm of human endeavor, is an unattainable ideal. You might further improve your prospects by mentioning some of the anomalies that are hard to reconcile with market efficiency, such as return reversals and the evidence on momentum.

Factor models offer a partial remedy to this shortcoming. In these models, returns are assumed to be a linear function of K systematic risk factors $F_k$,

$$r_j = \mu_j + \beta_{1j}F_1 + \cdots + \beta_{Kj}F_K + e_j \qquad (20.5)$$

where $\mu_j$ is the expected return on asset j, the $\beta_{kj}$ are asset j's sensitivities to the K systematic risk factors, and $e_j$ is firm-specific random error. Studies of domestic and international stock returns have identified macroeconomic factors such as industrial production, inflation, risk premia on corporate over government bonds, and the term structure of interest rates. Other well-documented factors in international stock returns include global, national, and industry indices, and size and value factors. Momentum effects are also present.

The chapter also included a discussion of the currency risk factor in international stock returns. Exposure to currency risk appears to be more important in non-U.S. markets than in the U.S. market, both in the percentage of firms that are exposed to currency risk and the effect on investors' required returns. It also appears to be important to recognize the conditional or time-varying nature of currency risk exposure in international markets. This is an area of active academic and professional inquiry, so stay tuned for further developments.

## KEY TERMS

*arbitrage pricing theory (APT)*
*beta (β)*
*capital asset pricing model (CAPM)*
*capital market line (CML)*
*country-specific risk*
*expropriation*
*factor models*
*growth stock*
*hedge portfolio*
*integrated market*
*international asset pricing model (IAPM)*
*market model (one-factor market model)*
*market portfolio*
*market risk premium*
*momentum strategies*
*one-factor market model*
*perfect market assumptions*
*political risk*
*security market line (SML)*
*segmented market*
*size effect*
*systematic versus unsystematic risk*
*value premium*
*value stock*

## CONCEPTUAL QUESTIONS

20.1 What is the CML? Why is it important?

20.2 What is the SML? Why is it important?

20.3 What is beta? Why is it important?

20.4 Does political risk affect required returns?

20.5 What assumptions must be added to the traditional CAPM to derive the IAPM?

20.6 What is the hedge portfolio in IAPM?

20.7 What is the difference between an integrated and a segmented capital market?

20.8 What is the APT? In what ways is it both better and worse than the IAPM?

20.9 What four factors did Roll and Ross (1995) identify in their study of U.S. stocks?

20.10 Are individual stock returns more closely related to national or industry factors? What implication does this have for portfolio diversification?

20.11 What is the value premium? What is the size effect? Do international stocks exhibit these characteristics? Are these factors evidence of market inefficiency?

20.12 What is momentum? Can it lead to profitable investment opportunities for international investors?

20.13 Are individual stocks exposed to currency risk? Does currency risk affect required returns?

## PROBLEMS

20.1 Calculate equity required return under each of the following, assuming the CAPM holds:

a. The risk-free rate is 8 percent, beta is 1.5, and the market risk premium is 8.5 percent.
b. The risk-free rate is 4 percent, beta is 1.2, and the market risk premium is 8.5 percent.

20.2 The correlation between returns to BMW stock on the Deutsche Börse and the German DAX stock market index is 0.44 when all returns are calculated in euros. The standard deviations of monthly returns to BMW stock and the DAX are 10.5 percent and 4.6 percent, respectively.

a. What is the beta of BMW relative to the DAX stock market index?
b. If the euro risk-free rate is 5 percent and the DAX market risk premium is 6 percent, what is the required return on BMW stock when measured against the DAX stock market index?
c. The correlation between the DAX and world stock market indices is 0.494. The standard deviations of monthly returns to the DAX and world indices are 4.13 percent and 5.26 percent, respectively. What is the beta of the DAX stock market index relative to the world stock market index?

20.3 As a security analyst for the London branch of Merrill Lynch, you have identified the following factors and factor sensitivities for British Petroleum (BP):

$$E[r] = \mu + \beta_{Prod}F_{Prod} + \beta_{Oil}F_{Oil} + \beta_{Spot}F_{Spot} \qquad (20.12)$$

Factors and factor sensitivities are as follows:

| Factors | Betas | |
|---|---|---|
| $F_{Prod}$ | change in world industrial production | $\beta_{Prod} = +1.50$ |
| $F_{Oil}$ | change in crude oil prices | $\beta_{Oil} = -0.80$ |
| $F_{Spot}$ | change in the exchange rate ($s^{£/f}$) against a basket of foreign currencies f with which BP trades | $\beta_{Spot} = +0.01$ |

a. All else constant, is BP's share price likely to go up or down with an increase in world industrial production? With an increase in crude oil prices? With an increase in the pound?
b. What is the expected return on BP stock in a year when world industrial production is 2 percent above the expectation, oil prices rise unexpectedly by 10 percent, and the spot rate $S_t^{£/f}$ goes down by 5 percent?
c. If BP stock rises by 4 percent during this period, by how much does BP over- or underperform its expectation?

20.4 As a security analyst for the Paris branch of Morgan Stanley Dean Witter, you've identified the following factors and factor sensitivities for Elf Acquitaine ("Elf"):

$$E(r) = \mu + \beta_{Prod}F_{Prod} + \beta_{Oil}F_{Oil} + \beta_{Term}F_{Term} + \beta_{Risk}F_{Risk} + \beta_{Spot}F_{Spot}$$

Elf's functional currency is the euro. Factors and factor sensitivities in euros are as follows:

| Factors | Betas | |
|---|---|---|
| $F_{Prod}$ | change in world industrial production | $\beta_{Prod} = +1.10$ |
| $F_{oil}$ | change in crude oil prices | $\beta_{Oil} = +0.60$ |
| $F_{Term}$ | long minus short government bonds | $\beta_{Term} = -0.05$ |
| $F_{Risk}$ | corporate minus government bonds | $\beta_{Risk} = -0.10$ |
| $F_{Spot}$ | change in the euro value of a basket of foreign currencies ($s^{€/f}$) with which Elf trades | $\beta_{Spot} = -0.02$ |

Elf's expected return is $\mu = 12$ percent if all factors are equal to their expectation.

a. State whether Elf's shares are likely to go up or down with an increase in world industrial production, crude oil prices, the slope of the term structure, the risk premium, or the euro?
b. Given these parameters, what is the expected return on Elf stock in a year when each factor is 10 percent higher than its expectation?
c. If Elf stock falls by 12 percent during this period, by how much does Elf over- or underperform its expectation given each of the factors was 10 percent higher than its expectation during the period?

20.5 As a security analyst for the New York branch of Deutsche Bank, you have identified the following factors and factor sensitivities for Amazon.com: $r = \mu + \beta_M F_M + \beta_{SMB} F_{SMB} + \beta_{HML} F_{HML}$.

Amazon.com's factor sensitivities in dollars are

| Factors | Betas | |
|---|---|---|
| $F_M$ | market factor $(r_M - \mu_M)$ | $\beta_M = +1.00$ |
| $F_{SMB}$ | firm size factor (small minus big stock returns) | $\beta_{SMB} = +0.10$ |
| $F_{HML}$ | relative financial distress (value minus growth stock returns) | $\beta_{HML} = +0.05$ |

Amazon.com's expected return is $\mu = 10$ percent if all factors are equal to their expectation.

a. What is Amazon.com's expected return in a year when each factor is 1 percent lower than its expectation?
b. If Amazon.com's stock price rises by 12 percent during this period, by how much does Amazon.com over- or underperform its expectation?

20.6 Two mutual fund managers are discussing their investment strategies over lunch. The first manager follows a value-oriented strategy of selectively buying stocks with high equity book-to-market ratios. The second manager prefers firms with high earnings growth that hopefully will lead to high stock price appreciation.

a. Which manager is likely to see higher returns over a 1-year investment horizon? Why?
b. Which manager is likely to see higher returns over a 10-year investment horizon? Why?
c. Which manager is likely to see higher returns on a risk-adjusted basis over a 10-year investment horizon? Explain your answer.

20.7 The regional directors of a major investment bank are discussing investment strategies for their respective countries.

a. As director of North American investments, describe to your foreign colleagues an investment strategy based on momentum.
b. As director of European investments, do you think such a momentum-based strategy will work in your markets? Why or why not?
c. As director of Latin American investments, do you think a momentum-based strategy will work in your markets? Why or why not?
d. Should momentum-based investment strategies continue to work if markets are efficient? Should investors continue to see above-average returns to momentum investing?

20.8 Suppose a fund manager places equal weights on each publicly traded stock in the world. Support your answers to each of the following by citing the relevant empirical asset pricing literature:

a. Would the fund's expected return be more or less than on a similar value-weighted portfolio?
b. Would investors prefer this fund to a value-weighted portfolio invested in the same assets?
c. How should the fund manager benchmark the performance of the fund?

## SUGGESTED READINGS

### The international CAPM (IAPM) is developed and tested in

Michael Adler and Bernard Dumas, "International Portfolio Choice and Corporation Finance: A Synthesis," *Journal of Finance* 38 (June 1983), 925–984.

Ines Chaieb and Vihang Errunza, "International Asset Pricing under Mild Segmentation," *Journal of Financial Economics* 86 (November 2007), 543–578.

### Factor models are developed and applied to asset pricing and capital market integration in

Andrew Ang, Robert J. Hodrick, Yuhang Xing, and Xiaoyan Zhang, "High Idiosyncratic Volatility and Low Returns: International and Further U.S. Evidence," *Journal of Financial Economics* 91 (January 2009), 1–23.

Geert Bekaert, Campbell R. Harvey, and Christian Lundblad, "Liquidity and Expected Returns: Lessons from Emerging Markets," *Review of Financial Studies* 20 (November 2007), 1783–1832.

Geert Bekaert, Robert J. Hodrick, and Xiaoyan Zhang, "International Stock Return Comovements," *Journal of Finance* 64 (December 2009), 2591–2626.

Lawrence Booth and Wendy Rotenberg, "Assessing Foreign Exchange Exposure: Theory and Application Using Canadian Firms," *Journal of International Financial Management and Accounting* 2 (Spring 1990), 1–22.

Nai-Fu Chen, Richard Roll, and Stephen A. Ross, "Economic Forces and the Stock Market," *Journal of Business* 59 (July 1986), 383–404.

Bernard Dumas and Bruno Solnik, "The World Price of Foreign Exchange Risk," *Journal of Finance* 50 (June 1995), 445–479.

Claude B. Erb, Campbell R. Harvey, and Tadas E. Viskanta, "Expected Returns and Volatility in 135 Countries," *Journal of Portfolio Management* 22 (Spring 1996), 46–58.

Eugene F. Fama and Kenneth R. French, "The Cross-Section of Expected Stock Returns," *Journal of Finance* 47 (June 1992), 427–465.

Eugene F. Fama and Kenneth R. French, "Multifactor Explanations of Asset Pricing Anomalies," *Journal of Finance* 51 (March 1996), 55–84.

Eugene F. Fama and Kenneth R. French, "Value Versus Growth: The International Evidence," *Journal of Finance* 53 (December 1998), 1975–1999.

Miguel Almeida Ferreira and Paulo Miguel Gama, "Have World, Country, and Industry Risks Changed over Time? An Investigation of the Volatility of Developed Stock Markets," *Journal of Financial and Quantitative Analysis* 40 (March 2005), 195–222.

Martin Glaum, Marko Brunner, and Holger Himmel, "The DAX and the Dollar: The Economic Exchange Rate Exposure of German Corporations," *Journal of International Business Studies* 31, No. 4 (2000), 715–724.

John M. Griffin, "Are the Fama and French Factors Global or Country Specific?" *Review of Financial Studies* 15 (Summer 2002), 783–803.

Jia He and Lilian K. Ng, "The Foreign Exchange Exposure of Japanese Multinational Corporations," *Journal of Finance* 53 (April 1998), 733–753.

Philippe Jorion, "The Exchange-Rate Exposure of U.S. Multinationals," *Journal of Business* 63, No. 3 (1990), 331–346.

Kuntara Pukthuanthong and Richard Roll, "Global Market Integration: An Alternative Measure and Its Application," *Journal of Financial Economics* 94 (November 2009), 214–232.

Richard Roll and Stephen A. Ross, "The Arbitrage Pricing Theory Approach to Strategic Portfolio Planning," *Financial Analysts Journal* 51 (January/February 1995), 122–132.

Stephen A. Ross, "The Arbitrage Theory of Asset Pricing," *Journal of Economic Theory* 13 (December 1976), 341–360.

K. Geert Rouwenhorst, "European Equity Markets and the EMU," *Financial Analysts Journal* 55 (May/June 1999), 57–64.

K. Geert Rouwenhorst, "Local Return Factors and Turnover in Emerging Stock Markets," *Journal of Finance* 54 (August 1999), 1439–1464.

Giorgio De Santis and Bruno Gérard, "How Big Is the Premium for Currency Risk?" *Journal of Financial Economics* 49 (September 1998), 375–412.

### Momentum returns are discussed in

Mark M. Carhart, "On Persistence in Mutual Fund Performance," *Journal of Finance* 52 (March 1997), 57–82.

Andy C.W. Chui, Sheridan Titman, and K.C. John Wei, "Individualism and Momentum around the World," *Journal of Finance* 65 (January 2009), 361–392.

Narasimhan Jegadeesh and Sheridan Titman, "Returns to Buying Winners and Selling Losers: Implications for Stock Market Efficiency," *Journal of Finance* 48 (March 1993), 65–91.

Narasimhan Jegadeesh and Sheridan Titman, "Profitability of Momentum Strategies: An Evaluation of Alternative Explanations," *Journal of Finance* 56 (April 2001), 699–720.

Narasimhan Jegadeesh and Sheridan Titman, "Momentum," working paper (January 2011), available at www.ssrn.com.

K. Geert Rouwenhorst, "International Momentum Strategies," *Journal of Finance* 53 (February 1998), 267–284.

### The concept of 'cultural distance' is developed in

Geert Hofstede, *Culture's Consequences: Comparing Values, Behaviors, Institutions, and Organizations across Nations*, 2nd ed. (Beverly Hills, CA: Sage Publications, 2001).

# Notes

## CHAPTER 1 An Introduction to Multinational Finance

1. Mark Twain wrote: "Always do right. This will gratify some people, and astonish the rest."
2. An arbitrage profit is a sure profit obtained with no net investment and no risk.
3. Franco Modigliani and Merton Miller each won a Nobel Prize in Economics, largely for this insight.
4. The effect of global diversification on firm value is examined in Chapter 17 on "Corporate Governance and the International Market for Corporate Control."

## CHAPTER 2 World Trade and the International Monetary System

1. As Winston Churchill observed: "The problems of victory are more agreeable than the problems of defeat, but they are no less difficult."
2. *IMF Annual Report on Exchange Arrangement and Exchange Restrictions*, 2009.
3. The Group of Ten or "Paris Club" included Belgium, Canada, France, Italy, Japan, the Netherlands, Sweden, the United Kingdom, the United States, and West Germany. A related group—the Group of Eight (G8)—has held an annual meeting of government officials from Canada, France, Germany, Italy, Japan, Russia, the United Kingdom and the United States since 1974. Representatives of the European Union, Brazil, China, India, Mexico, and South Africa also attend.
4. Joseph E. Stiglitz, *Globalization and Its Discontents*, 1st edition (NY: W. W. Norton & Company, April 2003).
5. Carmen M. Reinhart and Kenneth S. Rogoff, "Is the 2007 U.S. Subprime Crisis So Different? An International Historical Comparison," *American Economic Review* 98 (May 2008), 339–344.

## CHAPTER 3 Foreign Exchange and Eurocurrency Markets

1. Philippe Jorion, "How Informative Are Value-at-Risk Disclosures?" *Accounting Review* 77 (October 2002), 911–931.
2. Quotes such as "SFr1.7120/$ Bid and SFr1.7130/$ Ask" are called *outright* quotes. Traders often use an abbreviated *points* quote, such as "1.7120 to 30." Although they are a little less obvious than outright quotes, points quotes save time—and time is money in the fast-moving interbank currency markets.
3. Percentage changes in currency values are symmetric when stated in continuously compounded returns. This convenient property of continuously compounded returns is developed in Appendix 4-A.
4. Timothy Bollerslev, "Generalized Autoregressive Conditional Heteroskedasticity," *Journal of Econometrics* 31 (April 1986), 307–328.

## CHAPTER 4 The International Parity Conditions and Their Consequences

1. Note that the currency units cancel each other in these equations. Keep track of your currency units to ensure that each variable always appears in its proper place.
2. The nominal interest rates $i^d$ and $i^f$ in Equation 4.4 are geometric mean interest rates satisfying $(1 + i)^t = (1 + i_1)(1 + i_2)\ldots(1 + i_t)$, where each $i_t$ term represents an interest rate over a single future period t.
3. $E[S_t^{d/f}]/S_0^{d/f} = E[(P_t^d/P_t^f)]/(P_0^d/P_0^f)(E[P_t{}^d]/P_0{}^d)/(E[P_t{}^f]/P_0{}^f) = [(1 + E[p^d])/(1 + E[p^f])]^t$, where $(E[P_t]/P_0) = (1 + E[p])^t$ is one plus the expected geometric mean t-period inflation rate such that $(1 + E[p])^t = (1 + E[p_1])(1 + E[p_2])\ldots(1 + E[p_t])$.
4. Kenneth Froot and Richard Thaler, "Anomalies: Foreign Exchange," *Journal of Economic Perspectives* 4 (1990), 179–192.
5. Richard T. Baillie and Tim Bollerslev, "The Forward Premium Anomaly Is Not as Bad as You Think," *Journal of International Money and Finance* 19 (August 2000), 471–488; and Michael J. Moore and Maurice J. Roche, "Less of a Puzzle: A New Look at the Forward Forex Market," *Journal of International Economics* 58 (December 2002), 387–411.
6. A discount bond pays no interest and sells at a discount to face value.
7. For a discussion of deviations from uncovered interest parity, see James R. Lothian and Liuren Wu, "Uncovered Interest-Rate Parity over the Past Two Centuries," *Journal of International Money and Finance* 30 (April 2011), 448–473.
8. James R. Lothian and Mark P. Taylor, "Real Exchange Rate Behavior: The Recent Float from the Perspective of the Past Two Centuries," *Journal of Political Economy* 104 (June 1996), 488–509. Rogoff arrives at a similar estimate in Kenneth S. Rogoff, "The Purchasing Power Parity Puzzle," *Journal of Economic Literature* 34 (June 1996), 647–668.
9. In continuously compounded returns (Appendix 4-A), the strength of the forecast from the international parity conditions is linear in time T. If exchange rates are a random walk, then exchange rate volatility (standard deviation) increases with the square root of time. The ratio of the parity condition "signal" divided by the "noise" from exchange rate volatility then increases at the rate T/°T = °T. This "signal-to-noise ratio" ($\sqrt{T}$) improves as the forecast horizon T increases. This is why the international parity conditions provide more reliable long-term forecasts than they do short-term forecasts.
10. Mark P. Taylor and Helen Allen, "The Use of Technical Analysis in the Foreign Exchange Market," *Journal of International Money and Finance* 11 (June 1992), 304–314.
11. Kenneth Froot and Richard Thaler, "Anomalies: Foreign Exchange," *Journal of Economic Perspectives* 4 (1990), 179–192. See also Jamil Baz, Francis Breedon, Vasant Naik, and Joel Peress, "Optimal Portfolios of Foreign Currencies," *Journal of Portfolio Management* 28 (Fall 2001), 102–111.
12. Christopher J. Neely and Paul A. Weller, "Technical Trading Rules in the European Monetary System," *Journal of International Money and Finance* 18 (June 1999), 429–458.
13. See Nelson C. Mark and Donggyu Sul, "Nominal Exchange Rates and Monetary Fundamentals: Evidence from a Small Post-Bretton Woods Panel," *Journal of International Economics* 53 (February 2001), 29–52.

## CHAPTER 5 Currency Futures and Futures Markets

1. See Kenneth R. French, "A Comparison of Futures and Forward Prices," *Journal of Financial Economics* 12, No. 3 (November 1983), 311–342.
2. Try solving Problem 5.6 at the end of the chapter if you are still unconvinced that it is basis risk and not the spot rate change that is the source of risk in a futures hedge.

3. Ederington develops the properties of the delta hedge ratio in Louis Ederington, "The Hedging Performance of the New Futures Markets," *Journal of Finance* 34, No. 1 (1979), 157–170.

## CHAPTER 6 Currency Options and Options Markets

1. Early exercise of an American put is valuable when the future value of exercising early and investing the exercise price at the risk-free rate is greater than the expected value of the put at expiration. Consequently, American puts can sell at a slight premium to European puts. We'll leave this complicated topic to a specialized course in option pricing.
2. This table is true for American options priced according to the models developed in the appendix to this chapter.
3. These spot prices correspond to ±10 percent in continuously compounded returns from the current spot rate of $S^{¥/\$} = ¥100/\$$: $(¥100/\$)e^{(-0.10)} = ¥90.484/\$$ and $(¥100/\$)e^{(+0.10)} = ¥110.517/\$$. See Section 6.5.
4. These closing spot rates correspond to ±20 percent in continuously compounded returns; $(¥100/\$)e^{(-0.20)} = ¥81.873/\$$ and $(¥100/\$)e^{(+0.20)} = ¥122.140/\$$.
5. If continuously compounded returns are normally distributed, then changes in price are lognormal with larger price increases than decreases for continuously compounded returns of the same magnitude. See Section 6.5.
6. This hedge ratio is similar to the delta hedge of Chapter 5. In each situation, the hedge ratio identifies the ratio of assets that minimizes the variability of the hedged position.
7. In calculus terminology, delta is the first derivative of option value with respect to the underlying asset price. Gamma is the second derivative.
8. Continuous compounding also is discussed in the appendix to this chapter.
9. See T.M. Andersen and T. Bollerslev, "Answering the Skeptics: Yes, Standard Volatility Models Do Provide Accurate Forecasts," *International Economic Review* 39 (1998), 885–905.
10. A more complete discussion of the GARCH model appears in Chapter 3.
11. Recall that continuously compounded returns are additive. The average of a $(0.4)^2 = 0.16$ variance over the first month with a $(0.10)^2 = 0.01$ variance over the subsequent four months is $[0.16 + 4(0.01)]/5 = 0.04$. This is equivalent to a standard deviation of $\sigma = \surd(\sigma^2) = \surd(0.04) = 0.20$, or 20 percent per month with continuous compounding.
12. A spreadsheet with the Black-Scholes and Biger-Hull option pricing models can be downloaded as a part of "A financial toolkit" from the author's website at www.msu.edu/~butler/.
13. Since we're making up the rules as we go, let's assume that call options are infinitely divisible, so that you can split them up into as many pieces as desired. If you don't like this assumption, you can multiply all contracts and prices by 10,000 and achieve a similar result.
14. If you are still uncomfortable with the assumption of infinite divisibility, compare the payoffs to buying a call option on \$10,000 versus buying \$5,249.80 and borrowing ¥452,400 at 5 percent. The larger the transaction, the less we have to worry about an asset's divisibility.
15. You can verify this on a spreadsheet. Allow the ¥100/\$ exchange rate to vary by ±1% successively over eight periods and calculate the standard deviation of the resulting exchange rate distribution.
16. The instantaneous change in the exchange rate is $dS/S = \mu dt + \sigma dz$, where $\mu$ and $\sigma$ are the instantaneous mean and standard deviation of the exchange rate, dt is an instant of time, and $dz \sim N(0,1)$ is i.i.d. over time.
17. Nahum Biger and John Hull, "The Valuation of Currency Options," *Financial Management* 12 (Spring 1983), 24–28. See also Mark Garman and Steve W. Kohlhagen,

"Foreign Currency Option Values," *Journal of International Money and Finance* 2, No. 3 (1983), 231–237.

18. For an adaptation of the Black-Scholes model to options on futures, see Fischer Black, "The Pricing of Commodity Options," *Journal of Financial Economics* 3, No. 1/2 (1976), 167–179.

## CHAPTER 7 Currency Swaps and Swaps Marketss

1. Litzenberger discusses the default risk of swaps along with applicable portions of the U.S. bankruptcy code in Robert H. Litzenberger, "Swaps: Plain and Fanciful," *Journal of Finance* 47 (July 1992), pp. 831–850.
2. All-in cost is the percentage cost of a financing alternative, including any placement fees, calculated as an internal rate of return on incremental cash flows associated with the financing alternative.
3. The payoffs on interest rate swaps can be replicated by a portfolio of Eurodollar futures contracts. See Bernadette A. Minton, "An Empirical Examination of Basic Valuation Models for Plain Vanilla U.S. Interest Rate Swaps," *Journal of Financial Economics* 44 (May 1997), 251–277.
4. Firm-specific counterparty risk and industry-wide default risks in credit default swaps are discussed in Robert A. Jarrow and Fan Yu, "Counterparty Risk and the Pricing of Defaultable Securities," *Journal of Finance* 55 (October 2001), 1765–1799; and Philippe Jorion and Gaiyan Zhang, "Good and Bad Credit Contagion: Evidence from Credit Default Swaps," *Journal of Financial Economics* 84 (June 2007), 860–883.
5. Another type of swap, the *LDC debt-equity swap* or *debt swap*, allows investors to trade the external debt obligations of less-developed countries (LDCs) for equity positions in government-owned companies based in the issuing country. Don't confuse these LDC debt swaps with the debt-for-equity swap of Bull and Bear.

## CHAPTER 8 Multinational Treasury Management

1. Continuous updating is, of course, unattainable in the real world. Let us say that updates to the strategic plan should be made at periodic, but frequent, intervals.
2. Under U.S. law, the buyer can prevent the issuing bank from honoring the letter of credit if the buyer can demonstrate fraud (e.g., shipment of substitute or inferior goods). This is the only exception to the independence and strict compliance principles. Commercial banks thus have a stake in ensuring that the terms of trade are met by all parties.
3. See the *International Reciprocal Trade Association* website (www.irta.com) for details.
4. Multinational netting is discussed in detail in Chapter 9 on transaction exposure to currency risk.
5. National tax codes (e.g., Section 486 of the U.S. Internal Revenue Code) typically require transfer prices be set as if they were arm's-length transactions between unrelated parties.
6. Futures, options, and swaps are discussed in detail in Part II of the book.
7. This is strictly true only for payments that are independent of exchange rates. If payment depends in some way on exchange rates, then domestic monetary contracts may be indirectly exposed to currency risk. For example, a domestic receivable might not be paid if an adverse exchange rate movement forces a domestic customer out of business.
8. Henri Servaes, Ane Tamayo, and Peter Tufano, "The Theory and Practice of Corporate Risk Management," *Journal of Applied Corporate Finance* 21, No. 4, (2009), 60–78.
9. Lewent and Kearney describe the use of simulation in currency risk management in "Identifying, Measuring, and Hedging Currency Risk at Merck," *Journal of Applied Corporate Finance* 2, No. 4 (1990), 19–28.
10. Christopher C. Géczy, Bernadette A. Minton, and Catherine M. Schrand, "Taking a View: Corporate Speculation, Governance, and Compensation," *Journal of Finance* 62, No. 5 (2007), 2405–2443.

11. Smithson and Simkins survey the evidence in "Does Risk Management Add Value? A Survey of the Evidence," *Journal of Applied Corporate Finance* 17 (Summer 2005), 8–17.
12. George Allayannis and James P. Weston, "The Use of Foreign Currency Derivatives and Firm Value," *Review of Financial Studies* 14 (Spring 2001), 243–276.
13. Yanbo Jin and Philippe Jorion, "Firm Value and Hedging: Evidence from U.S. Oil and Gas Producers," *Journal of Finance* 61 (April 2006), 893–919.
14. See Henk Berkman and Michael L. Bradbury, "Empirical Evidence on the Corporate Use of Derivatives," *Financial Management* 25 (Summer 1996), 5–13; and Deanna R. Nance, Clifford W. Smith, Jr., and Charles W. Smithson, "On the Determinants of Corporate Hedging," *Journal of Finance* 48 (March 1993), 267–284. Tax loss carry-forwards and carry-backs also play a role (John R. Graham and Clifford W. Smith, Jr., "Tax Incentives to Hedge," *Journal of Finance* 54 (December 1999), 2241–2262).
15. Volatility and option valuation are discussed in Chapters 6 and 16.
16. See Stuart C. Gilson, "Managing Default: Some Evidence on How Firms Choose Between Workouts and Chapter 11," *Journal of Applied Corporate Finance* 4 (Summer 1991), 62–70; and John J. McConnell and Henri Servaes, "The Economics of Pre-Packaged Bankruptcy," *Journal of Applied Corporate Finance* 4 (Summer 1991), 93–97.
17. Eisdorfer ("Empirical Evidence of Risk Shifting in Financially Distressed Firms," *Journal of Finance* 63 (April 2008), 609–637) finds evidence consistent with risk-shifting behaviors among firms in financial distress.
18. John R. Graham and Daniel A. Rogers, "Do Firms Hedge in Response to Tax Incentives?" *Journal of Finance* 57 (April 2002), 815–839.
19. Peter Tufano, "Agency Costs of Corporate Risk Management," *Financial Management* 27 (Spring 1998), 67–77.
20. See, for example, Arturo Bris, Ivo Welch, and Ning Zhu, "The Costs of Bankruptcy: Chapter 7 Liquidation versus Chapter 11 Reorganization," *Journal of Finance* 61 (June 2006), 1253–1303.

## CHAPTER 9 Managing Transaction Exposure to Currency Risk

1. Chapters 5–7 provide detailed treatments of currency derivatives (futures, options, and swaps).
2. Gordon M. Bodnar, Gregory S. Hayt, and Richard C. Marston, "1998 Wharton Survey of Financial Risk Management by U.S. Non-Financial Firms," *Financial Management* 27 (Winter 1998), 70–91.
3. Note that these examples have the currency of reference (i.e., the U.S. dollar) in the denominator of the FX quotes, following Rule #2 from Chapter 3.
4. For example, see Peter MacKay and Sara B. Moeller, "The Value of Corporate Risk Management," *Journal of Finance* 62 (June 2007), 1379–1419.
5. S. Öhnke M. Bartram, Gregory W. Brown, and Frank R. Fehle, "International Evidence on Financial Derivatives Usage," *Financial Management* 38 (Spring 2009), 185–206.
6. Gordon M. Bodnar, Gregory S. Hayt, and Richard C. Marston, "1998 Wharton Survey of Financial Risk Management by U.S. Non-Financial Firms," *Financial Management* 27 (Winter 1998), 70–91.
7. See, for example, Gordon M. Bodnar and Gunther Gebhardt, "Derivatives Usage in Risk Management by U.S. and German Non-Financial Firms: A Comparative Survey," *Journal of International Financial Management & Accounting* 10 (Autumn 1999), 153–187.
8. Christopher C. Géczy, Bernadette A. Minton, and Catherine M. Schrand, "Taking a View: Corporate Speculation, Governance, and Compensation," *Journal of Finance* 62 (October 2007), 2405–2443.

## CHAPTER 10 Managing Operating Exposure to Currency Risk

1. Recall that $V_t^d = V_t^f S_t^{d/f}$. For a contractual amount $V_0^f = V_1^f = V^f$ that is fixed in value in currency f, $\Delta V^d = (V_1^d - V_0^d) = (V_1^f S_1^{d/f} - V_0^f S_0^{d/f}) = V^f(S_1^{d/f} - S_0^{d/f}) = V^f(\Delta S^{d/f})$.
2. Marston shows that—in many forms of competition—an exporter's exposure is proportional to net foreign revenues in "The Effects of Industry Structure on Economic Exposure," *Journal of International Money and Finance*, Volume 20 (April 2001), 149–164.
3. This model of exposure to currency risk is developed in depth in Chapter 20 on international asset pricing.
4. The r-square of the regression $r_t^d = \alpha^d + \beta^f s_t^{d/f} + \varepsilon_t^d$ can be used as a measure of the quality of the hedge. Chapter 5 discusses this measure of hedge quality in the context of currency futures contracts.
5. These variations are described in Judy C. Lewent and A. John Kearney, "Identifying, Measuring, and Hedging Currency Risk at Merck," *Journal of Applied Corporate Finance* 2, No. 4 (1990), 19–28.
6. Young Sang Kim, Ike Mathur, and Jouahn Nam, "Is Operational Hedging a Substitute for or a Complement to Financial Hedging?" *Journal of Corporate Finance* 12 (September 2006), 834–853.
7. Wayne R. Guay and S.P. Kothari, "How Much Do Firms Hedge with Derivatives?" *Journal of Financial Economics* 70 (December 2003), 423–461.
8. George Allayannis, Jane Ihrig, and James P. Weston, "Exchange-Rate Hedging: Financial Versus Operational Strategies," *American Economic Review* 91 (May 2001), 391–395.
9. The assumption of perpetual cash flows simplifies our algebra. Recall that the value V of a perpetual cash flow CF discounted at a rate i is simply $V = CF/i$.
10. Marston studies the relation of price elasticities and industry structure in "The Effects of Industry Structure." *Journal of International Money and Finance*, Volume 20 (April 2001) 149–164.
11. Exceptions to this rule include high-status goods or services for which quantity demanded *increases* with price, such as some expensive wines or consulting services.
12. The interaction of the firm's pricing decisions and its exposure to currency risk is studied in Gordon M. Bodnar, BernardDumas, and Richard C. Marston, "Pass-Through and Exposure," *Journal of Finance* 57 (February 2002), 199–231.

## CHAPTER 11 Managing Translation Exposure and Accounting for Financial Transactions

1. The impact of market imperfections on the firm's cash flow-based incentives to hedge are discussed in Appendix 8A.
2. Peter M. DeMarzo and Darrell Duffie, "Corporate Incentives for Hedging and Hedge Accounting," *Review of Financial Studies* (Fall 1995), 743–771.
3. P.A. Belk and M.Glaum, "The Management of Foreign Exchange Risk in U.K. Multinationals: An Empirical Investigation," *Accounting and Business Research* 21 (Winter 1990), 3–14.
4. See Antti Hakkarainen, Nathan Joseph, Eero Kasanen, and Vesa Puttonen, "The Foreign Exchange Exposure Management Practices of Finnish Industrial Firms," *Journal of International Financial Management & Accounting* 9, No. 1 (1998), 34–57.
5. Gordon M. Bodnar and Gunther Gebhardt, "Derivatives Usage in Risk Management by U.S. and German Non-Financial Firms: A Comparative Survey," *Journal of International Financial Management & Accounting* 10 (Autumn 1999), 153–187.
6. Carol Olson Houston and Gerhard G. Mueller, "Foreign Exchange Rate Hedging and SFAS No. 52 – Relatives or Strangers?" *Accounting Horizons* 2 (December 1988), 50–57.

7. Jayne M. Godfrey and Benita Yee, "Mining Sector Currency Risk Management Strategies: Responses to Foreign Currency Accounting Regulation," *The Accounting Review* 26 (Summer 1996), 200–214.
8. Raj Aggarwal, "Management of Accounting Exposure to Currency Changes: Role and Evidence of Agency Costs," *Managerial Finance* 17, No. 4 (1991), 10–22.
9. Laurent L. Jacque and Paul M. Vaaler, "The International Control Conundrum with Exchange Risk: An EVA Framework," *Journal of International Business Studies* 32, No. 4 (2001), 813–832.
10. Gordon M. Bodnar, Gregory S. Hayt, Richard C. Marston, and Charles W. Smithson, "Wharton Survey of Derivatives Usage by U.S. Non-Financial Firms," *Financial Management* 24 (Summer 1995), 104–114.
11. Gordon M. Bodnar, Gregory S. Hayt, and Richard C. Marston, "1995 Wharton Survey of Derivatives Usage by US Non-Financial Firms," *Financial Management* 25 (Winter 1996), 113–133.
12. The difference between hedging and speculating is something like pornography. Although it's difficult to define, you usually know it when you see it.
13. Some of the issues in qualifying a hedge are discussed in Kawaller, "What Analysts Need to Know about Accounting for Derivatives," *Financial Analysts Journal* 60 (March/April 2004), 24–30; and Kawaller, "Interest Rate Swaps: Accounting vs. Economics," *Financial Analysts Journal* 63 (March/April 2007), 15–19.
14. Shivaram Rajgopal, "Early Evidence on the Informativeness of the SEC's Market Risk Disclosures: The Case of Commodity Price Risk Exposure of Oil and Gas Producers," *Accounting Review* 74 (July 2002), 251–280.
15. Thomas J. Linsmeier, Daniel B. Thornton, Mohan Venkatachalam, and Michael Welker, "The Effect of Mandated Market Risk Disclosures on Trading Volume Sensitivity to Interest Rate, Exchange Rate, and Commodity Price Movements," *Accounting Review* (April 2002), 343–377.
16. Christian Leuz and Robert E Verrecchia, "The Economic Consequences of Increased Disclosure," *Journal of Accounting Research* 38 (Supplement 2000) 91–124.
17. Li Wang, Pervaiz Alam, and Stephen Makar, "The Value-Relevance of Derivative Disclosures by Commercial Banks: A Comprehensive Study of Information Content under SFAS Nos. 119 and 133," *Review of Quantitative Finance and Accounting* 25 (December 2005), 413–427.
18. Warren B. Bailey, George Andrew Karolyi, and Carolina Salva, "The Economic Consequences of Increased Disclosure: Evidence from International Cross-Listings," *Journal of Financial Economics* 81 (July 2006), 175–213.
19. Gordon M. Bodnar, Gregory S. Hayt, and Richard C. Marston, "1998 Wharton Survey of Financial Risk Management by U.S. Non-Financial Firms," *Financial Management* 27 (Winter 1998), 70–91.
20. Gordon M. Bodnar, Gregory S. Hayt, and Richard C. Marston, "1995 Wharton Survey of Derivatives Usage by US Non-Financial Firms," *Financial Management* 25 (Winter 1996), 113–133.

## CHAPTER 12 Foreign Market Entry and Country Risk Management

1. Claude Erb, Campbell Harvey, and Tadas Viskanta, "Political Risk, Financial Risk, and Economic Risk," *Financial Analysts Journal* 52 (November/December 1996), 28–46.
2. A procedure for valuing blocked funds is presented in Chapter 13.
3. Investment decisions in the presence of real options are discussed in Chapter 16.
4. The sensibility of using inflated hurdle rates in uncertain environments is discussed in Chapter 16 on real options.

5. C.K. Prahalad and Gary Hamel, "The Core Competence of the Corporation," *Harvard Business Review* 68 (May–June 1990), 79–91.
6. Author Jean Kerr wrote: "Marrying a man is like buying something you've been admiring for a long time in a shop window. You may love it when you get it home, but it doesn't always go with everything else."
7. Gary Hamel, Yves L. Doz, and C. K. Prahalad, "Collaborate with Your Competitors–and Win," *Harvard Business Review* 67 (January–February 1989), 133–139.

## CHAPTER 13 Multinational Capital Budgeting

1. The expectation of the product of two random variables A and B is E[AB] = E[A] E[B] + Cov(A,B). Consequently, expected cash flow in the domestic currency is in fact $E[C_t^{d}] = E[CF_t^{f}S_t^{d/f}] = E[CF_t^{f}]\ E[S_t^{d/f}] + Cov(CF_t^{f},\ S_t^{d/f})$. The covariance of project cash flows with the exchange rate $Cov(CF_t^{f},\ S_t^{d/f})$ is ignored on the grounds that the exposure is difficult to estimate and typically is small in magnitude.
2. If interest rate parity holds, then $(1 + i^{d})^{t} = (1 + i^{f})^{t}(F_t^{d/f}/S_0^{d/f})$ can be substituted into Equation 13.4, leading directly to Equation 13.2: $V_0^{d}|i^{d} = \Sigma_t E[CF_t^{f}]F_t^{d/f}/(1 + i^{d})^{t} = \Sigma_t E[CF_t^{f}]F_t^{d/f}/[(1 + i^{f})^{t}(F_t^{d/f}/S_0^{d/f})] = S_0^{d/f}\Sigma_t[E[CF_t^{f}]/(1 + i^{f})^{t}] = S_0^{d/f}(V_0^{f}|i^{f})$.
3. Can you imagine a world with no hypothetical situations?
4. We've assumed an all-equity project, so $i^{£} = 20$ percent is the required return on equity in pounds sterling. In the more general case, this would be the weighted average cost of capital in pounds sterling.
5. Taxation of foreign source income is discussed in Chapter 15.
6. Some of these strategic considerations are addressed in Chapter 16 on real options.
7. For example, see Charles Smithson Betty J. Simkins, "Does Risk Management Add Value? A Survey of the Evidence," *Journal of Applied Corporate Finance* 17 (Summer 2005), 8–17.
8. Problem 13.12 at the end of the chapter relaxes the assumption that Hook's treasure chest is risk-free.
9. Although nothing is certain in life except death and taxes, at least taxes are occasionally negotiable.

## CHAPTER 14 Multinational Capital Structure and Cost of Capital

1. Franco Modigliani and Merton Miller, "The Cost of Capital, Corporation Finance and the Theory of Investment," *American Economic Review* 48 (June 1958), 261–297.
2. Franco Modigliani and Merton Miller, "Corporate Income Taxes and the Cost of Capital: A Correction," *American Economic Review* 53 (June 1963), 433–442.
3. Appendix 8A discusses the impact of these market imperfections on the firm's hedging policy.
4. John R. Graham and Campbell R. Harvey, "The Theory and Practice of Corporate Finance: Evidence from the Field," *Journal of Financial Economics* 61 (2001), 187–243.
5. Strictly speaking, markets are integrated when real *after-tax* returns on equivalent assets are equal. We'll add differential taxes in Chapter 15. For now, we assume that taxes are the same in the domestic and foreign markets.
6. John R. Graham and Campbell R. Harvey, "The Theory and Practice of Corporate Finance: Evidence from the Field," *Journal of Financial Economics* 61 (2001), 187–243.
7. Kees G. Koedijk, Clemens J.M. Kool, Peter C. Schotman, and Mathijs A. van Dijk, "The Cost of Capital in International Financial Markets: Local or Global?" *Journal of International Money and Finance* 21 (2002), 905–929.
8. Currency risk exposure is discussed in more depth in Section 20.3.
9. For example, the July 2008 issue of the *Review of Financial Studies* examines the predictability of the equity premium.

10. Jeremy Siegel, "The Equity Premium: Stock and Bond Returns Since 1802," *Financial Analysts Journal* 48 (January/February 1992), 28–38.
11. Elroy Dimson, Paul Marsh, and Mike Staunton, "Equity Premia Around the World," presented at the 2012 AFA Annual Conference (available at www.ssrn.com).
12. Philippe Jorion and William N. Goetzmann, "Global Stock Markets in the Twentieth Century," *Journal of Finance* 53 (June 1999), 953–980.
13. John R. Graham and Campbell R. Harvey, "The Equity Risk Premium in 2010," working paper available at www.ssrn.com (2010).
14. There are a variety of algebraic adjustments for unlevering and relevering betas, but these adjustments almost always are based on models that ignore costs of financial distress (as does the MM capital structure model). At the target capital structure, costs of financial distress should be just as important as interest tax shields.
15. Inselbag and Kaufold apply the APV approach to the present value of interest tax shields in "Two DCF Approaches for Valuing Companies Under Alternative Financing Strategies," *Journal of Applied Corporate Finance* 10, No. 1 (1997), 114–122.
16. Geert Bekaert, Campbell R. Harvey, Christian T. Lundblad, and Stephan Siegel, "What Segments Equity Markets?" *Review of Financial Studies* 24 (December 2011), 3841–3890.
17. Campbell Harvey, "Predictable Risk and Returns in Emerging Markets," *Review of Financial Studies* 8 (Fall 1995), 773–816.
18. Claude B. Erb, Campbell R. Harvey, and Tadas E. Viskanta, "Political Risk, Financial Risk and Economic Risk," *Financial Analysts Journal* 52 (November/December 1996), 29–46.
19. Andrew Ang, Robert J. Hodrick, Yuhang Xing, and iaoyan Zhang, "High Idiosyncratic Volatility and Low Returns: International and Further U.S. Evidence," *Journal of Financial Economics* 91 (January 2009), 1–23. This article also discusses the influence of total risk in emerging market returns.
20. Claude B. Erb, Campbell R. Harvey, and Tadas E. Viskanta, "Expected Returns and Volatility in 135 Countries," *Journal of Portfolio Management* 22 (Spring 1996), 46–58.
21. Geert Bekaert and Campbell Harvey, "Foreign Speculators and Emerging Equity Markets," *Journal of Finance* 55 (April 2000), 565–613.
22. de Jong and de Roon estimate an 11-basis-point decrease in capital costs in "Time-Varying Market Integration and Expected Returns in Emerging Markets," *Journal of Financial Economics* 78 (December 2005), 583–613.
23. Geert Bekaert, Campbell R. Harvey, and Christian Lundblad, "Does Financial Liberalization Spur Growth?" *Journal of Financial Economics* 77 (July 2005), 3–56. See also Geert Bekaert, Campbell R. Harvey, Christian Lundblad, and Stephan Siegel, "Global Growth Opportunities and Market Integration," *Journal of Finance* 62 (June 2007), 1081–1137.
24. John R. Graham and Campbell R. Harvey, "The Theory and Practice of Corporate Finance: Evidence from the Field," *Journal of Financial Economics* 61 (2001), 187–243.
25. Compiled from Feldstein, "The Effects of Outbound Foreign Direct Investment on the Domestic Capital Stock," in *The Effects of Taxation on Multinational Corporations*, edited by Martin Feldstein, James R. Hines, Jr., and R. Glenn Hubbard, (Chicago: University of Chicago Press, 1995).
26. Chapter 15 discusses transfer prices.
27. A rights offering gives current shareholders the option of investing additional funds and maintaining their percentage ownership in the firm, or selling the rights to external investors.
28. Prior to the Tax Reform Act of 1986, U.S. corporations could issue bearer securities to foreign investors only through an offshore finance subsidiary.
29. Timothy Loughran and Jay R. Ritter, "The New Issues Puzzle," *Journal of Finance* 50 (March 1995), 23–52.

30. Stephen R. Foerster and G. Andrew Karolyi, "The Effects of Market Segmentation and Investor Recognition on Asset Prices: Evidence from Foreign Stocks Listing in the United States," *Journal of Finance* 54 (June 1999), 981–1013.
31. Susan Chaplinsky and Latha Ramchand, "The Impact of Global Equity Offerings," *Journal of Finance* 55 (December 2000), 2767–2789.
32. Sergei Sarkissian and Michael J. Schill, "Are There Permanent Valuation Gains to Overseas Listing?" *Review of Financial Studies* 22 (January 2009), 371–412.
33. Raghuram G. Rajan and Luigi Zingales, "What Do We Know About Capital Structure? Some Evidence from International Data," *Journal of Finance* 50 (December 1995), 1421–1460.
34. Stewart C. Myers and Nicholas S. Majluf, "Corporate Financing and Investment Decisions When Firms Have Information That Investors Do Not Have," *Journal of Financial Economics* 13, No. 2 (1984), 127–221.
35. Michael C. Jensen, "Agency Costs of Free Cash Flow, Corporate Financing, and Takeovers," *American Economic Review* 76, No. 2 (1986), 323–339.
36. Laurence Booth, Varouj Aivazian, Asli Demirguc-Kunt, and Vojislav Maksimovic, "Capital Structures in Developing Countries," *Journal of Finance* 56 (February 2001), 87–130.

## CHAPTER 15 Taxes and Multinational Corporate Strategy

1. See *The U.S. International Tax Rules: Background and Selected Issues Relating to the Competitiveness of U.S. Business Abroad* (JCX-68-03), Joint Committee on Taxation, July 14, 2003.
2. Mihir Desai and James R. Hines, Jr., "Basket Cases: Tax Incentives and International Joint Venture Participation by American Multinational Firms," *Journal of Public Economics* 71 (March 1999), 379–402.
3. Ernst & Young, "Transfer Pricing 2010 Global Survey" (www.ey.com).
4. Michael J. Smith, "Ex Ante and Ex Post Discretion over Arm's Length Transfer Prices," *Accounting Review* 77 (January 2002), 161–184.
5. Julie Collins, Deen Kemsley, and Mark Lang, "Cross-Jurisdictional Income Shifting and Earnings Valuation," *Journal of Accounting Research* 36 (Autumn 1998), 209–229.
6. Matteo P. Arena and Andrew H. Roper, "The Effect of Taxes on Multinational Debt Location," *Journal of Corporate Finance* 16 (December 2010), 637–654.
7. Kaye J. Newberry and Dan S. Dhaliwal, "Cross-Jurisdictional Income Shifting by U.S. Multinationals: Evidence from International Bond Offerings," *Journal of Accounting Research* 39 (December 2001), 643–662.
8. Dan Dhaliwal, Kaye J. Newberry, and Constance D. Weaver, "Corporate Taxes and Financing Methods for Taxable Acquisitions," *Contemporary Accounting Research* 22 (Spring 2005), 1–30.
9. Gil B. Manzon, Jr., David J. Sharp, and Nickoloas G. Travlos, "An Empirical Study of the Consequences of U.S. Tax Rules for International Acquisitions by U.S. Firms," *Journal of Finance* 49, No. 5 (1994), 1893–1904.
10. Harry P. Huizinga and Johannes Voget, "International Taxation and the Direction and Volume of Cross-Border M&As," *Journal of Finance* 64 No. 3 (2009), 1217–1249.

## CHAPTER 16 Real Options and Cross-Border Investment Strategy

1. This chapter values real options without the use of formal option pricing theory. Interested readers should consult the suggested readings at the end of the chapter.

2. Gordon M. Bodnar and Joseph Weintrop, "The Valuation of the Foreign Income of U.S. Multinational Firms: A Growth Opportunities Perspective," *Journal of Accounting & Economics* 24 (December 1997), 69–97.

3. See Peter Carr, "The Valuation of Sequential Exchange Opportunities," *Journal of Finance* 43 (December 1988), 1235–1256.
4. Deep-sea oil rigs and sunk costs? Sorry about that. Hanging is too good for a man who makes puns; he should be drawn and quoted.
5. Recall that the value of a perpetual cash flow that begins in one year and continues forever is $V = CF/i$.
6. As it turns out, systematic risk has no place in option pricing models. Instead, options are valued with a risk-free arbitrage position using a *replicating portfolio* that mimics the payoffs of the option. This topic is discussed in more detail in Appendix 6A in the chapter on currency options.
7. Exit and abandonment options can be valued as put options in which managers can sell or dispose of an existing project for a (perhaps time-varying) exercise price. See Philip G. Berger, Eli Ofek, and Itzhak Swary, "Investor Valuation of the Abandonment Option," *Journal of Financial Economics* 42 (October 1996), 257–287.
8. Christophe documents hysteresis in U.S. firms at a time when the dollar was at a relative high in real terms in "Hysteresis and the Value of the U.S. Multinational Corporation," *Journal of Business* 70 (July 1997), 435–462.
9. Depletion of the oil reserve has been omitted from our analysis. Depletion of a natural resource can be treated in the same way that dividends on a dividend-paying stock are treated in the valuation of a stock option.
10. Nalin Kulatilaka and Alan J. Marcus, "Project Valuation and Uncertainty: When Does DCF Fail?" *Journal of Applied Corporate Finance* 5 (Fall 1992), 92–100.
11. It is simplest to focus on the intrinsic value of the option. The general result prevails when the time value is included; the volatility of an option is greater than the volatility of the underlying asset.
12. The only exception to this rule is in the trivial case of a risk-free asset. This is the reason the investments in this chapter are assumed to be zero-beta, risk-free assets.
13. Appendix 6-A provides an example of a replicating portfolio for a currency option.

## CHAPTER 17 Corporate Governance and the International Market for Corporate Control

1. Bebchuk and Weisbach survey the literature in an article ("The State of Corporate Governance Research") that introduces a special issue of the *Review of Financial Studies* (March 2010) devoted to corporate governance research.
2. Rafael La Porta, Florencio Lopez-de-Silanes, Andrei Shleifer, and Robert W. Vishny, "Investor Protection and Corporate Governance," *Journal of Financial Economics* 58 (October/November 2000), 3–27.
3. Rafael La Porta, Florencio Lopez-de-Silanes, and Andrei Shleifer, "Corporate Ownership around the World," *Journal of Finance* 54 (April 1999), 471–517.
4. Rafael La Porta, Florencio Lopez-de-Silanes, Andrei Shleifer, and Robert W. Vishny, "Law and Finance," *Journal of Political Economy* 106 (December 1998), 1113–1155.
5. Larry Fauver and Michael E. Fuerst, "Does Good Corporate Governance Include Employee Representation? Evidence from German Corporate Boards," *Journal of Financial Economics* 82 (December 2006), 673–710.
6. Jun-Koo Kang and Anil Shivdasani, "Firm Performance, Corporate Governance, and Top Executive Turnover in Japan," *Journal of Financial Economics* 38 (May 1995), 29–58.
7. See Clifford G. Holderness, "The Myth of Diffuse Ownership in the United States," *Review of Financial Studies* 22 Issue 4 (April 2009), 1377–1408.
8. Christian Leuz, Karl V. Lins, and Francis E. Warnock, "Do Foreigners Invest Less in Poorly Governed Firms?" *Review of Financial Studies* 23 (March 2010), 3245–3285.

9. For example, Gary Gorton and Frank A. Schmid, "Universal Banking and the Performance of German Firms," *Journal of Financial Economics* 58 (October 2000), 29–80.
10. Julian Franks and Colin Mayer, "Ownership and Control of German Corporations," *Review of Financial Studies* 14 (Winter 2001), 943–977.
11. Financing considerations are discussed in Appendix 8A and Chapter 14.
12. Alexander Ljungqvist and Tim Jenkinson, "The Role of Hostile Stakes in German Corporate Governance," *Journal of Corporate Finance* 7 (December 2001), 397–446.
13. William Megginson, "Privatization and Finance," *Annual Review of Financial Economics* Vol 2 (December 2010), 145–174.
14. The joke at the time was "the only thing worse than having to take a capitalist's money is not being offered a capitalist's money."
15. Nandini Gupta, "Partial Privatization and Firm Performance," *Journal of Finance* 60 (April 2005), 987–1015.
16. George Alexandridis, Dimitris Petmezas, and Nickolaos G. Travlos, "Gains from Mergers and Acquisitions around the World: New Evidence," *Financial Management* Vol 39, Issue 4 (Winter 2010), 1671–1695.
17. Anusha Chari, Paige P. Ouimet, and Linda L. Tesar, "The Value of Control in Emerging Markets," *Review of Financial Studies* 23 (March 2010), 1741–1770.
18. For evidence from non-U.S. markets, see Faccio and Masulis, "The Choice of Payment Method in European Mergers and Acquisitions," *Journal of Finance* 60 (June 2005), 1345–1388.
19. Jun-Koo Kang, Jin-Mo Kim, Wei-Lin Liu, and Sangho Yi, "Post-takeover Restructuring and the Sources of Gains in Foreign Takeovers: Evidence from U.S. Targets," *Journal of Business* 79 (September 2006), 2503–2539.
20. Isil Erel, Rose C. Liao, and Michael S. Weisbach, "Determinants of Cross-Border Mergers and Acquisitions," *Journal of Finance* 66, (forthcoming June 2012).
21. Jun-Koo Kang and Anil Shivdasani, "Firm Performance, Corporate Governance, and Top Executive Turnover in Japan," *Journal of Financial Economics* 38 (May 1995), 29–58. "Does the Japanese Governance System Enhance Shareholder Wealth? Evidence from the Stock-Price Effects of Top Management Turnover," *Review of Financial Studies* 9 (Winter 1996), 1061–1095.
22. Julian Franks and Colin Mayer, "Ownership and Control of German Corporations," *Review of Financial Studies* 14 (Winter 2001), 943–977.
23. Joseph P.H. Fan, T.J. Wong, and Tianyu Zhang, "Politically Connected CEOs, Corporate Governance, and Post-IPO Performance of China's Newly Partially Privatized Firms," *Journal of Financial Economics* 84 (May 2007), 330–357.
24. Paolo F. Volpin, "Governance with Poor Investor Protection: Evidence from Top Executive Turnover in Italy," *Journal of Financial Economics* 64 (April 2002), 61–90.
25. Tatiana Nenova, "The Value of Corporate Votes and Control Benefits: A Cross-Country Analysis," *Journal of Financial Economics* 68 (June 2003), 325–351.
26. Christian Leuz, Karl V. Lins, and Francis E. Warnock, "Do Foreigners Invest Less in Poorly Governed Firms?" *Review of Financial Studies* 23 (March 2010), 3245–3285.
27. Reena Aggarwal, Isil Erel, René Stulz, and Rohan Williamson, "Differences in Governance Practices between U.S. and Foreign Firms: Measurement, Causes, and Consequences," *Review of Financial Studies* 23 (March 2010), 3245–3285.

## CHAPTER 18 International Capital Markets

1. In 2012, the Eurozone included 17 countries: Austria, Belgium, Cyprus, Finland, France, Germany, Greece, Ireland, Italy, Latvia, Luxembourg, Malta, Netherlands, Portugal, Slovakia, Slovenia, and Spain.
2. Although Bombay is now called Mumbai, the Bombay Stock Exchange chose to retain its traditional English name.

3. Michael S. Rozeff, "Closed-End Fund Discounts and Premiums," *Pacific-Basin Capital Markets Research* II (1991), 503–522.
4. Investing in a hedge fund is like buying a yacht. If you have to ask how much it costs, you probably can't afford it.
5. For a review, see Paul Gompers and Josh Lerner, "The Venture Capital Revolution," *Journal of Economic Perspectives* 15 (Spring 2001), 145–168.
6. For details, see Philippe Jorion and Leonid Roisenberg, "Synthetic International Diversification: The Case for Diversifying with Stock Index Futures," *Journal of Portfolio Management* 19 (Winter 1993), 65–74.
7. Geert Bekaert, Campbell R. Harvey, Christian T. Lundblad, and Stephan 0Siegel, "What Segments Equity Markets?" *Review of Financial Studies* 24 (December 2011), 3841–3890.
8. Kalok Chan, Albert J. Menkveld, and Zhishu Yang, "Informational Asymmetry and Asset Prices: Evidence from the China Foreign ShareDiscount," *Journal of Finance* 63 (February 2008), 159–196.
9. See, for example, Vihang Errunza and Etienne Losq, "Capital Flow Controls, International Asset Pricing, and Investors' Welfare: A Multi-Country Framework," *Journal of Finance* Vol 44, No. 4 (September 1989), 1025–1037.
10. Kalok Chan, Albert J. Menkveld, and Zhishu Yang, "Informational Asymmetry and Asset Prices: Evidence from the China Foreign ShareDiscount," *Journal of Finance* 63 (February 2008), 159–196.
11. Warren Bailey, Y. Peter Chung, and Jun-Koo Kang, "Foreign Ownership Restrictions and Equity Price Premiums: What Drives the Demand for Cross-Border Investments?" *Journal of Financial and Quantitative Analysis* 34 (December 1999), 489–511.
12. Susan Chaplinsky and Latha Ramchand, "The Impact of Global Equity Offerings," *Journal of Finance* 55 (December 2000), 2767–2789.
13. Stephen R. Foerster and G. Andrew Karolyi, "The Effects of Market Segmentation and Investor Recognition on Asset Prices: Evidence from Foreign Stocks Listing in the United States," *Journal of Finance* 54 (June 1999), 981–1013.
14. Darius P. Miller, "The Market Reaction to International Cross-listings: Evidence from Depositary Receipts," *Journal of Financial Economics* 51 (January 1999), 103–123.
15. Sergei Sarkissian and Michael J. Schill, "The Overseas Listing Decision: New Evidence of Proximity Preference," *Review of Financial Studies* 17 (Autumn 2004), 769–809.
16. Karl V. Lins, Deon Strickland, and Marc Zenner, "Do Non-U.S. Firms Issue Equity on U.S. Stock Exchanges to Relax Capital Constraints?" *Journal of Financial and Quantitative Analysis* 40 (March 2005), 109–133.
17. Warren Bailey, G. Andrew Karolyi, and Carolina Salva, "The Economic Consequences of Increased Disclosure: Evidence from International Cross-listings," *Journal of Financial Economics* 81 (July 2006), 175–213.
18. Vihang Errunza, Ked Hogan, and Mao-Wei Hung, "Can the Gains from International Diversification Be Achieved Without Trading Abroad?" *Journal of Finance* 54 (December 1999), 2075–2107.
19. William F. Sharpe, "Asset Allocation: Management Style and Performance Measurement," *Journal of Portfolio Management* 18 (Winter 1992), 7–19.
20. Some fund managers try to "game the system" by claiming one style and following another so that their performance is benchmarked to a standard that earns a lower rate of return. See Stephen J. Brown and William N. Goetzmann, "Mutual Fund Styles," *Journal of Financial Economics* 43 (March 1997), 373–399.
21. Cheng-Few Lee and Shafiqur Rahman, "Market Timing, Selectivity, and Mutual Fund Performance: An Empirical Investigation," *Journal of Business* 63 (April 1990), 261–278.
22. Connie Becker, Wayne Ferson, David H. Myers, and Michael J. Schill, "Conditional Market Timing with Benchmark Investors," *Journal of Financial Economics* 52 (April 1999), 119–148; William N. Goetzmann, Jonathan Ingersoll, Jr., and Zoran Ivkovic,

"Monthly Measurement of Daily Timers," *Journal of Financial and Quantitative Analysis* 35 (September 2000), 257–290.

23. Here we go again. To a U.S. resident, the term *table* means to "discontinue discussion." To a U.K. resident, it means to "put it on the table" and open the topic for discussion. Two nations divided by a common tongue.
24. Reverse this perspective if you are from the U.K. Assume you're assigned to the U.S. branch of Standard Chartered Bank in New York and must review Red Dog's loan. From a U.S. perspective, Red Dog appears to lack liquidity when in fact the balance sheets of the two firms are the same.

## CHAPTER 19 International Portfolio Diversification

1. The term *American* properly refers to all of the Americas (North, South, and Central). My apologies for using it here in a parochial way to refer only to U.S. equities.
2. As an exercise, verify that $\sigma_P = 0$ using these weights and Equation 19.3.
3. Don't confuse mean-variance efficiency with market efficiency. Mean-variance efficiency refers to the return-risk performance of an asset or a portfolio. Market efficiency refers to how well the market performs its operational, allocational, or informational (pricing) functions.
4. $(1+r^d) = (P_t{}^d/P_{t-1}{}^d) = [(P_t{}^f S_t{}^{d/f})/(P_{t-1}{}^f S_{t-1}{}^{d/f})] = (P_t{}^f/P_{t-1}{}^f)(S_t{}^{d/f}/S_{t-1}{}^{d/f}) = (1+r^f)(1+s^{d/f})$.
5. Continuous compounding eliminates the cross-product term, so that $r^d = r^f + s^{d/f}$ where $r^d$, $r^f$ and $s^{d/f}$ are continuously compounded rates of change. See Appendix 4A.
6. In continuously compounded returns, $Var(r^d) = Var(r^f) + Var(s^{d/f}) + 2Cov(r^f, s^{d/f})$.
7. *RiskMetrics'* conditional variance estimate puts a 97% weight on the previous month's conditional variance and a 3% weight on the square of the most recent spot rate change: $\sigma_t = \sqrt{}(0.97\sigma_{t-1}{}^2 + 0.03s_{t-1}{}^2)$. See Chapter 3.
8. See Weng-Ling Lin, Robert F. Engle, and Takatoshi Ito, "Do Bulls and Bears Move Across Borders? International Transmission of Stock Returns and Volatility," *Review of Financial Studies* 7 (Fall 1994), 507–538; Jonathan Lewellen, "The Time-Series Relations among Expected Return, Risk, and Book-to-Market," *Journal of Financial Economics* 54 (October 1999), 5–43.
9. See Eugene F. Fama and Kenneth R. French, "Business Conditions and Expected Returns on Stocks and Bonds," *Journal of Financial Economics* 25 (November 1989), 23–50.
10. Geert Bekaert, Robert J. Hodrick, and Xiaoyan Zhang, "International Stock Return Comovements," *Journal of Finance* 64 (December 2009), 2591–2626.
11. See William N. Goetzmann, Lingfeng Li, and K. Geert Rouwenhorst, "Long-Term Global Market Correlations," *Journal of Business* 78 (January 2005), 1–38.
12. Bruno Solnik, "Why Not Diversify Internationally Rather Than Domestically?" *Financial Analysts Journal* 30 (July/August 1974), 48–54. Reprinted in *Financial Analysts Journal* 51 (January/February 1995), 89–94. More recently, see Cliff S. Asness, Roni Israelov, and John M. Liew, "International Diversification Works (Eventually)," *Financial Analysts Journal* 67 (May/June 2011), 24–38.
13. Haim Levy and Zvi Lerman, "The Benefits of International Diversification in Bonds," *Financial Analysts Journal* 44 (September/October 1988), 56–64.
14. Philippe Jorion, "Asset Allocation with Hedged and Unhedged Foreign Stocks and Bonds," *Journal of Portfolio Management* 15 (Summer 1989), 49–54.
15. David J. Denis, Diane K. Denis, and David Yost, "Global Diversification, Industrial Diversification, and Firm Value," *Journal of Finance* 57 (October 2002), 1951–1979.
16. See Michael Adler and Bernard Dumas, "International Portfolio Choice and Corporation Finance: A Synthesis," *Journal of Finance* 38 (June 1983), 925–984.
17. Timothy M. Craft, "Home Bias Makes Sense for U.S. Pension Plans," *Journal of Portfolio Management* 32 (Spring 2006), 26–33.

18. Marianne Baxter and Urban J. Jermann, "The International Diversification Puzzle Is Worse Than You Think," *American Economic Review* 87 (March 1997), 170–180.
19. Magnus Dahlquist, Lee Pinkowitz, René M. Stulz, and Rohan Williamson, "Corporate Governance and the Home Bias," *Journal of Financial and Quantitative Analysis* 38, Special Issue on International Corporate Governance (March 2003), 87–110.
20. See Daniel Kahneman and Amos Tversky, "Prospect Theory: An Analysis of Decision Under Risk," *Econometrica* 47 (March 1979), 263–292.
21. Terrance Odean, "Do Investors Trade Too Much?" *American Economic Review* 89 (December 1999), 1279–1298.
22. Brad M. Barber and Terrance Odean, "Boys Will Be Boys: Gender, Overconfidence, and Common Stock Investment," *Quarterly Journal of Economics* 116 (February 2001), 261–292.
23. Hersh Shefrin and Meir Statman, "The Disposition to SellWinners Too Early and Ride Losers Too Long: Theory and Evidence," *Journal of Finance* 40 (July 1985), 777–782.
24. Mark Grinblatt and Matti Keloharju, "How Distance, Language, and Culture Influence Stockholdings and Trades," *Journal of Finance* 56 (June 2001), 1053–1073.
25. Joshua D. Coval and Tobias J. Moskowitz, "Home Bias at Home: Local Equity Preference in Domestic Portfolios," *Journal of Finance* 53 (December 1999), 2045–2074.
26. Chaieb and Errunza ("International Asset Pricing under Segmentation and PPP Deviations," *Journal of Financial Economics* 86 (November 2007), 543–578.) demonstrate this in an international asset pricing model that allows for market imperfections as well as deviations from purchasing power parity.
27. Kalok Chan, Vicentiu Covrig, and Lilian Ng, "Does Home Bias Affect Firm Value? Evidence from Holdings of Mutual Funds Worldwide," *Journal of International Economics* 78 (July 2009), 230–241. Sie Ting Lau, Lilian Ng, and Bohui Zhang, "The World Price of Home Bias," *Journal of Financial Economics* 97 (August 2010), 191–217.

## CHAPTER 20 International Asset Pricing

1. This is because both the portfolio's expected return $E[r_P] = x_F E[r_F] + x_A E[r_A]$ and the standard deviation of return $\sigma_P = [x_A{}^2 \sigma_A{}^2]^{1/2} = x_A \sigma_A$ are proportional to the percentage invested in the risky asset A.
2. A t-test comparison of means can be used as a test of statistical significance.
3. The classic reference is Michael Adler and Bernard Dumas, "International Portfolio Choice and Corporation Finance: A Synthesis," *Journal of Finance* 38 (June 1983), 925–984. For a more recent rendition, see Ines Chaieb and Vihang Errunza, "International Asset Pricing under Mild Segmentation," *Journal of Financial Economics* 86 (November 2007), 543–578.
4. See Kuntara Pukthuanthong and Richard Roll, "Global Market Integration: An Alternative Measure and Its Application," *Journal of Financial Economics* 94 (November 2009), 214–232.
5. Eugene F. Fama and Kenneth R. French, "The Cross-Section of Expected Stock Returns," *Journal of Finance* 47 (June 1992), 427–465.
6. Stephen A. Ross, "The Arbitrage Theory of Asset Pricing," *Journal of Economic Theory* 13 (December 1976), 341–360.
7. Nai-Fu Chen, Richard Roll, and Stephen A. Ross, "Economic Forces and the Stock Market," *Journal of Business* 59 (July 1986), 383–404.
8. The model in Equations 20.7 and 20.8 is a simplified version from Richard Roll and Stephen A. Ross, "The Arbitrage Pricing Theory Approach to Strategic Portfolio Planning," *Financial Analysts Journal* 51 (January/February 1995), 122–132.
9. Useful recent studies of market integration and stock market correlations include Kuntara Pukthuanthong and Richard Roll, "Global Market Integration: An Alternative Measure and Its Application," *Journal of Financial Economics* 94 (November 2009), 214–232.

Geert Bekaert, Robert J. Hodrick, and Xiaoyan Zhang, "International Stock Return Comovements," *Journal of Finance* 64 (December 2009), 2591–2626; and Miguel Almeida Ferreira and Paulo Miguel Gama, "Have World, Country, and Industry Risks Changed over Time? An Investigation of the Volatility of Developed Stock Markets," *Journal of Financial and Quantitative Analysis* 40 (March 2005), 195–222.

10. Eugene F. Fama and Kenneth R. French, "The Cross-Section of Expected Stock Returns," *Journal of Finance* 47 (June 1992), 427–465. "Multifactor Explanations of Asset Pricing Anomalies," *Journal of Finance* 51 (March 1996), 55–84.
11. Eugene F. Fama and Kenneth R. French, "Value Versus Growth: The International Evidence," *Journal of Finance* 53 (December 1998), 1975–1999.
12. K. Geert Rouwenhorst, "Local Return Factors and Turnover in Emerging Stock Markets," *Journal of Finance* 54 (August 1999), 1439–1464.
13. John M. Griffin, "Are the Fama and French Factors Global or Country Specific?" *Review of Financial Studies* 15 (Summer 2002), 783–803.
14. Hedging can increase firm value if it increases expected cash flows, say, through lower costs of financial distress. See Appendix 8A.
15. See Bernard Dumas and Bruno Solnik, "The World Price of Foreign Exchange Risk," *Journal of Finance* 50 (June 1995), 445–479.
16. Philippe Jorion, "The Exchange-Rate Exposure of U.S. Multinationals," *Journal of Business* 63, No. 3 (1990), 331–346.
17. Jia He and Lilian K. Ng, "The Foreign Exchange Exposure of Japanese Multinational Corporations," *Journal of Finance* 53 (April 1998), 733–753. Lawrence Booth and Wendy Rotenberg, "Assessing Foreign Exchange Exposure: Theory and Application Using Canadian Firms," *Journal of International Financial Management and Accounting* 2 (Spring 1990), 1–22. Martin Glaum, Marko Brunner, and Holger Himmel, "The DAX and the Dollar: The Economic Exchange Rate Exposure of German Corporations," *Journal of International Business Studies* 31, No. 4 (2000), 715–724.
18. Narasimhan Jegadeesh and Sheridan Titman, "Returns to Buying Winners and Selling Losers: Implications for Stock Market Efficiency," *Journal of Finance* 48 (March 1993), 65–91.
19. K. Geert Rouwenhorst, "International Momentum Strategies," *Journal of Finance* 53 (February 1998), 267–284.
20. K. Geert Rouwenhorst, "Local Return Factors and Turnover in Emerging Stock Markets," *Journal of Finance* 54 (August 1999), 1439–1464.
21. Narasimhan Jegadeesh and Sheridan Titman, "Profitability of Momentum Strategies: An Evaluation of Alternative Explanations," *Journal of Finance* 56 (April 2001), 699–720. Jegadeesh and Titman update their analysis in "Momentum," working paper (January 2011), available at www.ssrn.com.
22. Andy C.W. Chui, Sheridan Titman, and K.C. John Wei, "Individualism and Momentum around the World," *Journal of Finance* 65 (January 2009), 361–392.
23. Geert H. Hofstede, *Culture's Consequences: International Differences in Work-Related Values* (Beverly Hills CA: Sage Publications, 1980). Hofstede's other cultural dimensions are power distance, masculinity/femininity, uncertainty avoidance, and long-term/short-term orientation. Hofstede maintains an interesting website on national cultural differences at www.geert-hofstede.com.
24. See Mark M. Carhart, "On Persistence in Mutual Fund Performance," *Journal of Finance* 52 (March 1997), 57–82.
25. Geert Bekaert, Campbell R. Harvey, and Christian Lundblad, "Liquidity and Expected Returns: Lessons from Emerging Markets," *Review of Financial Studies* 20 (November 2007), 1783–1832. Andrew Ang, Robert J. Hodrick, Yuhang Xing, and Xiaoyan Zhang, "High Idiosyncratic Volatility and Low Returns: International and Further U.S. Evidence," *Journal of Financial Economics* 91 (January 2009), 1–23. Claude B. Erb, Campbell R. Harvey, and Tadas E. Viskanta, "Expected Returns and Volatility in 135 Countries," *Journal of Portfolio Management* 22 (Spring 1996), 46–58.

# Solutions to Even-Numbered Problems

## CHAPTER 3: FOREIGN EXCHANGE AND EUROCURRENCY MARKETS

3.2 The ask price is higher than the bid, so these are rates at which the bank is willing to buy or sell dollars (in the denominator). You're selling dollars, so you'll get the bank's dollar bid price. You need to pay SKr10,000,000/(SKr7.5050/$) ≈ $1,332,445.

3.4 a. The forward premium is equal to $(F_1^{\$/¥} - S_0^{\$/¥})$ = ($0.008772945/¥ − $0.009057355/¥) = −$0.000284410/¥, or −2.8441 basis points. As a percentage over the 90-day period, this is $(F_1^{\$/¥} - S_0^{\$/¥})/S_0^{\$/¥} = -0.031401$, or −3.1401 percent.

b. As an annualized forward premium following the U.S. convention, this is equal to

$(n)(F_1^{\$/¥} - S_0^{\$/¥})/S_0^{\$/¥} = (4)(-0.031401) = -0.125604$,
or −12.5604 percent.

c. As an APR, the premium is $(F_1^{\$/¥}/S_0^{\$/¥})^4 - 1 = -0.119811$, or −11.9811 percent.

3.6 a. (PZ5,000,000) / (PZ4.0200/$) = $1,243,781. Warsaw's bid price for PZ is its ask price for dollars. So, PZ4.0200/$ is equivalent to $0.2488/PZ.

b. (PZ20,000,000) / (PZ3.9690/$) = $5,039,053
PZ3.9690/$ is equivalent to $0.2520/PZ
Payment is made on the second business day after the 3-month expiration date.

3.8 When buying one currency, you are simultaneously selling another, so a yen bid price is a euro ask price. Yen quotes yield $S^{¥/€} = 1/S^{€/¥}$ = 1/(€0.007634/¥) = ¥130.99/€ and $S^{¥/€}$ = 1/(€0.007643/¥) = ¥130.84/€, so euro quotes (in the denominator) are ¥130.84/€ Bid and ¥130.99/€ Ask.

3.10 The 90-day dollar forward price is 33 bps below the spot price: $F_1^{SFr/\$} - S_0^{SFr/\$}$ = (SFr0.7432/$ − SFr0.7465/$) = −SFr0.0033/$. The percentage dollar forward premium is $(F_1^{SFr/\$} - S_0^{SFr/\$})/S_0^{SFr/\$}$ = (SFr0.7432/$ − SFr0.7465/$) / (SFr0.7465/$) = −0.442% per 90 days, or (−0.442%) × 4 = −1.768% on an annualized basis.

3.12 DKr is at a forward discount

30 day: ($0.18519/DKr − $0.18536/DKr)/$0.18536/DKr = −0.092%
90 day: ($0.18500/DKr − $0.18536/DKr)/$0.18536/DKr = −0.194%
180 day: ($0.18488/DKr − $0.18536/DKr)/$0.18536/DKr = −0.259%

3.14 $(F_t^{d/f} - S_0^{d/f})/S_0^{d/f} = [(1/F_t^{f/d}) - (1/S_0^{f/d})]/(1/S_0^{f/d})$
$= [(S_0^{f/d}/F_t^{f/d}) - (S_0^{f/d}/S_0^{f/d})]/(S_0^{f/d}/S_0^{f/d})$
$= [(S_0^{f/d}/F_t^{f/d}) - 1] = (S_0^{f/d} - F_t^{f/d})/F_t^{f/d}$.

## CHAPTER 4: THE INTERNATIONAL PARITY CONDITIONS AND THEIR CONSEQUENCES

4.2 $S^{SFr/\$} S^{\$/¥} S^{¥/SFr} = 1.0326 > 1$. Spot rates are "too high" relative to the parity condition, so you should sell the currencies in the denominators for the currencies in the numerators at the relatively high prices. This means that you should (a) sell dollars for francs, (b) sell yen for dollars, and (c) sell francs for yen. Alternatively, (a) buy francs with dollars, (b) buy dollars with yen, and (c) buy yen with francs. Triangular arbitrage would yield a profit of 3.26 percent of the starting amount. For triangular arbitrage to be profitable, transactions costs on a "round turn" cannot be more than this amount.

4.4 The forward price is at a 9 bp discount over six months, or 18 bps on an annualized basis. The 6-month percentage premium is $(F_1^{£/\$} / S_0^{£/\$}) - 1 = (£0.6352/\$) / (£0.6361/\$) - 1 = 0.9986 - 1 = -0.14\%$, or a discount of 0.28% on an annualized basis. Because $F_t^{£/\$} = E[S_t^{£/\$}]$ according to forward parity (the unbiased forward expectations hypothesis), the spot rate is expected to depreciate by 0.14% over the next six months.

4.6 From the Fisher relation: $(1 + i^{CNY}) = (1 + E[p^{CNY}])(1 + E[R^{CNY}]) \Leftrightarrow$
$E[R^{CNY}]) = (1 + i^{CNY}) / (1 + E[p^{CNY}]) - 1 = (1.071/1.05) - 1 = 0.0200$, or 2 percent.

4.8 a. In this problem, we know the spot and forward rates and U.S. inflation. The real and nominal interest rates are not needed: $F_1^{\$/£}/S_0^{\$/£} = (\$1.20/£)/(\$1.25/£) = 0.96 = E(1 + p^{\$})/E(1 + p^{£}) = (1.05)/E(1 + p^{£}) => E(p^{£}) = (1.05/0.96) - 1 = 9.375\%$

b. From the Fisher equation: $i^{£} = (1 + p^{£})(1 + R^{£}) - 1 = (1.09375)(1.02) - 1 = 11.56\%$.

4.10 a. A 7% annualized rate with quarterly compounding is equivalent to 7%/4 = 1.75% per quarter. From interest rate parity, the 3-month MR interest rate is $F^{MR/\$} / S^{MR/\$} = (MR3.9888/\$) / (MR4.0200/\$) = (1 + i^{MR}) / (1 + i^{\$}) = (1 + i^{MR}) / (1 + 0.0175) => i^{MR} = 0.009603$, or 0.9603% per three months. Annualized, this is equivalent to $(0.9603\%) \times 4 = 3.8412\%$ per year with quarterly compounding. Alternatively, the annual percentage rate is $(1.009603)^4 - 1 = 0.03897$, or 3.897% per year.

b. \$10,000,000 invested at the 3-month U.S. rate yields \$10,175,000. Changed into MR at the forward rate, this is worth (\$10,175,000)(MR3.9888/\$) = MR40,586,040. You can finance your \$10,000,000 by borrowing MR40,200,000. Your obligation on this contract will be (MR40,200,000)(1.009603) ≈ MR40,586,040 which is exactly offset by the proceeds from your forward contract.

4.12 $F_1^{MXN/\$} / S_0^{MXN/\$} = (MXN11/\$) / (MXN10/\$) = 1.1 < 1.1132 = (1.18) / (1.06) = (1 + i^{MXN}) / (1 + i^{\$})$. The ratio of interest rates is too high and must fall, so borrow at the relatively low dollar rate and invest at the relatively high peso rate. Similarly, the forward premium is too low and must rise, so buy dollars (and sell pesos) at the relatively low forward rate for the dollar and sell dollars (and buy pesos) at the relatively high dollar spot rate.

- Borrow \$1 million so that \$1,060,000 is due in six months.
- Sell \$1 million and buy MXN10,000,000 at the relatively high spot price.
- Invest MXN10,000,000 at 18% to yield MXN11,800,000 in six months.
- Cover by selling MXN11,800,000 at the MXN11/\$ forward rate to yield \$1,072,727.

This leaves a profit of \$1,072,727 − \$1,060,000 = \$12,727 at time t = 1 in six months.

4.14 a. $E[P_1^F] = P_0^F(1 + p^F) = 1.21$
$E[P_1^D] = P_0^D(1 + p^D) = 110$
$E[S_1^{D/F}] = (S_0^{D/F})(1 + p^D)/(1 + p^F) = (D100/F)(1.10/1.21) \approx D90.91/F$.

b. Because nominal exchange rates should adjust to reflect changes in relative purchasing power, the expected real exchange rate is 100% of the beginning rate: $E[X_1^{D/F}] = (E[S_1^{D/F}]/S_0^{D/F})((1 + p^F)/(1 + p^D)) = ((D90.91/F) / (D100/F))(1.21/1.10) = 1.00$, or 100%.

c. $E[P_2^F]) = P_0^F(1 + p^F)^2 = F1.4641$
$E[P_2^D]) = P_0^D(1 + p^D)^2 = D121$
$E[P_2^F]) = P_0^F(1 + p^F)^2 = F1.4641$
$E[P_2^D]) = P_0^D(1 + p^D)^2 = D121$
$E[S_2^{D/F}] = S_0^{D/F}((1 + p^D)/(1 + p^F))^2 = (D100/F)(1.10/1.21)^2 \approx D82.64/F$

The real exchange rate is not expected to change: $E[X_2^{D/F}] = (E[S_2^{D/F}]/ E[S_0^{D/F}])[(1 + p^F)/(1 + p^D)]^2 = ((D82.64/F)(D100/F)) / (1.21/1.10)^2 = 1.00$, or 100%.

4.16 a. technical / b. technical / c. fundamental / d. fundamental / e. technical

## APPENDIX 4A CONTINUOUS COMPOUNDING

4A.2 Inflation rates are $p^D = \ln(1 + p^D) = \ln(1.10) = 9.531\%$ and $p^F = \ln(1 + p^F) = \ln(1.21) = 19.062\%$ in continuously compounded returns. Expected price levels and spot rates are:

$E[P_1^D] = P_0^D e^{(0.09531)} = (D100)(1.10) = D110$

$E[P_2^D] = P_0^D e^{(2)(0.09531)} = (D100)(1.21) = D121$

$E[P_1^F] = P_0^F e^{(0.19062)} = (F1)(1.21) = F1.21$

$E[P_2^F] = P_0^F e^{(2)(0.19062)} = (F1)(1.4641) = F1.4641$

$E[S_1^{D/F}] = E[P_1^D]/E[P_1^F] = D110/F1.21 = D90.91/F$

$E[S_2^{D/F}] = E[P_2^D]/E[P_2^F] = D121/F1.4641 = D82.64/F$

## CHAPTER 5: CURRENCY FUTURES AND FUTURES MARKETS

5.2 The U.S. MNC will need (S$3,000,000)/(S$125,000/contract) = 24 futures contracts to cover its forward exposure. The underlying position is long S$, so the MNC should *sell 24 S$ futures contracts*. A short futures position in S$ gains from a depreciation of the S$. If the spot rate closes at $0.5900/S$ on the expiration date, then the gain accumulated over the three months of the contract (as the contracts are marked-to-market each day) will be ($0.6075/S$ − $0.5900/S$)(S$3,000,000) = $52,500.

5.4 a.

Expected future cash flows +S$125,000

−Sh500,000

b.

Buy shekels in the U.S. dollar futures market +Sh500,000

−$81,250

Sell Singapore dollars in the U.S. dollar futures market +$81,250

−S$125,000

Net payoff on futures hedge +Sh500,000

−S$125,000

These ending values exactly hedge the currency exposures of the expected cash flows. Any changes in spot rates $S^{Sh/\$}$ and $S^{S\$/\$}$ would be received over the 90-day life of the futures contract according to the daily settlement procedures.

c. Cotton Bolls could take out a 90-day futures contract to sell S$ for Israeli shekels. Because the ratio of exposed amounts (S$125,000/Sh500,000) = S$0.2500/Sh = $F^{S\$/Sh}$, the underlying exposures can be matched exactly. The implied forward rate is S$0.25/Sh. Cotton Bolls would save on commissions, having to buy one futures contract rather than two.

5.6 a. Profit/loss on each of the positions is as follows:

Scenario #1 $S_t^{\$/S\$} = \$0.6089/S\$$ and $i^{\$} = 6.24\%$ and $i^{S\$} = 4.04\%$

$Fut_{t,T}^{\$/S\$} = (\$0.6089/S\$)\,[(1.0624)/(1.0404)]^{(51/365)} \simeq \$0.6107/S\$$

| | | |
|---|---|---|
| Profit on futures: | +($0.6107/S$ − $0.6107/S$) | +$0.0000/S$ |
| Profit on spot: | −($0.6089/S$ − $0.6089/S$) | −$0.0000/S$ |
| Net gain | $0.0000/S$ | |

Scenario #2 $S_t^{\$/S\$} = \$0.6089/S\$$ and $i^{\$} = 6.24\%$ and $i^{S\$} = 4.54\%$

$Fut_{t,T}^{\$/S\$} = (\$0.6089/S\$)\,[(1.0624)/(1.0454)]^{(51/365)} \simeq \$0.6102/S\$$

| | | |
|---|---|---|
| Profit on futures: | +($0.6102/S$ − $0.6107/S$) | −$0.0004/S$ |
| Profit on spot: | −($0.6089/S$ − $0.6089/S$) | −$0.0000/S$ |
| Net gain | −$0.0004/S$ | |

Scenario #3 $S_t^{\$/S\$} = \$0.6089/S\$$ and $i^{\$} = 6.74\%$ and $i^{S\$} = 4.04\%$
$Fut_{t,T}^{\$/S\$} = (\$0.6089/S\$)\ [(1.0674)/(1.0404)]^{(51/365)} \simeq \$0.6111/S\$$

| | | |
|---|---|---|
| Profit on futures: | −($0.6111/S$ − $0.6107/S$) | + $0.0004/S$ |
| Profit on spot: | +($0.6089/S$ − $0.6089/S$) | − $0.0000/S$ |
| Net gain | +$0.0004/S$ | |

The profit spread is ±$0.0004/S$. This is about the same as in the example in Figure 5.6. This shows that basis risk exists even if the spot exchange rate does not change.

b. Profit/loss on each of the positions is as follows:

Scenario #1 $S_t^{\$/S\$} = \$0.6089/S\$$ and $i^{\$} = 6.24\%$ and $i^{S\$} = 4.04\%$
$Fut_{t,T}^{\$/S\$} = (\$0.6089/S\$)\ [(1.0624)/(1.0404)]^{(51/365)} \simeq \$0.6107/S\$$

| | | |
|---|---|---|
| Profit on futures: | +($0.6107/S$ − $0.6107/S$) | + $0.0000/S$ |
| Profit on spot: | −($0.6089/S$ − $0.6089/S$) | − $0.0000/S$ |
| Net gain | $0.0000/S$ | |

Scenario #2 $S_t^{\$/S\$} = \$0.6255/S\$$ and $i^{\$} = 6.24\%$ and $i^{S\$} = 4.04\%$
$Fut_{t,T}^{\$/S\$} = (\$0.6255/S\$)\ [(1.0624)/(1.0404)]^{(51/365)} \cong \$0.6273/S\$$

| | | |
|---|---|---|
| Profit on futures: | +($0.6273/S$ − $0.6107/S$) | − $0.0166/S$ |
| Profit on spot: | −($0.6255/S$ − $0.6089/S$) | − $0.0166/S$ |
| Net gain | $0.0000/S$ | |

Scenario #3 $S_t^{\$/S\$} = \$0.5774/S\$$ and $i^{\$} = 6.24\%$ and $i^{S\$} = 4.04\%$
$Fut_{t,T}^{\$/S\$} = (\$0.6089/S\$)\ [(1.0624)/(1.0404)]^{(51/365)} \simeq \$0.5791/S\$$

| | | |
|---|---|---|
| Profit on futures: | −($0.5791/S$ − $0.6107/S$) | + $0.0315/S$ |
| Profit on spot: | +($0.5774/S$ − $0.6089/S$) | − $0.0315/S$ |
| Net gain | $0.0000/S$ | |

Part b shows that the futures hedge provides a perfect hedge against changes in the spot rate of exchange if the basis does not change.

## CHAPTER 6: CURRENCY OPTIONS AND OPTIONS MARKETS

6.2 An exercise price of DKK8.45/£ is equivalent to £0.11834/DKK. The corresponding krone put values are:

| Spot rate (£/DKK) | 0.12500 | 0.11905 | 0.11876 | 0.11848 | 0.11820 | 0.11792 |
|---|---|---|---|---|---|---|
| Krone put value (£/DKK) | 0.00 | 0.00 | 0.00 | 0.00 | 0.14 | 0.42 |

The profit/loss graph is as follows:

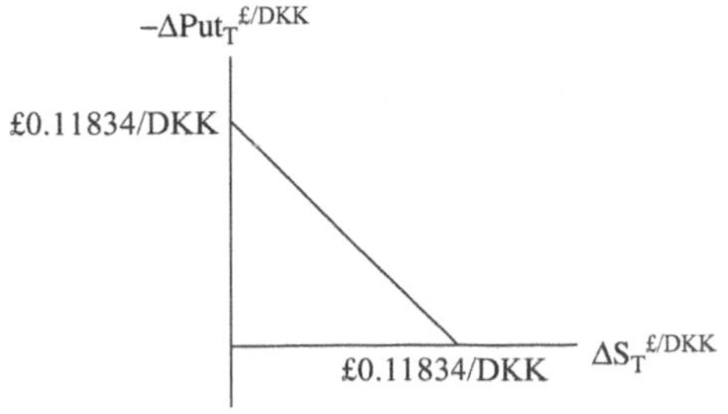

6.4 Buy an A$ call and sell an A$ put, each with an exercise price of $F_1^{\$/A\$} =$ \$0.75/A\$ and the same expiration date as the forward contract. Payoffs at expiration look like this:

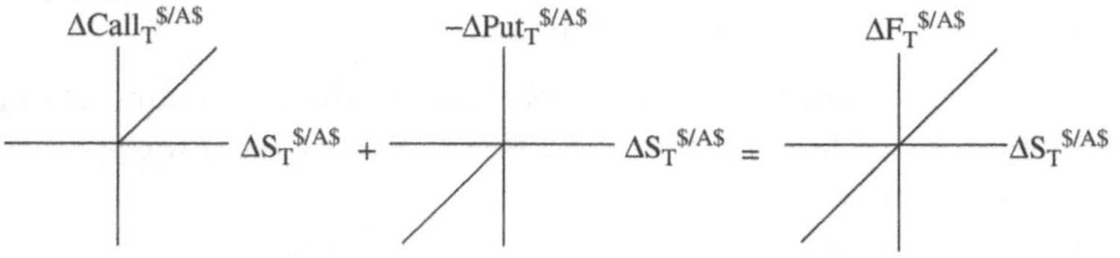


6.6 The payoff profile of a purchased straddle at expiration is shown below.

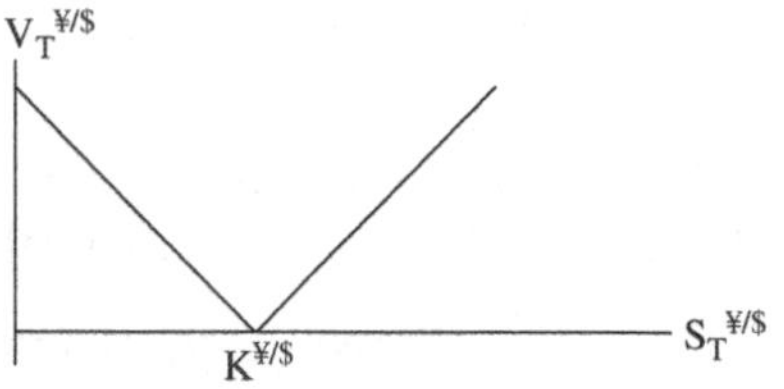


A purchased straddle has more value the further from the exercise price it expires. This combination will allow you to place a bet that the market has underestimated the volatility of the yen/dollar exchange rate. Of course, if the market is informationally efficient, then volatility is correctly priced in the market and this position (net of the costs of the options) will have zero net present value.

6.8 $\ln[(¥156.64/\$) / (¥105/\$)] = \ln(1.49181) = +0.40 = +40\%$
$\ln[(¥70.38/\$) / (¥105/\$)] = \ln(0.50819) = -0.40 = -40\%$

## APPENDIX 6A: CURRENCY OPTION VALUATION

6A.2 Option determinants are as follows: $i^{¥} = i^{\$} = 0.05$, $T = 0.5$ year, $S^{¥/\$} = \$80$, $K^{¥/\$} = \$100$, and $\sigma = 0.20$. Assume these are continuously compounded rates calculated from holding period rates according to $i = \ln(1 + i)$. Then,

$$
\begin{aligned}
d_1 &= [\ln(S^{d/f}/K^{d/f}) + (i^d - i^f + \sigma^2/2)T]/(\sigma\sqrt{T}) \\
&= [\ln((¥80/\$)/(¥100/\$)) + (0.05 - 0.05 + (0.20)^2/2)(0.5)] \\
&\qquad /(0.20)(0.5)^{1/2} \\
&= -1.5071 => N(d_1) = 0.065886 \\
d_2 &= d_1 - \sigma\sqrt{T} = -1.5071 - (0.20)(0.5)^{1/2} \\
&= -1.6486 => N(d_2) = 0.049617
\end{aligned}
$$

$$\begin{aligned}\text{Call}^{d/f} &= e^{(-i^fT)}[S^{d/f}N(d_1)] - e^{(-i^dT)}[K^{d/f}N(d_2)]\\ &= e^{(-0.05\times.5)}[(¥80/\$)(0.065886)] - e^{(-0.05\times.5)}[(¥100/\$)(0.049617)]\\ &= ¥0.3015/\$.\end{aligned}$$

With 10% volatility as in Problem 6A.1, the call option pricing model yields a value of ¥0.0013/\$. If the true volatility is 20% per year and this option is priced as if the volatility is 10% per year, then the option will be undervalued by (¥0.3015/\$ – ¥0.0013/\$) = ¥0.3015/\$ – ¥0.0013/\$ = ¥0.3002/\$.

6A.4 a. Interest rate parity provides forward rates according to: $F_t^{d/f}/S_0^{d/f} = [(1 + i^d)/(1 + i^f)]^t$.

A problem arises because the options are on Danish krone but the krone appears in the numerator of the ***FX*** rates. This is not unusual, as the pound is often left in the denominator of a currency quote. Historically, the pound was composed of shillings and pence rather than decimal units. (Nobody understands cricket, either.) The table below includes forward rates in £/DKK and quotes option prices in direct £/DKK terms from a Londoner's perspective. The spot rate is $S_0^{£/DKK}$ = 1/(DKK8.4528/£) = £0.11830/DKK and the exercise price is $K^{£/DKK}$ = 1/(DKK8.5/£) = £0.11765/DKK.

| | 1-month | 3-month | 6-month | 1-year |
|---|---|---|---|---|
| Forward rate (DKK/£) | 8.4404 | 8.4157 | 8.3787 | 8.3053 |
| Forward rate (£/DKK) | 0.11848 | 0.11883 | 0.11935 | 0.12040 |
| Call option value (£/DKK) | 0.00180 | 0.00294 | 0.00412 | 0.00583 |
| Put option value (£/DKK) | 0.00100 | 0.00178 | 0.00247 | 0.00326 |

b. Here is a sample calculation for the 3-month (= one period) call and put values:

$$\begin{aligned}d_1 &= [\ln(S^{d/f}/K^{d/f}) + (i^d - i^f + \sigma^2/2)T]/(\sigma\sqrt{T})\\ &= [\ln((£0.11830/DKK)/(£0.11765/DKK)) + (0.0174 - 0.0130\\ &\quad + (0.05)^2/2)(1)]/(0.05)(1)^{1/2} = +0.2244\\ d_2 &= d_1 - \sigma\sqrt{T} = +0.2244 - (0.05)(1)^{1/2} = +0.1744\end{aligned}$$

$$\begin{aligned}\text{Call}^{d/f} &= e^{-i^dT}[F_t^{d/f}N(d_1) - K^{d/f}N(d_2)]\\ &= e^{(-0.0174\times1)}[(£0.11883)(0.5888) - (£0.11765)(0.5692)]\\ &= £0.00294/DKK.\end{aligned}$$

c. Call option payoff profiles prior to expiration: The 1-year option is plotted as the highest line in the graph. The 1-month option is the lowest (curved) line in the graph. The darkened 45-degree line is the intrinsic value of the option.

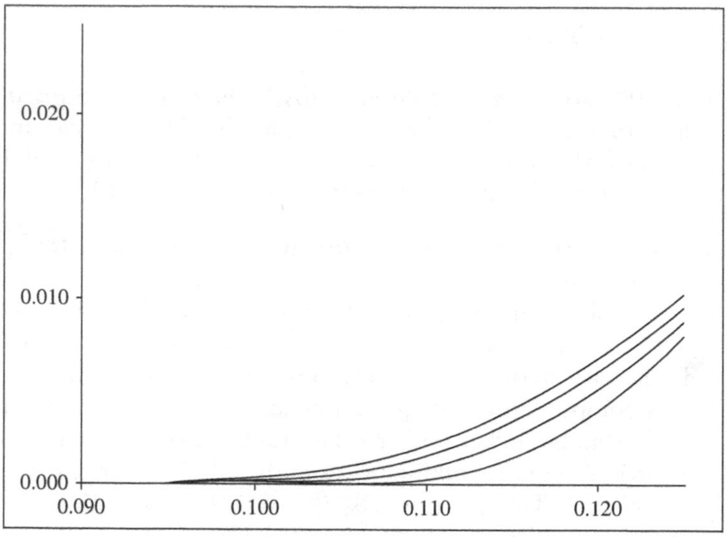


d. Put option payoff profiles prior to expiration: The 1-year option has a higher value at high spot rates and a lower value at low spot rates. The 1-month option has lower value at high spot rates and a higher value at lower spot rates. The darkened 45-degree line is the intrinsic value of the option. European put option values can be below the intrinsic value because they cannot be exercised until expiration; that is, the exercise price cannot be sold or captured until expiration.

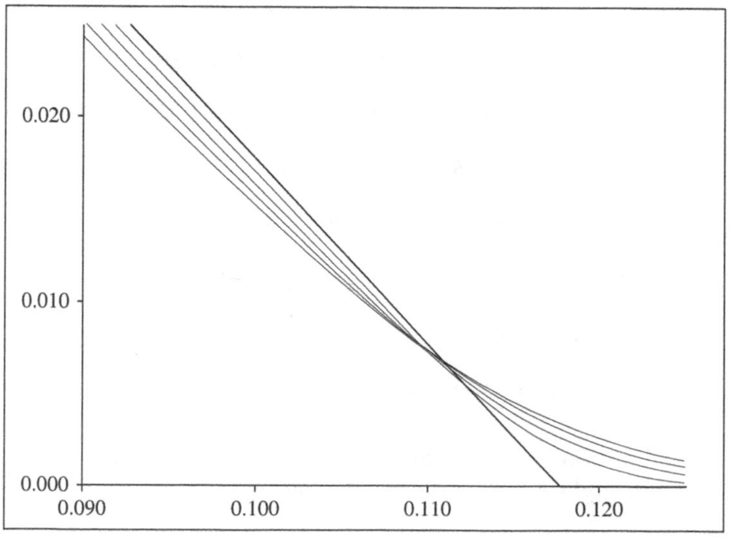

## CHAPTER 7: CURRENCY SWAPS AND SWAPS MARKETS

7.2 a. Ford pays fixed rate zloty interest at a bond equivalent yield of 7.98% + 0.78% = 8.76% and receives floating rate zloty interest at the 6-month LIBOR rate. After converting the 45 bps premium above LIBOR to a bond equivalent yield, Ford's cost of fixed rate zloty debt is 8.76% + 0.45%(365/360) ≈ 9.22% in semiannually compounded bond equivalent yield.

b. PM receives fixed rate zloty interest from the swap bank at 7.98% + 0.24% = 8.22%. PM pays floating rate zloty interest at 6-month LIBOR flat. After converting the difference between PM's fixed rate outflows and inflows (9.83% − 8.22% = 161 bps) to a money market yield, PM's cost of floating rate zloty debt is LIBOR + (161 bps)(360/365) = LIBOR+159 bps in money market yield.

c. The swap bank pays LIBOR to Ford and receives LIBOR from PM for no net gain or loss in floating rate zlotys. The swap bank receives 8.76% (sa) from Ford and pays 8.22% (sa) to PM for a net gain of (8.76% − 8.22%) = 54 bps in bond equivalent yield on the notional principal.

7.4 a. The dollar interest rate that corresponds to the zloty swap mid-rate is $((1+i^Z)/(1+i^\$))^t = F_t^{Z/\$}/S_0^{Z/\$} \Rightarrow i^\$ = (1+i^Z)/(F_t^{Z/\$}/S_0^{Z/\$}) - 1 = (1.079)/(1.038) - 1 = 0.03949904$, or about 3.95 percent. The corresponding annuity factors are PVIFA($i^Z$ = 7.9%,5) = 4.00325549 and PVIFA($i^\$$ = 3.949904%,5) = 4.45809446.

Usually, we know the notional principal and need to calculate payments based on the swap pricing schedule. In this problem, GE knows the payments and needs to calculate the notional principal. GE wants zloty cash outflows of Z5 million per year to hedge one-half of its Z10 million expected after-tax operating cash flow. GE will be paying the fixed zloty cash flow, and so will pay the swap bank's ask rate of 8.10%. This requires notional principal of $PV_0^Z = PMT^Z$ PVIFA($i^Z$ = 8.1%,5) = (Z5 million)(3.98220886) = Z19,911,044 to generate a 5-year annuity of Z5 million. This is equivalent to $7,111,087 at the Z2.80/$ spot rate.

Step (1): GE's cost of floating rate dollar debt is at LIBOR + 32 bps, or (32 bps)(365/360) = 32.4444 basis points in (dollar) bond equivalent yield.

Step (2): The zloty spread to LIBOR is $r^Z$ = (32.4444 bps)(4.45809446/4.00325549) = 36.1307 bps (BEY).

Step (3): GE's all-in cost of fixed rate zloty debt is then (8.10% + 36.1307 bps) = 8.461307% (BEY).

b. Step (1): SP is paying 10.24% on its existing zloty debt, compared with the 7.70% it'll receive from the swap bank, for a premium of (10.24% − 7.70%) = 254 bps.

Step (2): The equivalent dollar premium is $r^\$ = r^Z$ PVIFA($i^Z$ = 7.9%,5)/PVIFA($i^\$$ = 3.949904%,5) = (2.54%)(4.00325549/4.45809446) = 228.0855 bps in BEY, or (228.0855 bps)(360/365) = 224.9611 bps in MMY.

Step (3): SP's all-in cost of floating rate dollar financing is LIBOR + 224.9611 bps (MMY), or about 2.25 percent over the LIBOR Eurodollar rate.

c. The swap bank earns an (8.10% − 7.70%) = 40 bps in BEY on the notional principal. When the bank quotes fully covered rates, it adds a premium to both the fixed and floating rate sides of its swaps that leaves its net position unchanged.

7.6 a. GE pays a floating rate dollar cash flow of LIBOR + 32.4444 bps (BEY) of the $7,111,087 notional principal on its existing debt, for an annual payment of (0.00324444)($7,111,087) = $23,072 over the 1-year LIBOR Eurodollar rate.

| | |
|---|---|
| −$ LIBOR (MMY)<br>−$23,072 | −$ LIBOR (MMY)<br>−$23,072 |

The swap offsets the dollar spread to LIBOR with fixed rate zloty CFs of the same present value through Equation 7.2, or an annual spread of (0.00361307)(Z19,911,044) = Z71,940. GE pays the 8.1% swap rate, for a fixed rate payment of (0.081)(Z19,911,044) = Z1,612,795.

| | |
|---|---|
| +$ LIBOR (MMY)<br>+$23,072 | +$ LIBOR (MMY)<br>+$23,072 |
| −Z71,940<br>−Z1,612,795 | −Z71,940<br>−Z1,612,795 |

The total fixed rate zloty payment is Z1,684,735 each year.

| | |
|---|---|
| − Z1,684,735 | − Z1,684,735 |

This is indeed an all-in cost of (Z1,684,735)/(Z19,911,044) = 0.08461307 per year (or about 8.46 percent) on GE's fixed rate zloty debt.

b. SP's underlying fixed rate zloty payments are (10.24%)(Z19,811,044) = Z2,038,891 per year.

| | |
|---|---|
| −Z2,038,891 | −Z2,038,891 |

The swap offsets these fixed rate zloty CFs with floating rate dollar payments over LIBOR. The corresponding $ spread over LIBOR is (0.02280855)($7,111,087) = $162,194 as a BEY.

| | |
|---|---|
| +Z2,038,891 | +Z2,038,891 |
| −$ LIBOR (MMY)<br>−$162,194 | −$ LIBOR (MMY)<br>−$162,194 |

When combined with the underlying zloty obligation, this leaves net cash flows of

| | |
|---|---|
| −$ LIBOR (MMY)<br>−$162,194 | −$ LIBOR (MMY)<br>−$162,194 |

This is a money market spread of (228.0855 bps)(360/365) = 224.8611 bps, or about 2.25% over the 1-year LIBOR Eurodollar rate.

## CHAPTER 8: MULTINATIONAL TREASURY MANAGEMENT

8.2 a. The 2%/month factoring fee of (\$10 million)(0.02/month)(3 months) = \$600,000 is due at the time the receivables are factored. Fruit of the Loom is giving up accounts receivable with a face amount of \$10 million due in three months in exchange for a net amount of \$9,400,000.

b. The all-in cost to Fruit of the Loom is (\$10,000,000)/(\$9,400,000) – 1 = 0.06383 per quarter or an effective annual rate of $(1.06383)^4 - 1 = 0.2808$, or 28.08% per year. While this all-in cost seems high, note that Fruit of the Loom has no collection expenses or credit risk on this nonrecourse sale of receivables.

8.4 a. Cash flows faced by Savvy Fare include the following:

| | |
|---|---|
| Face amount of receivable | \$1,000,000 |
| Less 4% nonrecourse fee | –\$40,000 |
| Less 1% monthly factoring fee over six months | –\$60,000 |
| Net amount received | \$900,000 |

b. The all-in cost to Savvy Fare is (\$1,000,000)/(\$900,000) – 1 = 11.11% per six months or an effective annual rate of $(1.1111)^2 - 1 = 23.46\%$ per year.

## APPENDIX 8A: THE RATIONALE FOR HEDGING CURRENCY RISK

8A.2 a.

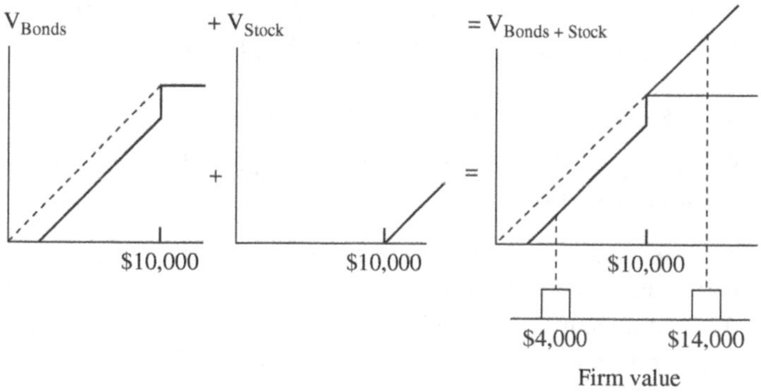


b. Unhedged $E[V_{Bonds}] = (1/2)(\$4,000 - \$2,000) + (1/2)(\$10,000) = \$6,000$

$+E[V_{Stock}] = (1/2)(\$0) + (1/2)(\$4,000) = \$2,000$

$E[V_{Firm}] = (1/2)(\$4,000 - \$2,000) + (1/2)(\$14,000) = \$8,000$

In this example, hedging can keep the firm solvent and avoid all of the costs of bankruptcy. Hedged value is then \$11,000 with certainty as in Problems 9.2 and 9.3. Payoffs are as follows:

$$\text{Hedged } E[V_{Bonds}] = \$10,000$$
$$+E[V_{Stock}] = \$1,000$$
$$E[V_{Firm}] = \$11,000$$

c. Hedging avoids the \$2,000 indirect cost as well as the ½ probability of a \$2,000 direct cost, resulting in a stakeholder gain of \$3,000. Bondholders would prefer to hedge and lock in \$10,000, resulting in a gain of \$4,000 over the unhedged situation. Equity locks in a value of \$1,000, resulting in an expected loss of \$1,000 relative to the unhedged situation. If equity is risk neutral, it will prefer to remain unhedged and face a 50 percent chance of having a \$4,000 payout.

Equity can gain from hedging in this situation. In particular, if equity can renegotiate the bond contract in these examples, then it can more evenly share the gain in firm value with the debt. Alternatively, equity can prenegotiate a smaller promised payment to debt (resulting in a lower required return and hence cost of capital) by establishing and maintaining a risk-hedging program. Again, this will allow equity to share in any gain from reducing the probability and costs associated with financial distress.

## CHAPTER 9: MANAGING TRANSACTION EXPOSURE TO CURRENCY RISK

9.2

| | Paying affiliate | | | | Total | Net | Net |
|---|---|---|---|---|---|---|---|
| Receiving affiliate | U.S. | Can. | Mex. | P.R. | receipts | Receipts | Payments |
| United States | 0 | \$800 | \$300 | \$400 | \$1500 | \$600 | \$0 |
| Canadian | \$600 | 0 | \$300 | \$700 | \$1600 | \$0 | \$700 |
| Mexican | \$100 | \$900 | 0 | \$800 | \$1800 | \$600 | \$0 |
| Puerto Rican | \$200 | \$600 | \$600 | 0 | \$1400 | \$0 | \$500 |
| Total payments | \$900 | \$2300 | \$1200 | \$1900 | 0 | \$1200 | \$1200 |

Here is one possible set of settling transactions:

[Canada pays U.S. \$600] + [Canada pays Mexico \$100] + [Puerto Rico pays Mexico \$500]

9.4 a. Not necessarily. From interest rate parity, $F_t^{A\$/\$}/S_0^{A\$/\$} = [(1 + i^{A\$})/(1 + i^{\$})]^t$, the forward premium says only that interest rates are higher in Australia than in the United States.

b. Rupert is short the U.S. dollar, so he might want to leave some of his exposure uncovered if he expects the dollar to close below the forward price. How much he leaves uncovered depends on his risk tolerance and on his corporate hedging policy.

c. By hedging at a forward price of A\$1.6035/\$, Rupert avoids having to buy U.S. dollars at the higher expected spot price.

d. Rupert should ask himself: "Do I feel lucky?" Over-hedging in this way is a form of currency speculation. Rupert is surely better off sticking to the beer business.

e. This differs from the situation in d. because Rupert has a legitimate business reason for buying more than \$5 million forward. Hedging an anticipated transaction makes good business sense when the anticipated transaction is highly likely to occur. If Rupert is not sure that he'll actually incur this additional dollar exposure, he probably should wait before hedging.

9.6 a. You are receiving £100,000 in one year, so sell £100,000 forward and buy dollars. In one year, you will receive £100,000 from your album sale. You can then convert this amount into (£100,000)($1.20/£) = $120,000 through the forward contract. You have eliminated your exposure to the value of the pound.

b. A money market hedge borrows in one currency, invests in another, and nets the transactions in the spot market. The result is the equivalent of a forward contract. The forward contract that you want to replicate is a forward sale of £100,000. This can be replicated as follows:

Borrow (£100,000)/$(1 + i^{£})$ = £89,638 at the $i^{£}$ = 11.56% pound sterling interest rate.

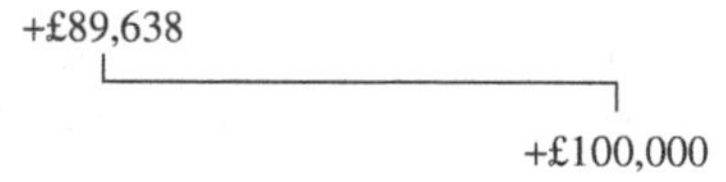


Convert to (£89,638)($1.25/£) = $112,047 at $S_0^{\$/£}$ = $1.25/£.

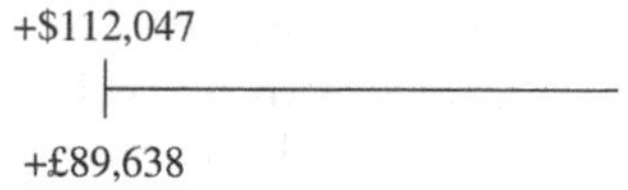


Invest in dollars at the U.S. dollar rate of $i^{\$}$ = 9.82%.

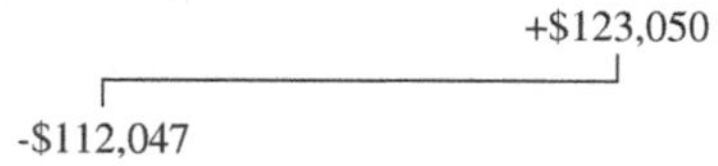


The net result is a forward contract to buy dollars with pounds.

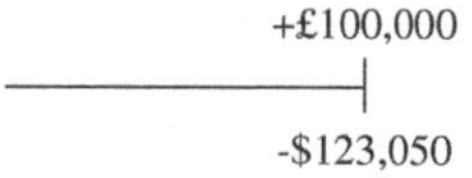


This is on more favorable terms than the forward contract. In this disequilibrium case, it is cheaper to hedge through the money markets than through the forward market.

c. These markets are not in equilibrium. $F_1^{\$/£}/S_0^{\$/£}$ = ($1.20/£)/($1.25/£) = 0.96 <= 0.98440 = (1.0982)/(1.1156) = $(1 + i^{\$})/(1 + i^{£})$, so you should buy pounds at the relatively low forward price, sell pounds at the relatively high spot price, invest in dollars at the relatively high dollar interest rate, and borrow pounds at the relatively low pound interest rate.

## CHAPTER 10: MANAGING OPERATING EXPOSURE TO CURRENCY RISK

10.2 a. Sterling & Co. has exposed monetary assets of $30,000 and exposed monetary liabilities of $45,000 + $90,000 = $135,000. Net monetary assets of −$105,000 are exposed to the dollar.

b. A 10 percent dollar appreciation will change the pound value of Sterling & Co. by (0.10)(£0.66667/$)(−$105,000) = −£7,000. Exposed monetary assets and liabilities change in value one-for-one with changes in exchange rates, so the r-square of this relation is +1, or 100 percent.

c. The sensitivity of plant and equipment to the value of the dollar is $\beta^{\$} = \rho_{r,s}(\sigma_r/\sigma_s) = (0.10)(0.20/0.10) = +0.2$. A 10 percent appreciation of the dollar is likely to increase the pound value of Sterling's plant and equipment by 0.2(10%) = 2 percent or \$1,600, from £80,000 to £81,600. The relation between real asset value and the exchange rate is not very strong. The r-square is $(0.10)^2 = 0.01$, so 1 percent of the variation in real asset value is explained by variation in the value of the dollar.

d. Equity exposure is equal to the net exposure of monetary assets and liabilities plus the exposure of real assets, or (−£7,000) + £1,600 = −£5,400.

e. Sterling's use of long-term dollar liabilities tends to offset the positive exposure of its real assets. However, the quality or effectiveness of this hedge is poor because the low r-square on the real asset side does not exactly match the one-for-one exposure on the liability side.

f. The sunk entry costs of this operating hedge are high. Opening a U.S. plant would entail renting or buying a U.S. site, hiring local (U.S.) artisans or bringing U.K. expatriates into the United States, and perhaps moving an existing supervisor from the United Kingdom to the United States as well. It will be difficult for Sterling & Co. to manage its U.S. operations as effectively as it manages its U.K. operations. Sterling should undertake this operating hedge if and only if it makes good business sense. The dollar exposure should not be the deciding factor.

10.4 Low currency risk exposures for U.S. firms means that U.S. investors are more likely than investors in other countries to be able to diversify away currency risk. This also suggests that currency risk management is more important outside the United States than within the United States.

10.6 Figure 10.6 is reconstructed for this problem as follows:

| | | | Twenty percent depreciation of the pound to \$1.20/£ | | | | | |
|---|---|---|---|---|---|---|---|---|
| | | | Maintain £4 price | | Maintain \$6 price | | | |
| | | | Sales volume | | Elastic demand | | Inelastic demand | |
| | Base case \$1.50/£ | | remains constant | | Sell 50% less | | Sell 10% less | |
| | £ | \$ | £ | \$ | £ | \$ | £ | \$ |
| Price | £4.00 | \$6.00 | £4.00 | \$4.80 | £5.00 | \$6.00 | £5.00 | \$6.00 |
| Cost | £2.00 | \$3.00 | £2.50 | \$3.00 | £2.50 | \$3.00 | £2.50 | \$3.00 |
| Volume | 20,000 | 20,000 | 20,000 | 20,000 | 10,000 | 10,000 | 18,000 | 18,000 |
| Rev | £80,000 | \$120,000 | £80,000 | \$96,000 | £50,000 | \$60,000 | £90,000 | \$108,000 |
| -COGS | −40,000 | −60,000 | −50,000 | −60,000 | −25,000 | −30,000 | −45,000 | −54,000 |
| EBT | 40,000 | 60,000 | 30,000 | 36,000 | 25,000 | 30,000 | 45,000 | 54,000 |
| -Tax | −20,000 | −30,000 | −15,000 | −18,000 | −12,500 | −15,000 | −22,500 | −27,000 |
| NCF | 20,000 | 30,000 | 15,000 | 18,000 | 12,500 | 15,000 | 22,500 | 27,000 |
| Value | £200,000 | \$300,000 | £150,000 | \$180,000 | £125,000 | \$150,000 | £225,000 | \$270,000 |
| Percentage change | | | −25% | −40% | −37.5% | −50% | 12.5% | −10% |

a. If Dow maintains its £4 price, value will fall by 25 percent in pounds and by 40 percent in dollars. This sets the benchmark for proposed changes in the pound price.
b. If Dow maintains its $6 price (resulting in a £5 price in the U.K.), value will fall by 37.5 percent in pounds and by 50 percent in dollars. With price elastic demand, Dow should maintain its £4 price to minimize the impact on its dollar value.
c. If Dow maintains its $6 price, value will rise by 12.5 percent in pounds and fall by 10 percent in dollars. With price inelastic demand, Dow should maintain its $6 price to minimize the impact on its dollar value.

## CHAPTER 11: MANAGING TRANSLATION EXPOSURE AND ACCOUNTING FOR FINANCIAL TRANSACTIONS

11.2 Translated value at C$1.50/$:

| Assets | C$ value | Value at C$1.60/$ | Current/ Noncurrent | Temporal | Current |
|---|---|---|---|---|---|
| Cash | C$320,000 | $200,000 | $213,333 | $213,333 | $213,333 |
| A/R | C$160,000 | $100,000 | $106,667 | $106,667 | $106,667 |
| Inventory | C$640,000 | $400,000 | $426,667 | $426,667 | $426,667 |
| P&E | C$480,000 | $300,000 | $300,000 | $300,000 | $320,000 |
| Total assets | C$1,600,000 | $1,000,000 | $1,046,667 | $1,046,667 | $1,066,667 |
| **Liabilities** | | | | | |
| A/P | C$320,000 | $200,000 | $213,333 | $213,333 | $213,333 |
| Wages | C$160,000 | $100,000 | $106,667 | $106,667 | $106,667 |
| Net worth | C$1,120,000 | $700,000 | $726,667 | $726,667 | $746,667 |
| Total liabilities & net worth | C$1,600,000 | $1,000,000 | $1,046,667 | $1,046,667 | $1,066,667 |

a. Net exposed assets:

= ($200,000 + $100,000 + $400,000 + $300,000) – ($200,000 + $100,000)

= $1,000,000 – $300,000 = $700,000.

b. The Canadian dollar has appreciated by $(S_1^{\$/C\$}/S_0^{\$/C\$}) - 1$ = (C$1.60/$)/(C$1.50/$) – 1 = 6.67 percent. Translation gains from the appreciation of the C$ are then: (+0.066667)($700,000) = +$46,667.

11.4 a. If a forward hedge of this euro receivable were capitalized on the balance sheet, the balance sheet would look like this:

| Assets | | Liabilities and Owners' Equity | |
|---|---|---|---|
| **Current assets** | | **Current liabilities** | |
| Accounts receivable | $60,000 | Accounts payable | $30,000 |
| (€60,000 at $1.00/€) | | (MXN300,000 at MXN0.10/$) | |
| Forward asset | $60,000 | Forward liability | $60,000 |
| (long $60,000) | | (short €60,000 at $1.00€) | |
| **Fixed assets** | | **Long-term liabilities & owners' equity** | |
| Furnishings (beds & blankets) | $30,000 | Long-term debt | $170,000 |
| Property and buildings | $910,000 | Owners' equity | $800,000 |
| Total assets | $1,060,000 | Total liabilities & owners' equity | $1,060,000 |

b.

| | Current ratio | Debt-to-assets |
|---|---|---|
| Before | $60,000/$30,000 = 2.000 | $200,000/$1,000,000 = 0.200 |
| After | $120,000/$90,000 = 1.333 | $260,000/$1,060,000 = 0.245 |

c. As in Problem 11.3 b, both debt and current ratios have deteriorated. However, Silver Saddle is actually less risky after the hedge than before. Silver Saddle can qualify this hedge under FAS #133. However, because this is only an anticipated transaction, the forward position has an element of speculation in it. The speculative element depends on the probability of not receiving the anticipated euro payment.

Upon further review: Note in passing that the exposure of the peso payable partially offsets the exposure of the euro receivable. If the euro-per-peso spot rate $S^{€/MXN}$ does not change, then a depreciation of the dollar (and hence an appreciation of the foreign currency in the denominator of the spot rate) will increase the dollar value of the euro receivable and—at the same time—increase the dollar value of the peso payable. Conversely, if the dollar appreciates, then the peso and euro depreciations will reduce the dollar value of the euro receivable at the same time that it reduces the dollar value of the peso payable. With no change in the $S^{€/MXN}$ exchange rate, the dollar value of Silver Saddle's net exposure to currency risk is ($60,000 – $30,000) = $30,000. Of course, the peso payable will not be a perfect hedge of one-half of the euro receivable because there is a chance that the euro-per-peso spot rate $S^{€/MXN}$ will change. (For those of you that studied the chapter on currency futures, note that Silver Saddle's offsetting euro and peso exposures are similar to a currency futures cross hedge where the exposure of the Mexican peso payable partially offsets the exposure of the euro receivable.)

11.6 a. The translated value is $P_1^{\$} = P_1^{W}/S_1^{W/\$}$ = (W1 billion)/(W1250/$) = W800,000.

b. The parent firm sees a translation loss of $200,000. The market value of the asset remained $1 million, so this translation loss is not an economic loss.

c. Selling W1 billion forward creates a $200,000 gain on the forward hedge. This exactly offsets the $200,000 translation loss on the underlying exposure. However, the net result in economic terms is a $200,000 gain on the forward hedge without a corresponding loss on the underlying exposure. The forward "hedge" actually increases the real or economic exposure of the firm to currency risk.

d. This forward hedge nevertheless would qualify for the hedge accounting rules under FAS #133 because it is tied to an underlying exposure—even though it is a translation and not an economic exposure.

## CHAPTER 12: FOREIGN MARKET ENTRY AND COUNTRY RISK MANAGEMENT

12.2 Although the most obvious form of expropriation occurs when a host government confiscates a firm's assets, in fact each type of political risk is a form of expropriation. Host governments can appropriate foreign assets for themselves or for local companies through actions that differentially impair nonlocal firms, including protectionism, blocked funds, or theft or misappropriation of intellectual property rights.

12.4 Although the answer to this question will be specific to the chosen country, country risks that turn up usually include factors from the ICRG political risk categories. These factors include political risk (leadership, government corruption, internal or external political tensions), economic risk (inflation, current account balance, or foreign trade collection experience), and financial risk (currency controls, expropriations, contract renegotiations, payment delays, loan restructurings or cancellations). Other political risk information providers use these same types of factors.

## CHAPTER 13: MULTINATIONAL CAPITAL BUDGETING

13.2 a. Expected future cash flows in euros are as follows:

| **Investment cash flows** | 0 | 1 | 2 | |
|---|---|---|---|---|
| Land | −100,000 | | 121,000 | grows at 10% inflation |
| tax on capital gain | | | −8,400 | |
| Plant | −50,000 | | 25,000 | market value at t = 2 |
| tax on capital gain | | | −10,000 | |
| NWC | −50,000 | | 60,500 | grows at 10% inflation |
| tax on capital gain | | | −4,200 | |
| **Operating cash flows** | 0 | 1 | 2 | |
| Rev (Price = 100, Q = 5,000) | | 550,000 | 605,000 | grows at 10% inflation |
| Variable cost (20%) | | −110,000 | −121,000 | |
| FC (20,000 at t = 0) | | −22,000 | −24,200 | grows at 10% inflation |
| Depreciation | | −25,000 | −25,000 | |
| Earnings before tax | | 393,000 | 434,800 | |
| Tax (at 40%) | | −157,200 | −173,920 | |
| Net income | | 235,800 | 260,880 | |
| Net cash flow (euros) | | 260,800 | 285,880 | CF = NI + depreciation |

**Sum of investment/disinvestment and operating cash flows**
Total net CFs −200,000 260,800 469,780
$V^{€}$ at $i^{€} = 20\%$ +€343,569

b. If the international parity conditions hold, then 20% interest rates in both the foreign and domestic currencies imply that forward (and expected future spot) exchange rates will equal the current spot rate of \$10/€. So,

**Sum of investment/disinvestment and operating cash flows**
Expected dollar CFs −2000000 2608000 4697800
$V^{\$}|i^{€}$ at $i^{\$} = 20\%$ \$3,435,694

13.4 a.

| t=1 | Bt3.4m | Bt3.4m | Bt3.4m | Bt6,913,840 |
|---|---|---|---|---|
| −Bt4m | t=2 | t=3 | t=4 | t=5 |

$i^{Bt} = 20\%$

Initial outlay = Bt4m at time t = 1
After-tax cash flows over t = 2,...,5 = (Bt100m − Bt90m − Bt5m)(1 − 0.40) + (Bt1m × (0.4)) = Bt3,400,000
Terminal CF = (Bt4m × $(1.10)^4$) − {[(Bt4m × $(1.10)^4$) − 0] × (0.4)} = Bt3,513,840
$V^{Bt}$ = Bt5,413,548

b. $(1 + i^{Bt}) = (1 + R^{Bt})(1 + p^{Bt}) \Rightarrow R^{Bt} = (1.20/1.10) - 1 = 0.0909091 \Rightarrow R^{Bt} = 9.09091\% = R^{¥} \Rightarrow i^{¥} = (1 + R^{¥})(1 + p^{¥}) - 1 = (1.0909091)(1.05) - 1 = 0.1454545$, or 14.54545%
Alternatively, $i^{¥} = (1 + i^{Bt})(1 + p^{¥})/(1 + p^{Bt}) - 1 = 1.20(1.05/1.10) - 1 \Rightarrow i^{¥} = 14.54545\%$

c.

$$E(S_1^{Bt/¥}) = (Bt0.25/¥)(1.20/1.1454545) = Bt.2619048/¥$$

$$E(S_2^{Bt/¥}) = (Bt0.25/¥)(1.20/1.1454545)^2 = Bt.2743764/¥$$

$$E(S_3^{Bt/¥}) = (Bt0.25/¥)(1.20/1.1454545)^3 = Bt.2874420/¥$$

$$E(S_4^{Bt/¥}) = (Bt0.25/¥)(1.20/1.1454545)^4 = Bt.3011297/¥$$

$$E(S_5^{Bt/¥}) = (Bt0.25/¥)(1.20/1.1454545)^5 = Bt.3154692/¥$$

d. Recipe #1: $V^{¥}|i^{Bt} = (V^{Bt})/(S_0^{Bt/¥}) = (Bt5,413,548)/(Bt0.25/¥) =$ ¥21,654,192
Recipe #2:

| t=1 | ¥12,391,736 | ¥11,828,475 | ¥11,290,817 | ¥21,916,055 |
|---|---|---|---|---|
| −¥15,272,727 | t=2 | t=3 | t=4 | t=5 |

$$V^{¥}|i^{¥} = ¥21,654,192 \text{ at } i^{¥} = 14.54545\%$$

The answers are the same because the international parity conditions hold.

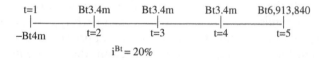

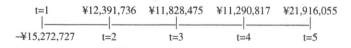

13.6 a. Interest rate parity requires a 2.913 percent forward premium $F_t^{ILS/CNY} / S_0^{ILS/CNY} = (1 + i_F^{ILS})^t / (1 + i_F^{CNY})^t = (1.0812)^t/(1.0506)^t = (1.02913)^t$. Forward rates are as follows:

$$F_1^{ILS/CNY} = (\text{ILS } 0.5526)[(1.0812)/(1.0506)]^1 = \text{ILS } 0.5687/\text{CNY}$$

$$F_2^{ILS/CNY} = (\text{ILS } 0.5526)[(1.0812)/(1.0506)]^2 = \text{ILS } 0.5853/\text{CNY}$$

$$F_3^{ILS/CNY} = (\text{ILS } 0.5526)[(1.0812)/(1.0506)]^3 = \text{ILS } 0.6023/\text{CNY}$$

$V(\text{Hedged}) = \Sigma_t\{F_t^{ILS/CNY} E[CF_t^{CNY}])/(1 + i^{ILS})^t\}[(-{}^{CNY}600\text{ m})(\text{ILS } 0.5526/\text{CNY}) + ({}^{CNY}200\text{ m})(\text{ILS } 0.5687/\text{CNY})/(1.16) + ({}^{CNY}500\text{ m})(\text{ILS}0.5853/\text{CNY})/(1.16)^2 + ({}^{CNY}300\text{ m})(\text{ILS } 0.6023/\text{CNY})/(1.16)^3] = \text{ILS } 99.72$ million

b. Relative purchasing power parity states $E[S_t^{ILS/CNY}] = S_0{}^{ILS/CNY}[(1 + i^{ILS})/(1 + i^{CNY})]^t$, so . . .

$$E[S_1^{ILS/CNY}] = (\text{ILS } 0.5526)[(1.16)/(1.12)]^1 = \text{ILS } 0.5723/\text{CNY}$$

$$E[S_2^{ILS/CNY}] = (\text{ILS } 0.5526)[(1.16)/(1.12)]^2 = \text{ILS } 0.5928/\text{CNY}$$

$$E[S_3^{ILS/CNY}] = (\text{ILS } 0.5526)[(1.16)/(1.12)]^3 = \text{ILS } 0.6139/\text{CNY}$$

$V(\text{Unhedged}) = \Sigma_t\{E[S_t^{ILS/CNY}]E[CF_t^{CNY}]/(1 + i^{ILS})^t\} = [(-{}^{CNY}600\text{ m})(\text{ILS } 0.5526/\text{CNY}) + ({}^{CNY}200\text{ m})(\text{ILS } 0.5723/\text{CNY})/(1.16) + ({}^{CNY}500\text{m})(\text{ILS } 0.5928/\text{CNY})/(1.16)^2 + ({}^{CNY}300\text{ m})(\text{ILS } 0.6139/\text{CNY})/(1.16)^3] = \text{ILS } 105.38$ million

c. V(Unhedged) > V(Hedged) > 0, so the project is worth pursuing. Hedging the project results in a lower expected value, albeit with less risk. The hedging decision will depend on the firm's risk management policy.

d. Shekel (yuan) borrowing costs are high (low) relative to the forward premium: $(1 + i_B^{ILS})/(1 + i_B^{CNY}) = (1.10/1.06) \approx 1.0377 > 1.029$. This firm should borrow in yuan and use the yuan interest payments to reduce the project's exposure to currency risk.

13.8 The funds are invested with the China Construction Bank, so the appropriate opportunity cost of capital is the (risky) bank rate of 6.09 percent. It is easiest to focus on the funds that are blocked and exclude other cash flows (in particular, the initial investment) from the analysis. The after-tax cost of debt is $6.09\%(1 - 0.25) = 4.5675\%$. The after-tax opportunity cost of blocked funds is as follows:

a. The present value of blocked funds assuming they are not blocked is ${}^{CNY}200\text{m}(1.045675)^{-1} + {}^{CNY}500\text{m}(1.045675)^{-2} + {}^{CNY}300\text{m}(1.045675)^{-3} = {}^{CNY}910.92$ million.

b. Blocked funds will delay the project cash flows for a year, so the present value of blocked funds is really only ${}^{CNY}200\text{m}(1.045675)^{-2} + {}^{CNY}500\text{m}(1.045675)^{-3} + {}^{CNY}300\text{m}(1.045675)^{-4} = {}^{CNY}871.13$ million.

c. The opportunity cost of the blocked funds is the difference between project value with and without the blocked funds: $V_{\text{SIDE EFFECT}} = V_{\text{PROJECT WITH SIDE EFFECT}} - V_{\text{PROJECT WITHOUT SIDE EFFECT}} = {}^{CNY}871.13$ million $-$ ${}^{CNY}910.92$

million = $-^{CNY}39.79$ million. At the $^{ILS}0.5526$/CNY spot rate, this is worth $^{ILS}21.99$ million.

Alternatively, incremental cash flows can be valued directly. Yuan flows in years 1–4 in the original case are (200,500,300,0). In the alternative case with blocked funds, yuan cash flows in years 1–4 are (0,200,500,300). The change in cash flow created by the blockage of funds is then (actual – expected) = (0–200, 200–500, 500–300, 300–0) = (–200, –300, +200, +300). The present value of incremental cash flows at the after-tax cost of debt is equal to $(-^{CNY}200m)(1.045675)^{-1} + (-^{CNY}300m)(1.045675)^{-2} + (+^{CNY}200m)(1.045675)^{-3} + (+^{CNY}300m)(1.045675)^{-4} = -^{CNY}39.79$ million, or $^{ILS}21.99$ million at the $^{ILS}0.5526$/CNY spot rate of exchange.

13.10 $V^{CNY} = {}^{CNY}194.39$ million without the side effect. The airport project reduces this value by $^{CNY}100$ million, but the NPV with the side effect is still positive. You should accept the project, even if the Chinese authorities are not willing to renegotiate.

13.12 *Step 1: Calculate the value of blocked funds assuming they are not blocked.* If blocked funds had been invested at the *risky* after-tax croc rate of 40%(1 – 0.5) = 20% per year, they would have grown in value to $Cr8{,}000(1.20)^3 + Cr13{,}819.5(1.20)^2 + Cr19{,}573.5(1.20) \approx Cr57{,}212$. Discounted at the 20% after-tax croc rate, this would have been worth Cr27,591 in present value. This is equivalent to discounting blocked funds back to the beginning of the project at the 20% risky after-tax croc discount rate, so this is a zero-NPV investment at the 20% after-tax croc interest rate.

*Step 2: Calculate the opportunity cost of blocked funds.* With blocked funds earning no interest, the accumulated balance of Cr41,393 has an after-tax present value of $(Cr41{,}393)/(1.20)^4 = Cr19{,}962$. The opportunity cost of blocked funds is (Cr19,962 – Cr27,591) = –Cr7,629.

*Step 3: Calculate project value including the opportunity cost of blocked funds.*

$V_{\text{project with side effect}} = V_{\text{project without side effect}} + V_{\text{side effect}} = -Cr137 - Cr7{,}629 = -Cr7{,}766$.

The opportunity cost of blocked funds at the 20% (forgone) risky after-tax discount rate is even higher than the Cr7,410 value in the text example using a $i_F^{Cr}(1 - T) = (37.5\%)(1 - 0.5) = 18.75\%$ risk-free, after-tax discount rate. Blocked funds make the Neverland project look even worse than when Hook's treasure chest is riskless.

## CHAPTER 14: MULTINATIONAL CAPITAL STRUCTURE AND COST OF CAPITAL

14.2 a. $r = r_F + \beta\,(E[r_W] - r_F) = 5\% + (0.8)(10\% - 5\%) = 9\%$

b. $r = r_F + \beta\,(E[r_M] - r_F) = 5\% + (1.2)(10\% - 5\%) = 11\%$

14.4 a. Grand Pet's debt ratio is $(B/V_L) = 33/(33 + 100) = 0.25$. The required return on Grand Pet's equity is $r_F = + \beta(E[r_M] - r_F) = 5\% + (1.2)(15\% -$

5%) = 17%. Grand Pet's WACC is $i_{WACC} = (B/V_L)i_B(1 - T_C) + (S/V_L)i_S = (0.25)(6\%)(1 - 0.33) + (0.75)(17\%) = 13.755\%$.

b. The debt-to-equity ratio is 0.50, so $(B/V_L) = 1/(1 + 2) = 0.33$. Equity required return is $r = r_F + \beta(E[r_W] - r_F) = 5\% + (0.8)(15\% - 5\%) = 16\%$, and the WACC is $i_{WACC} = (B/V_L)i_B(1 - T_C) + (S/V_L)i_S = (0.33)(6\%)(1 - 0.33) + (0.67)(16\%) = 12.007\%$.

c. In the United Kingdom, Grand Pet's value is $V = CF_1 / (i - g) = (£1\ \text{billion})/(0.13755 - 0.03) = £9.298$ billion.

If Grand Pet raises funds globally, $V = CF_1/(i - g) = (£1\ \text{billion}) / (0.12007 - 0.03) = £11.103$ billion.

Grand Pet can increase its value nearly 20% by raising funds internationally.

14.6 a. All-equity value is $APV = V_U - CF_0 = (CF_1)/(1 + i_U) - CF_0 = (£108\ \text{million}/1.08) - £100\ \text{million} = £0$.

b. APV = $V_U$ + PV(financing side effects) – Initial investment. Borrowing £25 million at 6% results in interest of $i_B B = £1.5$ million. The annual tax shield is $T_C i_B B = £500{,}000$. The PV of the tax shield is $(T_C i_B B)/(1 + i_B) \approx £467{,}000$. Since the unlevered investment has zero value, £467,000 is the APV of the 1-year investment after including the interest tax shield from the debt.

c. As a perpetuity, the all-equity value is still £0. The levered value is:

$APV = V_U + (T_C i_B B)/i_B - CF_0 = V_U + T_C B - CF_0 = £100{,}000{,}000 + £8{,}250{,}000 - £100{,}000{,}000 = £8{,}250{,}000$. The value continues to arise solely from the interest tax shield.

14.8 a. $E[r] = r_F + \beta(E[r_W] - r_F) = 3\% + 1.2(5\%) = 9\%$

b. $E[r] = r_F + \beta(E[r_W] - r_F) + \delta(E[r_{Region}] - E[r_W]) = 3\% + 1.2(5\%) + 1.5(4\%) = 15\%$

c. $E[r] = E[r_W] + CR = \{r_F + (E[r_W] - r_F)\} + CR = (3\% + 5\%) + 4\% = 12\%$

d. $E[r] = E[r_W] + S = \{r_F + (E[r_W] - r_F)\} + S = (3\% + 5\%) + 2\% = 10\%$

e. $E[r] = r_F + S\ (\sigma_{Br\text{-}stocks}/\sigma_{Br\text{-}bonds}) = 3\% + 2\%\ (30\%/10\%) = 9\%$

## CHAPTER 15: TAXES AND MULTINATIONAL CORPORATE STRATEGY

15.2 Here are parts a, b, and c:

| | Part a. | | Part b. | | Part c. | |
|---|---|---|---|---|---|---|
| | Poland | NZ | Poland | NZ | Poland | NZ |
| a Dividend payout ratio | 100% | 100% | 100% | 100% | 100% | 100% |
| b Foreign dividend withholding rate | 0% | 30% | 0% | 30% | 0% | 30% |
| c Foreign tax rate | 19% | 28% | 19% | 28% | 19% | 28% |
| d Foreign income before tax ($1000s) | 10,000 | 10,000 | 20,000 | 0 | 0 | 20,000 |
| e Foreign income tax (d × c) | 1,900 | 2,800 | 3,800 | 0 | 0 | 5,600 |
| f After-tax foreign earnings (d – e) | 8,100 | 7,200 | 16,200 | 0 | 0 | 14,400 |
| g Declared as dividends (f × a) | 8,100 | 7,200 | 16,200 | 0 | 0 | 14,400 |

| | | | | | | | |
|---|---|---|---|---|---|---|---|
| h | Foreign dividend withholding tax (g × b) | 0 | 2,160 | 0 | 0 | 0 | 4,320 |
| i | Total foreign tax (e + h) | 1,900 | 4,960 | 3,800 | 0 | 0 | 9,920 |
| j | Dividend to U.S. parent (d – i) | 8,100 | 5,040 | 16,200 | 0 | 0 | 10,080 |
| k | Gross foreign income before tax (line d) | 10,000 | 10,000 | 20,000 | 0 | 0 | 20,000 |
| l | Tentative U.S. income tax (k × 35%) | 3,500 | 3,500 | 7,000 | 0 | 0 | 7,000 |
| m | Foreign tax credit (i) | 1,900 | 4,960 | 3,800 | 0 | 0 | 9,920 |
| n | Net U.S. taxes payable [max(l – m,0)] | 1,600 | 0 | 3,200 | 0 | 0 | 0 |
| o | Total taxes paid (i + n) | 3,500 | 4,960 | 7,000 | 0 | 0 | 9,920 |
| p | Net amount to U.S. parent (k – o) | 6,500 | 5,040 | 13,000 | 0 | 0 | 10,080 |
| q | Total tax as separate subsidiaries (sum(o)) | | 8,460 | | 7,000 | | 9,920 |
| | Parent's consolidated tax statement | | | | | | |
| r | Overall FTC limitation (sum(k) × 35%) | | 7,000 | | 7,000 | | 7,000 |
| s | Total FTCs on consolidated basis (sum(i)) | | 6,860 | | 3,800 | | 9,920 |
| t | Additional U.S. taxes due [max(0, r – s)] | | 140 | | 3,200 | | 0 |
| u | Excess tax credits [max(0, s – r)] (carried back 1 year or forward 10 years) | | 0 | | 0 | | 2,920 |

d. In equilibrium, implicit taxes will force pretax returns lower in Poland and higher in New Zealand. Implicit taxes often result in lower sales (perhaps from higher competition), higher wages, and higher asset values in low-tax countries, at least relative to what these countries would experience with higher tax rates.

## CHAPTER 16: REAL OPTIONS AND CROSS-BORDER INVESTMENT STRATEGY

16.2 We know from Problem 16.1 that investment in one brewery has value. The issue is whether to invest in all five breweries today or invest in a single exploratory brewery and then make a decision on the four additional breweries in one year after receiving information about the price of beer produced by the exploratory brewery.

a. Decision tree:

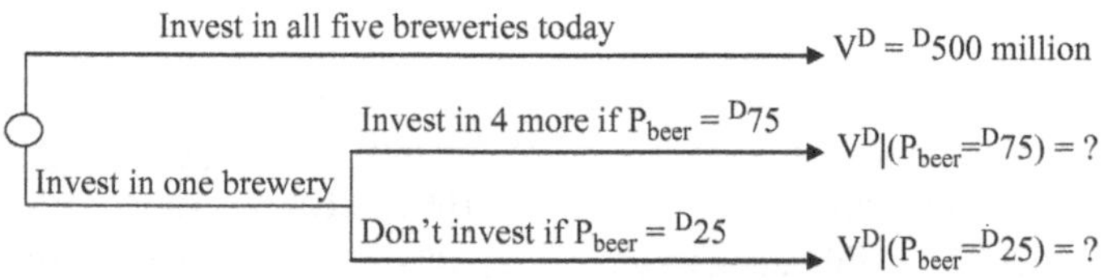


b. At the expected end-of-year price of $^D$50/btl, the NPV of a single brewery is $^D$100m as in Problem 16.1. The PV of the perpetual stream of cash inflows is either [(($^D$75 – $^D$10)(1m) – $^D$10m)/0.10] = $^D$550m or [(($^D$25 – $^D$10)(1m) – $^D$10m)/0.10] = $^D$50m with equal probability, for an expected value of

$^{D}$300m. Net of the required $^{D}$200m investment, this has a NPV of $^{D}$100m. Therefore, V(invest in all 5 breweries today) = 5×V(invest in 1 today) = $^{D}$500 million.

c. If Grolsch management waits one year before making its investment decision, beer prices will be either $^{D}$25 or $^{D}$75 with certainty in this problem. Of course, it won't know this until it invests in the first, exploratory brewery. The NPV of *each* of the four additional breweries at a price of $^{D}$75/bottle is $^{D}$300,000,000, as in Problem 16.1. At a price of $^{D}$25/bottle, the optimal strategy is to forgo further investment. The NPV of sequential investment is then

V(invest in exploratory brewery and continue to invest if it is positive-NPV)
=V(invest in one brewery today) + 4 [Prob($P_{beer}$ = $^{D}$75)] (V|invest in 1 year if $P_{beer}$ = $^{D}$75)
= $^{D}$100m + 4 (½) ($^{D}$300m) = +$^{D}$700 million > $^{D}$0 ⇒ Invest in an exploratory brewery

Alternatively, V(invest in exploratory brewery)
= [Prob($P_{beer}$ = \$25)](V|$P_{beer}$ = \$25) + [Prob($P_{beer}$ = \$75)](V|$P_{beer}$ = \$75)
= (½)[(($^{D}$25 − $^{D}$10)(1m) − $^{D}$10m)/(0.1) − $^{D}$200m]
+ (½)[(($^{D}$75 − $^{D}$10)(1m) − $^{D}$10m)/((0.1) − $^{D}$200m) + (4)($^{D}$300m) ]
= (½)[−$^{D}$150m] + (½)[($^{D}$350m) + (4)($^{D}$300m)]
= $^{D}$700 million > $^{D}$0 ⇒ Invest in an exploratory brewery

d. Option Value = Intrinsic Value + Time Value
V(wait one year) = V(invest today) + Opportunity cost of investing in four additional breweries today

$^{D}$700,000,000=$^{D}$500,000,000 + $^{D}$200,000,000

The NPV of investing in all five breweries today is −$^{D}$200,000,000. By investing today, Grolsch would forgo the flexibility provided by the timing option on this sequential investment.

e. Invest in an exploratory brewery and continue to invest if warranted by the quality (price) of the output. Endogenous uncertainty has created an incentive to hasten the first investment.

16.4 a. At production of 150 oz, the NPV of one mine is V(now-or-never) = (¥5,000/oz − ¥1,000/oz)(150 oz) − ¥600,000 = ¥0. The NPV of investing in all five mines as a now-or-never decision is also ¥0.

b. If you invest in an exploratory mine and then reconsider based on the revealed information about yield, then the NPV of the first mine is ¥0. The NPV of each additional mine is conditional on the yield of the first mine:

V|(Q = 200 oz) = [(¥5,000/oz − ¥1,000/oz)(200 oz)] − ¥600,000
= ¥200,000
V|(Q = 100 oz) = [(¥5,000/oz − ¥1,000/oz)(100 oz)] − ¥600,000
= −¥200,000

so don't invest at the lower guano yield. Then, V(sequential investment) = V(exploratory mine) + Prob(Q = 200 oz) × (4) × V| (Q = 200 oz) = ¥0 + (½)[(4)(¥200,000)] = ¥400,000.

c. The best strategy is to invest in an exploratory mine today and continue to invest if yield is high.

16.6 a.

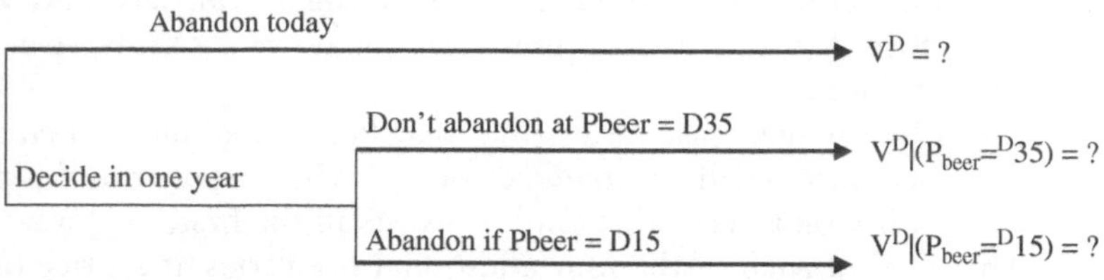


b. If the project is abandoned today at a cost of $^D$10,000,000, cash flows from the project will be forgone and there will be a minus sign on operating cash flow in the NPV equations that follow. At the expected end-of-year price of ½($^D$15/btl + $^D$35/btl) = $^D$25/btl, the NPV of the "abandon today" alternative is: V(abandon today) = −[($^D$25/btl − $^D$20/btl)((1,000,000 btls) − $^D$10,000,000)/0.10] − D10,000,000 = $^D$40,000,000 > $^D$0 ⇒ abandon today?

c. If Grolsch management waits one year before making its abandonment decision, beer prices will be either $^D$15 or $^D$35 with certainty.

$V|P_1 = {}^D35$ = −[(($^D$35/btl − $^D$20/btl)((1,000,000 btls) − $^D$10,000,000)/0.10)/(1.10)] − $^D$10,000,000 = −$^D$55,454,545 ⇒ don't abandon if price rises to $^D$35

$V|P_1 = {}^D15$ = −[(($^D$15/btl − $^D$20/btl)((1,000,000 btls) − $^D$10,000,000)/0.10)/(1.10)] − $^D$10,000,000 = $^D$126,363,636 ⇒ abandon if price falls to $^D$15

V(wait 1 year) = [Prob($P_1 = {}^D35$)](V|$P_1 = {}^D35$) + [Prob($P_1 = {}^D15$)](V|$P_1 = {}^D15$) = (½)($^D$126,363,636) + (½)($0) = $^D$63,181,818 > V(abandon today) > $^D$0

d. Option Value=Intrinsic Value+Time Value
V(wait one year)=V(abandon today)
+ Opportunity cost of abandoning today
+ $^D$63,181,818=+$^D$40,000,000+ $^D$23,181,818

e. Wait one year before making the abandonment decision.

16.8 This provocative question goes well beyond the material in the chapter. It turns out that the impact of a real investment opportunity depends on whether it is firm-specific or shared with other firms in an industry. If a firm has a real investment option that only it can exercise, such as a patent-protected drug that effectively combats prostate cancer, then the analysis in this chapter is appropriate. There will be an optimal time to invest and perhaps to exit, and it might pay to make a sequential investment to gain more information.

In a situation in which the entire industry shares an investment option (such as Grolsch's proposed investment in Eastern Europe), investment returns are sensitive to competitors' actions. When exit costs are zero, the effect of a shared investment opportunity is spread across all firms in the industry and results in a lower value to each firm. When there are exit costs, competitive response to uncertainty is asymmetric and firms must be more cautious in their investment decisions. As in the case of hysteresis, firms might stay invested in unprofitable situations in the hope that other less-profitable firms will exit first.

## CHAPTER 17: CORPORATE GOVERNANCE AND THE INTERNATIONAL MARKET FOR CORPORATE CONTROL

17.2 The preacquisition value of the two firms is \$3 billion + \$1 billion = \$4 billion. Synergy is 10% of this value, or (0.1)(\$4 billion) = \$400 million. After subtracting the (0.2)(\$1 billion) = \$200 million acquisition premium, Agile shareholders are likely to see a \$200 million appreciation in the value of their shares.

17.4 A real increase in the value of the domestic currency increases the purchasing power of domestic residents. When the domestic currency is strong, domestic firms are more likely to acquire foreign targets, and shareholders of the acquiring firm are more likely to benefit from the acquisition.

## CHAPTER 18: INTERNATIONAL CAPITAL MARKETS

18.2 With the actual/365 convention, 31 days out of 182.5 days would have accrued by July 31. This is $(31/182.5) \approx 16.986\%$ of the semiannual interest payment.

18.4 a. $8\frac{1}{2}\%$ compounded semiannually (or 4.25% semiannually).
b. Effective annual yield $= (1.0425)^2 - 1 \approx 8.6806\%$.

18.6 Countries with large stock markets tend to have large domestic bond markets as well. However, there are exceptions. For example, stock markets in China and India are large relative to their bond markets.

18.8 a. The argument for regulation is that hedge funds are exerting an increasing influence over financial markets and hence should be regulated to avoid a situation in which they precipitate a market collapse. The argument against regulation is that they are private investment partnerships and hence should not be subject to public disclosure requirements.
b. The arguments for and against public disclosure are the same as those for and against increased regulation.

## CHAPTER 19: INTERNATIONAL PORTFOLIO DIVERSIFICATION

19.2 $E[r_P] = (\frac{1}{2})(0.139) + (\frac{1}{2})(0.130) = 13.45\%$
$Var(r_P) = (\frac{1}{2})^2(0.300)^2 + (\frac{1}{2})^2(0.337)^2 + 2(\frac{1}{2})(\frac{1}{2})(0.402)(0.300)(0.337) = 0.0712$
$\Rightarrow \sigma_P = (0.0712)^{1/2} = 0.2669$, or 26.69%
$SI = (0.1345 - 0.061)/(0.2669) = 0.2754$, which exceeds that of Germany (0.230) or Japan (0.231) alone.

19.4 $E[r_P] = (\frac{1}{3})[(0.139) + (0.134) + (0.102)] = 0.125$, or 12.5%
$Var(r_P) = (\frac{1}{3})^2[(0.337)^2 + (0.283)^2 + (0.180)^2]$
$+ 2(\frac{1}{3})^2[(0.403)(0.337)(0.283) + (0.355)(0.337)(0.180)$
$+ (0.582)(0.283)(0.180)] = 0.0450$
$\Rightarrow \sigma_P = (0.0450)^{1/2} = 0.2122$, or 21.22%

SI = (0.1257 − 0.061)/(0.2122) = 0.302, which is superior in return-risk performance to the Japanese (0.231), U.K. (0.258), and U.S. stocks (0.228) alone.

19.6 $E[r_p] = X_A E[r_A] + X_B E[r_B] + X_C E[r_C] = 0.2(0.08) + 0.3(0.1) + 0.5(0.13) = 11.1\%$

19.8 $s^{d/f} = (S_t^{d/f}/S_{t-1}^{d/f}) - 1 = (€0.7182/\$)/(€0.7064/\$) - 1 = 1.0168 - 1 = 1.68\%$
$r^{€} = r^{\$} + s^{€/\$} + r^f s^{€/\$} = 0.1600 + 0.0168 + (0.1600)(0.0168) = 17.94\%$

19.10 $Var(r^{\$}) = Var(r^{Peso}) + Var(s^{\$/Peso}) = (0.248)^2 + (0.327)^2 = 0.1684$, so the standard deviation of dollar return on the Philippine stock market is $(0.1684)^{1/2} = 0.4104$, or 41.04 percent.

19.12 Because Greenland is less diversified than the United States, stocks in Greenland are relatively highly correlated with other domestic stocks. Hence, more of the total risk (variance) of individual stocks within Greenland will be systematic and less will be diversifiable. The extent to which international diversification can eliminate diversifiable risk depends on the correlation of Greenland's equities with the rest of the world.

19.14 Your return statistics will have a great deal of statistical *precision* in the sense that you'll have a large number of observations. However, these statistics won't be very *timely* in the sense that they'll be estimated over periods (of war, economic expansion or contraction, oil crisis, etc.) that might not match the current period. Market returns vary with inflation and the business cycle, and return statistics (correlations in particular) fluctuate over time. In addition, past performance is no guarantee of future results. Even if your estimates are accurate, performance over the coming year will have a large element of chance and will surely diverge from the past.

## CHAPTER 20: INTERNATIONAL ASSET PRICING

20.2 a. $ß_{BMW} = \rho_{BMW,DAX} (\sigma_{BMW}/\sigma_{DAX}) = (0.44)(0.105/0.046) \approx 1.00$ relative to the DAX index.

b. $r_{BMW} = r_F + \beta_{BMW} (E[r_M] - r_F) = 0.05 + (1.00)(0.06) \approx 0.110$, or 11.0%

c. $ß_{DAX,World} = \rho_{DAX,World} (\sigma_{DAX}/\sigma_{World}) = (0.494)\ (0.0413/0.0526) = 0.3879$ relative to the world.

20.4 a. According to Elf' factor sensitivities, Paribas shares should rise with an increase in industrial production or with an increase in the price of oil. Share price should fall with an increase in the term premium, the risk premium, or the value of the foreign currencies in Paribas' trading basket in the denominator of the foreign exchange quote.

b. $E(r) = \mu + \beta_{Prod} F_{Prod} + \beta_{Oil} F_{Oil} + \beta_{Term} F_{Term} + \beta_{Risk} F_{Risk} + \beta_{Spot} F_{Spot} = 12\% + (1.10)(10\%) + (0.60)(10\%) + (-0.05)(10\%) + (-0.10)(10\%) + (-0.02)(10\%) = 12\% + 11\% + 6\% - 0.5\% - 1\% - 0.2\% = 27.3\%$.

c. Surprise = actual − expected = (−12%) − (27.3%) = −39.3%; Paribas underperformed its expectation.

20.6 a. Over a single year, it is difficult to say which manager is likely to see higher returns. Returns to value (and other) investment strategies vary from year to year.

b. If the value premium persists over the next 10 years as it has in the past, then the value-oriented strategy of investing in stocks with high equity book-to-market value ratios is likely to lead to higher returns over 10-year investment horizons.

c. It is difficult to say whether higher returns to value strategies are truly superior risk-adjusted returns or merely a systematic risk for which investors demand compensation, such as a premium for relative financial distress.

20.8 a. By placing an equal weight on each asset, smaller cap firms will receive a larger weight. Smaller firms have higher expected returns, so this will increase the expected portfolio return. The equal-weighted portfolio also will benefit from the value premium (the higher expected return of firms with high equity book-to-market ratios) to the extent that value firms also tend to be smaller firms.

b. The answer is "it depends" on whether the investor believes that size and value premiums reflect compensation for bearing higher systematic risks.

c. Performance should be benchmarked to a similarly constructed equal-weighted portfolio. Otherwise, the comparison would be "apples and oranges."

# Symbols and Acronyms

Uppercase letters are used for asset prices, including currency values.

Lowercase letters are used for rates of change.

Superscripts indicate currency units.

Subscripts indicate a point in time (for prices) or a period of time (for returns).

Return statistics are either Greek letters or abbreviated in English (e.g., variance is denoted $\sigma_j^2$ or $Var(r_j)$).

***Continuously compounded returns are in italics.***

| | |
|---|---|
| $P_t^d$ and $P_t^f$ | Price of an asset at time t in the domestic (d) and foreign (f) currencies. |
| $p^d$ and $p^f$ | Domestic and foreign inflation (i.e., the percentage change in the Consumer Price Index). |
| $S_t^{d/f}$ | Spot exchange rate between currencies d and f at time t. |
| $s_t^{d/f}$ | Percentage change in the spot exchange rate between currencies d and f during period t. |
| $F_t^{d/f}$ | Forward exchange rate between currencies d and f priced at time 0 and for delivery at time t (sometimes denoted $F_{0,t}^{d/f}$). |
| $Fut_t^{d/f}$ | Price in currency d of a futures contract on currency f priced for delivery at time t (sometimes denoted $Fut_{0,t}^{d/f}$). |
| $fut_t^{d/f}$ | Percentage change in the futures price with maturity t between currencies d and f. |
| $i^d$ and $i^f$ | Nominal interest rates in currencies d and f. |
| $R^d$ and $R^f$ | Real interest rates in currencies d and f. |
| $Call_t^{d/f}$ | Domestic currency value of a call option (at option to buy) on currency f at time t. |
| $Put_t^{d/f}$ | Domestic currency value of a put option (at option to sell) on currency f at time t. |
| $K^{d/f}$ | The exercise (or strike) price of a currency call or put option on currency f. |
| $X_t^{d/f}$ | Real exchange rate at time t. |
| $x_t^{d/f}$ | Percentage change in the real exchange rate during period t. |
| V | Value of an asset or security (e.g., $V_{Firm} = V_{Debt} + V_{Equity}$). |
| $r_t^d$ and $r_t^f$ | Percentage return during period t in currencies d and f. |

| | |
|---|---|
| $E[r_j]$ | Expected return on asset j. |
| $\mu_j$ | Mean (historical) return on asset j. |
| $\sigma_j$ | Standard deviation of return on asset j (variance is denoted $\sigma_j^2$ or $Var(r_j)$). |
| $\rho_{j,k}$ | Correlation of returns to assets j and k, such that $\rho_{j,k} = \sigma_{j,k}\, \sigma_j \sigma_k$. |
| $\sigma_{j,k}$ | Covariance of returns to assets j and k, such that $\sigma_{j,k} = \rho_{j,k}\sigma_j\sigma_k$. |
| $\beta_j$ | Systematic risk of asset j (e.g., $\beta_j = \rho_{j,m}(\sigma_j\sigma_m)$ for the one-factor market model). |
| $\sigma_t$ | Conditional (time-varying) volatility of an asset. |

### *Continuously Compounded Rates of Change*

| | | | | |
|---|---|---|---|---|
| $i$ | = | $\ln(1+i)$ | = | Continuously compounded nominal interest rate |
| $p$ | = | $\ln(1+p)$ | = | Continuously compounded inflation rate |
| $r$ | = | $\ln(1+\iota)$ | = | Continuously compounded real interest rate |
| $s_t^{d/f}$ | = | $\ln(1+s_t^{d/f})$ | = | Continuously compounded percentage change in a nominal spot rate |
| $x_t^{d/f}$ | = | $\ln(1+x_t^{d/f})$ | = | Continuously compounded percentage change in a the real exchange rate |

# Useful Rules and Formulas

## CHAPTER 3 FOREIGN EXCHANGE AND EUROCURRENCY MARKETS EQUATION

Rule #1: Keep track of your currency units.

Rule #2: Think of buying or selling the currency in the denominator of a foreign exchange quote.

Foreign currency premium or discount (periodic) = $(F_t^{d/f} - S_0^{d/f})/S_0^{d/f}$ (3.1)

Percentage change in a foreign currency value: $s^{d/f} = (S_1^{d/f} - S_0^{d/f})/S_0^{d/f}$ (3.4)

Variance of a GARCH conditional volatility process: $\sigma_t^2 = a_0 + a_1\,\sigma_{t-1}^2 + b_1\,s_{t-1}^2$ (3.6)

## CHAPTER 4 THE INTERNATIONAL PARITY CONDITIONS AND THEIR CONSEQUENCES

Exchange rate determination: $P^d = P^f\,S^{d/f}$ (4.1)

Cross exchange rate equilibrium: $S^{d/e}\,S^{e/f}\,S^{f/d} = 1$ (4.3)

Interest rate parity: $F_t^{d/f} / S_0^{d/f} = [(1 + i^d)/(1 + i^f)]^t$ (4.4)

Relative purchasing power parity: $E[S_t^{d/f}] / S_0^{d/f} = [(1 + E[p^d])/(1 + E[p^f])]^t$ (4.5)

Forward parity: $F_t^{d/f} / S_0^{d/f} = E[S_t^{d/f}] / S_0^{d/f}$ (4.6)

Fisher equation: $(1 + i) = (1 + p)(1 + R)$ (4.8)

International Fisher relation: $[(1+i^d)/(1+i^f)]^t = [(1+E[p^d])/(1+E[p^f])]^t$ (4.9)

Uncovered interest parity: $E[S_t^{d/f}]/S_0^{d/f} = [(1 + i^d)/(1 + i^f)]^t$ (4.10)

Percentage change in a real exchange rate: $(1 + x_t^{d/f}) = (S_t^{d/f} / S_{t-1}^{d/f})[(1 + p_t^f)/(1 + p_t^d)]$ (4.13)

## CHAPTER 5 CURRENCY FUTURES AND FUTURES MARKETS

Relation between futures and spot prices: $Fut_{t,T}^{d/f} = F_{t,T}^{d/f} = S_t^{d/f}\,[(1 + i^d)/(1 + i^f)]^{T-t} = S_T^{d/f}$ as $t \to T$ (5.2)

Delta hedge: $s_t^{d/f} = \alpha + \beta fut_t^{d/f} + e_t$ where $\beta = \rho_{s,fut}(\sigma_s/\sigma_{fut})$ (5.7)

Hedge ratio: $N_{Fut}^* =$ (Amount in forward position)/(Amount exposed to currency risk) $= -\beta$ (5.9)

Delta-cross hedge: $s_t^{d/f1} = \alpha + \beta\,fut_t^{d/f2} + e_t$ (5.10)

Cross hedge: $s_t^{d/f1} = \alpha + \beta\,s_t^{d/f2} + e_t$ (5.11)

## CHAPTER 6 CURRENCY OPTIONS AND OPTIONS MARKETS

Put-call parity: $Call^{d/f} - Put^{d/f} = (F_T^{d/f} - K^{d/f})/(1 + i^d)^T$ (6.1)

Continuously compounded changes in an exchange rate: $s = \ln(1 + s) \Leftrightarrow (1 + s) = e^{\ln(1+s)} = e^s$ (6.2)

Return variance over T periods (assuming an iid normal return distribution): $\sigma_T^2 = T\sigma^2$ (6.3)

Historical exchange rate volatility: $\sigma = \sqrt{[(1/T)\sum_t (s_t - \mu)^2]}$ (6.4)

Black-Scholes Option Values

$Call = P\,N(d_1) - e^{(-iT)}\,K\,N(d_2)$ (6A.1)

$Put = Call - P + e^{(-iT)}\,K$ (6A.2)

where

$d_1 = [\ln(P/K) + (i + (\sigma^2/2))T]/(\sigma\sqrt{T})$ and $d_2 = (d_1 - \sigma\sqrt{T})$

Biger-Hull Currency Option Values

$Call^{d/f} = e^{(-i^f T)}\,[S_0^{d/f}\,N(d_1)] - e^{(-i^d T)}\,[K^{d/f}\,N(d_2)]$ (6A.4)

$Put^{d/f} = Call^{d/f} - e^{(-i^f T)}\,S_0^{d/f} + e^{(-i^d T)}\,K^{d/f}$ (6A.6)

where

$d_1 = [\ln(S^{d/f}/K^{d/f}) + (i^d - i^f + (\sigma^2/2))T]/(\sigma\sqrt{T})$ and $d_2 = (d_1 - \sigma\sqrt{T})$

## CHAPTER 7 CURRENCY SWAPS AND SWAPS MARKETS

Relation between bond equivalent yield and money market yield: $BEY = MMY\,(365/360)$ (7.1)

"Fully covered" swap quote equivalence: $\Sigma_t\,[r^d/(1 + i_t^d)^t] = \Sigma_t\,[r^f/(1 + i_t^f)^t]$ (7.2)

## CHAPTER 10 MANAGING OPERATING EXPOSURE TO CURRENCY RISK

Exposure as a regression coefficient: $r_t^d = \alpha^d + \beta^f s_t^{d/f} + e_t^d$ where $\beta^f = \rho_{r,s}(\sigma_r/\sigma_s)$ (10.3)

Price elasticity of demand $= -(\Delta Q/Q)/(\Delta P/P)$ (10.9)

## CHAPTER 13 CROSS-BORDER CAPITAL BUDGETING EQUATION

Net present value (NPV): $V_0^d = \sum_t E[CF_t^d] / (1 + i^d)^t$ (13.1)

NPV discounted in the foreign currency: $V_0^d|i^f = S_0^{d/f}\,V_0^f = S_0^{d/f}\,[\sum_t E[CF_t^f] / (1 + i^f)^t]$ (13.2)

NPV valued at forward rates and discounted in the domestic currency: $V_0^d|i^d = \sum_t E[CF_t^f]\,F_t^{d/f} / (1 + i^d)^t$ (13.4)

Value of project side effects: $V_{\text{PROJECT WITH SIDE EFFECT}} = V_{\text{PROJECT WITHOUT SIDE EFFECT}} + V_{\text{SIDE EFFECT}}$ (13.8)

## CHAPTER 14 MULTINATIONAL FINANCIAL STRUCTURE AND COST OF CAPITAL

MM's irrelevance proposition: If financial markets are perfect, then corporate financial policy is irrelevant.

Weighted average cost of capital: $i_{WACC} = [(B/V_L)i_B(1 - T_C)] + [(S/V_L)i_S]$ (14.2)

Market model regression: $r_i = \alpha_i + \beta_i\, r_M + e_i$ where $\beta_i = \rho_{i,M}(\sigma_i/\sigma_M)$ (14.4)

Security market line: $r_i = r_F + \beta_i\,(E[r_M] - r_F)$ (14.6)

Adjusted present value: APV = $V_U$ + PV(financing side effects) − Initial investment (14.7)

## CHAPTER 15 TAXES AND MULTINATIONAL CORPORATE STRATEGY

Purchasing power parity and equivalent *after-tax* returns: $i_H(1 - t_H) = i_L(1 - t_L)$ (15.1)

## CHAPTER 16 REAL OPTIONS AND CROSS-BORDER INVESTMENT

Value of an option: Option value = Intrinsic value + Time value (16.4)

Value of the firm: $V_{ASSET} = V_{ASSETS\text{-}IN\text{-}PLACE} + V_{GROWTH\ OPTIONS}$ (16.5)

## CHAPTER 17 CORPORATE GOVERNANCE AND THE INTERNATIONAL MARKET FOR CORPORATE CONTROL

Synergy = $V_{AT} - (V_A + V_T)$ (17.1)

Acquisition premium = Purchase price − $V_T$ (17.2)

Gain to acquiring firm = Synergy − Acquisition premium (17.3)

## CHAPTER 19 INTERNATIONAL PORTFOLIO DIVERSIFICATION

Expected return on a two-asset portfolio: $E[r_P] = x_A E[r_A] + x_B E[r_B]$ (19.1)

Variance of a two-asset portfolio: $Var(r_P) = \sigma_P^2 = x_A^2\sigma_A^2 + x_B^2\sigma_B^2 + 2x_A x_B \sigma_{AB}$ (19.3)

Covariance and correlation: $\sigma_{AB} = \rho_{AB}\,(\sigma_A\sigma_B) \Leftrightarrow \rho_{AB} = \sigma_{AB}/(\sigma_A\sigma_B)$ (19.4)

Variance of return on an N-asset portfolio: $Var(r_P) = \sigma_P^2 = \sum_i \sum_j x_i x_j \sigma_{ij}$ (19.5)

Sharpe index: $SI = (r_j - r_F)/\sigma_j$ (19.6)

Total risk = Systematic risk + Unsystematic risk (19.7)

Domestic currency return on a foreign asset: $(1 + r^d) = (1 + r^f)(1 + s^{d/f})$ (19.10)

Expected return on a foreign investment: $E[r^d] = E[r^f] + E[s^{d/f}] + E[r^f s^{d/f}]$ (19.11)

Variance of return on a foreign investment: $Var(r^d) = Var(r^f) + Var(s^{d/f})$ + interaction terms (19.12)

## CHAPTER 20 INTERNATIONAL ASSET PRICING

Security market line: $r_j = r_F + \beta_j(E[r_M] - r_F)$ (20.1)

Excess returns (CAPM): $e_j = r_j - E[r_j] = r_j - [(r_F + \beta_j(r_M - r_F)]$ (20.2)

One-factor market model: $r_j = \alpha_j + \beta_j r_M + e_j$ where $\beta_j = \rho_{j,M}(\sigma_j/\sigma_M)$ (20.3)

K-factor model: $r_j = \mu_j + \beta_{1j}F_1 + \cdots + \beta_{Kj}F_K + e_j$ (20.5)

One-factor market model in excess return form: $r_j = \mu_j + \beta_j F_M + e_j$ where $F_M = (r_M - \mu_M)$ (20.6)

Currency risk exposure: $r_j^d = \alpha_j^d + \beta_j^f s^{d/f} + e_j^d$ (20.10)

Multiple currency risk exposures in factor model form: $r_j^d = \mu_j^d + \beta_j^f s^{d/f1} + \beta_j^f s^{d/f2} + \cdots + e_j^d$ (20.11)

# Useful Websites

**Global Economic Agencies and Trade Associations**

| | | |
|---|---|---|
| Bank for International Settlements | Monetary cooperation | www.bis.org |
| International Chamber of Commerce | International conventions | www.iccwbo.org |
| International Labor Organization | International agency | www.ilo.org |
| International Monetary Fund (IMF) | Monetary cooperation | www.imf.org |
| Michigan State University Global Edge | International analyses | globaledge.msu.edu |
| United Nations | International cooperation | www.un.org/en/ |
| United Nations Commission on International Trade Law | International conventions | www.uncitral.org/uncitral/en/index.html |
| World Bank | Monetary cooperation | www.worldbank.org |
| World Bank's Multilateral Investment Guarantee Agency | Political risk insurance | www.miga.org |
| World Economic Forum | Economic cooperation | www.weforum.org |
| World Trade Organization (WTO) | Economic cooperation | www.wto.org |

**Regional Economic Agencies and Trade Associations**

| | | |
|---|---|---|
| Asia-Pacific Economic Cooperation (APEC) | Economic cooperation | www.apec.org |
| Association of South-East Asian Nations (ASEAN) | Economic cooperation | www.aseansec.org |
| European Union (EU) | Economic cooperation | http://europa.eu/index_en.htm |
| Organization for Economic Co-Operation and Development (OECD) | Economic cooperation | www.oecd.org |
| Organization of Petroleum Exporting Countries (OPEC) | Economic cooperation | www.opec.org |

**Economic and Financial Data**

| | | |
|---|---|---|
| FTSE (Financial Times/London Stock Exchange) | Economic data | www.ftse.com |
| Ibbotson Associates | Financial data | www.ibbotson.com |
| Social Science Research Network | Research articles | www.ssrn.com |
| Union Bank of Switzerland | Cost-of-living indices | www.ubs.com |
| United States Bureau of Economic Analysis | Economic data | www.bea.gov |
| United States Federal Reserve Board of St. Louis | Economic data | www.stlouisfed.org/ |
| United States Federal Reserve Systems | Economic data | www.federalreserve.gov |

**Financial Exchanges and Related Websites**

| | | |
|---|---|---|
| Chicago Board of Trade | United States | www.cbot.com |
| Chicago Mercantile Exchange | United States | www.cme.com |
| Eurex | Europe | www.eurexchange.com |
| Euronext | Europe | www.euronext.com |
| Tokyo Financial Exchange | Japan | www.tfx.co.jp |

**Trade Associations**

| | | |
|---|---|---|
| Futures Industry Association | Futures and options | www.futuresindustry.org |
| International Capital Market Association | Eurobond dealers | www.icmagroup.org/ |
| International Swaps and Derivatives Association | Swaps | www.isda.org |

**Risk Management Specialists**

| | | |
|---|---|---|
| JPMorgan | Data and tools | www.jpmorgan.com |
| Morgan Stanley Capital International | Data and tools | www.msci.com |

**National and Iternational Accounting Standards**

| | | |
|---|---|---|
| International Accounting Standards Board (IASB) | International standards | www.iasb.org.uk |
| U.K. Accounting Standards Board (ASB) | U.S. standards | www.frc.org.uk/asb/ |
| U.S. Financial Accounting Standards Board (FASB) | U.K. standards | www.fasb.org |

# Glossary

*The next best thing to knowing something is knowing where to find it.*
—Blaise Pascal

**Accounting (translation) exposure:** Changes in a corporation's financial statements as a result of changes in currency values. (Contrast with *economic exposure.*)

**Acquisition:** Acquiring control of an asset through purchase of the asset or the equity that controls the asset.

**Acquisition of assets:** In an acquisition of assets, one firm acquires the assets of another company. None of the liabilities supporting that asset are transferred to the purchaser.

**Acquisition of stock:** In an acquisition of stock, one firm buys an equity interest in another.

**Acquisition premium:** In a merger or acquisition, the difference between the purchase price and the pre-acquisition value of the target firm.

**Active fund management:** An investment approach that actively shifts funds either between asset classes (asset allocation) or between individual securities (security selection).

**Active income:** In the U.S. tax code, income from an active business. (See *general limitation income.*)

**Active security selection:** An investment strategy that attempts to identify individual securities that are underpriced relative to other securities in a particular market or industry.

**Adjusted present value:** A valuation method that separately identifies the value of an unlevered project from the value of financial side effects.

**Adverse selection costs:** Costs incurred as uninformed investors attempt to protect themselves against trading with informed investors. Adverse selection costs can impair liquidity, inflate bid-ask spreads, depress share prices, and increase the corporation's cost of capital.

**Agency costs:** The loss in value from conflicts of interest between managers and other stakeholders (particularly equity), including the costs of monitoring managers to ensure they act in the interests of other stakeholders.

**Agent:** Someone who represents another. In corporate governance terminology, management is the agent of the principal stakeholders in a principal–agent relationship.

**All-in cost:** The percentage cost of a financing alternative, including any placement fees, calculated as an internal rate of return on incremental cash flows associated with the financing alternative.

**Allocation-of-income rules:** Rules that define how income and deductions are to be allocated between domestic-source and foreign-source income.

**Allocational efficiency:** The efficiency with which a market channels capital toward its most productive uses.

**Alternative Investment Fund Managers Directive (AIFMD):** The EU regulatory framework for private investment funds (e.g., hedge funds).

**American depository receipt:** A derivative security issued by a non-U.S. borrower through a U.S. trustee representing ownership in non-U.S. shares held by a trustee.

**American option:** An option that can be exercised anytime until expiration. (Contrast with *European option.*)

**American shares:** Shares of a foreign corporation issued directly to U.S. investors through a transfer agent in accordance with SEC regulations.

**American terms:** A foreign exchange quotation that states the U.S. dollar price per foreign currency unit. (Contrast with *European terms.*)

**Andean Pact:** A regional trade pact that includes Venezuela, Colombia, Ecuador, Peru, and Bolivia.

**Appreciation:** An increase in a currency value relative to another currency in a floating exchange rate system.

**Arbitrage:** Simultaneous purchase and sale of the same or equivalent security in order to ensure a profit with no net investment or risk.

**Arbitrage Pricing Theory (APT):** An asset pricing model that assumes a linear relation between required return and systematic risk as measured by one or more factors according to $r_j = \mu_j + \beta_{1j}F_1 + \cdots + \beta_{Kj}F_K + e_j$.

**Arbitrage profit:** Profit obtained through arbitrage.

**Arm's-length pricing:** Prices that would be negotiated between independent parties. Arm's-length transfer prices are required by Section 486 of the U.S. Internal Revenue Code, Article 9 of the OECD Model Tax Convention, and other national and international tax standards.

**Asia-Pacific Economic Cooperation Pact (APEC):** A loose economic affiliation of Southeast Asian and Far Eastern nations. The most prominent members are China, Japan, and Korea.

**Ask (offer) rates:** The rate at which a market maker is willing to sell the quoted asset.

**Asset allocation policy:** The target weights given to various asset classes in an investment portfolio.

**Assets-in-place:** Those assets in which the firm has already invested. (Compare with *growth options.*)

**Association of Southeast Asian Nations (ASEAN):** A loose economic and geopolitical affiliation that includes Singapore, Brunei, Malaysia, Thailand, the Philippines, Indonesia, and Vietnam. Future members are likely to include Burma, Laos, and Cambodia.

**At-the-money option:** An option with an exercise price that is equal to the current value of the underlying asset.

**Balance-of-payments (BoP) statistics:** The International Monetary Fund's accounting system that tracks the flow of goods, services, and capital in and out of each country.

**Bank-based corporate governance system:** A system of corporate governance in which the supervisory board is dominated by bankers through their equity ownership in the firm.

**Banker's acceptance:** A time draft drawn on and accepted by a commercial bank.

**Basis:** The simple difference between two nominal interest rates.

**Basis point:** Equal to 1/100 of 1 percent.

**Basis risk:** The risk of unexpected change in the relationship between futures and spot prices.

**Basis swap:** A floating-for-floating interest rate swap that pairs two floating rate instruments at different maturities (such as 6-month LIBOR versus 30-day U.S. T-bills).

**Basel Accords:** International recommendations to ensure that financial institutions retain sufficient capital to protect themselves against unexpected losses.

**Bearer bonds:** Bonds that can be redeemed by the holder. The convention in most West European countries is to issue bonds in registered form. (Contrast with *registered bonds.*)

**Behavioral finance:** The study of the impact of psychological factors on investor behavior and asset prices.

**Beta (β):** A measure of an asset's sensitivity to changes in the market portfolio (in the CAPM) or to a factor (in the APT). The beta of an asset j is computed as $\beta_j = \rho_{j,k}\ (\sigma_j/\sigma_k)$, where k represents a market factor (such as returns to the market portfolio in the *capital asset pricing model*).

**Bid rate:** The rate at which a market maker is willing to buy the quoted asset.

**Bid-ask spread:** The dealer's profit margin on currency transactions, equal to the ask price minus bid price.

**Blocked funds:** Cash flows generated by a foreign project that cannot be immediately repatriated to the parent firm because of capital flow restrictions imposed by the host government.

**Bond equivalent yield:** A bond quotation convention based on a 365-day year and semiannual coupons. (Contrast with *effective annual yield.*)

**Bretton Woods Conference:** An international conference held in 1944 at Bretton Woods, New Hampshire, that established the International Monetary Fund and the World Bank.

**Business risk:** The risks of operating cash flows.

**Call option:** The right to buy the underlying currency at a specified price and on a specified date.

**Capital account:** A measure of change in cross-border ownership of long-term financial assets, including financial securities and real estate.

**Capital asset pricing model (CAPM):** An asset pricing model that relates the required return on an asset to its systematic risk.

**Capital market line:** The line between the risk-free asset and the market portfolio that represents the mean variance efficient set of investment opportunities in the CAPM.

**Capital markets:** Markets for financial assets and liabilities with maturity greater than one year, including long-term government and corporate bonds, preferred stock, and common stock.

**Capital (financial) structure:** The proportion of debt and equity and the particular forms of debt and equity chosen to finance the assets of the firm.

**Cash in advance:** Payment for goods prior to shipment.

**Chaebol:** A family-controlled horizontally diversified group of companies in South Korea.

**Check-the-box regulations:** Regulations that allow a U.S. parent to choose whether a foreign corporation is treated as a corporation or as a flow-through entity for tax purposes.

**CHIPS (Clearing House Interbank Payments System):** Financial network through which banks in the United States conduct their financial transactions.

**Closed-end fund:** A mutual fund in which the amount of funds under management is fixed and ownership in the funds is bought and sold in the market like a depository receipt.

**Collateralized debt obligation (CDO):** A special-purpose entity that owns a pool of mortgages as collateral and issues bonds against these assets, often in credit tranches of various maturities and credit risks.

**Commodity price risk:** The risk of unexpected changes in a commodity price, such as the price of oil.

**Commodity swap:** A swap in which the (often notional) principal amount on at least one side of the swap is a commodity such as oil or gold.

**Comparable uncontrolled price:** A transfer pricing method based on independent market transactions.

**Comparative advantage:** The rule of economics that states that each country should specialize in producing those goods that it is able to produce relatively most efficiently.

**Compound option:** An option on an option.

**Consolidated income:** The sum of income across all of the multinational corporation's domestic and foreign subsidiaries.

**Consolidation:** A form of corporate reorganization in which two firms pool their assets and liabilities to form a new company.

**Continuous quotation system:** A trading system in which buy and sell orders are matched with market makers as the orders arrive, ensuring liquidity in individual shares.

**Controlled foreign corporation (CFC):** In the U.S. tax code, a foreign corporation owned more than 50 percent either in terms of market value or voting power.

**Convertible bonds:** Bonds sold with a conversion feature that allows the holder to convert the bonds into common stock on or prior to a conversion date and at a prespecified conversion price.

**Convex tax schedule:** A tax schedule in which the effective tax rate is greater at high levels of taxable income than at low levels of taxable income. Such a schedule results in progressive taxation.

**Copyright:** A government-approved protection against the unauthorized reproduction of creative works, such as books, paintings, video recordings, and computer software.

**Corporate governance:** The way in which major stakeholders exert control over the modern corporation.

**Correlated default:** The tendency of asset prices to fall in unison.

**Correlation:** A measure of the comovement of two assets that is scaled for the standard deviations of the assets ($\rho_{AB} = \sigma_{AB}/\sigma_A\sigma_B$ such that $-1 < \rho_{AB} < +1$).

**Cost of capital:** Investors' required return given the risk of an investment.

**Cost plus:** The most common transfer pricing method, based on cost plus a profit margin.

**Costs of financial distress:** Costs associated with financial distress, including direct costs such as court costs and attorney fees incurred during bankruptcy or liquidation, and indirect costs incurred prior to formal bankruptcy or liquidation.

**Countertrade:** Exchange of goods or services without the use of cash.

**Country risk:** The political and financial risks of conducting business in a particular foreign country.

**Coupon swap:** A fixed-for-floating interest rate swap.

**Covariance:** A measure of the comovement of two assets ($\sigma_{AB} = \sigma_A\sigma_B\ \rho_{AB}$).

**Covered interest arbitrage:** Arbitrage that takes advantage of a disequilibrium in interest rate parity.

**Credit default swap:** A credit derivative in which a protection buyer pays a protection seller a periodic fee for a specified contract life for assuming the credit exposure of an underlying reference entity.

**Credit derivative:** A derivative instrument that synthetically transfers credit risk from one party to another.

**Cross exchange rates (cross rates):** Exchange rates that do not involve the domestic currency.

**Cross hedge:** A futures hedge using a currency that is different from, but closely related to, the currency of the underlying exposure.

**Cumulative translation adjustment:** An equity account under FAS #52 that accumulates gains or losses caused by translation accounting adjustments.

**Currency coupon swap:** A fixed-for-floating rate nonamortizing currency swap traded primarily through international commercial banks.

**Currency of reference:** The currency that is being bought or sold. It is most convenient to place the currency of reference in the denominator of a foreign exchange quote (see Rule #2 in Chapter 3).

**Currency option:** A contract giving the option holder the right to buy or sell an underlying currency at a specified price and on a specified date. The option writer (seller) holds the obligation to fulfill the other side of the contract.

**Currency (foreign exchange) risk:** The risk of unexpected changes in foreign currency exchange rates.

**Currency swap:** A derivative instrument in which two counterparties exchange a stream of cash flows in one currency for a stream of cash flows in another currency. The cash flows can comprise interest or principal. The most common currency swap is a fixed-for-floating currency coupon swap. The notional principal may or may not be exchanged.

**Current account:** A measure of a country's international trade in goods and services.

**Current account balance:** A broad measure of import-export activity that includes services, travel and tourism, transportation, investment income and interest, gifts, and grants along with the trade balance on goods.

**Current rate method:** A translation accounting method, such as FAS #52 in the United States, that translates monetary and real assets and monetary liabilities at current exchange rates. FAS #52 places any imbalance into an equity account called the "cumulative translation adjustment."

**Day count:** The day count defines the way in which interest accrues on a bond.

**Dealer:** In the currency market, a financial institution that makes a market in foreign exchange.

**Dealing desk (trading desk):** The desk at an international bank that trades spot and forward foreign exchange.

**Debt capacity:** The amount of debt that a firm chooses to borrow to support a project.

**Debt-for-equity swap:** A swap agreement to exchange equity (debt) returns for debt (equity) returns over a prearranged length of time.

**Decision trees:** A graphical analysis of sequential decisions and the likely outcomes of those decisions.

**Deliverable instrument:** The asset underlying a derivative security. For a currency option, the deliverable instrument is determined by the options exchange and is either spot currency or an equivalent value in futures contracts.

**Delta-cross hedge:** A futures hedge that has both currency and maturity mismatches with the underlying exposure.

**Delta hedge:** A futures hedge using a currency that matches the underlying exposure and a maturity date that is different from, but preferably close to, the maturity of the underlying exposure.

**Depository receipt:** A derivative security issued by a foreign borrower through a domestic trustee representing ownership in the deposit of foreign shares held by the trustee.

**Depreciation:** A decrease in a currency value relative to another currency in a floating exchange rate system.

**Derivative security:** A financial security whose price is derived from the price of another asset.

**Devaluation:** A decrease in a currency value relative to another currency in a fixed exchange rate system.

**Difference check:** The difference in interest payments that is exchanged between two swap counterparties.

**Direct costs of financial distress:** Costs of financial distress that are directly incurred during bankruptcy or liquidation proceedings.

**Direct terms:** The price of a unit of foreign currency in domestic currency terms, such as $1.10/€ for a U.S. resident. (Contrast with *indirect quote*.)

**Discounted cash flow:** A valuation methodology that discounts expected future cash flows at a discount rate appropriate for the risk, currency, and maturity of the cash flows.

**Discounted payback:** The length of time needed to recoup the present value of an investment; sometimes used when investing in locations with high country risk.

**Discounting:** A form of factoring in which a trade acceptance is sold at a discount to face value.

**Discretionary reserves:** Balance sheet accounts that are used in some countries to temporarily store earnings from the current year or the recent past.

**Diversification discount:** Diversified (both industrially and globally) firms usually sell at a discount to portfolios of single-segment firms operating in the same industries.

**Domestic bonds:** Bonds issued and traded within the internal market of a single country and denominated in the currency of that country.

**Domestic tax neutrality:** A situation in which incomes arising from the foreign and domestic operations of a domestically based multinational are taxed similarly by the domestic government.

**Draft (trade bill, bill of exchange):** A means of payment whereby a seller draws a draft that instructs the drawee (the buyer or its bank) to pay the seller according to the terms of the draft .

**Economic exposure:** Change in the value of a corporation's assets or liabilities as a result of changes in currency values.

**Economic value added:** A method of performance evaluation that adjusts accounting performance with a charge reflecting investors' required return on investment.

**Economies of scale:** Lower average cost per unit achieved through a larger scale of production.

**Economies of scope:** Lower average cost per unit achieved through joint production across product lines.

**Economies of vertical integration:** Achieving lower operating costs by bringing the entire production chain within the firm rather than contracting through the marketplace.

**Effective annual yield:** Calculated as $(1 + i/n)^n$, where i is the stated annual interest rate and n is the number of compounding periods per year. (Contrast with *bond equivalent yield* and *money market yield.*)

**Efficient frontier:** The mean-variance efficient portion of the investment opportunity set.

**Efficient market:** A market in which prices reflect all relevant information.

**Efficient market hypothesis:** A supposition that a market is informationally efficient.

**Emerging stock markets:** The stock markets of emerging economies. These markets typically have higher expected returns than established markets but also higher risk.

**Endogenous uncertainty:** Price or input cost uncertainty that is within the control of the firm, such as when the act of investing reveals information about price or input cost.

**Equity premium:** Expected stock market return relative to a risk-free benchmark, such as short-term U.S. T-bills.

**Equity-linked Eurobonds:** A Eurobond with a convertibility option or warrant attached.

**Eurobonds:** Fixed rate Eurocurrency deposits and loans and Eurocurrencies with longer maturities than five years.

**Euro Interbank Offered Rate (Euribor):** The offer rate on euro-denominated term deposits between major banks within the euro zone.

**Eurobonds:** Bonds that trade in external markets; that is, outside the borders of the country in which the bonds are denominated.

**Eurocurrencies:** Deposits and loans denominated in one currency and traded in a market outside the borders of the country issuing that currency (e.g., Eurodollars).

**Eurodollars:** Dollar-denominated deposits held in a country other than the United States.

**European currency unit (ECU):** A trade-weighted basket of currencies in the European Exchange Rate Mechanism (ERM) of the European Union.

**European exchange rate mechanism (ERM):** The exchange rate system used by countries in the European Union in which exchange rates were pegged within bands around an ERM central value.

**European Monetary System (EMS):** An exchange rate system based on cooperation between European Union central banks.

**European monetary union (Emu):** All 27 countries in the European Union participate in European monetary union. Seventeen EU states have entered the third stage of Emu and have adopted the euro as their currency.

**European option:** An option that can be exercised only at expiration. (Contrast with *American option.*)

**European terms:** A foreign exchange quotation that states the foreign currency price of one U.S. dollar. (Contrast with *American terms.*)

**European Union (EU):** Formerly the European Economic Community, a regional trade pact that includes 27 European countries.

**Eurosterling:** Pound-denominated deposits held in a country other than the United Kingdom.

**Euroyen:** Yen-denominated deposits held in a country other than Japan.

**Eurozone:** Refers to European Union countries that have adopted the euro as their currency, including Austria, Belgium, Cyprus, Estonia, Finland, France, Germany, Greece, Ireland, Italy, Luxembourg, Malta, the Netherlands, Portugal, Slovakia, Slovenia, and Spain, with several other EU members set to join in the future.

**Exercise price:** The price at which an option can be exercised (also called the *striking price*).

**Exogenous uncertainty:** Price or input cost uncertainty that is outside the control of the firm.

**Expiration date:** The date on which a contract (such as a currency futures contract or a currency call option) expires.

**Explicit tax:** A tax that is explicitly collected by a government; includes income, withholding, property, sales, and value-added taxes and tariffs.

**Export:** An entry mode into international markets that relies on domestic production and shipments to foreign markets through sales agents or distributors, foreign sales branches, or foreign sales subsidiaries.

**Export financing interest:** In the U.S. tax code, interest income derived from goods manufactured in the United States and sold outside the United States as long as not more than 50 percent of the value is imported into the United States.

**Export management company:** A foreign or domestic company that acts as a sales agent and distributor for domestic exporters in international markets.

**Exposure to currency risk:** Change in the value of assets or liabilities in response to exchange rate changes.

**Expropriation:** A specific type of political risk in which a government seizes foreign assets.

**External market:** A market for financial securities that are placed outside the borders of the country issuing that currency.

**Factor model:** A model that assumes a linear relation between an asset's expected return and one or more systematic risk factors.

**Factoring:** Sale of an accounts receivable balance to buyers (factors) that are willing and able to bear the costs and risks of credit and collections.

**Financial engineering:** The process of innovation by which new financial products are created.

**Financial innovation:** The process of designing new financial products, such as exotic currency options and swaps.

**Financial markets:** Markets for financial assets and liabilities.

**Financial policy:** The corporation's choices regarding the debt-equity mix, currencies of denomination, maturity structure, method of financing investment projects, and hedging decisions with a goal of maximizing the value of the firm to some set of stakeholders.

**Financial price risk:** The risk of unexpected changes in a financial price, including currency (foreign exchange) risk, interest rate risk, and commodity price risk.

**Financial risk:** Financial risk refers to unexpected events in a country's financial, economic, or business life.

**Financial service income:** In the U.S. tax code, income derived from financial services such as banking, insurance, leasing, financial service management fees, and swap income.

**Financial (capital) structure:** The proportion of debt and equity and the particular forms of debt and equity chosen to finance the assets of the firm.

**Financial services income:** In the U.S. tax code, income from offshore banking, shipping, or airline operations.

**Financial strategy:** The way in which the firm pursues its financial objectives.

**Fisher equation:** The relation of a nominal interest rate i to inflation p and a real interest rate R: $(1 + i) = (1 + p)(1 + R)$.

**Fixed exchange rate system:** An exchange rate system in which a government maintains an official exchange rate.

**Floating exchange rate system:** An exchange rate system in which currency values are allowed to fluctuate according to supply and demand forces in the market without direct interference by government authorities.

**Flow-through entity:** A legal entity whose taxable income "flows through" to the U.S. parent. The parent consolidates this with income from other foreign and domestic sources.

**Foreign base company income:** In the U.S. tax code, a category of Subpart F income that includes foreign base company sales income, foreign base company services income, and foreign personal holding company income.

**Foreign bonds:** Bonds that are issued in a domestic market by a foreign borrower, denominated in domestic currency, marketed to domestic residents, and regulated by the domestic authorities.

**Foreign branch:** A foreign affiliate that is legally a part of the parent firm. In the U.S. tax code, foreign branch income is taxed as it is earned in the foreign country.

**Foreign corporation:** In the U.S. tax code, any business entity that is not created or organized under U.S. laws.

**Foreign direct investment (FDI):** The act of building productive capacity directly in a foreign country.

**Foreign exchange brokers:** Brokers serving as matchmakers in the foreign exchange market that do not put their own money at risk.

**Foreign exchange dealers:** Financial institutions making a market in foreign exchange.

**Foreign exchange (currency) risk:** The risk of unexpected changes in foreign currency exchange rates.

**Foreign shares:** Shares of a foreign corporation issued directly to domestic investors through a transfer agent in accordance with local (domestic) regulations.

**Foreign subsidiary:** A legal entity that is incorporated in a host country. In the U.S. tax code, income from a foreign subsidiary typically is taxed as it is repatriated to the parent company.

**Foreign-source income:** Income earned from foreign operations.

**Foreign tax credit (FTC):** In the U.S. tax code, a credit against domestic U.S. income taxes up to the amount of foreign taxes paid on foreign-source income.

**Foreign tax credit limitation (FTC limitation):** In the U.S. tax code, a limitation on the FTC equal to taxable foreign-source income times the U.S. tax rate.

**Foreign tax neutrality:** A situation in which taxes imposed on the foreign operations of domestic companies are similar to those facing local competitors in the foreign countries.

**Forfaiting:** A form of factoring in which large, medium- to long-term receivables are sold to buyers (forfaiters) that are willing and able to bear the costs and risks of credit and collections.

**Forward contract:** A commitment to exchange a specified amount of one currency for a specified amount of another currency on a specified future date.

**Forward discount:** A currency whose nominal value in the forward market is lower than in the spot market. (Contrast with *forward premium.*)

**Forward market:** A market for forward contracts in which trades are made for future delivery according to an agreed-upon delivery date, exchange rate, and amount.

**Forward parity:** When the forward exchange rate is an unbiased predictor of future spot rates.

**Forward premium:** A currency whose nominal value in the forward market is higher than in the spot market. (Contrast with *forward discount.*)

**Forward premium anomaly:** The widespread empirical finding that the slope coefficient in a regression of the change in the spot exchange rate on the forward premium is less than unity (as suggested by forward parity) and often is negative.

**Franchise agreement:** An agreement in which a company (the franchisor) licenses its trade name or business system to an independent company (the franchisee).

**Free cash flow:** Cash flow after all positive-NPV projects have been exhausted in the firm's main line of business.

**Free float (or float):** Shares available for trade. Free float capitalization based on available shares differs from market capitalization based on issued shares when controlling shareholders (such as a founding family) do not trade their shares.

**Freight shippers (freight forwarders):** Agents used to coordinate the logistics of transportation.

**Fundamental analysis:** A method of predicting exchange rates using the relationships of exchange rates to fundamental economic variables such as GNP growth, money supply, and trade balances.

**Futures contract:** A commitment to exchange a specified amount of one currency for a specified amount of another currency at a specified time in the future. Futures contracts are marked to market periodically, so that changes in value are settled throughout the life of the contract.

**General Agreement on Tariffs and Trade (GATT):** A worldwide trade agreement designed to reduce tariffs, protect intellectual property, and set up a dispute resolution system. The agreement is overseen by the World Trade Organization (WTO).

**General limitation income:** In the U.S. tax code, income earned from participation in an active business (including foreign branches).

**Generalized autoregressive conditional heteroskedasticity (GARCH):** A time series model in which returns at each instant of time are normally distributed but volatility is a function of recent history of the series.

**Global bond:** A bond that trades in the Eurobond market as well as in one or more national bond markets.

**Global depository receipt:** A depository receipt that trades in more than one foreign market.

**Global shares (global equity):** A foreign share that trades in more than one foreign market.

**Gold exchange standard:** An exchange rate system used from 1925 to 1931 in which the United States and England were allowed to hold only gold reserves while other nations could hold gold, U.S. dollars, or pounds sterling as reserves.

**Gold standard:** An exchange rate system used prior to 1914 in which gold was used to settle national trade balances. Also called the "classical gold standard."

**Goodwill:** The accounting treatment of an intangible asset such as the takeover premium in a merger or acquisition.

**Growth options:** The positive-NPV opportunities in which the firm has not yet invested. The value of growth options reflects the time value of the firm's current investment in real assets as well as the option value of the firm's potential future investments.

**Growth stocks:** Stocks with low equity book-to-market ratios or high price/earnings (P/E) ratios.

**Hedge:** A position or operation that offsets an underlying exposure. For example, a forward currency hedge uses a forward currency contract to offset the exposure of an underlying position in a foreign currency. Hedges reduce the total variability of the combined position.

**Hedge funds:** Private investment partnerships with a general manager and a small number of limited partners.

**Hedge portfolio:** The country-specific hedge portfolio in the International Asset Pricing Model serves as a store of value (like the risk-free asset in the CAPM) as well as a hedge against the currency risk of the market portfolio.

**Hedge quality:** Measured by the r-square in a regression of spot rate changes on futures price changes.

**Hedge ratio:** The ratio of derivatives contracts to the underlying risk exposure.

**High-withholding-tax interest income:** In the U.S. tax code, interest income that has been subject to a foreign gross withholding tax of 5 percent or more.

**Historical volatility:** Volatility estimated from a historical time series.

**Home asset bias:** The tendency of investors to over-invest in assets based in their own country.

**Horizontal keiretsu (kinyû):** Japanese industrial groups, typically centered on a main bank and featuring extensive share cross-holdings between firms in different industries.

**Hysteresis:** The behavior of firms that fail to enter markets that appear attractive and, once invested, persist in operating at a loss. This behavior is characteristic of situations with high entry and exit costs along with high uncertainty.

**Implicit tax:** Lower (higher) before-tax required returns on assets that are subject to lower (higher) tax rates.

**Implied volatility:** The volatility that is implied by an option value given the other determinants of option value.

**Income baskets:** In the U.S. tax code, income is allocated to one of a number of separate income categories. Losses in one basket may not be used to offset gains in another basket.

**Index futures:** A futures contract that allows investors to buy or sell an index (such as a foreign stock index) in the futures market.

**Index option:** A call or put option contract on an index (such as a foreign stock market index).

**Index swap:** A swap of a market index for some other asset (such as a stock-for-stock or debt-for-stock swap).

**Indirect costs of financial distress:** Costs of financial distress that are indirectly incurred prior to formal bankruptcy or liquidation.

**Indirect diversification benefits:** Diversification benefits provided by the multinational corporation that are not available to investors through their portfolio investment.

**Indirect terms:** The price of a unit of domestic currency in foreign currency terms such as €0.9091/$ for a U.S. resident. (Contrast with *direct terms*.)

**Informational efficiency:** Whether or not market prices reflect information and thus the true (or intrinsic) value of the underlying asset.

**Instantaneous variance:** The variance of return at an instant of time in a continuous-time model, such as Brownian motion.

**Integrated financial market:** A market in which there are no barriers to financial flows, and purchasing power parity holds across equivalent assets.

**Intellectual property rights:** Patents, copyrights, and proprietary technologies and processes that are the basis of the multinational corporation's competitive advantage over local firms.

**Interbank spread:** The difference between a bank's offer and bid rates for deposits in the Eurocurrency market.

**Interest rate parity:** The relation between spot and forward exchange rates and nominal interest rates.

**Interest rate risk:** The risk of unexpected changes in an interest rate.

**Interest rate swap:** An agreement to exchange interest payments for a specific period of time on a given principal amount. The most common interest rate swap is a fixed-for-floating coupon swap. The notional principal is not exchanged.

**Internal market:** A market for financial securities that are denominated in the currency of a host country and placed within that country.

**International Asset Pricing Model (IAPM):** The international version of the CAPM in which investors in each country share the same consumption basket, and purchasing power parity holds.

**International Bank for Reconstruction and Development:** Also called the World Bank, an international organization created at Breton Woods in 1944 to help in the reconstruction and development of its member nations.

**International bonds:** Bonds that are traded outside the country of the issuer. International bonds are either foreign bonds trading in a foreign national market or Eurobonds trading in the international market.

**International Fisher relation:** The nominal interests rate $i$ is related to the real (or inflation-adjusted) interest rate $\iota$ and inflation rate $p$ according to $(1 + i) = (1+p)(1+R)$.

**International Monetary Fund (IMF):** An international organization that compiles statistics on cross-border transactions and publishes a monthly summary of each country's balance of payments.

**International monetary system:** The global network of governmental and commercial institutions within which currency exchange rates are determined.

**International parity conditions:** The relations between spot and forward exchange rates, Eurocurrency interest rates, and inflation.

**In-the-money option:** An option that has value if exercised immediately.

**Intrinsic value of an option:** The value of an option if exercised immediately.

**Investment agreement:** An agreement specifying the rights and responsibilities of a host government and a corporation in the structure and operation of an investment project.

**Investment opportunity set:** The set of possible investments available to an individual or a corporation.

**Investment philosophy:** The investment approach—active or passive—pursued by an investment fund and its managers.

**Investment Securities Directive (ISD):** The so-called European "passport" that allows investment services companies based in EU member states to operate in other EU countries so long as they have the approval of regulatory authorities in their home country.

**Irrelevance proposition:** The proposition (following Miller-Modigliani) that corporate financial policy is irrelevant if financial markets are perfect. The corollary is: If financial policy is to increase firm value, then it must either increase the firm's expected future cash flows or decrease the discount rate.

**Joint venture:** An agreement of two or more companies to pool their resources to execute a well-defined mission. Resource commitments, responsibilities, and earnings are shared according to a predetermined contractual formula.

**Keiretsu:** Collaborative groups of vertically or horizontally integrated firms with extensive share cross-holdings. Horizontal keiretsu have a major Japanese bank or corporation at the center.

**Kurtosis:** A measure of the size or probability mass of a distribution's tails. Distributions with fat tails relative to the normal distribution are said to be leptokurtic. Thin-tailed distributions are called platykurtic. Most assets have return distributions that are leptokurtic.

**Law of one price (purchasing power parity):** The principle that equivalent assets sell for the same price and have the same required return. Market participants promote the law of one price through arbitrage and through speculation.

**Lead manager:** The lead investment bank in a syndicate selling a public securities offering.

**Leading and lagging:** Reduction of transaction exposure through timing of cash flows within the corporation.

**Less developed country (LDC):** A country that has not yet reached the level of industrial organization attained by developed countries.

**Letter of credit (L/C):** A letter issued by an importer's bank guaranteeing payment upon presentation of specified trade documents (invoice, bill of lading, inspection and insurance certificates, etc.).

**Liberalization:** A decision by a government to allow foreigners to purchase local assets.

**License agreement:** A sales agreement in which a domestic company (the licensor) allows a foreign company (the licensee) to market its products in a foreign country in return for royalties, fees, or other forms of compensation.

**Liquid market:** A market in which traders can buy or sell large quantities of an asset when they want and with low transaction costs.

**Liquidity:** The ease with which an asset can be exchanged for another asset of equal value.

**Loanable funds:** The pool of funds from which borrowers can attract capital; typically categorized by currency and maturity.

**Locational arbitrage:** Arbitrage conducted between two or more locations.

**Location-specific advantages:** Advantages (natural and created) that are available only or primarily in a single location.

**Lognormal distribution:** The distribution in prices (e.g., exchange rates) that corresponds to a normal distribution in continuously compounded rates of return.

**London Interbank Bid Rate (LIBID):** The bid rate that a Euromarket bank is willing to pay to attract a deposit from another Euromarket bank in London.

**London Interbank Offer Rate (LIBOR):** The offer rate that a Euromarket bank demands in order to place a deposit at (or, equivalently, make a loan to) another Euromarket bank in London.

**Long position:** A position in which a particular asset (such as a spot or forward currency) has been purchased.

**Macro country risks:** Country (or political) risks that affect all foreign firms in a host country.

**Managerial flexibility:** Flexibility in the timing and scale of investment provided by a real investment option.

**Margin requirement:** A performance bond paid upon purchase of a futures contract that ensures the exchange clearinghouse against loss.

**Market-based corporate governance system:** A system of corporate governance in which the supervisory board represents a dispersed set of largely equity shareholders.

**Market failure:** A failure of arm's-length markets to efficiently complete the production of a good or service.

**Market internalization advantages:** Advantages that allow the multinational corporation to internalize or exploit the failure of an arm's-length market to efficiently accomplish a task.

**Market maker:** A financial institution that quotes bid (buy) and offer (sell) prices.

**Market model (one-factor market model):** The empirical version of the security market line: $r_j = \alpha_j + \beta_j r_M + e_j$, or $r_j = \alpha_j + \beta_j F_M + e_j$ where $F_M = (r_M - \mu_M)$.

**Market portfolio:** A portfolio of all assets weighted according to their market values.

**Market risk premium:** The risk premium on an average stock; $(E[r_M]—r_F)$.

**Market timing:** An investment strategy of shifting among asset classes in an attempt to anticipate which asset class(es) will appreciate or depreciate during the coming period.

**Marking-to-market:** The process by which changes in the value of futures contracts are settled.

**Mean-variance efficient:** An asset that has higher mean return at a given level of risk (or lower risk at a given level of return) than other assets.

**Mercosur:** The "common market of the South," which includes Argentina, Brazil, Paraguay, and Uruguay in a regional trade pact that reduces tariffs on intrapact trade.

**Merger:** A form of corporate acquisition in which one firm absorbs another, and the assets and liabilities of the two firms are combined.

**Merger waves:** The long-term ups and downs in merger and acquisition (M&A) activity.

**Method of payment:** The way in which a merger or an acquisition is financed. Gains to acquiring firm shareholders are related to the method of payment.

**Micro country risks:** Country risks that are specific to an industry, company, or project within a host country.
**Ministry of Finance, Japanese:** The regulatory body that oversees securities regulation in Japan.
**Momentum (or relative strength) strategy:** An investment strategy that selectively buys or sells securities based on their recent return performance.
**Monetary assets and liabilities:** Assets and liabilities with contractual payoffs.
**Money market hedge:** A hedge that replicates a currency forward contract through the spot currency and Eurocurrency markets.
**Money market yield:** A bond quotation convention based on a 360-day year and semiannual coupons. (Contrast with *bond equivalent yield.*)
**Money markets:** Markets for financial assets and liabilities of short maturity, usually defined as less than one year.
**Moral hazard:** The risk that the existence of a contract will change the behaviors of parties to the contract.
**Multinational corporation:** A corporation with operations in more than one country.
**Multinational netting:** Elimination of offsetting cash flows within the multinational corporation.
**National tax policy:** The way in which a nation chooses to allocate the burdens of tax collections across its residents.
**Nationalization:** A process whereby privately owned companies are brought under state ownership and control. (Contrast with *privatization.*)
**Negative-NPV tie-in project:** A negative-NPV infrastructure development project that a local government requires of a company pursuing a positive-NPV investment project elsewhere in the economy.
**Negotiable acceptance:** A banker's acceptance that is: (1) in writing, (2) signed by a bank representative, (3) an unconditional payment guarantee once trade documents are received, (4) a sight or time draft, and (5) payable to either order or bearer.
**Net asset value (NAV):** The sum of the individual asset values in a closed-end mutual fund. Closed-end funds can sell at substantial premiums or discounts to their net asset values.
**Net currency exposure:** Exposure to foreign exchange risk after netting all intracompany cash flows.
**Net exposed assets:** Exposed assets less exposed liabilities. The term is used with market values or, in translation accounting, with book values.
**Net monetary assets:** Monetary assets less monetary liabilities.
**Net position:** A currency position after aggregating and canceling all offsetting transactions in each currency and maturity.
**No-arbitrage condition:** An absence of arbitrage opportunities, so that the law of one price holds within the bounds of transaction costs.
**Nonmonetary (real) assets and liabilities:** Assets and liabilities with noncontractual payoffs.
**North American Free Trade Agreement (NAFTA):** A regional trade pact among the United States, Canada, and Mexico.
**Notional principal:** In a swap agreement, a principal amount that is only "notional" and is not exchanged.
**Offer (ask) rates:** The rate at which a market maker is willing to sell the quoted asset.
**Offering statement:** In the United States, a shortened registration statement required by the Securities and Exchange Commission on debt issues with less than a 9-month maturity.
**Official settlements balance (overall balance):** An overall measure of a country's private financial and economic transactions with the rest of the world.
**Open account:** The seller delivers the goods to the buyer and then bills the buyer according to the terms of trade.

**Open-end fund:** A mutual fund in which the amount of money under management grows/shrinks as investors buy/sell the fund.

**Operating exposure:** Changes in the value of real (nonmonetary) assets or operating cash flows as a result of changes in currency values.

**Operating leverage:** The tradeoff between fixed and variable costs in the operation of the firm.

**Operational efficiency:** Market efficiency with respect to how large an influence transaction costs and other market frictions have on the operation of a market.

**Opportunity cost:** The value of the next best alternative; that is, the value forgone as the result of making a decision.

**Opportunity set:** The set of all possible investments.

**Options:** Contracts giving the option holder the right to buy or sell an underlying asset at a specified price and on a specified date. The option writer (seller) holds the obligation to fulfill the other side of the contract.

**Out-of-the-money option:** An option that has no value if exercised immediately.

**Outright quote:** A quote in which all of the digits of the bid and offer prices are quoted. (Contrast with *points quote.*)

**Overall balance:** (See *official settlements balance.*)

**Overall FTC limitation:** In the U.S. tax code, a rule that limits the foreign tax credit (FTC) to the amount of U.S. tax attributable to foreign-source income.

**Ownership-specific advantages:** Property rights or intangible assets, including patents, trademarks, organizational and marketing expertise, production technology and management, and general organizational abilities, that form the basis for the multinational's advantage over local firms.

**Passive income:** In the U.S. tax code, income (such as investment income) that does not come from active participation in a business.

**Patent:** A government-approved right to make, use, or sell an invention for a period of time.

**Payoff profile:** A graph with the value of an underlying asset on the x-axis and the value of a position taken to hedge against risk exposure on the y-axis. Also used with changes in value. (Contrast with *risk profile.*)

**Pecking order:** A frequently observed preference for financing assets with internally generated funds, followed in order by external debt and equity.

**Pension liabilities:** A recognition of future liabilities resulting from pension commitments made by the corporation. Accounting for pension liabilities varies widely by country.

**Perfect market assumptions:** A set of assumptions under which the law of one price holds. These assumptions include frictionless markets, rational investors, and equal access to market prices and information.

**Periodic call auction:** A trading system in which stocks are auctioned at intervals throughout the day.

**Points quote:** An abbreviated form of the outright quote used by traders in the interbank market.

**Political risk:** The risk that a sovereign host government unexpectedly will change the rules of the game under which businesses operate. Political risk includes both macro and micro risks.

**Price elasticity of demand:** The sensitivity of quantity sold to a percentage change in price; $-\%\Delta Q/\%\Delta P$.

**Price uncertainty:** Uncertainty regarding the future price of an asset.

**Principal–agent relationship:** The relationship between a principal and an agent, such as between equity shareholders and management. Aligning the interests of principals and their agents can be difficult, especially under conditions of incomplete or asymmetric information. Also see *agency costs.*

**Private placement:** A securities issue privately placed with a small group of investors rather than through a public offering.

**Privatization:** Government sales of assets or common stock to private investors. (Contrast with *nationalization.*)

**Progressive taxation:** A convex tax schedule that results in a higher effective tax rate on high income levels than on low income levels.

**Project finance:** A way to raise nonrecourse financing for a specific project characterized by the following: (1) the project is a separate legal entity and relies heavily on debt financing and (2) the debt is contractually linked to the cash flow generated by the project.

**Prospectus:** A description of a mutual fund's investment objectives, strategies, and position limits.

**Protectionism:** Protection of local industries through tariffs, quotas, and regulations that discriminate against foreign businesses.

**Public securities offering:** A securities issue placed with the public through an investment or commercial bank.

**Purchasing power parity (law of one price):** The principle that equivalent assets sell for the same price. Purchasing power parity is enforced in the currency markets by financial market arbitrage.

**Pure-play firm:** A firm with the same systematic business risk and debt capacity as a project.

**Put option:** The right to sell the underlying asset at a specified price and on a specified date.

**Put-call parity:** The relation of the value of a long call, a short put, the exercise price, and the forward price at expiration; $Call_T^{d/f} - Put_T^{d/f} + K^{d/f} = F_T^{d/f}$.

**Rainbow option:** An option with multiple sources of uncertainty.

**Random walk:** A process in which instantaneous changes in exchange rates are normally distributed with a zero mean and constant variance.

**Real asset:** Productive technologies and capacities, whether tangible (land or a factory) or intangible (a patent).

**Real appreciation/depreciation:** A change in the purchasing power of a currency.

**Real exchange rate:** A measure of the nominal exchange rate that has been adjusted for inflation differentials since an arbitrarily defined base period.

**Real interest parity:** Real required returns on equivalent foreign and domestic assets are equal; $\iota^d = \iota^f$.

**Real options:** An option or option-like feature embedded in a real investment opportunity.

**Realized volatility:** A volatility estimate that averages squared returns measured over short (e.g., 15-minute) intraday intervals.

**Registered bonds:** Bonds for which each issuer maintains a record of the owners of its bonds. Countries requiring that bonds be issued in registered form include the United States and Japan. (Contrast with *bearer bonds.*)

**Registration statement:** In the United States, a statement filed with the Securities and Exchange Commission on securities issues that discloses relevant information to the public.

**Relative financial distress factor:** The difference in mean return between deciles of firms with the highest and lowest ratios of book-to-market equity (book value divided by market value), abbreviated *HML* for "high-minus-low."

**Relative purchasing power parity:** Expected change in the spot exchange rate is determined by the inflation differential according to $E[S_1^{d/f}]/S_0^{d/f} = (1 + p^d)/(1 + p^f)$.

**Reliability (accounting definition):** The quality of information that ensures that information is reasonably free from error and bias and faithfully represents what it purports to represent.

**Relevance (accounting definition):** The capacity of information to make a difference in a decision by helping users to form predictions about outcomes of past, present, and future events or to confirm or correct prior expectations.

**Repatriation:** The act of remitting cash flows from a foreign affiliate to the parent firm.

**Replicating portfolio:** A portfolio that mimics the payoffs on an option. Replicating portfolios are used in option pricing models to circumvent the problem of identifying the opportunity cost of capital.

**Reservation price:** The price below (above) which a seller (purchaser) is unwilling to go.

**Restricted shares:** Shares that may be held only by domestic residents.

**Revaluation:** An increase in a currency value relative to other currencies in a fixed exchange rate system.

**Risk:** The possibility that actual outcomes might differ from expectations.

**Risk exposure:** Changes in the value of the firm's assets or liabilities as a consequence of unexpected changes in some underlying factor, such as general business conditions or a financial price variable (exchange rates, interest rates, or commodity prices).

**Risk profile:** A graph with the value of an underlying asset on the x-axis and the value of a position exposed to risk in the underlying asset on the y-axis. Also used with changes in value. (Contrast with *payoff profile.*)

**R-square (the coefficient of determination):** The percent of the variation in a dependent variable that is "explained by" variation in an independent variable.

**Rule #1:** Always keep track of your currency units.

**Rule #2:** Always think of buying and selling the currency in the denominator of a foreign exchange quote.

**Sales agent:** A representative—such as a distributor—that promotes sales. Sales agents can be based in the domestic or a foreign market.

**Scenario analysis:** A process of asking "What if?" using scenarios that capture key elements of possible future realities.

**Securities and Exchange Commission (SEC):** The regulatory body that oversees securities regulation in the United States.

**Security market line (SML):** In the CAPM, the relation between required return and systematic risk (or beta): $r_j = r_F + \beta_j\,(E[r_M]—r_F)$.

**Segmented market:** A market that is partially or wholly isolated from other markets by one or more market imperfections.

**Semi-strong form efficient market:** A market in which prices fully reflect all *publicly* available information.

**Sharpe index:** A measure of risk-adjusted investment performance in excess return per unit of total risk: $SI = (r_P—r_F)/(\sigma_P)$.

**Short position:** A position in which a particular asset (such as a spot or forward currency) has been sold.

**Short selling:** Selling an asset that you do not own.

**Side effect:** Any aspect of an investment project that can be valued separately from the project itself.

**Sight draft:** A draft that is payable on demand.

**Signaling:** The use of observable managerial actions in the marketplace as an indication of management's beliefs concerning the prospects of the company.

**Simple option:** An option that has no other options attached.

**Size effect:** The finding that small firms tend to have higher mean returns than large firms.

**Size factor:** The difference in mean return between the smallest and the biggest 10 percent of firms, abbreviated *SMB* for "small-minus-big."

**Skewness:** A measure of asymmetry around a sample mean. The normal distribution is symmetric and has zero skewness. Positive skewness is an indication of large positive returns. Conversely, negative skewness is an indication of large negative returns.

**Sovereign yield spread:** The difference in yield to maturity between local government debt and risk-free debt (e.g., U.S. treasury debt) with similar characteristics.

**Special drawing right (SDR):** An international reserve created by the International Monetary Fund and allocated to member countries to supplement foreign exchange reserves.

**Spot market:** A market in which trades are made for immediate delivery (within two business days for most spot currencies).

**Stakeholders:** Those with an interest in the firm. A narrow definition includes the corporation's debt and equity holders. A broader definition includes labor, management, and perhaps other interested parties, such as customers, suppliers, and society at large.

**Stamp tax:** A tax on a financial transaction.

**State-owned enterprises (SOEs):** Enterprises that are partially or wholly owned by a national government; common in China and India. SOEs often are run as policy arms of the government, in which case they have objectives other than shareholder wealth maximization.

**Stationary time series:** A time series in which the process generating returns is identical at every instant of time.

**Stock index futures:** A futures contract on a stock index.

**Stock index swap:** A swap involving a stock index. The other asset involved in a stock index swap can be another stock index (a stock-for-stock swap), a debt index (a debt-for-stock swap), or any other financial asset or price index.

**Strategic alliance:** A collaborative agreement between two companies designed to achieve some strategic goal. Strategic alliances include international licensing agreements, management contracts, and joint ventures.

**Striking price:** The price at which an option can be exercised (also called the *exercise price*).

**Subprime loan:** A loan to a borrower of poor credit quality.

**Subsidized financing:** Financing that is provided by a host government and that is issued at a below-market interest rate.

**Sunk costs:** Expenditures that are at least partially lost once an investment is made.

**Supervisory board:** The board of directors that represents stakeholders in the governance of the corporation.

**Swap:** An agreement to exchange two liabilities (or assets) and, after a prearranged length of time, to re-exchange the liabilities (or assets).

**Swaption:** A derivative contract granting the right to enter into a swap.

**Swap book:** A swap bank's portfolio of swaps, usually arranged by currency and by maturity.

**Swap pricing schedule:** A schedule of rates for an interest rate or currency swap.

**SWIFT (Society for Worldwide Interbank Financial Transactions):** Network through which international banks conduct their financial transactions.

**Switching options:** A sequence of options in which exercise of one option creates one or more additional options. Investment–disinvestment, expansion–contraction, entry–exit, and suspension–reactivation decisions are examples of switching options.

**Syndicate:** The selling group of investment banks in a public securities offering.

**Synergy:** In an acquisition or a merger, when the value of the combination is greater than the sum of the individual parts: Synergy = $V_{AT} — (V_A + V_T)$.

**Synthetic forward position:** A forward position constructed through borrowing in one currency, lending in another currency, and offsetting these transactions in the spot exchange market.

**Systematic business risk (unlevered beta):** The systematic risk (or beta) of a project that is financed with 100 percent equity.

**Systematic risk:** Risk that is common to all assets and cannot be diversified away. Systematic risk in the CAPM is measured by beta. Factor models measure systematic risk as sensitivity to a factor such as relative financial distress.

**Tangibility:** Tangible assets are real assets that can be used as collateral to secure debt.

**Targeted registered offerings:** Securities issues sold to "targeted" foreign financial institutions according to U.S. SEC guidelines. These foreign institutions then maintain a secondary market in the foreign market.

**Tax arbitrage:** Arbitrage using a difference in tax rates or tax systems as the basis for profit.

**Tax clienteles:** Clienteles of investors with specific preferences for debt or equity that are driven by differences in investors' personal tax rates.

**Tax havens:** Countries offering low tax rates on corporate income and low withholding tax rates for dividend and interest distributions to nonresidents.

**Tax holiday:** A reduced tax rate provided by a government as an inducement to foreign direct investment.

**Tax neutrality:** Taxes that do not interfere with the natural flow of capital toward its most productive use.

**Tax preference items:** Items such as tax-loss carryforwards and carrybacks and investment tax credits that shield corporate taxable income from taxes.

**Technical analysis:** Any method of forecasting future exchange rates based on the history of exchange rates.

**Term structure of interest rates (yield curve):** The relation of interest rates or yields to maturity over various horizons for a particular class of debt.

**Territorial tax system:** A tax system that taxes domestic income but not foreign income. This tax regime is found in Hong Kong, France, Belgium, and the Netherlands.

**Time draft:** A draft that is payable on a specified future date.

**Time value:** The difference between the value of an option and the option's intrinsic value.

**Timing option:** The right to choose when to exercise an option. In particular, the ability of the firm to postpone investment or disinvestment and to reconsider the decision at a future date.

**Total return swap:** A credit derivative in which one party makes payments based on the total return of a reference entity and the other party makes interest payments that are unrelated to the reference asset.

**Total risk:** The sum of systematic and unsystematic risk (measured by the standard deviation or variance of return).

**Trade acceptance:** A time draft that is drawn on and accepted by an importer.

**Trade balance:** A country's net balance (exports minus imports) on merchandise trade.

**Trade secret:** An idea, process, formula, technique, device, or information that a company uses to its competitive advantage.

**Trademark:** A distinctive name, word, symbol, or device used to distinguish a company's goods or services from those of its competitors.

**Trading desk (dealing desk):** The desk at an international bank that trades spot and forward foreign exchange.

**Transaction exposure:** Changes in the value of contractual (monetary) cash flows as a result of changes in currency values.

**Transfer prices:** Prices set on intracompany sales.

**Translation (accounting) exposure:** Changes in a firm's financial statements as a result of changes in currency values.

**Triangular arbitrage:** Arbitrage conducted between three exchange rates.

**Tunneling:** The expropriation of corporate assets from minority shareholders by controlling shareholders or management, by legal or illegal means.

**Unbiased expectations hypothesis:** The hypothesis that forward exchange rates are unbiased predictors of future spot rates. (See *forward parity*.)

**Uncovered interest parity (UIP):** The nominal interest rate differential equals the expected change in the exchange rate.

**Universal banking:** A banking system (such as Germany's) in which banks offer a full range of banking and financial services to their individual and corporate clients.

**Unlevered beta (systematic business risk):** The beta (or systematic risk) of a project as if it were financed with 100 percent equity.

**Unlevered cost of equity:** The discount rate appropriate for an investment assuming it is financed with 100 percent equity.

**Unrestricted shares:** Shares that may be held only by anyone, including foreigners.

**Unsystematic risk:** Risk that is specific to a particular security or country and that can be eliminated through diversification.

**Value premium:** The finding that value stocks tend to have higher mean returns than growth stocks.

**Value stocks:** Stocks with high equity book-to-market ratios or low price/earnings (P/E) ratios.

**Value-added tax (VAT):** A sales tax collected at each stage of production in proportion to the value added during that stage.

**Value-at-risk (VaR):** Value-at-risk is an estimate of potential loss with a certain level of confidence and over a certain time horizon due to adverse price movements in an underlying asset.

**Vertical keiretsu (sangyô):** Japanese industrial groups with extensive cross shareholdings in related businesses. Vertical keiretsu are led by a major manufacturer in electronics (Hitachi, Sony, Toshiba) or automotive (Honda, Nissan, Toyota).

**Warrant:** An option issued by a company that allows the holder to purchase equity from the company at a predetermined price prior to an expiration date. Warrants frequently are attached to Eurobonds.

**Weak form efficient market:** A market in which prices fully reflect the information in past prices.

**Weighted average cost of capital (WACC):** A discount rate that reflects the after-tax required returns on debt and equity capital.

**Withholding tax:** A tax on dividend or interest income that is withheld for payment of taxes in a host country. Payment typically is withheld by the financial institution distributing the payment.

**World Bank:** See *International Bank for Reconstruction and Development.*

**World Trade Organization (WTO):** Created in 1994 by 121 nations at the Uruguay Round of the General Agreement on Tariffs and Trade (GATT). The WTO is responsible for implementation and administration of the trade agreement.

**Worldwide tax system:** A tax system that taxes worldwide income as it is repatriated to the parent company. Used in Japan, the United Kingdom, and the United States.

**Yield curve:** The term structure of interest rates or yields over various horizons for a particular class of debt.

**Yield to maturity:** The discount rate that equates the present value of promised future interest payments to the current market value of the debt.

**Zaibatsu:** Large family-owned conglomerates that controlled much of the economy of Japan prior to World War II.

# Index